THREE AMERICAN INDIAN WOMEN

POCAHONTAS
→ GRACE STEELE WOODWARD ←

SACAJAWEA
→ HAROLD P. HOWARD ←

SARAH WINNEMUCCA
OF THE NORTHERN PAIUTES
→ GAE WHITNEY CANFIELD ←

MJF BOOKS

NEW YORK

Front Jacket Illustrations:
1. National Portrait Gallery, Smithsonian Institution/Art Resource, NY. S0034873 NPG.82.137 Norval H. Busey, Photograph of Sarah Winnemucca (c. 1844-1891). National Portrait Gallery, Washington, DC, U.S.A.

2. Lewis and Clark with Sacajawea at Three Forks of Missouri, 1805. The Granger Collection, NY.

3. *Pocahontas and John Smith* (detail from the painting), Victor Nehlig © Courtesy Museum of Art, Brigham Young University. All rights reserved.

Published by MJF Books
Fine Communications
Two Lincoln Square
60 West 66th Street
New York, NY 10023

Library of Congress Catalog Card Number 95-80192
ISBN 1-56731-089-3

Pocahontas Copyright © 1969; *Sacajawea* Copyright © 1971; *Sarah Winnemucca of the Northern Paiutes* Copyright © 1983 by the University of Oklahoma Press, Norman, Publishing Division of the University.

Printed by arrangement with the University of Oklahoma Press, Norman

Manufactured in the United States of America

MJF Books and the MJF colophon are trademarks of Fine Creative Media, Inc.

10 9 8 7 6 5 4 3 2 1

Pocahontas
by Grace Steele Woodward

Acknowledgments

I WISH TO THANK the many thoughtful people who assisted me as I gathered information and data for this book. During the course of my research, both in the United States and in England, seeking out all known historical material relating to Pocahontas' life, I was given great help and guidance by many gracious librarians, scholars, and curators. And though I am indebted to so large a number of institutions and individuals that I cannot name them all, I would like to acknowledge my special gratitude to the following:

The director and staff of the Thomas Gilcrease Institute of History and Art, Tulsa, Oklahoma, and Mrs. Marie E. Keene, the research librarian of the institute; Mrs. Marydell Bradfield, of the Tulsa Central Library; T. Dale Stewart, acting curator of Physical Anthropology, Smithsonian Institution, Washington, D.C.; Robert A. Elder, Jr., museum specialist, Department of Anthropology, U.S. National Museum, Washington, D.C.; the staff of the Library of Congress; the late Eleanor Pitcher, of the Folger Shakespeare Library, Washington, D.C.; the staff of the Virginia State Library, Richmond, Virginia, and the library's archaeologist, Howard A. MacCord; Ben C. McCary, professor of modern languages, the College of William and Mary, Williamsburg, Virginia; The Rev. George J. Cleaveland, registrar of the Diocese of Virginia; Mrs. Wilmer N. Stoneman, present owner of "Varina-on-the-James"; Mary Isabel Fry of the Henry E. Huntington Library and Art Gallery, San Marino, California; His Grace, the Duke of Northumberland, K.G.; A. E. Gunther, collateral descendant of John Rolfe and official historian of the Rolfe family; the staff of Her Majesty's Public Record Office, London; the staff of the British Museum, London, and Edward Croft-Murray of the museum's Department of Prints and Drawings; the staff of the Ashmolean Museum, Oxford University; the staff of the Department of Western Manuscripts of the Bodleian Library, Oxford University; the staff of Magdalene College Library, Cambridge University; Osmond Tudor Francis, friend and guide through England; and Mrs. G. A. Tatchell, wife of the rector of St. George's Church, Gravesend.

I also extend my humble thanks and appreciation to my friends and to the members of my family, who gave me patient understanding and encouragement during the years that were devoted to the research and writing of this biography.

Tulsa, Oklahoma   GRACE STEELE WOODWARD

Contents

Illustrations and Map

MAP

CHAPTER I

An Introduction

FOR ABOUT TEN YEARS early in the seventeenth century, Pocahontas, a young Powhatan Indian princess, effected a remarkable and significant relationship first with the small group of English settlers at Jamestown and later with the English rulers and financiers who were sponsoring the colonization of the New World. It was a perceptive and creative relationship that was to help shape the course of American history, for, in her remarkable way, the Powhatan princess helped bring about the ultimate co-operation between her people and the English that was to

3

permit the successful founding of Virginia and lead ultimately to the making of a new nation.

For almost a century before 1607, when the London Company fleet of three small ships landed at Jamestown, the Spaniards had been busy colonizing the New World. They had been active in South America. Cortés had conquered Montezuma and established the rich colony of Mexico. Coronado and De Soto had pushed Spanish claims northward from Florida to California. France had also been deeply interested in the New World. French explorers had moved down the St. Lawrence and into the Great Lakes region, asserting the claims of France to that vast area. England's one small effort at colonization, Roanoke, had disappeared into the caverns of history, a lost and obliterated cause.

For reasons perhaps never to be completely understood, Pocahontas, daughter of Chief Powhatan, negotiated the success of Jamestown and saved it from the fate of the Lost Colony. She saw to it that corn, venison, and other foods were brought to the "gentlemen" colonists, who were ill-prepared to face the hardships of the new land. On a number of occasions she intervened on behalf of the colonists as inevitable conflicts arose between them and the Powhatans. She united her people and the English by her conversion to Christianity and her marriage to John Rolfe. And she represented both English colonist and American Indian when she traveled to the court of James I, there to inspire a greater economic support of colonization in the New World and to educate the British to the reality of a distant place and people.

Pocahontas could not have been much more than ten years old in 1607, when the Jamestown colonists, busily felling trees, clearing ground for gardens, and building their fort, first saw her playing in prenubial nakedness within their settlement, leapfrogging and turning cartwheels with four young cabin boys off

4

the *Susan Constant*, the *Godspeed*, and the *Discovery*.[1] William Strachey, appointed recorder of the colony in 1610, wrote down the stories he heard from earlier colonists about the young girl's visits to Jamestown and her uninhibited game playing with Nathaniel Peacock, James Brumfield, Richard Mutton, and Samuel Collier.[2] After their five-month voyage across the Atlantic (from December 20, 1606, to May 12, 1607), the cabin boys were more than willing to frolic with the energetic Indian princess, who, as Captain John Smith observed, frequented Jamestown in its early days with her "wild traine" as freely as she did her own father's habitation.[3]

Strachey referred to Pocahontas as "a well featured, but wanton yong girl."[4] Smith, on the other hand, apparently saw her not as wanton but as naturally precocious: ". . . a child of tenne years old, which not only for feature, countenance, and proportion exceedeth any of the rest of her people but for wit and spirit [is] the non-pareil of his [Powhatan's] countrie."[5] In light of the events that followed in the ten remaining years of Pocahontas' life, it is understandable that Smith's phrase rather than Strachey's came to be used to describe her. The aristocratic members of the Virginia Company were to appropriate it, and even in later days, when meeting at Sir Thomas Smythe's house on Philpott Lane in London to discuss the management of the

[1] William Strachey, "The First Booke of the Historie of Travaile into Virginia Britania . . .," Cap. 5, 29, MS 1622, Sloane Collection, Department of Manuscripts, Library, British Museum; hereafter cited as "The First Booke." (See also William Strachey, *Historie of Travaile into Virginia Britannia* (ed. by R. L. Major), Cap. V, 65; hereafter cited as *Historie.*)

[2] Strachey, "The First Booke," Cap. 5, 29.

[3] John Smith, *The Generall Historie of Virginia, New-England, and the Summer Isles . . . .*, Book IV, 122; hereafter cited as *Generall Historie.*

[4] Strachey, "The First Booke," Cap. 5, 29.

[5] Edward D. Neill, *Historie of the Virginia Company of London, with Letters to and from the First Colony Never Before Printed*, 83; hereafter cited as *History of the Virginia Company.*

5

Jamestown colony, the silken-clad members referred to Pocahontas as the "non-pareil of Virginia."

Certainly Pocahontas, from her earliest encounter with the English, was "without equal" among her people as far as her attitude toward the colonists was concerned. The Powhatans in general were fearful and suspicious of the newcomers, and consequently hostile. As early as May 26, only fourteen days after the English arrived, two hundred Paspaheghs, a tribe of Powhatans living near the juncture of the James and Chickahominy rivers, attacked Jamestown, killing Eustis Clovell and wounding eleven other colonists, one of whom later died of his wounds. Throughout the summer of 1607 the deaths of colonists—announced by the booming of artillery from the ships or by cannon or musket fire—prompted the Powhatans to mock and taunt the English. Powhatan warriors yelled and danced in the marsh grass outside the Jamestown fort to celebrate the colony's disasters; the horrendous shrieks and cries of "Yah, ha, ha!" and "Whe, Whe, Whe, Tewittowah"[6] bespoke the Powhatans' contempt for the colonists. In their mocking celebrations the Powhatans would implore their devil-god to plague and destroy the Tassantasses, as they called the English.[7]

Pocahontas did not share her people's hostility, and it is that fact that catapulted her into history. She was a woman who acted contrary to the manner of her people. She made manifest a different attitude, not only toward the English but also toward her own life.[8] Encountering a new culture, she responded with curiosity and concern, and she accepted the potential for change and development within herself. She rose, surely and dramatically, above the ignorance and savagery of her people, whom

[6] Strachey, "The First Booke," Cap. 6, 54.

[7] Strachey, *Historie*, Cap. VI, 79.

[8] An attitude that Smith tried to convey by saying, "God made Pocahontas." (John Smith, *New England Trials*, C2.)

the Jamestown colonists termed "naked slaves of the devill."[9] Her story is one of growth—cultural, intellectual, and spiritual. Her achievement as human being and as maker of history is extraordinary, and has for too long been obscured in the mists of legend. It is an achievement that warrants a modern telling and a new evaluation.

[9] Alexander Whitaker, *Good Newes from Virginia*, 23–24.

CHAPTER II

The Powhatans

To UNDERSTAND POCAHONTAS, one must first understand the Powhatan culture from which she emerged, a culture of dark superstitions and devil worship, a culture of easy cruelty and primitive social accomplishments. Although Pocahontas was exceptional within this culture, nevertheless, in her childhood, she accepted its values and was certainly a witness to, and participant in, the Powhatan way of life. She was, after all, a full-blooded Indian, and, though extremely individualistic within Powhatan society, she was not immune to it. Her later cultural

8

readjustment is all the more significant because she was born when and where she was.

Sometime long before the seventeenth century Pocahontas' people had migrated from the north into the coastal region that is today called Tidewater Virginia, but they kept no historical records carved in stone or inscribed on sticks, nor, unlike many other aboriginal American tribes, did they preserve any legends of their past in oral accounts recited to the succeeding generations. They were a people without a sense of origin or a sense of history.[1]

By Pocahontas' time the Powhatans were established as part of the late Woodland culture that flourished in the southeastern part of what is now the United States. It was a culture of pressure-flaked projectile points, stone-headed hatchets and war clubs, and primitive farm tools constructed of stone or bone. The Woodland "culture" was actually an amalgam of various tribes that belonged to different linguistic families not related by blood, their only common ties being certain tools and implements and other artifactual adaptations to a common environment marked by great stands of pine, cypress, and walnut trees and productive in cleared areas of pumpkin, maize, and beans (*peccatoas*).

The Powhatans lived on the northeastern edge of the Woodland territory. In the coastal and inland areas south and west of the Powhatans were the Cherokees, linguistically linked to the Iroquoian family; the Monacans, linked to the Siouan family; and the Choctaws, Creeks, and Chickasaws, linked to the Muskhogean family. The Powhatans, tied linguistically to the

---

[1] The prehistoric relics scattered above and below the Powhatan villages do not illuminate the Powhatans' origin. Used, but not made, by Powhatans, these relics—delicately chipped blades in the shape of laurel leaves and finely wrought spears—are thought to have been made by tribes who lived in the Tidewater region more than seven thousand years ago.

9

Algonquians, spoke—slowly and with great deliberation—a dialect derivative of the language spoken by the Algonquians living on the eastern shore of Chesapeake Bay and in the basins of the Delaware and Hudson rivers. The Tidewater Powhatans were distant kinsmen of the Lenape, whose Walam Olum, or "Painted Tally," told how between 1500 and 1600 bands of Algonquians settled along the Atlantic Coast from the Strait of Belle Isle, off the coast of Newfoundland, south to the Savannah River and also told of the relations among the Mahicans, Munsees, Manhattans, and other Indian tribes living along the Hudson River and near the bays and coastal areas of present-day New York State.[2]

Not only in language but also in other ways the Powhatans revealed their Algonquian ties. Like their northern kinsmen, the Powhatans lived in long, arbor-like houses made by implanting a double row of saplings in the ground and bending the tops into an arched roof. The sides of the houses were covered with mats woven of reeds or with large patches of bark that could be rolled up or removed in warm weather to permit air to circulate through the dwellings. The roofs were thatched with marsh grass or bark. A smoke hole was left in the center of the roof. Most Powhatan houses had but one large room, though some tribes built communal houses with one large central room flanked by several smaller rooms. Houses of these designs were common among all Algonquian tribes wherever they lived.[3]

There is evidence that sometime before Pocahontas' birth the Powhatans had established close relations with other displaced Algonquian tribes living in the Roanoke area in recognition of

[2] Congress, House of Representatives, 82 Cong., 2 sess., *House Report No. 2503*, 509–10; John L. Cotter, *Archeological Excavations at Jamestown*, 6–8; Ben C. McCary, *Indians in Seventeenth-Century Virginia*; Daniel G. Brinton (ed.), *The Lenape and Their Legends, with the Complete Text and Symbols of the Walum Olum.*

[3] McCary, *Indians in Seventeenth-Century Virginia*, 14–16.

and response to their kinship. The Powhatans' primitive swords, usually made of wood or bone, were occasionally made of bog iron similar to that found in deposits near the Outer Banks of North Carolina, not far from Roanoke Island.[4] And the magnificent water-color drawings of the Roanoke Algonquians made by John White in 1585[5] show the similarity of the Powhatans to their Algonquian cousins; the Roanoke tribes pictured in White's seventy-five drawings could easily be mistaken for Powhatans.

A comparison of the water colors with the Jamestown colonists' descriptions of the Powhatans reveals that the appearance and behavior of Roanoke and Powhatan tribes were much the same. For example, the Roanoke warriors depicted by White and described by Thomas Hariot in 1585 were remarkably like the Powhatan warriors described by George Percy two decades later. "The Princes of Virginia," wrote Hariot, . . . "weare the haire of their heads long and bynde opp the ende of the same in a knott under their eares. Yet they cutt the topp of their heads from the nape of the necke in manner of cokscombs."[6] Twenty years later George Percy wrote about the Powhatans: "They shaved the right side of their heads with a shell, the left they weare of an ell [forty-five inches] long tied up with an artifyciall knot, with as many of fowles feathers sticking into it."[7]

According to White's water colors and the Jamestown records, the men and women of both the Roanoke and the Tidewater

[4] Though there were such bog-iron deposits at the falls near Powhatan, a village near the present Richmond (ruled by Parahunt, Pocahontas' half-brother), they were not being extensively mined by the Powhatans at the time Jamestown was founded. It must be concluded that the Powhatans had procured most of the iron for their swords from the Roanoke Island area.

[5] John White, American Drawings, Department of Royal Manuscripts, Library, British Museum.

[6] Thomas Hariot, *A Briefe and True Report of the New Found Land of Virginia*, Chap. III.

[7] Samuel Purchas, *Purchas His Pilgrimes*, IV, 1687.

areas had tawny skin shading into light-reddish shades.[8] The men of both areas were about six feet tall, agile, and strong. According to Strachey, the Powhatans had round heads, wide, full-lipped mouths, and broad noses that were "either flatt or full at the end,"[9] characteristics closely resembling those of White's earlier Roanoke models.

Both the White drawings and the Jamestown records indicate that throughout most of the year the Algonquian males wore only breechcloths, consisting of pelts of medium-sized animals with heads and tails intact, fastened to belts and barely covering their "privities," as Strachey expressed it.[10] In winter, however, the men sometimes wore buckskin leggings and moccasins. Elderly men of both the Roanoke and the Tidewater areas wore feather mantles or the skins of wolves, bears, or deer over their shoulders, fastened in such a way as to leave a shoulder and arm bare.

Priests of both regions signified their status by wearing headdresses of dyed deer hair gathered into a topknot crowned with feathers, from which dangled a dozen or more snakeskins stuffed with moss. Knee-length shifts of quilted rabbitskins were their only coverings. In their ears they wore various ornaments: dangling claws of fowls inset with copper, live green garter snakes, or long strands of fresh-water pearls. Their bodies were usually painted black, or black with red or white.

Lesser tribesmen also painted themselves. Even when they were not at war, the tribesmen applied clay mixed with pulverized bloodroot to their faces and bodies. On special occasions walnut oil, blue clay sprinkled with particles of silver ore, white clay, and other ingredients were used for face and body paint.

---

[8] Strachey wrote, "They are generally of a collour brown or rather tawney." ("The First Booke," Cap. 6, 28.)

[9] *Ibid.*

[10] *Ibid.*

When they prepared for war, warriors of both areas painted identification marks on their shoulders to denote their tribe or village.

On special occasions the women also painted their faces, using a bright-scarlet mixture of berry juice, bloodroot, and other ingredients. Like the men, the women of both regions had long, straight black hair, small black eyes interestingly elongated at the corners, and handsome rather than pretty features. Fond of ornaments, they wore bone necklaces and, depending on their rank, feathers, beads, and other decorations. The chiefs' wives decorated themselves with many strands of pearls interspersed with copper.

Female dress in both the Roanoke and Tidewater areas consisted of a short, apron-like garment of dressed skins, fringed at the lower edges. According to Strachey, upper-class Powhatan women also wore mantles woven of feathers. Strachey described the wife of Pipisco, one of the Powhatan chiefs: ". . . as handsome a salvadge woman as ever I did see," with her mantle of blue feathers "so arteficyally and thick sowed together that it seemed like purple sattan."[11]

Married women of both regions wore their hair "all the same length" over their heads. Unmarried women kept their hair short at the front and sides, "grating it off," as Strachey said,[12] with shells. "Pouncing," or tattooing, the faces, breasts, thighs, and legs in flower, fish, or animal designs was a common practice among the women of both regions.[13]

The striking and picturesque Powhatans practiced a polytheistic religion. According to their creation myth, the Powhatans had been created by a giant hare, who had kept them in a huge bag in a far-distant land where they were constantly

[11] Strachey, *Historie*, Cap. VI, 57–58.
[12] *Ibid.*
[13] *Ibid.*

13

attacked by a group of aged women. Finally growing weary of the attacks, the hare released the prisoners, who then became earth dwellers. As for death and its aftermath, the Powhatans believed to a certain extent in reincarnation: for werowances, or chiefs, and priests especially, there was to be a continuation of existence; at death their privileged spirits would climb to the top of a tall tree supporting a bridge that led into the sky, where they would live until, after dying a second time, they would be reborn from the womb of an earth woman, to experience a second life on earth.

The most powerful of the Powhatan deities was Okeus, a devil-god, represented by a four-foot idol made of wooden crosspieces padded with moss, the body painted black, the face flesh-colored or white. Decorated with strands of pearls, the idol occupied the holiest area in each of the Powhatan temples: the chancel at the east and where the priests kept a fire burning to placate the god.

The priests taught that Okeus was responsible for all the evil in the world and that if he was not appeased he would wreak vengeance on the people, visiting sickness upon them, destroying their ripening corn, stirring up wars, making wives false to husbands, and sending storms to ravage their lands. To avoid such catastrophes, the Powhatans made an annual sacrifice of children to the devil-god. The priests would gather the entire Powhatan community in the woods and, after chanting their supplications to Okeus around a great fire, would present two or three of the Powhatan children to the god. Okeus would then mysteriously communicate to the priests the names of those to be sacrificed, and not even the son of a werowance was spared from death on the sacrificial altar if he was unfortunate enough to be selected.

Less powerful than Okeus was Ahone, the Powhatans' beneficent god. Associated with the sun, Ahone did not require placating, but each Powhatan paid homage to the god by bathing in a river or stream each morning at sunrise, following this ritual with another in which he placed dried tobacco in a circle around him, raised his arms skyward to the sun, and then, prostrating himself slowly lowered his hands to the earth. (The colonists, commenting on this ritual, observed that the men howled like wolves and foamed at the mouth.) The Powhatans would also cast bits of deer suet or tobacco into the water before bathing and before eating would spit a fragment of food into the fire as a tribute to Ahone.

The Powhatan religion was one of ritual—and their ritualistic sense extended to a general delight in celebrations of any kind. In *taquitock*, or autumn, they celebrated the harvest. They observed with dancing and feasting a marriage, the arrival of spring, the appearance of milk in the maize, the flight of wild fowl. Gathering in a circle around a fire, men and women—painted, feathered, and beaded—would dance sensual dances and sing erotic songs, so marking the vital affairs of their lives and the events of nature.

Perhaps the most revealing of their celebrations was the ritualistic torture of captives, a traditional ceremony held by all the Powhatan tribes and on an especially grand scale at the principal Powhatan settlement, Werowocomoco. In preparing for the ceremony, the Powhatan women, who were noted for their cookery, baked maize cakes, broiled fish on hurdles over outdoor fires, roasted joints of venison and wild fowl on spits, and baked fresh oysters in their shells. Wild mulberries, strawberries, and blackberries were included in the menu.

The torture ceremony at which the elaborate meal was served consisted of dismembering bodies of the captives piece by piece while they yet lived. The parts of the bodies were thrown into the fire and eventually reduced to ashes. Sometimes a captive was tied hand and foot and his head laid on a block of stone and

15

beat to a pulp with a stone mallet or a wooden war club. Scalps salvaged from the ceremony were hung on a line stretched between trees—to be admired and appreciated.

Among the Powhatans—savage, ritualistic, and flamboyant—the most powerful and representative figure at the beginning of the seventeenth century was Pocahontas' father, Chief Powhatan himself. He was described by John Smith as "a tall well proportioned man with a sower look, his head somewhat gray, his beard so thin it seemeth none at all, his age near sixtye of a very capable and hardy body to endure any labour."[14] Powhatan was a law unto himself, ruling with dictatorial powers throughout the Tidewater country—as the Jamestown colonists discovered soon after their arrival. After meeting Powhatan, William Strachey remarked that "it is strange to see what great favor and adoration all his people doe obey this Powhatan, for at his feete they present whatsoever he commandeth, and at the least froun of his brow the greatest will tremble, yet may be because he is very terrible and inexorable in punishing such as offend him."[15]

Powhatan had become head of the Powhatans' monarchical government about 1570, succeeding an older brother.[16] Upon his accession Powhatan inherited a small number of tribes and villages: Arrohattoc, twelve miles below the site of present Richmond, on the north bank of the James; Appomattoc, on Swift Creek near present-day Petersburg; Pamunkey, on the neck of land between the Pamunkey River (named the York by the English) and the Mattaponi River; Mattaponi, on the Mattaponi River in what is now King William County; Youghtanund, at the

[14] *Generall Historie*, Book II, 37.

[15] "The First Booke," Cap. 3, 24.

[16] Among the Powhatans the line of succession passed from the oldest brother to the next-oldest. Upon the death of the last brother the succession passed to the oldest sister and her male and female heirs.

16

head of the Pamunkey River; and Powhatan, a village near the present Richmond and probably Powhatan's birthplace. Apparently about the time of his accession Powhatan changed his name from Wahunsonacock and adopted the name of the village in which he was born.

Soon after 1570, not satisfied to rule the small kingdom he had inherited, Powhatan had conquered twenty-two or more Algonquian tribes in the Tidewater country, annexing their lands. And in the decades before the arrival of the Jamestown colonists, he had welded both inherited and conquered provinces into the powerful Powhatan Confederacy. As the absolute ruler of the confederacy, Powhatan shrewdly placed kinsmen—brothers, sons, and sisters—at the heads of his inherited territories and intimidated the werowances of the conquered tribes until they dared not oppose him.

An example of his intimidation was the night attack he made on the Piankatanks after they resisted his authority. Powhatan slaughtered all the men and carried off the women as captives. On another occasion, when the elderly chief at Kecoughtan (the site of present Hampton) died, Powhatan confiscated his lands, killed the Kecoughtan inhabitants who resisted him, and moved the survivors to Piankatank; then Powhatan transplanted a colony of his own people to Kecoughtan, appointing Pochins, his son, to rule the province.

By 1600 the powerful Powhatan Confederacy, encompassing about 8,500 square miles—about one-fifth of the present state of Virginia—embraced all the lands east of a line from what is now Washington, D.C., through Fredericksburg, Richmond, and Petersburg, Virginia. Southeast along the Blackwater River, the confederacy lands took in that part of coastal North Carolina to the Neuse River. Also included in the confederacy were the present Accomac and Northampton counties, on the eastern shore of Virginia. By 1607 the total population of the confederacy was between 8,500 and 9,000 persons, approximately 3,000 of whom were warriors.[17]

Powhatan ruled the confederacy like a despot. He demanded military support and taxes from all the tribes. The taxes, paid annually, consisted of eight parts out of ten of all the commodities Powhatan's subjects made, grew, or acquired. The skins they trapped, the fish they dried, the crops they raised, the copper they discovered, the pearls they found in oyster and mussel shells, the roanoke (shell beads used as currency) they bartered for—all were taxed.

The pelts, copper, and pearls that Powhatan acquired went into one of his three royal temples at Uttamussack,[18] where they were stored for the day of his death and burial. Piled high within the temple were caskets of pearls, thousands of skins, copper, bows, arrows, elaborately embroidered mantles, and pots of war

[17] The conquered tribes joined the inherited tribes in providing almost complete military protection of the confederacy's boundaries. By the early 1600's, Powhatan had nothing to fear from neighboring enemies, the confederated Manahoacs, a tribe belonging to the Siouan linguistic family, living at the head of the Rappahannock River, and the confederated Monacans, also of the Siouan linguistic family, living at the head of the James River.

Nor did the giant-sized Susquehannas, reputed to be seven feet tall, any longer threaten Powhatan's domain. Belonging to the Iroquoian linguistic family, the Susquehannas were kinsmen of the Iroquois tribes living south and west of the Powhatans, toward the Blue Ridge Mountains. In 1607 the Susquehannas lived north and a little west of the Powhatans. (McCary, *Indians in Seventeenth-Century Virginia*, 81. McCary refers to the Susquehannas [Conestogas] of Maryland, the assumption being that they lived in the Powhatans' area but not in Tidewater Virginia proper. See also Smith, *Generall Historie*, Book III, 60; Strachey, *Historie*, Cap. II, 39; and Charles C. Willoughby, "The Virginia Indians in the Seventeenth Century," *American Anthropologist*, Vol. IX, No. 1 [January–March, 1907], 57. Willoughby points out that the Powhatans were "hemmed in on the south and west by tribes of Iroquoian and Siouan stocks, and were separated on the north from the Canai, or Conoy, and Nanticoke, kindred of the Lenape, from the Susquehannocks, an Iroquoian people, by the Potomac River and Chesapeake Bay.")

[18] Spellings of Indian names are McCary's (*Indians in Seventeenth-Century Virginia*).

paint. Closely guarded on the outside by forty of Powhatan's fiercest warriors, the temple was protected inside by four huge wooden statues, carved in the likeness of a man, a bear, a dragon, and a leopard, standing menacingly in the corners. The taxes paid in grain, fish, dried venison, and other foods went into Powhatan's private storehouse at Werowocomoco, to feed his large family and his guests.

Powhatan not only taxed but also passed laws and issued decrees, one of which was that a man could have as many wives as he could afford. Powhatan himself was reputed to have had more than one hundred wives at one time or another, paying for them with roanoke or with copper, prized by all the Powhatans because of its scarcity. When Strachey visited Powhatan at the chief's large house at Orapaks, sometime between 1611 and 1613, he counted thirty-odd wives, among them Ashetoiske, Amopotoiske, Ponnoiske, Winganucki, and Ottopomtacks.[19]

All in all, Powhatan was a remarkable and powerful leader—fierce, clever, and unscrupulous. By the beginning of the seventeenth century he had made his people not less primitive but certainly more potent and formidable than they had ever been before. He had added ruthless organization and totalitarian methods to their lives. He had aggrandized himself, and he was ready to deal in his own confident and often cruel way with anyone who might challenge his authority.

It was into this world, into the household of Chief Powhatan and into the Powhatan culture, that Pocahontas was born, probably in 1596 or 1597. The colonists believed that Pocahontas' birthplace was Werowocomoco, Powhatan's principal residence until 1609.[20] Which of Powhatan's many wives was Pocahontas' mother is unknown; the mother's name and whereabouts were never ascertained by the colonists, who, in the process of found-

[19] Strachey, *Historie*, Cap. III, 54.
[20] In that year Powhatan became annoyed by the proximity of the colonists

ing Virginia, gathered as many vital statistics about the Powhatans as they could. For all the colonists knew, Powhatan could have had Pocahontas' mother put to death—or, growing tired of her, could have sold her or given her to a werowance in his confederacy to whom he owed some favor. It is more likely that the mother simply went away, since each of Powhatan's wives usually bore him but one child. A century after Pocahontas' death it was rumored that her mother was of "Runic," or Scandinavian, origin—but that is a theory with no real basis and has never been taken seriously by historians or ethnologists.

According to the early colonists, Pocahontas, like all other Powhatans, had two names. Pocahontas, the name given to her by her father, was translated by the English to mean "Bright Stream Between Two Hills" but in the Powhatan tongue perhaps meant "Little Wanton." Her secret name, known only among her own tribesmen, was Matoax, "Little Snow Feather," a name conjuring up the image of a slim, amber-skinned girl enveloped from neck to knee in a mantle woven of snow-white feathers plucked from the breast of a wild swan. Such a mantle, worn by Pocahontas in winter with moccasins and leggings of finely dressed white skins, would have given her people ample reason for calling her Matoax.

Pocahontas had her public and her secret names. She had her place in the Powhatan tribe. She was a favorite daughter in her father's home. As a princess, she was as privileged within the Powhatan world as anyone besides her father could be. And certainly she was heiress—indeed a royal heiress—to her people's attitudes, beliefs, and prejudices. It would be expected, therefore, that she would share in the general Powhatan distrust of white-skinned strangers and in her father's particular hatred of anyone who came to his land from across the sea.

---

and moved to Rasawrack, near Orapaks, his former hunting lodge, located between the Chickahominy and Pamunkey rivers, in what is now New Kent County.

Color Plates and Map

Village of Secoton. Water color by John White, 1585. All the White drawings were made of Indians living in the Roanoke region.

Indians dancing around a circle of posts. Water color by John White, 1585.

Man and woman eating. Water color by John White, 1585.

Indians fishing. Water color by John White, 1585.

Group of Indians around a fire. Water color by John White, 1585.

Village of Pomeioc. Water color by John White, 1585.

Pocahontas ("Lady Rebecca") in English court dress (the Bootan Hall Portrait).

Ruth window, St. George's Church, Gravesend, England.
In the lower right corner of the window is a portrait of
Pocahontas in court dress.

Rebecca window, St. George's Church, Gravesend, England, presented by the Colonial Dames of America in 1914. Below the figure of Rebecca is a representation of the baptism of Pocahontas. In the lower right corner is a portrait of Pocahontas in baptismal attire.

Pocahontas and her son, Thomas Rolfe
(the Sedgeford Hall Portrait).

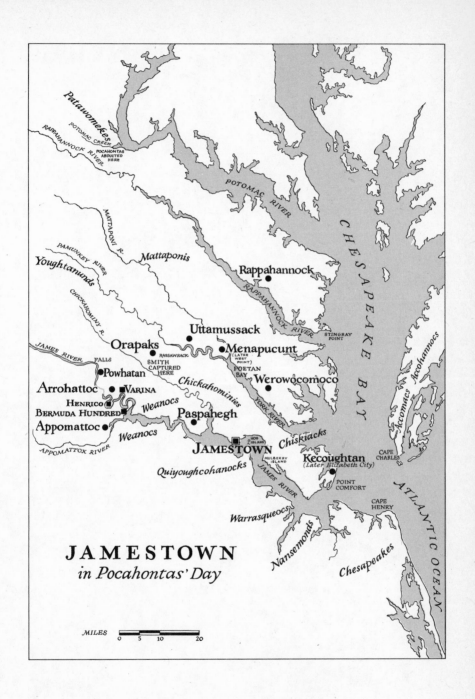

Patawomekes
POTOMAC CREEK
RAPPAHANNOCK RIVER
POCAHONTAS ABDUCTED HERE
POTOMAC RIVER
MATTAPONI R.
PAMUNKEY RIVER
Mattaponis
Rappahannock
RAPPAHANNOCK RIVER
CHESAPEAKE BAY
Youghtanunds
CHICKAHOMINY R.
Uttamussack
STINGRAY POINT
Orapaks
RASSAWACK
Menapucunt
(LATER WEST POINT)
Accomacs Accohannocs
JAMES RIVER
FALLS
SMITH CAPTURED HERE
POETAN BAY
Werowocomoco
Powhatan
Arrohattoc
VARINA
Chickahominies
YORK RIVER
HENRICO
Weanocs
BERMUDA HUNDRED
Paspahegh
Appomattoc
Weanocs
HOG ISLAND
Chiskiacks
APPOMATTOX RIVER
JAMESTOWN
CAPE CHARLES
MULBERRY ISLAND
Kecoughtan
(Later Elizabeth City)
Quiyoughcohanocks
JAMES RIVER
POINT COMFORT
CAPE HENRY
Warrasqueocs
Nansemonds
ATLANTIC OCEAN
Chesapeakes

JAMESTOWN
in Pocahontas' Day

MILES
0   5   10   20

The Invaders

By the time the English colonists arrived on the Virginia shore in 1607, the Powhatans were smoldering with a resentment that had its roots in a number of earlier visits by white men to their territories. For almost a century Europeans had been making sporadic visits to Powhatan country, and though some of the encounters had been amicable, others had resulted in misunderstanding at the best and sharp enmity at the worst.

Aged Powhatans living near the mouths of the four great rivers—the Potomac, the Rappahannock, the Pamunkey, and

41

Powhatan's Flu[1]—that striped the Powhatans' domain and emptied into Chesapeake Bay could remember seeing throughout their lifetimes various ships, flying French, Spanish, and possibly English flags, anchored offshore. Throughout the sixteenth century explorers from Europe had been attracted to the excellent natural harbors of the Powhatans. In 1524, Giovanni da Verrazano, the dark-bearded Florentine explorer who had been commissioned by Francis I of France to explore the New World, had led his fleet into Chesapeake Bay. His stay was short and disinterested, however, for he had already planted the French flag on the windswept sand dunes of the North Carolina coast near Cape Hatteras and Cape Fear.

A more colorful visit was that made in 1525 by Estéban Gómez, who arrived on Powhatan soil to claim the land for Spain.[2] The military drums, the clang of armor, the flash of silver helmets, the gleaming tips of spears, glaives, and maces, the harquebusiers in their slashed and ribbed uniforms—all these sights and sounds on the wilderness shore made an impressive spectacle for the Powhatans watching from hiding places behind sand dunes and in the marsh grasses. In a ceremony epitomizing the glory and power of Spain, the "conquerors" stood at attention as Gómez exclaimed proudly, "I possess all the new western world, in the name of our Lord Charles V." Gómez did not stay to exploit or administer the Powhatan territory, however, and the Powhatans were not yet faced with the problem of dealing with Europeans.

The Spanish were to return. Around 1560 Captain-General Pedro Menéndez de Avilés and his Spanish adventurers landed

[1] The James River, called Powhatan's River or Powhatan's Flu on the maps drawn by Captain John Smith.

[2] Reuben Gold Thwaites (ed.), *The Jesuit Relations and Allied Documents, 1612–1614*, II, 251–52; J. Bartlett Brebner, *The Explorers of North America, 1492–1806*, 115; James Mooney, "The Powhatan Confederacy, Past and Present," *American Anthropologist*, Vol. 9, No. 1 (January–March, 1907), 123–29.

on the Powhatan coast, captured the son of a werowance, and made him a slave. Menéndez became interested in the youth and took him to Cuba, to Mexico, and finally back to Spain, where the boy was educated in the finest schools and converted to the Roman Catholic faith. Upon his conversion he was given the name Don Luis de Velasco, in honor of the Spanish viceroy in Mexico. Pensioned by Philip II, Don Luis for a time lived the life of a Spanish grandee. Then in 1565 he returned to the New World to serve in Florida as interpreter for Menéndez during the construction of the fort at St. Augustine. Because of his outward conformity to Spanish customs, Don Luis was next chosen by Menéndez to help establish the Roman Catholic faith in Powhatan country—a country Don Luis had not seen since his abduction.

Don Luis was sent with an expedition headed by Father Juan Segura, a Jesuit missionary, who, refusing a military escort entered Indian country with nine other missionaries. The expedition entered Chesapeake Bay in the fall of 1570 and landed to celebrate Mass at the site of present-day Newport News, Virginia. Then, guided by Don Luis, Father Segura and the other missionaries, accompanied by a Spanish youth named Alonzo de Olmos, sailed up the James to the mouth of College Creek. Crossing the site of present-day Williamsburg, they eventually reached a point at the mouth of Queens Creek adjacent to the Pamunkey River. Here, with the help of Don Luis, Father Segura built a house to be used both as a residence and as a mission—the first such building on Powhatan land.

But the Spanish missionaries had not reckoned on Don Luis' reaction to his return to the land of his people. Instead of helping convert the Powhatans, Don Luis reverted to savagery. Using the Jesuits' own axes, he and several Powhatan accomplices murdered all the members of the expedition except Olmos, who escaped and found shelter with friendly Indians in the present

Hampton, Virginia, area. In 1572, Olmos was rescued by a Spanish relief ship whose captain avenged the murder of the missionaries by hanging a number of innocent Indians from the ship's yardarms before setting sail for Cuba.[3]

This episode marked the end, for the time being, of Spain's interest in colonizing the Powhatan region. It also marked the growing shadow of conflict between the indigenous Indian and the invading European, a conflict whose outcome was not yet predictable.

By the 1580's the Powhatan priests were prophesying that enemies would someday invade from the east through Chesapeake Bay and destroy the Powhatan people. Chief Powhatan, busy at the task of building and ruling his confederacy, was determined to prevent the fulfillment of the prophecy. He launched a campaign that eliminated nearly all the Chesapeake Indians living east of him, and he may well have been instrumental in the extermination of the Roanoke colony as well. That colony, founded on Roanoke Island in 1584, was re-established in 1587 (after all the original colonists had returned to England), but had disappeared by 1591, when its former governor, John White, returned from a stay in England. Certainly the Powhatans had had reason to hate the Roanoke colonists. Sir Richard Grenville, whose crested silver goblet had been stolen by an Indian, had retaliated by burning the offender's village to the ground. Ralph Lane, during his terms as governor of Roanoke Island, had burned a great many more native villages in reprisal for minor thefts.[4] Later colonists in Virginia were convinced that Powhatan —to avenge these deeds or to prevent further conflict—had been involved in what was probably a massacre of the entire Roanoke community.[5]

[3] Clifford M. Lewis, S.J., and Albert J. Loomis, S.J., *The Spanish Jesuit Mission in Virginia, 1570–1572,* 15–55.
[4] *History of the Thirteen Colonies,* 44.

44

By the beginning of the seventeenth century, during the years of Pocahontas' infancy and early childhood, the Powhatans' apprehensions about the Europeans had matured into an easily inflamed hostility. In 1604 a white man—his name unknown to history—was to provide one more aggravating event that led eventually to the drama in which Pocahontas played a leading role.

Paddling up the Rappahannock and Pamunkey rivers, the white man and his companions accepted the hospitality of a number of Powhatan werowances along their route, particularly the werowances of the Pamunkey, Rappahannock, and Chickahominy tribes. The hospitality offered to the party was not unusual, according to later accounts, even though the Powhatans were as a group fearful and anxious about strangers. Certain Powhatans were willing to observe and make contact with visi-

[5] Strachey, *Historie*, Cap. VIII, 101–102. The Jamestown colonists, having been so instructed by James I, made a serious effort to solve the mystery of Raleigh's second colony, though their only clue was the word "Croatoan" carved on a tree on Roanoke Island. When rumors reached the Jamestown colonists that Powhatan himself had been involved and that four men, two boys, and one girl had survived Powhatan's massacre of the colony, the colonists became increasingly watchful for English survivors. One rumor persisted that the survivors had been whisked off to an out-of-the-way village, where they were engaged in teaching Powhatan's people how to make brick and glass, later they heard the disheartening rumor that Powhatan, fearing the Roanoke survivors would be rescued by the Jamestown colonists, had ordered them killed.

Around May 20, 1607, while exploring the James River, Christopher Newport, captain of the *Susan Constant*, and his party made an exciting discovery, as recorded by George Percy, a member of the party: "At Port Cotáge in our voyage up the River we saw a Savage Boy about the age of tenne yeares which had a head of haire of perfect yellow and reasonable white skinne which is a miracle amongst all savages." (Purchas, *Purchas His Pilgrimes*, IV, 1689.) The Newport party believed that the boy was a Roanoke descendant but failed to make contact with him.

Discouraged by their failure to learn anything definite, and busy with their own settlement, the Jamestown colonists finally gave up their search for the Roanoke survivors.

tors to their country. On this occasion the visitors were beckoned to shore by the hospitable (and curious) chief of the Rappahannocks and seated on mats of woven reeds. Then the chief delivered an oration with great gusto and much gesticulation. Tubular clay pipes filled with tobacco grown and dried by the Powhatans were lighted and passed to the visitors. Then came feasting, dances, and games.[6]

The visitors, however, were little interested in entertainments or feasting. Their primary purpose was to abduct likely-looking young Powhatan boys to be sold as slaves to West Indies plantation owners. On this occasion they abducted a young Powhatan, apparently the son of the werowance who had entertained them. As the story was later told, the wrathful father and his warriors shot at the escaping whites, but their arrows broke against the enemies' metal armor. The whites then turned their guns on the Indians, killing the werowance and many of his warriors.[7] After this incident, and others like it, the Powhatans seized every opportunity to procure the white men's weapons, especially their guns. In later encounters with white men, the Powhatan chiefs signaled them to lay down their arms before coming ashore, promising that their warriors would do the same. But the command was seldom heeded.

It is not surprising that the Powhatans were resentful and suspicious when in 1607 a new group of Europeans arrived on their shores—the Englishmen who were to found Jamestown. The Powhatans recalled the Spanish and English slave hunters who had preyed upon them. They recalled their difficulties with the Roanoke colonists. They recalled the syphilis that the white men had brought to them, a disease against which the Powhatans' remedies of herbs and roots and incantations and sacrifices had been unavailing and which had brought suffering and

[6] Smith, *Generall Historie*, Book II, 30–34; Strachey, *Historie*, Cap. VI, 78.
[7] Philip Barbour, *The Three Worlds of Captain John Smith*, 163.

death to many Indians.[8] With the arrival of a new group of Europeans, the tribal priests reiterated their warnings to Chief Powhatan. If he did not resist the "enemies from the east," his people would be compelled to sacrifice thousands of their male children to Okeus. All the people of the Powhatan Confederacy would be in great danger if the new invaders were not resisted and driven out.

The English colonists were not aware of the difficult situation in which they were placing themselves. Even with the Roanoke disaster in mind, the Jamestown colonists were filled with hope as they ventured into what they considered to be an inevitable and necessary historical experience. With the accession of James I to the throne of England in 1603, New World colonization had become a matter of intense concern to the English. They had long worried about Spain's power in the New World, but because of internal strife and foreign wars their exploration and colonization efforts had largely been restricted to private ventures. By the early 1600's many powerful arguments were put forth to justify government-supported colonization: England, with a population of four million, was overcrowded. The defeat of the Spanish Armada had forced Spain to retreat from her century-long leading role in New World colonization. The time was ripe to assert England's rights to part of the wealth across the ocean. Moreover, the conversion of the Indians to the Anglican faith was imperative if the New World was not to fall under the hegemony of the Roman Catholic Church.

Consequently, on April 10, 1605,[9] the Great Seal of England was affixed to the first Virginia charter, and the stage was prepared for an encounter not only between individual Europeans

[8] Letter from George Thorpe to John Ferrar, 1621, MS 1019, John Ferrar Papers, Department of Manuscripts, Library, Magdalene College, Cambridge University; Strachey, *Historie*, Cap. IV, 110; Cotter, *Archeological Excavations at Jamestown*, 23–24.

[9] William W. Abbot, *A Virginia Chronology, 1585–1783*, 2.

and Indians but also between the English government and the Powhatan Confederacy.

The charter actually provided for two colonizing groups, one to settle North Virginia (New England) and the other to settle South Virginia (the present Tidewater Virginia region). The colonization of South Virginia was backed primarily by Londoners: Sir George Somers, an expert navigator; Richard Hakluyt, the renowned geographer; Edward Maria Wingfield, an experienced military leader; and Sir Thomas Smythe, one of the most astute businessmen of the day. Smythe was made treasurer of the group, which was henceforth known as the Virginia Company of London.

Soon after the charter was signed, King James issued the Articles and Instructions for the Virginia colony.[10] Described by his enemies as "the wisest fool in Christendom," James had one real gift—the ability to concentrate on an issue long enough to produce a treatise of intellectual and practical worth. With the help of Sir John Popham, lord chief justice of England, and other English intellectuals, James outlined clearly and concisely the procedure for the colonists to follow in establishing the settlements in North and South Virginia.

The instructions for South Virginia were sealed in three boxes, one of which was placed aboard each of the three outward-bound ships. When the ships dropped anchor in Chesapeake Bay, near present Cape Henry, in April, 1607, the instructions were opened and read. They dealt with, among other things, the choice of a site for settlement; the treatment of the Indians, or "naturals"; the exploration of the rivers and lands of the region; the fortification of the settlement; the recovery of the lost Roanoke colony; the search for natural resources that would bring wealth to England; and the discovery, if possible, of a route to the "Indian Sea." The instructions also contained the names of

[10] MS 21993, fol. 187, British Museum Archives; Abbot, *Chronology*, 2.

48

the members of the Jamestown council, as well as the name of its first president, Edward Maria Wingfield. To prevent the seeds of Catholicism from being planted in the new colony, each member of the council was required to take an oath of allegiance to King James, thereby renouncing allegiance to the pope.[11]

Thus well instructed, officially chartered, properly sworn, and representing the English nation and culture more explicitly than any group had ever done before, the Jamestown colonists confronted the Powhatan Indians, who were prepared, for their own reasons and in their own fashion, to complicate the English goal of an easy, immediate, reasonable, and rewarding establishment of the English way of life in the New World.

For the first days after the Jamestown colonists arrived, there were no overt acts of hostility. The Quiyoughcohanocks (Tapahanocks), who lived on the south bank of the James River, seemed friendly, as did the Paspaheghs, who lived west of the Chickahominy River near the point where it joined the James. Moreover, Pochins, Pocahontas' half-brother and the werowance at Kecoughtan, entertained the colonists lavishly when they visited his village while seeking a site for the settlement.

Then on May 18, four days after the colonists' arrival, an incident occurred that tragically altered relations between the Powhatans and the English—an incident that might have been

[11] Manuscript Records of the Virginia Company, Vol. III, Part i, 20, 20a, Library of Congress List of Records No. 5. The oath of Allegiance reads: "I, M_____ doe utterlie testifie & declare in my conscience y^t y^e kings highnes y^e onlie supreame Governor of Great Brietaine and of all the Collony . . . in all spirituall [and] ecclesiasticall things (or causes) as temporall. . . ." The oath of Supremacye reads: "I _____ M_____ doe trulie and sincerely acknowledge, professe testifie and declare in my Conscience before God & the world, That our Soveraigne Lord King . . . ys lawful and rightfull King of great Britaine and of the Colony of Virginia, and of all other his Maiesties Dominions and Countries. And that y^e pope neither of himselfe, nor by any Authoretie of the Church or See of Rome, or by any other meanes . . . hath any power or authorietie to depose the King or to dispose of any of his Maiesties Kingdomes or Dominions. . . ."

avoided if the colonists had been wiser and more tolerant of Powhatan ways and if the Powhatans had not been prepared to see in these particular Englishmen the enemies they desperately feared.

On that day the werowance of Paspahegh, accompanied by one hundred warriors, paid an ostensibly friendly visit to the colonists, bringing with him "a fat Deare"[12] for a feast. As the incident was recorded by George Percy, at first all went well at the meeting between the werowance and the colonists. The chief asked the white men to lay down their guns but did not seem particularly upset when they refused to do so. He even made signs—or so it seemed to the colonists—that he would give them all the land they wanted for their settlement. At that moment one of the settlers caught sight of a warrior making off with his English hatchet. According to Percy, the colonist "tooke it from him by force, and also strooke him over the arme. Presently another Salvage seeing that, came fiercely at our man with a wooden sword thinking to beat out his braines. The werowance of Paspahegh saw us take to our arms, and went suddenly away with all his company in great anger."[13]

It was an ominous beginning for the colonists, and to the Powhatans it was the long-dreaded invasion from the east. On May 26 the Paspaheghs attacked Jamestown. Thus the conflict was engaged, producing hostility that sometimes flared into warfare. The fate of Jamestown and Virginia, and all that they were finally to represent, depended upon a resolution that in 1607 was nowhere in sight.

[12] Purchas, *Purchas His Pilgrimes*, IV, 1688.
[13] *Ibid.*

CHAPTER IV

The Beginning of Jamestown

DURING THE FIRST DIFFICULT DAYS, weeks, and months of the English settlers' efforts to establish their colony, Pocahontas began what was to be her education in a new way of life and also began, to the future benefit of the English, what was to be her comprehension of that way of life and its relationship to the life of her people. Even in the midst of potential war and various acts of divisiveness between her people and the colonists, she ventured onto Jamestown Peninsula—a low-lying, unpleasant place abandoned by the Powhatans untold years earlier because of its vulnerability to hurricanes—to observe with her perceptive eyes the behavior and activity of the men from across the sea, struggling to build an orderly community.

No doubt Pocahontas watched in some amazement as the colonists erected a church, a fort, and habitations unlike anything she had seen before. Actually the buildings that impressed Pocahontas were by English standards quite primitive. According to Captain Smith, "For a Church we did hang an awning (which is an old sail) to three or foure trees to shadow us from the sunne. Our walls were rales of wood, our seats unhewed trees, till we cut plankes, our Pulpit a bar of wood nailed to two neighboring trees."[1] The fort itself was somewhat more substantial. It was built by laborers such as John Laydon, William Cassen, and "Old Edward," who felled tall trees for lumber and, with the help of the carpenters—William Laxton (or Laxon), Edward Pising, Thomas Emry, and Robert Small—completed the fort, which enclosed a storehouse, a market place, and several streets. When the fort was finished on June 15, George Percy noted that it was "triangle wise, having three Bulwarkes at every corner like a Halfe Moone, and foure or five pieces of Artillerie mounted in them."[2] No doubt Pocahontas was intrigued by the white men's buildings and also by their tools— the metal axes, hatchets, knives, and saws—and the weapons they kept close at hand—guns, poleaxes, pikes, demiculverins, and cannon. Certainly for Pocahontas the Jamestown settlement was a center of strange and exciting activity and, since she was but a child, a center of friendly attention from a remarkable and fascinating people.

Pocahontas may or may not have seen white men before 1607,

[1] John Smith, *Advertisements for the Unexperienced Planters of New England, or Anywhere: Or, the Path-Way to Experience to Erect a Plantation, 32;* hereafter cited as *Advertisements.*

[2] Purchas, *Purchas His Pilgrimes,* IV, 1689.

but even if she had, the English colonists would still have been curiosities. The English were shorter than the Powhatan men, and many of them had beards and mustaches. They dressed in peculiar ways, the Powhatans derisively called them "coat-wearing people." The colony's laborers wore jerkins of coarse homespun linen or canvas with matching breeches or hose, the dress prescribed by Parliament for their class in the time of Elizabeth I. The everyday dress of the Jamestown gentlemen, though not elaborate, was noticeably finer than the clothes the laborers wore on the Sabbath. The gentlemen's Sunday clothes were the finest in Jamestown: satin or taffeta lavishly decorated with slashes, pinking, and embroidery. The gentlemen's Sunday hats were plumed, while the laborers wore either small, flat berets like those worn by London craftsmen and known as "city flat caps" or brimmed hats with the severest of crowns, which had come into style in the latter part of the sixteenth century. On Sundays the gentlemen wore shoes of cordovan leather, while the laborers exchanged their sturdy boots for clumsy, heavy-soled shoes. When summer arrived, the gentlemen were compelled to shed their heavy, lined doublets, and the laborers, their jerkins.[3]

When Pocahontas first began visiting the colony, it contained more than one hundred Englishmen, and she soon became known to them all: the forty-eight English gentlemen, the Anglican chaplain, and the twelve laborers, the four carpenters, the bricklayer, the mason, the tailor, the blacksmith, the barber, and "divers others"[4] whose names, for some reason, were not listed on the ships' passenger lists.

Among the colonists were a number of especially interesting

[3] "Bill for Necessaries Bought by Mr. George Percy for His Voyage to the West Indies," MS Aln 114/5, Manuscripts, Dukes of Northumberland, Library of Congress (microfilm); Virginia A. LaMar, *English Dress in the Age of Shakespeare*.
[4] Smith, *Generall Historie*, Book III, 43–44.

and enterprising men. Among them was George Percy, a lean-faced, clean-shaven (except for a small mustache), member of the English aristocracy.[5] Percy had left England to escape persecution by King James. He was the younger brother of the ninth Earl of Northumberland—called the "Wizard Earl" because of his interest in science—who had been imprisoned for several years in the Tower of London for alleged participation in the Gunpowder Plot to blow up the House of Lords—and also the king. George Percy, knowing that he had no future in England while James ruled, preferred seeking his fortune elsewhere to joining his brother in the Tower. Another prominent colonist was John Ratcliffe, captain of the *Discovery* and a member of the Jamestown council, a man whom John Smith dubbed a "counterfeit Impostor"[6] after it was discovered that Ratcliffe's real name was Sicklemore. Though he was surrounded by an aura of mystery, apparently Ratcliffe had not adopted the alias for any ulterior purpose; Ratcliffe was the name of his stepfather, and Sicklemore, that of his true father, who was dead.

The newly elected president of the council, forty-seven-year-old Edward Maria Wingfield,[7] a member of an aristocratic Catholic family, was perhaps the most prestigious of the colonists. A military man who had served in Ireland and the Low Countries, Wingfield had been considered by the King's Council sufficiently experienced to carry out its instructions. However, Wingfield's Catholicism was held against him by the colonists, even though he had joined the other council members in taking the oath of allegiance.

There were other reasons for Wingfield's unpopularity. He

[5] MSS Aln 114/5, Aln 3/2, Aln 4/1, Aln 4/2, Manuscripts, Dukes of Northumberland, Library of Congress (microfilm); *Syon House*, 16–18.

[6] Smith, *Generall Historie*, Book III, 72.

[7] Henry Chandlee Forman, "Jamestown and St. Mary's Buried Cities of Romance," 35n.

was opinionated and brusque and impractical. At first he had been reluctant to fortify Jamestown for fear that to do so would wound the sensibilities of the Indians. When the Paspaheghs attacked the colony, Wingfield had second thoughts, reinforced by a Paspahegh arrow that hissed through his well-tended beard.

By far the most intriguing personality in the Jamestown colony was Captain John Smith, a dashing young bachelor of twenty-six, with twirled mustache and neatly trimmed beard. Smith had been a soldier of fortune in foreign lands before coming to Jamestown. He later boasted that "the warres in Europe, Asia, and Africa taught me how to subdue the Salvages in Virginia."[8] En route to Jamestown on the *Susan Constant* he had been arrested and put in irons by Captain Newport, who had accused him of inciting mutiny among some of the ship's passengers. Smith was released soon after the colonists landed at Jamestown, but he was not permitted to take the oath of allegiance to King James or to sit with the council, of which Newport was an honorary member, until June 10, when he was cleared of the charges against him.[9]

John Smith was not only the most intriguing of the colonists but also, as far as the young Pocahontas was concerned, the most approachable. From the time he began participating in colonial affairs, Smith was aware of the need for communication between the English and the Indians. He took the initiative in learning the Powhatan language so that he and the other colonists could talk with their hostile neighbors. For her part, while most of the Powhatans were uninterested in communicating with the English, Pocahontas also tried to penetrate the language barrier. Using the signs of her language, she would place her left hand over her heart and raise her right arm, a sign taken by the col-

[8] Smith, *Advertisements*, 1.
[9] John Smith, *Travels and Works of Captain John Smith* (ed. by Edward Arber and A. G. Bradley), II, 388.

onists to mean, "I am your friend," "I speak the truth," or "I will keep my promise."[10]

Smith's interest in learning the Powhatan language, and Pocahontas' youthful willingness to communicate, enabled him to learn from her a number of Powhatan words, phrases, and sentences, such as *tomahacks*, meaning "axes"; *monacookes*, meaning "swords"; *pawpecones*, meaning "pipes"; and *pawcussacks*, meaning "guns." Smith also learned that Pocahontas' people could count to one thousand, by ones to ten, and then by tens to one thousand.[11] His study of the Powhatan language lasted from 1607 to 1609 and resulted in a Powhatan vocabulary that he included in his *Generall Historie*. Smith composed sentences in English and then translated them into Powhatan. One of the most interesting of his practice sentences was, "Kekaten Pokahontas Patiaquagh niugh tanks Manotyens neer mowchick rawrenock Audough," which meant, according to Smith, "Bid Pokahuntas bring hither two little baskets, and I will give her white beads to make her a chaine."[12]

It was from Smith that Pocahontas learned her first English words—and received her first English "jewels." Both gifts, intellectual and material, marked the beginning of Pocahontas' friendship with Smith, the friendship that was later to prove invaluable to the dashing young captain.

Smith's concern with language was, of course, utilitarian, part of his plan for accommodation to the New World. The colonists' gifts to the Indians (the treasurer of the Virginia Company had seen to it that they had plenty of glass beads, bells, brass pans, metal hatchets, axes, and saws for trading) were also part of the design for success in the colonization effort. But words and beads alone were not to be adequate in the face of obstacles as formidable as the American wilderness and the recalcitrant natives.

[10] Purchas, *Purchas His Pilgrimes*, IV, 1690.
[11] Smith, *Generall Historie*, Book II, 40.   [12] *Ibid.*

In a very short time the colonists realized that their survival was threatened and that some determined counter measures were in order. The primary problem was the Indians, of course, and one measure that seemed to be indicated was the conversion of the Powhatans to Christianity. The Reverend Robert Hunt, the Anglican chaplain, believed that the way to tame the savages was to bring them into the Anglican faith, with its services centered around the Bible, the Book of Common Prayer, and the Constitution and Canons of the Province of Canterbury, from which Mr. Hunt read to his congregation on the Sabbath and other holy days. A special prayer had been composed for the colonists, and by the king's command it was said each morning and evening. The prayer clearly revealed the attitude of the English toward their pagan neighbors:

> Almighty God, . . . seeing that thou hast honoured us to choose us out to bear thy name unto Gentiles, we therefore beseech thee to bless us and this plantation which we and our nation have begun in thy fear and for thy glory . . . and seeing Lord, the highest end of our plantation here is to set up the standard and display the banner of Jesus Christ, even here where Satan's throne is, Lord let our labour be blessed in labouring for the conversion of the heathen. . . . Lord sanctify our spirits and give us holy hearts, that so we may be thy instruments in this most glorious work.[13]

Other colonists, among them Captain Smith, were not convinced that religious conversion would eliminate the problem with the Powhatans. They believed that it was necessary to subdue the Indians, though that would not be easily achieved either, for the colonists were not especially effective as soldiers in the Powhatans' native territory. The colonists had brought with them suits of light armor, which were impractical in the hot,

[13] Rev. G. Maclaren Brydon, *Highlights Along the Road of the Anglican Church*, 8.

57

humid weather that enveloped Jamestown Peninsula. The metal skirts, breastplates, and helmets were not only uncomfortably hot but also difficult to get into quickly during an Indian attack. The colonists' heavy matchlock muskets, which had to be propped on rests to be fired, were suitable for formal European warfare but as impractical as armor for informal combat with Indians, who, hiding in the tall marsh grass, sent arrows flying into the midst of the colonists as they worked in their gardens, gathered reeds, or felled trees. Long before a colonist could pour black powder into the muzzle of his musket, follow it with a two-ounce lead ball, and ram the charge home with a long iron ram-rod, he was dead from Indian arrows. So many colonists died in the early months of the settlement that the artillery in the fort and on the ships had to be pressed into service to repel the Indians. Poleaxes, pikes, and swords were also useless in the kind of warfare waged in the Virginia wilderness. How could one charge an enemy who was lying on his belly in the swamp, hidden from view by grass?

At the same time the colonists were confronted with the seemingly unresolvable Indian problem, they were also confronted with the problem of depleted supplies and provisions. It was decided that Captain Newport would return to England with the *Susan Constant* and the *Godspeed* and bring back sorely needed supplies. On Sunday, June 21, 1607, the colonists celebrated Communion, and the gentlemen finished off the day at a farewell dinner given by Captain Newport in his quarters aboard the *Susan Constant*. The next day Newport sailed.[14]

[14] Abbot, *A Virginia Chronology, 1585–1783*, 3. Captain Newport, who had lost an arm in the service of his country, was a capable man, and his qualifications for his job were a matter of record, as was his discipline of his ship. His main responsibility was to ferry colonists and supplies across the Atlantic, and between voyages he was to explore the surrounding country, looking for the natural wealth the New World offered. On this return voyage Newport's ships carried pine planks to be used for wainscoting in English manor houses (planks

The day after the ships departed, George Percy noted in his diary: "Captain Newport being gone for England, leaving us (one hundred and foure persons) verie bare and scantie of victualls, furthermore in warres [among ourselves] and in danger of the Salvages. We hoped after a supply which Captaine Newport promised within twentie weeks."[15] Thomas Studley, who was in charge of the storehouse at Jamestown, noted that the food remaining for the colonists was scanty and unappetizing. He reported that "there remained neither taverne, beerhouse, nor place of reliefe but the common Kettle . . . and that was halfe a pint of wheat, and as much barley boyled with water, for a man a day."[16] Percy tried to be optimistic, describing in his diary the "fruitfulness" of the new country and praising the James River: "If this river which wee have found had beene discovered in the time of warre with Spaine, it would have beene a commoditie to our Realme, and a great annoyance to our enemies."[17] But Percy's optimism could not hide the fact that provisions were fast disappearing.

In addition to the problems of the Powhatans and the lack of food, the colonists were beset with yet another difficulty, strife among themselves. After Newport's departure, Wingfield grew more unpopular than ever. He bunged up the two gallons of sack and aqua vitae left by Newport for the Communion table. He showed little concern for the colonists' hunger, suggesting that if they wanted more food they could fish or hunt for it. Sturgeon, pike, and other varieties of fish were available, and there was plenty of wild game and fowl. But because of the increasing hos-

cut by colonists who were still sleeping on the ground at Jamestown), as well as specimens of earth obtained around Jamestown to be analyzed for gold, and batches of sassafras to be tested for its curative powers in the treatment of syphilis.

15 Purchas, *Purchas His Pilgrimes*, IV, 1689.
16 Smith, *Generall Historie*, Book III, 44.
17 Purchas, *Purchas His Pilgrimes*, IV, 1689.

tility of the Indians few colonists dared venture beyond the fort. In various ways Wingfield proved an unsatisfactory leader, and finally he was removed from his office as president of the council by vote of John Smith, John Ratcliffe, and John Martin. Ratcliffe was elected president in his place.[18]

Also contributing to the strife among the colonists was the realization that a certain amount of subversion was taking place. The Spanish government was learning a good deal about the Jamestown settlement from reports originating within the colony itself. Soon after the *Susan Constant* and the *Godspeed* arrived in England, one Captain Waiman (or Warman) was taken into custody for carrying coded messages from the Jamestown settlement addressed to Philip III of Spain. In Jamestown council member George Kendall, suspected from the start by James Read, the blacksmith, of being a spy in the employ of Philip III, was finally openly accused, convicted, and executed.[19] Even Wingfield, after his recall from the council presidency, was charged with mutinous intentions and was imprisoned on the *Discovery*, the pinnace which had been left at Jamestown. The charge against Wingfield was never proved, however, and he was eventually released.

Conditions in the colony worsened as the summer wore on. Beginning in August there were deaths every few days. On August 6, John Asbie died of "the bloody flux"; three days later George Flowre died of "the swelling." William Bruster died on August 10 from arrow wounds, as did Jeremy Alicock four days

[18] Abbot, *A Virginia Chronology, 1585–1783*, 3–4.

[19] An account of Waiman's espionage for Spain may be found in Alexander Brown, *The Genesis of the United States*, I, 113, which contains the text of a letter from Sir Dudley Carleton in London to John Chamberlain, dated August 18, 1607. The letter reads, in part: "One Captain Waiman a special favorite of Sir William Copes was taken this weeke in a port in Kent shipping himself for Spaine, with intent it is thought to have betraied his friends and shewed the Spaniards a meanes how to defeat the Virginia attempt."

later. On August 22 the *Discovery's* guns announced the death of Captain Bartholomew Gosnold.[20] By the end of summer, the colony's population had been reduced by half.

Percy recorded the distress of the colonists:

> There were never Englishmen left in a forreigne Countrey in such miserie as wee were in this new discovered Virginia. Wee watched every three nights lying on the bare cold ground . . . which brought our men to bee most feeble wretches, our food was but a small can of Barlie sod in water to five men a day, our drinke cold water taken out of the River, which was at floud verie Salt, at a low tide full of slime and filth, which was the destruction of many of our men. Thus we lived for the Space of five moneths in this miserable distresse, not having five able men to man . . . [our] Bulwarkes upon any occasion. If it had not pleased God to have put terror in the Savage hearts, we had all perished by those wild and cruell Pagans, being in weakened estate as we were.[21]

Because of her regular visits to Jamestown, Pocahontas was inevitably aware of the destitution of the colonists and of the decimation of their numbers from disease. It was at this time that she began her ministrations to them, repaying the kindness and attention shown to her by John Smith and others. In September she persuaded some of her people to bring half-ripe corn to the fort. She was unquestionably responsible for directing Smith to those Powhatans who were less unfriendly than others and might give some assistance to the colony. Her half-brother Pochins supplied Smith with maize and fish. The Quiyoughcohanocks gave him maize and wild game.

---

[20] Smith, *Generall Historie*, Book III, 43–44; Purchas, *Purchas His Pilgrimes*, IV, 1691. Captain Bartholomew Gosnold (or Gosnoll), who brought the *Godspeed* to the New World, was Newport's second-in-command. He remained in Jamestown to serve as a member of the council.

[21] Purchas, *Purchas His Pilgrimes*, IV, 1690.

Pocahontas

In his later writings, Smith referred to Pocahontas' efforts on behalf of the colonists in those difficult times and in subsequent years. Writing to Queen Anne in 1616, he declared that "[Pocahontas] was . . . the instrument to prusurve this colonie from death, famine, and utter confusion."[22]

[22] Smith, *Generall Historie*, Book IV, 122.

CHAPTER V

The Rescue

BESIDES BRINGING FOOD TO THE COLONISTS and directing John Smith to more or less hospitable areas within the Powhatan Confederacy, Pocahontas performed yet another important service for the colonists, the act for which she has been immortalized in history. Her rescue of John Smith from a ritualistic Powhatan execution kept alive the hope of Powhatan-English co-operation and served to strengthen the colonists' morale.

Early in December, 1607, Smith decided to venture into the Chickahominy River country to procure corn from the inhabitants, who were presumably more or less hospitable, and also to explore the Chickahominy to its headwaters in hopes of discovering a great lake that would open into the "Indian Sea," a discovery greatly desired by the English. With Smith on the expedition were seven other colonists, among them John Robinson, George Cassen, and Thomas Emry.

Leaving Jamestown around December 10 in a shallop, Smith's party traveled up the river to the present Windsor Shades, at which point the river narrows into a shallow stream. Smith decided to leave the shallop there, guarded by four members of the party, whom he cautioned not to wander into the woods and run the risk of encountering hostile Indians. Then Smith, Emry, and Robinson continued upstream in a small dugout canoe manned by two seemingly peaceful Powhatans whom the party had met after leaving Jamestown and who had agreed to guide Smith on a "fowling expedition."

Upon reaching Bottom Bridge, near the present Providence Forge, Smith and one of the Powhatan guides left the canoe and set out on foot to explore the nearby countryside, leaving Robinson, Emry, and the second guide to make camp. A quarter of an hour later, when he was in the vicinity of White Oak Swamp, Smith heard a savage yell. Seizing his guide and using him as a shield, Smith whipped out his pistol and held it against the guide's back, threatening to kill the Indian if anything happened to Robinson and Emry. At that moment, an arrow shot from a nearby thicket grazed Smith's thigh, and in the distance he saw two Indians with drawn bows pointed in his direction. Quickly Smith fired at the Indians, missing both. Reloading the pistol, a French wheel lock, he succeeded in killing three or four bowmen who sprang from the woods. Before he could escape, however, a much larger number of Powhatans appeared and surrounded him.

After closing in on Smith and his guide, the Powhatan bowmen threw down their weapons and waited for Smith to discard his own arms. However, having been instructed by His Majesty —as were all the colonists—never to abandon weapons in the presence of savages, Smith ignored the invitation. Using his limited Powhatan vocabulary, he was finally able to learn that George Cassen had wandered away from the shallop and had been killed after divulging Smith's whereabouts.[1] Robinson and Emry, surprised by the Indians while making camp, had also been killed, Emry's body having been pierced by more than twenty arrows.

Smith gathered that he, being a captain, was to be spared the fate of his fellow colonists. Yet he realized that there would be a final reckoning for him, too, and he decided to try to retreat to the shallop. Pistol in hand, he began backing away from his captors toward the campsite, but he had not gone far when he slipped off the edge of an embankment into an icy bog, taking the guide with him. There the two remained hopelessly caught until "being near dead with cold he [Smith] threw away his arms."[2]

The Indians pulled him and his guide from the bog and conducted them to the campsite. There, before the campfire kindled by Robinson and Emry, Smith's captors chafed his numbed legs until circulation was restored. Then, obeying his demands to be presented to their werowance, they brought him before one of Pocahontas' more warlike uncles, Opechancanough.[3]

[1] The aftermath of Cassen's capture was not pleasant. He was tied to a tree and brutally mutilated, his fingers, hands, and legs hacked off with the Powhatans' torture weapons, mussel shells and reeds rendered razor sharp by much honing on rock or flint. Thrown into a nearby fire, the members were yet burning when Cassen, still alive, was disemboweled, and his remains were burned with the tree.

[2] Smith, *Generall Historie*, Book III, 46.

[3] Smith and other colonists had given the title King of Pamunkey to Opechancanough, after encountering him at the Weanocs' village seven months earlier.

Smith, though weaponless, was not lacking in resourcefulness. He presented to Opechancanough an ivory compass he was carrying, hoping to divert the chief and gain his good will. The tactic proved to be a clever one, as Smith's account of the episode reveals:

> . . . Much they marvailed at the playing of the Fly and Needle, which they could see so plainly and yet not touch it, because of the glass that covered them. But when he [Smith] demonstrated by that Globelike jewell the roundness of the earth, and skies, the spheare of the sunne, moone, and starrs, and how the sun did chase the night round about the world continually; the greatness of the Land and Sea, the diversitie of nations, varietie of complexions, and how we were to them Antipodes, and many other such like matters, they all stood as amazed with admiration. Not withstanding, within an hour after they tyed him to a tree, and as many as could stand about him prepared to shoot him, but the King holding up the compass in his hand, they all laid down their bows and arrows, and in a triumphant manner led him to Orapaks.[4]

Smith described the six-mile march to Orapaks, a Powhatan hunting preserve: ". . . drawing themselves all in fyle, the King in the midst had all their Peeces and Swords bore before him. Captain Smith was led after him by three great Savages holding him fast by each arme: and on each side six went in fyle with their Arrows nocked."[5]

Arriving at Orapaks, situated between the upper Chickahominy and Pamunkey rivers, Smith saw thirty or forty temporary shelters[6] from which streamed a large number of women and

---

[4] Smith, *Generall Historie*, Book III, 47.

[5] *Ibid.*

[6] The women of the tribe made the temporary hunting shelters by bending saplings into the shapes of beehives and covering the frameworks with removable mats. At the end of a hunt they dismantled and rolled up the shelters and carried them on their backs to another location.

children to stare at him as he was led to Powhatan's lodge, Rasa-wrack, about a mile from Orapaks. There Smith was encircled by Opechancanough's screeching warriors, who danced about him three times[7] and then led him into the lodge, which was some "fiftie or sixtie yards in length." There he was kept under guard by forty or fifty "tall fellows." Later his guards brought him venison and bread, which he could not eat, his stomach being at that time "not very good." The food that he could not eat "they put in baskets and tied over his head. About midnight they set the meate again before him, all this time not one of them would eat a bit with him, till the next morning they brought him as much more."[8]

While Smith was imprisoned in the lodge, the father of a young Powhatan whom Smith had wounded earlier in the day tried to kill him but was stopped by one of the guards. Smith was taken to see the dying youth, and, aware of the Powhatans' superstitions and their belief in wizardry, he promised to restore the youth's health if his captors would let him go to Jamestown for a vial of curative water. The Powhatans refused his offer and instead made one of their own. They offered Smith "life, liberty, land, and women"[9] if he would betray his fellow colonists by advising the Powhatans on how best to make an attack on the Jamestown fort. Smith, of course, refused the offer.

[7] The dance, composed of frenzied gyrations, was already familiar to Smith, who had seen similar dancing outside the Jamestown fort. He described the dancers thus: "Everyone his quiver of Arrows, and at his backe a club; on his arme a Fox or an Otter's skin, or some such matter for his vambrace; their heads and shoulders painted red . . . made an exceeding handsome show . . . with Bow in his hand, and with the skinne of [a] Bird with her wings abroad dried, tyed on his head, a peece of copper, a white shell, a long feather, with a small rattle growing at the tayles of their snakes tyed to it, or some such toy." (*Generall Historie*, Book III, 47.)

[8] *Ibid.*

[9] *Ibid.*

Finally, after several days had passed,[10] the Powhatans decided to exhibit Smith to the inhabitants of the region that, in 1604, had been visited by the white man who on his kidnapping expedition had killed the werowance of Rappahannock. The Powhatans were eager to know whether Smith was the same person.

Around December 18 he was taken from Orapaks and conducted by water and over land to Menapucunt (Menapacant),[11] and then to other towns and villages of the Pamunkeys. Then he was exhibited among the Youghtanunds, a tribe living in what is today King William County. He was also taken to the region of the Piankatanks, on the north side of the Piankatank River in Middlesex County. And he was taken to Rappahannock, on the north side of the Rappahannock River in Richmond County.

It was at Rappahannock that Smith's "exhibition" took its most serious turn. He sensed that his life depended on whether or not the Rappahannock tribe identified him as the slayer of their werowance. Fortunately, Smith was a short man, and the

[10] During this confinement Smith made claim to another kind of wizardry: "In part of a Table booke he [Smith] writ his minde to them at the Fort what was intended . . . and without fayle send him such things as he writ for." Inducing the Indians to deliver the note, he told them about the great guns and machines that they would encounter upon their arrival at the Fort. "Yet they went to Jamestown in as bitter weather as could be of frost and snow, and within three days returned with an answer." (*Ibid.*) To Smith's captors the answer was proof that the note he had written could speak, and they were convinced that he possessed occult powers akin to those of their own priests.

[11] The Pamunkey tribe, the largest single tribe in the Powhatan Confederacy, occupied the land around the junction of the Mattaponi and Pamunkey rivers, in present King William County. The Pamunkeys were ruled by Pocahontas' three uncles, Opechancanough, Kecatough, and Opitchapan. Called the "triumvirate" by the English, the three werowances ruled with powers second only to Powhatan's and were in turn to succeed Powhatan as rulers of the confederacy. Opechancanough's residence, Menapucunt (or Menapacant), was above the present West Point. Kecatough's residence was at nearby Cinquoteck, at West Point. Opitchapan's province was further upstream on the Mattaponi and upper Pamunkey rivers.

Rappahannocks remembered that the slayer had been much taller. Smith was exonerated of the 1604 crime.

However, the Powhatans were not yet ready to free him. They kept him prisoner in hope that he would provide information about Jamestown and its form. The final decision about his fate was apparently to rest with the great Chief Powhatan himself at Werowocomoco. Returned to Menapucunt about December 25, Smith was hurried off to Uttamussack to be interrogated in one of Powhatan's royal residences.

About December 29, after being thoroughly prepared by Powhatan's head priest in an elaborate ritual[12] designed to ascertain whether or not he "intended them well," Smith was taken to Werowocomoco, by dugout canoe in bitter, damp winter weather. Upon his arrival he was greeted by two hundred grim "Courtiers," staring at him "as [though] he had been a monster."[13] He was brought before the great Powhatan as the chief

[12] According to Smith, his guards seated him on a mat before a fire in the house temple and left, whereupon there "came skipping in a great grim fellow, all painted over with coale mingled with oyle; and many Snakes and Weasel's skins stuffed with moss, and all their tayles tied together, so as they met on the crowne of his head in a tassel; and round about the tassel was a Coronet of feathers." Powhatan's head priest then danced around the fire, uttering strange invocations, to the accompaniment of a rattle. Next he sprinkled corn meal around the fire after which he was joined by "three more such like devils," who sang and danced and then were joined by three more dancers, all of whom "with their rattles began a song, which ended, the chief priest layd down five wheat cornes: then strayning his arms with such violence that he sweat and his veins swelled, he began a short Oration,: at the conclusion they all gave a short groan; and then layd down three grains more. After that they began their song again, and then another Oration, laying doune so many cornes as before, till they had twice incirculed the fire; that done, they took a bunch of little sticks prepared for that purpose. . . . and at the end of every song and Oration they laid down a stick between the divisions of the corn." The ritual, Smith learned, was highly symbolic. "The circle of meal signified their country, the circles of corn the bounds of the sea, and the sticks his [Smith's] country. They imagined the world to be round, like a trencher, and they in the midst." (*Generall Historie*, Book III, 48.)

[13] *Ibid.*, 49.

sat majestically before a fire inside his dwelling "upon a seat like a bedstead, . . . covered with a great robe, made of rarowcun [raccoon] skins, and all the tayles hanging by."[14] The chief was surrounded by a large number of Powhatans. Seated on either side of him was a young woman "of 16 or 18 years, and along on each side [of the room] two rows of men, and behind them as many women, with all their heads bedecked with the white down of birds."[15]

Smith was the first of the Jamestown colonists to lay eyes on Pocahontas' father and the first to penetrate, albeit unwillingly, into the very heart of Powhatan society and culture. As for the Powhatans, Smith was the first of the Jamestown settlers to enter their midst. Upon Smith's entrance into the royal presence, a shout went up among the people, and Queen Oppussoquionuske, the werowance of Apamatuks and Pocahontas' aunt, brought Smith water in which to wash his hands, after which he was brought "a bunch of feathers instead of towel to dry them."[16] Then followed a great feast—venison, bread made from maize, a stew made with corn, and wild turkey poults—in preparation for the disposition of Smith that was to follow. For it was clear that Smith was to be put to death.

When the feast ended, Powhatan and his advisers held a lengthy parley, after which "two great stones were brought before Powhatan: then as many as could laid hands on him [Smith], dragged him to [the stones] and thereon laid his head." The execution was to be the evening's entertainment—and was to rid Chief Powhatan not merely of a white man but of an especially clever and industrious white man who had had the audacity to venture deep into Powhatan territory and to ask the

14 *Ibid.*
15 *Ibid.*
16 *Ibid.*

Powhatans to aid the English, the people Chief Powhatan most despised and feared.

But the father had not reckoned on his compassionate daughter. As the Powhatan warriors were about to fall on Smith with their clubs, the young princess, doubtless out of gratitude to Smith for his kindness to her, stepped from the crowd of Powhatans who had come to witness the execution. Quickly she took Smith's "head in her armes and laid her owne upon his to save him from death."[17]

Powhatan responded to the impulsive action of his favorite daughter and ordered Smith spared. The captive was brought "to a great house in the woods," where he was seated on a mat before a fire and left alone for a time. But "not long after from behind a mat that divided the house, was made the dolefulest noise he ever heard; then Powhatan more like a devil than a man with some two hundred more as black as himself, came unto him [Smith] and told him now they were friends and presently he should go to Jamestown to send him two great guns and a grind-stone for which he would give him the country of Capahowosick [Capahowasic] and forever esteem him as his son Nantaquoud!"[18]

Obviously Chief Powhatan had discovered an advantage to himself in sparing Smith's life and bringing him into the Powhatan fold. Powhatan's announcement of the "adoption" coupled with the request for guns was a transparent piece of political

---

[17] *Ibid.* Strangely enough, Smith did not immediately publicize the story of his rescue by Pocahontas. His failure to include this dramatic episode in his first published accounts of his capture and imprisonment by the Powhatans has never been explained. Smith's English publishers, fearful that his story of near death might discourage other colonists from going to Virginia, may have deleted the event from Smith's narrative. Or Smith himself omitted the story. The account of his rescue was not published until 1624, when it appeared in the *Generall Historie*, Book III, 46–49.

[18] *Ibid.*

strategy. Smith agreed to the proposal, and the adoption ceremony took place two days later at Werowocomoco, after which
Smith was sent on his way back to Jamestown, accompanied by
twelve Powhatan guides.[19]

Smith and his escort arrived at Jamestown early on the morning of January 2, 1608. Smith, again relying on his store of wit
and ingenuity to satisfy Powhatan's demand for weapons, offered to give Rawhunt, Powhatan's chief representative, two
demiculverins and a millstone to take back to Powhatan. Each
of the demiculverins weighed between 3,000 and 4,500 pounds,
and, of course, Rawhunt and his companions could not move
them. Then Smith demonstrated the power of the demiculverins:
"When they did see him discharge them, being loaded with
stones, among the boughs of a great tree loaded with icicles, the
ice and branches came so tumbling down that the poor savages
ran away half dead with fear. But at last we regained some conference with them and gave them such toys: and sent Powhatan,
his women, and children such presents as gave them in general
full content."[20]

So ended Smith's capture, trial, rescue, and adoption—a series
of events that marked the beginning of an even closer relationship between Pocahontas and the English settlers. According to
Powhatan custom, Pocahontas was now Smith's guardian. Like
any other captive turned over to the custody of a female, Smith
had become her special ward or possession. As a result, Pocahontas would play an even greater role in maintaining communication with the colonists in general and with Smith in
particular, and in achieving liaison between her father, who had
not yet abandoned his intention to rid himself of the English,
and the colonists, who were equally determined to remain in the
New World. Pocahontas was to remain a ministrant to the col-

[19] *Ibid.*
[20] *Ibid.*

ony, but now her activities would be expanded. She was to become much more openly a negotiator recognized by both sides, each using her talents and energies to bargain with the other.

CHAPTER VI

Negotiations

ON THE EVENING OF Saturday, January 2, 1608—the same day Smith returned to Jamestown—the *Susan Constant*, under the command of Captain Newport, dropped anchor at the James-town waterfront.[1] Earlier in the day Pocahontas and her retinue of attendants had brought provisions to Jamestown, and she may well have been on hand to watch the debarkation of nearly one hundred new colonists, as well as the unloading of long-awaited supplies and provisions for the Jamestown survivors, whose

[1] Abbot, *A Virginia Chronology, 1585–1783,* 4.

74

number had dwindled to scarcely more than thirty. Among the supplies Newport had brought were trade goods for the Indians.

Pocahontas may also have witnessed Newport's immediate intervention in a crisis that had arisen during the day between Smith on the one hand and John Ratcliffe (the new president of the council), Gabriel Archer, and Captain John Martin on the other. Ratcliffe, Archer, and Martin had seriously questioned Smith's story about his sojourn among the Powhatans[2] and had accused him of being responsible for the deaths of Emry and Robinson. His accusers had arranged a hasty trial. Archer, the prosecutor, who had studied law at Gray's Inn, based his case on the Levitical law. Ratcliffe, the civil authority of the colony, pronounced Smith guilty and condemned him to death by hanging. The noose had actually been placed around Smith's neck when Newport's booming cannon salute from the waterfront stayed the execution. After Newport came ashore and learned of the situation, he persuaded the council members to let Smith go free, reminding them of the services Smith had performed for the colony.

Upon seeing the arrival of the new colonists, Pocahontas must have been aware of the inevitable difficulties they would face because of her father's enmity. At Werowocomoco, Smith had implied that the colonists would soon depart from Powhatan shores. A question Powhatan had repeatedly asked Smith was why the English had settled at Jamestown in the first place. Smith's temporizing answer was that they had merely sought refuge at Jamestown because they were being pursued by the Spaniards and that the colonists would depart when Newport came back. Then Powhatan would ask why the English did not leave on their pinnace, to which Smith would reply that the *Discovery* leaked and could not be used by the colonists until it was repaired. Powhatan had naturally concluded that the English

[2] *Ibid.*

would depart as soon as some means of transportation presented itself. Now the *Susan Constant* had arrived with more colonists and fresh provisions.

The arrival of the new colonists undoubtedy boded further trouble with the Powhatans, and an event that occurred a week later placed the colonists in an even more precarious position. On January 7 a fire broke out at Jamestown, destroying a good part of the fort, the colonists' thatched huts and their crude little church—along with Mr. Hunt's cherished theological library—and, most disastrously, the roof of the storehouse and most of the food supplies that Newport had just brought from England. Once again the English were in the difficult position of needing help from Indians who had expected to witness their departure.

Pocahontas responded to the situation: "Now ever[y] once in four or five days Pocahontas and her attendants brought . . . so much provision that saved many of their lives."[3] Pocahontas presented the provisions not only to Smith but also to Captain Newport, for in his conversations with Powhatan, Smith had referred to the captain as "Father Newport" to indicate his important position. Acting now not simply as a friend of the colonists but also as a representative of her father, Pocahontas included Newport in her special attention, realizing that, since he had been influential in saving Smith from hanging, the Powhatans might profitably negotiate with him.

As far as the Powhatans were concerned, their primary interest in negotiation lay in bartering advantageously to acquire as many English goods as possible. Such negotiation was indicative of a change in the Indians' policy. Chief Powhatan had decided that the most effective means of eliminating the English was to acquire the materials and weapons that the English used. By his orders the colonists' near neighbors, the Quiyoughcohanocks, Paspaheghs, Weanocs, and Chickahominies, no longer attacked

[3] Smith, *Generall Historie*, Book III, 49.

every colonist they encountered outside the fort; instead they began visiting the colony, bartering for trade goods—and bartering with greater expertise than heretofore. To Smith's disgust, Newport's mariners traded the Indians one pound of copper for Indian produce that before Newport's arrival in January could have been bought for one ounce of the metal.

Most significantly, Chief Powhatan sent word by Pocahontas that he would like "Father Newport" to visit him at Werowocomoco. Late in February, after the rebuilding of the fire-damaged fort and repairs to the palisades enclosing it, Smith and Newport, with a bodyguard of thirty or forty colonists, journeyed to Werowocomoco, sailing the *Discovery* down the James River to Kecoughtan, rounding the tip of the peninsula, and, directed by their compasses, sailing twenty miles or more up the Pamunkey River to Poetan Bay.[4]

Though Chief Powhatan had asked specifically to see Newport, as the chief's adopted son, Smith took charge of the visit. He left Newport in the pinnace with a bodyguard, while he and eighteen other colonists went ashore in small boats to prepare for the meeting. Pocahontas had already informed Powhatan of the impending visit, and an escort of some two hundred warriors met Smith when he landed at Poetan Bay, conducting him and the other colonists over a series of primitive bridges to Powhatan's lodge at Werowocomoco. At the lodge Smith noted that "more than fortie platters of fine bread stood . . . in two files on each side of the doore. Four or five hundred people made a guard behind them for our passage: and Proclamation was made, none upon pain of death to presume to doe us any wrong of discourtesie."[5]

Chief Powhatan received his visitors in full ceremonial dress

[4] Smith made mental notes of the water route to Werowocomoco so that he could reproduce it accurately on the map he planned to make of the Powhatan country.

[5] Smith, *Generall Historie*, Book III, 51.

and "strained himselfe to the utmost of his greatnesse to entertaine them with great shouts of joy, Orations of protestation; and with the most plenty of victualls he could provide."[6] Smith, in turn, presented to Powhatan "a suit of red woolen cloth, a white greyhound, and a sugar loaf hat such as King James himself wore."[7] The white greyhound was a special novelty for Powhatan, and all the gifts were appropriately acknowledged, though not by the great Powhatan himself but by three minor werowances. With many gestures, grimaces, and flowery orations the chiefs assured Smith of Powhatan's friendship and of his willingness to provide the colonists with corn until they could harvest their crops.

Then Powhatan himself entered the conversation, asking Smith about the cannon and the grindstone that had been promised earlier. Smith explained that he had offered Rawhunt and the other Powhatans four demiculverins but that they had refused them. Powhatan laughed, acknowledging that the demiculverins had been too heavy to transport and added that he would be willing to accept a smaller cannon.

Next Powhatan asked Smith and the other Englishmen to put aside their guns and other arms while they were in his house. He pointed out that the walls of the house were hung with the Powhatan bows, arrows, and other war weapons. Why should the English not also lay down their arms in Powhatan's presence? Smith replied that laying down their arms "was a ceremony our enemies desired, never our friends."[8] Quickly changing the subject, Smith assured Powhatan that the colonists and their guns would be ready to serve Powhatan in any future wars he might wage against his Siouan enemies the Monacans and the Manahoacs.

6 *Ibid.*, 51–52.
7 Barbour, *The Three Worlds of Captain John Smith,* 178.
8 *Ibid.*, 179.

Smith and the eighteen men who had accompanied him spent the night in Powhatan's lodge. The next day Captain Newport came ashore and was duly presented to Chief Powhatan. As a gesture of good will, Newport had brought along a young English boy named Thomas Savage,[9] whom he proposed to "loan" to the Powhatans so that the boy might learn their language and eventually act as an interpreter between the two peoples. Powhatan was impressed by this act and insisted that Newport accept in exchange a young Powhatan boy named Namontack, who could in turn learn the colonists' language—and could even go back to England with Newport when next he sailed. After the exchange of "sons," Powhatan climaxed the ceremony by bestowing upon each of his visitors a large basket filled to overflowing with dried beans.

Newport invited Chief Powhatan to come aboard the *Discovery* and examine the trade goods that he had brought along to barter, but Powhatan made it clear that he had no intention of boarding the pinnace; the trade goods would have to be brought ashore. "It is not agreeable to my greatness," Powhatan said haughtily, "in this trifling manner to trade for trifles; and I esteeme you also a great werowance. Therefore lay me downe all your commodities together; what I like I will take, and in recompense give you what I think fitting their value."[10]

The store of copper kettles, hatchets, knives, scissors, and blue glass beads were brought from the pinnace and spread before Powhatan in his long house, whereupon Powhatan estimated their value in corn and other provisions in Powhatan's storehouse.

To Smith's dismay, Newport agreed to exchange twelve great copper kettles for the same amount of corn that Powhatan had

[9] Powhatan was confused about Thomas Savage's name and called the boy Thomas Newport.

[10] Smith, *Generall Historie*, Book III, 52.

earlier bartered to Smith for one small kettle. To compensate for Powhatan's inflated valuation of the corn, Smith began extolling the virtues of the glass beads, telling Powhatan that blue beads were very rare, being the color of the sky, and that they were not to be worn by any but the greatest kings. According to Anas Todkill, a member of the party, Smith was so convincing in his praise of the beads that Powhatan was "halfe madde to be the owner of such strange Jewells; so ere we departed, for a pound or two of blue beads Powhatan paid Newport and Smith two or three hundred bushels of corn, Yet parted good friends."[11]

After his visit with Powhatan, Newport felt that he had ingratiated himself quite satisfactorily with the Indians and was inclined to pursue a more liberal policy toward them. Later, when Powhatan sent twenty turkeys to the colonists, Newport complied with Powhatan's request for twenty English swords in return. On April 20, 1608, feeling confident that relations between the Powhatans and the colonists were cordial, Newport sailed for England in the *Susan Constant*.[12]

For his part, Smith had been dismayed by Newport's liberality with the Powhatans. Now once again the colony's chief representative to the Indians, he decided to return to a harder line. When Powhatan sent another twenty turkeys and demanded again an equal number of swords, Smith refused to make the exchange. Then Powhatan undertook to procure the swords by

[11] *Ibid.* After leaving Powhatan, Smith and Newport also visited Opechancanough and the other brothers. On those occasions Smith also bartered the blue glass beads. "None durst wear them," Smith told Opechancanough, "but their great kings, their wives, and children." So impressed was Opechancanough that he, too, paid extravagantly in corn for the beads.

[12] Wingfield, the deposed president of the local council at Jamestown, sailed with Newport. In reporting on activities in the Jamestown colony, Wingfield failed to mention the part that Smith had played in the procurement of provisions from the Indians, probably because it had been Smith, together with Ratcliffe, Martin, and Archer, who had brought about Wingfield's removal from office and his subsequent imprisonment on the *Discovery*.

stealth. "He caused his people with twentie devices to obtaine them," Anas Todkill later reported. "At last by ambuscadoes at our very ports . . . Powhatan's warriors would take them perforce, surprise us at worke or anyway."[13] These acts infuriated Smith, who "without further deliberation gave them such an encounter that this thievery of swords came to an end."[14]

Suppression of the thievery brought on new difficulties with the Indians. "Some he [Smith] so terrified with whipping, beating, and imprisonment" that the Indians sought revenge and threatened the fort gates in an effort to force Smith to give up seven Powhatan prisoners he had captured. If the prisoners were not released, the Powhatans warned the colonists "were all but dead men."[15] Smith refused to give up the prisoners and ordered "several vollies of shot" fired inside the fort to make the Indians think one of the captives had been executed.

The Indians retreated, but for a time barter ceased, and now that Newport had left, Powhatan's plan to acquire English weapons was being foiled. It was clear that new negotiations must be arranged. Once again Pocahontas was called upon to mediate between Smith and her father—two equally temperamental, clever, and stubborn men.

Early in May, 1608, Pocahontas came to Jamestown as her father's emissary, bringing presents for the colonists, whose number had once again been augmented by the arrival of forty new colonists in the *Phoenix*, under the command of Captain Francis Nelson. Pocahontas had come to negotiate the release of the seven Indians imprisoned in the fort. She begged Smith to "excuse him [Powhatan] of the injuries done by some rash and untoward captaines [warriors], desiring their liberties this time, with the assurance of his love."[16] Smith pondered the matter and

[13] Smith, *Generall Historie*, Book III, 54.
[14] *Ibid.*   [15] *Ibid.*
[16] *Ibid.*

then "corrected" the prisoners and released them to Pocahontas, "for whose sake onely," reported Todkill, "he fayned to have saved their lives."[17]

Pocahontas' intervention restored peace, at least for the time being, and brought to the Jamestown colonists the first really calm days they had had since their arrival twelve months before. Food was plentiful, the fort was in good condition, and new colonists had arrived. The Englishmen could venture outside the palisades with less fear of being attacked. Harsh winter weather had given way to spring. The colonists were busy planting gardens, fishing, and searching for gold and other precious metals in the Virginia soil.[18]

Spring and summer passed. Pocahontas continued her ambassadorial work, bearing messages and bringing provisions to Jamestown. In the autumn Pocahontas, now eleven or twelve years old, at an age when Powhatan girls were "shamefacd to be seene bare,"[19] began to appear dressed in a short, apron-like skirt of buckskin fringed at the lower edge, modestly folding her arms across her breasts when she was in the presence of strangers, and frequently repeating, as did the Indian girls who accompanied her, the English phrase she had learned: "Love

[17] *Ibid.*

[18] From the time of their arrival in Jamestown the colonists had had great hopes of finding gold. Smith felt that too much attention was given to searching for the "gilded durt." Others, such as Captain John Martin, the son of a London goldsmith, was much more enthusiastic about the possibility, and under his direction the hold of the *Phoenix* was loaded with dirt—rather than cedar, as Smith wished—to be taken to London for assay. Martin's departure for London did not displease Smith or Todkill, who commented, "Captain Martin being always very sickly and unserviceable, and desirous to injoy the credit of his supposed act of finding the golden mine, was most willingly admitted to return for England." (*Ibid.*)

[19] Strachey, *Historie*, Cap. V, 65.

you not me? Love you not me?"[20] Pocahontas was coming of age, and although she had already played an important part in Jamestown's settlement, she was soon to play an even more complex and difficult role.

[20] Smith, *Generall Historie*, Book III, 67.

CHAPTER VII

Powhatan's Coronation

IN THE AUTUMN OF 1608, Pocahontas must have felt that her conciliatory efforts had borne fruit. On September 8, John Smith, her friend and adopted brother, was elected president of the Jamestown council, and a month or so later the colonists staged an event especially designed to please her father. The cordiality was not to endure, but for a span of a few short months in the fall of the year, Pocahontas had reason to be optimistic.

Upon his election Smith made a vigorous effort to ensure the colony's continued progress and to correct some of the weaknesses of previous administrations. He was especially eager for increased colonization in the Jamestown area. In a series of expeditions during the summer of 1608 through the Chesapeake Bay area,[1] he had found evidence of French "infiltration" as close as the Susquehanna River. There the hospitable seven-foot-tall Susquehannock Indians had shown Smith metal hatchets given to them by Frenchmen from settlements in Canada.[2] Smith was convinced that it was now a matter of urgency for England to establish a truly permanent foothold in the New World, not only to provide wealth for the mother country and relieve the overpopulation at home but also to serve as a symbol of territorial expansion that would impress rival European powers.

With this goal in mind Smith took stock of what needed to be done and put all hands to work:

The Church was repaired;[3] the Store-house was recovered; buildings prepared for the Supplies we expected; the Fort reduced to five-square forme; the order of the Watch renewed; the squadrons (each setting of the Watch) trained; the whole Company every Saturday exercised, in the plaine by the West Bulwarke, prepared for that purpose . . . where sometimes more than a hundred Salvages

[1] Shortly after Newport's departure for England in April, 1608, Smith and fourteen other colonists set off again to search for the "Indian Sea." On June 16 they entered the Potomac River and traveled upriver to a point beyond present-day Washington, D.C. En route back to Jamestown, at the mouth of the Rappahannock River Smith was attacked by a sting ray while spear fishing and severely wounded in one arm. The injury was treated by Dr. Walter Russell, and the colonists named the site of the accident Stingray Point, the name it still bears today. (Abbot, *A Virginia Chronology, 1585–1783*, 4.)

[2] Smith, *Generall Historie*, Book III, 67.

[3] The church had fallen into disuse after Mr. Hunt's death in July. After it was repaired, Smith described it thus: "[It] was a homely thing like a barne set upon Crachets, covered with rafts, sedge, and earth, so was also the walls: the best of our houses of the like curiosity. . . . Yet wee had daily Common Prayer . . . and surely God did most mercifully heare us." (*Advertisements*, 32.)

would stand in amazement to behold, how a file would batter a tree, whereby he [Smith] would make them a mark to shoot at.[4]

On October 8 Captain Newport arrived at Jamestown on the *Mary and Margaret*, bringing seventy new colonists—including the colony's first women, a Mrs. Forest and her maid, Anne Burras. Smith was pleased by the arrivals, but he well knew that additional colonists would make more difficult his task of maintaining peaceful relations with Chief Powhatan. This problem had been anticipated by the Virginia Company, and the method of handling it was not left to Smith's discretion. Upon landing at Jamestown, Newport handed Smith an official packet of orders composed by Virginia Company officers and also by King James.

Though the orders pertained to several matters,[5] the most important one was designed to win over Chief Powhatan to accept the new colonists. Smith and Newport were to arrange to crown Powhatan as king of the Powhatan nation in an elaborate and colorful ceremony at Jamestown. The coronation was to impress Chief Powhatan so deeply that he would approve of the colonists ever after.[6] Reading these instructions, Smith bluntly declared that the august members of the Virginia Company were "fools" and that King James was no better. The whole idea "was gro-

[4] The Powhatan marksmen could hit Smith's metal target, of course, but an arrow shaft would break into splinters and the point would fall to the ground. When the colonists fired their guns at the target, their shot penetrated the metal, thereby proving to the Powhatans the superiority of the colonists' guns—a point Smith wanted to drive home, for the Powhatans' fear of the colonists' weapons was an important part of his program for dealing with the Indians. (Smith, *Generall Historie*, Book III, 66.)

[5] Smith and Newport were directed to make further efforts to find the survivors of the Roanoke colony; to see that the "Poles" and "Dutch-men" sent to Jamestown with Newport began making pitch, tar, glass, and "soape ashes"; to explore the Monacan country above the falls near Richmond; and to continue searching for gold and other minerals. (Smith, *Generall Historie*, Book III, 66–67.)

[6] *Ibid.*

tesque enough to have emanated from the teeming brain of James I after a nickle noggin of his native usequebaugh."[7]

Yet the order must be obeyed. For the ceremony Newport had brought from England "a scarlet cloke and apparell, a bason, ewer, bed, and furniture." The ewer, basin, and bed were presents from King James. To furnish the bed there were curtains, canopy, and coverlets made of rich damask lined with buckram —typical furnishings for the beds of English royalty.

While Newport went off to explore the Monacan country in accordance with Virginia Company orders, Smith reluctantly set out for Werowocomoco to arrange for Powhatan's visit to Jamestown. On the fifteen-mile journey he was accompanied by Andrew Buckler, Captain Richard Waldo, Samuel Collier, Edward Brinton, and the Indian ward Namontack, who had returned to Jamestown with Newport. Upon his arrival at Powhatan's lodge Smith was told that the chief was about thirty miles away. A runner was sent to inform Powhatan about his visitors.

Meanwhile, Pocahontas, who had remained at Werowocomoco, provided entertainment for Smith and his companions. The entertainment, which Smith later called "A Virginia Mask," was apparently both pleasurable and shocking. He and his companions were conducted by Pocahontas and her attendants to "a fayre plaine field" and seated on mats before a fire, around which were gathered a goodly number of Powhatan men, women, and children. Suddenly "amongst the woods was heard such a hydeous noise and shreeking, that the English betooke themselves to their armes and seized on two or three old men by them, supposing Powhatan with all his power was come to surprise them."[8]

But the Englishmen's fears were soon allayed by Pocahontas, who, with one hand over her heart and the other raised skyward,

[7] John Fiske, *Old Virginia and Her Neighbors*, I, 133.
[8] Smith, *Generall Historie*, Book III, 67.

willed Smith "to kill her if any hurt was intended." The Powhatans seated near him also assured him that he had nothing to fear.

Then the colonists were diverted by a brief drama:

> . . . thirtie young women came naked out of the woods, onely covered behind and before with a few greene leaves, their bodies all painted, some of one colour, some of another, but all differing, their leader had a fayre payre of Bucks hornes on her head, and an Otter's skinne at her girtle, and another at her arme, a quiver of arrowes at her backe, a bow and arrowes in her hand; the next had in her hand a Sword, another a club, another a pot-sticke; all horned alike: the rest everyone with their severall devises. These fiends with most hellish shouts and cryes, rushing from among the trees cast themselves in a ring around the fire, singing and dauncing with most excellent ill varietie, of falling into their infernal passions, and solemnly againe to sing and daunce; having spent neare an houre in this mascarado, as they entered in like manner they departed.
>
> Having reaccomodated themselves, they solemnly invited him [Smith] to their lodgings, where he was no sooner within the house, but all these Nymphes more tormented him then ever, with crowding, pressing, and hanging about him, most tediously crying, Love you not me? Love you not me?
>
> This salutation ending, the feast was set, consisting of all the Salvage dainties they could devise: some attending, others singing and dauncing about him . . . this . . . being ended, with firebrands instead of Torches, they conducted him to his lodging.[9]

Pocahontas' entertainment, though evidently embarrassing to the Englishmen, was a genuine gesture of good will. Just as Pocahontas had shared provisions with the English, now she shared with them a ritualistic celebration that expressed in its unique way both the passion and the dignity of life. Pocahontas,

[9] *Ibid.*

the girl becoming woman, drew from the cultural storehouse of her people a display of their capacity for self-expression.

The next day Powhatan returned to Werowocomoco, and Smith relayed the news of the forthcoming coronation. Using both Thomas Savage and Namontack as interpreters, Smith described the ceremony to the chief and invited him to come to Jamestown for the event. However, Powhatan was well aware of his royal prerogatives. He replied that "if your King have sent me presents, I also am a King and this is my land: Eight dayes will I stay to receive them. Your Father [Newport] is to come to me, not I to him, nor yet to your Fort, neither will I bite at such a bait. . . ."[10] Even when Pocahontas added her pleas to Smith's, Powhatan stubbornly refused to go to Jamestown. All Smith could do was return to the settlement and make arrangements with Newport to hold the ceremony at Werowocomoco.

A few days later Newport, Smith, other members of the council and "fiftie good shot" set out overland on the journey to Werowocomoco. They had dispatched Powhatan's copper crown, the bed, and other presents from King James by boat. When the boat reached Werowocomoco after a circuitous eighty-mile voyage, the presents were brought ashore. With much ado the canopy bed was set up in Powhatan's long house. Then the chief was persuaded to don the fine scarlet cloak. Newport wore full-dress sea captain's regalia. Smith and the other council members wore their Sabbath best.

Powhatan was then instructed to bend his knee and incline his head to receive the copper crown, but at this request Powhatan balked; never in his life had he bent knee or head to anyone. Offshore, the boat's gunners awaited a signal from Newport to fire the cannons at the close of the coronation ceremony. Powhatan's refusal to bend and bow delayed the signal, and, try as they would, none of the English could overcome Powhatan's

[10] *Ibid.*, 68.

resistance. Demonstrations, persuasion, and explanations were in vain. Finally, in desperation, someone came up behind Powhatan and pressed so hard on his shoulders that he was compelled to stoop whether he willed it or not, and quickly the crown was popped on his head. Newport fired a pistol to announce to the world that Powhatan was now "king." And the gunners on the boat fired the cannons.

Terrified by the salvos, Powhatan leaped into the air "in horrible fear" that the colonists' king was attacking Werowocomoco with a fleet of ships. But after being assured by Namontack that his fears were groundless, he recovered his dignity and presented to Newport his own buckskin mantle and moccasins, to be taken to the English king.[11]

When the colonists returned to Jamestown, Smith registered his protest against the proceedings in a rude letter addressed to King James and the "Royal Council of Virginia sitting in London":

RIGHT HONOURABLE LORDS AND GENTLEMEN
. . . Expressly to follow your directions [sent] by Captain Newport, though they be performed, I was directly against it . . . . I feare to the hazard of us all; which now is generally confessed when it is too late. . . . I have . . . crowned Powhatan according to your instructions. . . .

For the Coronation of Powhatan by whose advice you sent him such presents, I know not; but this give me leave to tell you, I feare they will be the confusion of us all ere we heare from you againe.[12]

Smith's fears were reasonable ones. Knowing that the colonists

---

[11] Powhatan's buckskin mantle is on exhibit at the Ashmolean Museum, Oxford University. The mantle is large enough to fit a broad-shouldered man six feet tall or taller. The great number of shells sewed into patterns on the mantle are indicative of Powhatan's enormous wealth at the time of his coronation.

[12] Smith, *Generall Historie*, Book III, 70–72.

were not yet self-sufficient (the storehouses could be filled with grain one month and empty the next) and were therefore dependent upon the Powhatans for much of their food, he felt that by being too generous the English would simply be placing the Indians in a stronger position to hinder the colony's development. Smith's attitude was much more aggressive; he believed in impressing upon the Indian the power and might of the English. In his view, displays of firepower were more effective than gifts of scarlet cloaks and copper crowns.

Unfortunately, Smith's fears proved well founded. The newly crowned king of the Powhatan Confederacy grew increasingly difficult. His coronation did not so much placate him as elevate him to a new position of power and self-confidence. As the English catered to him, Powhatan's generosity diminished. The price of Powhatan corn went up. Even more ominously, late in 1608, Powhatan forbade Pocahontas—the one really effective link between the Indians and the English—to communicate further with the Jamestown colonists, on penalty of death.[13]

[13] *Ibid.*, Book IV, 77.

CHAPTER VIII

The Contest Quickens

ALTHOUGH COMMANDED BY POWHATAN to sever her relations with the colonists, Pocahontas remained sympathetic to them, helping them in countless ways whenever she encountered them in Powhatan territory. Though her task grew considerably more difficult as the struggle between her father and the colonists moved toward its climax and she no longer openly aided the colonists or served as emissary, nevertheless, on at least two occasions in 1609 she intervened to save English lives.

Newport departed for England in December, 1608, leaving

Smith the task of dealing with the aggrandized Powhatan. Once again it was a difficult time for the colonists, with food shortages their most serious problem. Smith had sent word with Newport that the colony's harvest was not "halfe sufficient for so great a number. As for the . . . Corne Newport promised to provide us from Powhatan, he brought us but fourteene Bushels; and from the Monacans nothing. . . . From your Shipe we had not provision in victuals worth twenty pound, and we are more than two hundred to live upon this: the one halfe sick, the other little better."[1] There were fish in the sea, fowl in the air, and game in the woods, but Smith acknowledged that the colonists were "so weake and ignorant, we cannot much trouble them."[2]

Powhatan predictably took advantage of the situation. Increasingly fearful of the growing numbers of colonists at Jamestown and aware of their vulnerability, he began making a number of threatening moves.

Before Newport's departure Smith, growing desperate for provisions, had sent young Matthew Scrivener to Werowocomoco to trade English goods for corn. But Scrivener's mission had not been successful: "Master Scrivener . . . sent with the barges and pinnace to Werowocomoco . . . found the Salvages more ready to fight than trade," and it was only through the intervention of Namontack that Scrivener was able to acquire even "three or four hogsheads of Corne, and as much Pocones which is a red roote, which then was esteemed as a valuable dye."[3]

No longer interested in bartering and negotiation, Powhatan was once again listening to his priests' prophecies about the tribe that would "arise . . . and give end to his empire."[4] He adopted a suspicious and militant attitude toward the colonists, spying

[1] Smith, *Generall Historie*, Book III, 70–72.
[2] *Ibid.*
[3] *Ibid.*, 70.
[4] Strachey, *Historie*, Cap. VIII, 101–102.

upon them "from . . . [his] own courte down almost to our palisado gates."[5]

Nevertheless, Smith had to obtain food. Just before Christmas, 1608, he set out with two barges for the Nansemonds' country to collect four hundred bushels of corn which the tribe had earlier promised him in exchange for the usual English goods—copper, glass beads, brass, and cloth. But upon reaching the Nansemonds' territory, southeast and east of present Suffolk County on the Nansemond River, Smith learned that Powhatan had commanded them to keep their corn and to prevent the English from coming up the river.

Enraged by the refusal and desperate for food, Smith and his men resorted to violence, setting fire to the first Nansemond house they saw. The Indians fearfully and reluctantly gave Smith half the corn in their storehouse, loading it on the barges before nightfall.[6]

The grain was soon eaten, and again the colony was faced with starvation. In subsequent weeks Smith sent Waldo, Scrivener, and Percy to Powhatan villages in search of more corn. Waldo obtained a little corn from the Appomattocs; Percy and Scrivener "could . . . find nothing."[7]

At this critical time several messengers arrived from Powhatan with the surprising news that if Smith would come to Werowocomoco his boats would be loaded with corn from the royal storehouse. In return Smith was to build for Powhatan an English-style house near Werowocomoco and to give Powhatan "a gryndstone, fifty swords, some peeces [guns], a cock and a hen, with much copper and beads."[8] Though Powhatan was driving a hard bargain, Smith had no choice but to accept. What little

---

[5] *Ibid.*
[6] Smith, *Generall Historie*, Book III, 73.
[7] *Ibid.*
[8] *Ibid.*

grain remained in the Jamestown storehouse was rotting or being devoured at an alarming rate by rats that had arrived on the English ships and had since multiplied by the thousands.

Two barges and the pinnace were provisioned, and Smith selected twenty-seven fellow colonists to go with him by the water route. Fourteen colonists, including four Dutch carpenters, were to make the shorter journey overland so that they could begin construction of the house immediately and thereby more speedily fulfill Powhatan's conditions.[9]

Leaving Matthew Scrivener as acting president in his absence, Smith sailed for Werowocomoco, spending the first night with the Warrasqueocs, a friendly Powhatan tribe living near present Smithfield in the northern part of Isle of Wight County.[10] Tackonekintaco, chief of the Warrasqueocs, gave the colonists as much corn as he could spare and tried to dissuade Smith from going on to Werowocomoco, warning him that Powhatan intended to cut his throat.[11]

Smith disregarded the warning and continued downstream to Kecoughtan, Pochins' province at the mouth of the James. There the weather turned bad. Harsh, cold winds off the bay lashed Kecoughtan with sleet and snow, and Smith was forced to remain with Pochins until the weather cleared. Pochins was much friendlier to the English than his father. During the colonists' stay he provided food and shelter and entertainment. The colonists reported that they were "never more merry, nor fed on more plentie of good Oysters, Fish Flesh, Wild—fowle and good bread."[12] The colonists stayed at Kecoughtan into the new year, until January 6, 1609.

[9] *Ibid.*, 73, 74. Smith gives conflicting counts of the total number of colonists who participated in this expedition. At one point he states that forty-six men were involved; later he lists only forty-two.

[10] McCary, *Indians in Seventeenth-Century Virginia*, 7.

[11] Smith, *Generall Historie*, Book III, 74.

[12] *Ibid.*

At last the weather cleared, and the expedition made its way around Point Comfort, the pinnace and barges bobbing like corks on the turbulent waters of the bay, and began the arduous journey up the Pamunkey River. So labored was the passage upriver that Smith and his men were forced to go ashore near the Chiskiacks' villages, where they received a much less cordial reception than the Kecoughtans had given them. The Chiskiacks, apparently acting on orders from Chief Powhatan, displayed if not actual hostility certainly petulance toward the colonists, granting them shelter only after repeated requests and then making stealthy attempts to steal guns and powder from the boats. Smith frequently had to order his men to beat drums and discharge weapons to keep the Indians at a distance. Smith commented that, like most of the other Powhatan tribes, the Chiskiacks were afraid "of the noyse of our drums, of our shrill trumpetts and great ordinaunce."[13]

Smith and his men soon pushed on up the Pamunkey River, arriving at Werowocomoco on January 12, 1609. The river at Poetan Bay was frozen over for about half a mile from shore. One of the barges tried to break through the ice but was stranded on a shelf of mud at ebb tide, and Smith and his men were forced to wade ashore. The colonists took up quarters in an unoccupied shelter near the shore and then sent a messenger into Werowocomoco to tell Powhatan of their arrival. Powhatan sent back venison, turkey, and bread and on the following day granted Smith an audience.

Pocahontas was present at the meeting between her father and Smith[14] and was apparently privy to her father's strategy for

[13] Strachey, *Historie*, Cap. VIII, 102.

[14] The conversation between Pocahontas and Smith in London in 1616 furnishes evidence that she was present when Smith and Powhatan held their parley at Werowocomoco in 1609. Though seven years had elapsed, Pocahontas could quote verbatim certain things that had been said at the parley. Smith, *Generall Historie*, Book IV, 122.

dealing with the Jamestown colonists. It was obviously a strategy born of frustration. Seated on his bed-throne with Pocahontas by his side, and surrounded by wives, children, other relatives, and warriors, Powhatan bluntly asked Smith what he was doing in Werowocomoco, denying that he had extended an invitation or made any promise of corn. If Smith wanted corn, he would have to pay for it—one sword or gun for every bushel. Smith chided Powhatan for his "forgetfullness," pointing out to him the very warriors who had come to Jamestown bearing Powhatan's invitation, at which Chief Powhatan gave out with "a merry laughter."[15]

Then Powhatan agreed to look at the commodities the colonists wished to trade for corn, though he repeated firmly that "none he liked without gunnes and Swords."[16] Smith, growing irritated, reminded Powhatan that the colonists were neglecting the work of their "glass factory" at Jamestown by sending laborers to build Powhatan's house. Yet the colonists were being denied provisions because Powhatan had told the tribes living near Jamestown not to trade with the colonists. "As for swords and gunnes," Smith said, "I told you long agoe I had none to spare; and you must know those I have can keepe me from want; yet stele or wrong you I will not, nor dissolve that friendship we have mutually promised, except you constrain me by your bad usage."[17]

Powhatan listened attentively to Smith's words. Then he made his standard play: "Some doubt I have of your coming hither, that makes me not so kindly seeke to relieve you as I would: for many doe informe me, your coming hither is not for trade but to invade my people, and possess my Country, who dare not come to bring you Corne, seeing you thus armed with your men. To

[15] *Ibid.*, 75.
[16] *Ibid.*
[17] *Ibid.*

free us of this feare, leave abbord your weapons, for here they are needless."[18] It was clear that to disarm the English was still Powhatan's one desire.

Powhatan and Smith continued their verbal exchange, matching wits to determine who was going to govern the other. Both men employed flattery and threats. Lay down your arms, Powhatan said, "we being all friends and forever Powhatans."[19] Smith said that he would not yield an inch on that matter. The Powhatan warriors were never asked to discard their bows and arrows when they came to Jamestown. Besides, Smith loftily announced, trying to bluff the chief, the Powhatan's "friendly care"[20] was needless, for the colonists had other ways of procuring food that Powhatan did not know about. Then Powhatan, with sorrowful countenance, ordered his people to bring some corn from the royal storehouse but qualified the order: "Captain Smith, I never used any werowance so kindly as yourselfe, yet from you I receive the least kindness of any . . . if you intend so friendly as you say, send hence your armes that I may beleeve you."[21] Smith again refused. Powhatan's people carried the corn from the storehouse but made no effort to load it onto the barges, and Smith had to summon the crewmen to shore to see to the loading themselves.

Powhatan, realizing that the battle of wits was getting him nowhere, arose and departed, to continue his machinations from afar. He left some warriors milling about outside his palace, and Smith and John Russell, still inside and fearing they were in danger, rushed out and drove the warriors away. Then they returned to their quarters near shore. That evening Powhatan sent Smith "a great bracelet and chaine of pearle" with the mes-

[18] *Ibid.*
[19] *Ibid.*
[20] *Ibid.*, 76.
[21] *Ibid.*

98

sage that he had left the conference because he was afraid of the guns, and "knowing when the ice was broken there would come more men, sent these numbers but to guard his corn from stealing, that might happen without your knowledge: now though some bee hurt by your misprision [bad behavior], yet Powhatan is your friend, and so will forever continue."[22] Then Powhatan gave Smith permission to send the corn back to Jamestown but said that if he himself wished to stay at Werowocomoco he would have to put away his arms. Once again Smith refused to do so.

The next day Smith supervised the loading of the barges, but the task was not finished by nightfall, and the colonists were compelled to spend another night among the Powhatans. Since their provisions were exhausted, Smith sent word to Chief Powhatan asking for food. While the colonists were waiting for a reply, Pocahontas arrived at their quarters. She came, as William Phettiplace, Anas Todkill, Jeffry Abbot, and Richard Wiffin later testified, to save their lives.

When she arrived, having come "that darke night . . . through the irksome woods," she warned Smith that the chief would send them food but that "Powhatan and all the power he could make, would after[ward] come kill us all, if they that brought it could not kill us with our owne weapons when we were at supper."[23]

Smith now realized, if indeed he had not done so earlier, that Powhatan's protestations of friendship and concern were merely deceptive rhetoric and that the concessions he had made to the colonists—the food he had given them, the hospitality he had provided—were part of a strategy leading not to any ultimate reconciliation between Indian and colonist but, at the advantageous moment, to the extermination of the English.

Smith was deeply grateful for Pocahontas' warning and for

[22] *Ibid.*, 77.
[23] *Ibid.*

her intervention in the contest she had tried on so many earlier occasions to bring to an end. He tried to thank her, and "such things as shee would have delighted in, he would have given her: but with the teares running downe her cheekes she said she durst not be seene to have any: for if Powhatan should know it, she were but dead."[24] And so, having once again played her part in the Jamestown drama, "shee ranne away by herselfe as she came."[25]

Shortly thereafter, eight or ten stalwart Powhatans arrived, bringing food. Smith insisted that the Powhatans taste each dish of food before he and his companions ate from it. Then he sent the Indians back to their chief with a message that if the chief had anything further to add to their earlier conversation he must come to the colonists' hut immediately, for Smith was preparing to leave. Powhatan, probably sensing that Smith was prepared to do battle, did not come to the hut or send warriors in his stead. Smith departed the next day. The two men never met again.

Soon after Smith and his companions left Werowocomoco, Pocahontas saved the life of still another Englishman, colonist Richard Wiffin. Wiffin had set out from Jamestown alone to report to Smith the grim news of the deaths of Captain Scrivener, Richard Waldo, Anthony Gosnold, and eight other colonists.[26] Scrivener, temporary president of the colony, had ignored express instructions to remain in Jamestown until Smith's return, and had delegated Captain Peter Winne to act as commandant of the fort while he took a party of colonists to the Isle of Hogs in the James River to shoot fowl, wild hogs, and other game. The skiff in which they sailed had sunk, and all members of the party had drowned.[27]

24 *Ibid.*
25 *Ibid.*
26 *Ibid.*, 86.
27 *Ibid.*, 73.

En route to Werowocomoco with news of the disaster, Wiffin "was encountered with many dangers and difficulties in all parts as he passed" surreptitiously among the Powhatans, who kept watch for "such straungers as should invade their territories."[28] By the time Wiffin reached Werowocomoco, he was half-frozen and ill from hunger, and all he could perceive in the Powhatan capital were "preparations for warre." There was no sign of Captain Smith.[29]

Fortunately for Wiffin, Pocahontas discovered his presence at just about the same time the Powhatan warriors did. Realizing that "some mischiefe was intended" toward him, she "hid him for a time, and sent them who pursued him the cleane contrary way to seek him," saving him from capture and probable death "by her meanes and extraordinary bribes, and much trouble."[30]

Then Pocahontas told Wiffin how to reach Smith, who was on his way to Menapucunt, Opechancanough's village, in search of more provisions. Wiffin reached Menapucunt without mishap. There he found Smith and his men in the midst of "turmoyles."[31] On their arrival they had observed that Opechancanough's warriors outnumbered them by hundreds. Certain that the formidable chief would imitate Powhatan's increasingly overt treachery, Smith, John Russell, and George Percy had rushed into his lodge, where Smith, in his own words, "did take this murdering Opechancanough . . . by the long locke on his head, and with my pistole at his breast, I led him before his greatest forces, and before we parted made him fill our Bark of twenty tuns of corne."[32] It was while Smith, gun in hand, was supervising the loading of the corn and "200 weight of venison and suet" that Wiffin arrived with his news. Smith quickly brought his dealings

[28] Strachey, *Historie*, Cap. VIII, 101–102.
[29] Smith, *Generall Historie*, Book III, 80.
[30] *Ibid.*
[31] *Ibid.*
[32] Smith, *New England Trials*, C2.

with Opechancanough to an end and hastened back to James-town.

Smith was to make no more food-gathering expeditions among the Powhatans. For the remainder of the time he served as the administrator of Jamestown, he was to concentrate upon making the colony as nearly self-sufficient as possible. From his last expedition among the Powhatans he had reached two conclusions. First, the colonists could "dreame no longer of this vain hope from Powhatan"[33] of peaceful and constructive co-operation. Second, without the support of their one real friend among the Powhatans, the young Pocahontas, he and many other Englishmen would have been killed, and the Jamestown colony would have been doomed.

[33] Smith, *Generall Historie, Book* III, 86.

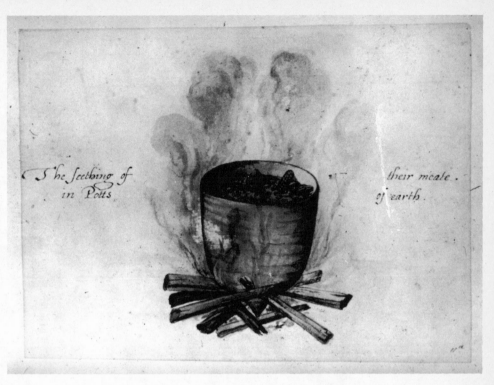

The seething of in Potts · their meate · of earth ·

Cooking in a pot. Water color by John White, 1585.

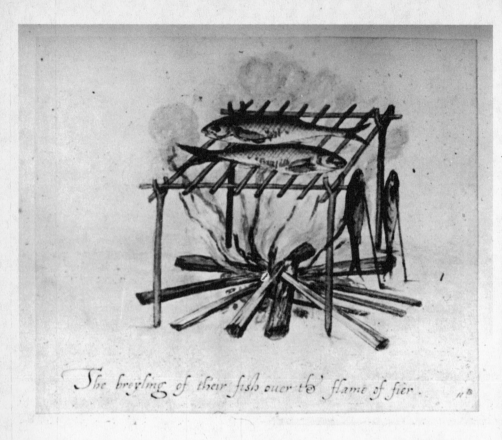

The breyling of their fish ouer the flame of fier.

Cooking fish. Water color by John White, 1585.

Indian charnal house. Water color by John White, 1585.

The "Lyte Jewel," seventeenth-century gold pendant, enameled and set with diamonds, containing a miniature portrait of King James I. In the British Museum, London.

Captain George Percy, twice governor of Jamestown and younger brother of the ninth Earl of Northumberland. Original in Syon House, Brentford, England.   Courtesy The College of William and Mary in Virginia

107

Thomas West, Third Lord de la Warr. From the original portrait by Wybrandt De Geest.

Sir Thomas Dale, governor of Virginia.

Eustace Rolfe, grandfather of John Rolfe.

CHAPTER IX

The Starving Time

As Jamestown entered its third year of existence, Smith inaugurated a new work program to strengthen the colony, hoping to make it invulnerable to the growing militancy of the Powhatans. Chief Powhatan was making ever bolder moves against the colonists. While Smith was taking the long water route home, Powhatan persuaded the colonists who were building his house to return to Jamestown overland to obtain swords, pikes, muskets, and hatchets on the pretext that Smith had requisitioned them. Captain Peter Winne, who was in charge of supplies at

Jamestown, believed the request legitimate and had sent back the weapons and tools, inadvertently contributing to Powhatan's arsenal.

Anxious for the future, Smith decided to enlarge the fort and to dig a deep well that would supply enough water to serve an even larger number of colonists than were presently at Jamestown. He also ordered laborers to clear, plow, and plant thirty acres of ground on the high ridges of the island. Tassore and Kemps, two Powhatan prisoners, were pressed into service to teach the colonists the Indian way of planting beans, corn, and pumpkins.

English gentlemen who had never done a day's labor in their lives were ordered to fell trees and split logs,[1] and Smith supervised the building of a blockhouse on the neck of land at the north end of Jamestown Peninsula, hoping thus to prevent the Chickahominies from entering Jamestown by its back door and stealing the colonists' supplies. The men stationed at the blockhouse were "to entertaine the Salvages trade . . . [but permit] none to passe nor repasse Salvage nor Christian Without the President's order."[2] In the spring of 1609, trying to prove to the Powhatans that the colonists could indeed supply their own needs, Smith sent "60 or 80 [colonists] with Ensign Laxon . . . down the river to live upon Oysters, and 20 with lieutenant Percy to try for fishing at Poynt Comfort, Master West with as many went up the falls, but nothing could be found there but acorns."[3]

Smith's strengthening of the colony was his last official service for Jamestown. In July, 1609, Captain Samuel Argall arrived from England and gave Smith the news that on May 23, 1609, a second charter had been granted to the Virginia Company of

[1] When the axes the gentlemen wielded blistered their hands, they sometimes "blasphemed their creator." As punishment Smith ordered his soldiers to dash a dipper of cold water down their sleeves.
[2] Smith, *Generall Historie*, Book III, 86.
[3] *Ibid.*

London, unyoking it from the North Virginia Company and abolishing the Jamestown council. The new company, the Treasurer and Company of Adventurers and Planters of the City of London for the First Colony in Virginia,[4] would govern Jamestown through its Supreme Council, sitting in London, and direct rule of the colony would be vested in a governor, with lifetime tenure of office. Lord De La Warr had been appointed to the office but had not yet left England for Jamestown. Argall reported, moreover, that nine ships had been scheduled to sail from England on June 1 as a demonstration of the new company's optimistic plans for revitalizing Jamestown.

Smith did not wait for the arrival of the new governor but immediately relinquished the presidency to George Percy and made plans to build himself a home away from Jamestown, near the falls at Parahunt's village. Smith had always been extraordinarily independent and had seldom been able to work successfully under another's command. When he learned of the return to the colony of Gabriel Archer and John Ratcliffe, with whom he had quarreled and who had returned to London and charged him with mismanaging the colony and leading it to failure,[5] Smith simply decided to set himself apart and live on his own terms. He went to the falls and obtained some land from Parahunt, but while returning by boat to Jamestown to arrange for the construction of a house (which he planned to call "Nonesuch"), a bag of gunpowder he was carrying exploded, burning him severely. His injuries were slow to heal, and finally he was compelled to return to England for medical treatment. He set sail on October 1, 1609, probably on board the *Falcon*, one of

---

[4] Virtually independent of either Parliament or king, the newly organized company was sponsored by Sir Francis Bacon and Robert Cecil, Earl of Salisbury, together with 21 peers, 96 knights, 10 clergymen and physicians, 53 officers, 28 members of the gentry, and 110 merchants. (Brown, *The Genesis of the United States*, I, 206–30; Neill, *History of the Virginia Company*, 32.)

[5] Smith, *Travels and Works of Captain John Smith*, I, 168–69.

seven ships that had recently brought hundreds of new colonists to Virginia.[6]

Smith's departure marked the beginning of the colony's most grievous days, though none in Jamestown realized it at the time. His absence and that of Pocahontas meant that the colony was deprived of the two people who had most earnestly struggled for accommodation between the English and the Powhatans. Though Smith had been aggressive and militant, he had earned the Indians' respect, if not their love, and certainly his friendly association with Pocahontas had for a time helped lessen the tensions between the colonists and the natives. Smith was never to return to Virginia, and three long years were to pass before Pocahontas would be seen in Jamestown again.

Without the peace-keeping influence of Smith and Pocahontas the latent hostility of the Indians flared into overt acts of destruction. Richard Potts and William Tankard, the new recorders of the colony, attested that "the salvages no sooner understood Smith was gone but they all revolted and did spoile and murther all they encountered."[7]

Powhatan's War had begun. According to George Percy, Indians in war paint made ferocious attacks on the colony. Howling Weanocs, Chickahominies, and Chiskiacks preyed on the colonists and made their lives miserable. The Indians sang a new song, composed, it was said, by Parahunt's people, the message of the song being that the savages now killed the colonists not because they were a foreign people but "for all their poccasacks [guns]" and for their other weapons, their hatchets, poleaxes, and English pikes. Indeed, it was a war for the acquisition of power and weaponry.

[6] Smith's arrival in England in December, 1609, made King James exceedingly happy. In accordance with instructions from Robert Cecil, the Lord Treasurer, Smith had brought along a pair of flying squirrels which the king very much wanted.

[7] Smith, *Generall Historie*, Book IV, 105.

With the opening of hostilities the Powhatans boasted that "for all that Captain Newport had brought them copper, they could kill 'Symon,' a youthful prisoner."[8] To assure their victory, they held the elaborate ritualistic sacrifice of youths of the tribe.

Chief Powhatan directed the war from his new seat of government at Rasawrack. There he conceived a plot to kill a number of the colonists in one blow. The plot involved young Thomas Savage, the English boy who had been left with Powhatan to learn the Indians' language and culture. Savage had become a favorite of Powhatan's; the chief called him "my boy," employed him as an interpreter, and permitted him to eat from his own royal platter.

In the autumn of 1609, Powhatan sent Savage to Jamestown accompanied by several Indians carrying provisions for the colony—wild turkeys, venison, and baskets heaped high with maize. Savage presented the gifts to Percy, the temporary council president, who interpreted them as a hopeful sign that Powhatan's War might soon end. Certainly Percy, not yet thirty years old, in ill-health himself and watching helplessly as his fellow colonists died of plague and yellow fever, yearned for peace with the Indians. He accepted Powhatan's provisions with gratitude and arranged for some blue glass beads and woolen fabrics to be sent to the chief in return.

Young Savage did not return to Rasawrack with the Indians. Though he had seemed satisfied among the Indians, now he was reluctant to return to them unless accompanied by one of his own countrymen.[9] Percy agreed to send young Henry Spelman with him—much to Spelman's annoyance. Spelman, the scapegoat son of an English aristocrat, had arrived only recently in Jamestown. Soon after his arrival he had accompanied Smith on his journey to Parahunt's village to arrange for the land for his

[8] Strachey, "The First Booke," Cap. 5, 34.
[9] Brown, "Spelman's Relation," *The Genesis of the United States*, I, 483–88.

new home. Smith had left Spelman at the falls with Parahunt when he went back to Jamestown,[10] expecting, of course, to return. After waiting in vain, Spelman had had to make his way back to Jamestown on his own. He had no desire to become another Thomas Savage, living among the natives and learning their languages and ways.

Nevertheless, Spelman accompanied Thomas Savage to Rasawrack, and found the Indian capital not too unpleasant. Warmly welcomed by Powhatan, Spelman was accorded the same honors as those bestowed on Savage. He was permitted to eat with the chief, and was waited upon by Powhatan's slaves. The two boys roamed Rasawrack at will, wandering as far as Uttamussack, on the Pamunkey River,[11] and even entering one of Powhatan's house temples, where Spelman saw the English bed, the copper crown, and the basin and ewer that King James had sent from England the year before.[12]

After remaining about three weeks at Rasawrack, Spelman returned to Jamestown, carrying a message from Powhatan to Captain Percy and other members of the council: If the colonists would "bring ther ship and sum copper he [Powhatan] would fraught [freight] her backe with corn."[13] Percy, hopeful that Powhatan might be genuinely interested in a peaceful relationship with the colonists, sent Spelman back to inform the chief that he would send the ship to Werowocomoco, where the royal storehouses were still located.

Without delay sixty-two colonists in two boats, one manned by Captain Ratcliffe and the other by William West, the nephew of Lord De La Warr, started up the Pamunkey River. Reaching

[10] *Ibid.*, 484.

[11] McCary, *Indians in Seventeenth-Century Virginia*, 57. McCary's identification of early Powhatan sites in Tidewater Virginia has been of great value to historians and archaeologists.

[12] Brown, "Spelman's Relation," *The Genesis of the United States*, I, 483–88.

[13] *Ibid.*, 484–85.

Werowocomoco, they went ashore, "Captain West and Captain Sicklemore [Ratcliffe] each with a small ship and each with thirtie or fortie men well appointed sought abroad to trade."[14]

But the colonists were to find not trade but ambush and death. "Sicklemore . . . with about thirtie others as careless as himself were all slaine; only Jeffry Shortridge escaped."[15] Sixty colonists were massacred by the Powhatans. A boy named Samuel was taken prisoner. Shortridge brought back the tragic news to Jamestown.

The massacre was a devastating blow to Jamestown. It seemed almost impossible to continue after such a loss, which robbed the colonists of much of their will to survive. Without corn there was no sustenance, and with the Powhatans' hostility now so intense there was little reason to seek help from the natives. Never since the founding of Jamestown had the colony been in such desperate straits. That bleak winter of 1609–10 was ever afterward to be known as the "starving time." In six months the population dropped from 490 to 60. In their last extremities the colonists revealed their agonies in tragic and erratic ways. One colonist killed his wife and was found eating her salted remains.[16] His trial and execution did not deter other colonists from roasting and eating an Indian killed during an attack on the fort.

So appalling did the situation become, while Powhatan waged war against them and they huddled in the final stages of starvation, that one Jamestown colonist, in utter despair, cast his Bible into the communal fire, crying out, "Alas, there is no God!"[17]

14 *Ibid.*; see also Smith, *Travels and Works of Captain John Smith*, I, 498.

15 Brown, "Spelman's Relation," *The Genesis of the United States*, I, 484–85.

16 Neill, *History of the Virginia Company*, 32; Purchas, *Purchas His Pilgrimes*, IV, 1759.

17 Brown, *The Genesis of the United States*, II, 996; Fiske, *Old Virginia and Her Neighbors*, I, 182; Purchas, *Purchas His Pilgrimes*, IV, 1757; Neill, *History of the Virginia Company*, 32.

CHAPTER X

A Second Chance

JAMESTOWN WAS DYING. England's great hopes for colonizing in
the New World seemed to be coming to nought. Sir Walter
Raleigh's enthusiastic claim of 1602, "I shall yet live to see in
Virginia an English Nation,"[1] rang hollow, and the optimism of
the backers of the effort appeared unlikely to save the distant
settlement. In 1609 the Lord Mayor of London was urging the
great livery companies of London to buy shares in the new Virginia Company, to rid the city of "a swarm of unhappy persons

[1] Alexander Wilbourne Weddell (ed.), *Virginia Historical Portraiture*, 70.

118

who infested their streets, the cause of plague and famine, and entice them to Virginia,"[2] and such publications as *Nova Britannia, Good Speed to Virginia,* and *Virginia Richly Valued*[3] were encouraging Englishmen to seek their fortunes in the New World.[4] Meanwhile, the Jamestown colony was suffering what seemed to be its final death agonies.

Yet Jamestown had never been more important to England. Her old enemy Spain had been deeply concerned about the attempt at colonization and had kept close watch on her successes and failures in the New World. Pedro de Zúñiga, the Spanish ambassador to the Court of St. James's, sent frequent reports in code to his ruler, Philip III, to which Philip would respond, as he did on May 14, 1609: "All that you say touching Virginia is well understood here and attention is paid to what may be proper to do in this matter."[5] Philip was indeed interested in knowing whether Protestant England was going to succeed in the New World. Whenever he learned of ships leaving for Virginia, he asked for details: "Concerning what you say of the progress made there in fortifying Virginia, and the number of people whom they wish to send there, you must be on the look out, to report when those will depart who are to settle that country, with what forces they go, and what route they will have to take in their voyage hither—so that here, such orders may be given as will be necessary."[6]

[2] Neill, *History of the Virginia Company*, 25.

[3] *Ibid.*, 25–26.

[4] Obviously weary of reading the many tracts designed to encourage emigration to Virginia, the Most Reverend Tobias Matthew, Archbishop of York, petulantly wrote to the Earl of Somerset (then a favorite of King James's): "Of Virginia there are so many tractates divine, human, historical, political, or call them as you please, as no further intelligence I dare desire." Neill, *History of the Virginia Company*, 26.

[5] Brown, *The Genesis of the United States*, I, 311.

[6] *Ibid.*

Thus, in 1610, Philip was delighted to hear from his new ambassador to England, Alonso de Velasco, that the Jamestown attempt seemed to have ended in total failure, a failure that perhaps prepared the way for Spanish acquisition of the Virginia territory:

The Indians hold the English surrounded in the strong place which they had erected there, having killed the larger part of them, and the others were left, so entirely without provisions, that, they thought it impossible to escape, because the survivors eat the dead, and when one of the natives died fighting, they dug him up again, two days afterwards to be eaten. The swine which they carried there . . . the Indians killed and almost all who came . . . died from having eaten dogs, Cat skins and other vile stuff. Unless they succour them with some provisions in an English ship . . . they must have perished before this. Thus it looks as if the zeal for this enterprise was cooling off and it would . . . on this account be very easy to make an end of it altogether by sending out a few ships to finish what might be left in that place.[7]

But while Philip was contemplating the invasion of Virginia, other events were occurring that were to give Jamestown a new lease on life. English luck and English determination combined to save the colony.

On May 23, 1610, the colonists who had survived the horrors of the previous winter saw two ships drop anchor off the Jamestown Peninsula. The ships were English, and they were appropriately named: the *Deliverance* and the *Patience*. The arrival of the ships marked the end of a six-month nightmare.

The *Deliverance* and the *Patience* had come to Jamestown only by the most difficult route and under the most unlikely circumstances. Almost a year before, on June 1, 1609, the *Sea Ven-*

[7] *Ibid.*, 392.

ture, flagship of the Virginia Company's nine-ship fleet, set sail from England bound for Virginia. Flying both the Union Jack and the flag of Scotland, the *Sea Venture* carried such distinguished passengers as Sir Thomas Gates, the newly elected deputy governor of the Virginia colony; Sir George Somers, the commander of the fleet; Christopher Newport, who was making one more trip across the Atlantic; William Strachey, a member of the Children of the Queens Revels, the London acting company, and a friend of Shakespeare's; the Reverend Richard Bucke, who was to succeed Mr. Hunt; and the Indian boy, Namontack, returning with another Powhatan boy, Matchumps, from a visit to England. The *Sea Venture* carried about one hundred prospective colonists, as well as "all manner of directions and provisions." Sailing west for the New World, the *Sea Venture* encountered a hurricane, became separated from the fleet, and was presumed lost.[8] Actually the ship managed to reach Bermuda, where it foundered and was wrecked. The survivors spent nine or ten months building two pinnaces, the *Deliverance* and the *Patience*, from timber they salvaged from the flagship. William Strachey kept a record of the survivors' adventures in Bermuda, noting that during the time it took to build the ships Elizabeth Persons, Mistress Horton's maidservant, married Thomas Powell, Sir George Somer's cook; two children were born and christened; and two murders were committed, one by Robert Waters, a sailor, who killed a companion with a shovel,

[8] The Spanish ambassador, Zúñiga, reported the loss of the *Sea Venture* to King Philip in a letter dated December 19, 1609: "I have received a letter in which I am told that three vessles of those which sailed down here to Virginia have returned to the Downs. They confirm what I have written Y.M. that the Captain's ship was lost with the most distinguished people who went, and the *Orders* according to which they were to be governed in that part. . . . I shall continue to give an account of all I may hear to Y.M. whose Catholic Person Our Lord preserve as all Christendom needeth." (Brown, *The Genesis of the United States*, I, 336–37.)

and the other by Matchumps, who in a fit of anger killed Namontack.[9]

When the two pinnaces were completed, the survivors, somewhat depleted in numbers, sailed away from Bermuda, making their way to their original Virginia destination. Sir Thomas Gates had managed to save the administrative orders and instructions for the colony and planned to assume office and guide Jamestown toward the pre-eminence that the Virginia Company so eagerly envisioned for it.

Upon their arrival at Jamestown, Gates and his party were met by desperate colonists, many of them dying, others wandering desolately about the ruins of the settlement. Gates realized that his first duty was to save the people, even if it meant abandoning the colony. He inspected the settlement and reported:

> Viewing the Fort, we found the Pallisadoes torne downe, the Ports open, the Gates from off the hinges, and emptie houses (which Owners' death had taken from them) rent up and burnt rather than the dwellers would step into the woods a stones castoff from them, to fetch other fire-wood: and it is true, the Indians killed without, if our men stirred beyond the bounds of their Block-house, as [many as] Famine and Pestilence did within. . . . In this desolation misery our Governour found the condition and state of our Colonie.[10]

Gates conferred with Percy and the other survivors, hoping to find some way to preserve the colony, but he soon agreed with them that little could be done in the face of Powhatan's crushing hostility:

> The Indians . . . were forbidden likewise (by their subtile King at all to trade with us); and not only so, but to endanger and assault any Boate upon the River, or stragler out of the Fort by Land, by

[9] Purchas, *Purchas His Pilgrimes*, IV, 1746.
[10] *Ibid.*, 1749.

which (not long before our arrival) our people had a large Boate
cut off, and divers of our men killed, even within command of our
Block-house; as likewise, they shot two of our people to death, after
we had bin foure and five dayes come in . . . .[11]

Gates, Somers, and Newport were seasoned veterans of wars
in the Netherlands and in Ireland and were well qualified to
assess the military aspects of the situation. Grimly, they decided
to abandon Jamestown. The colony's survivors would be placed
aboard the *Deliverance* and the *Patience* and, together with the
survivors of the wreck of the *Sea Venture*, would return to
England.

On June 7, 1610, Gates ordered his men to strip the huts of
possessions and load them on the ships. To the accompaniment
of funereal drum rolls, the colonists boarded the ships, sixty survivors of the nine hundred men, women, and children who had
come to Jamestown since 1607. The ships weighed anchor and
started down the James River toward the sea. At nightfall the
ships' crews dropped anchor at Mulberry Island, planning to
head into the Atlantic at daybreak.

So it was that the colonists were saved, though Jamestown
itself seemed a dead cause. The nightmare on the peninsula had
ended but with it all England's hopes for colonial expansion in
the New World. Or so it seemed.

In the early-morning light of June 8, 1610, while still at anchor
at Mulberry Island, the *Patience* and *Deliverance* passengers
saw three ships silhouetted on the horizon, heading upstream
toward them. Within a few hours they had made contact with
the ships, and with Lord De La Warr, the governor of the Virginia Company, who had decided to come to the New World
to see for himself how matters stood in Jamestown. It was an
almost miraculously opportune meeting. Had De La Warr ar-

[11] *Ibid.*, 1750.

rived only hours later, he would not have found a single English-man to govern. As it was, he turned the ships around and recommenced the Jamestown experiment, instilling in the colonists once again the spirit of commitment that destitution had wrung from them.

De La Warr had been appointed supreme governor of the colony in 1609, and on February 21 of that year had listened to the admonishment of the Reverend William Crashaw, who preached at the Temple in honor of the appointment:

> And thou most noble Lord, whom God hath stirred up to neglect the pleasures of England, and with Abraham to go from thy country, and forsake thy kindred and thy father's house, to go to a land which God will show thee, give me leave to speak the truth. Thy ancestor many hundred years ago gained great honour to thy house but by this action thou augmenst it. . . . Remember, thou art a general of English men, nay a general of Christian men; therefore principally look to religion. You go to commend it to the Heathen, then practice it yourselves; make the name of Christ honourable, not hateful unto them.[12]

So inspired, and after ample preparation and long study, De La Warr finally sailed for the New World in April, 1610, with a fleet of three ships carrying 150 new colonists. The flagship, the *De La Warr*, carried the governor himself and fifty scarlet-liveried attendants.

After meeting the refugees, he ordered Sir Thomas Gates to conduct everyone back to Jamestown. Stepping foot onto the peninsula on June 10, De La Warr reportedly fell to his knees and thanked God that he had come in time to save Jamestown. He had to admit, however, that it was "a verie noysome and unholsome place,"[13] and he was deeply disturbed by the sight that presented itself at the abandoned colony.

[12] Neill, *History of the Virginia Company*, 35.

Entering the fort through the south gate with standards flying, De La Warr went immediately to the church, where amid the ruins Mr. Bucke delivered a sermon. Then De La Warr's commission was read, whereupon Gates relinquished to him the administration of the colony, and De La Warr made a speech of acceptance.[14] Next he summoned Gates, Percy, and others to a conference to assemble information about Jamestown for a report to be sent to the Supreme Council in England, along with his own plans for rehabilitating the colony.

In the report he observed that much of the misery he saw at Jamestown had, in part, been

> occasioned bie the mortalitie and Idleness of our owne people, whereupon the next Daie I sett the sailors to worke to unloade shippes and the landmen some to cleanse the towne, some to make cole for the forges. I sent fisherman out to provide fish for our men, to save other provision, but these had but ill success. Likewise I Dispached Sir George Sommers back Againe to the Barmudas . . . and if it please God, he doe Saflie return, he will store us with hoges . . . fleshe, and fishe enoughe to serve the whole colonie this wynter. Thus bie God's assistance I shall goe forwards Imploying my best indevors in settlinge and managing these affairs.[15]

De La Warr set working hours from six to ten in the morning and from two to four in the afternoon. The church bell summoned colonists to their respective tasks, as well as to the church itself for twice-daily services, as attested to by Strachey, now the recorder of the colony:

> First they enter into the Church and make their praiers unto God, next they returne to their houses and receive their proportion of

[13] Brown, *The Genesis of the United States*, I, 415.
[14] Smith, *Generall Historie*, Book IV, 106.
[15] *Ibid.*

125

food. Nor should it be conceived that this business excluded Gentlemen whose breeding never knew what a daies labour meant, for though they cannot dig, use the Spade, nor practice the Axe finde how to employ [their] knowledge.[16]

The church building was rebuilt and refurbished. It was now sixty feet long and twenty-four feet wide, with a cedar chancel, a black-walnut communion table, and cedar pews. There were "faire broad windowes to shut and open," as well as a pulpit, a font, and two bells at the west end.[17] On orders from De La Warr, there were wildflowers in the church at all times. Sunday services were elaborate. Mr. Bucke preached two sermons, and De La Warr and his officers dressed for the occasion, wearing slashed velvet, ruffs, and jeweled accessories. De Le Warr's chair was elegantly draped with green velvet, and at his feet was a scarlet kneeling cushion. Following the services the governor entertained on board the *De La Warr*, where he lived throughout his nine-month stay at Jamestown.

De La Warr left for England on March 28, 1611. De La Warr apprised Robert Cecil, the Earl of Salisbury (James's minister of the treasury) in June that "he is weak from sickness, but would not have returned so suddenly if the winds had [not] favoured his voyage for the West Indies, at his departure from Virginia. That country is in a most hopeful state."[18] His leadership had by no means solved all the problems of the colony. There were still problems of recurring food shortage, illness, accidental death, and Indian attacks. Somers had died on the way to Bermuda for provisions. De La Warr himself had suffered from gout, dysentery, and scurvy, though he had been well treated by Dr. Laurence Bohun, his private physician. None of the new leaders,

[16] *Ibid.*, 107.

[17] Fiske, *Old Virginia and Her Neighbors*, I, 160–61.

[18] Vol. LXIV, 518 State Papers Domestic James I, Public Record Office, London.

De La Warr or his assistants, had made significant progress in ending Powhatan's War.

Yet De La Warr's leadership had given Jamestown a second chance. He had restored order and stability to the colony, clarified its significance for its members, and once again formalized its institutions. Moreover, he had encouraged private enterprise, which had been provided for in the second charter. Each colonist had been given his own plot of ground to cultivate, and communal farming had been abolished. This improvement in the economic functioning of the colony raised morale at Jamestown and brought forth renewed effort by the members. When De La Warr left, Jamestown had new courage to face the future. Once again Captain Percy assumed temporary command of the colony, awaiting the arrival of the High Marshal of Virginia, Sir Thomas Dale, who was to arrive in May, 1611, and serve until Sir Thomas Gates, who had returned to England in September, 1610, arrived in Virginia again.

CHAPTER XI

Signs of Success

POCAHONTAS COULD NOT come to Jamestown Peninsula to examine the revived colony. Open contact with the English was prevented by the dictates of her father and by the war her people continued to wage against the English. Yet she did not willingly accept the limitations upon her activities and did not altogether acquiesce in her father's commands. Ever since the massacre of the sixty colonists in 1609, she had been at odds with her father's policies, and, as John Smith was to observe many years later, there was strife between her and Chief Powhatan during the "long and troublesome warre after my departure."[1]

Pocahontas spent an increasing amount of time away from Rasawrack, her father's new capital. Early in 1610, shortly after the massacre, she settled among the less militant and hostile Patawomekes (Potomacs), ostensibly as a tax collector for her father but also as a refugee from the conflict. The Patawomekes' principal villages were about ninety miles north of Rasawrack on a pleasant bluff overlooking an arm of Potomac Creek and the Potomac River beyond. The tribe, which numbered about 750 people, was one of the larger tribes in the Powhatan Confederacy—and one of the richest. The principal chief was Pasptanze.[2]

While among the Patawomekes, far removed from the affairs of Jamestown, Pocahontas had an opportunity to help at least one Englishman, young Henry Spelman, who had been stranded among the Powhatans after the massacre. Having inadvertently played a role in the massacre by acting as messenger of Powhatan, Spelman was eager to escape from the household of the chief. Soon after Pocahontas went to live among the Patawomekes, she and Pasptanze journeyed to Rasawrack, probably to deliver tax collections to the Powhatan storehouses, and there they learned that Spelman wanted to leave Rasawrack, as did young Thomas Savage and the boy named Samuel, who had been taken prisoner during the attack.

As Spelman was later to tell it, "The King of Patomeck came to visit the great Powhatan, when being awhile with him, he shewed such kindness to Savage, Samuell, and myself, as we determined to goe away with him."[3] On the day Pocahontas and

---

[1] Smith, *Generall Historie*, Book IV, 105.

[2] Thomas De La Warr, *The Relation of the Right Honourable the Lord De La Warre, Lord Governour and Captaine Generall of the Colonie Planted in Virginia*; hereafter cited as *Relation*. See also Brown, *The Genesis of the United States*, I, 483.

[3] Brown, *The Genesis of the United States*, I, 487.

Pasptanze set out on the return journey to Patawomeke, the three boys stole away with them. As chance and human nature would have it, however, the boys' escape was not to be so easy. "Having gone a mile or too on the way Savage fayned some excuse to stay and unbeknownst to us went back to the Powhatan and acquainted him with our departing with ye Patawomeke (Potomac)."[4] Young Savage, Powhatan's pet, had been with the Indians too long; he had transferred his loyalty to the chief. As a result, "The Powhatan presently sends after us commanding our returne, which we refusing, went still on our way: and those that weare sent went still on with us, till one of them . . . suddenly strooke Samuell with an axe and killed him, which I seenge ran away."[5]

Pocahontas and Pasptanze were unable to defend the boys from Powhatan's warriors, but after Spelman made his escape, they were able to provide sanctuary and care for him. According to Captain Argall, who later heard the story from Spelman himself, "Pokahontas the King's daughter saved a boy called Henry Spelman that lived many years afterwards by her meanes among the Patawomekes."[6] Spelman thus acknowledged that it was Pocahontas who was primarily responsible for his survival and for his friendly acceptance among the Patawomekes, with whom he stayed until he could rejoin his own countrymen.

The most significant aspect of Pocahontas' assistance to Spelman was that it gave the English an opportunity to report to London that there were some hopeful signs in English-Indian

[4] *Ibid.*

[5] *Ibid.*

[6] Smith, *Travels and Works of Captain John Smith*, II, 498. It is unlikely that a stranger would have been able to find the Patawomekes' villages without help from the Indians. The region was not frequented by explorers; ossuaries of the Potomacs found by T. Dale Stewart, who excavated the site, yielded very few white men's trade goods. (See T. Dale Stewart, "Excavating the Indian Village of Patawomeke," *Explorations and Field Work of the Smithsonian Institution in 1938*, 87–90.)

relations. Such a report would help persuade more Englishmen to venture across the Atlantic and to swell the numbers of colonists to a size large enough to overwhelm the Powhatans. Certainly one of the reasons for the colonists' difficulties in the early years was their small numbers. And as reports of their sufferings and hardships circulated in England, enthusiasm for colonization waned. Everyone concerned with colonizing the New World realized the advantage of favorable reports from Virginia.

Lord De La Warr had revitalized Jamestown and had given new life to the colonial experiment. But now there was need to make colonial life attractive. In September, 1610, during De La Warr's stay in Jamestown, Captain Argall sailed for Bermuda, became lost, and found himself on the Potomac River. He chanced upon a friendly village of Patawomekes with young Spelman safe and sound in their midst and Pocahontas, the friendliest of all Powhatans, exerting her influence among them. This was the sort of story that would be welcomed in London.

In his reports to the Supreme Council of the Virginia Company, Lord De La Warr did not dwell upon the difficulties and hardships of life in Jamestown nor upon Powhatan's War. He elaborated upon the friendship between the English and the Patawomekes and upon the great possibilities for settlement in the Potomac area:

The last discovery during my continuall sickness, was by Captain Argall who hath found trade with Patamack (a King as great as Powhatan, who still remaynes our Enemie, though not able to do us hurt.) This [the Potomac] is a goodly River upon the borders thereof there are grown the goodliest trees for Masts, that may be found elsewhere in the World: Hempe better than English growing wilde in aboundance: Mines of Antimonie and Leade without our Bay [Chesapeake] to the Northward. There is also found an excellent fishing banke of Codde, and Ling as good as can be eaten, and

131

of a kind that will keep a whole yeare, in shipp's hould, with little care; a tryall whereof I have brought over with mee.[7]

This glowing report was to become increasingly important to the managers of the Virginia Company. But for the Spelman rescue, Lord De La Warr would have had few encouraging words to carry back with him.

It was this growing concern with "public relations" that was to lead to Pocahontas' future contributions to the colonizing of Virginia. During the first three years she had made her contribution in a personal way, by assisting the settlers themselves. In the future her contribution was to be of a different order; she would become an ever more important instrument in a carefully outlined plan to unite the English and the Powhatans and to dramatize, and thereby promote, the Virginia Company's ambitious goal of establishing unchallenged claim to a part of the North American continent.

Pocahontas would not play her new role in the drama of Virginia until the stage could be set by the English—a task that would take almost two more years and involve the enlargement of the theater itself, as well as a strengthening of the cast of actors. However, by May, 1611, the Virginia Company had begun attending to these matters. In its second charter the company had prepared for the eventual extension of English holdings in the New World to include the territory two hundred miles north and south of Old Point Comfort, encompassing most of present-day Tidewater Virginia, Maryland, and Delaware, as well as a good part of North Carolina. The enlarged territory would increase the size of the colonizing area from ten thousand square miles to one million square miles. As the English saw it, in 1611 the task was not only to maintain the original settlement

[7] De La Warr, *Relation.*

on Jamestown Peninsula but also to enlarge as extensively and rapidly as possible the English commitment in America.

On May 19, 1611, Sir Thomas Dale arrived at Jamestown to assume temporary command of the colony, pending the arrival of the deputy governor, Sir Thomas Gates, later in the year. Dale, who was on a three-year leave of absence from military duties in the Low Countries, brought with him the skill and experience of a veteran military commander. More than any English leader in the colony before him, Dale erected in the Virginia wilderness an outpost of Old World civilization that could survive and prosper. Under his leadership the colonists would be able to meet all obstacles, including the militancy of Powhatan, with new and greater force.

From May 12 to May 19, 1611, Dale had supervised repairs at Fort Henry and Fort Charles, fortifications Lord De La Warr had built at the mouth of the James. Then he proceeded to Jamestown, relieved Percy of his interim command, and posted "for the publique view" the "Laws Devine, Morall, and Martiall"[8] established by the second charter but only now to be enforced within the colony. The laws were severe instruments of discipline (the colonists called them the "Laws of Blood") designed to strengthen the moral fiber of the colony and to make it an effective community. Among other things, the laws prohibited the use of profanity, the vilification of the Christian faith, and the belittlement of the king or of the officials of the Virginia Company. The first violation was to be punished by flogging; the second, by a bodkin thrust through the tongue; the third, by death.

Totalitarian rule had arrived at Jamestown, a rigid structuring of human lives that was necessary for the common good, according to the lights of the Virginia Company officials, who believed

[8] "The Copy of the Commission Granted to the Right Honourable Sir Thomas West (Knight), Lord De La Warr," Add. MS 21993, fol. 187; MS 12496, fol. 456, Department of Manuscripts, Library, British Museum.

that many of the failures in Jamestown could have been avoided if only the colonists themselves had been better prepared, spiritually and morally, to meet the inevitable hardships. The regulations designed to improve the "nature" of the colonists were also severe. The first time a man failed to attend church services without showing good cause he forfeited his week's allowance of food. The second time, he was soundly flogged. The third time, he was shot, hanged, or tied to a stake and burned. Desertion, theft, unauthorized harvesting of corn belonging to others, unauthorized picking of flowers, unauthorized gathering of grapes, unauthorized slaughtering of domestic animals—all these acts were offenses punishable by having one's ears cut off and being branded on the hand or by being forced to lie "head and heels together" all night. Refusal to accept a minister's spiritual advice was to be punished by flogging until the sinner either repented or died.[9]

Sir Thomas Dale enforced the laws vigorously. His goals were, first, to eliminate all idleness among the colonists and, second, to extend England's power beyond Jamestown. He attended to the idleness first. He wrote to the Supreme Council that, although the colonists kept their livestock in good condition, in Jamestown's fields he saw "no corn sett, some few seeds put into a private garden or two."[10] He began to work the colonists under the lash to get the fields planted before the hot, humid days of summer. He was convinced that military regimen was necessary to make the colony truly productive.

In his campaign to improve the colonists Dale was assisted by the Reverend Alexander Whitaker, a twenty-six-year-old friend and admirer who had left a prosperous parish in northern England to administer the Holy Sacraments of the Church of Eng-

[9] *Ibid.*
[10] Charles E. Hatch, Jr., *Jamestown, Virginia*, National Park Service *Historical Handbook Series No. 2*, 15.

land to the colonists and, he hoped, convert the Powhatans as well. Though Mr. Bucke was still principal minister at Jamestown, Mr. Whitaker was Dale's chief supporter, eager to serve "our religious and valiant Governour," whom he saw as "a man of great knowledge in Divinity, and of a good conscience in all his doings: both which Bee rare in a martial man."[11]

By June, 1611, Dale had imposed serenity and order on Jamestown and was ready to attend to his second goal, the establishment of a new town in Virginia. Dale's plan, approved by the Supreme Council in London, was to maintain Jamestown as a port of entry but to build the principal colonial settlement elsewhere. He set out in June in search of a townsite, leading an expedition by boat up the James River deep into Powhatan's country. The mission was a dangerous one, of course, and certainly William Strachey and the "Ancients"—as the original Jamestown settlers were now called—had warned Dale about the Powhatan menace. But Dale, who had not hesitated to yank Captain Newport's beard in public and threaten him with hanging,[12] was not one to be intimidated by savages.

Sailing up the James past the village of Apamatuks, which was governed by Queen Oppussoquionuske, Pocahontas' aunt, Dale selected a site for the new settlement about forty-five miles upstream from Jamestown on a high and healthful peninsula jutting out into the James like a great jaw. Dale studied the topography of the area with a keen military eye and planned how the defenses of the peninsula should be built. He decided that about seven acres at the point would have to be impaled, or enclosed in a stockade, and severed from the mainland. The

[11] Raphe Hamor, *A True Discourse of the Present Estate of Virginia, and the Successe of the Affaires There till the 18 June, 1614 . . .*, 59; hereafter cited as *A True Discourse.*

[12] Newport had angered Dale by belittling Sir Thomas Smythe, treasurer of the Supreme Council.

town would be built on the point and fortified with five block-houses.

Dale returned to Jamestown and throughout the summer of 1611 kept the men at work felling trees for posts and lumber for the new buildings. He also saw to it that millwrights, lime burners, and bricklayers were kept busy. By the time Sir Thomas Gates arrived in the middle of September, 1611, Dale was ready to take 350 laborers and builders up the James to start construction of the new town, which was to be called Henrico in honor of Prince Henry, King James's oldest son and heir apparent. With characteristic military precision and energy Dale divided the workmen into two companies. One group, under the command of Captain Edward Brewster, would take the land route to the building site. The other group, under Dale's own command, would take the water route, escorting barges loaded with building supplies.

Evidence that Powhatan was still waging war soon presented itself, and on the trip to the new townsite Dale may well have gained some insight into the grievous problems that had beset the earlier colonists. Captain Brewster's men had scarcely set out when they were attacked by Chief Munetute, a minor Powhatan chief, and his warriors. The chief was grotesquely painted and wore on each shoulder the wing of a swan, a decoration that earned him the nickname "Jack of the Feathers" among the colonists. Munetute's warriors killed several of the colonists before they could reach for match and powder. Only after a fierce encounter were the colonists finally able to drive the Indians away with guns, poleaxes, and pikes and continue on the way.

Dale's group was also attacked, but more treacherously. Upon reaching the village of Apamatuks, twenty of his men accepted the invitation of Indian maidens to lay down their arms and spend the night. The invitation proved to be a trap. All twenty men were slain by order of Queen Oppussoquionuske, who, after the killings, appropriated the colonists' weapons.

The rest of the men made their way to Henrico safely and began building the new town, despite almost daily attacks by Powhatans. Dale first had the men impale seven acres at the point of the peninsula, a task they completed in ten days. Then he directed them in severing the impaled land from the mainland, using techniques he had learned in the Low Countries. The severed and impaled land, where Henrico was to be built, is today called Farrar's Island. The gap between the island and the mainland was named Dutch Gap, the name it still bears today.

Raphe Hamor, a recently arrived colonist, was an eyewitness to the construction of Henrico. Three years after its completion, while serving as the colony's secretary, he wrote the following description of the town:

> There is in the town three streets of well framed houses, a hansome Church, and the foundations of a more stately one laid, of Brick, in length an hundred foote, and fifty foot wide, besides store houses, watch-houses, and such like: there are also ornaments belonging to the towne, upon the verge of the river, five fair Block houses wherein live the honester sort of people, as the Farmers in England, and there keep continuall centinall for the townes security. About two miles from the towne into the Main, a pale of two miles in length, cut over from River to River, guarded likewise with severall Block-Houses with a great quantity of corn ground impaled.[13]

[13] Smith, *Generall Historie*, Book IV, 111. For other accounts of the founding of Henrico, see Robert Hunt Land, "Henrico and Its College," *William and Mary Quarterly*, 2d Ser., Vol. VIII, 464–68; The Rev. George J. Cleaveland, "The Reverend Alexander Whitaker, M.A. Parson of Henrico, Apostle to the Indians, a Saviour of Virginia," *Virginia Churchman*, Vol. LXVI, No. 2 (June, 1957), 16–17; The Rev. George J. Cleaveland, "The Beginning of a Good Work," *Virginia Churchman*, Vol. LXX, No. 6 (December, 1961), 12–14.

Henrico was completed around January 15, 1612, and its completion marked the beginning of a new era for the English. The town came to represent the expansionist mood of the English and of their determination to establish their new "nation" in the face of opposition from the French and the Spaniards. Even before Henrico was completed, Dale had revealed plans for still more towns in Virginia. On Christmas Day, 1611, he had burned to ashes Queen Oppussoquionuske's village—as punishment for the slaughter of his men—and had announced that he would build a town on the site of the razed village, to be called Bermuda Hundred.[14]

Indeed, signs of success were beginning to appear in Virginia. Dale's achievements were important steps forward; the friendship with the Patawomekes assured for the colonists a continuing supply of grain. There were soon to be further promising developments, among them a new and elaborate charter, to be issued the London Company on March 12, 1612. Soon the tobacco industry would be introduced into Virginia, to serve as the economic foundation of the expanding colony. Only one dark shadow hovered over English advances in the New World— Powhatan's War that continued month in and month out, year in and year out, always threatening the colonists with imminent danger and ultimate defeat. The English could not claim a real success until they had come to terms, one way or another, with the Powhatans.

[14] Strachey, *Historie*, Cap. VI, 73–78; McCary, *Indians in Seventeenth-Century Virginia*, 3.

Frontispiece and title page of John Smith's *Generall Historie*, 1624.

John Smith as a prisoner of the Powhatans. From John Smith's *Generall Historie*, 1624. Top: "A Conjurer," "Their Idoll [Okeus]," "A Priest." Below: "Their Comunation [Conference] about John Smith 1609."

"John Smith taketh the King of Pamaunkee prisoner 1608."
From John Smith's *Generall Historie*, 1624.

King Powhatan comandi C Smith to be slayne, his
daughter Pokahontas beggs his life his thankfullnes
and how he subiected 39 of their kings reade history

printed by James Reve

Courtesy Thomas Gilcrease Institute of History and Art, Tulsa

Pocahontas rescues John Smith from Powhatan's warriors.
From John Smith's *Generall Historie*, 1624. Top: "The countrey wee now call Virginia beginneth at Cape Henry distant
from Roanoack 60 miles, where was Sᵣ. Walter Raleigh's
plantation and because the people differ very little from them
of Powhatan in any thing, I have inserted those figures in this
place because of the conveniency." Below: "King Powhatan
comands J. Smith to be slayne, his daughter Pokahontas beggs
his life his thankfullness and how he subjected 39 of their
kings reade history."

142

Chief Powhatan's mantle, decorated with figures embroidered in roanoke, which the chief gave to Captain Christopher Newport, to be presented to King James I. In the Ashmolean Museum, Oxford.

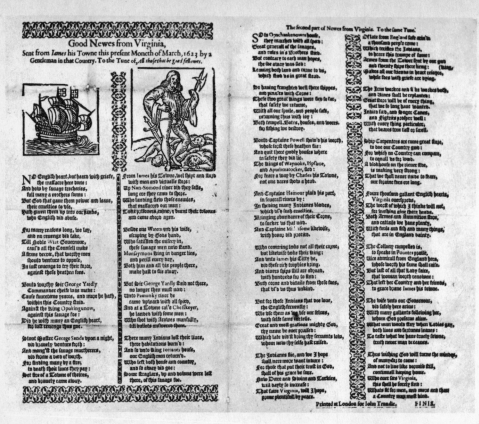

Broadside, "Good Newes from Virginia," sent to England in 1623.

Heacham Hall, the Rolfe manor house Pocahontas visited in 1616. In that year the house consisted of the central wing. The imposing wing at the left was added later. Heacham Hall was destroyed by fire in 1945.

St. George's Church, Gravesend, England, site of Pocahontas' burial in 1616.

Interior, new St. George's Church, Gravesend, England.

Statue of Pocahontas
in St. George's churchyard,
Gravesend, England.

Bas-relief of Pocahontas in the Church of St. Mary the Virgin, Heacham, Norfolk, England.

Village road sign commemorating Pocahontas at Heacham,
Norfolk, England.

Photograph by Mary E. Stith

Statue of Captain John Smith, Jamestown, Virginia.

CHAPTER XII

The Abduction and Conversion

WITH THE PROSPECTS NOW BRIGHT for permanent settlement in Virginia, serious efforts were made to resolve the Powhatan problem. In these efforts Pocahontas was to play a major part. For several years the English had contemplated capturing certain key Powhatans and using them as hostages to force Chief Powhatan to negotiate. Virginia Company officers had suggested one rather vague plan of abduction to Lord De La Warr:

> Yt is very expedient that your Lordship with all diligence endeavor the conversion of the natives and savages to the knowledge and

worship of the true God and their redeemer Christ Jesus as the most pius and noble end of this plantation, [which] the better to effect, you are to procure from them some of their Children to be brought up in our language and manners and if you think it necessary you first remove from them Quiacocks [quiyoughcosughes] or priests by a surprise of them and detayning them prisoners and in case they shall be wilful obstinate, then to send us some 3 or 4 of them into England, [so that] we may endeavor their conversion there.[1]

Perhaps abducting Indian children did not appeal to De La Warr, or perhaps he did not believe that converting three or four children and returning them to the Powhatans would necessarily transform the Indians into peaceful Christian neighbors. Whatever his objections, he ignored the plan, and no abductions took place.

Yet the idea lingered in colonial minds. The Virginia Company officials alluded to it in the Instructions, Orders, and Constitutions for the colony,[2] and the English clergy had supported the idea for some time, largely because of their interest in converting the Indians. In May, 1609, the Reverend William Symonds, preaching to Jamestown-bound colonists in Whitechapel, had ended his sermon by reminding his hearers that "a captive girl brought Naman to the Prophet. A captive woman was the means of converting Iberia. . . . God makes the weake things of the worlde confound the mighty, and getteth himselfe praise by the mouth of babes and sucklings."[3]

In one English mind in particular—that of Captain Samuel

---

[1] "The Copy of the Commission Granted to the Right Honourable Sir Thomas West (Knight), Lord De La Warr," Add. MS 21993, fol. 187; Add. MS 12496, fol. 456, Department of Manuscripts, Library, British Museum.

[2] *Ibid.*

[3] William Symonds, *A Sermon Preached at White-Chappel, in the Presence of Many Honourable and Worshipfull, the Adventurers and Planters for Virginia. 25 April, 1609* (photostat).

Argall—the idea of an abduction took root, and in 1613 he acted on the idea, confident that his scheme would greatly strengthen the colonists' influence over Chief Powhatan.

Argall had returned to Virginia from England in June, 1612. He was encouraged by the progress that was being made in the colony: "I found both the countrey and people in farre better estate there."[4] Soon after his arrival he busied himself "helping to repair such ships and Boats, as I found heere decayed for lack of Pitch and Tarre: and in pursuing the Indians with Sir Thomas Dale for their Corne, of which we got some quantitie, which we were like to have bought very deerely."[5] Argall also continued to explore the area and renewed his friendly contact with the Patawomekes. In December, 1612, he procured from them about eleven hundred bushels of corn.[6]

In April, 1613, Argall returned again to the Patawomekes' region, and it was on that visit that he decided to abduct Pocahontas, take her to Jamestown as a royal hostage, and then inform Powhatan that if he wanted her released he must agree to an enduring peace. The plot may have originated with Sir Thomas Gates and Sir Thomas Dale, both of whom were now living in Virginia, or perhaps even with London Company officials. At any rate, Argall was enthusiastic about the idea. He was resolved "to possess myself of her by any strategem that I could use."[7]

The abduction was a gamble. No one believed that Powhatan would end the war simply to rescue his daughter, even his favorite daughter. Yet her capture should serve to convince him that the English were now powerful enough to maintain the colony and determined to do so.

[4] In a letter to Master Nicholas Hawes. (Purchas, *Purchas His Pilgrimes*, IV, 1764).

[5] *Ibid.*

[6] *Ibid.*

[7] *Ibid.*, 1765.

While sailing up Potomac Creek, Argall learned from his Indian guides that Pocahontas was living in the region.[8] Then he launched his scheme:

> So soone as I came to an anchor before the Towne, I manned my Boate and sent on shore, for the King of Pastancy [Pasptanze] and Ensign Swift (whom I had left as a pledge of our love and truce, the Voyage before) who presently came and brought my pledge with him: Whom after I had received I brake the matter to this King, and told Him that if he did not betray Pokahuntis into my hands; wee would no longer be brothers nor friends.[9]

Argall's demand placed the chief of the Patawomekes in a difficult position:

> Hee alleaged, that if hee should undertake this businesse, then Powhatan would make warres upon him and his people; but upon my promise that I would joyne with him against him [Powhatan] hee . . . called his counsell together: and after some houres deliberation, concluded rather to deliver her into my hand, then [than] lose my friendship.[10]

According to Ensign Swift, who gave an eyewitness account of the affair to Raphe Hamor, the recorder at Henrico, the final details of the abduction were worked out with Captain Argall's special friend among the Patawomekes, one Jopassus (or Japazeus), his adopted "brother." Jopassus and his wife were won over to the plot by the promise of a copper kettle. Their role in the plot was to lure Pocahontas aboard the *Treasurer*, lying at anchor in the Potomac River, for what was ostensibly to be a tour of the ship.[11]

[8] Neill, *History of the Virginia Company*, 88–89.

[9] Purchas, *Purchas His Pilgrimes*, IV, 1765; Neill, *History of the Virginia Company*, 85.

[10] *Ibid.*

[11] *Ibid.*, 89–90.

Pocahontas was, of course, easy prey. She was "desirous to renue her familiarities with the English and delighting to see them would gladly visit. . . ."[12] On April 13, Pocahontas, Jopassus, and his wife boarded a waiting shallop in a cove near the mouth of Potomac Creek[13] and were rowed to the *Treasurer*, where they were conducted on the promised tour and afterward entertained at dinner served in Argall's quarters.

After dinner Jopassus and his wife led Pocahontas into the gunners' room and left her there, pretending that they would soon return. Instead, carrying their copper kettle, they hurriedly left the ship, and Pocahontas soon discovered that she was Argall's prisoner—whereupon, reported Argall, she grew "pensive and discontented." Argall did not relent and "presently departed from Patawomeke it being the 13 of Aprill, and repayred with all speed to Sir T. Gates [at Jamestown] to know of him upon what condition he would conclude this peace and what he would demand: to whom I also delivered my prisoner."[14]

Word quickly spread throughout Jamestown and the new settlements, Henrico, Bermuda Hundred, and Elizabeth City, that the royal princess, the "delight and darling" of Powhatan, had returned. Though Pocahontas had not visited the English for three years, she was well known among them, and Ensign Swift reported that her fame had "even bin spred in England."[15] She received a royal welcome from the Ancients who had known her in the early days.

Pocahontas' appearance had probably changed but little in the years since the colonists had last seen her. She was a small,

[12] *Ibid.*

[13] See Stewart, "Excavating the Indian Village of Patawomeke," *Explorations and Field Work of the Smithsonian in 1938*, 87–90. By following Stewart's directions, one can easily find this site, as well as the spring under the bluff known to be the scene of Pocahontas' abduction.

[14] Neill, *History of the Virginia Company*, 87.

[15] *Ibid.*, 89–90.

graceful young woman with alert dark eyes elongated at the corners, and lovely, expressive hands.[16] Her long, dark hair streamed down her back, though at the sides and over her forehead it was now cut short, in the fashion of unmarried Powhatan girls. Gentle and outgoing by nature, yet she was every inch a princess.

Soon after Argall had delivered Pocahontas to Gates, "an Indian was dispatched to Powhatan to let him know, that I had taken his Daughter and if he would send home the Englishmen (whom he deteined in slaverie with such armes and tooles, as the Indians had gotten and stolen) and also a great quantitie of Corne that then he should have his Daughter restored, otherwise not."[17]

At first Chief Powhatan seemed willing to meet these conditions: "This newes much grieved this great King, yet without delay, he returned the messenger with this answer. That he desired me to use his Daughter well, and bring my ship into his River, and there he would give mee my demands; which being performed, I should deliver him his Daughter and we should be friends."[18]

At this point Captain Argall turned the negotiations over to Sir Thomas Gates and Sir Thomas Dale, the two highest-ranking colonists in Virginia. Gates and Dale tried to persuade Powhatan to release the prisoners, return the weapons, and supply the grain that Argall had demanded. They also hoped, no doubt, for a settlement of Powhatan's War. But, as might be expected, the chief was not easy to deal with. A few days after Pocahontas was taken prisoner, he sent back to Jamestown seven of the Englishmen he had held captive, but kept all the stolen English goods,

[16] Portraits of Pocahontas by various artists show her hands as particularly graceful.
[17] Neill, *History of the Virginia Company*, 86.
[18] *Ibid.*, 87.

except for a broadax and a long whipsaw. He sent only one canoeful of grain, though he promised to try to send more after the harvest. There were no indications that he had decided to stop fighting.

In fact, it soon became apparent that Powhatan was not going to respond further to Pocahontas' abduction. Knowing full well that she was safe and well cared for, Chief Powhatan simply let the seasons pass away—spring into summer, summer into autumn, autumn into winter—without sending so much as a message to Gates or Dale. If the colonists' strategy had been to move Powhatan's fatherly heart toward peace and reconciliation, Powhatan's strategy was to ignore the colonists altogether or patiently wait them out. Gates and Dale soon realized that if Pocahontas was to be used as pawn in their political chess game with the Indians, the abduction in itself was not going to produce checkmate. Several other moves would have to be made.

At some point in the succeeding months it occurred to Gates and Dale that Pocahontas could be useful to them in other ways, to the ultimate benefit of the colony.[19] Thus, while they waited hopefully for some positive response from Chief Powhatan, they

[19] Before the end of the summer of 1613 news of Pocahontas' capture had reached England. In a letter dated August 1, Sir John Chamberlain wrote Sir Dudley Carleton the following: "There is a ship come from Virginia, with news of their well-doing, which puts some life into that action. . . . They have taken a daughter of a King, that was their greatest enemie as she was going a feasting upon a river to visit certain friends; for whose ransome the father offers whatsoever is in his power, and to become their friend, and to bring them where they shall meet with gold mines. . . ." (Letter from John Chamberlain to Sir Dudley Carleton, August 1, 1613, MS 4173, "Bibliotheca Birchiana," Department of Manuscripts, Library, British Museum; Thomas Birch, *Court and Times of James I*, I, 262–63.) Chamberlain's letter exaggerates the ransom that Powhatan was willing to pay for Pocahontas, but the letter is an important demonstration of the attitude that the English were taking toward Pocahontas—that she was the golden key to a prosperous future in the New World and a symbol of success that would be worthy of English support. Her abduction did indeed put "some life into that action."

attended more or less deliberately to the transformation of Pocahontas into a "model Indian princess."

Pocahontas was placed in the care of the Reverend Alexander Whitaker, who took her to his farm near Henrico.[20] His women parishioners taught her to wear English dress, and he undertook the Pygmalion-like role of molding the young savage into an English lady. No longer was she permitted to offer sacrifices to Ahone at mealtime or repeat traditional Powhatan chants to the god. Whitaker taught her to bow her head and thank the Christian God for what she was about to receive. "Every Sabbath day," he wrote his cousin, the minister of Black Friars in London, "wee preach in the forenoon and Chatechize in the afternoon. Every Saturday night I exercise in Sir Thomas Dale's house. . . . Once every moneth wee have Communion, and once a year a solemn Fast."[21] Pocahontas was soon attending the services, and under Whitaker's tutelage and that of Sir Thomas Dale she became a student of the faith of the Church of England. "Her desire to be taught and instructed in the knowledge of God, her capablenesse of understanding, her aptness and willingness"[22] made her a receptive student. She also accepted, though at first probably with little understanding, the Prayer Book admonition to "renounce the devil and all his works, the vain pomp and glory of the world, with all covetous desires of the same, and the carnal desires of the flesh, so that thou wilt not follow, nor be led by them."

[20] Whitaker's one-hundred-acre glebe farm was selected by Gates and Dale as a suitable abode for Pocahontas because of its well-guarded location on impaled land about two miles from Henrico. Nearby were Forts Charatie, Mount Malady, Elizabeth, and Patience. Whitaker's house, "Rocke Hall," a frame house despite its name, was but a short distance from Mount Malady, where there was a sixty-bed hospital.

[21] Hamor, *A True Discourse*, 60.

[22] Letter from John Rolfe to Sir Thomas Dale, MS Ashmolean 830, fol. 118–19, Department of Western Manuscripts, Archives, Bodleian Library, Oxford University.

Unable to read or write English, though she could speak and understand a fair number of English words, Pocahontas memorized the Apostle's Creed, the Lord's Prayer, and the Ten Commandments, and learned the answers to the questions of the short catechism. With great effort she learned to recite other creeds and prayers, "which thing," Whitaker wrote, "Sir Thomas Dale had laboured a long time to ground in her."[23]

Finally, in the spring of 1614, Whitaker reviewed her in the catechism, received her renunciation of paganism, heard her confession of faith in Jesus Christ, and through the sacrament of baptism renamed her Rebecca and welcomed her into the fellowship of the Church of England.

In Pocahontas' conversion a major step had been taken in the colonists' efforts to influence Powhatan to accept the fact of English settlement and to display a Christian Indian woman as a symbol of the cultural blending of Old and New Worlds. Pocahontas' conversion also revealed much about her personality and character. It was indicative of her capacity for entering new arenas of experience. Whether or not she fully understood or accepted her new faith cannot be known. But in her willingness to learn English ways, English words, and English rituals, she revealed an extraordinary ability to move from a culture grounded in sacrifice and superstition into a culture that was by contrast enlightened and sophisticated.

[23] Hamor, *A True Discourse*, 60; Purchas, *Purchas His Pilgrimes*, IV, 1770.

CHAPTER XIII

The Marriage

DURING THE TIME Pocahontas was held hostage in Henrico, she became acquainted with a twenty-eight-year-old widower named John Rolfe. Rolfe was an English gentleman, descendant of a family that had come to England from Scandinavia long before the arrival of William the Conqueror. John was greatly respected by his fellow countrymen both in Virginia and in his native Norfolk County. He was a handsome man, a little above medium height, with brownish hair streaked with gold, gray eyes, and the short nose that was the distinguishing feature of the Rolfe family. He was well educated and may have attended Cambridge University.[1] Rolfe was the grandson of Eustace Rolfe, who in 1587–88 had contributed £25 (the equivalent today of £1,000) to help build the ships that defeated the Spanish Armada.[2]

John Rolfe, one of the survivors of the shipwreck in Bermuda, arrived in Virginia in 1610.[3] His primary concern was to establish the tobacco industry in the colony. He discovered that tobacco could be obtained in the New World only by buying it from the Indians or by cultivating it; the plant did not grow naturally or untended. Almost as soon as he arrived in Jamestown, he began experimenting with the cultivation of Spanish, English, and Indian varieties of tobacco, hoping to make the crop commercially feasible. In June, 1613, he shipped samples of his new "West Indian" tobacco back to England on the *Elizabeth*,

[1] Little is known about Rolfe's formal education. His writings indicate that he was well schooled. He may have studied with private tutors at his ancestral home, Heacham Hall, near King's Lynn, and later may have attended not-far-distant Cambridge University, where he would have absorbed some of the Puritan ideas reflected in the "conscience searching" letter he was later to write to Sir Thomas Dale. (A. E. Gunther, *The Rolfe Family Records.* 2–4, 200–202.)

[2] Rolfe had two younger brothers, Edward and Henry, both of whom remained in England. Edward settled in King's Lynn. Henry went to London, where he became a prosperous merchant and a member of the Virginia Company. After the death of Rolfe's father, his mother married Robert Redmayne, chancellor of the Diocese of Heacham. (Gunther, *The Rolfe Family Records*, 1–4.)

[3] In his report concerning the *Sea Venture* survivors in Bermuda, Sir Thomas Gates wrote: "We had the childe of one John Rolfe christened . . ., to which Captain Newport and myselfe were Witnesses, and aforesaid Mistress Hortan and we named it Bermuda." The Rolfe infant was shortly thereafter listed by Gates among those who died in Bermuda. (Purchas, *Purchas His Pilgrimes*, IV, 1746.) Whether the first Mrs. Rolfe died in childbirth, in Bermuda, or on the way to Jamestown is unknown.

and he was soon making regular shipments of more than one ton of high-grade tobacco to the English market.[4]

Soon after their meeting, Pocahontas and Rolfe began seeing one another regularly not only at church and at Mr. Whitaker's home but also in Rolfe's tobacco fields, where Pocahontas demonstrated for him Powhatan methods of growing tobacco. When the eighteen-year-old Pocahontas revealed to Rolfe her capacity for adapting to English ways of life, including the Christian faith, the lonely Rolfe began pondering the possibility of marriage to this young, attractive woman.

Early in 1614, shortly before Pocahontas became a communicant of the Church of England, John Rolfe composed a long letter to Sir Thomas Dale, in which he requested approval of the union from the English community, for he was aware of the impact such a marriage might have upon his own people.

In the letter Rolfe expressed his earnest desire to marry

Pokanhuntas to whom my hartie and best thoughts are, and have for a long time been so intangled, and inthralled in so intricate a laborinth, that I was even awearied to unwind myselfe thereout. But Almighty God, who never faileth his, that truely invocate his holy name hath opened the gate, and led me by the hand that I might plainly see and discerne the safe paths wherein to tread.[5]

Rolfe admitted that the woman with whom he had fallen in love was

one whose education has bin rude, her manners barbarous, her generation accursed, and so discrepant in all nurtriture from myself

[4] For a thorough discussion of John Rolfe and the Virginia tobacco industry see Melvin Herndon, *Tobacco in Colonial Virginia, "The Sovereign Remedy."*

[5] Letter from John Rolfe to Sir Thomas Dale, MS Ashmolean 830, fol. 118–19, Department of Western Manuscripts, Archives, Bodleian Library, Oxford University.

that oftentimes with feare and trembling I have ended my private controversie with this: surely these are wicked instigations, hatched by him who seeketh and delighteth in man's destruction; and so with fervent praiers to be ever perserved from such diabolical assaults (as I tooke those to be) I have taken some rest.[6]

Rolfe was clearly aware of the long-standing taboo against such alliances. He was not oblivious, he said, to the punishment meted out by God to the sons of "Levie and Israel" for marrying "strange wives." Notwithstanding, he sought Dale's permission for the marriage: "And did not my case proceede from an unspotted conscience, I should not dare to offer to your view and approved judgement these passions of my troubled soule." So that Dale would not believe that the proposed marriage was based solely on "desire of carnal affection," Rolfe declared that it would be for the "good of this plantation, for the honour of our countrie, for the glory of God."[7]

Dale was quick to agree that the marriage would be good for the colony, though he had probably never counted on the good fortune of such an event. It must have astonished all the Virginia Company officials that Rolfe, scion of an old and respected family, would be the one to propose such a marriage. Needless to say, Dale gave his prompt and wholehearted approval.

Emboldened by Dale's consent, Rolfe pressed his suit to Pocahontas, and to his joy she accepted him. Then Dale took charge of matters, using the forthcoming wedding as justification for attempting once again to press Chief Powhatan for a peaceful settlement of hostilities. Dale decided to return Pocahontas to her father and demand the ransom of any Englishmen still held as prisoners and the return of all English weapons. Then he would present Powhatan with news of the proposed marriage, which he hoped would persuade Powhatan to agree to peace.

[6] *Ibid.*   [7] *Ibid.*

In March, 1614, Dale, Rolfe, and Pocahontas, with an escort of 150 men, boarded the *Treasurer*, still captained by Argall, and sailed from Point Comfort to Werowocomoco, which Powhatan had once again made his capital. In Poetan Bay, Dale's men informed Powhatan's warriors that the English had come "to deliver up the daughter of Powhatan and receive the promised return of men and arms."[8] The Indians' response was several light forays against the colonists. Finally, with the *Treasurer's* guns and cannons trained on the four hundred Powhatans on shore, a small group of Englishmen landed and burned several Powhatan houses near the water's edge. Then a brief truce was declared while two of Pocahontas' brothers, delegated by Powhatan, went aboard the *Treasurer* to see how their sister "had been used" by the English.

Pocahontas' appearance reassured the brothers. For her part, Pocahontas told them that she was deeply grieved by Powhatan's unwillingness to part with his English weapons in order to obtain her release, adding that because she had been so well treated by the English she intended to remain with them, now preferring them to her own people. Then Rolfe and another colonist, John Sparks, were sent ashore by Dale to negotiate with the chief himself. They were conducted not to the chief but to one of Powhatan's emissaries. Powhatan considered it beneath his dignity to negotiate with anyone but Dale himself.

Through the emissary, Rolfe and Sparks informed Powhatan about the proposed marriage. Much to their surprise, Powhatan sent back word that he gave his consent to the match and would be willing to make peace with the colonists. Rolfe and Sparks returned to the *Treasurer* with the good news. Though they returned without the ransom of all the white prisoners and the arms, there was general rejoicing over the chief's response. Rolfe and Pocahontas were no doubt pleased that the marriage would

[8] Neill, *History of the Virginia Company*, 90–91.

not offend Powhatan or arouse new hostilities. Dale was relieved by the prospect of peace at last with the Powhatans.

Ten days later, supposedly on the morning of April 5, 1614, John Rolfe and Pocahontas were married by Mr. Bucke, the senior minister in Virginia and a close friend of Rolfe's, in the little wild-flower-decorated church at Jamestown. Present at the wedding were Pocahontas' uncle Opitchapan, who gave her away, two of her brothers as Powhatan's representatives, and other guests, who had been summoned to the ceremony by church bells, whose chimes echoed pleasantly on the Jamestown air. The bride wore a "tunic of Dacca muslin, a flowing veil and long robe of rich material" from England. Encircling her neck was a chain of fresh-water pearls, a wedding gift from her father, who had refused to attend the ceremony.[9]

After their marriage John Rolfe and Pocahontas—now called Rebecca by the colonists—went to live in a house on the shore of the James River between Henrico and Bermuda Hundred. The land on which the house was built was another wedding gift from Powhatan. They called their new home "Varina," after a variety of tobacco that Rolfe had imported from Spain.

That the marriage symbolized for the colonists a lasting union between themselves and the New World was evident in comments Whitaker and Dale made shortly after the wedding. Whitaker wrote to his cousin in London: "Sir the Colony here is much better. Sir Thomas Dale . . . has now brought that to passe, which never before could be effected. For by warre upon our enemies, and kind usage of our friends, he hath brought them to seeke for peace of us, which is made, and they dare not breake."[10] Dale wrote to John King, the Bishop of London, that Pocahontas "is since married to an English gentleman of good understanding,

[9] Carolyn Thomas Foreman, *Indians Abroad*, 23; Smith, *Generall Historie*, Book IV, 113–14.

[10] Neill, *History of the Virginia Company*, 90–91.

and his letter to me contained the reason of his marriage to her. You may perceive another knot to bind the peace the stronger. Her father gave apprehension [consent] to it, and her uncle gave her to him in the church."[11]

There was an interesting confirmation that "another knot to bind the peace" had been tied. Dale, impressed by the Rolfes' compatibility and contentment, sent Raphe Hamor to Werowocomoco with an offer to "marry" Powhatan's youngest daughter. If Powhatan would consent to a union between Dale and the girl, then indeed "there could not be a truer assurance of peace and friendship."[12] But Powhatan told Hamor that he had already sold his youngest daughter "for two bushels of Rarwenoke"[13] to a great werowance "three daies journie from mee."[14] Powhatan evidently was not willing to give up another daughter to the English.

Then the chief asked about Pocahontas and Rolfe—"how they lived, loved, and liked." Hamor assured him that Pocahontas "was so contented she would not live again with him, whereat he laughed."[15] Most important, Powhatan confirmed the peace in a message he sent back with Hamor: "There have been too many of his [Dale's] men and mine slaine, and by my occasion there shall never be more . . . for I am now olde and would gladly end my daies in peace; if you offer me injurie, my countrie is large enough to goe from you. This much I hope will satisfie my brother."[16]

It was a message that the English had long awaited. And apparently Powhatan meant what he said. In the spring of 1614, seven years after the English had first arrived in Jamestown, the

11 *Ibid.*, 92.
12 Smith, *Generall Historie*, Book IV, 115.
13 *Ibid.*, 116.
14 *Ibid.*
15 *Ibid.*
16 *Ibid.*

struggle between the Powhatans and the colonists ceased. The marriage of Pocahontas and Rolfe did not herald a new day of mutual affection between Indians and Englishmen, and there would be isolated incidents of violence. But the English had established their foothold in the New World, and Chief Powhatan had at last recognized that he could not drive them away. The marriage of his daughter to an Englishman was a union he was not prepared to contest. Powhatan's War had come to an end.

CHAPTER XIV

A Matter of Money

Now THAT PEACE HAD DESCENDED upon Virginia, Sir Thomas Dale, Sir Thomas Gates, and other colonial leaders could turn to other vital matters, the most important of which was seeing to it that the colony was properly financed and adequately populated. The peace achieved with Powhatan presented a great opportunity to develop the colony to its fullest potential. Once again the English were to call upon Pocahontas to help assure Virginia's continued growth.

In 1615, Pocahontas gave birth to a son. Rolfe later wrote that the baby was the living image of his mother.[1] He was christened Thomas, possibly for Sir Thomas Dale. After his birth the Virginia Company, in appreciation of Pocahontas' many services to the colony, voted to provide an annual stipend for her and her son. To show its appreciation to John Rolfe, the company instructed Dale to appoint him recorder of the colony.

One important Englishman failed to share in the general enthusiasm over Rolfe's marriage. When King James was told of it, he was outraged and accused Rolfe of committing high treason in marrying the daughter of a savage king. James's Privy Council assured him that Rolfe's heirs would not inherit England's holdings in Virginia and further mollified him by reporting that the Chickahominies and other tribes in the Powhatan Confederacy were concluding separate peace treaties with Dale, who had promised each of eight Chickahominy chiefs a red coat or livery "from the King . . . [and] a picture of his majesty on copper, with a chain to hang around his neck." Thus bedecked, the chiefs were to be known as the "noblemen of King James I."[2] Reassured and flattered, James took a calmer view of events in Virginia.

James's reaction to the marriage was typical of the often irresponsible attitudes he had taken toward the colony and contributed to the problem of gaining the wholehearted support of the English people for the venture. James's unpredictability was a problem around which the colony's promoters had had to step cautiously for many years. He was an enigmatic man. On the one hand, he seemed to be fully aware of the importance of the Virginia colony and was eager to extend his domain beyond the seas and thereby become a more powerful Protestant monarch. On the other hand, he was quite capable of making overtures to

[1] Letter from John Rolfe to Sir Edwin Sandys, June 8, 1617, Box IX, Doc. 961, John Ferrar Papers, Department of Manuscripts, Library, Magdalene College, Cambridge University.

[2] Neill, *History of the Virginia Company*, 92.

Catholic Spain, which had consistently opposed England's colonial effort, with an eye to marrying his son Charles to the Spanish Infanta María. He could give his official blessing to the members of the Virginia Company and to their plans for Jamestown colonization and at the same time privately condemn the colonists for attempting to establish a Protestant colony in the face of papal bulls claiming the New World for Spain. He could be angered by the Rolfe marriage, seeing in it a threat to his "holdings" overseas, and at the same time be utterly indifferent to colonial affairs and refuse to become seriously committed to the success of the colonial experiment.

Moreover, James spent on frivolous causes money that could have been more usefully employed in support of colonization. He had inherited a debt of £400,000 from Queen Elizabeth, a debt which he could not discharge and over which he frequently quarreled with Parliament.[3] Yet he continued to spend great sums on inconsequential matters. Indeed, within five years of his coronation he had increased his debts to £700,000. Both he and his wife, Anne, spent money on elaborate masques and other frivolities, counting on replenishing their treasury through the marriages of their two sons and daughter to the wealthy offspring of European royalty.

In his indifference to the success of the Virginia colony, James hindered the efforts of both the clergy and the merchantmen. The planting of a Protestant colony was one of the most fervent wishes of such clergymen as Crashaw, Symonds, Donne, and John King, the Bishop of London, who were concerned with what they believed was their holy mission of converting the savages[4] and with saving the New World from Catholicism and

---

[3] William McElwee, *History of England*, 102–103; John Richard Green, *History of the English People*, II, 50.

[4] English clergymen were particularly stimulated to carry the faith to the New World when Mr. Whitaker sent to England an artificial toadstool (possibly

thereby putting a "bit" in their "ancient enemyes mouth."[5] The merchantmen, a comparatively new class in England, were searching for new markets and for cheaper and more abundant sources of raw material for home industries. Colonization of the New World was an obvious means of achieving those ends.

At length, realizing that no consistent backing would be forthcoming from James, a group of Virginia Company officers representing both clergy and merchantmen formed themselves into what became known as the Popular party, whose goal was to increase the company's capital and maintain its solvency. Among the members of the Popular party were Sir Edwin Sandys and the Earl of Southampton, Shakespeare's friend and patron. One of the tasks the party undertook was to collect monies already promised to the company (some stockholders had promised to "adventure" large sums of money in the Jamestown enterprise but had yet to honor their pledges[6]) and to encourage new investments.

Early in 1615 the group decided to hold a lottery in the churchyard of St. Paul's Cathedral, the proceeds from which were "to bring that work" in Virginia to a success as a "worthy Christian enterprise."[7] The lottery procedure was later described by the Reverend Samuel Purchas, the rector of St. Martin's:

> The great standing lottery was draine [drawn] in 1615 in the West end of Paul's churchyard . . . in which the Prizes were proportioned from two crowns (which was the least) to divers thousand . . . and

made of clay) painted in the image of Okeus as evidence of the Powhatans' pagan religion and their need of conversion.

[5] Brown, *The Genesis of the United States*, I, Preface, xiv.

[6] Neill, *History of the Virginia Company*, 84–85.

[7] To gain support for the lottery, Sandys and his friends solicited the consent of the church officials at Canterbury and of the city's lay officials as well, knowing that as Canterbury went so went England. Accompanying a letter sent to Canterbury's mayor and aldermen by members of the Popular party were blank books in which to register the sums to be "adventured" by Canterbury citizens.

paid in money or in Plate there set forth in view, provided that if any chose money rather than Plate or goods for paiment in summes above ten crownes, he was to abate [rebate] the tenth part. The orders of this lottery were published, and courses taken to prevent fraud.[8]

The lottery was highly successful and encouraged the Popular party to devise an even more elaborate fund-raising project, based on an idea that had originated among clerics of the Church of England. These worthies had proposed that a school of religious instruction should be established in Virginia for both white and Indian children. The idea was put forth that the recently converted Mrs. John Rolfe might pay a visit to England to help launch the school. The possibility of such a visit had first been mentioned by Sir Thomas Dale in a letter to the Bishop of London.[9]

In 1616 the Virginia Company appropriated the idea as an opportunity to dramatize in a startling and colorful way the story of Virginia. By bringing to England the Powhatan princess who had become an English lady,[10] to be shown off to royalty, clergy, and merchantmen, the Virginia Company hoped to attract more money and more colonists to Virginia. In seventeenth-century public relations fashion, plans were made for Pocahontas to sit for a formal portrait. Ben Jonson would devise a court masque

[8] Purchas, *Purchas His Pilgrimes*, IV, 1773.

[9] Neill, *History of the Virginia Company*, 92.

[10] Pocahontas was not the first Indian woman to visit England. Ten years earlier, Captain George Weymouth had arrived with five Abnaki Indians from Maine. Among the Indians was a comely young woman who was given the name "Mrs. Penobscot" upon her arrival in England. Mrs. Penobscot made no lasting impression upon the English, however, even though she donned Elizabethan dress, was presented at court, and sat for a portrait. After all, Mrs. Penobscot was not a royal princess, nor had she achieved fame. (See A. L. Rowse, "The Elizabethans and America," *American Heritage*, Vol. X, No. 5 (August, 1959), 24–25.

for her entertainment. She would be received at court and be welcomed by the great people of the day.

And so, in the spring of her nineteenth or twentieth year, Pocahontas was called from her peaceful life at "Varina" to give her final and most colorful performance in the drama of American history.

CHAPTER XV

The Visit to England

ON JUNE 12, 1616, Pocahontas, her husband, her son, and a retinue of ten or twelve tribesmen and tribeswomen[1] arrived at Plymouth on the *Treasurer*. There she was met with pomp and ceremony by Sir Lewis Stukley, the Vice-Admiral of Devon, and other gold-braided officials. Escorted to London and housed at

[1] Among Pocahontas' retinue were her half-sister Matachanna, who was serving as young Thomas Rolfe's nurse; Matachanna's husband, Tomocomo, who painted his face and body and wore native dress—a decorated scalplock, a breech-cloth ornamented with an animal's head and tail, and a fur mantle; another half-

174

the Bell Savage Inn on Ludgate Hill, Pocahontas began her visit, with all classes of English society prepared to pay her homage.

Virginia Company officials had made careful plans, designed "to advance the good of the plantation," calling for an enthusiastic welcome from the English people. The government would be represented by the king, the royal family, and the court; the church, by England's most distinguished divines; and the trades, by London's wealthy merchants and city companies. Her arrival was noted in a letter from John Chamberlain to Sir Dudley Carleton on June 22, 1616:

> Sir Thomas Dale is arrived from Virginia and brought with him some ten or twelve old and yonge of that countrie, among whom the most remarquable person is Poco-huntas (daughter of Pow-[h]atan a Kinge or Cacíque of that countrie . . . married to one Rolfe an English man.[2]

Perhaps the most important arrangements to be made were those for Pocahontas' presentation at court. The titled members of the Virginia Company, many of whom were not in royal favor, asked Captain John Smith to write a letter to Queen Anne calculated to interest her in receiving "Lady Rebecca." Though Smith was a commoner, he had dedicated his recently published *New*

sister; three Powhatan women servants, and four Powhatan men. The retinue had been organized by Sir Thomas Dale to enhance Pocahontas' status as a woman of royal birth.

Among those accompanying Pocahontas the most colorful was Tomocomo, who had been directed by Powhatan to count all the people he saw in England. As soon as he arrived at Plymouth, Tomocomo began making the count by notching a stick but soon abandoned the project because the people in England were as numerous, he later reported to Powhatan, "as the stars in the sky, the sand on English beaches, or the leaves on the trees." (Purchas, *Purchas His Pilgrimes*, IV, 1774.)

[2] Letter from John Chamberlain to Sir Dudley Carleton, June 22, 1616, Vol. LXXXVII, MS 375, State Papers Domestic James I, Public Record Office, London.

England Trials to Prince Charles, "the Most High and Excellent
. . . Prince of Wales . . . Heire to Great Britain, France and Ireland,"[3] and was at the moment in favor with the ruling family.

Respectfully addressed to "Most Admired Queene," Smith's
letter reviewed all the courtesies that Pocahontas had extended
to British subjects, including himself, since the founding of
Jamestown. He emphasized that if it had not been for Pocahontas "Virginia might [lie] as it was at our first arrival to this
day."[4] He described her "extraordinarie affection to our Nation,"
even after the onset of Powhatan's War terminated her visits to
Jamestown. He reviewed events of her life after her abduction
in 1613. Pocahontas, possessing far more wit and understanding
than others of her people, had rejected her barbarous condition,
and after accepting the Anglican faith

> had married an English Gentleman with whom at this present she
> is in England: the first Christian ever of that Nation, the first Vir-
> ginian ever spake English, or had a child in marriage by an English-
> man, a matter surely, if my meaning bee truly considered and well
> understood, worthy a Prince's understanding. . . . Thus most gra-
> cious Lady, I have related to Your Majestie what at your best leisure
> our approved Histories will account you at large and however this
> may be presented you from a more worthy pen, it cannot come
> from a more honest heart.[5]

In concluding his letter, Smith made bold to hint that if Pocahontas was not

> well received by Her Majesty her present love to us and Christi-
> anity might turn to such scorn and fury, as to divert all this good to

[3] Smith, *New England Trials*, C2. Charles, James's younger son, had become
heir apparent to the throne upon the death of Henry, the older brother, in 1612.
[4] Smith, *Generall Historie*, Book IV, 121–24.
[5] *Ibid.*

176

the worst of evil, where finding so great a Queene should do her some honor . . . would so ravish her dearest blood to effect that, Your Majestie and all the King's honest subjects most earnestly desires. And so I humbly kiss your Majestie's gracious hands.[6]

Smith's letter was hurriedly written and lacked grace,[7] but it apparently facilitated Pocahontas' presentation at court. Shortly after receiving it, Queen Anne selected Lord and Lady De La Warr to act as Pocahontas' social sponsors, to attend her at court, and to accompany her to state affairs and to the theater.

In the portrait painted of Pocahontas at the time of her presentation at court, she is shown wearing a mantle of red brocaded velvet richly ornamented with gold, possibly selected by Lady De La Warr. The dark underdress decorated with gold buttons is in keeping with the fashion of the day. In place of a ruff she wears an elaborate white lace whisk, or shoulder collar. In her right hand she holds a fan made of three ostrich feathers. Her dark, Stuart-style hat is richly banded with gold, giving the illusion of a coronet. Her hair is hidden beneath what appears to be a reddish-colored wig of the style popular among high-born Englishwomen of the day. Despite the wig and the English attire, however, Pocahontas retains her Indian appearance. Her smooth skin has the copperish tint of her people. Her high cheekbones, dark eyes, and Powhatan features are preserved, as are her dignity and royal bearing.[8]

[6] *Ibid.*

[7] Smith wrote the letter while engaged in organizing an expedition to New England—the fourth attempt he had made to colonize the area since his departure from Jamestown.

[8] The artist of the portrait is unknown. Engravings of the portrait were made by the distinguished artist Simon de Passe and circulated throughout London. Sir John Chamberlain received one of the engravings and sent it on to Sir Dudley Carleton with an accompanying letter dated March 29, 1617 (Old Style Calendar). The engravings, mere caricatures in comparison with the portrait itself, bore the following inscriptions in Latin and English: "Matoaka als Rebecka Filia

To Queen Anne and her ladies in waiting, Pocahontas' appearance and behavior were wholly acceptable. (It is possible that the Indian princess may have outshone the English queen in both qualities—which would not have been difficult, for, in the estimation of many, Queen Anne set a bad example for her subjects, being frivolous, vain, and too fond of spirits, as was the king, to suit the Puritan element of the time.)

After the presentation at court, the Virginia Company officials proceeded to display Lady Rebecca's virtues to the English people. John King, the Lord Bishop of London, entertained her at Lambeth Palace with pomp and festiveness that was, according to Samuel Purchas, a guest at the party, accorded no other lady of his acquaintance. Purchas later wrote that "Master Rolfe's wife did not only accustome herself to civilitie but carried herself as a Daughter of a King, and was accordingly respected not only by the great Virginia Company, which allowed provision for herself and her sonne, but of divers particular persons of Honour."[9]

When she was not being honored at affairs of state, Pocahontas received distinguished Englishmen at the Rolfes' quarters in the Bell Savage Inn. One such gentleman was Sir Walter Raleigh, whose presence at court was forbidden and who must thus meet the visitor privately.[10] Always the gallant, Raleigh knelt and kissed her hand, reputedly commenting afterward on his joy and good fortune in greeting so beautiful a princess.

Potentiss: Princ: Powhatani Imp: Virginiae"; "Aetatis suae 21. A°. 1616"; and "Matoaks als Rebecka daughter to the mighty Prince Powhatan Emperour of Attanoughkomouck als Virginia converted and baptized in the Christian faith, and Wife to the worh. Mr Tho: [John] Rolff."

[9] Purchas, *Purchas His Pilgrimes*, IV, 1774; Lucy Aiken, *Court of King James the First*, 334.

[10] Raleigh, freed from the Tower after a twelve-year imprisonment, was, with James's reluctant permission, preparing for an expedition to the West Indies.

Raleigh also escorted Pocahontas to the Tower of London to introduce her to his good friend, the Earl of Northumberland, the older brother of George Percy, whom, of course, Pocahontas had known in Jamestown.

Still a prisoner in the Tower, Northumberland, the Wizard Earl, was working among his crucibles, retorts, and other scientific apparatus when Pocahontas paid her visit. He invited her to leave with him the double-shell earrings that she was wearing so that he might reset them in silver rims.

Captain Percy himself visited Pocahontas at the inn, as did other early Jamestown settlers who were in England at the time. Another notable visitor was the poet and dramatist Ben Jonson, who, meeting Pocahontas in the inn parlor, questioned her rapidly for five minutes and then for the next forty-five minutes sat staring at her curiously until Pocahontas finally withdrew silently to her quarters upstairs, leaving Jonson to his bottle of sherry. Sir Thomas Dale, of course, visited the Rolfes regularly, though personal problems kept him from giving them his full attention,[11] and he left most of the details of their English visit in the hands of Sir Edwin Sandys and other titled members of the Virginia Company.

The reception at court, the gala affairs, and the visits from distinguished men were exciting new experiences for Pocahontas. But after a number of weeks the strain of the fast-paced, complex life took its toll of her health. Several times she was forced to bed with respiratory ailments. At length it was decided

[11] Upon his return to England in 1616 Dale found his wife, whom he had married shortly before his departure for Virginia in 1611, seriously ill, and he was heavily in debt. He showed little inclination to return to the New World and complained that he had no friends, money, or influence in England. Rolfe tried to help Dale by reporting to the king and to Sir Robert Rich that "Sir Thomas Dale's worth and name in managing the affairs of this Colony will outlast the standing of this plantation." (John Rolfe, "A True Relation of the State of Virginia by Mr. Rolfe," Box I, Doc. 208, Duke of Manchester Papers, Public Record Office, London.)

that the damp air of London did not agree with her, and the Rolfes moved to Brentford, a village about nine miles west of London where the Earl of Northumberland's handsome manor, Syon House, was situated. The Rolfes took quarters in the Brentford Inn, and slowly Pocahontas began to recuperate.

At Brentford she continued to receive a stream of courtiers, and it was there that she was reunited with Captain John Smith, whom she had not seen in eight years and whom until her arrival in England she had believed to be dead.[12] Upon seeing Smith at last, Pocahontas was at first too overcome with emotion to speak. According to Smith, "She turned about, obscured her face, as not seeming well contented; and in that humour with divers others we all left her two or three houres, repenting myself to have writ [the queen] she could speak English. But not long after that, she began to talk and remembered me well what courtesies she had done."[13]

At one point in their conversation she called Smith "father," a title he quickly rejected, explaining that he "durst not allow of that title, she being the daughter of a King." At this, "with well-set countenance," she spiritedly replied: " 'Were you not afraid to come into my father's Countrie, and caused feare in him and all of his people and feare you here I should call you father: I tell you I will, and you shall call mee childe, and so I will be for ever and ever your Countrieman.' "[14]

After the meeting ended, Smith wrote that "divers courtiers and others of my acquaintance [who] hath gone with me to see her generally concluded they did think God did have a great hand in her conversion, and they have seen many English ladies

[12] To ascertain whether Smith was dead or alive had been another commission given Tomocomo by Chief Powhatan, who had also commanded him to have Smith, if he was indeed alive, show him the English God and the English rulers, of whom Smith had so often spoken to the chief.

[13] Smith, *Generall Historie*, Book IV, 123.

[14] *Ibid.*, 121–23.

worse favored, proportioned, and behaviored."[15] Smith and Pocahontas never met again, but he was always to remember her as an important person in his life, and eight years later, in the Dedication of his *Generall Historie*, he gave her, "that blessed Pocahontas," equal listing with the "beautious Lady Tragabigzanda . . . the charitable Lady Callamata . . . and the good lady Madame Chanoyes" among the women who had most helped him in his lifetime.[16]

After Pocahontas had apparently recovered from her fatigue, she and her husband paid a visit to Heacham, the Rolfes' ancestral home. This visit was one of their own choosing and not a part of the Virginia Company's program. Rolfe felt the time was ripe to introduce "Lady Rebecca" and little Thomas to his family. Heacham was about a hundred miles from London, a week's journey by coach, on a route through Cambridge, Newmarket, Ely, and King's Lynn.

The Rolfe family's response to Pocahontas is unknown. The family records yield no information. The fact that the visit was made seems to indicate that it was a success. The appealing portrait of Pocahontas and her child (which later came to be known as the Sedgeford Hall Portrait) may have been painted at this time or from sketches made during the visit to Heacham. In the portrait mother and son are strikingly similar in features and expression. The eyes of both are dark and searching beneath their straight black brows. Pocahontas' hair hangs down her back. Her crimson bodice is embroidered with silver buttons and ornaments. Her skirt is olive green. She wears the double-shell earrings reset for her in silver by the Wizard Earl, and the pearls around her neck are presumably the wedding gift from her father. Her son, standing at her side, is dressed in frilled blouse and sashed breeches. His hand rests in his mother's.

15 *Ibid.*
16 *Ibid.*

The Heacham visit drew to an end, and Pocahontas and Rolfe returned to London, where Pocahontas again became a captive of the company. The officials, eager to display her as often as possible during her remaining weeks in England, were blind to her now obviously failing health. Many events were scheduled, one of which was Ben Jonson's Christmas masque performed on Twelfth Night at Whitehall in Pocahontas' honor. On January 18, 1616,[17] Sir Charles Chamberlain wrote his friend Sir Dudley Carleton: "On Twelfth Night there was a masque when the new made Earl [of Buckingham] and the Earl of Montgomery danced with the Queen. . . . The Virginian woman Pocahontas with her father counsellor [Tomocomo] have been with the King and graciously used, and both she and her assistant were pleased at the masque."[18] In the same letter Chamberlain announced the news that Pocahontas was soon to return to Virginia "though sore against her will, if the wind would about to send her away."[19]

Pocahontas' seven-month visit was drawing to a close. Her task was completed, or nearly so, and the company began making arrangements for the Rolfes' return to Virginia. In nearly every way Pocahontas' appearance had been a success. It had inspired Sir Thomas Smythe to promote a second and even more successful lottery in St. Paul's churchyard, which produced a great deal more money for financing the Virginia colony.[20] John Rolfe had seized the opportunity to support Sir Edwin Sandys, an enthusiastic backer of Virginia and a critic of the king's apathy, and also to write a tract entitled "A True Relation of the

[17] Old Style calendar.

[18] Letter from John Chamberlain to Sir Dudley Carleton, March 29, 1617 (Old Style Calendar), Vol. XC, MS 454, State Papers Domestic James I, Public Record Office, London.

[19] *Ibid.*

[20] The prizes in the second lottery were quite large: one of 4,500 crowns, two of 2,000 crowns, and four of 1,000 crowns, as well as numerous smaller consolation prizes. (Brown, *The Genesis of the United States*, I, 119.)

State of Virginia," addressed to the king, which invited prospective colonists to partake of the fruits of paradise in the virgin wilderness of Virginia, where every Englishman could "sit under his fig tree in safety, gathering and reaping his labors with much joy and comfort."[21] Moreover, the clergymen of London and environs had committed themselves to building a school at Henrico and had begun preaching sermons to that effect and taking up collections for the project throughout England.[22]

Pocahontas, her husband, her child, and her retinue had made real and tangible a distant world and had brought Virginia, and indeed the New World, nearer to the lives of Englishmen at home. They had turned many thoughts westward across the Atlantic to a land of new hope and incalculable opportunity.

[21] Rolfe, "A True Relation of the State of Virginia, by Mr. Rolfe," Box 1, Doc. 208, Duke of Manchester Papers, Public Record Office, London.

[22] Tomocomo had a part in eliciting church support for a religious school in Henrico. Fascinated by Tomocomo's barbarism, particularly in contrast to Pocahontas' gentility, the Reverend Samuel Purchas wrote to a fellow clergyman: "I have often conversed at my good friend's Master Doctor Goldstone's, where he [Tomocomo] was a frequent guest; and where I have both seen him dance his diabolical measures, and heard his discourse of his countrie, and religion, Sir Thos. Dale's man being the interpreter." Purchas described Tomocomo as "a blasphemer . . . preferring his God to ours because he taught them . . . to wear their Devill-lock at the left ear, . . . and [he] believed that this Okee or Devil had taught them their husbandry." (Purchas, *Purchas His Pilgrimes*, IV, 1874.)

CHAPTER XVI

Gravesend

POCAHONTAS, WITH HER HUSBAND, child, and escort, was booked to return to Virginia late in March, 1617, on the *George*, one of three ships scheduled to sail from Gravesend, at the mouth of the Thames. While she was waiting for the ship in Gravesend or shortly after she boarded the ship, Pocahontas became gravely ill, probably with pneumonia, or perhaps tuberculosis.[1] Rolfe,

[1] There is a tradition that when Pocahontas became ill she was staying in a small cottage at the foot of what is today Stone Street, in Gravesend, not far from the Thames.

184

aware for months of his young wife's declining health, was nevertheless unprepared for the possibility that she might die. In an effort to comfort her grieving husband, she reminded him that "all must die. 'Tis enough that the child liveth."[2] With those words Pocahontas died, in her twentieth year, far from home in an alien land.

Her body was prepared for burial, and on that same day, March 21, 1616 (Old Style Calendar), the funeral cortege wound its way up the hill to St. George's Parish Church, an ancient church standing near the water's edge. The Reverend Nicholas Frankwell, the rector of St. George's, met the procession at the entrance to the churchyard and escorted the coffin into the cold, damp, dimly lighted church. A medieval church of Saxon origin, St. George's had been stripped of its statuary in 1538 by order of the crown and converted into an Anglican church.[3] In this unlikely setting Pocahontas' funeral was held.

Attending the funeral with Rolfe and Pocahontas' retinue were Captain Argall, now deputy governor of Virginia and commander of the three ships that were scheduled to sail from Gravesend; Raphe Hamor; and the captain of the *Lizard*, another of the ships. In accordance with the custom of the parish at the time, the men sat with John Rolfe on one side of the church, and the women sat on the other.

Mr. Frankwell read from the Book of Common Prayer the traditional service for the burial of the dead. Afterward, Pocahontas was buried in the chancel of the church and Mr. Frankwell made the following entry in St. George's register: "1616 March 21. Rebecca Wrolfe, Wyffe of Thomas [John] Wrolfe Gent. a Virginia Lady Borne, was buried in ye Chancell."[4]

[2] Letter from John Rolfe to Sir Edwin Sandys, June 8, 1617, Box IX, Doc. 961, John Ferrar Papers, Department of Manuscripts, Library, Magdalene College, Cambridge University.

[3] Robert Heath Hiscock, *A History of the Parish Churches of Gravesend and the Burial Place of Princess Pocahontas*, 8–9, 12–13, 24–25.

[4] *Ibid.*, 24.

Captain Argall sent a message announcing her death to the Virginia Company in London.[5] On March 29, Sir John Chamberlain wrote to his friend Sir Dudley Carleton: "The Virginian woman whose picture I sent you died last week at Gravesend as she was returning home."[6] To those who did not know her well the death of Pocahontas was merely a matter of interest. However, to the Ancients who had been Pocahontas' first friends at Jamestown, her death was especially sad. Captain John Smith was said to have commented: "Poor little maid. I sorrowed much for her thus early death, and even now cannot think of it without grief, for I felt toward her as if she were mine own daughter."[7]

[5] Though Rolfe also signed the message, Argall evidently wrote it; it has the cold, matter-of-fact quality of his other writings. Rolfe was concerned with caring for his son, who was also ill, as was Matachanna, the nurse.

[6] Letter from John Chamberlain to Sir Dudley Carleton, March 29, 1617, Vol. XC, MS 454, State Papers Domestic James I, Public Record Office, London. (By the Old Style calendar the new year began on March 25.)

[7] Marguerite Stuart Quarles, *Pocahontas: Bright Stream Between Two Hills,* 29.

CHAPTER XVII

An Epilogue

IN HIS WRITINGS Captain Smith was to help make Pocahontas famous beyond her time, and as the Virginia Company went on to develop from their colony a New World empire, many more writers and commentators began to tell the story of Pocahontas in various ways. Though death cut short Pocahontas' life and though she played her role in history for only ten years, she was not to be forgotten. Her death at Gravesend marked the beginning of her immortality.

Not long after Pocahontas' death John Rolfe returned to Virginia. He left his son, Thomas, with Sir Lewis Stukley at Plymouth, who in turn placed young Thomas in the care of his physician, Dr. Manouri. Rolfe had wanted to take Thomas back to Virginia with him, but "by the advise of Captain Argall, and divers who also foresaw the danger and knew the inconvenience hereof, I was persuaded to do what I did."[1] Thomas was later entrusted to the care of Rolfe's youngest brother, Henry, in London. Rolfe never saw his son again.

Soon after his return to Virginia, Rolfe sent word to Chief Powhatan of Pocahontas' death. Shortly thereafter, Powhatan turned over leadership of the Powhatan Confederacy to his brother Opitchapan and went to live with the Patawomekes, as far as possible from the English settlements. He died a year later, in April, 1618,[2] at which time the Powhatan peace with the English was reconfirmed by Powhatan's brothers and successors, Opitchapan and Opechancanough.

Rolfe reported to his good friend Sir Edwin Sandys that Pocahontas' death was "much lamented" in Virginia. He wrote also of the "good estate of the colony (God be thanked)" and of the firm peace it enjoyed. "All men," he wrote, "now cheerefully labor about their grounds, their harts and hands not ceasing. . . . English wheate, flaxseed distributed to most men by the Govrnr and is putt in the ground: nothing neglected, wch in any waies may be avayleable to advance [the] Company. The Cattle thrive and increase exceeding well, the ploughes yerely worke and

[1] Letter from John Rolfe to Sir Edwin Sandys, June 8, 1617, Box IX, Doc. 961, John Ferrar Papers, Department of Manuscripts, Library, Magdalene College, Cambridge University.

[2] Powhatan's death was reported by John Rolfe on June 15, 1618, and the Reverend Alexander Whitaker published the news in a tract, which Purchas included in *Purchas His Pilgrimes*. (See also Smith, *Travels and Works of Captain John Smith*, II, 539.)

oxen are plentyfull."[3] There was also evidence that the Indians were willing "to Parte with their children"[4] and allow them to join white children in attending the school that was soon to be founded at Henrico.

Rolfe was concerned about his son's future welfare. The Virginia Company's stipend to Pocahontas had been provided for her lifetime only. In his letter to Sandys, Rolfe asked that the stipend

> may not die [with] my wife, but contynue for her childe's advancement wch will the better inable myself and him hereafter to undertake and execute what may be comaunded and requyred from us. Thus refering himself to yor approved wisdom craving pardon for my boldness, desyring no longer to live, then when I shall cease from studying and indeavoring to bend my best strength to [persevere] in this action for the advancement of . . . God, King, and Cuntry.[5]

Rolfe found consolation for his sorrow in devoting himself to the prosperity of the colony. For the next several years he worked to develop the tobacco industry. By 1619 tobacco, Virginia's "golden weed," had become the mainstay of the economy. In 1619 he also served as a member of the first representative legislative assembly in America, and helped shape Virginia's growth into an orderly and productive colony.

The only real tragedy of those prosperous years occurred in 1622, when Opechancanough, who had succeeded his less warlike brother Opitchapan, led an uprising against the colonists. By then the English population was so large and powerful that In-

[3] Letter from John Rolfe to Sir Edwin Sandys, June 8, 1617, Box IX, Doc. 961, John Ferrar Papers, Department of Manuscripts, Library, Magdalene College, Cambridge University.
[4] *Ibid.*
[5] *Ibid.*

dian opposition could not deter its growth, but in the uprising more than three hundred colonists were killed. One of them was John Rolfe.[6]

Thirteen years later, in 1635, Thomas Rolfe, now a young man of twenty, at last returned to Virginia, the land of his mother. The Powhatans had not forgotten that their royal princess had had a son who was in his own right a descendant of the Powhatan royal line. When Thomas arrived in Virginia, he found waiting for him not only "Varina," the plantation on which he was born, but also thousands of acres of land in the provinces originally inherited by his grandfather, Chief Powhatan.

As attested to by Surry County court records, "Mr. Thos. Rolfe" possessed "by Guifte of the Indian King"[7] about twelve hundred acres along the fertile south shore of the James River, the region commonly known as "Smith's Fort." His holdings in the area extended a mile or so inland from the high bluff along Gray's Creek directly opposite Jamestown. To make certain that there was no question about Thomas' ownership of the land, before his death John Rolfe had taken out a royal patent on it for his son.

Powhatan had also left Thomas hundreds of acres scattered elsewhere within a twenty-five-mile radius of Jamestown. More than four hundred acres were within the Chickahominies' boundaries and were adjacent to Fort James. In order to retain possession of the land, Thomas was required to maintain the fort for three years.[8]

[6] Christopher Brooke, *A Poem on the Late Massacre in Virginia*; Susan Myra Kingsbury (ed.), *The Records of the Virginia Company of London, 1607–1622*, III, 550–51.

[7] Ann Page Johns, *The Rolfe Property, Warren House, at "Smith's Fort Plantation," 1652–1935*, 8.

[8] According to the wording of Act II, October 5, 1646, of the Grand Assembly of Virginia: "And it is further enacted and granted, That Left. [Lieut.] Thomas Rolfe shall have and enjoy for himselfe and his heires forever Fort James alias

Thomas remained in Virginia the rest of his life, becoming, like his father, a tobacco planter. In 1641, Thomas petitioned the Virginia General Assembly for permission to visit his Indian kinsmen, mainly an aunt, "Cleopatre," and his formidable uncle, Opechancanough. Under ordinary circumstances colonists were forbidden by law to "speak or parley"[9] with the Powhatans, so strained had been relations between the English and the Indians since the 1622 massacre.[10]

Though Thomas visited among the Powhatans, he preferred English life and participated in colonial rather than Indian affairs. He married an Englishwoman, Jane Poythress, and from their union descended seven successive generations of educators, ministers, statesmen, and lawmakers, among whom were the Blairs, the Bollings, the Lewises, and the Randolphs. One of Thomas'—and therefore Pocahontas'—most distinguished descendants was John Randolph of Roanoke, who represented Virginia in the United States House of Representatives and in the United States Senate. Thus, through her son and his descendants, Pocahontas lived on in American history.

The people of England did not forget her contribution to New World colonization. The church in which she was buried is no

Chickahominy fort with foure hundred acres of land adjoyning to the same, with all houses and edifices belonging to the said forte. . . . Provided that he the said Left. Rolfe doe keepe and maintaine sixe men upon the place during the terme and time of three yeares, for which tyme he the said Lft. Rolfe for himselfe and the said sixe men are exempted from publique taxes." (William Waller Hening [ed.], *Statutes at Large: Being a Collection of All the Laws of Virginia from the First Session of the Legislature, in the Year 1619*, I, 327; hereafter cited as *Virginia Statutes at Large.*)

[9] Act XLVI, February, 1631–32, of the Grand Assembly of Virginia: "All trade with the Savages prohibited, as well Publique as private." (Hening, *Virginia Statutes at Large*, I, 173.)

[10] The colonists captured and executed Opechancanough on October 5, 1645, finally destroying the Powhatans' power in Tidewater Virginia. (Abbot, *A Virginia Chronology, 1585–1783*, 16–18.)

longer standing. In the present St. George's, built on the same site, is a memorial tablet placed in the chancel at the direction of the Reverend John H. Haslam, the rector of St. George's from 1892 to 1899. The inscription reads:

> This stone commemorates Princess Pocahontas or Metoaka daughter of the mighty American Indian Chief Powhattan. Gentle and humane, she was the friend of the earliest struggling English colonists whom she nobly rescued, protected, and helped.
>
> On her conversion to Christianity in 1613, she received in baptism the name Rebecca, and shortly afterwards became the wife of Thomas Rolfe, a settler in Virginia. She visited England with her husband in 1616, was graciously received by Queen Anne, wife of James I. In the twenty second year of her age she died at Gravesend, while preparing to revisit her native country, and was buried near this spot on March 21st 1617.[11]

A second memorial to Pocahontas was installed in St. George's in 1914, when two stained-glass windows were presented to the church by the Society of Colonial Dames of Virginia. The windows, dominated by the biblical figures of Ruth and Rebecca, also depict Pocahontas at the baptismal font and are bordered by plants and trees native to Virginia. On July 16, 1914, the windows were dedicated by the Bishop of Rochester in the presence of the American ambassador to Great Britain and visiting American Navy personnel.[12]

In the years during and after World War II, St. George's fell

---

[11] Hiscock, *A History of the Parish Churches of Gravesend and the Burial Place of Princess Pocahontas*, 25. Unfortunately, the error in referring to John Rolfe as "Thomas" was transferred from the church registry to the tablet in the chancel. The date given, 1617, is the New Style calendar date; by the Old Style calendar the year of Pocahontas' death was 1616. But since she died on March 21, the New Year (Old Style Calendar) was only four days away and was therefore referred to after March 25 as 1617.

[12] *Ibid.*, 25–26.

into disrepair, and in England and the United States a total of £4,000 was raised for its restoration and preservation as a memorial to Pocahontas and nondenominational chapel.[13] After its restoration the church was reopened by Nancy, Lady Astor— a descendant of Pocahontas—and the church was rededicated by the Bishop of Rochester on November 1, 1952, All Saints Day.[14]

On October 5, 1958, England and America again joined in paying tribute to Pocahontas when a bronze statue of Pocahontas, presented to St. George's Church by the people of Virginia, was unveiled in the churchyard by the Governor of Virginia, John S. Battle. Dogwood trees, representing the Virginia state tree, were planted in the churchyard by Governor Battle, assisted by the Mayor of Gravesend, Councillor L. Kempster; Lord Hailsham, Lord President of the Council; the Bishop of Rochester; and Lord Cornwallis, Lord Lieutenant of Kent.[15]

Elsewhere in England there are other memorials to Pocahontas. One is to be found in the Church of St. Mary the Virgin at Heacham, the church which members of the Rolfe family have attended since the sixteenth century. The memorial, carved in alabaster, is the work of Ottillea Wallace, a pupil of Rodin. According to A. E. Gunther, the memorial "takes the form of a bas-relief from a portrait of the Princess . . . showing the lady in the dress in which she attended Queen Anne of Denmark, consort of James I, at a masque."[16] Conceived and planned by Mrs. Charles Torrey (nee Neville Rolfe), whose husband was an American by birth, the memorial was unveiled on May 27, 1933, by the Lord Fermoy, M.P., and was dedicated by the Archdeacon of Lynn in the presence of representatives of the Rolfe family and of Americans descended from Thomas Rolfe.[17]

[13] *Ibid.*, 25–29.
[14] *Ibid.*, 25–26.
[15] *Ibid.*, 29.
[16] Gunther, *The Rolfe Family Records*, 89.
[17] *Ibid.*

At the request of Mrs. Torrey the memorial was placed in the north aisle of the church directly above the bronze memorial to John Rolfe's father.

Also in commemoration of Pocahontas' relationship with the Rolfes, in 1960 the Parish Council of Heacham erected a village road sign that

> depicts a relief in wood of Princess Pocahontas supported by a Norfolk hackney and by a seahorse. The ground shows the industries of Heacham in lavender, shellfish, and agriculture. An inscription on an oak support eight feet high, built into a brick and carstone base reads as follows:

> THIS SIGN WAS ERECTED BY PUBLIC SUBSCRIPTION
> 9TH APRIL 1960
> COMMEMORATING PRINCESS POCAHONTAS
> THE INDIAN PRINCESS
> WHO MARRIED JOHN ROLFE
> OF HEACHAM MANOR
> ALSO DEPICTING PAST AND PRESENT INDUSTRIES.[18]

In the United States, too, memorials have been erected to Pocahontas. Over the western rotunda of the Capitol in Washington is a marble frieze depicting Pocahontas' rescue of John Smith. At Jamestown stands a bronze statue of her, evidently a duplicate of the statue in St. George's churchyard at Gravesend. As recently as 1964 an exhibit was held at Jamestown of articles that Pocahontas once touched or wore, such as the white double-shell earrings that the Earl of Northumberland reset for her and an exquisite little sewing basket made of gaily dyed porcupine quills.

Because of the intrinsically romantic events of her life, Poca-

[18] *Ibid.*, 92.

hontas has been made the heroine of countless sentimental stories, plays, and poems that have had the unfortunate effect of making her seem more a figure of legend than one of history. Yet it is her true story, lived in a critical moment of history, that gives her enduring significance—the true story that took place many years ago, when the American adventure began.

Bibliography

I. MANUSCRIPT MATERIALS

Department of Western Manuscripts, Archives,
Bodleian Library, Oxford University

Descriptive Analytical and Critical Catalogus Codd. MSS Bibl. Bodl.,
XIV and XIX, Oxford MDCCC.
Letter from John Rolfe to Sir Thomas Dale, MS Ashmolean 830, fol.
118–19. (Physical description [p. 491]: "This seems to be a copy.

It is fairly written on two first leaves of two sheets and is neither dated, directed, nor indorsed. It is addressed to an English gentleman in the time of James I." The text of the letter is Rolfe's profession of love for and intent to marry Pocahontas.)

MS Tanneri, CLXVIII, fol. 2. (Handwritten MS arguing England's right to found a colony in the New World.)

Department of Manuscripts, Library, British Museum

Birch, Thomas. "Bibliotheca Birchiana" (Birch's MSS), MS 4173. (Relates to unpublished manuscript correspondence between John Chamberlain and Sir Dudley Carleton [1616–17] coincident with Pocahontas' visit to England. Utilized both by Thomas Birch, in *Court and Times of James I*, and by John Nichols, in *The Progresses, Processions and Magnificent Festivities of King James I . . . .*)

"Instructions Orders and Constitutions by Way of Advice Set Downe Declared by and Propounded to Sir Thomas Gates (Knight) Governour of the Virginia Colony Therein Planted . . .: Given by Virtue of His Majesty's Two Patents . . . ." 35 pp. (Included are "The Copy of the Commission Granted to the Right Honourable Sir Thomas West [Knight], Lord De La Warr," and "A Coppy of Old Instructions Given to Sir Thomas Gates Now Given to Lord La Warre Signed by 'A Constant and Perpetuall Servant Thomas Dale 9th August 1611,'" Add. MS 21993, fol. 187; Add. MS 12496, fol. 456).

Strachey, William. "The First Booke of the Historie of Travaile into Virginia Britania Expressing the Cosmographie and Commodities of the Country Together with the Manners and Customes of the People Gathered & Observed as Well by Those Who Went First Thither as Collected by William Strachey Gent: 3 Years Employed Secretarie State and of Counsaile with the Right Honorable the Lord LaWarre His Majesty's Lord Governour and Captain Generall of the Colony," Sloane Collection, MS 1622.

White, John. American Drawings (originals), Roy. 18 A XI. Box 1: Title and 4–8, 10–19; Box 2: 20–24, 30–31, 37–43; Box 3: 44–59. Department of Royal Manuscripts.

*John Ferrar Papers, Department of Manuscripts, Library,
Magdalene College, Cambridge University*

Letter from John Rolfe to Sir Edwin Sandys, June 8, 1617, Box IX, Doc. 961. (Apprises Sandys of Pocahontas' death and of Rolfe's decision to leave his son at Plymouth with Sir Lewis Stukley and also gives a description of the colony upon Rolfe's return to Virginia.)

Letter from George Thorpe to John Ferrar, 1621, MS 1019, Box X. (Urges Ferrar to have colonists examined by a physician before they embark for Virginia: "Of those few boys assigned to my oversight there are two that are so diseased . . . that one of them confessed he hath had [name of disease cut out of letter].")

Letter from William Turner to John Covett, December 20, 1606, Box X. (Gives details of delayed sailing of the *Susan Constant, the Godspeed,* and the *Discovery.* Difficult to decipher, it is the oldest letter pertaining to Virginia in the Ferrar Papers. It may have been deliberately vague in order to mislead Spanish spies whose duty it was to note dates of departure and return of ships to and from Virginia.)

Letter 1 to Sir Edwin Sandys (signature and date illegible), Miscellaneous Papers, Box XVI. (Relates to the making of iron. In the same folder is an undated, unsigned letter referring to Sir Thomas Gates and Sir Thomas Dale and to "the savages, and God.")

Letters from Sir George Yeardlye to Sir Edwin Sandys, 1249, imperfect, n.d.; 1250, July 20, 1619; 1251, June 7, 1620; 1252, May 11, 1621. Box XII. (Relate to Virginia colony.)

Public Record Office, London

"Grant to John Smith [of] 12d per Diem for Life (November, 19, 1616)," Grant Book, Vol. LXXXIX, MS 217.

Letter from John Chamberlain to Sir Dudley Carleton, June 22, 1616, State Papers Domestic James I, Vol. LXXXVII, MS 375.

Letter from John Chamberlain to Sir Dudley Carleton, January 18, 1617 (1616 Old Style calendar), State Papers Domestic James I, Vol. XC, MS 428.

Letter from John Chamberlain to Sir Dudley Carleton, March 29, 1617

(1616 Old Style calendar), State Papers Domestic James I, Vol. XC, MS 454.

Letter from Thomas De La Warr to Salisbury, June 3, 1611, State Papers Domestic James I, Vol. LXIV, 518.

Petition from George Yeardlye, George Thorpe, Sam Maycock, John Pory, John Rolfe, and other colonists to James I, January 21, 1620, Box 2, Doc. 290, Duke of Manchester Papers (classified under National Register of Archives). (Petitions James I to withdraw his "late proclamation" prohibiting the importation of tobacco into England.)

"A True Relation of the State of Virginia by Mr. Rolfe ni[nth] May, 1616," Box 1, Doc. 208, Duke of Manchester Papers. (One of three handwritten copies of a report concerning the Virginia colony by John Rolfe, recorder, addressed to "Ye right Hoble and Virtuous K^t Sir Robert Riche my singular good friend.")

Library of Congress, Archives and Photoduplication Service, Washington

"Early Records of Virginia," Safe 13. 2 vols. (Notes collected by Susan Myra Kingsbury, ed., for *The Records of the Virginia Company of London 1607–1622*.) Includes folio with Instructions to Colonists.

Virginia Miscellaneous (1606–1772), Box I. (Contains photostat of burial record of "Rebecca Wroth [Rolfe]," in St. George's Register, Gravesend, England.)

Microfilm copies of manuscripts, Dukes of Northumberland. Library (Alnwick Castle), British MS Project, as classified by Lester K. Born. Aln 114/5 (containing "Bill for Necessaries Bought by Mr. George Percy for His Voyage to the West Indies"); Aln 3/2 (F240) (Letters and Papers, 1600–1607); Aln 4/1 (F241) (Papers Relating to Military Affairs); Aln 4/2 (F241) (Letters and Papers, 1608–11, containing information about expenditures of George Percy and the payment by the Earl of debts incurred by Percy for clothing from London merchants); Aln 5/1 (F245) (Book of His Majesty's Offices, 1617, alluding to the tax of £30,000 levied on the Earl of Northumberland and his subsequent imprisonment in the Tower of London by order of James I for his alleged participation in the Gunpowder Plot).

Pamunkey Indian Reservation, King William County, Virginia

Cook, Tecumseh D. "Facts about the History of the Pamunkey Indian Tribe." Unpublished manuscript.

Varina-on-the-James, Richmond, Virginia

Stoneman, Janet Chase. "A History of Varina-on-the-James." Farmville, Va., Longwood College. Unpublished theme, 1957.

University of Pennsylvania, Philadelphia

Forman, Henry Chandlee. "Jamestown and St. Mary's Buried Cities of Romance." Unpublished Ph.D. dissertation, 1938.

II. UNITED STATES GOVERNMENT PUBLICATIONS, DOCUMENTS, AND RECORDS

Congress, House of Representatives. 82 Cong., 2 sess., *House Report No. 2503*, Ser. 11583.

Cotter, John L. *Archeological Excavations at Jamestown.* National Park Service *Archeological Research Series No. 4.* Washington, U.S. Government Printing Office, 1958.

Hatch, Charles E., Jr. *Jamestown, Virginia.* National Park Service *Historical Handbook Series No. 2.* Washington, U.S. Government Printing Office, 1957.

Hening, William Waller, ed. *Statutes at Large: Being a Collection of All the Laws of Virginia from the First Session of the Legislature, in the Year 1619.* 13 vols. New York, printed by the editor, 1819–23.

Hodge, Frederick Webb, ed. *Handbook of American Indians North of Mexico.* Bureau of American Ethnology *Bulletin 30.* 2 pts. Washington, U.S. Government Printing Office, 1907, 1910.

Holmes, William Henry. *Aboriginal Pottery of the Eastern United States.* Bureau of American Ethnology *Report 20.* Washington, U.S. Government Printing Office, 1903.

Index to the Writings on American History. Washington, U.S. Government Printing Office, 1956.

Kingsbury, Susan Myra, ed. *The Records of the Virginia Company of London 1607–1622.* 4 vols. Washington, U.S. Government Printing Office, 1906–35.

Lane, W. C., and N. E. Browne, eds. *Portrait Index.* Washington, U.S. Government Printing Office, 1906.

Swanton, John R. *The Indians of the Southeastern United States.* Bureau of American Ethnology *Bulletin 137.* Washington, U.S. Government Printing Office, 1902.

III. PRINTED PRIMARY SOURCES

Anonymous. *Good Newes from Virginia Sent from James His Towne This Present Month of March, 1623 by a Gentleman in That Country. To the Tune of, All Those That Be Good Fellowes. A Broadside Ballad from Virginia.* London, John Trundle, 1623. (Description: "This broadside ballad appears to be otherwise unknown; it is not recorded in *Short Title Catalogue*, Bishop, Sabin, Hazlett, B. A., Britwell or Bib Lindes *Catalogue of a Collection of Printed Broadsides in the Possession of The Society of Antiquitaries of London,* 1866." It antedates Anne Bradstreet's poetry and has the distinction of being the first poem written by an Englishman in the New World, since Christopher Brooke never visited America.)

Brinton, Daniel G., ed. *The Lenape and Their Legends, with the Complete Text and Symbols of the Walum Olum.* Philadelphia, 1885.

Brooke, Christopher. *A Poem on the Late Massacre in Virginia.* London, "Imprinted at London by G. Eld, for Robert Mylbourne and to be sold at his shop at the great South doore of Paul's [churchyard]," 1622. (From the Library of Lord Cromwell, Sprotborough Hall, Dorcaster, England, now in the Archives of the Thomas E. Gilcrease Museum of History and Art, Tulsa.)

Bry, Théodore de. *Historia Americae Sive Novi Orbis . . .* , Frankfurt, Matthew Meriani, 1590–1634.

Cotes, Richard. *James I, King of Great Britain.* London, Michael Sparkes, 1651.

De La Warr, Thomas. *The Relation of the Right Honourable the Lord*

De La Warre, Lord Governour and Captaine Generall of the Colonie Planted in Virginia. London, William Hall for William Welbie, 1611. (Photostat.)

Eburne, Richard. *A Plain Pathway to Plantations.* Ed. by Louis B. Wright. Ithaca, Cornell University Press, 1962. (Originally published in London in 1624.)

Gray, Robert. *A Good Speed to Virginia.* London, 1609.

Gunther, A. E. *A Guide to Heacham: Its History and Architecture.* Heacham, Norfolk, June, 1963.

———. *The Rolfe Family Records.* Vols. I and III in one volume. Heacham, Norfolk, and London, Litho Developments, Ltd., 1962.

Gunther, R. T., and A. Gunther. *The Rolfe Family Records.* Vol. II. Heacham, London, and Aylesbury, privately printed, 1914.

Hall, Joseph. *The Discovery of the New World.* London, for Ed. Blount and W. Barrett, 1609.

Hamor, Raphe. *A True Discourse of the Present Estate of Virginia, and the Successe of the Affaires There till the 18 June, 1614 . . . ,* London, "John Beale for William Welby dwelling at the signe of the Swanne in Paul's Church-yard," 1615. (Copy.)

Hariot, Thomas. *A Briefe and True Report of the New Found Land of Virginia.* London, 1588. (Description inside book: "A brief and true report of the new-found land of Virginia of the commodities and of the nature and manners of the naturall inhabitants. Discovered by the English Colony there seated by Sir Richard Grenville Knight in the yeere 1585 which Remained under the government of twelve moneths. At the Speciall charge and direction of the Honourable Sir Walter Raleigh Knight lord Warden of the Stanneries who therein hath been authorised by Her Majestie and her letters patents; This forebooke Is Made in English by Thomas Hariot, Servant to the above named Sir Walter, a member of the Colony. . . .")

Ingleby, Clement. *A Guide to the Rolfe Portraits, Formerly at Sedgeford Hall, Now Permanently in the Custody of the Urban District Council of Hunstanton.* Hunstanton, Witley Press, 1955.

Lorant, Stephen, ed. *The New World: The First Pictures of America Made by John White and Jaques Le Moyne and Engraved by*

Théodore de Bry with Contemporary Narratives of the Huguenots' *Settlement in Florida 1562–65 and the Virginia Colony 1585–90.* New York, Duell, Sloane & Pearce, 1946.

Percy, George. *Observations Gathered out of "A Discourse of the Plantation of the Southern Colony in Virginia by the English, 1606."* Ed. by David B. Quinn. Charlottesville, University Press of Virginia, 1967.

Purchas, Samuel. *Purchas His Pilgrimes.* 4 vols. London, William Stansbury for Henry Fetherstone, 1625.

Rich, R. *Newes from Virginia* (poem). New York, Scholars' Facsimilies & Reprints, 1937. (Originally published in London in 1610.)

Rolfe, John. *A True Relation of the State of Virginia Left by Sir Thomas Dale.* New Haven, Yale University Press, 1951. (Originally published in London in 1616.)

Smith, John. *Advertisements for the Unexperienced Planters of New England or Anywhere: Or, the Path-Way to Experience to Erect a Plantation.* London, John Haviland, 1631.

———. *The Generall Historie of Virginia, New-England, and the Summer Isles . . . .* London, printed by J. Dawson and J. Haviland for Michael Sparkes, 1624.

———. *A Map of Virginia. With a Description of the Countrey, the Commodities, People, Government and Religion. Written by Captaine John Smith Sometimes Governour of the Countrey, Whereunto Is Annexed the Proceedings of Those Colonies, Since Their First Departure from England, with the Discourses, Orations, and All Their Relations with the Salvages, and the Accidents That Befell Them in All Their Journies and Discoveries.* Oxford, Joseph Barnes, 1612. (Photostat.)

———. *New England Trials.* 2d ed. London, W. Jones, 1622.

———. *The True Travels, Adventures, and Observations of Captaine John Smith, in Europe, Asia, Affrica, and America, from Anno Domini 1593 to 1630.* London, "Printed by F. H. for Thomas Slater, and are to bee sold at the Blew Bible in Greene Arbour," 1630.

Strachey, William. *Historie of Travaile into Virginia Britannia.* Ed. by R. L. Major. Ser. I, Vol. VI. London, Hakluyt Society, 1849.

Symonds, William. *A Sermon Preached at White-Chappel, in the Presence of Many Honourable and Worshipfull, the Adventurers and Planters for Virginia. 25 April, 1609.* London, I. Windet, for Eleazer Edgar and William Welby, 1609. (Photostat.)

Wecheli, Joannis, and Théodore de Bry. *The American Indian as Depicted in a Collection of Plates Engraved by Théodore de Bry in the Year 1590; India Occident 1590–1602.* (A rebound volume of original De Bry engravings. Exact publication date unknown.)

Whitaker, Alexander. *Good Newes from Virginia.* Scholars' Facsimiles & Reprints, New York, 1937. (Originally printed in London in 1613.)

IV. BOOKS

Agar, Ben. *King James I King of Great Britain: His Apophthegmes or Table Talk.* London, printed by B. W., 1643.

Aiken, Lucy. *Court of King James the First.* 2 vols. London, 1822.

The American Heritage Book of Indians. New York, American Heritage Publishing Company, Inc., 1961.

America's Historylands. New ed. Washington, National Geographic Society, 1967.

Anonymous ("By the Author of *The Secret History of King Charles I and King James II*"). *The Secret History of King James I and King Charles I.* London, 1650.

Bancroft, George. *History of the United States.* Last rev. 5 vols. Boston, 1882.

Barbour, Philip L. *The Three Worlds of Captain John Smith.* Boston, Houghton Mifflin Company, 1964.

The Beauty of Britain. Intro. by J. B. Priestly. Rev. ed. London, B. T. Batsford, Ltd., 1962.

Bell, Adrian, George A. Birmingham, Edmund Blunden, Ivor Brown, Charles Bradley Ford, R. H. Mottram, and G. M. Young. *England's Heritage.* London, B. T. Batsford, Ltd., 1961.

Bemiss, S. M. *Ancient Adventurers.* Richmond, Va., Garrett & Massie, Inc., 1959.

Birch, Thomas. *Court & Times of James I.* 2 vols. London, Henry Colburn, 1849.

Bolton, Herbert Eugene. *Bolton and the Spanish Borderlands.* Ed. and with an introduction by John Francis Bannon. Norman, University of Oklahoma Press, 1964.

————, and Marshall Thomas Mailand. *The Colonization of North America, 1492–1783.* New York, 1920.

Brebner, J. Bartlett. *The Explorers of North America, 1492–1806.* London, 1933.

Brown, Alexander. *The Genesis of the United States.* 2 vols. Boston, Houghton Mifflin Company, 1890.

Burk, John. *The History of Virginia.* 4 vols. Petersburg, Va., Dickson and Pescud, 1822.

Chatterton, Edward Keble. *Captain John Smith.* New York, Harper & Brothers, 1927.

Churchill, Winston. *The New World (1485–1688).* Vol. II in *A History of the English-speaking Peoples.* 4 vols. New York, Dodd, Mead & Company, Inc., 1956.

Chute, Marchette. *Shakespeare of London.* New York, E. P. Dutton & Co., Inc., 1949.

Cotterill, R. S. *The Southern Indians: The Story of the Civilized Tribes Before Removal.* Norman, University of Oklahoma Press, 1954.

Cox, J. C., and C. B. Ford. *Parish Churches.* Rev. by Bryan Little. London, B. T. Batsford, Ltd., 1966.

Davidson, Marshall B. *The American Heritage History of Colonial Antiques.* New York, American Heritage Publishing Company, Inc., 1967.

Davis, J. *The First Settlers of Virginia.* New York, Riley and Company, 1806.

Devon, Frederick. *Pell Records James I.* London, John Rodwell, 1836.

Dickens, Charles. *A Child's History of England.* New York, G. W. Carleton & Co., 1878.

Drake, Francis S., ed. *The Indian Tribes of the United States.* Philadelphia, J. B. Lippincott and Company, 1884.

Drake, Samuel G. *The Aboriginal Races of North America*. 15th ed. New York, Hurst and Company, 1880.

Dutt, W. A. *The King's Homeland*. London, Adam and Charles Black, 1904.

Dutton, Ralph. *The English Country House*. Rev. ed. London, B. T. Batsford, Ltd., 1962.

Embrey, Alvin T. *History of Fredericksburg, Virginia*. Richmond, Va., Old Dominion Press, 1937.

Fiske, John. *Old Virginia and Her Neighbors*. 2 vols. Boston, Houghton Mifflin Company, 1897.

Force, Peter. *Tracts and Other Papers, Relating Principally to the Origin, Settlement, and Progress of the Colonies in North America from the Year of Discovery of the Country to the Year 1776*. 3 vols. Washington, Force, 1836.

Foreman, Carolyn Thomas. *Indians Abroad*. Norman, University of Oklahoma Press, 1943.

Garnett, David. *Pocahontas, or the Nonparell of Virginia*. London, Chatto and Windus, 1933.

Goodman, Godfrey. *The Court of King James The First*. 2 vols. London, 1839.

Green, John Richard. *History of the English People*. 2 vols. New York, American Book Exchange, 1881.

Groves, G. I. *Famous American Indians*. Chicago, 1944.

Gruden, Robert Pierce. *History of Gravesend*. London, William Pickering; James Johnston, Gravesend, 1843.

Guide Book King's Lynn England. King's Lynn, King's Lynn Publicity Committee, 1933.

Hamer, Philip M., ed. *A Guide to Archives and Manuscripts in the United States*. New Haven, Yale University Press, 1961.

History of the Thirteen Colonies. New York, American Heritage Publishing Company, Inc., 1967.

Horgan, Paul. *The Habit of Empire*. Santa Fe, N.M., Rydal Press, Inc., 1939.

Hotten, John Camden. *The Original Lists of Persons of Quality . . . and Others Who Went from Great Britain to the American Planta-*

tions, 1600–1700 (compiled from "MSS. Preserved in the State Paper Dept. of Her Majesty's Public Record Office, London"). New York, G. A. Baker Company, 1874.

Hyde, George E. *Indians of the Woodlands: From Prehistoric Times to 1725.* Norman, University of Oklahoma Press, 1962.

Irving, Washington. *The Life and Voyages of Christopher Columbus.* ("Arundel Series," No. 134.) New York, United States Book Company, 1891.

Jacobson, Jerome, S.J. *Educational Foundations of the Jesuits in Sixteenth Century New Spain.* Berkeley, University of California Press, 1938.

———. *James I, King of Great Britain.* 1690.

Jones, Mrs. Herbert. *Sandringham Past and Present.* London, Sampson Low, Marston, Searle, and Livingston, 1883.

King's Lynn, England. London, for John Franke, 1642.

Knight, Frank, and Rutley Knight. *Heacham Hall.* London, Waterlow & Sons, Ltd., 1929.

Larned, Josephus Nelson. *The New Larned History for Ready Reference.* 6 vols. Springfield, Mass., 1901.

———, ed. *The Literature of American History.* Boston, Houghton Mifflin Company, 1902.

Lewis, Clifford M., S.J., and Albert J. Loomis, S.J. *The Spanish Jesuit Mission in Virginia 1570–1572.* Chapel Hill, University of North Carolina Press, 1953.

Linklater, Eric. *Ben Jonson and King James.* London, 1931.

McElwee, William. *History of England.* New York, Barnes & Noble, Inc., 1960.

McKenney, Thomas L., and James Hall. *The Indian Tribes of North America.* Intro. by H. S. Braunholtz. Edinburgh, John Grant Publishers, 1934.

McSpadden, J. Walker. *Indian Heroes.* New York, 1928.

Mason, Frances Norton. *My Dearest Polly.* Richmond, Va., Garrett & Massie, Inc., 1961.

Meade, William. *Old Churches, Ministers and Families of Virginia.* 2 vols. Philadelphia, J. B. Lippincott Company, 1894.

Neill, Edward D. *History of the Virginia Company of London, with Letters to and from the First Colony Never Before Printed.* Albany, Joel Munsell, 1869. (From first relation of the colony, published in 1608 and attributed to John Smith.)

Nichols, John. *The Progresses, Processions and Magnificent Festivities of King James I . . . .* 4 vols. London, J. B. Nichols, 1828.

Nicholson, Nigel. *Great Houses of Britain.* New York, G. P. Putnam's Sons, 1965.

Nutting, Wallace. *Virginia Beautiful.* New York, Garden City, New York, Publishing Company, 1930.

Parley, Peter. *Lives of Celebrated American Indians.* Boston, Bradbury, Soden & Company, 1843.

Petrie, Sir Charles. *The Stuarts.* London, Eyre and Spottiswoode, 1937.

Price, Andrew. *The Princess Pocahontas.* Marlinton, W.Va., 1924.

Robertson, Wyndham. *Pocahontas and Her Descendants.* Richmond, Va., J. W. Randolph and English, 1887.

Scherman, David E., and Rosemarie Redlich. *Literary America.* New York, Dodd, Meade & Company, Inc., 1952.

Schoolcraft, Henry, *Algic Researches.* New York, Harper & Brothers, 1839.

Seelye, Elizabeth Eggleston, and Edward Eggleston. *Pocahontas.* New York, 1879.

Shelley, Henry C. *Inns and Taverns of Old London.* London, Sir Isaac Pitman and Sons, Ltd., 1809.

Smith, John. *Travels and Works of Captain John Smith.* Ed. by Edward Arber and A. G. Bradley. 2 vols. Edinburgh, John Grant Publishers, 1910.

Smith, Lacey Baldwin. *The Horizon Book of the Elizabethan World.* New York, American Heritage Publishing Company, Inc., 1967.

Stacy, John. *A General History of the County of Norfolk.* 2 vols. London, John Stacy, 1829.

Stith, William. *The History of the First Discovery and Settlement of Virginia.* Williamsburg, William Parks, 1746.

Swem, E. G. *Virginia Historical Index.* 2 vols. Roanoke, Stone Printing and Manufacturing Company, 1934.

Taylor, William. *The History and Antiquities of Castle Rising*. London, J. Masters; [King's] Lynn, W. Taylor and Thew and Son, 1850.

This England. Foreword by Melville Bell Grosvenor. Washington, National Geographic Society, 1966.

Thwaites, Reuben Gold, ed. *The Jesuit Relations and Allied Documents, 1612–1614*. Vol. II. Cleveland, Burrows Brothers Company, 1896.

Weddell, Alexander Wilbourne, ed. *A Memorial Volume of Virginia Historical Portraiture 1558–1830*. Richmond, Va., 1930.

Willson, George F. *Saints and Strangers*. New York, Reynal & Hitchcock, 1945.

Wilson, Arthur. *The History of Great Britain*. London, for Richard Lownds, 1653.

Wilson, John Dover. *Life in Shakespeare's England*. Baltimore, Penguin Books, Inc., 1959.

Winsor, Justin, ed. *Narrative and Critical History of America*. Vol. IV. Boston, 1884.

Woods, George B., Homer A. Watt, and George K. Anderson. *The Literature of England*. Rev. ed. Vol. I. Chicago, Scott, Foresman & Company, 1941.

Wright, Louis B. *Shakespeare for Everyman*. New York, Washington Square Press, Inc., 1964.

V. BOOKLETS

General History

Abbot, William W. *A Virginia Chronology, 1585–1783*. Richmond, Garrett & Massie, Inc., 1957.

Bland, Edward (Merchant), Abraham Woods, Captaine Sackford Brewster, and Elias Pennant, Gentlemen. *A Discovery of New Britaine*. Ann Arbor, reprinted for the Clements Library Associates, 1960. (Originally published in London in 1651).

Brydon, Rev. G. Maclaren (historiographer of the Episcopal Diocese of Virginia). *Highlights Along the Road of the Anglican Church*. Richmond, Va., Virginia Diocesan Library, 1957.

————. *Religious Life of Virginia in the Seventeenth Century*. Richmond, Va., Garrett & Massie, Inc., 1957.

The Church of Saint Mary, the Virgin, Heacham, Bishop's House, Norwich, England, Heacham Parochial Church Council, 1963.

Harrison, Caroline Rivers. *Historic Guide Richmond and James River*. 9th ed. Richmond, 1961.

Henrico County Primary and Secondary Highway Systems. Richmond, Va., Department of Highways, January 1, 1963.

Herndon, Melvin. *Tobacco in Colonial Virginia, "The Sovereign Remedy."* Richmond, Va., Garrett & Massie, Inc., 1957.

Hiscock, Robert Heath. *A History of the Parish Churches of Gravesend and the Burial Place of Princess Pocahontas*. Gloucester, England, n.d.

Hughes, Thomas P. *Medicine in Virginia 1607–1699*. Richmond, Va., Garrett & Massie, Inc., 1957.

Hunt, David C. *Reports from the New World*. Tulsa, Thomas Gilcrease Institute of American History and Art, 1966.

Johns, Ann Page. *The Rolfe Property, Warren House, at "Smith's Fort Plantation" 1652–1935*. Richmond, Va., Association for the Preservation of Virginia Antiquities, 1938.

McCary, Ben C. *Indians in Seventeenth-Century Virginia*. Richmond, Va., Garrett & Massie, Inc., 1957.

————. *John Smith's Map of Virginia, with a Brief Account of Its History*. Richmond, Va., Garrett & Massie, Inc., 1957.

Quarles, Marguerite Stuart. *Pocahontas: Bright Stream Between Two Hills*. Richmond, Va., Association for the Preservation of Virginia Antiquities, 1939.

Syon House. Northhampton, England, Syon House Estate, 1950.

Williams, Frances Leigh. *A Tour of Historic Richmond*. Richmond, Va., 1937.

Tudor and Stuart Civilization

LaMar, Virginia A. *English Dress in the Age of Shakespeare*. Washington, Folger Shakespeare Library, 1958.

————. *Travel and Roads in England*. Washington, Folger Shakespeare Library, 1960.

Penrose, Boies. *Tudor and Early Stuart Voyaging.* Washington, Folger Shakespeare Library, 1962.

Schmidt, Albert J. *The Yeoman in Tudor and Stuart England.* Washington, Folger Shakespeare Library, 1961.

Stone, Lilly C. *English Sports and Recreations.* Washington, Folger Shakespeare Library, 1960.

Thompson, Craig R. *The English Church in the Sixteenth Century.* Ithaca, Cornell University Press, 1958.

VI. ARTICLES

Andrews, K. R. "Christopher Newport of Limehouse, Mariner," *William and Mary Quarterly*, 3d Ser., Vol. XI, No. 1, 28–41.

Anonymous. "Orapax," *Virginia Magazine of History and Biography*, Vol. XXXV (1937), 78.

Bushnell, David I., Jr. "John White—the First English Artist to Visit America, 1585," *Virginia Magazine of History and Biography*, Vol. XXXV (1937), 419–30.

———. "Virginia—from Early Records," *American Anthropologist*, Vol. 9, No. 1 (January–March, 1907), 38–41.

Carter, Charles S. "Gondamar: Ambassador to James I," *Historical Journal*, Vol. VII, No. 2 (1964), 189–208.

Cleaveland, The Rev. George J. "The Beginning of a Good Work," *Virginia Churchman*, Vol. LXX, No. 6 (December, 1961), 12–14.

———. "The Reverend Alexander Whitaker, M.A. Parson of Henrico, Apostle to the Indians, a Saviour of Virginia," *Virginia Churchman*, Vol. LXVI, No. 2 (June, 1957), 15–24.

Fisher, Allen C., Jr. "The City—London's Storied Square Mile," *National Geographic*, Vol. 129, No. 6 (June, 1966), 743–91.

Fishwick, Marshall. "Was John Smith a Liar?" *American Heritage*, Vol. IX, No. 6 (October, 1958), 28–33, 110–11.

Goodwin, Mary F. "Virginia Ever Missionary," *Virginia Churchman*, Vol. LXVI, No. 2 (June, 1957), 19–24.

Grossman, Mary Louise. "A Heritage in Peril," *American Heritage*, Vol. XVII, No. 5 (August, 1966), 4–14, 68–69.

Hanke, Lewis. "Conquest and the Cross," *American Heritage*, Vol. XIV, No. 2, (February, 1963), 5–17.

Hume, Ivor Noel. "Digging Up Jamestown," *American Heritage*, Vol. XIV, No. 3 (April, 1963), 66–77.

Kenney, Nathaniel T., and Bates Littlehales. "Chesapeake Country," *National Geographic*, Vol. 126, No. 3 (September, 1964), 370–411.

Land, Robert Hunt. "Henrico and Its College," *William and Mary Quarterly*, 2d Ser., Vol. VIII, 464–68.

Mooney, James. "The Powhatan Confederacy, Past and Present," *American Anthropologist*, Vol. 9, No. 1 (January–March, 1907), 123–29.

Morton, Louis, "The End of Formalized Warfare," *American Heritage*, Vol. VI, No. 5 (August, 1955), 12–15, 18–19, 95.

Price, Willard, and Robert F. Sisson, "The Thames Mirrors England's Varied Life," *National Geographic*, Vol. CXIV, No. 1 (July, 1958), 45–95.

Robinson, Morgan P. "Henrico Parish in Diocese of Virginia and the Parishes Descended Therefrom," *Virginia Magazine of History and Biography*, Vol. XLIII, No. 1 (January, 1935).

Rolfe, John. "John Rolfe's Will, of James City in Virginia, Dated 10 March 1621 . . . ," *Virginia Magazine of History and Biography*, Vol. XXI (1913), 209.

Rowse, A. L. "The Elizabethans and America," *American Heritage*, Vol. X, No. 3 (April, 1959), 4–15, 94–98; Vol. X, No. 4 (June, 1959), 4–19, 105–11; Vol. X, No. 5 (August, 1959), 22–29, 105–11; Vol. X, No. 6 (October, 1959), 48–53, 78–83; Vol. XI, No. 1 (December, 1959), 46–48, 57–59.

Russell, Frances. "Apostle to the Indians," *American Heritage*, Vol. IX, No. 6 (December, 1957), 4–9, 117–19.

Smythe, Clem T. "The Burial of Pocahontas," *Virginia Historical Register*, Vol. II (1849), 187–89.

Villiers, Alan, and Bates Littlehales. "Channel Cruise to Glorious Devon," *National Geographic*, Vol. 124, No. 2 (August, 1963), 208–59.

Willoughby, Charles C. "The Virginia Indians in the Seventeenth Century," *American Anthropologist*, Vol. 9, No. 1 (January–March, 1907), 57, 53n.

Wright, Louis B. "The Ancestors and Descendants of John Rolfe with Notices of Some Connected Families," *Virginia Magazine of History and Biography*, Vol. XXI (1913), 209–12.

———. "The Britain That Shakespeare Knew," *National Geographic*, Vol. 125, No. 5 (May, 1964), 613–67.

VII. INTERVIEWS

The Rev. George J. Cleaveland (registrar of the Episcopal Diocese of Virginia), Richmond, June, 1964.

Robert A. Elder, Jr. (museum specialist, Department of Anthropology, U.S. National Museum), Washington, June, 1964.

A. E. Gunther (author of *The Rolfe Family Records*, Vols. I and III), Heacham, Norfolk, England, May 20, 1968.

John Waverly Lindsey (owner and occupant of site of Werowocomoco), June, 1964.

Ben C. McCary (professor of modern languages in the College of William and Mary), Williamsburg, June, 1964.

Howard A. MacCord, Sr. (archaeologist, Virginia State Library, Richmond), June, 1964.

Relatives of Tecumseh Cook, chief of the Pamunkey Indians, living on the Pamunkey Reservation: Mrs. Jayce Bradby, a niece; Mrs. Dora Bradby, a sister; and Pocahontas Cook, a sister, June, 1964.

T. Dale Stewart (acting curator, physical anthropology, Smithsonian Institution, and author of "The Finding of an Indian Ossuary on the York River in Virginia," *Journal of the Washington Academy of Science*, Vol. XXX [1940], 356–64; and of "Excavating the Indian Village of Patawomeke [Potomac]," *Explorations and Field Work of the Smithsonian Institution in 1938* [1938–40], 87–90), June, 1964.

VIII. ETHNOLOGICAL SPECIMENS FROM TIDEWATER VIRGINIA

Department of Antiquities, Ashmolean Museum, Oxford

Powhatan's mantle, heavily embroidered with roanoke figures of animals and men.

Pocahontas

Bow, arrows, quivers, darts (*ca.* 1607–1608).

Purse, typical of those worn by Powhatan males in Pocahontas' era, embroidered in roanoke perforated with an awl and sewed to purse with sinew thread.

Tobacco pipes.

Smithsonian Institution, Washington

Beads (bone and shell).

Imprinted pottery fragments.

Pipes.

Miscellaneous artifacts.

Jamestown, Virginia

Double white shell earrings edged with silver, supposedly reset for Pocahontas by the Earl of Northumberland when she visited him at the Tower of London in 1616.

Pocahontas' small sewing basket, ornamented with porcupine quills.

Indian trade artifacts relating to English-Indian trade in the seventeenth century: beads, bells, hatchets, scissors, knives.

English artifacts: metal farming tools; hardware for houses; brick and other building materials; military weapons (fragments), such as gun parts, polearms, cutlasses, and broadswords; suits of mail and armor; and earthenware, glass, and metal objects of English manufacture.

Pamunkey Indian Reservation, King William County, Virginia

From private collection of Tecumseh Cook, chief of the Pamunkey Indians:

Pottery.

Pipes.

Bows, arrows, clubs, and other early Pamunkey weapons.

Awls, scrapers, stone chisels, and other tools, both artifacts and reproductions.

Index

Sacajawea

HAROLD P. HOWARD

Preface

FEW personalities in American history have been more idealized—or more controversial—than Sacajawea, the Shoshoni Indian girl who accompanied Meriwether Lewis and William Clark on their expedition to the Pacific Coast in 1804–1806. Some historians, among them Samuel Eliot Morison and LeRoy R. Hafen, refer to her as a guide or interpreter for the party. Others call her an unofficial "ambassadress" to the Indians living in the regions through which the explorers passed. Her importance to the expedition has also been disputed. Early twentieth-century historians tended to glorify her role. More recent writers are inclined to minimize her contribution and even to adopt a somewhat scornful view of her assistance to the explorers. It is the purpose of this book to review what has been learned and conjectured about her life before, during, and after the expedition and to accord to this appealing woman her rightful place in the westward expansion of the United States.

Sacajawea's life, like that of other native Americans who played brief but important roles on the stage of American history, must be largely pieced together from contemporary accounts—from the journals, diaries, and notes of Lewis and Clark and other members of the expedition. From those records it seems clear that Sacajawea joined the expedition largely by accident. She was allowed to accompany her French-Canadian husband, Toussaint Charbonneau, who was hired in the Mandan villages in North Dakota to serve as an interpreter on the journey westward. Sacajawea was one of the two unofficial members of the party, the other being Clark's black servant, York. Moreover, she was an unlikely member: she carried a newborn son. Yet it may be that her greatest service, among the many she performed, was simply her presence among the hardy band of explorers. The Indians the expedition encountered along the way knew that a woman with a baby never accompanied a war party. Her presence assured them that the explorers' intentions were peaceful.

After the Lewis and Clark party returned to North

Dakota, Sacajawea's service to the expedition ended. For many years afterward her name was almost lost to history. Contemporary records indicate that she died in her twenties in South Dakota. Indian tradition gives her a long life, the latter part spent in Wyoming with her people.

Contemporary records make it fairly easy to trace the later life of Sacajawea's husband, Charbonneau. Sacajawea's subsequent life is much more difficult to ascertain. Over the years the mists of legend tended to obscure the real woman. All that is known today about her and her family can be found in the pages that follow, with due attention to what many accept as authentic Indian oral tradition.

Americans are sentimental about their heroines. More memorials honor Sacajawea than any other American woman. Monuments, markers, and shafts have been erected in her honor, and parks, lakes, and mountain peaks have been named for her. This book, the product of many years spent in research and in sifting fact from romance, represents an effort at an unbiased appraisal of Sacajawea and her achievements.

To make clear Sacajawea's contribution to the success of the Lewis and Clark Expedition, I have found it necessary to retrace the path of the expedition in some detail, relating events in which Sacajawea took no direct or recorded part. Her daily assistance to the explorers—primarily as a provider of edible wild food—was often accepted without comment. Only in moments of crisis or times of deprivation was her aid acknowledged. Yet the explorers were aware of and grateful for her presence—as I hope to make clear in the pages that follow.

I wish to express thanks to many persons who have helped

Sacajawea

in the preparation of this book by offering useful advice and criticism—especially Ardis Edwards Burton, of Crockett, California; T. A. Larson, of the University of Wyoming; and Will G. Robinson, former secretary of the South Dakota Historical Society.

HAROLD P. HOWARD

Stickney, South Dakota

Contents

PART TWO. *Sacajawea's Later Life*

PART ONE: *The Lewis and Clark Expedition*

SACAJAWEA, *by Henry Lion, after a sketch by Charles M. Russell*
COURTESY OF NATIONAL COWBOY HALL OF FAME AND WESTERN
HERITAGE CENTER, OKLAHOMA CITY

The Expedition Sets Out

THE Lewis and Clark Expedition was a favorite project of President Thomas Jefferson. He had dreamed of this journey of exploration long before 1803, when his emissaries managed to buy the Louisiana Territory from Napoleon I of France for fifteen million dollars.

Before he received congressional approval of the Louisiana Purchase, and almost before the ink was dry on the document of sale, Jefferson set in motion his plan to explore the vast wilderness northwest of the Mississippi River. The land included in the Louisiana Purchase extended to the western border of what is now Montana. He expected the explorers to go beyond the limits of the newly acquired territory, and he hoped that they would find a traversable land or land-and-river route to the Pacific Ocean.

Jefferson had already decided who would lead this proposed expedition—Captain Meriwether Lewis, whom Jefferson first employed as his secretary, probably in anticipation of the expedition. Captain Lewis in turn had already decided whom he wanted to share the command if he could be persuaded to go—Captain William Clark, the younger brother of the famed Revolutionary War general George Rogers Clark. Lewis wrote to Clark from Washington on June 19, 1803, and received a favorable reply from Kentucky on July 26. Lewis insisted upon joint command of the expedition, wanting Clark to have authority equal to his own and to share equally in all decisions.

The expedition assembled in the fall of 1803 near St. Louis, Missouri, a village then consisting of just three streets. To begin with, the party numbered, besides the two captains, nine young Kentucky volunteers; fourteen soldiers, also volunteers; two French rivermen; one hunter; and Clark's Negro servant, York. To accompany them by water as far as the Mandan Indian villages in what is now North Dakota, nine more boatmen were employed, along with seven more soldiers. Winter quarters were established at Wood River on the eastern side of the Mississippi, opposite the mouth of the Missouri.

Jefferson's instructions said: "The object of your mission

is to explore the Missouri River, & such principal streams of it, as by its course & communication with the waters of the Pacific Ocean, may offer the most direct and practicable water communication across this continent, for the purpose of commerce." Lewis and Clark were expected to learn about the Indians, draw maps, find specimens of everything new to them—minerals, trees, flowers, animals, birds—and keep journals. Their cataloguing of these discoveries, and much more, is incredibly detailed. For the journey the explorers received altogether a niggardly appropriation of twenty-five-hundred dollars from Congress. Fortunately, they were able to draw on army depots for additional supplies.[1]

The materials most necessary for the expedition were divided into bales and boxes, one box containing a little of everything in the case of accidents. The men packed clothing, fine instruments, tools, locks, flints, powder, ammunition, medicines, and articles of a critical nature in seven bales and one reserve box. To these were added fourteen bales and one box of Indian presents—fancy coats, medals, flags, knives, tomahawks, ornaments, looking glasses, handkerchiefs, paints, and beads. The heaviest single item was lead for bullets. Spirits and tobacco were also included.

The party pulled away from the Wood River base on May 14, 1804, and proceeded up the Missouri River past a few small settlements. Very infrequently were they entirely

[1] The expedition finally cost more than $38,000, including army pay, subsistence, bounties, clothing, special uniforms, disbursements for horses, and so on, as well as the cost of outfitting and conducting a party of Mandan Indians to Washington in 1806 and returning them to Mandan country.

waterborne, since some members of the party usually walked along the shore. The plan was to go up the Missouri to its headwaters, which were thought to be several thousand miles away, and then strike off across the mountains, if necessary, to find a river leading to the Pacific Ocean.

For this water journey the men had procured a fifty-five-foot keelboat with a small sail and twenty-two oars. The men added two boats called pirogues, forty to fifty feet long, twelve feet wide, pointed at the prow, and square-sterned. Two horses, for hunting or carrying meat, were led or ridden along the banks of the river. The party pulled, poled, rowed, or sailed the boats up the river, always against the current.

The difference between this expedition and earlier and subsequent efforts to make the transcontinental journey was that the Lewis and Clark Expedition was well equipped and well planned. At times it would seem that there was too much baggage and that too much time was spent taking notes. But the result of the expedition was the opening of a land-and-river route across the United States—not the best or the shortest, but a good one—and the accumulation of a wealth of scientific information. The captains also drew the first good maps of the region.

A comparison of the Lewis and Clark trip, which was made into a completely unknown area, with the Astorians' trip of 1811, seven years later, points up how well Lewis and Clark managed. The Astorians tried to make the trip partly by water and partly by land, and they nearly failed to reach their destination, although Lewis and Clark had opened the way.

Another reason for the success of the Lewis and Clark Expedition was the alertness of the leaders. They always posted guards, and they seemed to be able to anticipate trouble. Lewis brought along his big Newfoundland, Scannon, who proved useful as a watchdog and hunter. Most of the Indian tribes ate dog meat, and Lewis and Clark did too; at times they even considered it a delicacy. But because of his value to the expedition Scannon never became a stew, and once a search party was sent out to find him when he was stolen by Indians.

Sir Alexander Mackenzie, an intrepid Scottish explorer, had reached the Pacific Ocean through the Canadian Rockies about a dozen years before the Americans arrived there. Responsible for only a boatload of men, Mackenzie followed such a mountainous route that it could not be developed. Although he moved 17,500 miles up and down Canadian rivers and another 500 miles on foot, he collected little scientific information, and by comparison with Lewis and Clark's journals his reports make dull reading.

Mackenzie's home base was at Lake Athabasca, near the Canadian Rockies, to which he could repair when he went in the wrong direction in his search for the Pacific Ocean. Mackenzie went northwest in 1789, all the way up the river that now bears his name and to the Arctic Ocean. In 1792 he explored the Peace River and found a short portage route across the mountains, reaching the Pacific above Vancouver Island, but no highway follows that route today.

Lewis and Clark were expected to succeed the first time, and the key to their success was skillful preparation. To begin with, they made few mistakes in calculating the amount of supplies necessary. One of their misjudgments was to carry too few blue beads, which the far-western Indian tribes cherished. Another was to haul halfway across the continent an iron framework for a boat, which Lewis planned to cover with skins or bark. The idea was a failure. Otherwise, the leaders' logistics were infallible. One of their most important precautions was to take along a full assortment of gun parts, even though they started with new guns. They lost some supplies, but accidents could not be foreseen or avoided.

In preparing for the rest of their journey, the captains made several fortunate decisions after they reached the Mandan villages, thereby proving they were good geographers who made no serious errors in their route.

The journey did not become a true exploration until the explorers reached the Mandans. All of the lower part of the Missouri River had been traveled by traders. The explorers passed through regions (later to be part of ten states of the United States), starting by crossing what is now the state of Missouri. From the west edge of the Missouri, the river flows from the north between Missouri and Iowa, between Missouri and Nebraska for a short stretch, and between Iowa and Nebraska. At the southeastern tip of South Dakota the river angles northwest into North Dakota, and near present-day Bismarck it passes through what was then the land of the Mandans and the Hidatsas.

The diaries kept by members of the expedition call attention to storms, heat, sandbars, snags, and treacherous currents, but in the early stages of their journey (across present-day Missouri, Iowa, Nebraska, and Kansas) they also remark on the beauty and richness of the countryside beyond the Missouri River bluffs.

The adventurers met few Indians and fewer white traders on their laborious trip upriver. To the Indians they gave variations of their "Great White Father" speech, urging them to discard Spanish and French medals and flags and to accept American medals and flags. Before they reached the Mandans, lack of an interpreter handicapped them.

There were some lapses of discipline. The "Corps of Discovery" was not yet a tightly integrated group.[2] In each instance the captains court-martialed the offending men and flogged them when necessary. Before long the men were under military control. There was one death, early in the journey, the only death throughout the course of the expedition. Sergeant Charles Floyd, of Kentucky, died on August 20, 1804, near present-day Sioux City, Iowa, probably from a ruptured appendix and peritonitis. The captains named a river for him, and today a monument to him stands in the vicinity.

The first crisis that threatened the progress of the expedition began on September 25 and continued for three days. A series of confrontations took place with the warlike Teton Sioux in what is now south-central South Dakota. The captains slept little during this crisis. Trouble was expected with the Indians, and the men were prepared for it, for the Sioux had stopped earlier trading parties and had forced them to dispose of their goods for little or nothing.

On September 25, Lewis and Clark faced the Sioux, turning swivel guns on them. The following three days were mostly anticlimactic, and from that time on the Tetons did not molest them.

On October 27 the expedition reached the Five Villages

2 The Corps of Discovery was a title probably suggested by Captain Lewis. Lewis signed his papers as "Captain, 1st Infantry" and Clark as "Captain of Corps of Discovery."

of the Mandans in North Dakota. In the 1730's the Mandans had lived in the region around present-day Bismarck. It was there that white men first encountered them. They later retreated upriver about sixty miles to avoid the Sioux. Lewis and Clark found them near the mouth of the Knife River. Besides a village of Mandans there were two villages of Hidatsas and a settlement of relatives of the latter, whom the journals refer to as "Wettersoons." These Indians had substantial, livable dwellings, lodges made of timber, sunk partly into the ground and covered with thick roofs of earth. Most important, they were friendly.

The Journals and Diaries

IN accordance with President Jefferson's instructions, everyone on the Lewis and Clark Expedition was urged to keep a diary. Besides the two captains, apparently three of the twenty-three privates and four sergeants did so. The members of the party had been selected for their ability to withstand the rigors of life on the trail, rather than for their writing ability. Sometimes it was more important to kill game or find one's way back to camp than to compose a narrative or keep a diary. It must have been a great effort not only to write by firelight at the end of a difficult day's travel but also to protect notes from the elements.

The journal that Captain Clark kept is more nearly complete than that of Captain Lewis. It contains a daily record for all but ten days of the entire journey (a single entry covers those ten days). The records of 441 days of the expedition are missing from Lewis' journal. Often the two captains' records parallel each other, occasionally making it appear that one of the men copied from the other's log—borrowing perhaps made necessary by accident or illness.

Privates Joseph Whitehouse, Robert Frazier (or Frazer), and George Shannon recorded some of their experiences. Whitehouse's writings cover the period from May 14, 1804, to November 6, 1805. His journal was given to someone who later sold it to a private collector in 1894. Reuben Gold Thwaites, the famed Wisconsin historian, found and purchased the Whitehouse journal in the early 1900's. Frazier's diary was lost, and only a few of his maps were found.

The journal of one of the four sergeants, Nathaniel Pryor, was also lost. Sergeant Charles Floyd kept a faithful record until his death on August 20, 1804, mentioned earlier. His journal, lost for eighty-five years, was found by Thwaites in 1895. Patrick Gass, who was elected sergeant after Floyd's death and who had attended school only fourteen days in his life, kept a journal that was edited and embellished by a schoolmaster and published in 1807. It gives a great deal of useful information about the expedition.[1]

[1] Gass gave his book a splendid title: A *Journal of the Voyages and Travels of a Corps of Discovery Under the Command of Captain*

The journal of Sergeant John Ordway, for many years believed lost, was also found by Thwaites. Parts of it were owned by the heirs of Captain Clark, and other parts eventually became part of the Nicholas Biddle estate. Biddle, a prominent Philadelphia lawyer, publisher, and diplomat, edited the notes for the first official narrative of Lewis and Clark's travels, having been persuaded to do so by Captain Clark. Biddle's work was completed by Paul Allen, a writer whom he asked to assist him. George Shannon, one of the privates who kept a diary, was employed to help Biddle and Allen interpret the notes. Biddle was a well-educated scholar, and he was thorough. He could write in Latin as well as English, and when he found descriptions of Indian rituals offensive, he put them in Latin in his narrative, although his notes are in English.

Ordway fortunately bridges most of the gaps left by the other diarists. He was one of the better educated of the enlisted men. He guarded his manuscript carefully through the whole arduous journey, keeping it inside his shirt most of the time. Eventually he sold it to Clark for ten dollars.

After the expedition Gass's diary, published in 1810, was the first to be published. Lewis' untimely death in 1809 delayed publication of an "official" account of the expedition, which was finally issued in 1814 in two volumes and became known as the Biddle edition. Two thousand copies

Lewis and Capt. Clark of the Army of the United States, from the Mouth of the River Missouri Through the Interior Parts of North America to the Pacific Ocean, During the years 1804, 1805 and 1806, Containing an Authentic Relation of the Most Interesting Transactions During the Expedition, a Description of the Country and an Account of Its Inhabitants, Soil, Climate and Curiosities and Vegetable and Animal Production.

were to have been printed, but only fourteen hundred copies were actually issued. As far as the records show, Biddle never received any payment for his work.[2]

The Biddle edition was re-edited in 1893 with many notes by Elliott Coues, an army surgeon, naturalist, and surveyor from New Hampshire. Coues retraced many miles of the Lewis and Clark trail, and his geographical notes are of great interest, although he tended to overedit the diaries.

In the years 1904–1906, Thwaites, secretary of the Wisconsin Historical Society, published his eight-volume work on Lewis and Clark, including everything then available on the expedition, in addition to scientific notes and letters, in unabridged form.[3]

[2] Since Biddle was married to a very wealthy woman, payment was probably not important to him.

[3] The quotations in subsequent pages are largely taken from the diaries of Meriwether Lewis or William Clark, and occasionally from the diaries of other members of the expedition. The unedited journals, as published by Thwaites, have a flavor of their own, but they are not easy to read. Spelling is phonetic, punctuation is largely absent, and capitalization follows no rules. Coues re-edited Biddle in 1893, adding a great many useful notes explaining names and locations that would otherwise mean little to the general reader.

Sacajawea Comes to Visit

"WE commence building our cabins," Clark wrote on November 3, 1804. The day before he had gone downriver from the Mandan village where they had stopped to look for a suitable campsite with timber nearby. On November 4, Clark mentioned visitors: "A Mr Chaubonie, interpeter for the Gross Ventre nation Came to See us, and informed that [he] came Down with Several Indians from a hunting expedition up the river, to here what we had told the Indians in Council   this man wished to hire as an interpiter."

Thus is introduced Toussaint Charbonneau, Sacajawea's French-Canadian husband. The "Several Indians" referred to by Clark included at least two Indian women. Ordway wrote on the same day: "Frenchman's squaw came to our camp who belongs to the Snake nation. She came with our interpreter's wife and brought with them four buffalo robes and gave them to our officers." The interpreter was a French Canadian named Réné Jussome, a local trader and a friend of Charbonneau's. Jussome was the first interpreter hired by Lewis and Clark, and it is likely that his wife and Sacajawea were the visitors to the camp.[1]

Charbonneau, well known to the Indians of the region,

[1] For one hundred years after the expedition, the Indian girl's name was spelled Sacajawea and pronounced either with both the *Sa* and *we* syllables accented, or with the *ja* syllable accented, as the Shoshonis pronounced it. In time, etymologists decided that the spelling should be Sacagawea or Sakakawea. The phonetic rendering of the name in Hidatsa is Tsi-ki-ka-wi-as, which has apparently become Sakakawea. In Hidatsa the name means Bird Woman. In Shoshoni it means Boat Pusher. The spelling Sacagawea doubtless stems from a reference to her by Clark in his journal. On April 7, 1805, Clark, a phonetic speller, made what appeared to be a special notation in his journal: "Sah-kah-gar-we-a." He may have intended a hard g sound in the third syllable. One cannot rely on Clark's spelling, however. In his notes he managed to spell the name Sioux twelve different ways. Ordway, in his diary, makes a reference to Sah-ka-gah. But it appears that Shannon advised Biddle and Allen, who prepared the first official edition of the journals, to spell the name Sacajawea. Shannon was one of the expedition's better spellers and was attending college when he was called upon to assist in editing the journals. In 1893, Elliott Coues, who added many notes to the Biddle edition of the journals, retained the spelling Sacajawea. For historical purposes I have also chosen to use this spelling.

16

had lived among them for about eight years. Before that he had been with the Northwest Fur Company, and in 1803 he had been at Fort Pembina. The Indians regarded him with some amusement, and through the years they gave him several nicknames, most of them derisive.[2]

Sacajawea must have been a pathetic sight at this time— young (about sixteen years old), small, forlorn. A long way from her home in Idaho, she had been the property of the Hidatsas, who had stolen her from her people, the Shoshonis, and she was now one of Charbonneau's chattels. He had probably acquired her in a gambling game or by barter when she was ten or twelve years old. She was pregnant. Charbonneau had another Shoshoni wife, whose name may have been Otter Woman. He may also have had a Mandan wife; he was constantly marrying Indian girls. It is quite possible that he took both Shoshoni girls as wives at their own request, perhaps because they hoped to stay together. This was marriage *à la façon du pays* ("after the fashion of the country"), as the French said. "Man and wife" simply lived together.

On this occasion the two female visitors to the camp were given some provisions and sent home by the captains. On November 11, Clark noted, "Two Squars of the Rock[y] mountains, purchased from the Indians by a frenchman came down." The younger of the girls on this visit was again Sacajawea.

On November 20 the members of the expedition moved into their winter quarters, which they had named Fort Mandan. They had built two rows of sheds, adjoining at a

[2] Some of the Indian names for Charbonneau were Chief of the Little Village, Great Horse from Afar, and Forest Bear.

right angle. Each row contained four rooms, fourteen feet square and seven feet high, with plank ceilings and slanting roofs. The walls behind the huts were eighteen feet high. Fort Mandan was to be the men's home until April, 1805.

The Indians were interested in the building operations. Clark wrote that three chiefs from one of the Mandan villages stayed all day on November 20. "They are very curious in examining our works."

Winter arrived, and the weather grew increasingly cold. On the morning of December 10 the temperature stood at ten degrees below zero. Nevertheless, the men at the fort tried to preserve the amenities of home. They held a Christmas party, which Sacajawea and other Indian wives attended out of curiosity. On December 25, Gass wrote: "At half past two another gun was fired, as a notice to assemble at the dance, which was continued in a jovial manner till eight at night; and without the presence of any females except three squaws, wives to our interpreter, who took no other part than the amusement of looking on."[3] No other Indians were invited.

Lewis and Clark had employed Jussome, who was familiar with the Mandan tongue, to interpret for them. Charbonneau was employed to accompany the expedition because he could make himself understood by most of the river Indians. He communicated with them chiefly by sign language; he freely admitted that he could not pronounce

[3] The favorite musical instruments in the wilderness were the jew's-harp and the harmonica. On this occasion Peter Cruzatte had his violin, and Ordway mentioned "a fiddle, tambereen & a sounden horn," the last probably a bugle or trumpet. The men evidently danced their square dances without women partners.

Indian words correctly. Neither Charbonneau nor Jussome was very highly thought of by the fur traders of the region, who often referred to them as knaves, sneaks, and scoundrels. The captains thought that they could handle Charbonneau, and they were already contemplating Sacajawea's possible usefulness to them later on, if they encountered her tribe.

Lewis and Clark interviewed the Indians who came to their camp out of curiosity or in hope of presents. From their visitors they learned something about the country up-river. They concluded that they would have to portage the Rocky Mountains. Some of the Indians knew about the Great Falls of the Missouri in Montana. Beyond that they were not too informative, but the Hidatsas, who ranged widely, knew that the Shoshoni Indians had horses. It was the Hidatsas who had brought the Shoshoni girls back from present-day southwestern Montana (Sacajawea had been kidnapped by the Hidatsas near the headwaters of the Missouri, at a spot she would later point out to Lewis and Clark).

Some of the Indians were attached to the Fort Mandan garrison during the winter, and the interpreters and their wives were allowed within the stockade. Lewis wrote on February 7: "The sergeant of the guard reported that the Indian women (wives to our interpreters) were in the habit of unbarring the fort gate at any time of night and admitting their Indian visitors." Probably these guests were other women. Lewis directed the men to put a lock on the gate.

One or more of the Indian wives at Fort Mandan may have been present to aid Sacajawea in the delivery of her baby. Lewis and Clark wanted to start up the Missouri as soon as the ice broke up in the spring. They had by now agreed to let Sacajawea accompany Charbonneau, and they hoped that her baby would arrive before the departure. The much anticipated birth occurred on February 11 or 12, 1805. The baby, Sacajawea's first, was a boy. Four diaries, those of Lewis, Ordway, Gass, and Whitehouse, mention his birth. Lewis writes: ". . . her labor was tedious and the pain violent." Although he had brought along a variety of medicines and cures, he was not prepared for childbirth. Everyone made suggestions. Jussome said that he had heard of powdered rattlesnake rattle for difficult births. Wrote Lewis:

Having the rattle of a snake by me, I gave it to [Jussome], and he administered two rings of it to the woman, broken in small pieces with the fingers, and added to a small quantity of water. . . . I was informed that [Sacajawea] had not taken it ten minutes before she brought forth. Perhaps this remedy may be worthy of future experiments, but I must confess that I want faith as to its efficacy.

Ordway did not mention Sacajawea's difficulty in delivery. He wrote only: "An interesting occurrence of this day was the birth of a son of the Shoshone squaw." Gass commented: "On the twelfth we arrived at the fort and found that one of our interpreter's wives had, in our absence, made an addition to our number." The baby was christened Jean Baptiste, later nicknamed "Pomp," Shoshoni for "firstborn."

Leaving the Mandans

4

IN the spring of 1805 the Lewis and Clark party, to which Sacajawea and Charbonneau—and the new baby—had now been attached, were ready to set out through country almost completely unknown to white men.

The captains had been able to secure information about the Missouri River's main tributaries, the first of which was the Yellowstone (from the south). They had a clear idea of the distant Great Falls of the Missouri. From the Hidatsa tribe they had learned that there were several possible routes across what came to be known as the Continental Divide, which led to northward-flowing rivers that Lewis and Clark thought might be southern branches of the Columbia River. These routes were described so vaguely to them that the explorers were seldom sure of their actual direction.

The men expected to cross mountains somewhere, and they knew that they would have to acquire some horses. The Shoshonis had horses. The captains concluded that Sacajawea could prove a real asset to the expedition.

By April 7 they were ready to move. Six soldiers and two French hunters were sent downriver to St. Louis in a barge and a canoe to take back papers and reports for President Jefferson and various items the party had collected, among them buffalo robes, Mandan corn, a set of mountain ram horns, a live prairie dog, and four magpies. On the same day the main, or "permanent," party, pushed off upriver for the unknown.

In command was Captain Lewis, a frontiersman of Welsh stock, a moody, introspective young man, thirty years old, a "rambler," as he called himself. He was a lover of nature, a dreamer, and an amateur doctor. He could write a connected narrative, albeit with individualistic spelling and punctuation, for he had had little formal education. He was a serious, dedicated man.

Captain Clark, Lewis' partner in command, was of Scots descent, a frontiersman like Lewis, a good-natured, outgoing man. He was red-headed but notably even-tempered withal. He was thirty-four years old, an experienced geographer, surveyor, and map maker. He expressed himself satisfactorily in writing, though, like Lewis, his spelling was inventive.

These two young captains successfully directed, without serious friction, a group made up of Americans, French Canadians, and Indians—and one Negro, Clark's personal servant, York.

The personnel the two captains led included Sergeants John Ordway, Nathaniel Pryor, and Patrick Gass; Privates William Bratton, John Colter (later to achieve fame as the first white man to discover Jackson Hole, Wyoming[1]), Reuben Fields, Joseph Fields, (brothers), John Shields, George Gibson, George Shannon, John Potts, John Collins, Joseph Whitehouse, Richard Windsor, Alexander Willard, Hugh Hall, Silas Goodrich, Robert Frazier, Peter Cruzatte, Baptiste LePage, Francis Labiche, Hugh McNeal, William Werner, Thomas P. Howard, Peter Wiser, and John B. Thompson. The interpreters were George Drewyer (or Drouillard), Toussaint Charbonneau (at forty-six the oldest member of the expedition), and York (the foregoing names are given variant spellings in the diaries).

A few specialists were included in the party. Gass was an expert carpenter. Drewyer was not only an interpreter but also a skilled hunter. Shields was a gunsmith. Cruzatte was a veteran riverman.

The vessels consisted of six small canoes and two large pirogues, one red and one white. Lewis was pleased to be starting, as he wrote in his diary, and he thought that his little fleet would weather the trip without trouble, although it was "not quite so respectable as that of Columbus or Captain Cook."

[1] See David J. Saylor, *Jackson Hole, Wyoming: In the Shadow of the Tetons*, Norman, 1970.

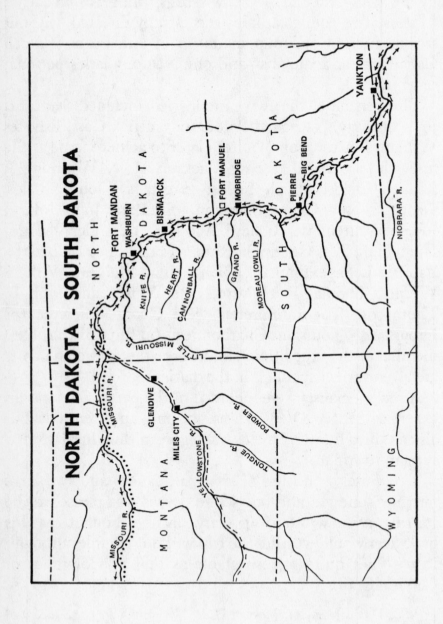

NORTH DAKOTA—SOUTH DAKOTA

After spending the first winter on the trail at Fort Mandan, on the Missouri River, the Lewis and Clark Expedition set out in the spring of 1805 for the West.

The Missouri River was the route of the expedition from Wood River, Illinois, north of St. Louis, where the Missouri joins the Mississippi, through all the states since created west of that point, to southwestern Montana, where the explorers left the Missouri and its tributaries to turn west through Lemhi Pass in the Rocky Mountains.

On the return trip from the Pacific Ocean, the party divided. In the summer of 1806, Clark and his men proceeded east from Three Forks, Montana, to the Yellowstone River and followed that river to its junction with the Missouri. Part of Lewis' party went downriver from Great Falls, while another group made a trip up the Marias River, joined the river party at the junction of the Marias with the Missouri, and proceeded down the Missouri for a reunion with Clark and his men.

To orient the reader, present-day state lines and towns have been added to this and subsequent maps.

The men's armament consisted of short rifles made especially for the expedition, pistols, fusils (light flintlock muskets), blunderbusses, a swivel cannon, and an air gun.[2] They also had knives, axes, and spontoons, the last a combination short pike and ax. To the Indians the swivel gun and the air gun were the "big medicine" of the expedition.

York was also of endless interest to the Indians. He entertained them with feats of strength and permitted them to try rubbing off his "black paint." When this pastime became monotonous, he pretended to be ferocious and untamed. Indian women thought that he was a spectacular warrior.

Scannon, Lewis' Newfoundland dog, who weighed 140 pounds, was useful to have along for a trip upriver, for he was a water dog. Still, he must have been weighty baggage for a canoe. On the journey he frequently distinguished

[2] The rifles were half-stock weapons (short) with ribs soldered beneath the barrels, about .52-caliber. The pistols were probably .69-caliber, with walnut stocks, brass mountings, and brass frames, each weighing about three pounds and more than a foot long. The fusils, muskets of a type used by the English, were not very accurate. The blunderbusses were short guns with bell-shaped mouths. The swivel cannon could be turned any direction and was usually loaded with miscellaneous metal pieces. It pivoted on a V bracket which held the barrel. At Fort Mandan such guns were used to defend the stockade. Only one was taken west from Fort Mandan. The air gun was a novelty that Captain Lewis had paid for out of his own pocket. It looked like an ordinary musket. Air was forced into a chamber with bellows, and a large copper ball held back the compressed air until it was released by a trigger. When it was being tested along the Ohio River before the party left St. Louis, it was discharged accidentally and stunned a woman standing forty yards away. Powder for the weapons was packed in lead canisters. There were flints for the rifles, pistols, and fusils.

himself, sometimes for bravery, sometimes for foolishness. He was big enough to kill an antelope swimming in the river and haul it in. Yet when he first met a harmless-looking beaver, he was badly bitten.[3]

On this well-equipped expedition a few items were included that were not ordinarily found on a wilderness journey, among them Cruzatte's violin and the captains' writing desks. The violin survived the journey and made music for dancing around many a campfire. Some of the Indians even said politely that they enjoyed violin music. Clark's desk lasted until September 15, 1805, when one of the pack horses slipped on the perilous Lolo Trail from Montana to Idaho, fell down an embankment, rolled on the desk, and smashed it. That was only one of many accidents. Lewis' desk was cached before the expedition crossed the mountains.

One can imagine that Sacajawea was excited by the trip. She was no longer a prisoner of the Hidatsa tribe that had taken her captive five or six years earlier. Now she was the wife of an interpreter—however few privileges that gave her —and she had a baby. Most important, the expedition was heading toward the land of her birth and her native tribe.

In their entries for the day of departure, April 7, both captains mentioned the Indian girl and her husband. Lewis wrote: "Our party now consists of the following individuals: interpreters George Drewyer and Taussan Charbono; also a black man of the name of York, servant to Captain Clark, and an Indian woman, wife to Charbono, with a young child." Clark, naming the personnel of the party, referred to

[3] On April 26, 1805, Ordway wrote: "Capt Lewises dog Scamon [Scannon] took after [a flock of goats] and caught one in the River."

"Sharbonah and his Indian Squaw to act as interpreter and interpretress for the Snake Indians."

Lewis was optimistic on starting day. He wrote:

Entertaining as I do the most confident hope of succeeding in a voyage which had formed a darling project of mine for the last ten years, I could esteem this moment of departure as among the most happy of my life.

We were about to penetrate a country at least two thousand miles in width on which the foot of civilized man has never trodden.

The Rescue

5

FOR a month the party made fifteen to twenty miles a day. The captains frequently walked on shore, but there were few trees or shrubs for Lewis to examine. The men had some variety in their diet: goose eggs one day, beaver tails and liver another.

Almost immediately Sacajawea proved useful. On April 9 she busied herself in a search for "wild artichokes which the mice collect and deposit in large hordes," as Lewis explained. "This operation she performed by penetrating the earth with a sharp stick about some collection of driftwood. Her labors soon proved successful and she procured a good quantity of these roots."

On April 10, Clark went on foot across a great bend of the Missouri River, taking Charbonneau, Sacajawea, and her baby along. On April 18, Clark walked on shore with Charbonneau, and "the squar followed on with her child." On April 30, Lewis mentioned that Clark spent the greater part of each day walking along the shore accompanied by Charbonneau and Sacajawea. This practice became commonplace.

Having passed the junction of the Yellowstone (near the North Dakota–Montana line) they stopped briefly to celebrate. Each man had one gill of whisky, and all "made merry, fiddled and danced, etc.," Ordway wrote.

May 14 was an exciting day. Both the land and the water parties had hair-raising experiences. The former tried to kill a grizzly bear. Six men, all good hunters, converged on the beast. Four of them fired the first volley, but the bear ran them off a cliff into the river, jumped in after them, and pursued them. When the grizzly was finally killed, eight balls were found to have passed through him.

The water party had enjoyed an easy day. Everything had gone so well that both captains were ashore near the boats when the white pirogue, under full sail, was struck by a sudden squall. Charbonneau was at the helm, although he was, according to Lewis, "the worst steersman of the party" and "perhaps the most timid waterman in the world."

When the wind struck the pirogue, the two captains, looking across three hundred yards of river, saw the craft heel over and then lie agonizingly on her side among the waves. The man handling the brace of the sail clung to it until the wind jerked it out of his hands. The boat was filling as water poured over the gunwale. Charbonneau dropped the tiller and began "crying to his God for mercy" in a scene of wild confusion. Both captains tried to make themselves heard across the water. They fired their rifles, hoping to attract the men's attention. Then Lewis threw down his rifle and shot pouch and was unbuttoning his coat to swim out when he realized that such action would be hopeless.

Cruzatte, in the bow, saved the day by bellowing a threat to shoot Charbonneau if he did not take hold of the rudder and try to right the boat. Cruzatte ordered two of the men to start bailing with kettles. The pirogue did not quite capsize, and the men, hauling in sail, slowly righted her. It was Sacajawea who saved what she could reach of the expedition's valuable supplies. Although burdened with her baby, trying to balance herself in the stern, the Indian girl calmly fished out of the river everything that floated near her. If the pirogue had capsized, the expedition would have been deprived of "nearly everything necessary for our purposes, at a distance of between two and three thousand miles from any place where we could supply the deficiency." Three of the men aboard, including Charbonneau, could not swim.

Lewis, who never became as fond of the Indian girl as Clark did, nevertheless wrote of her glowingly when he related the story of the day in his journal: "The Indian woman, to whom I ascribe equal fortitude and resolution with any person on board at the time of the accident, caught and preserved most of the light articles which were washed overboard."

The pirogue was finally rowed ashore, barely above water, and all the remaining articles were removed from the boat and dried. Apparently the expedition lost chiefly medicines in the accident. Sacajawea probably rescued cases of instruments, compasses, books, clothing—equipment that would float for a time. Many valuable instruments were included in the baggage—spirit levels, a magnet, a quadrant, a sextant, a microscope, a chronometer, a protractor, and platting instruments. There were also valuable books, such as a navigational book, called an ephemeris, giving the daily location of the sun, moon, and planets. Most of the instruments and books were probably packed in waterproof bags and would float briefly. Lewis would have been inconsolable if he had lost his copy of Benjamin Barton's *Elements of Botany*.[1]

Near the junction with the Musselshell River on May 17, three days later, the Corps of Discovery had further excitement. Clark narrowly escaped being bitten by a rattlesnake, and that night their campfire set a large tree ablaze. The trunk burned partly through, and a high wind brought the tree crashing down among the tents. No one was injured.

On May 20, Sacajawea received her first formal recognition: a river was named in her honor. The name, unfortunately, did not endure. As Ordway's journal notes: "With

[1] On one occasion the men upset their lead canisters of powder, but fortunately into shallow water. The canisters were recovered without damage to the contents. Andrew Ellicott, a surveyor, had warned President Jefferson to be sure to have Lewis store the chronometer in a "bladder" when it was not in use, in case a boat overturned.

less gallantry, the present generation call it Crooked Creek."[2]

Although the expedition had not yet encountered any Indians, and were not to see any until they reached the headwaters of the Missouri, there was evidence of Indians here and there—a recently occupied camp, an Indian ball, a moccasin. Sacajawea, who studied the moccasin, said that it did not belong to the Shoshoni.

On the morning of May 29 the party reached the mouth of the Judith River.[3] In the flats around the mouth of the river they found remnants of 126 Indian lodges, but no Indians. Along the bluffs beyond the mouth of the Judith were "buffalo leaps," places where the Indians stampeded buffaloes off the cliffs to their deaths. Lewis wrote that he counted at least one hundred carcasses at the base of the cliffs. The wolves around the carcasses were so tame that Captain Clark was able to kill one with his spontoon.

Next to come in sight along the Missouri were high limestone cliffs that reminded Lewis of "elegant ranges of lofty freestone buildings, having their parapets well stocked with statuary; columns of various sculpture, both grooved and plain."[4]

On June 3 the expedition reached the mouth of a river

[2] This is the first stream that enters the Missouri from the west, above the junction of the Musselshell from the south. Today, because of the widening of the river caused by waters from Fort Peck Dam, it is difficult to determine where the Musselshell entered the big V that the Missouri forms at this point.

[3] Named by Clark for Julia (or Judith) Hancock, of Fincastle, Virginia, whom he later married.

[4] The limestone cliffs decorate the river today just as they did in 1805. The stretch of the Missouri from the Musselshell to Fort Benton is still a primitive region.

flowing from the north. The men stopped there for nine days, while scouting parties went up both branches in an effort to determine which river would lead them to the Rocky Mountains. They named the new-found river the Marias.[5] The Missouri had been uniformly silty, and the Marias looked a good deal like it, but the river coming in from the south (the Missouri, as it proved) ran rapidly and had transparent waters. The captains decided that this branch came from the mountains and was therefore the one to follow. As the expedition left the eroded lands around the Missouri and the outlying rolling prairies, they also left a permanent name for the latter: the Great Plains.

[5] It was Lewis' turn to name a river, and he called it Maria's (the apostrophe has since been dropped). Several other names that Lewis and Clark bestowed on the rivers they discovered were changed by later geographers, for no apparent reason.

Portaging the Falls

THE Lewis and Clark Expedition faced a combination of crises after reaching the mouth of the Marias River. From June 3 to July 5 they experienced little but trouble. None of the journals of the expedition, all of which are generally matter-of-fact, really do justice to the men's predicament.

The men reached the Marias nearly exhausted, and exhaustion had spawned illness. They were at a low ebb mentally and physically. Perhaps it was just as well that a rest was taken at the Marias. From the start of the expedition the men had suffered from occasional boils and dysentery. Few days passed with everyone free of illness or injury. Colds, fevers, influenza, abdominal pains, lame backs, nausea, cuts, bruises, and sprains were common. Poor diet and muddy water probably caused some of the sickness. The men were bitten relentlessly by insects. Sometimes the mosquitoes were intolerable, and later gnats, flies, fleas, bugs, and snakes plagued them.

During the long journey to the Pacific Ocean and back, Lewis treated everybody in the party (including himself), for illness or injury, and by the time the return trip started, even Clark had gained a reputation as a doctor. Credit must be given to Captain Lewis for his folk remedies and his bagful of medicines. He hastened the recovery of every sick person on the expedition, despite periodic bleeding of patients and doses of purgatives.

The pause at the Marias was fortuitous for another reason. A mistake in direction at this point might have been fatal to the expedition. Gass, with two others, went up the southern branch, while Pryor, with two men, explored the northern river. For a water expedition the Lewis and Clark troops covered many miles on foot. Sometimes they walked miles away from the river. When Gass and Pryor reported on their exploratory trips, the captains were still uncertain and decided to investigate further. Lewis took a six-man party to explore the Marias, and Clark took five men upriver to the south. Between them they covered one hundred miles, sometimes across the rough country between the two rivers. After the second exploration everybody except the captains themselves thought that the Marias was the main river. Only the two leaders alone were convinced that the south river was the one to follow. As usual, time proved them right.

On June 9 the parties returned to the mouth of the Marias to confer again. It was decided to cache as many supplies as the men could spare,[1] find a hiding place for the red pirogue, and give Captain Lewis and four men time to return from a third exploration of the south branch of the river.

Meanwhile, Sacajawea had fallen ill. Notations in the journals indicate the captains' anxiety about her. They had to take care of her in relays, because first one and then the other captain was away exploring the rivers. On June 11, Lewis, trying to treat the sick girl, also became so unwell that he could not walk. He decided to treat himself, confident of the efficacy of his own concoctions, some of which his mother probably taught him to make.[2] Directing his men to make him a bitter brew of chokecherry twigs, he drank a whole quart of this "strong black decoction" in an hour. The next day he was much improved.

On June 13 Lewis decided to reconnoiter the south branch of the river again. He and four men walked southwest over comparatively level bluffs, overlooking a plain on which many buffaloes were grazing. On the south they saw

[1] A cache was made by digging a bottle-shaped excavation, six or seven feet deep; placing in it the supplies to be recovered later; covering them with turf; and destroying all signs of digging.

[2] Mrs. Lewis was known in Virginia as an "herb doctor."

two high buttes. As they continued, they heard a tremendous roar. They realized that they were approaching the Great Falls, which had been described to them by Indians, and that they were indeed on the Missouri River.

Walking another seven miles to the first falls, Lewis wrote, he saw:

Immediately at the cascade, the river is about 300 yards wide. About 90 or 100 yards of this next larboard bluff is a smooth, even sheet of water falling over a precipice of at least 80 feet. The remaining part of about 200 yards on my right forms the grandest sight I ever beheld. The height of the fall is the same as the other, but the irregular and somewhat projecting rocks below receive the water in its passage down, and break it into a perfect white foam which assumes a thousand forms in a moment—sometimes flying up in jets of sparkling foam to the height of 15 to 20 feet; and are scarcely formed before large rolling bodies of the same beaten and foaming water are thrown over and conceal them. In short the rocks seem to be most happily fixed to present a sheet of the whitest beaten froth 200 yards in length and 80 feet perpendicular. The water, after descending, strikes against the butment . . . on which I stand and seems to reverberate; and being met by the more impetuous current, they roll and swell into half-formed billows of great height which rise and again disappear in an instant.

The next day Lewis and his men continued upriver, discovering still more falls. A series of cascades brought the level of the river down about four hundred feet. While separated from his men temporarily, Lewis had one of his many narrow escapes. He encountered a grizzly bear when his gun was unloaded (he had just shot at a buffalo) and was chased into the river. Lewis suddenly turned and faced the bear with his spontoon. The animal wheeled and ran, a typical change of mind peculiar to the grizzly bear.

In the meantime, Clark, who was at the main camp, was trying to cope with Sacajawea's illness and other ailments. On June 12 he wrote: "The interpreter's woman very sick. One man has a felon rising on his hand; the other, with the toothache, has taken cold in the jaw."

The rest of the party was feeling well enough that evening to sing some songs and listen to Cruzatte's violin. But on June 13, Clark noted that Sacajawea was suffering from abdominal pains. Since the weather was turning hot, he laid her in the covered part of the white pirogue, gave her laudanum, and applied bark poultices. Still she grew weaker. When Lewis rejoined the party on June 16, he found the Indian girl extremely ill. He wrote:

About 2 p.m. I reached the camp, found the Indian woman extremely ill, and much reduced by her indisposition. This gave me some concern, as well as for the poor object herself, then with a young child in her arms, as from her condition of her being our only dependence for a friendly negotiation with the Snake Indians [Shoshonis], on whom we depend for horses to assist us in our portage from the Missouri to the Columbia River.

One of the small canoes was left below this rapids in order to pass and repass the river for the purpose of hunting as well as to procure water of the sulphur spring, the virtues of which I now resolved to try on the Indian woman.

... I caused her to drink the mineral altogether.... When I first came down I found that her pulse was scarcely perceptible, very quick; frequently irregular, and attended with strong nervous symptoms; that of the twitching of the fingers and the leaders of the arm; now the pulse has become regular, much fuller, and a gentle perspiration had taken place; the nervous system has also in great measure abated, and she feels herself much freer of pain.

Lewis continued to apply the "cataplasms" (poultices) of bark and laudanum that had previously been used by Captain Clark. "I believe her disorder originated principally from an obstruction of the mensis in consequence of taking could."

Gradually Sacajawea grew better. By June 18 she was sitting up. She soon felt well enough to go out and gather "a considerable quantity of white apples," which she ate, and also a considerable quantity of dried fish. Soon she was sick again, suffering from pain and fever, and Lewis rebuked Charbonneau sharply for letting his wife "indulge herself with food." Yet the next day Sacajawea was better again and celebrated by going fishing. Lewis reported on June 24 that she was fully recovered.

The next crisis was the portage around the series of falls. The men hauled their canoes through water as far upriver as they could go and then set to work to build wagon frames. There was no suitable wood for axles. In fact, they had no material for wheels, and so they cut cross sections of a cottonwood tree, the only one they could find.

The portage of eighteen miles began on June 21, the men pulling their loaded canoes on primitive carts across rough ground carpeted with prickly pear (cactus) that pierced their moccasins and inflamed their feet. Axles cracked; wagon tongues broke. Some of the ground had been crossed and recrossed by thousands of buffaloes, whose rough, scraggy tracks had dried hard as rock.

In the middle of the difficult portage a storm blew up. Captain Clark, Charbonneau, Sacajawea, and her baby were almost swept away by a flood that followed a sudden cloudburst while they were making their way along a creek. Clark exhibited his usual presence of mind, Sacajawea her customary coolness in emergency, and Charbonneau his usual panic. Clark and his small group scrambled for shelter along the riverbank when the heavy rain started. About a fourth of a mile above the falls Clark ordered them under a shelving rock on the upper side of a creek. There was a torrent of rain, and suddenly a wall of water came down the creek.

Clark wrote:

I took my gun and shot pouch in my left hand, and with the right scrambled up the hill pushing the interpreter's wife (who had the child in her arms) before me, the interpreter himself making attempts to pull up his wife by the hand, much scared and nearly without motion. We at length reached the top of the hill safe, where I found my servant in search of us, greatly agitated for our welfare. Before I got out of the bottom of the ravine, which was a flat dry rock when I entered it, the water was up to my waist and wet my watch. I scarcely got out before it raised ten feet deep with a torrent that was terrible to behold, and by the time I reached the top of the hill, at least fifteen feet of water.

The incident was also recorded by Captain Lewis, Gass, and Ordway. Sacajawea lost most of her baby's clothing. Clark lost his compass, and Charbonneau his gun (the compass was later recovered).

The men who had been hauling baggage in the open, hatless and shirtless, were pelted with heavy hailstones. Lewis said some of the stones bounced ten to twelve feet in the air as they landed and that one stone measured seven inches in diameter.

The bruised and battered party finally finished the portage, having spent ten days making eighteen miles, and established camp at White Bear Island. The camp received its name from the "white" (silver-tipped) grizzlies that infested the island and harassed the men in camp.

Now that the two pirogues were cached, Lewis tried to build his famous *Experiment*, the boat whose iron framework they had hauled all the way from the Mississippi River. There was no bark to cover the frame that they assembled and no tar to seal the sewed seams of animal skins that they tried to use instead of bark. The boat began leaking shortly after it was floated, and the project had to be abandoned.

July 4, Independence Day, was celebrated by consuming the last of the supply of whisky, and Cruzatte furnished music on his violin until a heavy shower stopped the concert.

Sacajawea Returns to Home Country

7

WITH the failure of the *Experiment*, Lewis and Clark found it necessary to build two more canoes to supplement the six they already had, all of them hollowed out of cottonwood logs. After a search through the rather scarce timber they found two cottonwood trees that would serve. They cut them down and built two dugouts, each about three feet wide, one twenty-five and the other thirty-three feet

43

long. Lewis suggested that the men discard some of their souvenirs to avoid overloading the boats. The canoes were ready by July 14. The next day the expedition set out again, going south (upstream) along the eastern edge of the Rockies.

Where were the Indians? Many times they saw "Indian sign," but no Indians. On July 16 some recently occupied willow shelters came into view and, a little farther on, the remains of eighty "leathern lodges."

Despite their preoccupation with Indian sign, the captains did not fail to make notes about the flora and fauna. Lewis wrote in detail about shrubs and berries. To save their parched meal and corn, they subsisted largely on meat and berries.

Some members of the party walked, and some poled and pulled the canoes. Those who were on foot were busy hunting game, but Lewis and Clark alternately looked for Indians. On July 19, Captain Clark passed the site of several Indian camps. Sacajawea, who was walking with Clark, pointed out where the pine trees had been stripped of their bark and explained that the Indians had been hunting for the soft underparts of the wood for food. It was hard walking. Clark reported extracting seventeen cactus needles from his feet that night.

The boats went through the gorge northeast of present-day Helena, Montana, which they named the Gates of the Mountains. On July 20 they emerged into a valley and saw smoke from an Indian camp rising in the distance. The green valley bred hordes of mosquitoes, and they observed that without their "biers" they would have had little sleep.[1]

[1] The biers were frameworks for the gauze used to keep off mos-

Sacajawea recognized the countryside on July 22. She said that her tribe made visits to the banks of one of the creeks they were passing to get white earth for paint. The captains named it White Earth Creek. She also told them that the Three Forks of the Missouri were not far away. This news cheered the party.[2]

Captain Clark was still walking energetically, wearing out his companions on the trail. Lewis was helping pole the boats through uncounted islands and around endless bends in the river. He wrote that he had learned "to push a tolerable pole." He wrote of the excessive fatigue of all the party and remarked sadly: "Our trio of pests still invade and obstruct us on all occasions. These are the musquetoes, eye knats and prickley pears, equal to any three curses that ever poor Egypt laiboured under, except the Mahometant yoke."

By July 25, Clark had worn out one companion, Charbonneau, and by the next day Clark was sick himself. But he had finally reached the Three Forks of the Missouri. Several days later the captains decided to name the three rivers after Jefferson and two of the President's cabinet members, Madison and Gallatin.

Clark's ill-health was not improved by having to rescue

quitoes and other insects. They were "like a trunk to get under," Clark wrote. Elliott Coues commented: "Many have thought that Lewis and Clark made too much of these insects, for such brave men as they were. But such critics as these know nothing of mosquitoes." He added that in some areas mosquitoes were so thick they killed horses, cattle, and caribou by clogging the animals' nasal passages.

[2] In January, 1944, C. S. Kingston wrote (in the *Pacific Northwest Quarterly*) that Sacajawea determined the route of the exploring parties on only one occasion (to be discussed later). It should be pointed out, however, that she gave them assurance that they were on the correct route and that she continued to do so on succeeding days.

Charbonneau, who could not swim and was nearly swept
away in the current when they waded a stream. By July 27,
Clark was so ill that Lewis was administering Dr. Rush's
Pills to his friend.[3] In a few days Clark had recovered and
was again taking his turn walking on shore or accompanying
the canoes.

Lewis wrote: "We begin to feel considerable anxiety with
respect to the Snake Indians. If we do not find them or
some other nation who have horses, I fear the successful
issue of our voyage will be very doubtful."

After investigating the three rivers, a tiresome procedure,
the expedition decided that the Jefferson, coming in from
the southwest, was the next river to follow. "Our consolation is that this southwest branch can scarcely head with
any other river than the Columbia." The captains had a
sixth sense when it came to choosing directions, and again
they were right, although there were still mountains between them and the Columbia.

The Indian girl reaffirmed that the party had reached
Shoshoni ground when she told the captains on July 28 that
they were camped on the precise spot where the huts of her
people had stood five years before, when the Hidatsas of
Knife River first came into sight.

Lewis, with Charbonneau, Sacajawea, and "two invalids,"
walked along the river and soon found the place where
Sacajawea told them the Shoshonis had hidden in the
woods when they were attacked. The women and children
had fled, leaving Sacajawea and other Indian girls to be
captured. She showed them the place where she was over-

[3] Dr. Rush's Pills, like most of the others the captains administered,
were a physic.

taken in midriver. Ordway writes: "... she was crossing at a shoal place to make hir escape, when caught." Thus the Indian girl who had been taken as a captive all the way to North Dakota had returned with Lewis and Clark to the scenes of her early childhood.

What were her thoughts as she neared the land of her people? "She does not ... show any distress at these recollections, or any joy at the prospect of being restored to her country," Lewis noted. "For she seems to possess the folly or the philosophy of not suffering her feelings to extend beyond the anxiety of having plenty to eat and a few trinkets to wear." But Sacajawea was more emotional than Lewis suspected, as her reunion with her tribesmen would soon demonstrate.

Where the Jefferson split into three rivers, the captains again had to decide which branch to follow. This time they chose what is now the Beaverhead, the central tributary. On August 8, Sacajawea recognized a high point on the plain on the right, which, she informed the captains, was not far from the summer retreat of her people, on a river flowing west beyond the mountains. She assured them that they would find her people on this river or on the river immediately west of its source, and she also said, correctly, that there were no more falls.

Meeting the Shoshonis

THE Lewis and Clark Expedition had been traveling south-ward since leaving the junction with the Marias River in June. It was apparent that they would soon have to turn west. The Missouri had given way to the Jefferson, the Jefferson to the Beaverhead.[1] The information they re-

[1] The ultimate source of the Missouri River is probably upper Red Rock Lake, where Red Rock Creek originates. It flows into the Beaver-

ceived from Sacajawea influenced the decision of the captains to turn toward the mountains on the first tributary of the Beaverhead that looked suitable.

Early in August, Clark was unable to walk very far because of a carbuncle on his ankle. He stayed with the water party while Lewis struck out cross-country with Drewyer (a half-blood French Canadian, who was useful as an interpreter, as well as a hunter), McNeal, and Shields. The Indian girl remained with the canoes.

Lewis was eager to make contact with any Indians he could find. He was reasonably certain that they would be Shoshonis. His hunters had to procure game for food, but their gunshots, Lewis knew, would frighten the Indians. It was necessary to get ahead of the water party, doing as little shooting as possible, so that they could tell the water party where to leave the water and start overland.

The Northern Shoshonis were a tribe of mountain Indians of the Shoshonean linguistic stock. They lived in the mountains because larger enemy tribes overran them whenever they ventured onto the plains. The Shoshonis were not warlike; they had almost no guns. They had fine horses, but even with horses they had difficulty obtaining large game with bows and arrows.[2] The Indians were probably half-

---

head at Dillon, Montana, where the Beaverhead is now considered to terminate.

[2] The Shoshoni horses were probably pintos and Appaloosas. Spanish explorers had brought horses to the southern regions of the United States, and the Indians had traded for them or captured strays. The Shoshonis may have acquired the Appaloosas from their neighbors, the Nez Percés, who were noted for breeding and training them.

A modern-day Indian artist's conception of Sacajawea. The clothing, decorations, and cradle are close approximations of Shoshoni dress and ornamentation. The horse's bit is the leather tie commonly used by Shoshonis and Nez Percés. Drawing by George Henry, Sioux City, Iowa.

starved, Lewis thought. Why else would they be stripping bark off trees and eating wood fiber?

When he reached the Beaverhead, Captain Lewis, ahead of the water party, decided to turn west on the tributary (later named Horse Prairie Creek) and look for Indian trails. On August 10 he followed the creek for four or five miles toward what is now the Montana–Idaho border and found

a beautiful and extensive plain about 10 miles long and five or six in width. This is surrounded on all sides by higher rolling or waving country, intersected by several little rivulets from the mountains, each bordered by its wide meadows. The whole prospect is bounded by these mountains, which nearly surround it, so as to form a beautiful cover, 16 or 18 miles in diameter.[3]

On the next day, Sunday, August 11, Lewis again set out early with his men to follow Horse Prairie Creek. They headed toward a narrow pass that they saw toward the west, and after walking about five miles, they sighted an Indian on horseback about two miles away. Lewis, studying the horseman through his glass, discerned that he was armed with bow and arrow and was dressed differently from other Indians the explorers had seen. The Indian, he also observed, was riding a good horse.

[3] This area, northwest of present Armstead, Montana, was to be called Shoshoni Cove and was to be an important point on the itinerary of the expedition. It was the camp from which the men searched for and found the Shoshoni Indians and the Continental Divide. Clark would return this way the following year from the Pacific Coast. The junction of Horse Prairie Creek with the Beaverhead was the head of navigation for the party. As soon as Clark's water party reached this junction, the expedition struck out overland.

There followed a dramatic and fruitless confrontation between white man and Shoshoni. As soon as he was near enough, Lewis took out a blanket and spread it out ceremoniously on the ground—a sign of friendship. He moved toward the Indian, waving a looking glass, beads, and other trinkets. Then he shouted "Ta-ba-bone," an Indian word which meant "white man" but probably did not have an equivalent in Shoshoni. Drewyer and Shields unfortunately kept moving around to each side of the Indian. Lewis' signals to them to stop went unheeded. The Indian reined in and watched all three uncertainly. Then he suddenly wheeled his horse, leaped a creek, and disappeared in the willows.

The men were gloomy that night. They set out the next day, following what appeared to be an Indian trail. Horse Prairie Creek divided, and they followed Trail Creek. They found signs indicating that the Indians had been digging up roots, and they continued on, tramped across high ground, and descended the other side. They had just surmounted the Continental Divide at Lemhi Pass. The ridge they crossed is now the boundary line between Montana and Idaho.

Lewis reports what he saw:

. . . I discovered immense ranges of high mountains still to the west of us, with their tops partially covered with snow. I now descended the mountain about three quarters of a mile, which I found much steeper than the opposite side, to a handsome bold running creek of cold, clear water. Here I first tasted the water of the great Columbia River.[4]

[4] It is now called the Lemhi River, a tributary of the Salmon and the Salmon of the Snake, before the Snake enters the Columbia. Lewis

Having killed nothing that day, the men ate a little of their remaining provisions (pork, flour, and parched meal) and found some currants. Early on the morning of August 13 they resumed their march along the Indian trail, found another creek, a tributary of the Lemhi River, proceeded along a rolling plain, and saw at a distance two Indian women, a man, and a few dogs. All were wary, disappearing before Lewis could reach them.

The dusty path led them unexpectedly upon two women and a little girl. The younger woman fled. The old woman and the little girl, perhaps feeling that they could not escape, sat quietly with bowed heads, expecting death. Captain Lewis spoke to them gently, producing presents, and asked the woman to call back the young woman. She did so, and Lewis distributed more presents and painted their cheeks with vermilion, to the Shoshonis emblematic of peace.

The women led Lewis and his men toward their camp, and soon about sixty warriors rode up to them. The chief spoke to the women, who told them that the white men were friends, and soon Captain Lewis was being enthusiastically embraced, cheek to cheek, as the Indians called out "Ah-hi-e! Ah-hi-e!" an exclamation of friendship. Lewis remarks, "We were all caressed and besmeared with their grease paint until I was heartily tired of the national hug."

There followed a pipe-smoking ceremony and distribution of a few gifts. Then everyone went to the Indian camp,

---

had crossed Lemhi Pass, and he and his men would camp on the western slope. The Lemhi River was so named in 1855, when Mormons established a settlement there (abandoned in 1858). The Mormon colony did not cross Lemhi Pass. They reached the area by way of Ogden, Utah, and Idaho Falls.

about four miles away, for more ceremonies. Drewyer, using sign language, served as interpreter during the conference that followed. Asked about the course of the Lemhi River, the Indians told Lewis that neither it nor the river into which it flowed was navigable. If this was true, Lewis realized, the party must obtain horses.

While these events were taking place, Captain Clark's party was toiling up the Beaverhead. The river was so crooked and full of shoals that progress was painfully slow. Lewis had to think of some way to convince the Indians that the men coming upriver were friendly, that they had a Shoshoni Indian girl with them, and that their hunters would kill some much-needed game. Both the Indians and Lewis' men were very hungry. The Shoshonis were valiantly trying to procure meat with their bows and arrows, and it was obvious to Captain Lewis that before he could discuss the purchase of horses he must produce something to eat. He sent out Drewyer and Shields on two borrowed horses, but to Lewis' embarrassment they returned with no game. The next day Lewis divided his few remaining provisions among some of the Indian chiefs.

Cameahwait, the head chief of the Shoshonis, was friendly to the white men. A few of the lesser chiefs and a good many warriors, however, were suspicious of the explorers and their story of a party coming up the Beaverhead. Were the white men in league with their Indian enemies? Lewis finally persuaded some of the warriors to accompany him back to the river fork, where he hoped Clark's party was waiting.

Drewyer and Shields went hunting again, this time with suspicious Indians trailing them. There was a stroke of luck:

Drewyer killed a deer. An Indian came galloping back happily to tell the others. Lewis, who could not see what the excitement was about, was carrying a young Indian behind him on his horse. The Indian boy, who wanted something to eat, lashed the animal at every jump for a whole mile before the captain could discover where everyone was hurrying.

The meat-starved Indians had a bloody feast at the spot where the deer was killed—devouring the meat and entrails raw. When two more deer were killed, Lewis' problems were partly solved.

The river party had not yet arrived at the fork, however. The men with Clark had found the river ever shallower and swifter. Ordway complained: "The water is very cold. We have to waid in it, which makes our feet and legs ake with cold. We expect it is made of springs."

On August 15 Clark's party passed two tall rock pillars, which they named Rattlesnake Clifts because they were crawling with snakes. Both Clark and Sacajawea narrowly escaped being bitten.

In the valley beyond, Sacajawea picked some serviceberries. Clark saw that they were approaching a fork in the river. He, Charbonneau, and the Indian girl walked through high, dew-covered grass, Clark behind because he was still lame. Suddenly he saw Sacajawea jump up and down, dancing, sucking her fingers, and pointing to Indians riding toward her.

"This is my tribe!" she was saying in sign language, as she danced ecstatically. Sacajawea had returned to her people.

Clark describes the reunion of the Indian girl with her people:

56

. . . I saw at a distance several Indians on horseback coming towards me. The interpreter and the squaw who were before me at some distance danced for the joyful sight, and she made signs to me that they were her nation. As I approached nearer them, I discovered one of Captain Lewis's party with them dressed in their dress. They met me with great signs of joy.

This meeting took place near present-day Armstead, Montana. In the Biddle edition of the journals appears a description of the conference which followed:

While Sacajawea was renewing among the women the friendships of former days, Captain Clark went on, and was received by Captain Lewis and the chief, who, after the first embraces and salutations were over, conducted him to a sort of circular tent or shade of willows. Here he was seated on a white robe, and the chief immediately tied in his hair six small shells resembling pearls, an ornament highly valued by these people, who procured them in the course of trade from the sea-coast. The moccasins of the whole party were then taken off, and after much ceremony, the smoking began. After this the conference was to be opened. . . . Sacajawea was sent for. She came into the tent, sat down, and was beginning to interpret, when, in the person of Cameahwait, she recognized her brother. She instantly jumped up, and ran and embraced him, throwing over him her blanket, and weeping profusely. The chief himself was moved, though not in the same degree. After some conversation between them she resumed her seat and attempted to interpret for us; but her new situation overpowered her, and she was frequently interrupted by her tears.

After the council was finished the unfortunate woman

learned that all her family were dead except two brothers, one of whom was absent, and a son by her eldest sister, a small boy, who was immediately adopted by her.

After the canoes arrived, chiefs, warriors, and members of the expedition met again for the customary smoking ceremony, where the captains spoke at some length, asking for horses to transport their equipment across the mountains, as well as for a guide. More presents were distributed—Jefferson medals, shirts, tobacco, and small articles. The air gun was shot off. Everything surprised the Indians—the appearance of the men, their arms, their clothing, the canoes, Clark's Negro servant, even the intelligence of Scannon, the dog. The hunters brought in four more deer and antelope.

On Sunday, August 18, the party traded for a few horses, and Clark set out to discover whether the Lemhi River was indeed unnavigable, as the Indians had said. Gass wrote in his diary:

A fine morning. We bought three horses of the Indians. Captain Clark and 11 more, with our interpreter and his wife and all the Indians, set out at 11 o'clock to go over to the Columbia [Lemhi]. The Indians went for horses to carry our baggage, and we to search for timber to make canoes for descending the Columbia.

On the same day Lewis wrote (poignantly, in retrospect, in view of his death at thirty-five in 1809):

This day I completed my thirty-first year, and conceived that I had in all human probability now existed about half the period which I am to remain on this sublunary world. I reflected that I had as yet done but little . . . to further the happiness of the human race. . . . I viewed with regret the many hours I have spent in indolence . . . but since they are past and cannot be recalled, I dash from me the gloomy thought and resolve in the future to redouble my exertions . . . or, in the future to live for mankind, as I have heretofore lived for myself.

Across the Divide to the Columbia

SACAJAWEA was elated by the reunion with her tribe. She had found a brother, Cameahwait, and her sister's son. She had been reunited with the girlhood companion who had been captured with her by the Hidatsas. (Unlike Sacajawea, this girl had escaped and made her way back to her tribe.)[1]

[1] During the stay with the Shoshonis, Sacajawea also encountered a

Yet despite her joy at being reunited with her people, it is apparent that Sacajawea's loyalties had been committed to the white men. Although she doubtless could have stayed with the Shoshonis, she chose to remain with Charbonneau and the expedition. She would go on to the Pacific with them.

It was decided that Clark would explore the Lemhi River to determine whether it was navigable. Before he left, he took Sacajawea and Charbonneau to the main Shoshoni camp to help hasten the collecting of horses.[2] Clark and eleven of the men were to build canoes, if the condition of the river and the supply of trees made it practicable. The captains suspected, however, that a portage of the Rocky Mountains would be necessary. They bartered for three horses before Clark's reconnaissance party set out.

Chief Cameahwait drew diagrams of the rivers for Clark. Although his information was vague and communication difficult, he indicated that the Lemhi River flowed into the Salmon, the Salmon into the Snake, the Snake into the Columbia, and the Columbia into the Pacific.

---

warrior who declared that in early childhood she had been promised to him as a wife. But upon learning that she was married to Charbonneau and had a son by him, the Indian renounced his claim to her.

[2] By her presence Sacajawea undoubtedly helped the expedition secure horses from her people, just as she undoubtedly helped maintain cordial relations between the captains and the chiefs. The Shoshonis had about seven hundred horses at this time, but the bartering situation was precarious because the items the Shoshonis wanted most —trade goods, guns, and ammunition—the men of the Lewis and Clark party did not have. They could only make small gifts, give speeches, and promise future trade between white men and the Shoshonis.

From August 19 to 26, Clark and his men investigated the Lemhi and Salmon rivers, finding them just as forbidding as the Indians had described them. The circle trip along the Lemhi and Salmon and back amounted to about seventy miles of rugged country. By August 24, Clark had decided that they should not try to take a water route.[3] The situation was serious, because fall was approaching and there was little game. The men would have to start soon.

By now the members of the expedition were used to hardships, as their journals frequently pointed out. But they were not used to going without food for days at a time or subsisting on only a few berries or roots or small fish, their present diet. The Shoshonis were on a meager diet too. Cameahwait pronounced a piece of dried squash which the expedition had brought from Mandan country, the best food he had ever tasted—except for sugar, a small lump of which Sacajawea had saved and given to him.

While Clark was on his reconnaissance, Lewis was trying to barter for horses with Indians who were more interested in hunting. Three deer, brought in on August 25 by his men, alleviated the food shortage temporarily, but on the same day Lewis had a bad scare. Sacajawea had told Charbonneau that all the Shoshoni hunters were leaving for buffalo country the next day. With his usual dull-wittedness, Charbonneau failed to relay this information to Lewis until that afternoon.

Lewis could foresee the results of such a caprice: he and his men would be left stranded in the mountains. He called together the three main chiefs and asked them whether they

[3] In 1893, Coues wrote: "Perhaps Captain Clark's good judgment in abandoning any route by way of the Salmon River saved the expedition."

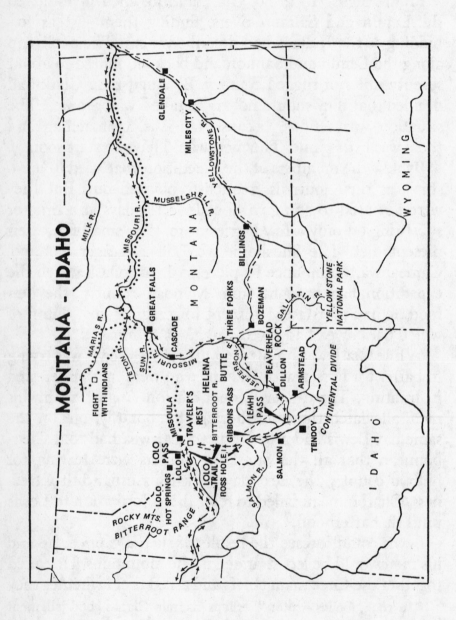

MONTANA—IDAHO

On the westward trip the Lewis and Clark Expedition followed the Missouri River to Three Forks and then followed the river they named the Jefferson, the most westerly branch of the three forks. They continued up the Beaverhead (the higher part of the Jefferson), branched off westward at Horse Prairie Creek, crossed Lemhi Pass, and entered the present state of Idaho. They crossed a mountain pass back into Montana, following the Lemhi River and the Bitterroot to what is now Missoula, Montana, where they turned west through Lolo Pass, followed the high "buffalo trail" of the Nez Percés, recrossed the Bitterroots again, came down into a broad, flat prairie, and again began traveling by water at the forks of the Clearwater near Lewiston, Idaho.

On their return trip they divided near Missoula, Lewis and his men going northeast to Great Falls, thence on an exploratory tour of the Marias River, turning back to the junction of the Marias with the Missouri after a skirmish with Blackfoot Indians. Clark and his men went southward in Montana, through Gibbon's Pass, back to the Beaverhead, crosscountry eastward at Three Forks to the Yellowstone, and down that river to its junction with the Missouri.

were men of their word. He reminded them of their promise to help his party cross the mountains. Cameahwait finally admitted that he was wrong, excusing himself by saying that his people were hungry. Lewis must have breathed a sigh of relief when on the next day, August 26, Cameahwait promised him at least twenty more horses.

"I directed the fiddle to be played," Lewis wrote, "and the party danced very merrily, much to the amusement and gratification of the natives, though I must confess that the state of my own mind at this moment did not well accord with the prevailing mirth."

By August 29, Lewis and Clark had bargained for twenty-nine horses, none in especially good flesh. The party then set out, accompanied by an old Indian guide, Toby, his four sons, and another Indian who went along out of curiosity. They started north along the Lemhi River. By September 2 all the Indians but their guide and one of his sons had left them. Progress had become extremely difficult. The horses, carrying baggage, frequently slipped and fell down the rocky slopes. One was crippled, two worn out. It was not an auspicious start.[4]

Bad weather was expected momentarily and it was no surprise when, on September 3, snow began to fall. Soon the surrounding mountaintops were white. The men shivered in the cold. They had broken their last thermometer and could not take temperature readings. About two inches of snow fell. Then it rained, and the rain turned to sleet.

[4] The party was now in the vicinity of present-day Gibbonsville, Idaho, a small town in the tip of the eastern bulge of lower Idaho. They were barely west of the Continental Divide, approaching Lost Trail Pass.

"We crossed a high mountain!" the journals exclaim on September 4, reporting the second crossing of the Bitterroot Range, a chain of mountains four hundred miles long. The men had crossed from Idaho back into Montana, traveling north.

In Ross's Hole, a wide valley, they encountered a large camp of Flathead Indians. Lewis and Clark called them Ootlashoots. They looked much like the Shoshonis and dressed a good deal like them, but their language puzzled the white men, who described it as like the "clucking of the fowl" or the "noise of a parrot." The Flatheads were friendly, shared berries and roots, and sold the expedition eleven more horses.

By the evening of September 7 the Corps of Discovery had progressed northward along the Bitterroot River to a point near present Grantsdale, Montana. They noted many creeks coming into the river, but not until September 9, when they reached a large creek joining the Bitterroot River on the west side, did their Indian guide notify them that the time had come to turn west. The explorers described the stream that they would follow as a "fine bold creek of clear water, about 20 yards wide, which we call Traveler's Rest creek." There they stayed two days, hunting and repairing clothing. From this point (Lolo) they would turn toward the Pacific Ocean over what came to be known as the Lolo Trail.

The men started up Traveler's Rest Creek on September 11. The valley grew narrower. Next day they made a difficult short cut across steep, stony hills to avoid the bends of the stream, and on Friday, September 13, they found some hot springs.[5] On that day the party had its share of bad luck: Lewis lost his horse, and Toby, the guide, mistakenly took them three miles out of the way on "an exceedingly bad route" before he found the right trail again. On that day they crossed the main divide of the Bitterroot Mountains and passed over from Montana again into what is now Idaho. It was their third crossing of the range. The expedition's drooping spirits were buoyed by the end of the day by the deer and several grouse that their hunters killed.

The main journals of the party are worded so tersely that it is difficult to imagine the agonizingly slow and painful progress across the mountains. Only occasionally do comments by some of the diarists reveal their sufferings. Gass described the terrain as a "horrible mountain desert." Ordway complained: "We eat our verry last morcil of our provisions except a little portable soup."[6] Later he entered: "We killed a wolf and eat it."

On Sunday, September 15, several of the packhorses lost their footing on the treacherous trail. One horse, carrying Clark's desk, rolled on top of it and smashed it. Despite these crises the headwaters of the Kooskooskie (Clearwater) River were reached that day.

Journal entries such as the following give a bleak picture of the next few days:

It began to snow and continued all day. . . . We were obliged to kill a second colt for our supper. . . . Our guns are scarcely of any service, for there is no living creature in these mountains except a few small pheasants [grouse], a small species

[5] Lolo Hot Springs.
[6] A dehydrated mixture which nobody liked and which was eaten only as a last resort.

of gray squirrel and a blue bird . . . about the size of a turtle dove or jay. . . . One of our horses slipped and rolled over with his load down the hillside. . . . The men are growing weak and losing their flesh very fast.

Clark, with an advance hunting party, named one stream Hungry Creek because there they had nothing to eat.

Such conditions prevailed until September 20. Clark's party, and later the other explorers, descended with relief out of the ridges and reached some flats, the favorite camas-root grounds of the Indians of the region. The plains were dotted with lodges of the Nez Percés.[7]

These Indians seemed well disposed, and on September 21, Captain Lewis made the acquaintance of Chief Twisted Hair. The chief gave Lewis the impression of being "cheerful and sincere."[8] The captains held a conference two days later and passed out more gifts and Jefferson medals. Great crowds of Indians gathered around.

There was more food in the region—camas roots, berries, and dried fish. On his map of 1814, Clark labeled this low

[7] Nez Percé is French for "pierced nose." Fur traders observed some members of the tribe wearing shells in their noses. The route the party had taken was known as the "upper Nez Percé buffalo trail," along the ridges of the mountains. Today a modern highway follows the route, but at a lower altitude. Since the days of Lewis and Clark the high ridges have been traversed by men with pack horses— all of whom have found the passage difficult. In recent years snowmobiles have tried the trail. The drivers are faced with the same problem that challenged Lewis and Clark—staying on the ridges.

[8] Apparently the captains thought that the Nez Percés were friendly from the start, but Indian tradition describes the tribe as suspicious of white men. These Indians apparently thought seriously of waylaying and killing the white men as they straggled through the mountains, but were dissuaded by an aged Indian woman, Stray Away, who had once been befriended by a white trader.

country Quamash (Camas) Flats. The change from a meat diet, together with the temptation to eat too much, made most of the explorers sick.[9] In an effort to restore some meat to their diet, the whites bought dogs from the Indians.[10]

A spell of hot weather followed the cold. It was not until October 3 that the men had sufficiently recovered from the trip to go to work. Cool winds on that day and the next helped. Captain Lewis, who had also been ill, could walk around a little by then.

The hunters tried to find game to shoot, and others of the party who felt well enough worked on canoes. They conserved their energy by burning out the tree trunks, Indian style. This spot was called Canoe Camp, at the forks of the "upper" and "lower" Clearwater River (about five miles west of present-day Orofino, Idaho), a stream that probably carried much more water in those days than it does now.

On October 6 the men of the expedition hid their saddles, along with some powder and bullets, branded their horses with an iron stirrup, and arranged for the Nez Percés to keep the animals until their return. The next day one small canoe and four large ones were loaded, and water travel once more was resumed. Old Toby, the Indian guide, had no fondness for this form of travel. He left, without collecting his pay.

On the night of October 9, as the explorers camped near

[9] Camas roots, eaten without other food, were both an emetic and a purgative to anyone whose stomach was not accustomed to them.

[10] Neither the Shoshonis nor the Nez Percés, although they sold dogs to the members of the expedition, cared about eating dog meat. Tradition says that Sacajawea was never hungry enough to partake of it.

the junction of the Clearwater and Snake rivers, the Indians gave them a final, noisy going-away party.[11]

[11] The white men, as usual, danced for the Indians, whose descendants could still describe the scene in the 1930's. Potts, whose monosyllabic name was easy for the Indians to remember, was apparently a star performer: "He boss other mans how to do funny dance and sing songs, all laugh" (apparently Potts called the figures for a square dance). "Negro York he do lots dance with feet and looks funny." John Bakeless, *Lewis and Clark: Partners in Discovery*, 268.

Past the Cascades of the Columbia

10

IT was to be expected that the voyage, downstream from now on, would be easy, without need for poles, towlines, or portages. That was the optimistic hope the members of the expedition held when they set off down the Clearwater River. There were some surprises in store for them.

At first the canoes floated down the river serenely, but soon they came to rapids. One of the canoes hung itself on a rock, and the men spent an hour disengaging it. That was just the beginning. The next day they passed the junction of the Clearwater and the Snake and encountered still more rapids.

Down the Snake and the Columbia the story was the same. Mileage was sure to be good each day, provided the canoes could survive the endless series of rapids. Many of the Indians the explorers met along the way were friendly, but some were terrified by the appearance of the strangers. When the Indians were frightened, they usually hid, but were soon reassured by seeing Sacajawea with her baby.

Along this river the staple of Indian diet was salmon, and along the banks the men saw groups of Indians drying fish. There were a few Indians on horseback and many in canoes. The latter obviously knew how to negotiate the rapids.

On October 14 three of the explorers' canoes hit rocks in the river. Cargoes spilled into the water, and one crew was forced to perch on a rock until rescued. Bedding and tomahawks were lost. Canisters of powder were dredged up from the riverbed. To dry out their baggage, the men had to break one of their rules—not to touch Indian property— "borrowing" a little split wood from an Indian cache to build a fire.

Three days later they reached the confluence of the Snake and the Columbia. They judged the Columbia to be 960 yards wide at that point, soon widening to a distance of one to three miles. There they found a tribe of Indians they called the Sokulks, who, along with most of the other tribes living along the river, fished in the glare of the sun and gazed constantly on snow in winter and consequently had chronically inflamed eyes. Those who subsisted chiefly on fish also had bad teeth, Lewis noted.

On October 19 the party met Chief Yellepit. He was perhaps a chief of the Cayuse Indians; the explorers referred to him as "the head of a band on the river below." He was a particularly intelligent and respected chief, "35 years of age, with a bold and dignified countenance." They would see him again the following spring.

On the same day they navigated Umatilla Rapids and saw Mount Adams and Mount Hood in the distance. Also on the same day Captain Clark unintentionally frightened a group of Indians. While rowing over to some houses along the shore, he shot a duck and a white crane, both of which fell into the water near the houses. It took him some time to convince the thirty-two terrified men, women, and children of the village that a man with so much magic at his command was friendly, especially when he took out his "burning glass" and, without thinking, lit his pipe. In the end presents pacified the Indians.

The next day, more rapids. They became an almost daily menace. On October 21, J. Collins presented the party with some acceptable beer that he had brewed from a bread made from roots. The explorers reached Celilo Falls on October 22 and portaged twelve hundred yards, descending more than thirty feet in two days, dropping their boats with elk-skin ropes over large rocks. At the upper end of the portage were new enemies—fleas. Waste left behind by Indians who had camped there had nourished a multitude of insects, which, the journals noted, "were so pleased to exchange the straw and fish skins . . . for some better residence, that we were soon covered with them."

On October 24 the party escaped destruction while bringing canoes and baggage successfully through six miles of rapids and whirlpools (the Short Narrows, forty-five yards wide), to the astonishment of the Indians below. The Indians there (Echeloots, or Wishrams) had the largest supply of dried salmon Lewis and Clark had yet seen, over ten thousand pounds. Most of the river Indians did not want to barter fish that they needed, and the explorers were not especially fond of fish anyway. They preferred to subsist on whatever they could shoot or on dogs they could buy. The Indians were willing to exchange dogs for such small articles as bells, thimbles, brass wire, and beads. They also prized fishhooks and needles.

On the next day the expedition encountered the Long Narrows. There the three-mile-long river channel, worn through hard, rough, black rock, was only fifty to one hundred yards wide. "The water swells and boils in a tremendous manner," it was noted. A canoe was damaged running this narrows. The men portaged most of their valuable stores and at last emerged into a fairly quiet basin. The campsite that night was a high point of rocks, which they named Fort Rock Camp (for the flat rocks forming the bed of the river, now called (The Dalles). It appeared that hunting, and consequently diet, might improve. Moreover, the men saw a deer, a goose, a beaver, and a sea otter—clearly the coast was near.

At this point along the Columbia were several Indian tribes, most of them friendly and helpful.[1] The Indians

[1] One of the men shot a goose that fell into the river. An Indian plunged into the channel, swam close to the rocks, where he could have been dashed to pieces, seized the goose, and swam to shore "with

knew a few English words and had learned to ask high prices for the few items they were willing to sell. Obviously they had had contact with men from trading ships.

Alternately quiet and noisy water appeared in the river as the expedition proceeded down the Columbia. At the "Great Shoot," the Cascades of the Columbia, it was wisely decided to portage, since the river was confined for a quarter of a mile within 150 yards and then dropped steeply over rocks in a 20-foot fall.[2] A mile and a half further on, the river was again confined within a narrow channel between large rocks. Unloaded canoes were sent down the second series of cascades on November 2, and a note was later made that this was the "last of all the descents of the Columbia." Camp was made twenty-nine miles farther down, on the Oregon side, at the edge of the Willamette Valley.

A little farther upriver on the Washington shore a perpendicular rock about eight hundred feet high created much interest. It was named Beacon Rock.[3] The explorers' first Oregon camp was somewhat more than halfway from the Cascades to the present city of Portland.

great composure." The men willingly gave the Indian the bird. He plucked about half the feathers and then, without opening the goose, ran a stick through it and carried it off to be roasted.

[2] The Cascades were the first series of rapids on the Columbia to be dammed and to furnish hydroelectric power. Other large dams on the river below the Snake are John Day, Bonneville, and McNary.

[3] Beacon Rock is perhaps the best-known landmark on the Columbia, standing at the head of tidewater and visible for some twenty miles below. Clark at first spelled it Beaten Rock.

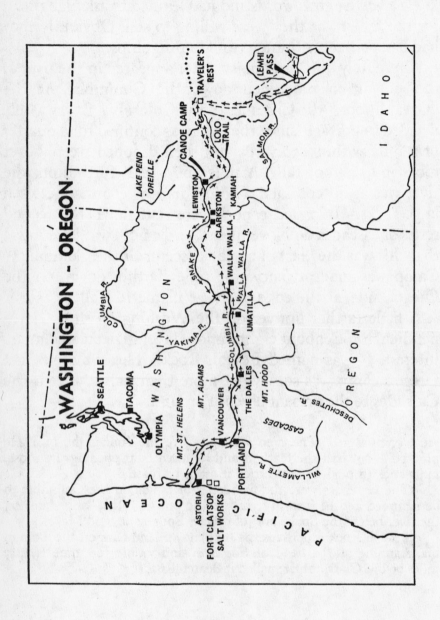

WASHINGTON—OREGON

Except for a few variations, the Lewis and Clark party followed the same route westward to the Pacific Coast and then back through Washington, after spending the winter at Fort Clatsop on the Oregon coast. From the forks of the Clearwater in Idaho to the Pacific Ocean near Astoria, they took the water route—the Clearwater, Snake, and Columbia rivers.

The Canoe Camp was at the forks of the Clearwater. There the men made dugout canoes after portaging the mountains on horseback and by foot. Beside the old trail near Canoe Camp stumps of trees from which the canoes were made were still being pointed out as late as 1900.

Camping on the Columbia

11

FROM this point on, the explorers would camp at relatively close distances along the upward bend of the Columbia, until they finally decided on November 24 to try the south side for a permanent winter camp. There was little promise of finding trading ships near the mouth of the Columbia.

They camped on the Oregon side on November 3, discovering that new obstacles and hardships awaited them.

The fog was so thick that they could not make out anything at a distance of fifty steps. They tried to wade across the mouth of the Sandy River, which joined the Columbia, only to discover that its bars were quicksand. They hastily returned to their canoes.

Nearly every day Indians came into camp to trade and observe the whites at work. One group brought with them a female prisoner who was supposedly Shoshoni. Sacajawea was introduced to her, but the two women could not understand each other. The prisoner had probably been taken captive by the Shoshonis from some other tribe.

Captain Lewis thought that some of the Indians' mode of dress, especially that of the women, was so unusual that he described it in detail:

The women are clad in a peculiar manner, the robe not reaching lower than the hip, and the body being covered in cold weather by a sort of corset of fur, curiously plaited and reaching from the arms to the hip; added to this is a sort of petticoat, or rather tissue of white cedar bark, bruised or broken into small strands, and woven into a girdle. . . . Being tied around the middle, these strands hang down as low as the knee in front, and to the mid-leg behind; they are of sufficient thickness to answer the purpose of concealment whilst the female is in an erect position, but in any other attitude form but a very ineffectual defense.

One day an Indian wearing a sailor's jacket offered to pilot them down the channel. Now the distant roar of breakers could be heard, and on November 7, after the fog cleared, they were charmed by the "mountainous high country" along the right bank. By nightfall it was raining again. Their camp that night was opposite a high rock in the water (Pillar Rock). High mountains could be seen in the southwest.

On November 8 the ocean was sighted. "Great joy in camp," wrote the usually unemotional Clark. "We are in view of the Ocian, this great Pacific Octian which we have been so long anxious to see, and the roreing or noise made by the waves brakeing on the rockey shores (as I suppose) may be heard disti[n]ctly." The estimated distance the explorers had traveled from St. Louis to the ocean was 4,100 miles.

Throughout the rest of the month the explorers moved uncertainly along the northern shore of the Columbia, trying to find a suitable site for a winter camp. It is natural to think of the Columbia as a wide, placid stream whose mouth could be explored at will under pleasant conditions. But at that time of year the river was whipped into high waves by the winds. Fogs shrouded the water, and debris was driven against the northern shoreline, where precipitous banks alternated with spits, points, and what Clark picturesquely called "nitches." Rain fell almost constantly. Few campsites were safe. The expanding mouth of the river varied from five to ten miles in width, depending upon what could actually be called the mouth.[1]

Conditions were wretched all through the month of November. The salty river water was almost undrinkable.

[1] Because the vast mouth of the Columbia is shrouded much of the time in fog, its discovery by Pacific mariners was delayed for some years—they sailed right by it. In 1791, Robert Gray, a Yankee shipmaster, found a bay into which an unknown river was discharging a current so strong that he could not ascend it. Again in 1792 he found the mouth and named it the Columbia after his ship. He also gave the name Cape Hancock to what is now Cape Disappointment.

The hills bordering the river were so steep that there was no storage place for the men's baggage at night. If the dugouts were left in the water, the waves dashed them against the shore and threatened to break them up. High tides washed in immense floating trees. Firewood was almost impossible to find. The men's clothes, tents, and baggage rotted in the rain.

More out of curiosity than a desire to help, small groups of Indians continued to visit the expedition from time to time by canoe. The Indians had lighter, more maneuverable canoes than those of the white party. "Those Indians are the best canoe navigators I ever saw," commented Clark.

Young females, blatantly offering to sell themselves to the men of the expedition, became a nuisance. The captains would have liked to obtain Indian goods, especially foods, but the natives wanted exorbitant prices. Usually they demanded blue, or "chief," beads, which all the coast Indians coveted, but unfortunately the expedition had exhausted its supply of blue beads. One visiting Indian had a gorgeous sea-otter robe that the captains were determined to secure. Sacajawea gave up her belt of blue beads so that a trade could be made for the robe. In compensation she was given a coat of blue cloth.

The captains finally reached the conclusion that the northern banks of the river were too unfriendly for occupation and that winter camp should be pitched somewhere else, perhaps on the south side. On November 26 they made a crossing, retreating fifteen miles upstream before finding a suitable place to paddle to the southern shore.

The decision to cross the Columbia had been duly voted upon by the whole party, including York and Sacajawea.

The Indian girl said that she favored going where there were "plenty of potatoes"—by which she meant wapatoo, an edible root.

Though the rain was heavy on the south side of the river, game was more plentiful there. Lewis, with three men, went on a three-day reconnaissance and found the elk abundant. Sacajawea showed the men what could be done with an elk after the meat had disappeared. She "broke two shank bones of the elk after the marrow was taken out; boiled them and extracted a pint of grease or tallow from them."

According to Gass, at length Lewis found a place for winter camp "about 15 miles from this camp, up a small river which puts into a large bay." The bay was named Meriwether's Bay, and to reach it the expedition rounded Smith's Point, on which Astoria was later founded. Living in this vicinity were various families from a group of Clatsop Indians. They were much neater in their persons and eating habits than most of the Indians the explorers had seen. Lewis and Clark got on well with them, and here they decided to build winter quarters—a fortification that they would call Fort Clatsop. The party moved to the new site on December 7.[2]

The men built eight cabins on high ground, avoiding the low areas, which were swampy. The cabins, each sixteen by thirty feet, were surrounded by a stockade. In one of the cabins was a tree stump so large that it could not be re-

[2] Before they moved, Clark autographed a pine tree with his famous legend: "William Clark December 3rd 1805. By land from the U. States in 1804 and 1805" (the United States was then considered to end at the Mississippi River). The party was outside the Louisiana Purchase from the time they left Montana.

moved. The men built around it, and Clark used it as a writing desk and drafting table.

The fort was nearly completed by Christmas. The men held a party and exchanged presents. Clark happily noted in his journal that he received fleece hosiery, shirt, drawers, and socks from Captain Lewis; a pair of "mockersons" from Whitehouse, and "two dozen white weazil tails" from Sacajawea. The Christmas feast consisted of little but "pore elk," however. Meanwhile, the fleas were still active, and the rain continued to fall.

By January 1 the winter quarters were finished—as snug as could be hoped for in that far outpost. The members of the expedition settled down to spend what was to be a winter of dampness, beautiful scenery, and skimpy diet. It was for the most part a monotonous winter. The men spent their time repairing gear, collecting salt, and striking up acquaintances with the Clatsop Indians and their likable chief, Yanakasac Coboway, whose name the captains rendered as Comowool. The fort was operated in military style, with sentries always on duty.

Winter at Fort Clatsop

12

"O! how disagreeable is our Situation dureing this dreadful weather," Clark complained.

The winter at Fort Clatsop was not severe, only miserable. At the first of the new year, 1806, a goodly number of the men were sick. Even York was ill with a cold from the strain of "carrying meat from the woods and lifting the heavy logs."

FORT CLATSOP

Southwest of Astoria, Oregon, where Lewis and Clark wintered in 1805–1806

Still, there were diversions. With ocean water available, a group of the men established an evaporation plant on a fine beach just north of present-day Tillamook Head. They boiled water in kettles, scraping salt from them and storing twenty gallons in iron-bound kegs.[1] "I care little wheather I have any with my meat or not," Clark observed, but most of the men found the salt a great treat.

One day the Indians who came to observe the salt workers reported that a large whale had been cast upon the shore of the ocean. Sacajawea, in one of her few recorded complaints, said that she had traveled a long way to see the

[1] A pile of rocks near the site, not far from Seaside, Oregon, is one of the few remaining physical signs of the expedition.

great waters and, now that a monstrous fish was also to be seen, she thought it "very hard" that she could not be permitted to see it, and the ocean too.

Sacajawea's complaint fell on sympathetic ears, and Clark took her, Charbonneau, and a group of men in two canoes to find the whale and, if possible, obtain some blubber. The explorers descended Tillamook Head, crossing an eighty-yard-wide stream, which they named Ecola, or Whale Creek. Tillamook Head and nearby Cannon Beach were the southernmost coastal points the expedition reached. By the time the men found the whale, all that remained of the monster was a skeleton, Clark ruefully noted. The Indians had almost stripped the bones. Clark and his party procured about three hundred pounds of blubber from the Indians, which they had to haul thirty-five miles back to Fort Clatsop. One member of the group, McNeal, nearly came to grief on the return trip as he was passing through an Indian village. One of the Indians became obtrusively friendly, inviting him into his lodge. A sympathetic Indian woman, who suspected that McNeal might be killed for the blanket he had around him, ran screaming for help. Clark, who was not far away, sent some men to the village to investigate. McNeal had escaped from the lodge, and was found hastily retreating, more surprised than alarmed. Clark named the neighboring creek McNeal's Folly (now called the Nehalem River).

Many Indian girls visited the fort, but the captains urged their men to avoid them, particularly those who were selling their "indulgencies." Lewis and Clark feared venereal disease, which was rife among the Indians. Contacts between the natives and maritime traders had spread various ailments among the natives and had also caused a general cultural decline. The men saw a red-haired, freckled-faced Indian boy whose father, probably a sailor long gone, had refused to let his mother flatten the boy's head—a common practice among some of the coastal Indians. One of the Indian girls had "J. Bowman" tattooed on her arm.

Game was short during the winter. The elk in the region were wary, and unfavorable weather constantly interfered with hunting. Among a group of expert riflemen Drewyer was the only hunter who brought in elk meat regularly. Their only beverage, Lewis remarked sadly, was "pure water."

Sacajawea, for whom the winter was equally hard, had saved a small piece of bread made from real flour—not native roots—which she had been keeping for her baby. She gave it to Captain Clark, who ate it with relish, even though, as he wrote, "it unfortunately got wet."

The captains took advantage of the lull in activities to write reports and catalogue the Indian subtribes around—dozens of them with—to the explorers—unpronounceable names.[2] Clark finished his maps. Lewis classified trees, shrubs, ferns, fish, reptiles, and birds. In the journal entries for this month are many observations of Indian dress and tribal life. The men made moccasins. In one way or another everyone marked time, waiting to start for home. Their

[2] One example will suffice: the "Cookoooose" (whose spelling would be somewhat improved by a hyphen: "Cookoo-oose"). It was later decided by etymologists that *coos* in one of the dialects meant "lake," "lagoon," or "inland bay."

primary mission had been fulfilled. They had found a route to the Pacific.

The men traded almost daily with the Indians, but they were nearly out of trade goods. In March they admitted having only enough to tie up in two handkerchiefs. For a little amusement some wore Indian hats made by the Clatsops—tall hats woven from cedar bark and bear grass with small brims "of about two inches and a high crown widening upward." Some preferred a neighboring tribe's conical hats, which had no brim and were held on the head by a string under the chin. At one time hats were bought for the whole party.

As spring drew near, game grew even scarcer.[3] Hunters had to go so far from camp that only with great effort could they haul back the game they managed to shoot.

Tobacco gave out. The men, thirty of whom either chewed or smoked tobacco, had to fall back on crab-tree bark for chewing and the inner bark of the red willow for smoking. There was general sickness. Willard cut his leg with a hatchet, Gibson and Bratton were so ill that they could do no work. Bratton was suffering from a back ailment. He did not recover until the men were on the homeward trail.

The main purpose in camping so near the coast had been to find a sailing vessel that might take the party home by

---

[3] Some historians have suggested that the men could have made an effort to kill seals. The only seal meat they ate was given to them by the Indians. According to Shoshoni stories, Sacajawea thought the seals were a strange race of human beings. When she tried to "talk" to them, they slipped away into the water.

water. President Jefferson, for some reason—perhaps wishing not to stir up the Spanish government—sent no ships to meet the explorers. The Indians told of trading vessels that had been seen along the coast but failed to mention the brig *Lydia*, commanded by Captain Samuel Hill, which was sailing along the coast of Oregon and Washington through parts of 1805 and 1806. In fact, the vessel was in the estuary of the Columbia for at least a month, and Captain Hill had taken a small boat one hundred miles upriver before Lewis and Clark arrived. The *Lydia* was standing offshore in November, but fog probably prevented those on board from seeing the campfires.

Thus Lewis and Clark had to return home overland. A plan to leave a few men on the Pacific Coast was considered and abandoned. All the men wondered whether they would make it back, particularly those who had been ill during the winter.

As March wore on, there was a bustle of preparation around Fort Clatsop. Damaged canoes were repaired; Lewis sacrificed his fancy gold-laced uniform coat in exchange for another canoe; the guns were overhauled by Shields; 440 pounds of lead and powder were packed.

By March 15 the captains were getting spring fever. They noted on that day that the sorrel had put forth some leaves and the birds were singing "very agreeably."[4] On March 22 they turned Fort Clatsop over to Chief Coboway, and on

---

4 Taken from "Remarks," notes appended to their daily weather reports, or "meteorological register." The notes were reprinted for the first time by Elliott Coues in *A History of the Expedition Under the Command of Captains Lewis and Clark*, III, 1293–94.

the next day the Lewis and Clark Expedition set out eastward.[5] Sacajawea and her family accompanied them.

[5] Chief Coboway, who lived until about 1825, used Fort Clatsop as a fall and winter hunting lodge for ten or fifteen years. The fort was still standing when the Canadian explorer Alexander Henry visited it in 1831. In 1836, John Kirk Townsend, the ornithologist, found the logs still sound but the roof gone. By about 1850 only two cabins and some ruins were left. It has since been rebuilt and is now a national memorial.

The Walla Wallas

13

IT was raining when the Corps of Discovery left Fort Clatsop. No matter—they were accustomed to rain by this time (Gass commented that there were only six entirely clear days between November 5 and March 25). March 24 was clear after a rain, but the next day there was a heavy rainfall with thunder and lightning and more rain.

Paddling along among the Seal Islands, where the channel narrows near present-day Cathlamet, Washington, they took the wrong channel, but a Cathlamet Indian pursued them and directed them to the right channel. Then he embarrassed them by claiming that one of their canoes, which they had taken from the Clatsops in reprisal for a theft, was his. The captains gave him an elk skin for it.

They discovered a large river, emptying into the Columbia from the south, about where Portland now stands, and the captains added it to their map. It was the Willamette, which had been hidden from their view by small islands as they went downriver the previous fall.

Until the expedition reached the Walla Wallas, they found the various tribes along the river sullen—not outwardly warlike, but uncooperative, perhaps because food was so scarce. Lewis had to resort to a demonstration of magic to trade with recalcitrant Indians for wapatoos. Unnoticed, he tossed an artillery fuse ("a port fire match") into an Indian campfire. The brilliant flame terrified them. Lewis then showed them his compass. Impressed and fearful, the Indians, to appease the wrath of the gods who seemed to be helping the captain, agreed to trade.

Thefts were a nuisance. The Indians went so far as to steal Scannon, who had faithfully served the explorers as a sentry. Lewis, who did not propose to let Scannon end his days in an Indian kettle, sent a rescue party to recover him.

The upriver trip in canoes was not an easy one. As soon as Indians with horses were encountered, trading began. By now the captains had almost nothing to trade. However, Clark treated the Indians for aches and pains, inflamed eyes, and other complaints in exchange for horses. Clark's "eye water" was especially in demand.[1] He complained on April 18 that one of his woman patients was a "sulky bitch," but he treated her anyway for back pains, since her husband, a chief, had some horses to trade.

As the men acquired horses, they discarded the canoes (one had already been lost in rapids). If the Indians would not trade horses for canoes, the boats were chopped up for firewood.

On April 27, Lewis and Clark revisited Yellepit, the friendly chief whom they had met the year before. Clark gave Yellepit his sword in exchange for an "elegant white horse." (A sword bearing the name Clark was found near Cathlamet, Washington, in 1904.)

Sick and injured Walla Wallas gathered in the explorers' camp. One had a broken arm that taxed Clark's skill as a physician. He undauntedly applied splints, and he treated others for colds, sprains, and rheumatism. The Walla Wallas were friendly and sociable, a welcome change from the hostile tribes between the ocean and the mouth of the Walla Walla River. The captains agreed to festivities, with square dancing and violin music. The next day the party was ferried across the river in canoes to resume travel on the south side of the Columbia. There they said good-by to one of their favorite Indian tribes and headed overland for the Snake (Lewis) River. At the Touchet River they found adequate firewood and game.

The men now had enough horses to journey cross-country. Charbonneau, not only the worst waterman of the expedi-

[1] A solution containing sugar of lead (lead acetate) and/or white vitriol (zinc sulphate).

tion but also a poor horseman, twice delayed the party by losing his horse. Sometimes Indian families would join them, breaking their line of march and slowing them down. But since the Indians were friendly and were trying to be helpful, they were allowed to remain.

As they moved up the Pataha Valley on May 1, the captains were astounded to be overtaken by three young Walla Walla braves, who returned a steel trap that had been overlooked on departure. "Hospitable, honest and sincere," was the praise given these Indians in the journals.

Among the Walla Wallas was a woman prisoner of the Shoshoni tribe. Although she belonged to a different group of Shoshonis, Sacajawea was able to communicate with her. "We were able to explain ourselves to the Indians, and answer all their inquiries with respect to ourselves and the object of our journey. Our conversation inspired them with much confidence."

Gradually Nez Percé Indians began to filter into camp. They too were friendly. On May 11, in order to address a number of Nez Percé chiefs, Lewis and Clark called in their battery of interpreters. The Nez Percés also had a Shoshoni prisoner. The captains gave their message, one sentence at a time, to a Frenchman of their party, who repeated it in French to Charbonneau. Charbonneau, who spoke broken English, relayed the message in Hidatsa to Sacajawea, who translated it into Shoshoni for the prisoner. By this roundabout method the captains communicated with the Nez Percés.

The Blue Mountains of northern Oregon were now in sight. The captains devoted some space in their journals to a description of the local hills in the spring:

We now find, for the first time since leaving Rock fort [The Dalles] an abundance of firewood. The growth consists of cottonwood, birch, crimson haw, red and sweet willow, chokecherry, yellow currants, gooseberry, the honeysuckle with a white berry, rosebushes, sevenbark and sumac, together with the corn grass and rushes.

Food was better too:

We were soon supplied by Drewyer with a beaver and an otter, of which we took only a part of the beaver and gave the rest to the Indians. The otter is a favorite food, though much inferior, at least in our estimation, to the dog, which they will not eat.

The men saw deer, curlews, cranes, ducks, and prairie larks along the way, but no herds of buffaloes or elk, so plentiful along the Missouri River. The expedition camped for a night at a site between what later would be the towns of Prescott and Waitsburg, Washington.

The Nez Percés

14

DURING May and part of June the Lewis and Clark Expedition traveled through Nez Percé country. They camped for some time on the South Fork of the Clearwater (in what is now Idaho County, Idaho), departing on June 10. No name is recorded for this stopping place, but it could well have been called Camp Chopunnish (near present-day Kamiah, Idaho).

Sacajawea continued to gather roots and to contribute substantially to the company's food supply. Lewis makes a journal entry under the date May 16: "Our sick men are much better today. Sahcargarweah gathered a quantity of the roots of a species of fennel, which we found very agreeable food. The flavor of the root is not unlike annis seed." On May 18 Clark noted that Sacajawea was gathering "year-pah" (yampa) roots, which could be eaten fresh, roasted, boiled, or dried and were "generally between the size of a quill and that of a man's finger, and about the length of the latter."

Game was easier to find but not plentiful until June; then bear meat and venison replaced the flesh of horses and dogs. The weather had improved somewhat, but every rain in the valleys meant snow on the heights. The Indians warned Lewis not to attempt the passage of the Bitterroots until June.

The captains continued to regard the Nez Percés as the most amiable and gentle Indians with whom they had associated. Indifferent to trinkets and baubles, the Nez Percés prized such useful items as knives, kettles, blankets, and awls.

Clark's medical practice grew much larger than he could handle. He did the best he could with the remedies at his disposal. It was not unusual for him to treat forty sick or injured Indians in one day. He remarked that, in any event, he did not give them anything that would hurt them. His eye water and liniments and laxatives must have been effective, for his reputation spread. "The extent of our medical fame is not a little troublesome," he lamented.

One of Clark's most worrisome patients was one of his

own men, Bratton, whose back was still so painful that he could scarcely sit up. For him the captains finally prescribed an Indian treatment—a sweat bath. The men dug a four-foot-deep pit, built a fire in it, and heated stones. The hot stones were placed in an enclosure, and water was poured on the stones. Bratton sat in the steam imbibing large quantities of horsemint tea. Periodically he was plunged into cold water and then returned to his steamroom. Finally he was wrapped in blankets. He began to improve the next day and soon recovered fully. After this success the captains gave an elderly chief, Tom-a-tap-po, who had suffered from partial paralysis for three years, the same treatment, and he too soon began to show improvement.

The most serious medical emergency at this time was the illness of Sacajawea's baby. Little Pomp, who had shared all the hardships of the journey, was now about fifteen months old. Both Pomp and his mother had seemed to be indestructible, but now he was suffering from a swollen neck and throat.

The captains poulticed his neck with wild onions and then tried a salve of resin, beeswax, and bear's oil. By May 25 the little boy was better.

During May the captains were busy rounding up the horses they had left with the Nez Percés the year before. They learned that three of the chiefs, Twisted Hair, Broken Arm, and Cut Nose, had quarreled over the care of the horses. All of them apparently anticipated rewards. Because of the quarrel the horses had been scattered during the winter. They were eventually rounded up, except for two that the Shoshoni guides of the year before had taken. The captains did not complain about it, since the guides had received no pay. Part of the cache of gear and supplies had been destroyed, but the chiefs had saved most of the saddles.

Mishaps were frequent. To get supplies for the mountain crossing, Charbonneau and LePage were sent out with meager trading goods to visit an Indian village. These two Frenchmen may have known how to deal with Indians, but they were inept with horses. They managed to let their packhorse fall into the river, lost some of their goods, and soaked the rest. Shannon, Collins, and Potts, also on a trading mission, upset their canoe and lost it, along with some of their clothing and blankets—a serious loss. Potts, unable to swim, barely escaped drowning.

One day a number of Nez Percé chiefs assembled at camp, probably for medicines and treatments. The captains decided that it was an opportune time to deliver one of their well-rehearsed orations. At least seven main chiefs and several subchiefs were present. Clark set out to tell the Indians all about the United States, the Great White Father, and the white men's desire for peace and trade with their Indian brothers.

The chain of interpreters again went into action. The message was passed from the captains to one of the more articulate Frenchmen, to Charbonneau, to Sacajawea, to the Shoshoni captive. He communicated the message to the assembled Indians. They seemed to understand. The principal chief harangued his men, urging them to agree to follow the advice of the white men, chiefly to keep peace. While the Indians debated this, a big meal of mush was being prepared in the kettles, and at the conclusion of his oration the chief instructed all those who wished to ratify the proceedings to join them in eating. The rest could abstain. Clark commented with dry humor: "There was not a dissenting voice on this great national question, but all swallowed their objections, if any they had, very cheerfully with their mush." For their co-operative attitude the chiefs received some medals.

On June 10 the expedition took to the trail again, going first to Quamash Flats, just west of Weippe Prairie (northwest of the present town of Weippe). Lewis wrote on that day: "At 11 a.m. we set out with the party, each man being well mounted, and a light load on a second horse; besides which we have several supernumerary horses, in case of accident or want of provision. We therefore feel ourselves perfectly equipped for the mountains."[1]

[1] From June 10 to 16, 1806, the Lewis and Clark party hunted in the area of Weippe Prairie. The camas plants were in bloom, as well as violets, honeysuckle, huckleberry, and white maple. The fields of camas were described as appearing, from a short distance, like "lakes of fine clear water."

Recrossing the Bitterroot Mountains

15

FIVE days were spent preparing for the mountain crossing. The men were in high spirits. They had enough surplus energy to engage in foot races, pitch quoits, and play "prisoner's base." Nothing seemed to dismay them, not even the prospect of wading into the mountain snows or failing to shoot enough game for the trip. They dried what meat they had, packed their baggage the night before departure, and were ready to start.

On June 15 the expedition commenced a swift, forced march eastward over the Bitterroots. They intended to take the same high "buffalo trail" that they had followed on the western trip and cross the mountains in five days—no more, because that was as long as the horses could go without forage.

By June 17 they had climbed into the high ridges of the mountains, and there they bogged down. Lewis reported: "We found ourselves enveloped in snow from 12 to 15 feet in depth, even on the south side of the mountain. . . . Winter now presented itself in all its rigors; the air was keen and cold, no vestige of vegetation was to be seen, and our hands and feet were benumbed." They were forced to backtrack, returning to Hungry Creek. After one camp they retreated to Weippe Prairie.[1] Drewyer and Shannon were sent back to try to find Nez Percés who would guide them over the mountains as far as Traveler's Rest Creek (near present-day Missoula, Montana).

Mishaps of the next day were described by Gass:

We proceed on [while waiting for a guide] with four men in front to cut some bushes out of the path; but did not go very far till one of the men [Potts] cut himself badly with a large knife; when we had to halt and bind up his wound. We went again forward, and in crossing the creek the horse of one of our men [Colter] fell with him, threw him off, hurt his leg and lost his blanket.

---

[1] Ordway liked the prairie and commented that he wished he could stay there. "Plenty of strawberries," he wrote.

These were the critical days of the journey home. The men were unable to proceed. No guides had been found. Two horses were lost, and a search party had set out to look for them. Two men were injured. There was almost nothing to eat. Cruzatte found some mushrooms, which the ravenous men ate without knowing whether they were poisonous. Fortunately, they were edible.

Another of their horses was injured on June 21, as the backtrack continued. About then two Indians rode up, leading four extra horses. They were setting out to cross the mountains in the direction Lewis and Clark wanted to go. They were persuaded to wait for the full party to reassemble. Drewyer and Shannon soon returned with three more Indians.

The next day one of the Indian guides fell behind, declaring that he was ill and unable to travel. The captains interpreted this to mean that he was not eager to cross the mountains. A companion turned back with him. As it turned out, the guide really was ill. He and his companion caught up with the party a few days later, the sick man so poorly clad—in only an elk-skin shirt and moccasins—that the captains gave him a buffalo robe.

On June 26 the men faced the mountain crossing again, finding that the snow banks had shrunk slightly and that there were a few patches of grass for the horses. But it was bear grass, which the horses disliked so much that they seemed to prefer to starve. By June 28 the party had plodded twenty-eight miles without taking the loads from the horses. A rest stop was made, and lunch was "bear's oil with some boiled roots." They pitched camp at midday because of the extreme fatigue of both men and beasts.

The mountains looked bleak and impassable to Lewis and Clark, but the native guides knew what they were doing. Lewis wrote that they "traverse this trackless region with a kind of instinctive sagacity; they never hesitate, they are never embarrassed; and so undeviating is their step, that wherever the snow had disappeared for even a hundred paces, we find the summer road."

The Corps of Discovery came out of the Bitterroot Mountains on June 29. Lewis reported: "We continued along the ridge which we have been following . . . till at the end of five miles it terminated; and bidding adieu to the snows in which we have been imprisoned, we descended to the main branch of the Kooskooskee." The party went wearily down Lolo Creek to Lolo Hot Springs, Montana. The short but torturous mountain crossing was over. The horses could feed on grass at last, and for the first time in two years the men had a hot bath at the springs. That night they reached Traveler's Rest Creek.

The Party Divides

WHILE at Traveler's Rest in the Bitterroot Valley, Lewis and Clark made the decision to divide the party for the remainder of the return trip. Lewis wanted to explore the sources of the Marias River. Clark would take the most direct route he could find—shorter, it was hoped, than the looping one followed on the way west—to the Beaverhead River, where the expedition had cached boats. Both parties would then subdivide. Lewis' party would divide at Great Falls, which Lewis would reach overland; Clark's at the Beaverhead. Lewis would leave some men at Great Falls. Clark would send some of his men downriver to Great Falls to help with the portage. Clark would then proceed to the Yellowstone River overland, sending from that point another group by land with the horses to the junction of the Yellowstone and the Missouri, while he took the river route. All would reassemble at the mouth of the Yellowstone (near the North Dakota line).

If all went well, Lewis' route would take him northeast to Great Falls, thence north to the Marias; Clark's route, southeast to the Beaverhead, thence east to the Yellowstone. Charbonneau and Sacajawea would accompany Clark. Both routes would be dangerous, and everyone knew that this separation might be a final one. Lewis wrote that he hoped it would be "only momentary."

Nez Percé guides were persuaded to travel for a day or two with Lewis and his party. Then they departed, a little fearful of the "Pahkees" (their enemies, the Hidatsas), not far from present-day Missoula. Lewis' route followed Hellgate Canyon, then up the Blackfoot River and north across the Dearborn River to the Sun River, which he followed east to the Missouri at present-day Great Falls. To follow this route, the party had to cross a low pass on the Continental Divide, which has since been known as Lewis and Clark Pass, although Clark never crossed it. Lewis' party would reach Great Falls on July 13.

Meanwhile, Clark's party followed the main fork of the Bitterroot River and on July 5 camped at Ross's Hole (near where the expedition had first met the Flatheads). Following an old buffalo trail, they found another pass across the Continental Divide (Gibbon's Pass), which would permit them to go directly southeast to the Beaverhead. Sacajawea recognized the plain; her tribe had gone there often to dig camas roots.

On July 7, Clark's men found some hot springs. Two of the men, experimenting, found it possible to cook meat in the bubbling spring waters. The next day they reached the junction of Horse Prairie Creek and the Beaverhead, the point at which they had left the Beaverhead the year before. They found the cache of canoes and supplies in good condition. The men were delighted to find their prized supply of chewing tobacco intact. Clark remarked with amusement that the tobacco chewers, who had been out of tobacco for half a year, scarcely gave themselves time to take the saddles from their horses before they were off for the cache.

Pausing for some preparations and repairs, Clark sent Sergeant Pryor and some of the men overland toward Three Forks with the horses, while he ventured onto the river downstream with the rest. Both groups would meet again at Three Forks on July 13.

When Lewis and his party arrived at Great Falls on July 13, they found game plentiful. It was mating season for the buffaloes, and great herds of them were milling around. The bellowing of the bulls created a constant roar, upsetting the horses, who were unused to buffaloes. Both parties complained of ever-increasing swarms of mosquitoes. Clark thought that the deer were thin because of the insects, and the horses had to be held within a circle of smoking campfires for protection. Sacajawea's son especially suffered from mosquito bites. Clark's party also had to endure cold, windy weather. Freezing rain fell and then turned to ice; snow appeared imminent—in July. The journals report three-quarters of an inch of ice on standing water on the night of July 10. Still there were mosquitoes aplenty until dark.

Sacajawea was familiar with this part of the country, and she was able to assure Clark that they were on the right route and could cross the Continental Divide by continuing in their present direction.

After reaching Three Forks, Ordway and nine others loaded baggage into six canoes and then started down the Missouri to join Lewis at Great Falls. Clark and the rest of his party (now consisting of Pryor, Shields, Shannon, Bratton, Labiche, Windsor, Hall, Gibson, Charbonneau, Sacajawea, Pomp, and York) started eastward overland, looking for the Yellowstone River.

Lewis Explores the Marias River

17

BETWEEN July 13 and July 17, Lewis and his men, camped at Great Falls, prepared to divide again, one group to go north and explore the Marias River, the other to proceed downstream on the Missouri. Some of Clark's men were expected momentarily from Three Forks. Clark himself and the rest of his group were moving eastward, cross-country, with a band of forty-nine horses and one colt.

Clark's journey toward the passes of the Rocky Mountains, through which they must find a route, provided the background for one of the controversies of the return journey: Did Sacajawea now guide the expedition? And did she pick the best route?

The party set out eastward on July 13 but journeyed only four miles that day, halting with lame horses on the north bank of the Gallatin River. By July 15, however, they had traveled nine miles beyond the top ridges of the Continental Divide and had reached the Yellowstone. Sacajawea recommended the pass now called Bozeman Pass.

Clark's exact route from Three Forks to the Yellowstone is relatively unimportant; he could have made the crossing through any of three different passes in the region. C. S. Kingston declared that "it was solely on [Sacajawea's] advice that Clark decided to go to the Yellowstone by the Bozeman Pass route. But he did not know when the party started for Bozeman Pass that there was a wide expanse of swamp ground which must be crossed . . . an intolerable route!"[1] Kingston thought that she should have suggested Flathead Pass.

Biddle's edition of the journals agrees that Sacajawea recommended Bozeman Pass:

The squaw now assured Captain Clark that the large road from Medicine (Sun) River to the gap they were seeking crossed the upper part of this plain. He therefore proceeded four miles up the plain and reached the main channel of the

[1] "Sacajawea as Guide," *Pacific Northwest Quarterly*, Vol. XXXV (January, 1944). Kingston was indulging in hairsplitting. Sacajawea recommended a trail followed by her tribe. More than that could hardly be expected of her.

river (West Gallatin), which is still navigable for canoes, though much divided and dammed up by multitudes of beaver. Having forded this river, they passed through a little skirt of cottonwood to a low open plain, where they dined.[2]

According to Biddle, Sacajawea added some information. She told the captains that, a few years before, buffaloes had been numerous not only in that region but even as far as the sources of the Jefferson River.

As Clark looked eastward on July 13, he saw the Bridger Range and, southward, the Gallatin Range. The East Gallatin River emerged from between the ranges, south of Bridger Peak and north of Mount Ellis. The gap "to the southward" was the one Sacajawea recommended. Clark took her advice and later wrote, "The Indian woman . . . has been of great service to me as a pilot through this country."

Coues commented that Clark "very sensibly followed the advice of the remarkable woman, who never failed to rise to the occasion, even when it was mountains high. He accordingly makes the Bozeman Pass . . . and strikes the Yellowstone at its nearest point, by the most direct route."[3] Sacajawea's route enabled the Clark party to proceed forty-

[2] Coues (ed.), A *History of the Expedition Under the Command of Captains Lewis and Clark*, III, 1132–33.

[3] Clark and his party did do some floundering around in the marshes of the West Gallatin River. Everything considered, however, they made remarkable time between Three Forks and the Yellowstone. Their route was later the one selected for the Northern Pacific Railroad and also for the main highway. Part of it was a buffalo road. Coues pointed out: "The other gap . . . would have taken [Clark] over Flathead Pass of the Bridger range, and so to Flathead creek and other upper tributaries of Shields' river, a good deal north of his best route." Coues (ed.), A *History of the Expedition*, III, 1132.

eight miles between July 13 and July 15, marshes and rivers notwithstanding. They were now in the Yellowstone Valley, not far from the present town of Livingston, Montana.[4]

Clark expected to find some Crow Indians in the valley. He did not actually see them, but he was soon convinced that they were nearby, for horses began to disappear nightly. Canoe travel would have been easier than overland travel, but no trees suitable for large canoes were to be found.

Accidents occurred. Charbonneau, always inept with horses, fell with his mount while pursuing a buffalo. The Frenchman was shaken up and bruised. Gibson, trying to mount a skittish horse, fell on a sharp charred snag that penetrated his thigh two inches, making it necessary to carry him on a litter. On July 21 the men found some timber and began building canoes. It was none too soon, for the next morning twenty-four horses were missing. By then travel by water seemed preferable.

On the morning of the twenty-fourth, near present Billings, Montana, Pryor, Shannon, and Windsor set out to take the remaining horses overland to Fort Mandan, while Clark and the rest of the men pushed off in loaded canoes down the Yellowstone. The canoes were so small that they were lashed in pairs. Both parties made camp together that night, but Pryor reported difficulty driving a band of horses with only three riders. The horses, trained by Indians, insisted on chasing buffaloes. Clark added Hall to Pryor's party, and since Hall was just about naked, he was given a spare shirt, leggings, and moccasins. By now all the men were ragged and insufficiently clothed.

Meanwhile, Lewis and his men were having considerably

[4] Bernard De Voto (ed.), *The Journals of Lewis and Clark*, 449.

more excitement. They too had lost some of their horses, and they almost lost McNeal, whose horse plunged into brush at the White Bear Island camp near Great Falls and found himself face-to-face with a grizzly bear. The horse wheeled and threw McNeal practically at the bear's feet. As the huge beast rose on his hind legs, McNeal swung his rifle and struck the bear over the head, breaking the weapon. As the stunned beast clasped his head, McNeal climbed the nearest tree and stayed there until the angry bear finally stalked away.[5]

On July 17, while Clark and his men were looking for timber along the Yellowstone, Lewis left Sergeant Gass and five others at Great Falls to portage supplies from the cache, with instructions to wait for the group coming downriver from Three Forks and then meet Lewis at the mouth of the Marias River. Lewis took with him only Drewyer and Joseph and Reuben Fields to investigate the sources of the river on the north.

For a week the Lewis party continued up the Marias after intersecting it overland and then turned back toward the Missouri. As Drewyer walked along the river bottom—the rest on higher ground—Lewis saw a group of horses about a mile away. He studied them through his glass and made out a small band of Indians standing silently, watching Drewyer. He was sure that they were Blackfeet—always harbingers of trouble—and they had horses.

[5] Sergeant Patrick Gass's published journals, which contained drawings of expedition episodes executed by an artist with only a vague conception of conditions, illustrates McNeal's plight with a sketch that shows a bear looking more like Lewis' Newfoundland than a grizzly, and McNeal sitting placidly on a tree limb wearing a high-crowned hat and a long-tailed coat.

Thus was the stage set for Lewis' only important error in judgment during the expedition—and a fight, by morning, which resulted in the certain death of one Indian and probably two. The date was July 26; the place, on the south fork of the Marias River, not far from present Cutbank, Montana.

A Skirmish with the Indians

18

LEWIS thought that he counted thirty horses or more as he studied the group of Indians on the hill through his glass. He determined that perhaps eight of the horses were saddled, indicating a larger party of Indians than he had at first supposed. He decided upon a friendly approach—especially since the Indians had spotted Drewyer. For their part, the Indians, who gave evidence of alarm and indecision on seeing the white men, rode toward Lewis and his two companions. At a distance of one hundred yards Lewis dismounted to meet one of the Indians who was approaching while the others waited.

Now began Lewis' most critical effort at diplomacy. He asked by signs whether the Indians were Hidatsas. The Indians indicated that they were Blackfeet. Lewis inquired whether any among the party were chiefs. They replied that three were chiefs. Not likely, Lewis thought. He gave away a flag, a medal, and a handkerchief. The two parties eyed each other for a while. The white men wondered nervously whether there were any more Blackfeet. The Indians appeared equally ill at ease, doubtlessly wondering whether another party of white men would appear.

Finally Lewis proposed that both groups camp together, probably because he wanted to keep an eye on the Indians. The Indians agreed. Both groups sought to convince each other that they were parts of large forces. Men were coming up the Missouri to the mouth of the Marias, Lewis informed the Indians solemnly. The Indians told him that two large bands of Blackfeet were nearby, one camped on the main branch of the Marias.

After having made the mistake of suggesting that they camp together, Lewis and his men compounded the error by not remaining alert. They smoked with the Indians until a late hour, and then Lewis ordered Joseph Fields to stand guard. Everything about camp was quiet until sunrise, when the Indians arose and crowded around a fire that Fields had built. He had carelessly left his rifle near his brother, who was still sleeping. One of the Indians slipped behind them, seizing both the brothers' guns. Two other Indians seized

the rifles belonging to Lewis and Drewyer, and one started
to run away. Lewis heard Drewyer yell, "Damn you, let go
of my gun!"

A furor erupted. The Fields brothers chased the nearest
Indian, overtook him, and wrestled with him for the gun.
Drewyer battled with the Indian who had taken his gun,
and Lewis, awakened by the commotion, drew his pistol and
ran after another Indian.

An Indian was stabbed in the scuffle with the Fields
brothers. The Blackfoot ran a little distance and fell dead.
Lewis overtook the Indian he was chasing and ordered him
to drop the gun or be shot. As the Fields brothers came
running up, Lewis called out to them to hold their fire and
try to recover the horses, which other Indians were running
off.

Lewis again set out with his pistol after the Blackfoot who
had stolen his gun and another Indian, who was attempting
to steal the horses still in camp. As Lewis later wrote:

I called to them as I had done several times before that I
would shoot them if they did not give me my horse and
raised my gun, one of them jumped behind a rock and
spoke to the other who turned around and stopped at the
distance of 30 steps from me and I shot him through the
belly, he fell to his knees and on his wright elbow from
which position he partly raised himself and fired at me, and
turning himself about crawled in behind a rock which was
a few feet from him. he overshot me, being bearheaded I
felt the wind of his bullet very distinctly.

Lewis' shot probably was fatal to the Indian, but the
journals do not verify his death.[1]

[1] Weapons were lethal enough in those days, but it took from

Drewyer soon returned from his pursuit of the Indians, and the Fields brothers returned shortly with four horses. In their flight the Blackfeet had left some of their belongings, including bows and arrows, which Lewis burned in the campfire. The men hastily saddled, taking one of their own horses and four of the Indians'. They lost no time heading for the mouth of the Marias. This was the longest almost continuous trail ride in the history of American expeditions. The men jolted for sixty-three miles the first day, stopping briefly at the Tanzy River to allow the horses a short rest, and then pushed on another seventeen miles. By 2:00 A.M. the next morning they had ridden almost one hundred miles. At last, feeling reasonably safe from pursuit by friends of the dead and wounded Blackfeet, they dismounted and slept.

The next morning the men were so stiff that they could scarcely move. Nevertheless they pressed on toward the Missouri. Near the hills along the banks of the river they heard gunshots. Was a fight already in progress? The shots proved to be those of Sergeant Ordway and nine men who on July 19 had joined Gass and those already at Great Falls after coming downriver from Three Forks.

Lewis and his men could have crossed the Marias River and put more distance between themselves and the Indians, but Lewis had decided to go to the mouth of the river, the agreed meeting place. His decision was based partly on his conviction that the Blackfeet would pick the junction as the

-----

twenty to thirty seconds to fire a second shot. Lewis did not have his powder with him and thus could fire only once with his pistol.

point to intercept them.[2] "I told [the men] that we owed much for the safety of our friends and that we must risk our lives on this occasion," the captain explained in his journal. Later he reported, "We had the unspeakable satisfaction of seeing our canoes coming down." The two parties saluted each other by gunfire, and the men in the canoes paddled to shore. All warmly shook hands.

[2] Many years later a Blackfoot in the group that had had the skirmish with Lewis said that the Indians were just as frightened as the white men and rode off in another direction to put as many miles between them and the white men as possible.

The Mouth of the Yellowstone

19

ON July 24, the day before Lewis and his friends met the Indians near the Marias River, Clark and his water party had started down the Yellowstone River and were making good time with the help of a swift current. They saw a now-famous rock "in an extensive bottom on the right, 250 paces from the shore." They estimated that it was about two hundred feet high. On the rock Indians had carved figures of animals and other objects. Clark named it Pompey's Pillar. After climbing it and looking over the countryside, Clark descended and cut his name and the day, month, and year on the face. His signature is still visible on the rock, protected by a grillwork—another of the few remaining physical signs of the expedition. A town named for the landmark stands nearby.

The party camped near the mouth of the Bighorn River on July 26, and on the next day, when Lewis and his men were involved in the shooting incident with the Indians, Clark's party made more than eighty miles downriver—practically flying, in comparison with the slow trip up the Missouri the year before. By July 30 they had reached the mouth of the Powder River.

From this point they began to see more buffaloes and some grizzly bears. Clark wrote: "The buffalo now appear in vast numbers. A herd happened to be on their way across the river. Such was the magnitude of these animals, that, though the river, including an island over which they passed, was a mile wide, the herd stretched, as thickly as they could swim, from one side to the other." The shaggy swimming animals caused an hour's delay.

Clark's party reached the mouth of the Yellowstone on August 3, and although this was the point where they were to meet Lewis, the mosquitoes were so troublesome in the windless heat that they decided to go farther downriver. Clark wrote a note to Lewis, fastened it to a pole at the confluence of the rivers, and then moved on to another camping place (which proved to be even more mosquito-infested). By now little Pomp's face was badly swollen,

Clark noted. Clark went out to shoot bighorns, but insects clouded the barrel of his rifle, making his gunsights useless.

The storms and rain of the next two days were welcome, for the mosquitoes disappeared temporarily. On August 8, to everyone's surprise, Sergeant Pryor, with Shannon, Hall, and Windsor, came paddling downriver in skin boats. At a point near Pompey's Pillar they had made themselves circular skin canoes like the Mandans' bull boats and had been happy to find the frail vessels ideal for skimming downstream. Unfortunately, Pryor had removed most of Clark's note to Lewis at the junction of the Yellowstone and the Missouri, but at least he and his men had learned from it where Captain Clark was, and they continued paddling downstream until they caught up with him.

Sacajawea continued gathering roots and berries for the party. Clark reported that she gathered "a large well-flavored gooseberry, of a rich crimson color, and a deep purple berry of a species of currant common on the river as low as the Mandans, and called by the engagees Indian currant."

Meanwhile, Lewis and his small party, exhausted by their headlong ride from the Blackfeet, had been joined by the men who had come downriver from Great Falls. They turned the horses loose and again set out on the Missouri from the mouth of the Marias River. They had hoped that the red pirogue they had cached there would still be usable, but it had rotted.

Sergeant Ordway's party, which had left the mouth of the Madison River on the thirteenth, had departed from Great Falls on the twenty-seventh in the white pirogue and five canoes. Sergeant Gass and Willard had set out from that point by land, taking horses with them. All the groups met at the mouth of the Marias and were headed down the Missouri, making rapid progress. The river was high, and game was plentiful. The Lewis party reached the junction of the Musselshell on August 1 and the mouth of the Milk River on August 4. The same hot weather that Clark complained of also oppressed Lewis' party on the Missouri. Later they were pelted by the same rains. At times the wind was so high that it was not safe to put loaded canoes into the water. Nevertheless, they reached the mouth of the Yellowstone on August 7, where Lewis was a bit puzzled to find a scrap of paper on a pole, with only his name on it, in Clark's handwriting.

Pressing on to catch Clark's waiting crew, on August 11 they saw some elk on a sandbar thick with willows. Lewis and Cruzatte landed to try to shoot one. Lewis, who had experienced most of the close escapes of the expedition, was now to experience one more. Both he and Cruzatte shot at an elk and then separated in the underbrush to find it. Just as Lewis was preparing to shoot again, he heard a rifle crack, and a ball struck him squarely in the backside. Cruzatte, who was nearsighted, had mistaken Lewis for an elk and had shot his captain. The ball passed through the left side of Lewis' buttocks, grazed the right one, and dropped into his breeches. Fortunately, it struck no bone or artery.

Lewis yelled, "Damn you, you have shot me!" Then, when Cruzatte did not answer, he wondered whether the shot might have come from Indians. Lewis hobbled back to the pirogue, fearing that Indians might attack at any time. Cruzatte finally appeared, apologizing profusely for his stupidity.

The bleeding wound was dressed, and Lewis lay down in the boat, ignominiously put out of action just before he and Clark were reunited. After the next day, August 12, Lewis, because of the pain of his wound, discontinued his journal.

Down to St. Louis

20

LEWIS' party caught up with Clark on August 12. Clark, looking across the water as shots were fired in salute, at first could not see the captain. Lewis' wound was so painful that he could barely move, and he had to stay in the pirogue, even at night.

The next day, aided by a stiff breeze, the reunited explorers made eighty-six miles downriver and felt that they were practically in home country as they drew near Fort Mandan. On August 14 they reached an encampment of Hidatsas.

Captain Clark called the Hidatsa chiefs together and addressed them through the interpreter Jussome, whom Drewyer had been sent to find at the Mandan villages. Clark wanted one of the chiefs to visit the Great White Father in Washington, but the chiefs were full of excuses—afraid to pass through the land of the Sioux. Despite Lewis' and Clark's arguments and hopes for peace, intertribal wars had continued. Charbonneau, visiting with the Indians, reported that the Hidatsas had been fighting both the Shoshonis and the Arikaras and had all but gone to war with the Mandans in an argument over a woman.

Clark went to see Le Borgne, "the great chief of all the Minnetarees" [Hidatsas], who at the time was living at one of the Mandan villages, and invited him to visit the Great Father, but he too said that the Sioux would prevent him from going.[1] Finally She-he-ke (Big White) of the Mandans agreed to go to Washington, provided he could take along his wife and son and also Jussome, his wife, and two children.

Colter, the only member of the expedition who appeared not to be eager to go home, asked permission to accompany two white traders named Dickson and Hancock into beaver country. Lewis and Clark gave him permission to leave.

[1] It is unlikely that Le Borgne was afraid of the Sioux or anyone else. He was a fearsome chief, a one-eyed giant with a violent temper. He was probably using the Sioux as an excuse for avoiding the journey to Washington.

At Fort Mandan the explorers bade farewell to Charbonneau and Sacajawea. On August 17, Clark wrote:

Settled with Touisant Charbono for his services as an
enterpreter the price of a horse and Lodge (leather tent)
purchased of him for public Service in all amounting to
500$ 33 1/3 cents. derected two of the largest of the Canoes
be fastened together with poles tied across them So as to
make them Study [steady] for the purpose of Conveying
the Indians and enterpreter and their families.

we were visited by all the principal Chiefs of the Menetarras to take their leave of us at 2 oClock we left our encampment after takeing leave of Colter who also Set out
up river in company with Messrs. Dickson and Hancock. we
also took our leave of T. Chabono, his Snake Indian wife
and their child who had accompanied us on our rout to the
pacific ocean in the capacity of interpreter. . . . T. Chabono
wished much to accompany us in the said Capacity if we
could have provailed (upon) the Menetarre Chiefs to
decend the river with us to the U. States, but as none of
those Chiefs of whoes language he was Conversent would
accompany us, his services were no longer of use to the U.
States and he was therefore discharged and paid up. we
offered to convey him down to Illinois if he chose to go, He
declined proceeding on at present, observing that he had no
acquaintance or prospects of makeing a liveing below, and
must continue to live in the way that he had done. I offered
to take his little son a butifull promising child who is 19
months old to which they both himself & wife wer willing
provided the child had been weened. they observed that in
one year the boy would be sufficiently old to leave his
mother & he would then take him to me if I would be so
friendly as to raise the child for him in such a manner as I
thought proper, to which I agreed &c.

Sacajawea received no pay, but Clark apparently expected to make it up to her later.

After much weeping by She-he-ke's friends and relatives, the stocky, prematurely gray Mandan chief and his entourage boarded the canoes, and the Lewis and Clark party glided downriver.[2] The swivel gun had been given to Le Borgne, who fired it and then took it with great ceremony to his village.

Lewis spent an uncomfortable two weeks nursing his wound. On the twenty-third, Clark noted that Lewis was recovering rapidly. But on the twenty-seventh Lewis did too much walking, and on the thirtieth Clark was a little more cautious in reporting that "Captain Lewis is mending slowly." Finally on September 9 he reported: "My worthy friend, Capt. Lewis, has entirely recovered. His wounds are healed up, and he can walk and even run nearly as well as he ever could."

All the members of the party except for Chief She-he-ke were happy as they floated down the Missouri toward St. Louis. The chief and his family were already weary of the journey. They soon met traders on the Missouri. A party

[2] The Mandan chief made a longer visit in the United States than anyone bargained for. In 1807, Clark arranged to send him back upriver with an escort under Nathaniel Pryor, but the Arikaras were hostile. One of their chiefs had died on such a visit. A fight developed along the river: Shannon, the former member of the expedition, suffered a bad leg wound, and his leg was later amputated. Jussome, the interpreter friend of the Mandan chief, was also injured in this encounter. She-he-ke refused to accompany the party overland to the Mandan villages. It was not until 1809 that he was finally delivered back to his people. His sojourn among the whites had given She-he-ke, already too talkative, a great deal to relate, which his tribesmen found hard to believe. The Mandans branded him a liar.

of Frenchmen, manning a boat owned by Auguste Chouteau, gave the returning explorers a gallon of whisky—only a sip for each person, but deeply appreciated—their only drink of "spirits" since July 4, 1805. A few days later traders LaCroy, Aiten, and Chouteau, commanding three boats, gave the thirsty men all the whisky they could drink. That evening they were very hilarious, singing songs until midnight.

Making fifty or more miles daily, by September 20 the Corps of Discovery was nearing St. Louis. The men saw cows grazing along the banks of the river. At sundown the town of La Charette came into view. People rushed to the riverbank to see the returning explorers; they had long since been given up for lost. Nothing had been heard from them since they left the Mandans more than a year and a half before.

The last half of September, 1806, was unusually warm. Clark had reported September 8 as the hottest day of the year, but September 16 was still warmer. Clark described it as "emencely worm." Thirty-two hard-rowing, bearded men in dugout canoes, their clothes ragged and their skin burned brown, were coming down the river, resting momentarily to fire volleys of rifle shots. They had traveled eight thousand miles.

Clark's notation on September 23 reads: "Descended to the Mississippi and down that river to St. Louis at which place we arrived at 12 o'clock. We suffered the party to fire off their pieces as a salute to the town." His shortest notation was made on September 26: "A fine morning. We commenced writing, etc."

The Expedition Ends

21

THE Lewis and Clark Expedition had ended. A postrider waited at Cahokia, Illinois, to take a letter to President Jefferson. As the news spread across the country, the importance of the Louisiana Purchase was realized. It had been proved that there was a land-and-water route to the Pacific Ocean.

The members of the expedition separated and went their

own ways, never again to reassemble. Lewis and Clark each received 1,600 acres of land from the government, and each of the other members were allotted 320 acres, though few settled on them. All were to receive double pay for the time they spent on the journey, about $166 for each man and $1,228 for each captain.

Meriwether Lewis was appointed governor of Louisiana Territory; William Clark was made brigadier general of the Louisiana militia. In 1809, while en route from St. Louis to Washington, Lewis died under mysterious circumstances in a dingy little roadside hostelry in frontier Tennessee. He may have been murdered; he may have taken his own life. At the time of his death Lewis was on his way to explain to Jefferson some of his problems as territorial governor.

Clark rejected the opportunity to succeed Lewis as governor of Louisiana Territory, but he later became governor of Missouri Territory and superintendent of Indian Affairs at St. Louis. He was universally admired and respected, had great personal influence among the Indians, and was responsible for thirty Indian treaties. After a long and useful life, Clark died in 1838 at the age of sixty-eight.

As for the other members of the famous expedition, some returned to the wilderness. John Colter opened the route to Jackson Hole, Wyoming. Some became farmers; others fought in the War of 1812.[1] Shannon became a judge; Willard settled in California; Drewyer and Potts lost their lives to the Indians; and some simply disappeared from history. One, Paddy Gass, lived to be almost one hundred years old. York died of cholera a few years after the expedition.

[1] Among them Bratton and Gass. Bratton married and fathered ten children. Gass married at sixty and fathered seven children.

But what of Sacajawea, Charbonneau, and little Baptiste? For a while they remained at the Mandan villages after the expedition went downriver to St. Louis. Then, on August 20, Captain Clark, writing from the Arikara village below future Fort Manuel, sent a letter to Charbonneau:

Charbono:

Sir: Your present situation with the Indians gives me some concern—I wish now I had advised you to come on with me to the Illinois where it would most probably be in my power to put you in some way to do something for yourself. . . . You may have been a long time with me and have conducted yourself in such a manner as to gain my friendship; your woman, who accompanied you that long and dangerous and fatiguing route to the Pacific Ocian and back, deserved a greater reward for her attention and service on that route than we had in our power to give her at the Mandans. As to your little son (my boy Pomp) you well know my fondness for him and my anxiety to take and raise him as my own child.[2] I once more tell you if you will bring your son, Baptiest, to me, I will educate him and treat him as my own child—I do not forget the promise which I made to you and shall now repeat them that you may be certain—Charbono, if you wish to live with the white people, and will come to me, I will give you a piece of land and furnish you with horses, cows and hogs—if you wish to visit your friends in Montrall, I will let you have a horse, and your family shall be taken care of until your return—If you wish to return as an interpreter for the Menetarras when the troops come up to form the establishment, you will be with me ready and I will procure you the place—or if you wish to

[2] Clark's affection for Baptiste is apparent throughout his journal.

return to trade with the Indians and will leave your little son Pomp with me, I will assist you with merchandise for that purpose . . . and become myself concerned with you in trade on a small scale, that is to say not exceeding a pirogue load at one time. If you are disposed to accept either of my offers to you, and will bring down your son, your femme Janey³ had best come along with you to take care of the boy until I get him. Let me advise you to keep your bill of exchange and what furs and peltries you have in possession and get as much more as you can, and get as many robes, and big horn and cabbra skins as you can collect in the course of this winter. And take them down to St. Louis as early as possible. . . . Inquire of the governor of that place for a letter which I shall leave with him. . . . I shall inform you what you had best do with your furs, peltries and robes, etc. . . . When you get to St. Louis write a letter to me by the post and let me know your situation—If you do not intend to go down either this fall or in the spring, write a letter to me by the first opportunity and inform me what you intend to do that I may know if I may expect you or not. If you ever intend to come down, this fall or the next spring will be the best time—this fall would be best if you could get down before winter. I shall be found either in St. Louis or in Clarksville at the falls of the Ohio.

Wishing you and your family great success, and with anxious expectations of seeing my little dancing boy, Baptiste, I shall remain your friend.

WILLIAM CLARK

Keep this letter and let not more than one or two persons see it, and when you write to me seal your letter. I think you best not determine which of my offers to accept until you

³ Clark's nickname for Sacajawea.

see me. Come prepared to accept . . . which you may choose after you get down.[4]

Thus Clark gave the family an opportunity to go to St. Louis and enter the white man's world. Charbonneau accepted the offer and took Pomp and Sacajawea to St. Louis. Later, when Charbonneau decided to return to the Upper Missouri, Sacajawea went with him, leaving her son in St. Louis.

[4] For ease of reading, Clark's spelling (except for names) has been corrected.

PART TWO: *Sacajawea's Later Life*

Sacajawea — What Was She Like?

22

MUCH of Sacajawea's life is shrouded in mystery. The year and a half she spent with the Lewis and Clark Expedition is the only documented period of her life. During that time she served the United States faithfully and without pay, although it is doubtful that she comprehended the significance of the expedition.

Of her life before and after the expedition much less is

known. She was born into a tribe of Northern Shoshonis somewhere in Idaho's Lemhi Valley. Her early days were spent wandering with her people through the mountains of Idaho and Montana. Kidnapped by a party of raiding Hidatsas, she was taken east to the Great Plains, hundreds of miles from her home.

The girl must have longed for her home and family, although, except for the moving story of her reunion with Cameahwait, there is no record that she ever gave expression to her longing.

Charbonneau, a rough, aging, unchivalrous fur trader, either bought Sacajawea from the Hidatsas or won her in a gambling game and took her for his wife. When she was only sixteen, Sacajawea lay in pain on buffalo robes in a fort in the wilderness, with only bearded men around—and perhaps an interpreter's wife—and in a difficult delivery gave birth to a baby boy. Less than two months later she set out for the Pacific with Lewis and Clark with her baby on her back.

Picture a slight, active Indian girl, with the black hair and copper skin of most Shoshonis of her time. This small Indian girl endured discomfort and semistarvation and survived a year and a half of rigorous travel, much of it afoot, caring for a baby, accepting her share of difficult tasks.

When the expedition started, Sacajawea was probably freshly clothed in fringed deerskin. As time went on and conditions of travel worsened, she no doubt wore any garments she could patch together. Even in the hardest times, however, she probably found ways to decorate her clothing. Like most girls, Sacajawea liked beads. But she gave her blue-beaded belt to the captains when they needed it for trade. She probably carried her belongings and those of her baby in a parfleche, a buffalo skin cut into a pattern and folded over, laced, decorated, and perhaps painted.

Any appraisal of Sacajawea must depend on the fragments of reference to her in the diaries and journals of the Lewis and Clark Expedition, plus statements made by explorers who said they knew her—though they did not refer to her by name—a few years afterward.

The first characteristic of Sacajawea's described in the journals was compassion. She tried to protect another Indian woman from an angry husband at Fort Mandan. Soon after the expedition was under way, she demonstrated coolness in emergency and courage in the face of danger. She won the admiration of the captains on the day the pirogue nearly capsized. Whenever the Indian girl appears in the journals, the reference is generally to her usefulness. No fault was ever found with her. She was alert and industrious, a busy berry and root gatherer. Sometimes she showed the men Indian ways of cooking and of eking out a scanty meal.

As the only woman on the expedition, it is certain that she helped nurse the sick and injured, mended clothes and moccasins, and scraped and tanned skins—at the same time caring for her tiny son.

The members of the party were half-starved throughout much of the mountain travel. Little surprise that after Sacajawea's one recorded sick spell she ate too much. Queasy stomachs were frequent on the expedition. There was too much to eat or too little, the weather was too hot or too cold, and the water supply in the plains was muddy.

Lewis, alone among the diarists in trying to describe

Sacajawea's nature, once wrote that she possessed a "folly or philosophy" that enabled her to accept life as she found it. Almost without fail she radiated cheerfulness. Captain Clark called her uncomplaining. This trait must have been conspicuous to have elicited such a comment.

Sacajawea was also impulsively generous, a girl who gave a lump of hoarded sugar to her brother and a precious piece of bread to Captain Clark.

On only one occasion, on November 14, 1805, during the interminably rainy stay at the mouth of the Columbia River, did Sacajawea display pique. Captain Clark wrote, "Squar displeased with me," but he failed to explain why.

It is obvious that even before the party left the Mandan villages, the captains had concluded that Sacajawea was going to be useful to them on the journey. She became much more useful than they expected.

No historian is likely to assert now that the Indian girl was indispensable to the party. The members might have survived without her root digging and berry picking, her cooking, sewing, and nursing. They might have succeeded in obtaining horses from her tribe without her help. Lewis might have forestalled the Shoshonis' departure to hunt buffalo without her warning. Yet there can be no question that her presence eased the way. As mentioned earlier, it may be that Sacajawea's greatest contribution was simply her presence. Tradition has it that the Nez Percé contemplated killing the straggling party as it crossed the Bitterroots on the way west but that an Indian girl who had been befriended by white men dissuaded her tribesmen by asking, "Why do these white men have an Indian girl with a baby along? Surely this cannot be a war party."

Historians disagree about how much help Sacajawea actually was in guiding the Clark party eastward through Bozeman Pass. No doubt Clark could have experimented with other routes, but he might have been later—much later—reaching the Yellowstone with horses whose hooves were already worn to the quick.

There were instances when Sacajawea strengthened morale. She reassured them, when the expedition was all but lost while trying to find a western Rocky Mountain crossing, "In that direction you are sure to find my tribe."

How did Sacajawea fare as the only woman member of a boisterous expedition made up almost entirely of bachelors? Indian girls were generally accorded little respect. It was customary to think of the girls as chattels. Charbonneau had the typical fur trader's careless attitude toward Indian womanhood. Not noted for refinement, delicacy, patience, or kindness—who among the fur traders was?—he may have quarreled with her frequently and may have mistreated her. He did indeed strike her in one recorded instance when Captain Clark intervened.

Fur traders married Indian girls because they needed them. It is not accurate to say that the women provided only sex. Wives were indispensable to the mountain men, and many wives were well treated. Some of the roughest characters of the plains and mountains were inconsolable when they lost their wives, and most of them loved their half-blood children. It was the pinnacle of many Indian girls' ambitions to marry a fur trader.

It is overstating the case to claim, as romanticizers tend to do, that Sacajawea suffered for a cause. Any reader of the journals of the expedition is impressed by her enjoyment of life. She had spunk and energy and endurance. Outdoor life was the only life she knew. It must be remembered that she was a Shoshoni, and Shoshonis came from a cold and inhospitable homeland in the Rockies. They were inured to hardship and lack of food and were seldom bowed by misfortune. The Shoshonis were often gay and carefree under conditions that white men found all but intolerable. It is probable that Sacajawea's life as a Hidatsa captive was not entirely unhappy, either. Probably she was permitted to enjoy some of the freedom of Hidatsa girls below the age of marriage.[1]

After she joined the expedition, the fact that Sacajawea was married and a mother doubtless restrained any amorous inclinations on the men's part. The journals indicate that Charbonneau and Sacajawea were permitted a certain amount of privacy; the interpreters and their wives shared a tent with the captains. As for Pomp, he was a favorite. As soon as he learned to toddle, the men played with him, danced around with him, or dandled him on their knees.

Thus it is likely that Sacajawea enjoyed a reasonably happy life with the Lewis and Clark party. In fact, her lot may have been an improvement over that of many another

---

[1] George Catlin told of crossing the Missouri River with two others in a bull boat, assisted by laughing, screaming Hidatsa maidens. He wrote: "We were soon surrounded by a dozen or more beautiful girls twelve to eighteen years of age. . . . They all swam in a bold and graceful manner, as confidently as so many otters or beavers; and with their long black hair floating on the water, whilst their faces were glowing with jokes and fun, which they were cracking about us and which we could not understand." Harold McCracken, *George Catlin and the Old Frontier*, 112.

Indian girl. She was in her most active years and should be pictured that way—not as a prematurely aging woman bowed down with burdens.

As for the often-repeated suggestion that Sacajawea had a romantic attachment for Captain Clark, it is indeed possible that she did. No doubt he was a much more attractive man than Charbonneau. But Lewis and Clark had to maintain a certain posture before their men. They were emissaries of the President and were under the constant observation of their men.

Many of the tribes were afflicted with venereal disease, the scourge left by coastal traders, for which the Indians had no cure. Both Lewis and Clark cautioned their men against relations with Indian women suspected of being diseased. Apparently the warning went unheeded. Clark mentioned the use of mercury in treating his men.

Though the captains evidently avoided any personal contact with Indian women, they observed them and often described them in their journals. Indian women were ranked from "handsome" to "disgusting." The captains thought that the Mandan girls were exceptionally good-looking. Some of the coastal tribes had pleasant enough faces but tied their ankles and feet so tightly as to restrict circulation and cause misshapen legs. Some of them had elongated heads, which were not attractive to white men. Others painted themselves too liberally, smeared their hair with bear oil, or wore costumes that appeared ludicrous to white men.

The captains did not think that in general Indian women were particularly chaste. Among the exceptions were the

Shoshonis and the Nez Percés. Of the Shoshonis, Lewis writes: "Some of their women appear to be held more sacred than in any nation we have seen."

To the end of her days Sacajawea continued to be held in unusually high esteem. Two contemporary writers spoke well of her. Henry Brackenridge, the author-explorer, who wrote that he met her on a boat going upriver from St. Louis in 1811, thought her "a good creature of mild and gentle disposition." John Luttig, the clerk at Fort Manuel, who tersely reported her death there, called her "the best woman at the fort."

At Fort Manuel

SACAJAWEA'S life after she parted company with the Lewis and Clark Expedition has been the subject of controversy among scholars and mythmakers. It appears almost certain, however, that in 1806, some months after the expedition ended, Sacajawea, Charbonneau, and Baptiste, at Clark's invitation, went down the Missouri to St. Louis, where they hoped to make a life for themselves. Grace

FORT MANUEL, 1812

Raymond Hebard, who wrote a popular account of Sacajawea's life, believed that Charbonneau took both of his
Shoshoni wives and two sons with him.[1] Leaving his family
there, the interpreter accepted an offer to trap for a fur
company on the rivers of the Southwest.

Miss Hebard identified the second boy as Baptiste's half-
brother, Toussaint. Later historians believe that there was
probably only one boy, Baptiste called by two different
names.

On October 30, 1810, Charbonneau purchased from Cap-

[1] Grace Raymond Hebard, *Sacajawea: Guide of the Lewis and
Clark Expedition.*

tain Clark, who was then Indian agent for Louisiana Territory, a tract of land on the Missouri River, in Saint Ferdinand Township, near St. Louis. In the spring of 1811, Charbonneau sold the land back to Clark for one hundred dollars, a transaction recorded on March 26, 1811. Charbonneau must have decided that he did not want to farm and was homesick for the plains, the fur traders, and his Indian friends. About the time he sold his tract of land, Charbonneau bought fifty pounds of "biscuit" (the hardtack of those days), apparently anticipating employment with Henry Brackenridge's party on the boat going upriver.

An entry in Brackenridge's journals reads:

We have on board a Frenchman named Charbonet, with his wife, an Indian woman of the Snake nation, both of whom accompanied Lewis and Clark to the Pacific, and were of great service. The woman, a good creature, of mild and gentle disposition, was greatly attached to the whites, whose manners and airs she tries to imitate; but she had become sickly and longed to revisit her native country; her husband also, who had spent many years amongst the Indians, was become weary of a civilized life.[2]

By providing Charbonneau with an extra wife and son in St. Louis, Miss Hebard was able to argue that Brackenridge mistakenly identified the Indian woman with Charbonneau as Sacajawea. She insisted that the woman mentioned by Brackenridge was not Sacajawea but another Shoshoni wife, the mother of the second Indian boy and that Baptiste, only six years old, was too young to be left in St. Louis without a mother. Thus, Miss Hebard claimed, "Sacajawea . . . re-

[2] Henry M. Brackenridge, *Journal of a Voyage Up the Missouri River in 1811.*

mained to care for her son and also to have oversight of the other boy, Toussaint."

John Bradbury, the English naturalist, confirmed Brackenridge's statement that Charbonneau and his wife went upriver in April, 1811. In view of the fact that Miss Hebard offered no proof for her version of events, there seems no reason to question Brackenridge's identification.

Two expeditions set out from St. Louis in the spring of 1811: Brackenridge with Manuel Lisa, the fur baron; Bradbury with the Astorians under Wilson Price Hunt. These men headed competitive parties, both after the fur trade. The Astorians left the Missouri River and reached the Pacific Coast by an overland route, suffering many hardships along the way. Bradbury left the party when it started overland and returned to St. Louis. Charbonneau traveled as far as Mandan country, and made various villages in the region his headquarters for many years. He also joined the Lisa expedition of 1812, although it is not clear at what point or whether Sacajawea accompanied him on a trip he made to St. Louis in 1812. Only Charbonneau's name appears on the list of *engagés* hired for the 1812 trip.[3]

Lisa's party was to build Fort Manuel (named for him) just below the North Dakota border in South Dakota, on the banks of the Missouri. John C. Luttig, a former Baltimore and St. Louis businessman, went along and became clerk for Lisa at Fort Manuel. Luttig kept a daily journal of activities at the fort until it was abandoned in 1813.

His journal, which is a primary source of information about the troubles with the British and Indians in the

[3] John C. Luttig, *Journal of a Fur Trading Expedition on the Upper Missouri, 1812–1813* (ed. by Stella M. Drumm), 158.

region in 1812, is also our main evidence that Charbonneau spent some time at the fort. Luttig mentioned Charbonneau several times, generally in a derogatory manner.

Luttig began his journal with the departure of the boat from St. Louis. He reported that eighty-seven persons were aboard and that the boat was accompanied by two barges loaded with goods, including the first domesticated animals other than horses to be taken to the Upper Missouri.

The fort was constructed on the present line between North and South Dakota, and its completion was celebrated on November 19. The festivities included a dance, attended by all the ladies of the fort. During its short life, the fort was the site of almost frenzied activity. People came on foot, on horseback, by boat. Indians of many tribes, traders, trappers, and hunting parties came on all kinds of missions. There were women, children, dogs, and horses in profusion. Drunken brawls, horse stealing, lost livestock, unwelcome campers, domestic quarrels, accusations, and suspicion abounded. Amid the general furor there was a busy traffic in goods of various kinds.

Luttig's daily log indicates that confusion—even pandemonium—prevailed much of the time. He must have been a busy man, and that may explain the terse, sometimes hurried entries in his journal:

August 13, 1812: At 10 P.M. 60 Rees composing a War party arrived. they requested something to eat. . . .

August 14: . . . last night about 40 Indians camped with us. they were gathering Cherries and other fruits about the Country.

August 26: Grey Eyes (Ree Chief) arrived with 100 men from a war tour. They had not killed or even seen an enemy.

In the evening a larger party passed by with Two Scalps. . . .

September 11: Mr. Lewis, two engages and the trappers for the little Horn, in all 18 Men [arrived]. At noon a Sioux Chief arrived. . . .

September 17: The Men who went to gett the Horses came back and told the sad news that 5 Indians, supposing Grosventers, had mounted the horses in their sight and rode them off.

September 21: . . . the Sioux after having taken a little mixed whisky, pretended to be drunk, and cut Capers about like mad men. . . .

October 15: A Band of Chajennes, about 12 Lodges arrived, their chief named Lessaroco. They had plenty of Women & Children and a great Number of Dogs. . . .

November 14: . . . the Saunie Sioux had arrived with about 150 Lodges at the Rees. . . . a band of Chajennes were camped about 5 miles above the fort. . . .

Luttig's entries reporting deaths at the fort were also brief. On December 20, 1812, he wrote: "This evening the wife of Charbonneau, a Snake squaw, died of a putrid fever. She was a good and the best woman in the fort, aged about 25 years. She left a fine infant girl." Luttig did not record the woman's name—perhaps because he, like the diarists of the Lewis and Clark Expedition, had trouble spelling it. Perhaps he did not even know it.

The fort itself did not survive long. The Indians were becoming hostile. On February 5, 1813, a young Hidatsa hunter was shot and killed just outside the gates. "The Sioux!" Luttig exclaimed. On February 22 one of the *engagés*, Archambeau, was hauling hay on a sled. As he approached the opposite shore of the river, he was shot by Indians. "They took the scalp and cut him nearly to pieces,"

Luttig reported. The fort's swivel guns could not be trained on the four or five hundred Indians Luttig claimed were poised across the river. Most of the men who had come upriver with Lisa were scattered for many miles, trapping or trading, and the fort was not well protected. Women and children outnumbered defenders. On February 26, Luttig complained that those remaining in the fort "are like Prisoners in Deserts to expect every moment our fate." His journal ends on March 5: "Snowstorm last night and continued snowing all this Day...."

Within a few days the fort was abandoned, and the occupants scattered. Luttig took with him the baby girl whom he called Sacajawea's Lizette. Luttig, a man of sympathetic feelings, felt a responsibility toward the child, even though he was not overly fond of her father. Fort Manuel was evidently burned by the Indians. Luttig arrived in St. Louis in June, 1813, and in August applied to the court to be appointed guardian for Lizette, as well as for "Toussaint," a boy about ten years old. In the court record the name Luttig was subsequently crossed out and William Clark's substituted. Luttig died in 1815.

Charbonneau, who was undoubtedly away from Fort Manuel when it was abandoned, can be traced in later diaries and journals of the western explorations and occasionally through official records. Although he survived until his eighties, he was never reunited with his children. He evidently did not return to St. Louis after 1816, when he left on a trading trip for Auguste Chouteau, until 1839.

Despite Luttig's journal record of Sacajawea's death at Fort Manuel, in Shoshoni oral tradition Sacajawea rejoined her tribe years later on the reservation. Baptiste, who was often called Toussaint, can be followed until 1866, the probable year of his death, although in Shoshoni tradition he too reappeared with his tribe and lived in Wyoming with his aged mother and Bazil, the son of her dead sister, whom she had adopted in 1805. By the latter account Baptiste lived until 1885, Bazil until 1886. Both briefly outlived their mother, who died in 1884. The Shoshoni tradition will be discussed in the chapters that follow.

There is no record of what became of Lizette. On April 23, 1843, the daughter of one Joseph Vertifeuille and Elizabeth Carboneau was baptized at Westport, Missouri. The little girl's name was Victoire. It is at least possible that Victoire's mother, Elizabeth (née "Carboneau"), was Sacajawea's daughter.

Toussaint Charbonneau

THE fairest appraisal of the fur trader and interpreter Toussaint Charbonneau was that of O. D. Wheeler, who wrote: "It has been rather the fashion of latter-day writers and critics to sneer at and decry the old interpreter. [But] . . . Charbonneau was, after all, a man of fairly commendable traits considering his environments."[1]

[1] O. D. Wheeler, *The Trail of Lewis and Clark, 1804–1806.*

It would be difficult to visualize Toussaint Charbonneau in "civilization." He was born in or near Montreal, Canada, about 1759. From the time he was in his twenties, he was making his fortune among the fur traders and Indians on the frontiers. In 1793 and 1794 he was employed by the Northwest Fur Company at Pine Fort, on the Assiniboine River. Several years later he went to North Dakota. He was staying with the Hidatsas near the Knife River when Lewis and Clark met him.

He could be pictured as short, swarthy, and bearded, talkative, perhaps boastful. Some said that he was high-strung and had a quick temper. The Indians regarded him with some amusement, and the nicknames they gave him, such as "Chief of the Little Village" and "Great Horse from Afar," were bestowed in mockery, but not necessarily in antagonism. The fact that he lived among the Indians until he was past eighty is proof enough that he was their friend. Unfortunately, he was a constant pursuer of Indian girls; when we first meet him in the journals of the fur traders, he is in the bad graces of an Indian girl's mother.

Charbonneau appealed to the western explorers and mountain men because he knew his trade. When his ability to translate Indian words failed him, he could interpret sign language. Those who sometimes called him a villain or a knave were generally his competitors. He had his failings. On the Lewis and Clark Expedition he proved to be accident-prone, a timorous waterman, a poor horseman, and at times slow-witted. He certainly did less for the party than his wife, Sacajawea, did. Yet, as the oldest member of the group, he endured hardships that exhausted men much younger than he. Although he was seldom praised by Lewis or Clark, he was sometimes commended for his on-the-trail cookery and his emergency meals. Coues was inclined to believe that Charbonneau was a "minus function" and described him as a "poor specimen, consisting chiefly of a tongue to wag in a mouth to fill." But Lewis and Clark referred to him as their "friend" and noted that he performed his duties satisfactorily, although he had no "peculiar merit."

Other notable explorers and adventurers took advantage of his skills. Prince Paul of Württemberg employed him in 1823. He was favorably mentioned by General Henry Atkinson in 1825, by Major Stephen Kearny, also in 1825, and by Captain Reuben Holmes, who met him in 1833. (Holmes commented that Charbonneau never carried a rifle—that a knife was his only weapon.)

In the 1830's, James Kipp, a Canadian with the American Fur Company, frequently employed Charbonneau as an interpreter. In the books of the Mandan Agency, it is recorded that from November 30, 1828, to September 30, 1834, Charbonneau was paid $2,437.32 for his services as an interpreter between the whites and the Mandans, Gros Ventres (Hidatsas), and Crows. He had his detractors, however. William Laidlaw, in a letter to Kipp from Fort Pierre, dated January 14, 1834, wrote: "I am much surprised at your taking old Charbonneau into favor after showing so much ingratitude upon all occasions."

Others were less critical. Prince Maximilian of Wied, a former Prussian army officer who traveled in the American West, met Charbonneau in 1833 and was favorably impressed by him. He expressed indebtedness to Charbonneau for many valuable accounts of the manners, morals, and habits of Indian tribes. Charbonneau was undoubtedly crude, but he was scarcely as inept as some writers have characterized him.

According to Stella M. Drumm: "Charbonneau had many friends among the traders, Indian agents and travelers of the West. In letter-books and manuscripts to be found among the archives of the Missouri Historical Society, as well as in many published narratives of travellers, are many favorable references to him."[2]

The old interpreter was durable. He was around Fort Clark and the Mandan villages through the years of cholera and smallpox (1835 to 1837), when he was apparently spared from either disease, although, according to the fort records, he lost still another Indian wife during the period.

All his life—into his eighties—he was marrying Indian girls. Typical of his experiences is one related by Chardon, the factor of Fort Clark, who wrote in his journals on October 22, 1834: "Charbonneau and his lady started for the Gros Ventres on a visit (or to tell you the truth) in quest of one of his runaway wives—for I must inform you he had two lively ones. Poor old man." Chardon also mentioned that in 1838, Charbonneau, at nearly eighty, married an Assiniboine girl of fourteen. He reported that the young men of the fort gave the couple a "splendid Charivaree." Of those years, Bernard De Voto wrote, Charbonneau was as "old as Rameses but active as ever."

In 1838, Charles Larpenteur and his fur traders met Charbonneau not far from Fort Clark. They said that the interpreter was wearing pants and a red flannel shirt. Evidently, despite his long years among the Indians, he never

[2] Luttig, *Journal of a Fur Trading Expedition*, 137.

adopted Indian dress. The last note that history took of Charbonneau was in 1839, when he appeared at the Office of Indian Affairs in St. Louis, tottering under the infirmities of eighty winters, to ask Joshua Pilcher, superintendent of Indian Affairs, for salary due him for services rendered the United States government. Apparently Charbonneau had been dismissed as interpreter after smallpox virtually wiped out the Mandan tribe in 1837, but the old man had continued to serve for some time, unaware of his dismissal. On August 26, 1839, Pilcher wrote to the Indian Department in Washington: "This man has been a faithful servant of the Government—though in a humble capacity. I . . . think it but right that he should be paid."

It may be assumed that the interpreter had had some narrow escapes during his lifetime on the plains (certainly he had had his share on the Lewis and Clark Expedition). The last documented one was revealed in a letter from Major David D. Mitchell to W. N. Fulkerson, Indian agent for the Mandans, dated June 10, 1836. Mitchell wrote that "old Charbonneau" had barely escaped death, "two balls having passed through his hat," when a Sioux shot at a Hidatsa boy in the interpreter's room at Fort Clark.

The date of Charbonneau's death and the site of his grave are unknown. Hebard says that he may have married a Ute woman and eventually died among the Ute Indians in Utah, but no Indian agency in Utah has a record of his death or burial.

Charbonneau's colorful life has been summed up as follows:

Toussaint Charbonneau: perhaps the first white man to

live in the Mandan-Minnataree towns, associated with the earliest traders at Pembina—Lewis and Clark, Sacajawea, Auguste Chouteau, Brackenridge, Luttig, Manuel Lisa, Jules de Mun, Long, Kearny, Prince Paul, Colonel Leavenworth, General Atkinson, Maximilian, John Jacob Astor, "the Liberator," Larpenteur, Pilcher—every name important on the Missouri prairies. The old Frenchman knew them all.

And just perhaps out there somewhere on those prairies where the buffalo bulls no longer stomp and roar, but where the long, lean coyote still cries across the snow—just perhaps, we say—the soul of old Charbonneau still wanders Missouri trails.[3]

[3] Gordon Speck, *Breeds and Half-Breeds*, 148.

Jean Baptiste Charbonneau

25

JEAN Baptiste Charbonneau, the son of Toussaint Charbonneau and Sacajawea, began his travels at the age of two months. He journeyed from the Mandan villages in North Dakota to the Pacific Ocean and back again with Lewis and Clark—by canoe, on his mother's back, on horseback, or in the arms of a bearded white explorer.

He accompanied his father and mother to St. Louis, probably in 1806, almost certainly before 1810. In 1811 his father, and apparently his mother too, left him there in the care of William Clark or someone designated by Clark. In 1813, John Luttig became the legal guardian of "Toussaint Charbonneau" and his sister, Lizette.

Several circumstances suggest that Toussaint was actually Baptiste. A son of Charbonneau, usually identifiable as Baptiste, can be traced with fur traders and explorers until 1846, the year of the Mexican War, and in California thereafter until 1866, when he set out on a trip to the Idaho or Montana gold fields and died on the way. No other son of Charbonneau's is mentioned in contemporary records. On the occasions when Toussaint (or "Tessou") is mentioned, the chances are that Baptiste was being given his father's name and that he was regarded as a "junior."

As late as 1820, Baptiste was being educated in St. Louis, for Clark's papers show sums for tuition paid during that year to both a Baptist minister and a Roman Catholic priest and other payments for school supplies, books, clothing, board, lodging, and laundry. The payments were made in behalf of "J. B. Charbonneau" or "Toussaint Charbonneau" (almost without doubt the same boy).[1]

In 1823, Prince Paul of Württemberg, a twenty-year-old explorer, was given permission to travel up the Missouri River. He met both Baptiste and old Charbonneau. In the prince's account of his travels, which was published in 1835,[2] he described his first meeting with Baptiste, near the mouth of the Kaw River, on June 21, 1823:

[1] American State Papers, 1820, Missouri Historical Society, St. Louis.
[2] *A Trip to North America*, Huntington Library, San Marino, Calif.

Here I found also a youth of sixteen,[3] whose mother was of the tribe of Sho-sho-ne, or Snake Indians, and who had accompanied the Messrs. Lewis and Clark to the Pacific ocean in the years 1804 to 1806 as interpretress. This Indian woman was married to the French interpreter of the expedition, Toussaint Charbonneau by name. Charbonneau rendered me service also, some time later in the same capacity, and Baptiste, his son (the youth of sixteen) of whom I made mention above, joined me on my return and followed me to Europe, and has remained with me ever since.

Prince Paul and Baptiste did not return to America until 1829. In that year Prince Paul received permission to make another trip into Indian country and traveled as far as the Mandan region. The journal of this expedition has never been found.

When he returned from Europe, Baptiste was well educated and could converse fluently in German, Spanish, French, and English. Despite his Continental education, on his return to America he apparently resumed life on the frontier. Up to 1846 western narratives mention him frequently and identify him clearly. Baptiste accompanied Prince Paul on the 1829–30 expedition. He was with the Robidoux Fur Brigade in 1830. In 1831 he may have been with Joseph Meek, who claimed that on his way from Powder River, Wyoming, to St. Louis he was accompanied by "a Frenchman, Cabenau."

W. A. Ferris, in his "Life in the Rocky Mountains," a memoir of his experiences in 1830–35, tells of an earlier experience, on the Lewis and Clark Expedition, with "Char-

[3] Baptiste was actually eighteen at the time.

171

bonneau, one of our men . . . the infant who, together with his mother, was saved from a sudden flood near the Falls of the Missouri." Nathaniel Wyeth mentioned Baptiste in his journal, saying that, after the Indians stole some horses, "Charbonneau pursued them on foot." Baptiste was also with Jim Bridger in 1832 and at the Green River traders' rendezvous in 1833. According to Walter S. Campbell, in *Kit Carson*, "Chabonard," Sacajawea's son, told Indian stories to Carson's company in 1839. In 1839, T. J. Farnham, in *Life, Adventures, and Travels in California*, mentioned meeting an educated Indian at Fort El Pueblo, five miles from Bent's Fort, in Colorado. The man was probably Baptiste.

According to E. Willard Smith, Charbonneau was with Vásquez and Sublette on the South Platte River in 1839. He mentioned two Indian traders and added: "One of them was a son of Captain Clark, the great Western traveler and companion of Lewis. He had received an education in Europe during seven years." Smith, who thought that Baptiste was Clark's son, spelled the trader's name "Shabenare." In 1842, Baptiste was in charge of a fur-trading party on the South Platte. In his journal of his expedition of 1842, John Charles Frémont mentioned "Chabonard's camp, on an island in the Platte." He said that the Frenchman was in the service of Bent and St. Vrain, and he praised his cooking ability.

A month or so later, Rufus B. Sage visited the men of the same party, who were waiting for high water to proceed downriver. He wrote: "The camp was under the direction of a half-breed, named Chabonard, who proved to be a gentleman of superior information."

In 1843 a party of more than eighty hunters on the Oregon Trail, led by Sir William Drummond Stewart, included one Baptiste Charbonneau, who was listed as a cart driver. In this group were also listed Captain Jefferson Kennerly Clark, a son of William Clark, and William Clark Kennerly, a nephew of Clark, for whom he was named.

Baptiste was apparently at Bent's Fort for a time. W. M. Boggs mentioned him in a chronicle covering the years 1844–45. Boggs wrote:

This Baptiste Charbenau, or half-breed son of the elder Charbenau that was employed by the Lewis and Clark expedition to the Pacific Ocean, had been educated to some extent; he wore his hair long so that it hung down to his shoulders. It is said that Charbenau was the best man on foot on the plains or in the Rocky Mountains.

Baptiste accompanied Lieutenant J. W. Abert on an exploring expedition down the Canadian River from Bent's Fort in 1845. Thomas Fitzpatrick, a mountain man with the party, praised the guide, "Mr. Charbonard," for his ability. Baptiste was included in George Frederick Ruxton's list of important fur traders in his book *Life in the Far West*. Ruxton described "Charbonar, a half-breed, . . . last in height, but first in every quality which constitutes excellence in a mountaineer."

In 1846–47, "Charbonneaux" accompanied Lieutenant Colonel Philip St. George Cooke and his troops through New Mexico to California. Cooke made a note in his journals that Baptiste could read and sign his name and was a skillful guide and hunter, like his mother before him. He could also speak Spanish. In Cooke's entry for November,

1846, he reported that "Charbonneaux" had encountered
three grizzly bears "far up among the rocks" and killed one
of them. Cooke gave his guide much credit for the success
of his expedition to California, which traversed some of the
most dangerous country in the Western world.

From these accounts one can construct a vivid picture of
Baptiste: a short, dark, rugged man, intelligent and coura-
geous, and a skilled guide, hunter, and mountaineer.

Baptiste apparently stayed in California. After the Mexican War he is said to have become alcalde of San Luis Rey.
Later he moved to Placer County, where he lived until
1866. In that year he started for the gold fields of Montana
and Idaho, contracted mountain fever, and died at Inskip's
Ranch and Stage Station on Cow Creek, near the present
town of Danner, Oregon.

On June 2, 1866, the *Owyhee Avalanche* of Ruby City,
Idaho, reported his death. His death was also recorded in
the *Placer Herald*, of Auburn, California, on July 7, and in
the *Butte Record*, of Oroville, California, on July 14, 1860.

The Two Versions

26

IN the early years of the twentieth century Grace Raymond Hebard and Charles A. Eastman pieced together, with similar conclusions, the traditional Shoshoni account of Sacajawea's later life.[1] In the 1900's, Miss Hebard corresponded

[1] Grace Raymond Hebard was a teacher of history and political economy at the University of Wyoming, Laramie. She was especially interested in the Shoshoni tribe and devoted many years to research

with Mrs. Eva Emery Dye, who in 1902 had published a novel about Sacajawea, *Conquest*. Miss Hebard also corresponded with the Reverend John Roberts, an Episcopal missionary to the Shoshonis. In the 1920's the Indian Bureau asked Eastman to try to trace Sacajawea's life. In Miss Hebard's book about Sacajawea, published in 1932, she seems to have relied partly on Eastman's investigations.

Miss Hebard suggested that, when Charbonneau went to St. Louis in 1806, he took with him a new wife, Eagle, of the Hidatsa tribe. Sacajawea apparently made no objection to sharing her home. According to Miss Hebard and Eastman, Charbonneau later obtained employment with a fur company and took with him two wives, Eagle and Sacajawea, and two sons, Baptiste and "Toussaint," one or both of whom Clark had been educating. Both Miss Hebard and Eastman were convinced that there were two sons.

According to Miss Hebard, somewhere in western Oklahoma or Kansas the "polygamous old interpreter" took still another wife, a Ute woman, young and beautiful. Before long she and Sacajawea were quarreling over domestic matters. One day Charbonneau whipped Sacajawea, and she left him. She wandered from tribe to tribe, finally making her home with the Comanches, a branch of the same linguistic stock as that of the Shoshonis. In time Sacajawea mar-

---

on the life of Sacajawea. She died in 1936. Charles A. Eastman was born in 1858. His father was a full-blood Santee Sioux, and his mother was half Sioux. He held various posts with the Bureau of Indian Affairs. In 1903 he was sent into the Sioux region to establish a system of recording Indian surnames. In 1925 he made his report on Sacajawea to the commissioner of Indian Affairs. In his last years he was a lecturer and a homeopathic physician.

ried a Comanche named Jerk Meat and "lived harmoniously for a number of years, giving birth to five children." Later Jerk Meat was killed in battle, and Sacajawea began wandering again. The Comanches, not knowing her whereabouts, referred to her as Wadze-wipe (Lost Woman). Her Comanche son Ticannaf searched for her in vain among the Wichitas and Kiowas.

With her daughter, Yago-Wosier, this version continues, the Indian woman, no longer young and wishing to return to her tribe, followed the explorer John Charles Frémont from Comanche territory to Fort Bridger, in Wyoming, where the Lemhi branch of the Shoshonis was now living.

In July, 1843, at St. Vrain's Fort, Frémont wrote an account of a Shoshoni woman with his party:

A French engage at Lupton's fort in Colorado had been shot in the back on July 4th, and died during our absence to the Arkansas. The wife of the murdered man, an Indian woman of the Snake nation, desirous, like Naomi of old, to return to her people, requested and obtained permission to travel with my party to the neighborhood of the Bear river, where she expected to meet some of their villages. Happier than the Jewish widow, she carried with her two children, pretty little half-breeds, who added much to the liveliness of the camp. Her baggage was carried on five or six pack-horses; and I gave her a small tent, for which I no longer had any use, as I had procured a lodge at the fort.

On July 18, near Ham's Fork of Black's Fork on the Green River, the Indian woman took leave of Frémont's expedition, expecting to find some of her people at Bridger's Fort, which had been established that year. She may have found some Shoshonis there, but after a time she left the

177

fort and again wandered for a number of years, finally settling down permanently with her tribe sometime between 1850 and 1870.

Home at last with the Shoshonis, Sacajawea was reunited with her son, Baptiste, by Charbonneau, and her adopted son, Bazil. Her brother, Cameahwait, had been killed in battle about 1840. In 1862, Bazil suffered a crippling leg wound. He became known to the Indians as the lame subchief of Chief Washakie. In substance, the foregoing is Miss Hebard's reconstruction of the Indian version of Sacajawea's later life.

In the 1920's, Eastman undertook investigations which led him to the Shoshonis, Comanches, and Gros Ventres in Wyoming, Oklahoma, and North Dakota. He concluded that there was indeed a happy family reunion at Fort Bridger:

Bazil, the older son, . . . was exceptionally devoted to [Sacajawea]. It was in this family that she lived and died. There are many instances among the Indians where a nephew or step-son has been more devoted to the mother than the real son. This was the case in the relation of Bazil to this mother. It is the Ben Hur of the Indians. A most remarkable romantic life of any age.

To try to establish that Sacajawea lived among the Shoshonis, Miss Hebard interviewed the Indian woman's supposed descendants, as well as missionaries and agents. In 1905 the Reverend John Roberts, who in 1884 had officiated at last rites for the Indian woman (whom he sincerely believed to be Sacajawea), wrote:

I do not think Sacajawea's picture was ever taken, but

178

some of the old people tell me that one of her granddaughters looks very like the heroine did in former days. . . . She understood French well. . . . The old lady was wonderfully active and intelligent, considering her age. She walked alone and was bright to the last.

The Indian agents credited this woman with much influence on her tribe until she reached old age. They said that she encouraged the Shoshonis to adopt white men's ways and learn to farm. According to them, she made her influence felt in the council at Fort Bridger in 1868, an unusual achievement for an Indian woman.

Fincelius G. Burnett, who went to the Shoshoni Indian Reservation in 1871 as agricultural agent ("boss farmer") to teach the Indians to farm, claimed to have known Sacajawea, her two sons, and many descendants. He said that she spoke both English and French and that she told him she had accompanied Lewis and Clark. She told of her capture by the Hidatsas, and she could describe "great fish" on the ocean shore and relate other incidents of the journey. Burnett described Sacajawea in old age as rather light in complexion, of medium size—"a very fine-looking woman and much thought of by the other Indians." She did not look her age: "You would have taken her son, Bazil, as the elder of the two."

James McAdams, a Shoshoni who attended Carlisle Indian School in Pennsylvania in 1881, told Miss Hebard that Porivo (the Shoshoni name for the woman who claimed to be Sacajawea) was his great-grandmother and Bazil his grandfather. He said that he had lived with his great-grandmother at one time and that she, Baptiste, and Bazil spoke French. Porivo had told him many times that she had "worked for the soldiers away off into the country clear to the big waters to the west." McAdams added that many persons had seen a gold-rimmed medal that Porivo cherished. The medal had Jefferson's likeness on it. He also said that his great-grandmother had given his grandfather Bazil some precious papers, which were placed in a leather wallet and, upon his death, were buried with him.

In 1926, Miss Hebard chanced to meet an old Indian woman who told her that she had met Porivo when she herself was only twelve years old. Porivo had told the girl's mother that she had traveled "with a large body of men over whom army officers were in charge, that the people became very hungry and killed some of their horses, and even dogs, for food."

In 1929, Tom Rivington, of Gering, Nebraska, wrote of this woman:

She was . . . not satisfied anywhere, and the stage companies helped to make her that way as they gave her free rides. . . . She told me she was as far south as the Gila river in Arizona. . . . She was over in California to see the Indians there, but said they were so poor, as the whites had taken all the country away from them, and she had been with the Nez Percé Indians in the state of Washington for several years. She had lived with different tribes up in Canada.

In 1871, James I. Patten became lay missionary to the Indians of the Wind River (Shoshoni) Reservation in Wyoming. There he saw and talked with the woman many were calling Sacajawea. He said that she spoke both English and French. In the late fall of 1874, Patten said, Bazil and Baptiste brought her to agency headquarters to be cared for while they were away on a buffalo hunt. They spoke of her as their mother. Patten said that during his long period of years on the reservation he daily saw Wadze-wipe, who was also called Lost Woman, Sacajawea, the Boat Pusher, Bah-ribo, and Water White-Man. She told him that she had accompanied Lewis and Clark on the expedition to the Pacific Ocean and that her son, Baptiste, was a "little papoose whom she carried on her back from the Mandan villages across the shining mountains to the great lake, as she called the Pacific ocean."

Patten also told a poignant story of a day when he and Bazil were walking together. They saw an aged Shoshoni woman lying on her back, her shoulders resting on a fifty-pound sack of flour around which a rope was looped. The ends were brought over her shoulders and held in her hands in front.

She was just ready to rise with her burden, and Bazil assisted her to her feet and she trudged off. I told Bazil I thought the load too heavy for such an old person to carry. "See, she is staggering," I said. "Yes, pretty old [replied Bazil]." "She is my mother," and spoke of her connection with Lewis and Clark.

Charles Bocker, a Wyoming pioneer who was driving spikes for the Union Pacific in 1868, wrote that he knew Sacajawea in 1866. He added:

When I was introduced to Sacajawea at Fort Bridger, . . . I should judge at this time she must have been an old woman of about seventy years, . . . quite lovely looking for an old woman, and she could ride horses as well as any of them. . . . I heard at that time when I was at Ft. Bridger, as many times, that she had been with the white men. Everybody all around everywhere knew it, and it was common talk.

This woman, whom many believed to be Sacajawea of the Shoshonis, died on April 9, 1884. Her body was taken from the tipi in which she died and wrapped in skins, which were sewed up for burial. She was placed on her favorite horse, led by Bazil, taken to a coffin, and placed in it. She was buried in the Shoshoni cemetery.

In 1885, the man known on the reservation as Sacajawea's son, Baptiste, died, and was buried by some of the agency Indians in the mountains west of the agency. In the winter of 1886, Bazil, Sacajawea's supposed adopted son, died. Since the ground was frozen, he was placed in a cave on a stream. A leather wallet containing papers, letters, and documents was buried with him. The cave later collapsed and covered the body. In 1924, Andrew, Bazil's son, offered to find the site of his father's grave and gave permission to have the grave opened by Eastman, who was searching for information about the Indian woman. The wallet containing the papers was found, but the papers had disintegrated; Eastman could discern only that there had once been writing on them.

Miss Hebard's first report about Sacajawea was published in the *Journal of American History* in September, 1907, five years after the publication of Mrs. Dye's novel, which had given the Indian girl her first claim to a place in American history. For twenty-five years Miss Hebard continued her efforts to prove that the old Shoshoni woman of the Wind River Reservation was Sacajawea. In 1910 the Bureau of American Ethnology, disregarding Brackenridge's account of meeting Sacajawea in 1811 on the Missouri River, accepted part of Miss Hebard's version of Sacajawea's life.[2] Then, in 1920, John Luttig's journal was published, and readers learned that a wife of Charbonneau's had died at Fort Manuel on December 20, 1812, soon after the birth of a daughter.

It was this publication and the attendant confusion that prompted the commissioner of Indian Affairs to assign Eastman the task of tracing the life of Sacajawea. Eastman made his report in March, 1925. His account largely agreed with Miss Hebard's conclusions, varying only in details. For example, Miss Hebard thought that Bazil was Sacajawea's adopted son; Eastman thought that he was "Toussaint," probably the son of Otter Woman.

Eastman and Miss Hebard had undertaken a nearly impossible task. The Indians had no written language and could only report their recollections orally. By the time the Indian woman's friends and relatives were interviewed, memories were dim. Mrs. James Irwin, wife of the one-time agent on the Wind River Reservation, learned the Shoshoni language, visited with the woman known as Sacajawea, and recorded some of her experiences, including stories she told about the Lewis and Clark Expedition and her later wanderings. Unfortunately a fire at the agency burned Mrs. Irwin's manuscript.

If Sacajawea wandered among the Comanches, as Eastman and Miss Hebard believed, she told them nothing of her experiences or her life with Charbonneau, according to Mr. and Mrs. W. H. Clift, who researched for Miss

[2] Frederick Webb Hodge, "Sacajawea," in *Handbook of American Indians North of Mexico,* II, 401.

Hebard.[3] The Clifts could only report that they encountered "everywhere in some form" the story of a woman who "might have been Sacajawea." The Comanches thought that she had had a Mexican husband at one time and had had at least one child by him. According to Eastman and Miss Hebard, Sacajawea had rejoined her tribe by traveling overland to Fort Bridger with Frémont in 1843. It seems more likely that she would have found her way to western Montana, to ascertain her tribe's whereabouts. Since the United States did not assume authority over the western tribes until 1862, the Shoshonis probably did not move very far east until that date.

The substance of the Shoshoni tradition and the reservation agents' comments was that Porivo was highly respected and that Bazil, the adopted son, was close to his mother, while Baptiste was indifferent to her. (According to those sources, Bazil was more than six feet tall and walked with a limp. Baptiste was short, dark, and uncommunicative.)

Bazil would have had to take his adoptive mother's word for her identity—if he was in truth the boy whom she had adopted when she was with Lewis and Clark. When she rejoined her tribe, Bazil would not have known her, and by then Cameahwait, her brother, was dead.

The Baptiste of this account was only semiliterate and was uncommunicative, preferring ease to activity, and was, in short, altogether different from the gregarious Baptiste whom explorers and fur traders called the best man on foot on the plains or in the Rocky Mountains.

[3] Mrs. Clift was the daughter of William Connelley, at one time secretary of the Kansas Historical Society. She and her husband interviewed many elderly Indians of the Comanche tribe.

The "Sacajawea" of the reservation apparently did not
volunteer information, but on occasion she would talk. The
sincerity of the people who interviewed her has never been
questioned, but they may have been gullible. Any Indian
girl who had known Sacajawea in St. Louis, Fort Mandan,
or Fort Manuel would have been able to repeat the stories
that had been told for years about Sacajawea. French was a
common tongue west of the Mississippi, and any Indian
who associated with fur traders would speak some French.
Charbonneau was known to have had many wives, any one
of whom could have claimed to be the wife who went with
him to the Pacific Ocean.

The "valuable papers" (the ones buried with Bazil)
would have been important evidence in establishing Sacajawea's identity, but unfortunately they proved unreadable.

An Indian woman of later days, Mrs. Esther Burnett
Horne, who identified herself as Bazil's great-granddaughter,
traveled through the country in the 1950's, speaking earnestly to audiences about her connection with Sacajawea. She
was undoubtedly convinced of the truth of the traditional
Shoshoni story and wanted to convince others, but she had
no further basis for her belief than the foregoing stories.

Eastman, in his report, and Miss Hebard, in her book,
elevated Sacajawea to a high position in history—which the
Indian girl undoubtedly deserved—but their error lay in
trying to reinterpret history. They assumed that Charbonneau came down from the Mandan to St. Louis with two
Indian wives and two children. They did not address themselves to the question of why he would do such a thing. He
had been invited by Captain Clark to bring one wife and
one child, Sacajawea and Baptiste (Pomp). Even if Clark

had permitted it, domestic arrangement involving two wives would have been frowned upon in St. Louis.

The record shows that Clark made good his promise to Charbonneau, starting the trapper in farming and, as late as 1820, contributing toward Baptiste's education.

There are two possible explanations for the fact that Sacajawea was not named by either Brackenridge or Bradbury in their journals of 1811. One is that, if only one Shoshoni wife went to St. Louis, then only one could have gone upriver again in 1811 with Charbonneau, and she would have been Sacajawea. Brackenridge, whose identification must carry some weight, said that the woman was the Frenchman's Snake Indian wife and that both she and Charbonneau had accompanied Lewis and Clark. Bradbury confirmed these statements. Sacajawea was generally known as the "Frenchman's squaw" at that time. There were so many fur traders with Indian wives that it did not seem necessary to give the wives first names. The other explanation is that Sacajawea's name was difficult to render in English. Both Lewis and Clark had difficulty pronouncing and spelling it. It was much easier for all concerned to refer to her simply as "Charbonneau's woman."

On December 20, 1812, a year after the boat journey up the Missouri, Luttig reported in his journal the death of the Snake wife of Charbonneau. If Luttig had given Charbonneau's wife a name, a good deal of latter-day speculation and argument would have been avoided. But these contemporary writings, even though incomplete, are persuasive.

It has been argued that Brackenridge's description of Charbonneau's wife failed to match the earlier picture of Sacajawea as an energetic and outgoing girl. He called her "a good creature, of a mild and gentle disposition."[4] It must be remembered that she had lived in St. Louis for five years among white people, whom she wished to emulate, as Brackenridge pointed out—plenty of time for an eager young woman to learn the "rules" of white women's deportment.

It has been questioned, too, whether Sacajawea could be called "sickly," as she was by Brackenridge, in view of the endurance she displayed on the long journey with Lewis and Clark. Such arguments again fail to consider the intervening years, in which Sacajawea matured from girlhood to womanhood—and in an unfamiliar environment, a frontier settlement, where she may easily have become victim to the many ills of so-called civilization. Indeed, the "fever" that Luttig reports as the cause of Sacajawea's death at Fort Manuel may very well have been caused by an infection to which the Indian girl (as well as another Shoshoni woman at Fort Manuel, the wife of Josef Elie) had no resistance. There is also the possibility that complications following the birth of the daughter, Lizette, caused her death.

No burial site has been discovered in the region of Fort Manuel, although it is known that several persons died there. The two Shoshoni wives no doubt received a burial

[4] Neta Lohnes Frazier has suggested that Brackenridge's description did not fit Sacajawea, who "so irritates her husband that he beats her," who "berates Clark when he displeases her," and who "demands her rights to go to the ocean to see the whale" (*Sacajawea: The Girl Nobody Knows*, 140). What we know of Sacajawea from the journals indicates that she was anything but irritating, quarrelsome, and demanding. Nor do we know that Charbonneau was a wife beater or that Sacajawea ever displeased Clark or that she "demanded her rights."

in the ground, after the manner of the white people, but excavations made around the site of the fort, which was abandoned and burned nearly one hundred and fifty years ago, have not revealed any human skeletons. Sacajawea may have been buried on one of the hills not far from the fort. However, with Sioux war parties so close in December, 1812, it would seem more likely that the burial place was near the stockade, though an armed party could have been sent to oversee interment in a more suitable area.

In 1883 the Reverend John Roberts, mentioned earlier, became missionary at the Shoshoni reservation in Wyoming and remained there for forty-nine years. In 1884 he officiated at the funeral of the woman he later identified as "Sacajawea of the Shoshonis." But he could have had only slight acquaintance with her. Moreover, at the time of her death he evidently did not know that she was reputed to be the Sacajawea of the famous expedition. The official form he completed at the time of her death states only that she was "Bazil's mother." Only later did Mr. Roberts comment on her supposed identity: "I read over her grave the burial services of the Episcopal church. I little realized that the heroine we laid to rest, in years to come would become one of the outstanding women of American history."

At the time of the woman's funeral a small wooden slab was placed at the head of her grave; later, boulders were set at the head and foot. A stone marker was erected there in 1909 by H. E. Wadsworth, the Shoshoni agent. The marker was the gift of Timothy F. Burke, of Cheyenne, Wyoming.

It appears certain that an estimable Shoshoni woman lies buried on the Wind River Reservation, with a son on each side of her. It is equally certain, however, no written evidence or surviving objects prove that she was Sacajawea of the Lewis and Clark Expedition.

In 1955 a notebook belonging to Clark was discovered.[5] The book was apparently used by Clark between 1825 and 1828. On the outside of the book, in his writing, appears a list of names of members of the expedition, with notations about what happened to each one after the journey or his residence at the time the notes were made. Beside Sacajawea's name, which Clark spelled "Secarjaweau," he wrote one word: "Dead."

He also listed Lewis, Odoway (Ordway), Floyd, Gass, Collins, Colter, J. Fields, Goodrich, McNeal, Shields, and LePage as "dead." He listed Cruzatte, Potts, Wiser, and Drewyer as "killed." Some others he named with a possible place of residence (as, "N. Pryor at Fort Smith; R. Fields near Louisville"); and some he named without further notations. He included others who were not members of the permanent party which left from the Mandan villages. He also wrote "Tous. Charbono Mand" (Mandans?), "Tousant Charbon in Wertenburgh, Gy." (by "Tousant Charbon" Clark unquestionably meant Baptiste). This notation dates the document between 1824 and 1829, since those are the years Baptiste was known to have been with Prince Paul in Württemberg.

Clark was wrong about one member of the expedition, Gass, whom he reported dead. Patrick Gass lived to be almost one hundred years old. In 1962, Donald Jackson wrote:

We are hardly justified in saying "If Clark was wrong about

5 Now in the Newberry Library, Chicago.

Gass, then perhaps he is wrong about Sacagawea," for the cases are different. Gass had gone back to Virginia and severed his contacts with the West, but Sacagawea, her husband, Charbonneau, and her children were Clark's concern for many years after the expedition. He cared about them and felt a kind of responsibility for them. It is difficult to believe he could have been wrong about Sacagawea's death.[6]

In 1956, Will G. Robinson, secretary for the South Dakota State Historical Society, wrote: "It seems most improbable that she was buried at any other place [than Fort Manuel]. . . . We think that the entry in the Clark Journal writes 'finis' to the controversy." He added:

I, for one, am much better pleased with a feeling that this truly great woman died at Ft. Manuel . . . rather than try to follow the vague and nebulous wanderings of a woman who had many husbands, followed the hard life of a drudge among the fur traders and died wholly unrecognized.[7]

Certainly this seems a reasonable conclusion. The traditional account of her quarrel with Charbonneau and her subsequent wanderings is vague and unsupported by written record. And yet, as Jack R. Gage has pointed out, even written records can be fallible. The journals of explorers

[6] Donald Jackson (ed.), *Letters of the Lewis and Clark Expedition,* 639.

[7] Many Indian women were reduced to drudges. Often they were substitutes for pack animals. At Fort Mandan Lewis and Clark reported that She-he-ke brought to the fort a quarter of beef on his wife's back. On another occasion a woman carried a canoe three miles on her back. When Clark's "whale party" was returning from Tillamook Head, he tried to help a Chinook woman whose load of blubber had slipped, but he found the load so heavy that he could barely lift it. Finally her husband came back to help her.

and mountain men have their share of errors.[8] All that the serious researcher can do is to judge, on the basis of verifiable fact and reliable documentation, what he believes to be the truth.

In this context, still another version of Sacajawea's death must be considered. In 1947, John Bakeless reported that a Hidatsa warrior, Bull's Eye, speaking in open council, where other Indians could hear (and correct) his story, claimed to be the grandson of Sacajawea, wife of "Sharbonish," with whom she went "far away somewhere." She was killed, Bull's Eye said, by hostile Indians near Glasgow, Montana, in 1869, when he himself was four years old.[9] This version of Sacajawea's death has never been authenticated.

In sum, documentary evidence seems to indicate clearly that Sacajawea died at Fort Manuel, South Dakota, in 1812 and lies buried there in some unmarked grave. The independent records of Brackenridge, Bradbury, Luttig, and later of Clark seem to permit no other reasonable conclusion. And yet, despite the evidence, there will always be those who prefer to believe that Sacajawea, the heroine of the Lewis and Clark Expedition, lived to be nearly one hundred years old and died venerated by her tribe on the Wind River Reservation in Wyoming. Each year many persons visit the reservation to see the stone erected in her memory in 1963 by the Wyoming State Organization of the National Society of Daughters of the American Revolution. The marker reads: "Sacajawea, Died April 9, 1884. A Guide with the Lewis and Clark Expedition, 1805–1806.

[8] Jack R. Gage, *Wyoming Afoot and Horseback: History Mostly Ain't True.*

[9] Bakeless, *Lewis and Clark*, 455.

Identified, 1907, by Rev. J. Roberts, Who Officiated at Her Burial."

It may never be known for certain whether Sacajawea lived a short life or a long one—whether she died in her twenties at a white men's fort in South Dakota or at an old age on a reservation in Wyoming. In a sense her chapter in history ended in 1806, with the successful conclusion of the Lewis and Clark Expedition. Perhaps the most enduring picture that can be conjured up of this remarkable woman is of an Indian girl bearing a baby on her back, gathering berries along a riverbank for a boatload of explorers bound on America's great westward adventure.

Appendices

A. MEMORIALS TO SACAJAWEA
River

Sacajawea Creek, Montana, named by Lewis and Clark. It flows into the Missouri River near the confluence of the Musselshell (now known as Crooked Creek).

Statues

Louisiana Purchase Exposition Grounds, St. Louis, Bruno Louis Zimm, 1904.

Lakeview Terrace, now in City Park, Portland, Oregon, Alice Cooper, 1905.

Indian girl pointing the way for Lewis and Clark, Cyrus Edwin Dallin, 1910.

Bronze statue, erected by Federation of Women's Clubs and school children of North Dakota, Capitol Building grounds, Bismarck, North Dakota, Leonard Crunelle, 1910.

Group, Lewis and Clark and Indian girl, Public Square, Charlottesville, Virginia.

Group, Sacajawea with Lewis and Clark, Charles M. Russell, National Cowboy Hall of Fame and Western Heritage Center, Oklahoma City.

Mountains

Sacajawea Peak, Bridger Range, Montana.

Sacagawea Peak, Wind River Range, Wyoming.

Sacajawea Peak, Wallowa Range, Oregon.

Sacajawea Peak, Lost River Range, Idaho.

Paintings

Sacajawea on Indian pony, with child in papoose cradle, Henry Altman, 1905.

Sacajawea, State University of Montana Library, Edward Samuel Paxson, 1906.

Mural, *Lewis and Clark at Three Forks*, Edward Samuel Paxson, Capitol, Helena, Montana.

The Shoshonis Naming Sacajawea, Tullius P. Dunlap, 1925.

Mural, Capitol, Helena, Montana, Charles M. Russell, 1912.

Painting, Sacajawea in boat meeting Chinook party, Amon Carter Museum of Western Art, Fort Worth, Texas, Charles M. Russell.

Markers

Grave of "Sacajawea of the Shoshonis," on the Shoshoni Reservation, near Lander, Wyoming, 1909.

Sacajawea marker, near Tendoy, Idaho, west of Lemhi Pass.

Bronze tablet on wall of Bishop Randall Chapel, Shoshoni Cemetery, Wyoming, 1931.

Granite marker, Shoshoni Cemetery, for Bazil, Baptiste, and Baptiste's daughter Barbara Meyers, 1932.

Boulder with bronze tablet, honoring meeting place of Sacajawea and her brother, Cameahwait, near the confluence of Horse Prairie and Red Rock creeks, Armstead, Montana, 1914.

Boulder and brass tablet erected by Daughters of American Revolution, near Three Forks, Montana, 1914.

Monument near Mobridge, South Dakota, 1929.

Lakes

Lake Sacajawea, Longview, Washington.

Lake Sakakawea (formerly Lake Garrison), North Dakota.

Music

"Sacajawea," intermezzo, Rollin Bond, bandmaster, New York City, 1904.

"Sacajawea," song, lyrics by Porter Bryan Coolidge, of Lander, Wyoming, music by Frederick Bouthroyd, Leicester, England, 1924.

"The Bird Woman, Sacajawea: A Legend of the Trail of the West," cantata, Toledo Choral Society, text by Evangeline Close, music by William Lester, 1932.

Miscellaneous

Silver service set, battleship *Wyoming*, 1912. Now at University of Wyoming.

Pageant, 1915, Beaverhead River valley.

Sacajawea Museum, Spalding, Idaho (destroyed by floods, 1964; see Appendix B).

Airplane, *Spirit of Sacajawea*, first flight, July, 1927, over Shoshoni National Forest, Wyoming.

Sacajawea State Park, near Pasco and Kennewick, Washington, including wooden marker and carved inscription.

Pageant, 1955, Three Forks, Montana.

Sacajawea Springs, south fork of Payette River, Idaho.

Camp Sacajawea for Girl Scouts, Casper Mountain, Casper, Wyoming.

Bronze casting of model by Henry Lion from sketch by Charles M. Russell for monument showing Sacajawea pointing the way for Lewis and Clark, Montana Historical Society Museum, Helena, Montana, 1958.

B. The Land of the Nez Percés

The area around Spalding, Idaho, is Nez Percé country. There Lewis and Clark first encountered Indians of that tribe. Today the area east of Spalding is the Nez Percé Reservation. The town was named for the Reverend Henry Spalding, who built his second mission, then called Lapwai, there in 1838.

Canoe Camp, at which Lewis and Clark built dugout canoes in the autumn of 1805 and cached supplies and from which they set off down the Clearwater, is about five miles west of Orofino in Canoe Camp State Park, on U.S. 12. Camas Prairie is about eight miles southwest of Grangeville on U.S. 95. It was once covered with grass and the blue-flowered camas. About a mile and a half north of the highway bridge at Kamiah, on U.S. 12, Lewis and Clark camped for the better part of a month in the spring of 1806, on their way home.

The Sacajawea Museum, once located at Spalding, was destroyed by flood in 1964. It contained equipment, including a canoe, said to have been used by members of the expedition. A Nez Percé National Historical Park in this region has been authorized by Congress but has not yet been established.

Bibliography

Alter, J. Cecil. *James Bridger*. Salt Lake City, 1925.
American State Papers, 1820. Missouri Historical Society, St. Louis.
Anderson, Irving W. "J. B. Charbonneau, Son of Sacaja-wea," *Oregon Historical Quarterly*, Vol. LXXI, No. 3 September, 1970).

Andrews, Wayne, ed. *The Concise Dictionary of American History*. New York, 1962.

Andrist, Ralph K. *To the Pacific with Lewis and Clark*. New York, 1967.

Bakeless, John. *The Journals of Lewis and Clark*. New York, 1964.

————. *Lewis and Clark: Partners in Discovery*. New York, 1947.

Bleeker, Sonia. *Indians*. New York, 1963.

Boggs, W. M. "Manuscript on Bent's Fort, 1844–1845," ed. by LeRoy R. Hafen, *Colorado Magazine*, Vol. VII, No. 2 (March, 1930).

Botkin, B. A. *Western Folklore*. New York, 1962.

Brackenridge, Henry M. *Journal of a Voyage up the Missouri River in 1811*. Pittsburgh, 1814. (Also in Thwaites, *Early Western Travels, q.v.*)

Bradbury, John. *Travels in the Interior of America in the Years 1809, 1810 and 1811*. London, 1819. (Also in Thwaites, *Early Western Travels, q.v.*)

Brown, James S. *Life of a Pioneer*. Salt Lake City, 1900.

Burnet, John C. Letters, manuscripts, photographs, and interviews. Hebard Collection, University of Wyoming, Laramie.

Burnett, F. G. Letters, manuscripts, and typed interviews. Hebard Collection, University of Wyoming, Laramie.

Campbell, Walter S. *Kit Carson*. New York, 1928.

Catlin, George. *Manners, Customs and Conditions of the North American Indians*. 2 vols. London, 1841.

Chandler, Katherine. *Bird Woman of the Lewis and Clark Expedition*. New York, 1905.

Chardon, Francis A. Fort Clark Journals. Ed. by Annie Heloise Abel. Pierre, S. Dak., 1932.

Chittenden, Hiram M. *The American Fur Trade of the Far West.* 3 vols. New York, 1902.

Clark, W. P. *Indian Sign Language.* Philadelphia, 1885.

Clarke, Charles G. *The Men of the Lewis and Clark Expedition.* Glendale, Calif., 1970.

Clift, Edith Connelley. Manuscripts. Hebard Collection, University of Wyoming, Laramie.

Clift, W. H. Manuscripts. University of Wyoming, Laramie.

Coues, Elliott. *A History of the Expedition Under the Command of Captains Lewis and Clark.* 3 vols. New York, 1965. (First published in 4 vols., 1893.)

Crawford, Helen. "Sakakawea," *North Dakota Historical Quarterly*, Vol. I, No. 3 (April, 1927).

Defenbach, B. *Red Heroines of the Northwest.* Caldwell, 1929.

De Voto, Bernard, ed. *The Journals of Lewis and Clark.* Boston, 1963.

Dye, Eva Emery. *The Conquest.* Chicago, 1902.

Eastman, Charles A. Original letters, 1925. Hebard Collection, University of Wyoming, Laramie.

Eidie, Ingvard Henry. *American Odyssey: The Journal of Lewis and Clark.* Chicago, 1969.

El Hult, Ruby. *Guns of the Lewis and Clark Expedition.* Washington State Historical Society, Tacoma.

Emory, W. H. *Notes on Cooke, Johnson, Abert. Ft. Leavenworth in Missouri to San Diego in California, 1804–1847.* Washington, D.C., 1848.

Ferris, W. A. "Life in the Rocky Mountains, 1830–1835," *Western Literary Messenger*, in *Wonderland*, 1901.

Frazier, Neta Lohnes. *Sacajawea: The Girl Nobody Knows.* New York, 1967.

Frémont, John C. *Report of the Exploring Expedition to the Rocky Mountains.* Washington, D.C., 1845.

Fuller, George W. *History of the Pacific Northwest.* New York, 1931.

Gage, Jack R. *Wyoming Afoot and Horseback: History Mostly Ain't True.* Cheyenne, 1966.

Gass, Patrick. *Journal of the Lewis and Clark Expedition.* Philadelphia, 1810; Chicago, 1904.

Ghent, W. J. *The Early Far West.* New York, 1936.

The Great West. New York, 1965.

Grinnell, George Bird. *Blackfoot Lodge Tales.* Lincoln, 1962.

Hafen, Ann W. "Baptiste Charbonneau, Son of Bird Woman," in *The Mountain Men and the Fur Trade of the Far West*, Vol. I. Glendale, 1965.

Hebard, Grace Raymond. *Sacajawea: Guide of the Lewis and Clark Expedition.* Los Angeles, 1957 (first published in 1932).

Henry, Alexander, and David Thompson. *Manuscript Journals, 1799–1814.* Ed. by Elliott Coues. 3 vols. New York, 1897.

Hodge, Frederick Webb. "Sacajawea," in *Handbook of American Indians North of Mexico*, Vol. II. Washington, D.C., 1910.

Hosmer, James K. *History of the Louisiana Purchase.* New York, 1902.

Hunt, Theodore. Minutes. Testimony Relating to Lands in the Towns and Villages of St. Louis, Etc., Feb. 13 to

May 25, 1825. Missouri Historical Society, St. Louis.

Indians. New York, 1961.

Indians of the Americas. Washington, D.C., 1967.

Indians of the Plains. New York, 1967.

Jackson, Donald, ed. *Letters of the Lewis and Clark Expedition.* Urbana, 1963.

Karsten, M. O. *Hunter and Interpreter for Lewis and Clark, George Drouillard.* Glendale, 1968.

Kennerly, William Clark. "Hunting Buffaloes in the Early Forties." Missouri Historical Society, St. Louis.

Kingston, C. S. "Sacajawea as Guide," *Pacific Northwest Quarterly,* Vol. XXXV (January, 1944).

Larpenteur, Charles. *Forty Years a Fur Trader on the Upper Missouri.* Ed. by Elliott Coues. 2 vols. New York, 1898.

Lewis, Meriwether. *The Lewis and Clark Expedition.* Ed. by Nicholas Biddle. 3 vols. Philadelphia, 1961 (originally published in 1814).

———, and William Clark. *Original Journals of the Lewis and Clark Expedition, 1804–1806.* Ed. by Reuben Gold Thwaites. 8 vols. New York, 1904.

Lisa, Manuel. Collection of letters, 1794–1820. Missouri Historical Society, St. Louis.

Lowie, Robert H. *Indians of the Plains.* New York, 1954.

Luttig, John C. *Journal of a Fur Trading Expedition on the Upper Missouri, 1812–1813.* Ed. by Stella M. Drumm. New York, 1964 (first published by the Missouri Historical Society, St. Louis, in 1920).

McCracken, Harold. *George Catlin and the Old Frontier.* New York, 1959.

Maximilian, Prince of Wied. *Travels in the Interior of North America.* London, 1843.

Meek, Joseph. *River of the West*. Ed. by Frances Fuller Victor. Hartford, Conn., 1870.

Mencken, Henry L. *The American Language*. 4th ed. New York, 1960.

Morison, Samuel Eliot. *The Oxford History of the American People*. New York, 1968.

O'Meara, Walter. *Daughters of the Country*. New York, 1968.

Ordway, John. Journal. Wisconsin State Historical Society, Madison.

Patten, James I. Letters and manuscripts. Hebard Collection, University of Wyoming, Laramie.

Poole, Edwin A. "Charbono's Squar," *Pacific Northwesterner*, Vol. VIII, No. 3.

Porter, Clyde H. "Jean Baptiste Charbonneau," *Idaho Yesterdays*, Vol. V, No. 3.

Quaife, M. M. *Journals of Captain Meriwether Lewis and Sergeant John Ordway*, Madison, 1916.

Rees, John E. "The Shoshoni Contribution to Lewis and Clark," *Idaho Yesterdays*, Vol. II, No. 2.

Rivington, Tom. Original letters and manuscripts. Hebard Collection, University of Wyoming, Laramie.

Roberts, John. Letters and manuscripts. Hebard Collection, University of Wyoming, Laramie.

Robinson, Doane. *Brief History of South Dakota*. New York, 1919.

———. "Sacajawea vs. Sakakawea" (address before the Academy of Science and Letters), Sioux City, Iowa, January 24, 1924.

Ruxton, George Frederick. *Adventures in Mexico and in the Rocky Mountains*. New York, 1848.

———. *Life in the Far West*. Norman, 1951.

Salisbury, Albert, and Jane Salisbury. *Two Captains West.* New York, 1950.

Schultz, J. W. *The Bird Woman: Guide of Lewis and Clark.* Boston, 1918.

Scott, L. T. *Sacajawea: The Unsung Heroine of Montana.* Armstead, 1915.

Siebert, Jerry. *Sacajawea.* Boston, 1960.

Smith, E. Willard. "Journal While with the Fur Traders, Vásquez and Sublette in the Rocky Mountain Region," *Oregon Historical Society Quarterly*, Vol. XIV, No. 3 (September, 1913).

Snyder, Gerald S. *In the Footsteps of Lewis and Clark.* Washington, D.C., 1970.

Speck, Gordon. *Breeds and Half-Breeds.* New York, 1969.

Thwaites, Reuben Gold, ed. *Early Western Travels, 1748–1846.* 32 vols. Cleveland, 1904–1906.

———. *Original Journals of the Lewis and Clark Expedition, 1804–1806.* New York, 1904.

Tomkins, Calvin. *The Lewis and Clark Trail.* New York, 1965.

U.S. Superintendent of Indian Affairs. *Correspondence of William Clark and Others at St. Louis, 1813–1855.* 29 vols. Kansas State Historical Society, Topeka.

Vestal, Stanley (pseud. of Walter S. Campbell). *The Missouri.* New York, 1945.

Wheeler, O. D. *The Trail of Lewis and Clark, 1804–1806.* 2 vols. Hartford, 1870.

Whitehouse, Joseph, ed. *Journal of the Lewis and Clark Expedition, 1804–1806.* New York, 1904. (Also in Thwaites, *Early Western Travels, q.v.*)

Wyoming State Journal, December 3, 1930.

Index

Sarah Winnemucca of the Northern Paiutes

To my family

Bob, Lynn, Noel, and my mother,
Fern Whitney, who gave me
a love of history

Contents

Illustrations

Maps

Preface

Sarah Winnemucca was a self-educated Northern Paiute Indian who, in the short span of her life, sparred with Indian agents, local politicians, and the United States government to try to improve the living conditions and the education of her people. She enlisted many influential citizens in her cause, partly through her autobiography, *Life Among the Piutes: Their Wrongs and Claims*, published in 1883, which was one of the first works of literature by an American Indian. She also made many spirited stage appearances in San Francisco and on the East Coast.

The Northern Paiutes are a desert-plateau people native to western Nevada, southeastern Oregon, and a strip of northeastern California east of the Sierra Nevada. In the 1860s, after the discovery of gold and silver in the Sierra, they found themselves in the path of white progress. The small, roaming Northern Paiute bands had two choices: they could seek friendship with the whites in hopes of becoming assimilated into the new order, or they could move north to hidden areas where there was still unspoiled land not yet desired by the emigrants.

Captain Truckee, Sarah Winnemucca's grandfather, chose the path of friendship. Because of his expansive nature and great curiosity, he continued his efforts to be friendly even when rebuffed by early explorers. On occasion he would remind his people of an ancient Paiute tale that prophesied the return of long-lost white brothers of the Paiutes, the reconciliation of the white and dark-skinned peoples, and lasting peace. This tale was later used by Sarah when she tried to influence the white world, as an admonition to the newcomers that the Paiutes had always expected great things of their white brothers.

Chief Winnemucca, Sarah's father, did not share Captain Truckee's innate trust of the emigrants. He had heard too many stories of outrage and murder. The Paiutes were well aware, for example, of the cannibalism in the Donner party near Truckee Lake in the winter of 1846–47. As a result Winnemucca guided his followers away from the Humboldt River emigrant trail. The white men had a penchant for burning Paiute villages and destroying food supplies. Many of them simply wanted to "get themselves an Injun."

Sarah Winnemucca was torn between those two philosophies. Her sympathy with her father's point of view contended with her own need to make an honest living within the white man's economy (which she sometimes did at the expense of her own people, as when she worked as a scout and interpreter for the United States Army). It was at great sacrifice that she made a decisive choice in favor of her people.

After reading Sarah's autobiography, I was intrigued by her personality and the sense of purpose emanating from her story. I wished for a larger understanding of her place in history. I soon found that I had to learn about the Northern Paiutes, her people. After considerable anthropological reading and several visits to the history collections of the Inter-Tribal Council of the Shoshoni, Washo, and Paiute peoples, at Pyramid Lake and Reno, Nevada, I began to develop some background. One particular book, Margaret W. Wheat's *Survival Arts of the Primitive Paiutes*, was of inestimable value in informing me of the old ways of the Northern Paiutes, because of its excellent photographs and explanations of house building; basketry; the making of rabbit-skin blankets, duck decoys, arrowheads, and tule boats; and the harvesting and preparation of foods.

The Bancroft Library of the University of California, Berkeley, was a haven for several years. There I started putting together the pieces of Sarah Winnemucca's puzzle from old newspapers, the National Archives microfilm records of the United States Bureau of Indian Affairs, and the published personal accounts by people who were important in Sarah's life—from Indian agents to army generals. The stage-costumed Indian woman became a person of flesh and blood. Although Sarah was slightly on the plump side with features not as refined as those of her younger sister, Elma, she still caught the attention of the public. She was a strong woman determined to succeed for her cause while essentially alone in a man's world. She had to fight for her own integrity as well as for a good life for her people.

Not all the pieces of the puzzle of Sarah Winnemucca have been found, and perhaps some are lost forever, but I hope that the voice of aboriginal America, the voice of another age that is gone may be heard in the pages that follow. Any words attributed to Sarah are quoted from her autobiography or another source indicated in the notes. I found her autobiographical account to be largely confirmed by other historical records except for inconsistencies in dates and the spelling of proper names.

Much that has been written about Sarah Winnemucca is not based on research from authentic documents, but is only a working of the same mistakes. This book brings together a useful bibliography for future writers, who can perhaps reveal more layers of her personality. I suspect, however, that, as time moves on from Sarah Winnemucca's lifespan, it will be more difficult to discover the truth. I hope that this book defines her rightful place in history and demonstrates the importance of the problems in assimilation that still face American Indians.

My special thanks to the Inter-Tribal Council, Reno-Sparks, Nevada, and to Winona Holmes, their historian, for permission to use their historical collection. I extend my appreciation to Carolyn Schooley, who introduced me to *Life Among the Piutes: Their Wrongs and Claims* in 1965, and to Elinor Richey for sharing her material on Sarah. Essential information on Sarah's later years came from Sam Eagle, historian of West Yellowstone, Montana, and Mrs. R. W. Talbot of Henry's Lake, Idaho. Also of service were James Abajian, archivist for the Archdiocese of San Francisco; Sister Mary Dominica McNamee, historian of College of Notre Dame, Belmont, California; Mrs. Donna Rob Spainhower of West Yellowstone, Montana; and the Oliver Historical Museum of Canyon City, Oregon. I thank Ella Thorpe Ellis, Celeste MacLeod, Betty Howell and Gail Landis for their helpful suggestions after reading the manuscript. My appreciation too for Carmilla Duran, Robert Emory Johnson, Dana Johnson, Joy Whitney Scott,

John Howell, and Joanne Richert for their contributions. I have been fortunate in having the outstanding support and assistance of my editor, Sarah Morrison. Most of all, I thank my husband, Robert Lane Canfield, for his continued enthusiasm throughout this enterprise and his help with photography and map reproduction.

It was a delight slowly to turn the microfilm reels, straining my eyes over page after page of dim letters and elaborate calligraphy, and suddenly come across another clue or a letter in Sarah's crimped handwriting. I hope that some of that excitement is conveyed in this biography and that readers will catch such a glimpse of Sarah Winnemucca, too.

GAE WHITNEY CANFIELD

Berkeley, California

Sarah Winnemucca of the Northern Paiutes

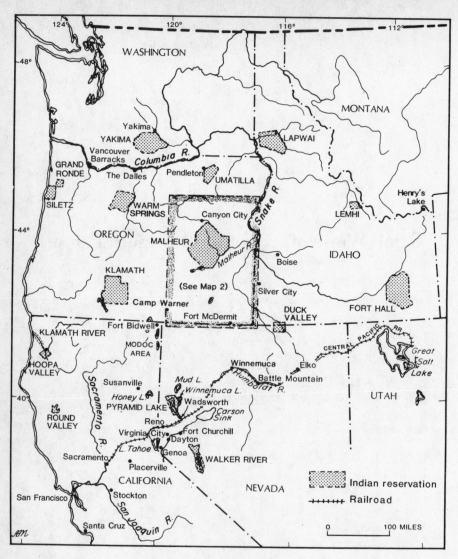

Map 1. *The Area of Sarah Winnemucca's Activity. (Map 2 is on page 95.)*

1

Early Years

Before the invasions of the white man in the mid-nineteenth century, Sarah Winnemucca's people, the Northern Paiute Indians, freely roamed the high deserts of the Great Basin of what is now western Nevada, northeastern California, and southern Oregon. Having no notion of themselves as a formal political unit,[1] they called themselves simply the Numa, or "People." In anthropological terms they were not a tribe, though history has accorded them tribal status. With the Bannock Indians on the east they constituted a Shoshonean dialectic group in the Uto-Aztecan Indian language family. Like most other Native American peoples they were unaware of the names that were bestowed on them by the first whites. In early accounts their name was spelled in a variety of ways, such as Piute, Pi-Utah, and Paviotso, and they were known as the Snake Indians in parts of Oregon. They were not related to the Southern Paiutes, whose language was very different.

Sarah was born about 1844, the fourth child and second daughter of the older Chief Winnemucca (who was called Old Winnemucca to distinguish him from a nephew of the same name).[2] Winnemucca's name meant "the giver" or "one who looks after the Numa."[3] As an antelope shaman he oversaw the communal antelope hunts. At other times he led his band as they

3

wandered in their searches for food. Even at an early age Sarah helped elevate her father so that he was regarded as the "Big Chief of the Paiutes." She recognized an opportunity in the white emigrants' desire to deal with a few leaders who could parley and answer for the Numa.

Winnemucca was not a war leader in the sense that the Plains Indian chiefs were, since the Paiutes possessed few horses and had no raiding tradition. Although there were occasional altercations, and there was fighting on a small scale, survival under hard living conditions was the Paiutes' prime object of attention. Bands shared food sources with other bands and, in times of abundance, even with neighboring tribes, including the Shoshonis on the east and the various California tribes on the west.

Sarah's Paiute name was Thocmetony, or Shell Flower. She was born in the vicinity of Humboldt Lake in present-day Nevada. Her mother, Tuboitonie,[4] like all other native women living in the Great Basin, spent much of her time gathering wild seeds, roots, and herbs and grinding and preparing them as food. It was a strenuous life; the women were accustomed to traveling miles each day to the sources of the foods as they came in season.

Single families might wander for days without seeing other Numa, but when food was in abundance, there were large gatherings. Bands would get together for games, gossip, and courtship when the leaders decided on a collective rabbit or mud-hen hunt and during the traditional pine-nut collecting in the fall. As antelope shaman Old Winnemucca first discovered the location of a herd in a dream. Then he would lead his band in a ritual preparing them to lure the animals (which appeared to be in a hypnotic state) into a brush corral, where they could be easily killed.

Sarah's maternal grandfather was Captain Truckee, for whom the Truckee River in California and Nevada is named. He had been a guide to early emigrants crossing the Great Basin. There is evidence that he acted as guide for the Stevens-Townsend-Murphy[5] party of 1844 and also for Captain Joseph Aram in 1846.[6] When Sarah was a baby, Truckee was away in California with General John C. Frémont's army and fought in the Bear Flag Rebellion against continued Mexican control of California.

Sarah Winnemucca spent her childhood in a time of great disruption in the life of the Numa. The activities of eastern emigrants on the sage plains of the desert were abruptly changing the conservative aboriginal existence based on a balance with nature. The Numa had either to move away from the roving cattle of the settlers, which decimated the grass seed and brought diphtheria and typhus to the alkaline waters of the Humboldt river, or adapt to the white man's ways, learn from him, and, unfortunately, accept him as master.

Sarah developed an early fear of white men, which was reinforced by the death of a favorite uncle, who was shot while fishing on the Humboldt.[7] At the time, emigrants had recently erected tents in the Humboldt meadows. Members of the band demanded revenge on them, but Captain Truckee reminded his followers that the same emigrants had given sacks of flour to the Numa and had welcomed Truckee and Winnemucca. They were not the transgressors who had killed Truckee's son.

As an adult Sarah remembered her father describing these early emigrants, the first white men whom Winnemucca had encountered close at hand. He called them "owls," because of their unfamiliar beards and light-colored eyes. Young Sarah connected this description of her father's with the Cannibal Owl,[8] a Paiute boogeyman who, in a well-known tale, carried away crying, misbehaving children, pounded them into a tender pulp, and ate them with relish.

Sarah's fear of the emigrants was increased by another traumatic experience. Once, when the cry had gone out that the whites were coming, Tuboitonie and a woman companion could not keep up with the other members of the band and carry the burden of their two young ones. Consequently they buried Sarah and her cousin in the sand, and the two children were left through the heat of the day, their heads protected from the sun by sagebrush. Sarah imagined that at any moment the "cannibal owls" would spring upon them. In the darkness of night Tuboitonie returned to rescue her, but the experience was an indelible memory for Sarah.[9]

For their part, the emigrants, observing the Paiutes in their insubstantial grass shelters and minimal clothing, thought of them as primitive "diggers." The word "digger" was used in a derogatory way to refer to the natives of the Great Basin and California, because the Indian women often dug with sticks for bulbs and roots. Also the whites were put off by the Paiutes' willingness to eat roasted crickets and grasshoppers and ground squirrels and other small desert rodents. The emigrants failed to appreciate the natives' ability to use all of their resources to avoid starvation in a sparse land. Existence required a keen observation of nature and remembrance from season to season when and where to find the natural harvests that were available.

Sarah's early childhood, while largely happy, was often intruded upon by the presence of her maternal grandfather, Captain Truckee, who frightened her with his strange ways and talk of "white brothers." Chief Truckee would return from trips to California with amazing stories of the abundance of food and horses there and the great towns and houses built by the white man, some of which floated on water.[10] The men who accompanied him to California returned with guns and ammunition and demonstrated their prowess with them by shooting mud hens. When the Paiute bands came together at harvest times, there was much talk of the experiences of the Numa who had gone to California. What they described was almost beyond the comprehension of those who had continued to lead the traditional life.

Captain Truckee had learned many English words. He proudly displayed what he called his "rag friend," a letter of introduction from General Frémont commending the Paiute leader for his active part in the war against Mexico.[11] Whenever Truckee presented it, emigrants were liberal with handshakes and gifts. The men of the Numa were tempted when Truckee explained that horses would be given to those who chose to return with him to California to work for white ranchers. Horses would greatly increase the food-gathering capabilities of the bands.

It was probably in the spring of 1850 when, contrary to Winnemucca's wishes, Truckee took his daughter Tuboitonie and her five children in a group of about thirty Paiutes on another journey to California.[12] Winnemucca remained behind with his second wife and her family. Six-year-old Sarah was placed on a horse behind her brother Tom, and Truckee's small band started from the Humboldt Sink toward the Carson River. There were many miles of emigrant tracks to follow, tracks strewn with broken wagons decaying in the sand and sun. Truckee used his rag friend to great advantage among the white travelers, and the Paiutes were treated to sacks of flour, shirts for the men, and dress goods for the women, some of whom still wore the traditional skirt of tule fiber that left them bare above the waist.

In the eyes of her grandfather Sarah behaved badly during her first encounter with the "cannibal owls," for she hid under her blanket and cried. Truckee took Sarah's new baby sister, Elma, from Tuboitonie's back and showed her to an emigrant woman. The woman offered them a powdery substance that Tom and Natchez tried and liked. Sarah finally had the courage to taste the sugar and found it sweet like the Paiutes' own *pe-har-be*,[13] which was taken from a cane growing along the Humboldt River.[14]

At Mormon Station, a settlement on the Carson River that later became Genoa in present-day Nevada, Sarah saw for the first time the manner of living of the whites. When the Paiutes crossed the Sierra into California, the newcomers were awe-struck with the thriving town of Stockton, on the San Joaquin River. Sarah saw brick buildings three stories high and the busy steamboat traffic between San Francisco and the gold fields.[15] Her grandfather had been right: the whites did build houses that made noises and moved up the river.

At six years old Sarah was at a sensitive age to assimilate such drastic change. She cried incessantly, calling her grandfather a bad man to have brought the family among the whites, and begged to return home. Finally she fell ill. Tuboitonie thought that Sarah had been poisoned by a gift of food, but her illness proved to be only a severe case of poison oak. An emigrant woman, who had just lost a child of her own, helped nurse Sarah back to health. With the care and kindness of this woman Sarah found a new trust in the white race. She was, however, terribly disappointed when she could not keep the lovely dresses that the grieving woman had given her, which had belonged to her own daughter. Captain Truckee insisted that the gifts be burned, for it was the Paiute custom that all possessions of the dead, including clothing, must be destroyed.

From their camp near Stockton the Paiutes moved up the San Joaquin River to the ferry crossing owned by Hiram Scott and Jacob Bonsall, who hired the men as vaqueros on their large ranch. Sarah's brothers, Tom and Natchez, worked on the Bonsall ferry.[16] It was an opportunity to learn English and become acquainted with white ways. The women worked in the ranch kitchen, where Sarah was attracted to the bright dishes in the

The Stockton, California, waterfront in the 1850s. Stockton was the first large white settlement that Sarah Winnemucca knew. (Courtesy of Bancroft Library, University of California, Berkeley.)

cupboards. Most of all she loved the red plush chairs around the dining table. She sat on them whenever she could, twisting in her seat to gaze at the tapestry pictures on the backs.

Sarah's older sister, Mary, would never forget the treatment that she received from some of the cowboys at the ranch. She continued to despise white men for the rest of her life. Tuboitonie desperately tried to protect Mary from their attentions. Finally Hiram Scott came to their aid by assigning the women a room in the ranch house. The other Numa remained in the Indian camp. Truckee was not aware of the situation, for he was tending cattle and horses in a camp miles from the home ranch.[17] Tuboitonie had reason to be concerned. In California, Indian women were commonly seized and forced to serve as servants and concubines. Some were cast aside after a time, while others became common-law wives. Legal marriage between whites and Indians was prohibited in both California and Nevada.

At the end of the work season the Numa brought in the stock that they had herded. The ranchers killed several beefs for the

Paiutes, and the Indians celebrated with a thanksgiving dance. If any horses had been missing, there could have been serious consequences for Truckee. Not long before, Jacob Bonsall had led twelve Americans in hanging five Mexicans for horse stealing, despite their protestations that they were not guilty. There had been no jury trial, and the bodies were simply left hanging.[18]

When the band returned to their homeland with their newly acquired horses, at the head of the Carson River they met some of their own people who had recently come from the Humboldt River region. They told a chilling story of the death of many of the Numa on the Humboldt. They were convinced that the emigrants had poisoned the waters of the river. Sarah learned with relief that her father and his band were safe. They had stayed in the mountains away from the river.[19]

The Numa mourned, cutting off their hair and brushing their faces and bodies with ashes. Truckee sent a message to Winnemucca, and his band hurried on their journey to Mormon Station, where they would eventually meet Winnemucca. There had been much activity in this settlement since their previous stop. Now there was a sawmill and a gristmill, and men were out in the plowed fields planting wheat and corn. Great logs had been cut and laid on the ground for fences between the fields.[20]

Hundreds of prospective gold miners were following the trail to California. They stopped at the Reese store in Mormon Station only long enough to buy provisions for the trip over the Sierra. A strong stockade had been built around the log store, but it was an unnecessary precaution. The Washos, the Indians who lived in that country, were peaceful. Though they occasionally drove off horses and cattle, this was really an uneven trade, since so much of their land was now possessed by the newcomers.[21]

Many days later Winnemucca came from the desert regions with a large band of his people. Their crying and wailing could be heard from afar. The two groups fell into each other's arms. Everyone was in mourning because whole families had died of typhus. Tuboitonie found that she had lost two sisters, their husbands, and all her nephews and nieces except for one niece. The Paiutes thought that the whites must have poisoned the Humboldt River. Truckee talked to his people for a long time, and they listened quietly as he defended the whites, saying:

"Oh, my dear children, do not think so badly of our white fathers, for if they had poisoned the river, why, . . . they too would have died when they drank of the water. . . . It must be some fearful disease or sickness unknown to us, and therefore, my dear children, don't blame our brothers."[22]

After his speechmaking Truckee went into Mormon Station with his rag friend. He procured sacks of flour for the hungry people, and Winnemucca received a new blanket and a shirt. Thus Truckee's interpretation of the situation prevailed, and the Numa moved on down the Carson River. On its green margins they found emigrants felling trees and building cabins. There were way stations and whiskey shops where wayfarers traded their run-down stock for fresh animals and supplies. Eventually the miners would invade the eastern foothills of the Sierra when gold was found on the Great Basin side. There was only a small quantity of the precious metal, but enough to keep a few men working. They established a settlement, which was christened Johntown, in Gold Canyon, one of the Paiutes' traditional pine-nut-gathering areas.[23]

While Truckee did not hesitate to bring his people in close proximity to the white miners during his band's annual pine-nut pilgrimage, Winnnemucca chose to take his people farther north, where there was less emigrant activity. The Winnemucca band pursued their wandering life on Smoke Creek in the vicinity of Honey Lake, in a remote area of northeastern California.[24] The country was high-plateau sage desert, but large game animals were still available. The Indians found grazing for their increasing herds of ponies along the banks of the rivers and lakes.

When Truckee made more trips into California with those of his people who wished to follow, Sarah and her brothers accompanied him. Some of their relatives had married Spaniards in the Santa Cruz area, and Sarah thus learned to speak Spanish before she was ten years old.[25] Truckee and his band were attracted to the Santa Cruz Mountains because there was much wild game there and space to wander freely as they had previously in the Great Basin.

The personable Truckee made friends at the old Santa Clara Mission. His friend Captain Aram, whom Truckee had guided across the Sierra in 1846, had fought near the mission ruins during the Mexican War. Now the Sisters of Notre Dame de

Namur were starting a school near the mission. Truckee found them friendly and willing to instruct him regarding their religious beliefs. Most of the Paiute men found jobs as ranch hands or agricultural workers, but Natchez and Tom continued to work for Scott and Bonsall on the San Joaquin River ferry.[26]

In 1873, Sarah told an interviewer that she owed a great deal to a Mrs. Roach, of Stockton, who adopted her, but we do not know how old Sarah was when that occurred.[27] She worked for several white families and was probably given her Christian name during this period. Then, in 1857, she and her younger sister, Elma, moved again to the eastern side of the Sierra to live in the household of Major William M. Ormsby in former Mormon Station, which was now a bustling town known as Genoa.[28] Ormsby's store was located on the main street and was also a stage stop for the Carson Valley Express, for which the major was an agent. Sarah and Elma worked at household chores and helped serve passengers. Sarah was now thirteen years old and, like most of the Paiute children who were adopted by settlers, was expected to earn her keep. Besides doing housework, the two girls were companions to Lizzie Ormsby, the only child of Major and Mrs. Ormsby. Lizzie was four years younger than Sarah. Although Major Ormsby did not share the religion of his Mormon neighbors, Genoa was a close-knit community, and Sarah grew to know the citizens well. When she wrote her autobiography twenty-five years later, she remembered the settlers' names (though she misspelled some of them) and where they lived.[29]

The Paiute sisters were separated from their family, but many other Paiutes lived in the Carson River valley, where they had proved most adaptable to white ways. The men were employed as herdsmen and laborers, and the women as cooks and household help. Generally they acquired some English and dressed as whites.[30] It was at this time that English became Sarah's major language, and she picked up the rudiments of reading and writing.

While Sarah was living with the Ormsbys, a tragic incident occurred that colored her view of white justice. The Washo Indian tribe was accused of killing two traders, James Williams and John McMarlin, who owned a store in Chinatown, now Dayton, Nevada (Sarah spelled their names MacWilliams and McMullen).[31] Both men were on their way to California in charge of separate packtrains when they were attacked. The white community demanded

Lizzie Ormsby at age thirteen. Sarah Winnemucca and her sister Elma were companions of Miss Ormsby while living in Genoa, Nevada, in 1857. (Courtesy of Mrs. Eleanor Johansen.)

that the guilty persons be found and prosecuted immediately. The bodies of the dead men were brought into Genoa, and the Washo arrows were removed and saved for evidence.[32]

Chiefs of the Paiute tribe were asked to come and identify the arrows. Sarah's brother Natchez was now a young man. He came to Genoa with his cousin, Young Winnemucca, who was respected by the whites as an important leader. The Paiutes identified the arrows as Washo to Major Ormsby's satisfaction, and he sent for Captain Jim, a leader of that tribe. Captain Jim admitted that the arrows were Washo but said that all of his people had been harvesting pine nuts and that they were innocent of the killing of the two white men. Major Ormsby said that Captain Jim must bring in the guilty parties or his tribe would find themselves at war. His threat was backed by the Paiutes, who regarded the deceased McMarlin as a loyal friend.[33]

In a few days three Washo men were brought in by Captain Jim. They were accompanied by their wives and mothers, who pleaded for their release, saying that they were innocent. Nevertheless, the three were taken into custody and held overnight. On the next day thirty men with arms came to take the prisoners to California for trial, but the Washos were so terrified that they broke and ran. The militia shot them down, and all three died of their wounds.

Sarah and Elma saw the bloodshed and ran crying to Mrs. Ormsby. Sarah said, "I believe those Washo women who say their men are innocent."

Mrs. Ormsby replied: "How could the Washo arrows be there if they are innocent? Their chief himself has brought them. Besides, my husband knows what he is doing."

One of the mourning women cried to Natchez and Young Winnemucca: "Oh, may the Good Spirit send the same curse upon you! You may all live to see the day when you will suffer at the hands of your white brothers, as you call them."[34]

The Washo bodies were burned, as was the tribal custom. Meanwhile the Washo chief confessed to Natchez that he had known that the men were innocent: "It is true what the women say—it is I who have killed them. Their blood is on my hands. I know their spirits will haunt me, and give me bad luck while I live."[35]

Elma was inconsolable for days after this event. Sarah explains

that two white men later were found with the money that had
been stolen from McMarlin and Williams. They admitted that
they had used the Washo arrows to make it appear that the Indians had murdered the two packers.[36]

The episode seemed to mark the beginning of new misunder-
standings and loss of faith in the tenuous relationship between
the newly established white settlers in the Great Basin and their
darker-skinned neighbors.

2

The Pyramid Lake War

In 1857, Sarah and Lizzie Ormsby were old enough to go from Genoa to the occasional square dances at Johntown, accompanied by Major and Mrs. Ormsby. There were not many women in the Utah Territory at this time, and even little Elma was sometimes brought in to round out a foursome and dance to the fiddle.[1] The Johntown gold miners knew Sarah as a Paiute girl with long raven hair and flashing eyes. They thought of her as a bit haughty and proud, which, of course, made her all the more attractive to them.

Major Ormsby was becoming a leading figure in the Carson River valley. He bought out John McMarlin's store downriver in Chinatown (later Dayton, Nevada)[2] and was made the chief judge of a murder case.[3] Meanwhile he continued to act as the agent for the stage company. Living with the Ormsbys acquainted Sarah with many important local people. Among them was a young man named Frederick Dodge, who was the first United States Indian agent to work exclusively in the western part of the Utah Territory. He set up his office in Genoa. Sarah was undoubtedly pleased to hear that he had distributed hickory shirts, overalls, and tobacco to many of her kinsmen.

In recent years Old Winnemucca had watched emigrants appropriate land and settle on his hunting grounds in the Honey Lake

Genoa, Nevada, in 1870. In this community, originally called Mormon Station, Major William Ormsby acted as the agent for the Carson Valley Express. A steep trail near the town led over the mountain to Lake Bigler (later renamed Lake Tahoe) in the Washo Indian country. (Courtesy of Nevada Historical Society, Reno.)

valley in northeastern California. Although the intrusions were unwelcome, the old leader found some loyal friends among the whites. One was old Peter Lassen, who had lived amiably with the Indians along Deer Creek farther west in California. Lassen often prospected and hunted near Honey Lake. Another was Warren Wasson, who had established a ranch in Long Valley, California, and had spent a good amount of his time working for the welfare of the Paiutes who roved in his area. He knew their language and was of significant help to Agent Dodge in gathering the various bands for a council rendezvous with their new agent.

At the rendezvous Dodge talked with the chiefs, estimated the numbers of the bands, and established himself as a representative of their interests.[4] In making his reports on the Indians, he wrote: "As near as I can ascertain at present, the Piute nation numbers some 6000 souls. I have seen and given presents to 3735. . . . Wun-a-Muc-a (The Giver) is the head chief of the nation. He generally stays on Smoke Creek: near Honey Lake. His family and small band that stays with him number 155." Dodge named twelve bands that he had visited. They included the band of Wa-he, or Fox (a brother of Old Winnemucca) at the big bend of the Carson River, numbering 130; San-Joaquin's band in the Carson valley, numbering 170; and Young Winnemucca's band along the shores of lower Mud Lake, numbering 300.[5]

As has been noted, there had been no head chief of the Paiutes up to this time. Since the settlers now felt a need to communicate with a responsible tribal representative, it is probable that Sarah, when she talked to Dodge in Genoa, gave him the impression that her father held the honors. She continued to support the notion of Old Winnemucca's predominance from this time on.[6] That is not to say that he did not deserve the status that was awarded him. He was well-known to the many Paiute bands and was a respected leader.

While Agent Dodge was with the Paiutes, he made a point of looking over the high plateaus of the Great Basin to determine what lands should most appropriately be set aside for future Paiute reservations. It was clear that the tribe's roaming way of life was necessarily changing. He found much of the best land already taken by settlers.

A third man who had a close acquaintance with Chief Winnemucca was Captain William Weatherlow. He praised the Paiutes because they did not beg for food or clothing, or steal, but brought furs and game to the homesteaders of Honey Lake in exchange for the articles that they wanted.[7] The Honey Lake settlers made an agreement with Winnemucca that, if Indians committed any depredations, the settlers would go to the chief to complain instead of taking revenge on the Indians. Similarly, if the Indians were molested by the whites, or their horses or cattle were stolen, the chief would come to the settlers for redress. The agreement was faithfully observed on both sides.

Major Ormsby's business affairs had so progressed that he took an interest in starting a new town in the Eagle River valley, called Carson City. In the growing little town he built himself a two-story adobe building that was both his hotel and residence, and in 1858 the Ormsby family moved there. The major had a hunch that settling closer to Chinatown and the gold fields would be to his advantage. He continued in the general-merchandising and hotel businesses.[8]

When Frederick Dodge frequented Carson City, he stayed either at the St. Nicholas Hotel or Major Ormsby's establishment. Dodge was an emotional, opinionated young man. He irritated the Mormons because of his outspoken criticism of the dominance of that religious group in the affairs of the Utah Territory. There was little doubt, however, that he had the interest of "his" Indian charges at heart. He spent $5,000 of his own money to purchase four mules, an ambulance, harness, packsaddles, presents for the Indians, provisions, and pay for employees. He expected to be reimbursed by his superior in Salt Lake City,[9] but Superintendent Jacob Forney did not respond to Dodge's requests for payment. After months of waiting and many requests Dodge made a trip to the seat of Mormonism and indignantly forced his way into the superintendent's private quarters to demand the money. Forney gave him a draft on a Saint Louis bank for the disputed amount, but it bounced. The frustrated Dodge still lacked the money that had been legally budgeted for his use. He took affidavits from citizens that Forney had made promises to the Indians to give them cattle and grain that Dodge could not possibly provide because of lack of funds.[10]

When Winnemucca's friend Peter Lassen was murdered while on a prospecting trip in the spring of 1859, some settlers suspected the Indians. Others remembered the warm friendship between the chief and Lassen. Although the Paiutes remained friendly, the question remained unresolved. As for Agent Dodge, he suspected the Mormons, whom he blamed for most Indian troubles.

Dodge foresaw that there would be another influx of whites to occupy more land when a new emigrant road was completed across the Great Basin. The road's destination was Genoa. Captain James H. Simpson, the road superintendent, spent an agreeable evening at the Ormsbys' in Carson City, where, for the first time since he had left Camp Floyd (west of Utah Lake), he encountered the society of ladies.[11] When he rode into Genoa on the following day, the citizens gave his company a thirteen-gun salute and ran up the American flag.

Then, in late June, 1859, the excitement of the discovery of the new Washoe silver mines stirred the country. Hundreds of miners left unpromising diggings in California and hurried on horseback, on foot, or with teams of horses or pack mules to lay claims in the Washoe district, which was just over the border in present-day Nevada. The black rocks that the gold miners around Johntown and Gold Hill had been throwing away for months as worthless debris were now recognized to be solid silver.[12] The Carson valley had been a bustling area before, but now it was a beehive. Towns expanded, new businesses opened, and, perhaps most important of all, there was talk of wresting the western part of Utah away from Mormon control and establishing a new territory.

In late September five wagons from the new mines at Virginia City passed through Carson City. They were en route to California loaded with silver ore. All along the main street people cheered and hollered after the procession. It would create even more excitement when it crossed the Sierra into California with the loads of sudden wealth.[13] At this time, however, Sarah and Elma were suddenly requested by Chief Winnemucca to return to him. Their father was concerned about the increased emigrant activity and sent Natchez to accompany them.[14]

Agent Dodge pleaded once more with the commissioner of Indian affairs in Washington, A. B. Greenwood: "Yesterday's overland mail brought me advices from Carson Valley that there was a general stampede of persons from California to the mining localities within my agency which devolves in me an additional reason for appealing to your kind consideration on behalf of my

Indians." He requested that land be set aside for the Pyramid
Lake and Walker River reservations and sent accompanying maps
to show the boundaries. He remarked:

These are isolated spots, embracing large fisheries, surrounded by mountains and deserts, and will have the advantage of being their home from
choice.
    The Indians of my agency linger about the graves of their ancestors—
"but the game is gone," and now, the steady tread of the white man is
upon them. The green valleys too, once spotted with game are not theirs
now.[15]

A traveler who met Sarah at this time wrote of her:

Near the sink of the Humboldt river a strange but interesting woman
visited our camp. She was a full blood Piute Indian woman, highly
intelligent and educated and talked the English language fluently. She
ate breakfast with me and became so interested in our conversation that
she offered to travel with me, across the desert to Carson Valley. Her
name was Sarah Winnemucca, the only daughter of Chief Winnemucca,
the great chief of the Piute Nations. There is a station on the Union
Pacific Railroad named Winnemucca in honor of her father. He was the
head to whom all sub-ordinate chiefs reported when anything was wrong
all the way from the Humboldt river to the sink of the Owens river,
four hundred miles south.[16]

Sarah had impressed this newcomer too with the importance of
her father's role in tribal affairs. It is doubtful that he had much
influence south of the Humboldt, since he and his band usually
moved north from that river, going as far as central Oregon.
Sarah's conversation with the traveler might have included information about Agent Dodge and the growing tensions between
the settlers and the Paiutes.
    The winter of 1859 was the worst that the Indians could re-
member. Large numbers of Washos died in Truckee valley. The
whites helped build fires for them and offered food, but the
starving Indians refused to eat. They thought that the bread was
poisoned and that the whites had brought the severe weather
upon them.[17] In January, while the fierce storms were still raging,
there was talk of an "Indian outrage" near Honey Lake. A young
man, named Dexter E. Demming, had been murdered, and his
horses and property stolen. The settlers at Honey Lake demanded
that Captain Weatherlow lead a company of men after the offenders, whom they were convinced had been Smoke Creek Paiutes.

The captain reasoned with the settlers that those Indians had always been friendly and had kept the Honey Lake treaty, but the tracks in the snow from the scene of the murder proved to be Paiute. A party came back and reported that the murderers were from the Smoke Creek band, who had drawn away from Winnemucca's control and recognized Smoke Creek Sam as their leader. An agreement was reached that Weatherlow should have a talk with Winnemucca, inform him of the murder, and demand that the guilty parties be given up. When the captain arrived at Pyramid Lake, he was accompanied by a representative of Provisional Governor Isaac Roop. The two men found themselves suddenly surrounded by Paiutes, who were well armed and mounted. The Indians took them prisoner and refused to let them interview Winnemucca.

Weatherlow recognized the men as Smoke Creek Paiutes. He parleyed with them, finally agreeing to return to Honey Lake. He and his companion set off in the direction of the white settlement, but they later took cover in a dense fog and changed their course again to Pyramid Lake. There they found Young Winnemucca, who invited them in to his *nobee*, or *karnee*, the rounded hut of woven rushes or cattails that was the traditional Paiute dwelling. Since Young Winnemucca had spread a blanket for them to sit upon, and had always been cooperative, Weatherlow was surprised to find that the chief would not agree to return to Honey Lake valley to settle their differences, nor would he admit that Paiutes had committed the murder. Weatherlow added, "We then asked him to appoint some future time for visiting us; he replied that he would not come at all, but that the people of Honey Lake must pay to his people $16,000 for their land."[18]

Weatherlow believed that the request for payment for the land did not originate with the Paiute leader, but that some white man had put the notion in Young Winnemucca's head. He concluded, "My belief was, from the manner and actions of Winnemucca that we were going to have trouble with the Pah-utes—he did not say in so many words that he was preparing for war, but from my knowledge of Indian character and from the excited and unusual manner of the warriors I was convinced that they contemplated mischief." The captain gave warning to the cattlemen in the vicinity of Pyramid Lake, who begged the Honey Lake settlers not to "demonstrate" against the Indians until they could remove their stock when the snows had melted in the spring.[19]

In late February, Old Winnemucca came with an interpreter into Virginia City, which is about fifty miles southeast of Honey Lake. He made bitter complaints to the citizens. Curious miners crowded around him on a saloon porch while he told them that the cattlemen at Pyramid Lake had threatened his men and taken his ponies. He said Agent Dodge had promised that the herders would pay for the use of the land, but now they would not because they claimed that the Paiutes had stolen some of their cattle: "They say they will bring down white men from this town and kill all the Indians at Pyramid Lake."[20] The citizens told him that nobody from Virginia City was going out to fight Indians, but Winnemucca was not satisfied with their assurances. In a few days the people of Virginia City noted that most of the Paiutes who lived on the outskirts of town had left, but they thought little of it because the Indians usually returned to Pyramid Lake for the spring fishing season.

Sarah must have been fully aware at this time of her people's disenchantment with the white invasion. Many bands came into Pyramid Lake in the early spring, even the Paiutes' distant relatives, the Bannocks of Idaho, whose appearance was more like that of Plains Indians because of their beaded leather clothing and long, braided hair. The abundance of cutthroat trout, called *hoopagaih*, meant that there was food for all. All the bands had their own camps, which were sometimes separated by miles of sagebrush, but the leaders met, and there was much talk.

Young Winnemucca's high qualities of leadership were generally recognized,[21] for he was a powerful man of intelligence and dignity. He spoke strongly for continued peace with the whites. He reminded the other leaders that Major Dodge had promised them a reservation and believed that they should turn to tilling the soil. Old Winnemucca also wanted peace, but he wished to continue the traditional hunting and gathering; he knew of land that could sustain his band where no white man had settled. His words were not favorably received by the majority, who were tired of being driven from their accustomed hunting areas.

The deliberations in council went on for many days, as the people continued to linger, waiting for something to be decided. Young Winnemucca was adamant for peace, and, when he saw that he was not winning, he fell in a coma and lay as though

Young Winnemucca, also called Numaga, a cousin of Sarah's and a respected leader of the Paiutes at Pyramid Lake. (Courtesy of Nevada Historical Society.)

dead.[22] Shamans did this, because it was thought that while in such a trance they could leave their bodies to call upon the dead or the Great Spirit.[23] When Young Winnemucca again stood before the council, there was new interest in what he had to say. His temperate words were lost, however, when a rider dashed up with solemn news.

Two young Paiute girls had been found in the Williamses' cellar at Williams Station, a whiskey shop on the Carson River that also provided provisions and water. Their parents had thought them drowned or lost, but now they were found, and, though still alive, they had been abused by the Williams brothers. A party of warriors, headed by Captain Sou, had burned the station and killed the two Williamses and a traveler with them. Thus an act had been committed that was an excuse for conflict, and the feelings of the Paiutes were inflamed for battle. When Young Winnemucca heard of the revenge that the Numa had taken on the Carson River, he knew that it would be only a matter of time before the whites descended upon the Paiutes. He became war chief and prepared his people for battle.[24]

Rumors circulated in the white settlements that besides the horror at Williams Station other settlers along the Carson River had been attacked and there was a general uprising of the Paiutes. Each town got up a company of volunteers to chastise the Indians, while riders raced through the countryside to warn isolated settlers of the danger. In Carson City on May 9 a company was organized of thirty mounted men, who were under the command of Major Ormsby. Genoa, Silver City, and Virginia City also formed motley companies, who were armed with firearms of all kinds and ages. The white men moved toward Williams Station with little plan and no central command, though it seems that in the end Major Ormsby accepted leadership through default.[25]

When they followed the Truckee River to the Paiute stronghold at Pyramid Lake, the volunteers found that their initially pleasurable Indian hunt turned into a nightmare. As they pursued them, the Paiutes would fade away behind sagebrush and rocks, only to reappear and move away again. Ormsby suspected an ambush and posted guards at a narrow spot on the trail that was blocked by high cliffs on the right and the Truckee River on the left. As the wary volunteers moved down the trail to a meadow that was surrounded on two sides by cottonwood trees and brush, the Indians attacked. Paiute horsemen charged from behind a line of trees, while other warriors opened fire from rocks and low vegetation on the hillside above. The volunteers found themselves in a well-conceived trap, with no way out but to go back the narrow trail along the Truckee River.

Many volunteers and their terrified, rearing horses lost their lives in the first minutes of the battle. A general white retreat followed. At the place where the trail narrowed, most of the men who had been in charge of covering their comrades fled for their lives, though a few stood their ground and died for their bravery.[26] The volunteers who reached the plateau were pursued for miles, and those whose horses gave out found death awaiting them. Major Ormsby was shot in the mouth and both arms. Attempting to ride a wounded mule, he climbed the trail to the plateau, but, when he saw that there was no hope, he turned to face his death. In her autobiography Sarah claims:

My brother [Natchez] had tried to save Major Ormsbey's life. He met him in the fight, and as he was ahead of the other Indians, Major Ormsbey threw down his arms, and implored him not to kill him. There was not a moment to be lost. My brother said, — "Drop down as if dead when I shoot, and I will fire over you," but in the hurry and agitation he still stood pleading, and was killed by another man's shot.[27]

Only the darkness of night saved many. In the next few days those who had hidden or outrun the Paiutes straggled back to the settlements. The news of the high number of casualties, which totaled close to eighty, plus the discipline of the Indians amazed and frightened the settlers. Expecting the worst, they sent to California for reinforcements and barricaded themselves in the strongest buildings in the towns. The residents of western Utah were panic-stricken. Some decided that California was a more promising place to reside and headed back over the Sierra. Four regular companies of United States troops were brought from San Francisco and Benicia to chastise the Paiutes.[28]

On June 1 over five hundred volunteers plus the regulars joined forces and began a second march to Pyramid Lake. When they reached the point where the narrow trail dropped to the wide meadow, scouts observed three hundred mounted warriors approaching and more Indians following on foot. After a furious battle the whites had to admire the tactics of the Paiutes: The

Major William Ormsby, the leader of an attack by settlers on the Northern Paiutes. He died along with more than eighty other whites in the Pyramid Lake War. (Courtesy of Nevada Historical Society.)

women and children had escaped behind the lines while the warriors kept the enemy occupied. A few days later, when they reached the main Paiute encampment, the soldiers found the village deserted.[29]

Meanwhile, Captain Weatherlow and his thirty-five Honey Lake volunteers had waited in a three-day sleet storm for the Indians to come through a pass on the northern end of the lake. They gave up just one day too soon.[30] A few white scouts pursued the retreating Indians as they moved toward the northern deserts, but, when one of their number was killed, they lost heart, and they returned to the settlements.

Before the year 1860 was over, the United States government had reacted to the battle of Pyramid Lake by building a fort on the Carson River, called Fort Churchill. It was meant to be a bulwark of defense against the Paiutes. The mutual trust of the days of Peter Lassen was no more. Yet Captain Weatherlow was convinced that, if Chief Winnemucca had been visited by Major Dodge with full power to make a treaty to create a reservation, the bloody massacre would never have occurred.[31] The Honey Lakers, now stranded in an isolated community far from the new fort on the Carson, were fortunate that Colonel Frederick Lander and his men were building a United States wagon road in the vicinity. Lander arranged a meeting with Young Winnemucca, and, though he could not treat with him in an official capacity, he offered to write about their conversations to Washington, D.C.[32]

Young Winnemucca greatly impressed Lander with his desire for peace and his understanding of the Paiutes' critical situation. The young chief complained that he was accused of killing Pete Lassen, who had been one of the best men he had ever known, and with whom he had slept in the same blanket. His people had shown the whites much kindness when the whites had nothing, but now there was no corresponding help from the whites. He spoke repeatedly of the promises that the whites had made and broken. The young chief was especially upset by the example of the California Indians, who had been put on reserved lands and promised food by the whites, only to find themselves starving. When they stole some cattle, the whites retaliated by murdering them all: men, women and children. Lander had no good rejoinder to Young Winnemucca's accusations, for he also knew of the massacre of reservation Indians in northern California. He reported to U.S. Commissioner Greenwood: "I told the Chief that his tribe was more like the whites than the Daggers [sic]. That much of the Pah-Ute territory, especially the mountain-sheep and antelope ranges, the whites would never covet, that their lakes were full of fish which the whites did not want."[33] Young Winnemucca was not persuaded. The good white man who was to teach him had never been sent, and a reservation had not been provided for his people.

Terms were negotiated for an armistice that was to last until the next summer when the grass was dry. The young chief sent for Old Winnemucca, who was on the Oregon border, and promised that the old leader would arrive in two weeks. He explained that Old Winnemucca had always been averse to war and would await Major Dodge's arrival at the Big Meadows on the Humboldt River.[34] Dodge had been in the East at the outbreak of the war. When he returned, Lander sent an urgent letter to him, asking him to treat with both Winnemuccas. Warren Wasson, who had been employed as a guide and scout for the army, arranged a meeting, which was held at Pyramid Lake. A peace settlement was finally negotiated.[35]

Agent Dodge was so delighted by Wasson's influence with the Indians that he engaged him in the Indian Service and left him in charge of his agency while he returned to Washington (where he was later recruited into the Civil War and killed). Dodge left behind him many white critics who felt he was too easy on the Indians and had an ulterior purpose in setting up the reservations: "It is known that he is on amicable terms with the Pah-Utes, and it is surmised that he wishes them to resist prospectors in the neighborhood of Pyramid Lake, where, it is said, he knows there is a rich mineral deposit—hoping, that when the Indians should get rid of all prospectors, he could get a large slice himself."[36] Warren Wasson refuted Dodge's critics, stating in a written report to the Office of Indian Affairs, "I may as well state from actual personal knowledge of Mr. Dodge, I know he was scrupulously honest and zealous in the discharge of his duties, but unacquainted with Indian character, and, therefore, unfit for the position of Indian agent."[37]

3

Growing Up Proud

It seems probable that Sarah Winnemucca was able to find a refuge during and after the Pyramid Lake War. She did not describe the hostilities in her autobiography as if she had actually experienced them with the "'squaws and papooses' who were hungry and tired of living in the rocks" whom Young Winnemucca reported at the close of the war.

In October, 1860, five months after the hostilities had ended,[1] Captain Truckee became ill with a serious infection in his hand caused, some sources say, by a tarantula bite. He and his band had been harvesting pine nuts in the Palmyra Mountains near Como, south of Dayton, Nevada. The miners nearby tried to alleviate his suffering with poultices and disinfectants, but Truckee's wives knew that he was dying. In her account of the death Sarah relates that signal fires were placed on the mountains to call in the Paiutes. As his granddaughter she was at Truckee's side, along with other members of the family.[2] She was about sixteen years old.

Captain Truckee asked one of his white friends, a Mr. Snyder, to come to him. Sarah quotes him as saying to Snyder:

There . . . are my sons' children, and the two little girls I want you to take to California, to Mr. Bonsal and Mr. Scott. They will send them to school to "the sisters," at San José. Tell them this is my last request to them. I shall soon die. I shall never see them in person; they have promised to teach my two little girls when they become large enough.[3]

Then Truckee spoke to Winnemucca: "He told him what he must do, as he was to be head chief of the Piute nation. He cautioned him to be a good father, as he had always been, and, after talking awhile, he broke down. We all cried."[4]

After a day and two nights Truckee's death was imminent. "He opened his eyes in his usual bright and beautiful way," Sarah recorded. After admonitions to all present he said, "Don't throw away my white rag friend; place it on my breast when you bury me." Then after a few more words, he died. Sarah described her feelings as follows:

I could not speak. I felt the world growing cold; everything seemed dark. The great light had gone out. I had father, mother, brothers, and sisters; it seemed I would rather lose all of them than my poor grandpa. I was only a simple child, yet I knew what a great man he was. I mean great in principle. I knew how necessary it was for our good that he should live.[5]

Truckee had always cautioned his people to be honest and never to take articles from the miners in the mountains that were around the new reservations even if they left them on the ground. The miners might return for them and think the Numa had stolen them.[6]

Sarah's tribute to her grandfather, written with genuine affection, emphasized his importance as a calming influence and as a leader who was well regarded by both races. In reality, however, Truckee had no authority to bestow the high chieftainship of the Paiute nation upon his son-in-law. Sarah was doing some wishful thinking in this regard. In the years to come Old Winnemucca would be a well-known chief to white society, but this was partly because of Sarah's insistence that he was such a personage.

In *Life Among the Piutes*, Sarah described her time at the San Jose convent school as brief:

In the spring of 1860, my sister and I were taken to San José, California. Brother Natchez and five other men went with us. On our arrival we were placed in the "Sisters' School" by Mr. Bonsal and Mr. Scott. We were only there a little while, say three weeks, when complaints were made to the sisters by wealthy parents about Indians being in school with their children. The sisters then wrote to our friends to come and take us away, and so they did,—at least, Mr. Scott did. He kept us a week, and sent word to brother Natchez to come for us, but no one could come, and he sent word for Mr. Scott to put us on the stage and send us back. We arrived at home all right.[7]

Inconsistently, in an 1873 interview Sarah said, "I was sent to the Convent of Notre Dame in San Jose in 1861 where I remained nearly three years."[8] In 1879 she related that she was educated by the Sisters of Charity at Saint Mary's in San Jose in 1858, 1859, and 1860,[9] though there were no Sisters of Charity and there was no Saint Mary's Church in San Jose in those years. It is hard to account for the discrepancies, since Sarah could well remember names and dates on other occasions.

The Academy of Notre Dame had been established by the Sisters of Notre Dame de Namur in San Jose in 1851.[10] It was a prestigious school for daughters of the wealthy, where girls were taught languages, science, literature and handiwork. Although the school possessed beautiful gardens and buildings and a fine music and drama department, all of that cultivation had grown from austere and primitive beginnings. In 1851 the sisters had been thankful to receive a bear haunch to supplement the cabbages from their garden.[11] Unfortunately, when Sarah and Elma arrived in 1860, the case of two Indian girls attempting to enter the academy presented problems. There are no records of the two Winnemucca sisters at the academy, though it is possible that they were at least admitted. It is likely that the Paiute girls were dismissed from the school after a short stay because of parents' complaints—as Sarah explained. The upper echelon of San Francisco society would have been offended by their presence, Indian princesses or no.[12] Both girls must have been deeply hurt by the affair. The Catholic sisters surely would have tried to disguise the insult, but it would have been apparent to Sarah that the equality and brotherly love that her dear grandfather had sought was not accessible to his granddaughters.

It is probable that Sarah claimed that she had attended the school for a longer period because she thought that it would strengthen her in white society. In fact, however, it is a credit to her individualism and character that she became culturally assimilated and educated by her own determination and persistence. The shame was not on her side in this affair.

Settlers in the Nevada Territory had generally been kind to

Academy of Notre Dame in San Jose, California, in the 1880s. (Courtesy of Bancroft Library, University of California.)

Sarah. She had lived with the Ormsbys and other white families, and, although her appearance and culture were different from theirs, that had been accepted. Many Paiute children had been adopted into settlers' homes, and, though it is true that they worked hard, so did everyone who was building the new towns, cultivating the soil for the first time, digging ditches for water, or searching for the riches of the mines. In Virginia City people had stared at Sarah, but she had known that that was because she was attractive and there were not many women in the populace. She was ambitious and had always had a sense of her own worth. That was not destroyed by the rejection from the sisters' school.

At about the time when the Winnemucca sisters returned to the Great Basin, President Abraham Lincoln appointed James W. Nye to be the first governor for the new Nevada Territory. When Nye visited Pyramid Lake Reservation on official business he was pleased with the war chief, Young Winnemucca: "I found him a most intelligent and appreciative man, one who reasons well and talks like a prudent, reflecting leader."[13] The governor found that white settlers had established themselves along the Truckee River on the most valuable reservation land. He ordered them off as soon as they could bring in their crops, but surely he must have known as well as the Paiutes that the settlers were there to stay unless dragged off by military force.

A pageant was prepared in honor of the arrival of the new territorial official, and Old Winnemucca, who always reveled in pomp and circumstance, made himself conspicuous in the proceedings. The *Carson City Silver Age* described the occasion as follows:

The visit is represented as being highly successful in every particular, and extremely gratifying to the old chieftain. Winnemucca, it seems, had been apprised of their approach, and with 150 of his picked warriors, "dressed from top to toe," met the Governor and party 20 miles this side of the Lake, and escorted them to his camp, where they were entertained in the most superb style known to the Pi-Utes. Captain Price and his soldiers were also partakers in the hospitalities of the tribe, and encamped at the lake during the sojourn of the Governor and suite. The Indians were greatly impressed with the importance of a visit from so many of our distinguished men, and used every means to render their stay agreeable, and the ceremonies that came off upon the separation are described as very appropriate and imposing. When the time approached for our men to depart, Winnemucca assembled his tribe, and compliments were freely exchanged, all of which wound up with a grand dance, soldiers, Indians and everybody else taking part. When the Governor and suite left, they were highly pleased with the manner in which they were entertained by the Indians and it is generally supposed that Old W nnemucca was much elated and considered himself about that time a leetle greater man than Governor Nye. This, we presume, will settle affairs in that quarter for at least six months and perhaps a year.[14]

Despite the attentive niceties of this ceremonial occasion the plight of the Numa continued to deteriorate. The general attitude of the whites toward the Indians was to "keep them on the reservations and let them take care of themselves," but various efforts were already underway to decrease the size of their reserve. The new Paiute agent, Jacob T. Lockhart, expressed the fear that the territorial legislature's grant of a franchise for a toll road across the southern end of the Pyramid Lake Reservation would introduce hotels and whiskey shops to a population that had not yet been greatly harmed by the evils of white society. The *Carson City Silver Age* quoted him as saying that the toll road was a beginning attempt to get the reservation abolished.[15]

Paiutes who wished to pursue their traditional roaming existence off the reservation were considered to be showing "unrest." The bands had to be careful about their movements. Changing campgrounds or kindling large fires at night caused wary settlers to believe that the Indians were getting ready for an uprising. The cavalry from Fort Churchill with Captain Almond B. Wells in charge moved through the country, reminding the Numa of their presence. Young Winnemucca spoke to the citizens of Como,[16] a community in the vicinity of Captain Truckee's grave, protesting the destruction of the pine-nut trees. He said that they were welcome to fallen or dead timber, but he would not permit the cutting of the living trees, which provided food for his people. The trees were cut down anyway.

In the spring of 1863 new gold and silver mines opened in southern Idaho. Agent John C. Burche, who lived in the Big Meadows on the Humboldt requested that Old Winnemucca go to the Bannock chief Pas-sé-quah in Idaho and ask that prospectors from California receive safe passage as they moved through his land. Winnemucca agreed to the proposal, and his son Natchez accompanied the old man to act as interpreter. Sometime later Burche received a telegram:

We are here one hundred miles from Star City and all is peace and quiet. I have been to see the Bannock Chief, Paseco; and all is right. If the whites wish to prospect through the country there is no danger from the Piutes or Bannocks; for there is an agreement with those tribes to that effect, and I am going north for the purpose of seeing that there is a perfect understanding with all the surrounding tribes.

The Young War Chief is within one day's ride of this place, and I am going to see him in a few days. He is not out on the Salt Lake Road fighting as was reported. . . .

Yours respectfully,
Winnemuc, Indian Chief
Per Natchez, Interpreter[17]

Old Winnemucca received a Spanish sombrero, a red silk sash, and a few blankets for his efforts as roving ambassador. Agent Burche on the Humboldt understood that the Indians needed food, not pretty dainties for their leaders. He wrote Governor Nye that, if he could not distribute supplies to the hungry Paiutes, whose traditional foods were disappearing, he could not guarantee future peace.[18]

Meanwhile Sarah and her father, confronted with the same facts, helped develop a plan that, they were determined, would save the Numa.

4

On Stage

It seems paradoxical that Old Winnemucca, who had shunned white society and searched for new hunting grounds in which to keep the traditional Paiute way of life, was the same person who enjoyed leading the ceremonies at Pyramid Lake at the time of Governor Nye's first visit. But there was pomp and circumstance in his nature, which Sarah understood. She once said, "The Indian is like my white brother, Emperor Norton: he likes epaulets."[1]

In 1864, Virginia City, Nevada, was a burgeoning town of 15,000 built atop the fabulous wealth of the Comstock mines. The city was completely overrunning the Johntown that Sarah had known when she went square dancing with the Ormsbys in her youth. Residents were familiar with the Paiutes, whose *nobees* were erected on the eastern fringes of the town, their frames covered with blankets, sacking, and sagebrush. When it was announced that Chief Winnemucca and his two pretty daughters were to appear on stage in a local theater, they were a major attraction. The performances were held at Sutcliff's Music Hall, where Max Walter, the manager, gave his seasoned advice to the inexperienced performers.[2] Jim Miller, a resident of the city, also took an interest in the proceedings. Sarah, with her quick ear for language probably helped with the dialogue.

Before performances Winnemucca appeared in the streets of Virginia City mounted upon a pony and surrounded by a cavalcade of his followers. He was described "as one used to authority and command, though the wrinkles in his full, heavy face showed the mark of age." On his head he wore a crown of feathers and on his shoulders brass epaulets. Two of his followers held a crescent above his head that was bound with red, white, and blue stripes. Elma sat behind him on his horse, and Sarah rode abreast on another pony.[3]

Before the first performance the old man addressed a large crowd who had assembled in front of the International Hotel to see them. Sarah interpreted for him in very good English, saying that her father and his tribe were friends of the white man. Winnemucca told how overtures had been made to him by the tribes on the plains to join them in their war against the whites. He had refused to do so. Though he and his tribe were poor, they would not fight against the palefaces. After his talk, hats were passed through the crowd, and a sum of money collected and given to him. The procession then turned and rode down B Street, as Winnemucca waved his hand to the people on the boardwalks, who were craning their necks for a better look at the Indians.[4]

A reporter interviewed Sarah later. She told him that the chiefs of some hostile tribes had endeavored to enlist Winnemucca in their cause, but that her father had said there was fighting enough in the country (the American Civil War) without the Indians adding to it, and he had refused. Sarah also reported that the hostile chiefs had told him to go to his friends the whites, because, if he or any of his tribe crossed a certain boundary line, they would kill them. "WINNEMUCCA WARNS THE WHITES AGAINST THE APPROACH OF THE HOSTILES,"[5] read the newspaper headlines.

The Bannocks were probably "the plains tribe" that had offered to join with the Paiutes in battle against the whites, despite the treaty that Burche had made with Pas-sé-quah. The agent recognized that the Bannocks were much more aggressive than the Paiutes or Shoshonis and that they were rich in ponies and weapons. Winnemucca tried to use this information to the advantage of the Paiutes by representing his tribe as the allies of the whites. Captain Truckee had followed a similar course, teaching his people to sing "The Star Spangled Banner" and to salute the flag. Nevertheless, when Sarah praised her father as a chief loyal

Virginia City, Nevada, a few years after Sarah Winnemucca's stage debut in 1864. Maguire's Opera House is in the background. (Courtesy of Nevada Historical Society.)

to the whites' interests, her advocacy, exaggerated or not, was met with indifference.

After their stage experience in Virginia City the performers moved on to San Francisco. Miller still backed the Paiutes' enterprise. On October 22 a San Franciscan might have noticed this unusual item in the amusement section of the *Daily Alta California*:

METROPOLITAN THEATRE

Unique Attraction
For Saturday Afternoon and Evening, Oct. 22
The Citizens of San Francisco are respectfully informed that:

Winnemucca
The Chief of the Piutes
Accompanied by his
Two daughters and eight braves
Now on their way to Washington, will at the request of numerous
citizens appear in a series of
Tableaux Vivants
Illustrative of Indian Life
A Descriptive Lecture and Appropriate Music
will accompany this romantic entertainment

Prices of Admission
Orchestra and Dress Circle $1.00
Parquette   50 cts.   Gallery   25 cts.[6]

"Romantic entertainment" was a good description of what followed on the stage in the Metropolitan, which was the most
popular theater in San Francisco. The program bore little relationship to the true life of the Paiutes, but it did fulfill the public's
notion of a good stage show, such as they might expect from an
Indian troupe.

Before the performance Winnemucca, Sarah, Elma, and six
warriors rode in open carriages through the crowds near the
theater on Montgomery Street.[7] The warriors were painted with
ochre and vermilion, and all of the party wore buckskins and
bright-colored feather headdresses that the *San Francisco Daily
Alta California* claimed resembled enormous mops more than
anything else. The latter description makes it appear that the
men wore California rather than Plains Indian headdresses.

On the next morning reporters had a heyday reviewing the
entertainment. They made slurring remarks about Indians in
general and these Paiutes in particular, ridiculing their costumes
and their names on the program:

The Royal Family were introduced to the audience by a gentleman
in black . . . as Winnemucca, Chief of the Piutes, and his two daughters.
Royal Family bowed. The audience returned a rapturous greeting. Warriors to the right and left of us also presented. The eight arose from
their seats as one man, made a mechanical, half-military salute, half-
Oriental salaam, and subsided. The gentleman in black then read a
lecture on Piutes "and any other Indians," which sounded in its delivery
like a school boy's production and spoke of pale faces, red men, tented
plains, warriors with a hundred wounds, etc.

Metropolitan Theatre, circa 1865, the location of Sarah's first performances in San Francisco. (Courtesy of California Historical Society, San Francisco.)

It was intended, however, to be highly eulogistic of the Great Chief. . . . The lecture finally came to an end, and after an intermission . . . the tableau vivante, with the accompaniment of forest scenery and Greek fire, were introduced in the following order: "The Indian Camp," "The Message of War," "The War Council," "The War Dance," "The Capture of a Bannock Spy," "Scalping the Prisoner," "Grand Scalp Dance," "Scalping of an Emmigrant Girl by a Bannock Scout," "The Wounded Warrior," "The Coyote Dance," and a series of five tableaux's representing Pocahontas saving the life of Captain John Smith. One of the "Flowers" acted the part of the famous Indian Maiden, and old Winnemucca the hard-hearted old parent, Powhatan. A white man in the costume of an "honest miner" did the John Smith. . . . Some of the tableaux were very good, the Indians seeming to possess the power to maintain an inanimate position as if carved of bronze. . . . Of the dances the Coyote was the best and was decidedly the favorite with the youngsters, especially when the "Flower" . . . got a back fall by pulling too hard on the tail of the Coyote.

The crowning feature of this unique entertainment was the address in the Pi-Ute dialect, by Winnemucca, and interpreted by one of his daughters. The old fellow came forward to the front of the stage, supported by the two daughters, Shell and Lattice, and with a self-possession and assurance that would do honor to a Copperhead stump speaker, spoke as follows:

> Rub-a-dub, dub! Ho-daddy, hi-daddy; wo-hup, gee-haw
> Fetch water, fetch water, Manayunk!

That's about as near as we could catch the words as they fell, and they were taken up and rendered by the Shell, in very good English thus:

"My father says he is very glad to see you. He has heard a great deal about San Francisco, and wanted very much to see it; so he has come to see it for himself!"

His part of the speech being loudly applauded by the appreciative audience, the old fellow became inspired and rattled off at such a telegraphic rate that we couldn't come up with him at all. Not so with Shell Flower: she had been there and knew just what to say, and it came to us in her sweet English voice to this effect, "My father says he is glad to see so many of you here, and he hopes there will be a great many more tonight when he hopes to accomodate you—I mean please you better." The curtain fell amidst the most rapturous applause from the ladies, and the Pi-Ute war whoop from the boys. The aboriginal entertainment was over. People like novelty, let them have it. Opera and minstrelsy will pall after a season or two, and if we do go now and then to see an aboriginal entertainment or a Chinese theatrical troupe, whose business is it? we would like to know.[8]

A woman, who had been a settler on the Carson River in 1853 and knew the Winnemuccas well, wrote an anonymous letter to the editor while the Paiutes were performing before the gaslights at the Metropolitan:

I did wonder, when I saw the accounts in the newspapers of the city, that Winnemucca—his daughters and braves, were exhibiting pantomimic scenes of Indian Life, if it could be the veritable Old Chief who was stooping from his dignity to become a common actor, for a "star" I knew he could never be, try however much he would. But now the secret is out. In passing down Kearny street, I met three Indians, who I knew belonged to the Piute tribe and Winnemucca family. . . . I concluded to go into the hotel and see the Chief, whom I had not seen since the Indian war of 1860. Glad was the old man to see me, and the young squaws, both of whom recognised me on the moment.

Well, as soon as I could hear myself speak, (for their chatter was not unlike that of a flock of magpies in spring time) I asked the chief why he had taken the white man's ways to show himself? Then came the story of his people's poverty, their suffering for food, and the cause of the distress now upon them. For this reason he had condescended to make a show of their habits, their pastimes, and among them, their time honored dances: and his object in so doing is to raise money to buy food and blankets for his people. But he sees, even now, that these exhibitions will not accomplish the great object he has at heart. . . .

The fact is that Winnemucca's tribe is starving because of our usurping of their right, and because, of the Chief's kindly feeling toward us. He has firmly refused all offers of assistance for himself and people, tendered as a bribe by numerous tribes more fortunately located, and richer in horses and all else that the Indian prizes. . . .

People of California! People of Nevada! You are those for whom this old chief refused all that would have made his people comfortable. . . . Now will you turn him away empty — tell him to go to his children without bread? . . . I have been acquainted with this aged chief and his family for more than 10 years, and I do not doubt in the least but in every respect his report is true. . . .

The 1st thing to be done is to rescue the Chief, his daughters and his native attenders from the present degrading exhibitions, and provide for their immediate wants. Afterwards such contributions in provisions and blankets should be furnished to his people over the mountains as may seem expedient to the enlightened charity of this community.[9]

We do not know if there was a concerted response to this appeal by a friend of the Paiutes, but it was a foregone conclusion that Winnemucca's debut on the San Francisco stage would produce little for them. The cost of theater rental, traveling expenses, hotel rooms and meals, promoter's cuts, and some minimal payment to the performers had to be deducted from the receipts. Winnemucca's first responsibility was to his own relatives and his band, and he can have done little more than help his needy people with a few sacks of flour and blankets. Still, it helped them to survive another winter.

When the Paiute troupe returned to their homeland, Nevada Territory had just been declared the thirty-sixth state in the union by President Abraham Lincoln. The wealth of Virginia City was needed to help finance the final days of the Civil War. Not much credence was given to Sarah's insistence, while she was in Virginia City, that her father was a friend of the whites and had turned down substantial offers from neighboring tribes who had asked him to participate in a general war. After all, Captain Wells from Fort Churchill was available to subdue the

Indians by the awe-inspiring presence of his cavalry. The four-year truce since the Pyramid Lake War perhaps could not be expected to last forever, but the following remark on Sarah's interview by a reporter in Virginia City reflected the attitude of many of the citizens, who felt secure because of the superior forces:

While it is well enough to keep an eye open upon the movements of the savages there is no occasion for the slightest alarm. Two or three thousand men fully armed and equipped could be raised almost at a moment's warning in this city alone, and perhaps it would be a good thing in the end if the opportunity could be had to give these redskins a lesson that would last them for a generation or two.[10]

There was no inclination to be concerned about hungry Paiutes.

The Pyramid Lake Reservation

In the early spring of 1865, Sarah was in the Indian camp at Dayton, Nevada, when a company of cavalry came through town. The leader, Captain Wells, accused the Paiutes of stealing cattle at Harney Lake in Oregon, and he threatened to kill every Indian that came in sight of his company. He was also looking for the Paiutes who had killed two white miners on Walker River.[1]

Sarah was very frightened for her father's band and lived in dread of bad news in the days that followed. Soon after his appearance at Dayton, Captain Wells and his men moved north onto the Pyramid Lake Reservation. At three o'clock one morning they found an encampment of thirty people on Mud Lake[2] (sometimes called Winnemucca Lake), which is produced by the overflow from Pyramid Lake. The camp was made up of old men, women, and children; Winnemucca had all the young men with him at Carson Sink on a hunting excursion. The soldiers killed all the Numa but one, set the camp afire, and threw babies, still in their baskets, into the flames. Sarah wrote that she had a baby brother killed at this time, who must have been the child of a younger wife of Winnemucca's, as Tuboitonie would no longer have been of child-bearing age. Mary, Sarah's oldest sister, jumped on Winnemucca's best horse and, though the soldiers chased her, made her escape.[3]

During this terrible winter of famine, cold, and unexpected

deaths, Mary and Tuboitonie both died. It is not certain whether they lost their lives as a result of the Mud Lake massacre. Two newspaper articles of the time indicate that both of Old Winnemucca's wives were among those killed:

CAPTAIN WELL'S INDIAN FIGHT

Mr. Gilson, Indian Agent, called at this office yesterday, and in course of conversation admitted that the two wives of Old Winnemucca were killed in the late fight of Captain Wells. He thinks they were killed in this desperate "hand to hand fight" at a distance of half a mile. Captain Wells says nothing in his official report about the slaughter of these women. Mr. Gilson also states that a party of Indians were sent out to bury the dead, and found 29 bodies. No white man has been on the ground he says since the fight.[4]

Another newspaper reported: "Young Winnemucca says Captain Wells did not kill Smoke Creek Indians but says they were some of his people—mostly women and children. It is ascertained on corroborative evidence that the two wives of Old Winnemucca were slain in this 'stubborn and sanguinary' battle, where the killing was all on one side."[5]

The Paiutes at Walker River delivered to Captain Wells two Indians who were supposed to be guilty of killing the miners, but the captain was not satisfied. There were rumors that the Indians in the Humboldt River country were threatening the settlements there, and he led his dragoons to "pacify" that area.[6] On May 20, with thirty-six men, Wells fought five hundred Paiutes, Bannocks, and Shoshonis, according to his report. The cavalry lost two men killed and four wounded. One of the soldiers who fought in the battle probably portrayed the number of Indians present more accurately: "They must have had fifty or sixty guns, perhaps a great many more; they used no bows or arrows."[7]

In the Paradise Valley, north of Winnemucca, the citizens were concerned about the Indian scare. They slept together in one cabin at night for protection, and, thinking that they had evidence of the presence of hostile Indians, one man decided to get military assistance. He happened onto the temporary camp of Colonel Charles McDermit, who sent some of his Nevada Volunteers to the settlers' aid. A group of the volunteers met a body of Indians in the valley, and, though the Indians raised a white flag, the commander concluded that they were not friendly. The sergeant ordered a charge, and in the battle that followed twenty-three Indians died. Five of them had taken cover in a house that caught fire; they were shot to death when they ran from the burning building. One citizen and one soldier were killed in the battle, and several whites were wounded.[8] Soon after, Colonel McDermit, who was in command of the Department of Nevada, was shot in ambush, presumably by an Indian, near Quin's River Station (which later became Fort McDermit).[9]

The Indian difficulties on the Humboldt River and northward to the Quinn, or Queen's, River halted a stagecoach line that some private companies had organized to service the new mines that were expanding in southern Idaho. As stations were destroyed, stock run off, and whites murdered, a war of extermination began. One writer of the time said, "I have seen many Indians by the wayside, where they fell by the unerring bullets of the Henry rifles in the hands of citizens."[10] Most of the depredations that were committed in the Paradise and Quinn River valleys and along the Oregon-Idaho border were executed by Black Rock Tom and his Smoke Creek band of Paiutes, joined by some Shoshonis and Bannocks.[11]

The continuing destitution of the Paiutes, the breakdown of peaceful relations with the whites, and above all the untimely deaths of Sarah's sister, mother, and little brother caused Sarah to remove herself at this time as far as possible from white society. Her recourse was to return to the Pyramid Lake Reservation and find a home there with her brother Natchez and his family.[12]

During the winter of 1865–66, Sarah and Natchez heard of the battles in the north and the decimation of the Numa. Their father had sent word after the deaths of his relatives at Mud Lake that he was taking the remainder of his band into the mountains, where he planned to stay for the rest of his life.[13] Sarah was fearful that the band would be surprised by the cavalry and forced into a battle, in which the Indians would be no match for the dragoons in the deep snow. When they were cornered, the Paiute women fought alongside the men. The soldiers seldom took captives. Instead they would leave the women and children to fend for themselves in the bitter cold, or occasionally they shot them down too.

The *Humboldt Register* described such a battle in January, 1866:

Life on the reservations was always difficult for the Paiutes. Here women and children pose in front of a summer shelter. (Courtesy of Special Collections, University of Nevada, Reno.)

At the close of the battle 35 dead Indians lay on the field with their bows and quivers still clutched in their hands. All were large, powerful men—a picked company of braves, prepared for battle. But 5 squaws were in the band, and they were acting in capacity of pack train. Two of these were killed in battle by mistake; the other three were furnished with some provisions and left unmolested.

Scouting parties made the entire circuit of the field and found that no living thing had escaped, as the snow was 3 inches deep and there were no tracks leading from the camp."[14]

In March the same newspaper described another battle:

At half past nine the order was given to charge. Right merrily the men obeyed. The Indians stood up bravely, fighting sullenly to the last— asking no quarter; but the charge was irresistible. The boys rode through the Indian ranks, scattering and shooting down everything that wore paint. At length the Indians sought shelter under a bluff of rocks. . . . Loss of the enemy, 80 warriors and 35 squaws. The latter were dressed the same as the bucks, and were fighting—and had to be killed to ascertain their sex. . . ."[15]

Captain Sou had been the leader of the raid on Williams Station that triggered the Pyramid Lake War,[16] but now he was working for the soldiers. He led many forays against his brother Paiutes, for which he was acclaimed as "the New Winnemucca" by the whites on the Humboldt River, who signed a petition on his behalf. His actions ensured the safety of his own band at the expense of other Paiutes.

The Humboldt River citizens' petition was published in the *Humboldt Register* on May 5, 1867:

Whereas, It having been satisfactorily proven that Old Winnemucca, the late Chief of the Piutes, has turned traitor to his tribe, deserted his Country and joined the hostile Indians of the North, and is now instigating and inciting said Indians to continue the war, for the avowed purpose of exterminating the whites and their allies, the friendly Indians; and Whereas Captain Sou has often attested his fidelity to his white brethren on the battle field, and has always been a devoted friend to peace and progress; and Whereas Every inhabitant of the State of Nevada manifestly has an interest in who shall govern and advise the Piute Nation: now, therefore, in order to secure a Chief faithful to the white inhabitants, and to prevent further hostilities in our midst.

Be it resolved, By the citizens of the State of Nevada (the friendly Piutes concurring), that Captain Sou be nominated and chosen Chief of the friendly Piutes to be known by the title of "Winnemucca", and to have supreme command of the Piute Nation; and that we the undersigned citizens of Nevada, and good Piutes, will sustain Sou in that exhalted position which he is by nature so well fitted to adorn.

(Numerously signed, and done up fantastically with the seals of the county (Humboldt) office.)[17]

The citizens' attitude toward Old Winnemucca was especially undeserved, as he had never harmed a white man, nor had he directed his people to do so, except perhaps at the time of the Pyramid Lake War. He had suffered great personal losses from actions led by the military and by white citizens while still keeping the peace.

Captain Sou made a speech to his people in which he argued that the whites were a friendly people, that they killed coyotes but did not eat many rabbits, that they discarded good clothing and threw out much good food, and, best of all, they kept away mean Indians. The whites, he concluded, had become a necessity to the "good" Indians who collaborated with them, and they should be encouraged to remain.[18]

This was a dark time in Sarah's life. She was not only hungry, for there was little to eat at the Pyramid Lake Reservation, but also most of her family were dead or gone. With regard to bands other than Captain Sou's, the "Humboldt code" had been adopted by the whites: "kill and lay waste everything pertaining to the tribes, whenever found—no trials, but at arms; no prisoners; no red tape."[19] Chief Winnemucca was hiding with his small band in the mountains of southeastern Oregon. Even Sarah's sister Elma was gone, for she had been adopted by a French family in Marysville, California.[20] Soon this younger sister would marry a white man, John Smith, with whom she would make her home first in Montana and then in Idaho, never to return to the Indian life. Natchez's main concern at this time was hunting and working to keep his young family alive through the harsh winter. His wife sometimes went to the house of the local subagent, Hugh Nugent, to wash clothes and clean house. She was paid in flour, which helped supplement the rabbits and fish that Natchez could bring in.[21]

There were about 600 Paiutes living on the Pyramid Lake Reservation at this time, including 250 Quinn River Indians who had been brought in by military authorities after their surrender on the Oregon border. All the Paiutes on the reserve were near starvation. Agent H. G. Parker in Carson City complained that because of bad weather he could not get goods distributed to the Indians at Pyramid Lake. Yet in February calico and blankets were provided for Captain Sou's band at the Big Meadows on Humboldt River in payment for some Paiute scalps that Sou had helped deliver.[22]

When spring came, the white men's cattle were herded in droves onto the reservation without any benefit to the Indians. A promised sawmill to produce lumber for houses did not materialize. Natchez and Sarah became convinced that life on the reservation did not hold promise. A ten-mile strip along the Truckee River had been removed from the reservation for the new railroad, and efforts were underway to reduce the reservation still further.

The 22,000 acres of land set aside for the needs of the Paiutes had been known as the United States Timber Reserve. Several entangling agreements had been made by the Interior Department with white lumbermen concerning the property.[23] The sawmill had been sold, along with all cut logs and lumber, on May 27, 1865, for $30,000, which was to have been paid to the Indians in lumber.[24] The lumber was never received.[25] Subsequently, the Central Pacific Railroad ran through the timber reserve and claimed alternate sections, and in 1867 the Nevada legislature passed a resolution that the United States Congress set aside the remainder for school lands for the state of Nevada.[26] Warren Wasson reported at the time that the timber reserve was worth over $100,000,[27] but the legislature decided that it was worthless to the Indians because they would never live on it. White settlers persisted in staying along the Truckee River on the most fertile reservation land despite their promise to Governor Nye in 1862 to quit the area. One might ask why the Paiutes did not force the squatters off the land that rightfully belonged to them, but they knew full well that, if they did so, they would pay with their lives.

The situation was very tense. A Paiute was shot and killed by one of the agent's men for possessing gunpowder (which had been purchased from the subagent, Nugent). Sarah's people were very angry. The relatives of the young man threatened to kill Nugent for his wrongdoing. Sarah and Natchez understood the peril that the band faced: if the subagent was harmed, there would be nothing to keep the soldiers from wiping out all the Paiutes on the reservation, for they needed little excuse.

Sarah tells us that she and Natchez saddled their horses and rode from the Paiute encampment to Nugent's house, crossing the Truckee River, which was swollen from spring storms. As her horse climbed the steep bank on the opposite side of the stream, Sarah fell into the swirling water, but Natchez jumped from his horse and pulled her to safety. She mounted again, and they hurried to Nugent's house, where they warned the subagent that some of their people were threatening to kill him and that he should leave at once.

Nugent did not care to listen to advice and instead told his men to get their guns ready. "We will show the damned red devils how to fight," he yelled. Natchez and Sarah pleaded with him, but he told them vehemently to go away. When the two returned to camp, Natchez called a council. He told the people that ten young men must guard the river crossing to Nugent's house, and, if any of the Paiutes tried to cross the river, they must try to catch them. He admonished, "If there is more than one kill them if you can; by so doing we will save ourselves, for you know if we allowed our people to kill the white men we should all be killed here."[28]

Later that night Natchez called the people together again. He looked very troubled as he told them that he had had a dream. In it the warriors who were coming to kill Nugent had instead killed two white men at the Wells and stolen many horses. The Wells was a whiskey shop about thirty miles from the reservation on the way to Virginia City. No one doubted Natchez's dream. Sometime later a runner came in and confirmed Natchez's vision. The messenger also brought the awesome news that Nugent had gone to the soldiers at Fort Churchill and would probably return with them ready for battle.[29]

While Natchez took thirty of his men toward the Wells, in hopes that they could intercept the killers, the subchief sent out scouts so that the Paiutes would be aware of the approach of the soldiers. Meanwhile, the men in camp prepared to fight. Late in the night two Paiutes brought a written message to Sarah from Fort Churchill:

Miss Sarah Winnemucca, — Your agent tells us very bad things about your people's killing two of our men. I want you and your brother Natchez to meet me at your place to-night. I want to talk to you and your brother.

> Captain Jerome
> Company M., 8th Cavalry.[30]

When Sarah had deciphered the writing she did not know what to do, as Natchez had not returned. The Paiutes urged her to talk to the soldiers "on paper," but there was nothing to write upon and no pen and ink. Finally she resorted to using a sharp stick dipped in fish blood, writing on the back of the original message:

Hon. Sir. — My brother is not here. I am looking for him every minute.

We will go as soon as he comes in. If he comes to-night, we will come some time during the night.

Yours,
S. W.[31]

The messenger had not been gone long before Natchez arrived with his men who had found many horse tracks near the Wells. Sarah told him that they must go speak to the captain. Natchez ordered two fresh horses, and the two of them rode with twenty men to the soldiers' camp, rushing "like the wind" through the dark night as Sarah reported later. When they arrived, Captain A. B. Jerome and a few of his men stepped away from the fire to meet them. He listened attentively while Sarah recounted the full story of how Nugent himself had sold the powder and how the subagent's own man had then killed the Indian possessing it. She explained how she and Natchez had begged Nugent to leave and that he had refused, talking to them in an insulting manner. The agent stood beside the soldiers and heard what Sarah said without refuting her.[32]

Captain Jerome inquired of Natchez how many horses he thought the Paiutes had stolen. "Maybe sixty or more," he said, "judging from the tracks." The captain then asked them to stay the night, but, since Sarah was afraid to do so, they returned to the Paiute camp. They promised that they would have another talk on the next day.

The Numa did not sleep well that night with the soldiers so close by, though Natchez told them they were their friends and that there would have been many more if they had planned to attack.[33] In the morning the Paiutes waited with apprehension as they watched the cavalry ride slowly to the camp and dismount. After blankets had been laid on the damp sand, another council was held. Captain Jerome told the Indians not to be afraid, that if they wanted more protection he would send for his company from Fort Churchill. Sarah and Natchez promptly told him that their people's biggest fear was the soldiers and not to send for more troops.[34]

When the captain investigated the condition of the Paiutes, he saw they had nothing to eat, though the Indians were waiting expectantly for the cui-ui fish (Chasmistes cujus) to come up the Truckee River to spawn. Jerome was determined to do something about this situation, and two days later the band received word that he was sending three wagonloads of provisions. While the flour and beef were distributed, Agent Nugent came around and offered to sell some cattle to add to the issue. The captain angrily told him to "be off."[35]

Sarah writes that while the Paiutes on the reservation were still enjoying the bounty from the soldiers, five dragoons came from Fort Churchill with a message from Captain Jerome. He asked for Natchez and Sarah and told them that he had received a letter from his commanding officer inquiring after the whereabouts of Chief Winnemucca. Sarah could not hold back her tears. She described her reply in her autobiography:

I told him father had not been in since the soldiers killed my little brother. I told him that he sent word to us some six months ago that he had gone to live in the mountains, and to die there. I was crying all the while I was talking to him. My people were frightened; they did not know what I was saying. Our men gathered all round us. They asked brother what was the matter. He told them what the officer said to me.[36]

Jerome told Sarah that his commanding officer, Capt. Dudley Seward of the Eighth Cavalry, wanted her and Natchez to go to Camp McDermit, where they could scout for Winnemucca and his band and bring them in. He said that the band would be fed and well treated, but Natchez and Sarah were dubious of the offer. When they consulted with the Pyramid Lake Paiutes, many said that the soldiers might kill Chief Winnemucca: "You and your sister know what liars the white people are. . . . His blood will be on you." Natchez said, "I believe what the officers say, and if father comes in they will take good care of us." They replied, "Well, it is your father, and you two know best what to do. If anything happens to him you will have no one to blame but yourselves."[37]

More serious trouble with the whites was to come before Sarah and Natchez would contact their father. A brother of Winnemucca's, Truckee John, had industriously started a farm at Pyramid Lake. He had built a cabin and fenced land, where he raised horses, grass, and grain with the help of an irrigation ditch that he had dug. On July 7, 1867, he was murdered by a white man, named Alexander Fleming. The excuse that Fleming gave was that he had recognized John as the Paiute who had killed his brother during the Pyramid Lake War.[38]

On the following day two Paiutes were shot and badly wounded on the road ten miles east of Virginia City. The settlers, fearful of Paiute retribution, left their farms on the Truckee River and assembled for defensive purposes. Franklin Campbell, a farmer on the Walker River Reservation, talked to the Paiutes and found that they had no intention of retaliating, but were worried that the whites would continue the violence.[39] As was the custom, the widow of Truckee John burned her house.

Young Winnemucca, wishing to hunt off the reservation, had used sensible caution. He stationed fifteen of his men on their ponies outside of the town of Susanville, in eastern California, before riding into town to show the hunting permit that he had received from Agent Parker. He was met by mounted citizens with Henry rifles, who chased his Paiute escort away and threw him in the local calaboose for several hours.[40] From then on the young chief attempted to survive living on the reservation.

6

Camp McDermit

When Sarah and Natchez accepted Captain Jerome's invitation to Camp McDermit it was in the heat of the summer of 1868. After an arduous journey to the Oregon border, the accompanying soldiers took them to Captain Dudley Seward, who advised them to bring in their father before Old Winnemucca's band was waylaid by General George Crook.[1] When Crook had taken command of the Department of the Columbia in 1867, his method of combating the numerous small bands of Northern Paiutes had been to establish Camp Harney in south-central Oregon at the center of their stronghold. Most of the Indians had been starved out or exterminated. When they did surrender, it was only after they had been reduced to eating their horses.[2]

By the summer of 1868 most of the bands had been accounted for to the army's satisfaction, but Winnemucca had not yet come in. Sarah explained to Seward that her father had wanted nothing to do with the whites since the Mud Lake massacre. The captain was sympathetic but firm. He advised Natchez to go with a company of cavalry to find his father. He would be paid five dollars a day while doing so. Sarah would remain at Camp McDermit as an interpreter and was offered sixty-five dollars per month for the position.[3]

The Quinn River Paiutes were already in the camp. When

Sarah and Natchez found that they were well treated, clothed, and fed, Natchez was willing to go for Old Winnemucca. He did not take the dragoons with him, however, for he was afraid his people would believe that the soldiers had come to fight them. He took only five Quinn River Indians who would testify to the kindness of the soldiers at the camp. He held a letter from Captain Seward for safe passage among the whites.

Natchez had left with the understanding that his sister would stay with the Quinn River women in the Indian camp. Sarah had many misgivings about finding herself in that situation. It had been years since she had seen many of the so-called "wild Indians," and now she was expected to live with the Quinn River women, who knew only a primitive life. Fortunately, they were very solicitous of her. Of necessity she requested that the commanding officer make the Indian camp off limits to the soldiers, and, when he complied, she rested much easier during Natchez's absence.[4]

Early in July, Old Winnemucca and 490 other Paiutes came into Camp McDermit, guided by Natchez.[5] The men, dressed in tattered clothing, were followed by groups of exhausted women, who were burdened with the baskets that held their few possessions. A scattering of almost naked children came with them. Old Winnemucca met his daughter with open arms. There were no words for those who were gone; one did not speak of the dead.

The soldiers found warm clothing for the men from their own issues, and the people were highly pleased, even though the blue uniforms did not fit properly. There was nothing with which to clothe the women and children, but Sarah suggested that, since the Paiutes were given ample food, they should sell some of it to the camp sutler. Thus they were able to buy yard goods and sewing notions to make their clothing.[6]

In council Old Winnemucca told the people that the band should continue to find their own food. In the summer there would still be deer and rabbit, and the women should continue in the old way to dig roots and gather seed. He was rightly concerned that the Numa would become dependent. Brevet Lieutenant Colonel James N. McElroy, who was in charge of the Paiutes at Camp McDermit, agreed to Winnemucca's request that the men be allowed to hunt and arranged for them to purchase ammunition at the sutler's store.[7]

Fort McDermit, in 1887, with snow on the hills. The long building on the left was the horse barn. The two-story structure on the right in the background was the hospital where Sarah served as matron for a time. (Courtesy of Nevada Historical Society.)

Both Sarah and Natchez were employed as scouts to bring other wandering bands to Camp Harney, Camp Smith, and Camp McDermit. This created enmity among certain segments of the Paiute population, who believed that the Winnemuccas exposed their people to surprise attacks.[8] Meanwhile, the army was criticized by some white citizens for harboring and feeding the Paiutes, who they felt should have been killed outright.

Sarah was asked to bring to Camp McDermit the bands who had surrendered at Camp Smith. At the time Colonel McElroy offered her several companies of soldiers, but, according to her account, Sarah took only her half brother Lee, who was also working as a scout, to accompany her. She and Lee found the starving bands collected at Camp Smith, and after parley they agreed to removal to Camp McDermit. Sarah sent for fifteen wagons to transport the children, and they were furnished rations for the two-day journey, which was made without incident.[9] Over eight hundred Paiutes were given issues every day at McDermit. Each family was furnished a canvas tent. The women lined up in the morning to receive their family's rations, and Sarah helped with the distribution.

General Crook claimed to have made peace with all the hostile Indians from the Humboldt River on the south to Fort Hall on the north.[10] He selected We-ah-wee-wah, a leader from the Malheur Lake area of central Oregon, as the principal chief. Since Paulina, the notorious leader of many fights against emigrant trains in Idaho, had been killed, his band was led by Ocheo.[11] In December, 1868, a peace treaty was negotiated with the Paiutes near Fort Harney by Superintendent J. W. Huntington. Though it was never ratified by the Senate,[12] Crook let most of the Indians return to their old places.

While the surviving Paiutes around Camp McDermit were encouraged to come into the military post for safety and sustenance, the Paiutes in Nevada at Pyramid Lake became increasingly dissatisfied, and many left the reservation. An epidemic of measles from infected cast-off clothing hit those who remained. The agent did nothing for these sick Indians and even refused to reimburse an army doctor who out of humanity had brought vaccine to the reservation. More than one hundred individuals died on the Pyramid Lake Reservation,[13] and about the same number died at the Walker River reserve from ague, typhoid fever, and consumption.[14]

Meanwhile Agent Parker at Pyramid Lake reported to his superior in Washington that the Indians "were never so happy, or so well provided for."[15] In reality, no produce had been raised on either reservation, so that there was no food available except from hunting and seasonal fishing. Later an epidemic of smallpox decimated the Indians who were living nearer civilization on the Humboldt.[16]

The Paiutes were greatly affected too by the new steam locomotives that crossed the iron bridge over the Truckee River into the growing town of Wadsworth, which was flourishing on productive land that formerly had been part of the reservation. Wadsworth was a typical railroad town with saloons and gambling halls. Its presence was felt by the Paiutes, whom a white neighbor had described only a few years earlier, in 1864, as follows: "As yet they [the Paiutes] have resisted the baneful influence of intoxicating drinks and have preserved with great tenacity the native virtue of their women."[17] Some Indians worked on the railroad. They were hired en masse, along with the Chinese, by Charles Crocker, who, it was said, never paid names and faces, but only counted numbers at the beginning and end of a day's work. Indian *nobees* were a permanent part of the landscape on the fringes of Wadsworth.

Paiutes could apply for free passage on the tracks, and whole bands might climb aboard empty flatbed cars. Thus ponies were no longer a necessity for the Humboldt River Indians in their wanderings. Women and young girls could sell their baskets and beadwork to gawking tourists along the railroad, and the men transported fish and game from Pyramid Lake to Lovelock or Winnemucca for the best market. For the Paiutes who were close to civilization, subsistence of a kind was available in the towns, though certainly not on the reservations.

In the fall of 1869, Major Henry Douglass was assigned as Indian superintendent to Nevada, under a policy of President Ulysses S. Grant that replaced civil agents with army officers after the Civil War.[18] Douglass was of a different stripe from his predecessor, Parker; for a true interest in the welfare of the Paiutes emanated from his agency office in Carson City. To the

A Northern Paiute family in Wadsworth, Nevada. (Courtesy of Nevada
Historical Society.)

satisfaction of Young Winnemucca and his followers, the major
ousted all the white fishermen from Pyramid Lake. Until then
the Indians had been compelled to fish from boats while the
nets of the white intruders had extended across the Truckee
River in at least twenty places. Most important, Douglass learned
after a council with the Paiutes of Young Winnemucca's band
that they would agree to remain at the Pyramid Lake Reservation
if they were assigned individual farms, and if they could expect
protection from intruders while receiving guidance in learning to
plant and harvest.

In his pursuit of the Paiute point of view Douglass wrote to
the commanding officer at Camp McDermit. Colonel McElroy
in turn laid Douglass's questions before his Paiute interpreter,
Sarah Winnemucca. She wrote Douglass on April 4, 1870, and
he was so happily impressed with her letter that he sent it on to
E. S. Parker, the commissioner of Indian affairs in Washington.
Sarah was very critical of the reservation system: "If this is the
kind of civilization awaiting us on the Reserves, God grant that
we may never be compelled to go on one, as it is much preffer-

able [sic] to live in the mountains and drag out an existence in our native manner." She did, however, write:

On the other hand, if the Indians have any guarantee that they can secure a permanent home on their own native soil, and that our white neighbours can be kept from encroaching on our rights, after having a reasonable share of ground allotted to us as our own, and giving us the required advantages of learning &eo, and I warrant that the savage (as he is called to-day) will be a thrifty and Law abiding member of the community fifteen or twenty years hence.[19]

The letter supported Douglass's plans to bring the wandering bands onto the reservation to work in agricultural pursuits and establish permanent homes where they could sustain themselves. The major wished to stem the tide of the white citizens who said that the reservations should be opened for settlement since the Paiutes did not live on their lands year-around or cultivate them. The letter was shown around in Washington circles, and in May, 1870, an article on Sarah appeared in *Harper's Weekly*.[20] Her letter was paraphrased in the article, and it was suggested that she should be given serious consideration: "If it should turn out there is no Sarah Winnemucca, and that no such letter was ever written, its statements will still remain as the plea and protest of thousands of the Indians." Later Sarah's entire letter was published in a popular book that received wide circulation, Helen Hunt Jackson's *A Century of Dishonor*.[21]

A Boise, Idaho, editor did not react favorably to the publicity that Sarah was receiving:

Miss Sarah, says Harper's Weekly, "has written(?) a very sagacious letter to Indian Comm. Parker, in which she has eloquently portrayed the wrongs of her race." What infernal noodles some of these Eastern people are. If we are not very much mistaken we had the pleasure of seeing some years ago, Miss S. at Camp McDermitt, Nev. She and a few other interesting relics of the "noble red man" were being fatted at the fort during that winter for the spring campaign against Idaho emigrants. The emigration having stopped for the season "there were no other worlds to conquer," so Sarah and her tribe were about to fare badly, as the supply of dried scalps, grasshoppers and lice had been exhausted. Their condition excited the sympathy of Uncle Sam's boys at the Fort, so they were taken in and cared for until spring when they resumed their favorite pasttime of stealing and murdering. But it is our recollections of Miss Sarah we propose to recite. Sarah was at that time sweet 16 or 20—it would be difficult to judge of her exact age from her appearance owing to a careless habit she acquired of never washing her beautifully chiselled features.

The article continued in the same vein, describing Sarah as an ungroomed, tattered, hungry Paiute. It was a general vilification of her and her father, saying, for example: "Mr. Winnemucca, Chief of the Paiutes, whose gallant exploits in stealing horses and cutting the tongues out of defenseless emigrants will long be remembered by the people of Nevada and Southern Idaho with feelings of just pride and admiration." The following description of Sarah was typical of the piece: "Her raven tresses, which had been permitted to coy with the sportive breeze, unbound, unwashed and uncombed, from her earliest childhood, stood out in elegant and awry confusion from her classically shaped 'cabeza', which contributed to her contour an air of romantic splendour." The article was reprinted in the *Humboldt Register* on May 28, 1870.

Douglass accompanied Natchez to Camp McDermit to induce the Numa there to come to the reservation at Pyramid Lake. He looked forward to meeting Natchez's sister, about whom he was curious after their correspondence. Soon after the encounter with Sarah he wrote:

Some Eastern newspapers . . . have greatly exaggerated her attainments and virtues. She is not by any means the Goddess, which some of the Eastern people imagine her to be (judging from their love letters to her and erudite epistles on Indian affairs), neither is she "a low, dirty, commerce Indian," as the papers of this country describe her to be, in order to counter the Eastern romance. She is a plain Indian woman, passably good looking, with some education and possesses much natural shrewdness and intelligence. She converses well and seems select in the use of terms. She conforms readily to civilised customs, and will as readily join in an Indian dance.[22]

Agent Douglass spoke to the separate Paiute bands, trying to convince them to come to Pyramid Lake. His efforts were not successful, as they were content to remain in their own territories and afraid of encroaching on Young Winnemucca's established hunting grounds.[23] Also the Paiutes could not expect to find *better* conditions on the reservation. Its-a-ah'-mah, the leader of the Quinn River Indians, said:

I was taken to the reservation three years ago with 250 other Indians from here. We had nothing to live on. Measles got among us—many suffered and died. I would not now take what few Quinn River Indians [are left] from here to Pyramid Lake. . . . Here are plenty of Antelope, game, roots and everything to live on. . . . I will stay here and lay my bones here with my dead children.[24]

Douglass's plans for improvements on the reservations under his charge were beginning to get underway when, a few months after his trip to Camp McDermit, he was suddenly informed that the American Baptist Home Mission Society had been given the authority to staff his agency with their own people. In his final report he wrote of his accomplishments and listed some of the problems facing the new agent. He had never been supplied with a map of the Walker River Reservation showing its boundaries. Thus it was extremely difficult to keep out white squatters and fishermen. He also explained that the former subagent under Parker (Nugent) had rented the reserve to cattlemen for $1.00 per head and collected $15,000 for his own pocket. The major suggested that this money would have been better used by the Paiutes. In conclusion he wrote:

It was my purpose next summer had I continued on duty, to organise two schools, one on Truckee [Pyramid Lake] and one on Walker river reserve. . . . It was my intention to place the first school on Truckee river reserve, and employ "Sarah Winnemucca" as instructress; the good elementary English education she has received, and her knowledge of Indian language and character, would make her invaluable as an instructress.[25]

If future agents on the reservation had possessed the integrity and foresight of Major Douglass, much of the problems and heartaches experienced by Sarah and her people would not have come to pass.

7

Marriage and New Agents

In 1870 rumours circulated among the soldiers and Indians at Camp McDermit that the fort was to be closed. Because of the attention of the public to her first letter to Agent Douglass, Sarah decided to write another, this time directly to the commissioner of Indian affairs in Washington.[1] If the military post was vacated, she was fearful that the Paiute bands who were sheltered there would have difficulty in finding safety and sustenance. She exaggerated the Paiutes' warlike intentions in order to make her point:

It will be not only criminal in the authorities to remove the troops now, but it will be far more expensive to the government to restore order and quiet after the Indians have once broken out, and it does not require much provocation to make them do so. I know more about the feelings and prejudices of these Indians than any other Person connected with them & therefore I hope this petition will be received with favor. Sir I am the daughter of the Chief of the Piutes I am living at Camp McDermit and have been in this employ of the U.S. government for nearly three years as interpreter and guide I have the honor to be, Sir, your

> most obedient servant
> Sarah Winnemucca
> Camp McDermit Nev.

PS   please answer this short Epistle if you consider me worthy and I

promise you that my next letters will be more lenghty [sic]. Direct to
Camp McDermit Nev.

Sarah Winnemucca
August 9th 1870[2]

A few weeks later Sarah was found in the railroad town of
Winnemucca by a correspondent from the Sacramento *Record*.
The newspaperman interviewed her and found her to be a well-
informed, wide-awake young woman

. . . and I think the most handsome Piute of her sex that I ever saw.
She conversed freely on the condition of her people and their future
prospects. . . . She said: I am glad to see you, although I have not now
a parlor to ask you into except the one made by nature for all. I like
this Indian life tolerably well; however, my only object in staying with
these people is that I may do them good. I would rather be with my
people, but not to live with them as they live. I was not raised so; . . .
my happiest life has been spent in Santa Clara while at school and
living among the whites.[3]

During this interview Sarah asked that old school books be sent
to her at Camp McDermit, as she and her father and brother
were interested in starting a school there for the Paiute children.

Despite those remarks, Sarah's concern for the Paiutes, which
all her life had overshadowed her destiny, was placed in the
background at this time. She was now twenty-six, but, since she
was a woman of two worlds, it had been doubly difficult to find
a mate. While the Indian men did not share her experience or
education, the whites were mostly repugnant to her, because
she knew that she often represented an exotic, available woman
to them. She was not available in that way, and she made that
clear on several occasions that were reported by the press, as we
shall see.

One newspaper writer stated that Sarah was married for a
time to a German, named Snyder, who died on a visit back to
his home country.[4] We know from Sarah's account that a white
man named Snyder was a friend of Captain Truckee and present
at his deathbed. In any case, this early marriage has not been
confirmed, and Sarah did not mention it in interviews or in her
autobiography.

Marriage entered Sarah's mind in 1870 because a man had
stolen her heart: First Lieutenant Edward C. Bartlett, who was

more expensive to the government to restore order and quiet
after the Indians have once broken out, and it does not require
much provocation to make them do so. I know more about
the feeling and prejudices of these Indians than any other
Person connected with them & therefore I hope this petition
will be received with favor. Sir I am the daughter
of the Chief of the Piutes I am living at Camp
McDermit and have been in this employ of the U.S.
government for nearly three years as interpreter and
guide I have the honor to be, Sir, your
                    most obedient Servant
                    Sarah Winnemucca
                    Camp McDermit Nev

P.S   please answer this short Epistle
    if you consider me worthy and
    I promise you that my next letters
    will be more lengthy Direct to
    Camp McDermit Nev
                    Sarah Winnemucca
                    Augt 9th 1870

Excerpt from Sarah Winnemucca's letter to Commissioner of Indian Affairs
E. S. Parker, who was himself of American Indian descent. (Courtesy of
National Archives.)

a native of New York and a fine horseman. Bartlett had been attracted to Sarah from the first time he saw her. He liked her flashing eyes and quick temper and was drawn to a woman who could mount a horse gracefully and stay in the saddle all day, not expecting any special consideration. He knew that she had a good mind and a keen interest in the politics and the events that were determining the future of her people.

Unfortunately Sarah had lost not only her heart but her senses too. Bartlett, though well liked by his men, was an irresponsible drunkard who took advantage of people with his charming manners and handsome face. Sarah knew this and had heard the story of Bartlett's short-lived command at Camp McDermit, where Captain Henry Wagner had placed him in charge of the soldiers during a brief absence. The lieutenant, instead of taking the responsibility seriously, had gotten drunk and, in a "frenzy of intoxication," had ridden through the Indian camp shooting off his revolver and shouting that the Paiutes had formed a conspiracy and were planning to massacre all the whites. His fellow officers, familiar with his condition, had rounded him up, undressed him, and put him to bed.[5]

Sarah and Bartlett took the stagecoach from Camp McDermit to Winnemucca, where they boarded the Central Pacific Railroad for Salt Lake City. There they were married by a justice of the peace on January 29, 1871. They could not have been legally married in Nevada, where there were laws against miscegenation. Bartlett turned out to be absent without leave from his company, and Sarah had not consulted Captain Wagner before her departure. The marriage was quite unacceptable to Chief Winnemucca and to Sarah's brother Natchez as well.

While still in Salt Lake, after some of her romantic delusions had been torn from her, Sarah knew that the marriage would not work and that she could not prevent Bartlett from drinking away any money that they might possess. From her work at Camp McDermit she had some savings and had bought some good jewelry, which her husband began pawning. A few weeks later, when she was most desperate, Natchez appeared at her hotel in Salt Lake City.[6] Perhaps Sarah had written him to come and bring her home again.

The army registers show that First Lieutenant Bartlett resigned from the army on November 15, 1871, within a year after his marriage. Sarah returned to her position at Camp McDermit and continued her work there, though from that time on her unsettled marital status would add to her personal problems and bring out more of her fiery nature.

A Baptist minister, George Balcom, was slated to take over Major Douglass's position in the Indian Service in Nevada. He arrived with his daughter, Flora, in early March, 1871. His first concern was to find suitable accommodations in Wadsworth for his large family. The house would also have to serve as a church in which to preach the gospel. He made plans for a day school and "sabbath school" at Pyramid Lake Reservation. They were to be established in a storage shed that Douglass had built. He sent a flurry of letters to Washington asking for subsidies to bring the remainder of his family from New York to Nevada, to buy furniture for a home and office, and to acquire a horse and conveyance for his transportation.[7] His letters were always faithfully signed, "Yours with Christ."

On his first visit to Pyramid Lake, Agent Balcom called the Indian men together, and about seventy-five knelt with him while he and his daughter sang hymns and prayed for the souls of the heathens. He used Natchez as his interpreter, but found that many of the Paiutes understood English. He reported to Commissioner Parker in Washington: "I told them I was born and raised a practical Farmer till about thirty years of age was then converted to God 'The Great Spirit' and belonged to Him ever since, and that now in the change of Administration our Governmental father at Washington had sent me to be their Minister and Agent and gave them quite an idea of work, Morality and Religion."[8]

Balcom was not aware that at this time on the Walker River the Paiute shaman Wodziwob was prophesying the return of the Paiute dead. In his trances Wodziwob was receiving signs that great changes would take place for the Indian peoples. He collected many followers, among whom was a Paiute, named Tavivo, who taught his son Wovoka some of the precepts of the new thought. As the prophet of the ghost-dance religion, Wovoka in turn would become a spiritual leader who influenced many

Indian tribes. Thus the Paiutes' discontent with their white-dominated life found a release in a religion of the Indians' own choosing.

On his next visit to Pyramid Lake Agent Balcom discovered that the Paiutes were holding a traditional "fandango," a dance celebration that was religious in nature. Thus Woziwob's influence was spreading. At the same time the preachings of Balcom may also have affected the Paiutes. About twelve hundred of them were encamped at Pyramid Lake in the spring of 1871. Balcom went two evenings and one afternoon to talk, pray, and sing for them. He wrote:

They got impressed with the idea that "God was coming" and are very susceptible of religious things, and very serious even in their monotonous dance, modifying it very much. Their criers go about the circular camp crying "God is coming" and all Indians must stop sinning against Him, by swearing, lying, gambling, chewing tobacco, smoking or keeping dogs. And all promise to break off as fast as possible. . . . Any quantity of them are ready to work to send their children to school. So I increase the rations somewhat, and will take the preliminary step to form a school District and school to begin May 1st."[9]

Unfortunately, Balcom was a naive, impractical man and did not know how to deal with the problems that confronted him as Indian agent. At the time of his arrival the settlers on the Truckee River were disgruntled over a dam that Douglass had built. Though it had a fish ladder, it still seemed to prevent the trout from moving up the river to spawn in Pyramid Lake. On March 27, 1871, Balcom hurried to the telegraph office at Wadsworth with an urgent message to the commissioner: "Two men from Reno have torn out part of dam what shall I do?"[10] Upon closer inspection the agent found that the dam was not materially damaged, even though giant powder had been used.

Two weeks later the agent received a threatening letter from white fishermen in Reno: "Will come down with force enough to take out the Dam and clean out the Indians, there is about 150 men armed and ready to turn out at any moment. . . . etc. N. B. This is no boys play. If you wish to reply address H. C. Reno."[11] Balcom sent for troops and was hopeful that the soldier guards would arrive before any trouble.

On April 29, Balcom sent the following telegram: "About twenty wild indians drove us from reservation House last night soldiers wanted."[12] Then, after sending this missive, Balcom's terror turned to sheepish apologies as he reported in a letter to Parker the explanation for the happenings of the previous night. The agency house had been surrounded by twenty Indians on horseback, who were shooting guns and yelling, "You go away, all." Two farmers, named Bass and McCormick, had been with Balcom inside the building, and the three whites had soon discovered that their own guns were gone: "One my 16 shooting improved Winchester costing me $45," complained Balcom, "the other McCormicks double barrelled shotgun well loaded for any emergency." Balcom confessed:

I locked myself into one room and held the door while the other men parlied with the Indians . . . but I utterly refused to leave (though I confess to the greatest fears of my life) until both the white men come and said they were going and had our horses saddled, so then I left, but as I was passing around the corner of the house an Indian shot at me, no more than 12 feet distant, but I recd no harm. I mounted the Govt horse who took me a mile pretty quick, but in going up a steep hill my saddle girt gave way and let me off dangerously, the horse kicking the saddle off and ran back until caught by friendly Indians who had gathered.[13]

Balcom hid in a "friendly" Indian camp until morning and asked for six escorts back to town. Later in the day Sheriff Doyle of Reno arrived with the missing guns and the explanation: Nugent, the former subagent on the reservation, had furnished the powder and the men to play the part of the wild Indians. They were opposed to the dam and the Indian fishing business.[14] Nugent was only reprimanded over the fiasco.

Agent C. A. Bateman, another Baptist missionary, arrived soon after Balcom's misadventure. His destination was the Walker River Reservation, where he had been assigned to find his field of Christian endeavor. After determining the immediate needs of the Paiutes there in a businesslike way, he made plans for buildings, sought out suitable farm land, and put to work as many Paiutes as he could afford to pay. It was apparent to him that because of a drought the grass seed and pine nuts would not provide sufficient food:

Indian women with their laundry at Hot Springs, Nevada. (Courtesy of Nevada Historical Society.)

No sooner than I commenced operations here in opening irrigating ditches—improving lands and planting etc. etc., than I found three times as many wanting to work as our monthly allowance of supplies would justify . . . and though we were obliged to turn many away before we were aware we found some of them with tools in their hands hard at work that they might thereby receive something to satisfy their cravings for food.[15]

Though Bateman and Balcom were brothers in the American Baptist Home Missionary Society, they did not see eye to eye on many issues. Bateman was distressed to find that Balcom had already overspent the monies available for the agency by $1,500. Balcom had made a trip to California to buy furniture, built a summer kitchen, privies, and a well at Pyramid Lake, and set up a school with a blackboard and a few desks. Bateman had starving Paiutes uppermost in his mind and was particularly upset that he could not purchase more of the supplies that were direly needed. Bateman confided to Commissioner Parker in Washington that the Indians at Pyramid Lake did not like Balcom and therefore came to Walker River to add to his own burdens.[16]

Many of the Paiutes who were normally at Pyramid Lake were observed by the military on the Fall River, in Big Valley, and near Camp Bidwell in northeastern California, collecting roots and hunting game.[17] General E. O. C. Ord, who was commander of the Pacific division, noted, "I think if the Indian Department of Nevada is powerless to give food to the starving Indians, military commanders should be authorized to issue to such in limited quantities, as much less expensive than having to fight them."[18]

At this time Sarah was still concerned about the possible closing of Camp McDermit. She and Natchez therefore made a trip to Carson City. Getting no satisfaction from the Nevada officials, the brother and sister then traveled to San Francisco to interview General John McAlister Schofield. The general was polite and sympathetic, but said that he could not provide a home for the Paiutes at Camp McDermit because only the politicians had the authority to determine what the Bureau of Indian Affairs might do with the Indians in the northern part of Nevada. He concurred with Sarah that Balcom had spent money unwisely on a school-house and the salary of a teacher while her people were starving. He recommended that she and Natchez contact Senator John P. Jones at Gold Hill, Nevada, who would be better able to help them.[19]

Sarah and Natchez returned to Nevada and took the stage up Mount Davidson to the mining town to seek out the wealthy senator. Jones received them. He was apparently concerned, because he asked polite questions, but he made no commitments to help them. Upon their leaving he gave them a twenty dollar bill. Perhaps this salved his conscience, for the portly gentleman did not manage to do anything else for the Paiutes.[20]

While she was still in San Francisco, Sarah had written a letter to General Ord that caused a sensation in Nevada. There were repercussions in Washington as well, as Balcom and Bateman had difficulty explaining the allegations that Sarah made against them. Bateman replied to the inquiries of the Indian commissioner that Sarah was a fake and not the daughter of Old Winnemucca, that she had not been on the reservation and had never held a council with the Paiutes there.[21] Balcom was even stronger in his vehemence against her, questioning her moral integrity rather than addressing the points of her argument.

This was the letter that understandably raised the agents' ire:

E. O. C. Ord. Esq.
Sir:

I have visited your City through the persuasion of my Indian Brothers and Sisters, for the purpose of asking if there is not some way by which our Indians can be provided for during the coming winter, as the dry season has caused a scarcity of Fish and other food which the Indians chiefly live upon. I being Chief Winnemuccas daughter they look to me for help, and I am afraid if there is not some notice taken of this appeal that there will be an insurrection amongst our people.

We held a Council at the Pyramid reservation and there were present sixteen hundred and ninety adults and it is to prevent this trouble if possible that I ask aid. We have asked the Agents of the different reservations to help us, but all to no avail, only to be put off with another promise, so that many of the Indians of the Pyramid reservation having become dissatisfied and being on the borders of starvation, have left their homes and wandered we know not where but they say they will not work for these Agents for by doing so they enrich these Agents, and come to absolute poverty and degradation themselves, and we would all much rather be slain and put out of our misery than to be lingering here, — each day bringing new sorrows — and finally die of hunger and starvation.

We know full well that the Government has been, and is still, willing to provide us with all we need, but I must inform you that it never gets past these Agents' hands, but they reap all the benefit whilst we have all the suffering.

Your's respectfully,
Sarah Winnemucca

San Francisco
July 1, 1871[22]

At about the time when the two agents were required to answer Sarah's charges, Agent Balcom explained to the commissioner that he wished to resign, for his position was not compatible with his higher call as a missionary. He wished to leave Nevada as soon as possible so that he could save his homestead on the Solomon River in Kansas. He hoped to settle his affairs speedily, draw his pay, and then rejoin his family.[23]

After Balcom's departure Bateman did not spare criticism of his administration, for he found that the Indians at Pyramid Lake had been criminally neglected. One Paiute died while he was present, and he ordered a physician to tend the others. He also found the dam broken and the crops beyond saving, though a few Paiutes were bringing in sand by boat, trying to repair the damage. He distributed clothing to them, as they were in tatters.[24]

The attending physician, E. S. Coleman, later noted that Bateman called a "council" of six old Indians on the reservation to make a show of inquiring into Sarah's assertions. The doctor thought it a little singular that Sarah had no notice of such a council, nor did Young Winnemucca, though the chief was at the time only five miles from the council house. Doctor Coleman wrote, "The report of the council is doubtless a curiosity."[25]

Young Winnemucca died in the fall of that year, on October 28, 1871. The agent first claimed that the Paiute leader had heart disease, but changed his story six months later, when he admitted that the chief had died of a lingering consumption.[26] In the *Sacramento Union* of May 16, 1872, Doctor Coleman wrote: "The Chief Winnemucca went up from the Reservation to Wadsworth, laid down in the sagebrush and died there for want of medicine and care. The Indians have no houses, not a single one and in case of sickness are exposed to rain and sun, with no one to care for them." Thus Young Winnemucca—who had held high hopes for the justice of the whites for his people, who had preached peace but was forced to lead his Paiutes in an unwanted war against the whites—had died in destitute and demeaning circumstances.

When the farmer Franklin Campbell at Walker River had become acquainted with the preachings of the shaman Wodziwob, he had told the Indians and the whites that the philosophy was good and no harm could come from it. Indian emissaries visited the reserve from Idaho, Oregon, and the plains states to observe and learn about the new religion. Campbell visited the Indian camp and watched the Indians gather around the shaman while he lay in a trance. They joined in a song that guided the spirit back to the body. When he awoke, the shaman gave a long account of his visit in spirit form to the "Supreme Ruler," who he believed was then on his way with all the spirits of the departed dead to reside again upon this earth and change it into a paradise. Life was to be eternal, and no distinction was to be made between races.[27]

The Paiutes would not preach insurrection. That was against their conservative way of life and not feasible. Still they desired equality and justice, both of which were to be attained, they believed, in the new era to come. In the quiet of the desert, where there were few whites, and where the rugged Sierra loomed large against the baking sun of noon or the low-hanging stars of a clear night, the spirits could seem near, very near, to them.

8

The Modoc War

Sarah continued working at Camp McDermit for almost a year after the breakup of her marriage in 1872. She was no longer employed as a scout but served as the hospital matron, with W. P. Corbusier as attending physician.[1] There are indications that Sarah made attempts to contact Edward Bartlett during this time. Perhaps there was even an effort at reconciliation.[2] Sarah's fall out of favor with her father because of her marriage took a great emotional toll on her. Chief Winnemucca and her people were the focus of her interest and love.

After an argument with Captain Wagner, the commander at Camp McDermit, with whom she had never gotten along very well, Sarah moved in 1873 to Winnemucca, which was eighty miles south of Camp McDermit on the Central Pacific Railroad.[3] She was in need of work, since her ill-fated marriage had taken so much of her funds. As she had a reputation for fine glove making and millinery, she relied upon those skills to support herself. She also acted as interpreter at Battle Mountain in the Shoshoni country of Nevada, while an issue of goods was distributed there.

Sarah ridiculed the agents for the meager issue, calling it "the saddest affair she ever saw," and she noted the abundance of ready-made clothes that were destined to go on farther east to the Indians on the borders of the state. During the issue Bateman arrived and gave the Shoshonis one ton of flour, which was more than Sarah had ever seen him give to the Paiutes. She said to him in front of the Shoshoni agent: "You come up here to show off before this man. Go and bring some flour to my people on the Humboldt River, who are starving, the people over whom you are agent. For shame that you who talk three times a day to the Great Father in Spirit-land should act so to my people."[4]

Sarah's criticism was warranted, but she did not know that in that year of unusually deep winter snows Agent Bateman found himself without funds for the Paiutes because of former Agent Balcom's overspending. Bateman had no response from Washington to his urgent pleas for help, and shipments could not get through the heavy snows in the Rocky Mountains in any case. He had no emergency budget. He did call on General Schofield to help the hungry Paiutes at Walker River Reservation, where the Indians had congregated in large numbers to hear of the coming apocalypse from the shaman Wodziwob. Bateman was given army flour to supply them.[5]

When Sarah returned to the town of Winnemucca, her fiery temper got her into difficult situations. The following article appeared in the *Humboldt Register:*

We witnessed a settlement of a slight misunderstanding between two of the gentler sex of the Piute persuasion, the other day. It seems that one of their sisterhood had been slandering the virtue of Mrs. S. W. Bartlett, who came here to attend the Piute dance. Mrs. Sarah caught her out, and went for her, and such scratching, biting and pulling of hair, we never did see; until, at last, Mrs. Bartlett got her traducer down, and sat upon her, bounced upon her, and at every bounce gave her a lick in the face, exclaiming, "there, talk so about me to white folks, will you?"[6]

Only a couple of weeks later Sarah again made the news. This time she did not wholly succeed in trouncing her foe, for it was a waiter at the Travelers Home:

The trouble occurred in the dining room of the hotel, with no one but the combatants themselves to witness the affair, consequently we can but give the sequel to the transaction. The young man got off with a black eye, and Salley [sic] with a severe jolt in the mouth, which split her lip badly, and caused the claret to flow most profusely. The barkeeper interfered and stopped the muss. Sally rushed across the street to procure a warrant for the arrest of her adversary, but before the papers could be made out, she went into spasms, and soon after was taken in charge by the Indians and carried off to camp. The whites, however, had her conveyed from there to a room at the French Hotel, where she lay for two days in a stupor, apparently more dead than alive. At one time her life was despaired of, but at last accounts however, she was rapidly convalescing. There are, of course, all sorts of rumors afloat. Some say Sally was the agressor, and others that she was not. Some say that she was drunk, while others contend that she never drank. Some who claim to know all about such things say she was drugged, while others who claim to be equally wise, say it was nothing but an overdose of "mad" that caused the stupor. Up to this time there have been no arrests, but it is expected there will be as soon as "Sally goes marching around."[7]

Sarah's volatile nature had been subdued in her earlier years. It was a facet of her personality that would be called upon to help her contend with the stresses of living in two worlds, an unhappy marriage, and the defense of her honor in a frontier society. She was essentially on her own, and she was an object of admiration or contempt, depending on the viewer's attitude toward race and the role of women. As an Indian she had no legal protection of her person or property. At this time she started carrying a small knife for protection.

Because of her prominence in Indian affairs in Nevada, Sarah had become a personage well known to the residents of the state. In the *Nevada State Journal*[8] a writer described her in February, 1872, as a woman of medium height:

 . . . Rather stout, but not too much so, and graceful in all her movements. Her jet black hair hangs in heavy curls, and her sparkling black eyes forbid anything tending to too much familiarity. She dresses very tastefully but not extravagantly—a la Americaine, upon this occasion, in a tight fitting suit of black alpaca, very prettily trimmed with green fringe—in all making a very attractive appearance.

When asked about the delicate question of her age and place of birth she laughed and said that was almost more than she knew herself. This I do know, I was born near the Humboldt Lake. As to the time . . . that it was during Captain Fremont's visit to California when my Grandfather, Captain Truckee accompanied him and took part in the Mexican war then going on.

After brief questioning on her work as a scout and interpreter with the army, Sarah was asked about the reservations. She described the agents as follows:

[They] are too anxious to keep the people down, or from doing anything to help themselves. If let alone they would go to work, as quite a number have done already. Our agent is continually promising farming implements, but they never come. He don't want them for should my people raise their own provisions his place would be worth but little. Then again, I know that the agent has been in the habit of renting the reservations to stockraisers, putting the rent in his own pocket. Last Fall, when I was there, there was an immense number of sheep pastured there. It seems to me high time that the Government should look into these matters, and see that my people shall not suffer that these agents may put money in their pockets.

When questioned about her marriage, Sarah replied:

My folks were very angry at my marriage, my father especially—he says he never will forgive me. They all knew the character of the man—he was nothing but a drunkard. He kept continually sending to me for money after my return home, and I supplied him as long as I could; but what makes me now so bitter against him is the fact that he finally sold all my jewelry. I never want to see him again.

The interview continued as follows:

Reporter—How long since you have seen your father—Winnemucca?

Miss W.—I have not seen him for two years, though he was at Camp McDermit the first of last month. He was so angry at my marriage that, though living but a short distance from me he would never send for me.

Reporter—There has been a report in circulation that he has gone to help the Modocs in Oregon; at any rate, that he has mysteriously disappeared from the reservation with a number of others. Do you know anything of this?

Miss W.—But little. During the late Indian fight in Oregon a cousin of ours, Jerry Long, was reported killed, and my father immediately wrote to my uncles to send him some of the best young men to go over there with him. . . . Quite a number went to him, and I think they went over into Oregon to join the Modocs. The death of Jerry seemed to raise quite a bitter feeling among some of the tribe.

Reporter—Could you have no influence with your people in this matter?

Miss W.—Very little; when once they imagine an insult they seem to lose all reason. . . . I have now told many of the utter foolishness of their taking part in this trouble, and am confident many have remained here through this. I cannot say that I know my father and his braves have gone to the Modocs, but that seems to be the general impression among us.

Old Winnemucca now subsisted with his small band in the Steens Mountain area of southern Oregon (which was known then as Stein's Mountains). He seldom came into Camp McDermit except to council with the soldiers, as rations were no longer provided to the Indians there.[9] There was unrest among the Paiutes, partly because of the recent arrest of two of their people.[10] Natchez was hired by cattlemen from southern Idaho to talk with Winnemucca when it was claimed that depredations had been committed by his band in the area around Steens Mountain.[11]

By the time of the interview with Sarah early in 1873, the Modoc war had raged for over two months. It was an embarrassment to the United States Army, for about 175 Modocs (two-thirds of them women and children) were holding off troops from their stronghold in the Lava Beds in northeastern California and causing many casualties among the soldiers. The Modocs were resisting a return to their reservation at Klamath, where they claimed that they had starved. They wanted their old tribal lands on the Lost River, Oregon for a reservation, but these were denied them.[12]

Both the military and white citizens were apprehensive that other tribes would revolt when they saw the Modocs' success. The interview with Sarah, which indicated that Old Winnemucca might join the Modocs, did not ease anyone's fears. Captain Jack, the Modoc leader, was known to have sold guns and ammunition to Paulina's band of Paiutes in 1865.[13] Would the Paiutes help him now?

A Nevada newsman observed:

For some time many of the old settlers who are familiar with the Indian character have believed that the Piutes, or a portion of the tribe, at least, were secretly aiding the Modocs. They knew all about the death of Canby and the Peace Commissioner within 24 hours after it occurred and before the San Francisco papers, with a detailed account of the affair, reached here. Whether the Piutes have assisted the Modocs or not, it is certain that by a system of telegraphing known to the Indian, they have kept themselves thoroughly posted on their movements and doings.[14]

Lieutenant Colonel Frank Wheaton, commander of the District of the Lakes, recognized Winnemucca's authority among the Paiutes and said that, though the chief was old and feeble, he was the acknowledged head of all the "Piute Snakes" tribe: "I have reason to believe that runners frequently pass from the Klamath Lake Basin to communicate with the heads of Winnemucca's different Bands, and I know they are promptly advised of everything of interest to them that occurs at Military Posts in Southern Oregon."[15] He pleaded for reinforcements at Camp Bidwell, as an unusually large number of Pyramid Lake Indians were in the Surprise valley:

The settlers in all the valleys between Yainax and Camp Harney are reported by several reliable parties to be greatly alarmed and excited dreading an outbreak of the several bands of Pi-u-tes off and on reserves in Southern Oregon. . . . Suspicious conduct of several bands, warrants me in suggesting that Camp Harney be largely reenforced at an early date and that there should be one company at Camp Bidwell as protection to Surprise and Goose Lake Valleys.[16]

One of the officers at Camp Warner in southern Oregon met with the Chief Ocheo, whose Paiutes had left their reservation at Yainax, Oregon (Ocheo had taken over the leadership of Paulina's band in 1867, when that chief was killed). The Paiute assured the Camp Warner representative that his band was not friendly with the hostile Modocs.[17] The officer reported: "We have thus far no occasion to doubt his sincerity, but it is thought his future conduct may be governed in some degree by the attitude assumed by Winnemucca the prominent chief of the tribe."

Sarah had commented to the *Nevada State Journal* reporter in February: "I cannot say that I know my father and his braves have gone to the Modocs, but that seems to be the general impression among us." Her remark was taken up by a Portland, Oregon, paper in April, but much distorted: "Mr. Jones, recently from Camp Warner, reports that Sally Winnemucca, an educated squaw and Government Interpreter at Warner, stated that her father's band (Winnemucca's) was in constant communication with Jack, and that it was agreed that if the soldiers did not whip Jack all the Indians would join in a general war of extermination."[18]

Lieutenant Colonel Wheaton had read the article in the Nevada paper and recognized the original context. He wrote to the assistant adjutant general of the Department of the Columbia:

The Indian Squaw referred to is not and never has been an interpreter at this post [Camp Warner]. . . . I understand she was at one time employed in that capacity at Boise or McDermit in 68 or 69. . . . Her home is near Winnemucca on the C. P. RR and February last I heard of her being in Reno Nevada. . . .

The nearest residence or settlement to Camp Warner is D. R. Jones' stock ranch in Warner Lake Valley, 18 miles from the post. The Indian referred to [Jones] is apt to know her further opinions, as she is living with him or was in March last.[19]

If Sarah was living with an Indian named Jones at this period in her life, she may have married him in an Indian ceremony, but not with any white formality. In a later interview in the *San Francisco Call* of November 2, 1879, she did relate that she was married to an Indian for a short time.

Wheaton's letter continued:

I cannot learn that any proposition has been made to O-che-ho to join other Piute Chiefs in any projected outbreak, but I believe the young men of the different Piute Bands to be greatly excited and elated at the delay in exterminating Jack's, renegade Modocs, and that if Egan their most popular and influential War Chief, or O-che-ho, probably the next best chief among them choose to become disaffected and lead them a very expensive and bloody war would ensue. . . . This Chief, Egan and We-ah-wa all Piute Snakes, Lalake the Klamath Chief, and the renegade Modoc Jack are all firm believers in the Smoholla or new Indian religion which instructs them that the time is not far distant when all dead Indians will be restored to life and that through their aid and the magical efforts of their Chief Medicine Men all white men will be Spirited away and the Country restored to its original Indian occupants.[20]

The curly headed Doctor the principal medicine man of Jack's Modoc Band induced and has through his influence on Jack kept up the Modoc War. O-che-ho cannot be convinced today that a bullet shot at his chief Medicine Man would harm or injure him in any way, and only a few weeks since, he kept a party of incredulous Klamaths waiting three days at his camp while his medicine man was arranging with the great Spirit to catch all bullets fired at him.[21]

On May 15, 1873, Captain Wagner's command from Camp McDermit met Chief Winnemucca at Steens Mountain. Captain Jack's surrender was only two weeks away, and the Modoc shaman's influence over his tribe had been broken by their losses in battle. Winnemucca appeared to have very few followers with him—only about twenty men—but they were young and capable warriors. He reiterated his desire to remain at peace with the whites, but seemed impatient and restless. He asked why troops were moving toward Camp Warner, saying, "There are no Indians that way." Wagner became suspicious that a runner had been dispatched to notify Winnemucca's friend Ocheo that the troops were coming near. There had been continued bad feeling between Winnemucca's band and the settlers around Steens Mountain. Winnemucca asked Captain Wagner to keep the stockmen away because local whites had threatened him.[22]

On June 1, Captain Jack of the Modocs surrendered. After a trial by a military tribunal at Fort Klamath in southern Oregon he and three of his followers were hung for the death of three United States peace commissioners. The remaining Modoc prisoners were sent to the Quapaw Reservation in Indian Territory. General W. T. Sherman telegraphed to General J. C. Davis: "I will submit [prisoners] to the War office for reference to the highest authority with a view to what disposition is to be made of prisoners according to law and Justice. Some should be tried by court martial and shot others to be delivered to the Civil authorities and the balance dispersed so that the name 'Modoc' should cease."[23]

9

Law and Order

Natchez had made a name for himself among the white citizens in western Nevada as a capable Paiute leader who spoke good English and was an excellent interpreter. He helped the Storey County authorities stop Chinese liquor sales to the Indians, and he adjusted difficulties not only between whites and Indians but also between Paiutes, Washos, and other Indian tribes.[1] He aided John Wesley Powell of the Smithsonian Institution in collecting Northern Paiute material goods, such as baskets and hunting paraphernalia, for museum specimens. He also transmitted an extensive Paiute vocabulary to Powell and explained Paiute customs, including burial methods and the marriage ceremony.[2]

In the fall of 1873 the Shoshonis were brought to a big council at Elko, Nevada, so that Agent Bateman could persuade them to go on a reservation. The tribe appeared to be seriously considering the proposition when Natchez spoke to a newspaper reporter about the foolishness of choosing reservation life: "The Truckee reservation [Pyramid Lake] is a cold, unhealthy place and we Paiutes can't be forced to stay there. The Paiutes never receive presents and do not expect any from Agent Bateman."[3] Natchez had observed that the Shoshonis were issued beef, potatoes, blankets, combs, utensils for cooking, and various trinkets. Distribution of goods was now a subject of controversy between Natchez and Bateman, as it had been between Sarah and Bateman.

The Paiutes heard that Agent G. W. Ingalls was distributing blankets at Stone House, a Southern Pacific Railroad stop in the Shoshoni country, nineteen miles west of Battle Mountain. Some of the Paiutes took advantage of the free rail transportation and went there to receive their share. They were perhaps testing the agents to see what would happen. Ingalls told them to go see Bateman.

When they did, Bateman told them that he would have nothing to do with them and that they should see Ingalls. The Paiutes could not understand why they should be so pushed about and get nothing. When they asked for an explanation from Bateman, he forgot his "Christian character and allowed his evil spirit to rise." Natchez "got his injun up" too, and high words passed between them. It seems that Natchez threatened to go to Washington with other Paiute leaders if Bateman would not distribute goods to them as the agents had done to the Shoshonis. Bateman told Natchez that he would have him arrested and sent away from his tribe where he would never come back.[4]

Natchez, worried by that threat, spoke to the editor of the *Humboldt Register* about the altercation. The newspaper people told him that they thought no harm would come of it. Bateman, however, informed General Schofield that Natchez was inciting the Indians against him. Under instructions from Schofield, Captain Wagner came from Fort McDermit, obtained evidence to issue a warrant for Natchez, and then arrested him and delivered him to Fort Alcatraz in San Francisco Bay.[5]

The white community of eastern Nevada came to Natchez's defense. Newspapers headlined the story, blaming Bateman for the trouble:

We have no doubt that the arrest of Natchez was a very needless if not outrageous piece of official tyranny. . . . We suspect the trouble is that Natchez knows too much to suit the purposes of Mr. Indian Agent Bateman. . . . He is not to be galled by any humbuggery of the Agency to which the affairs of his tribe are referred. An Indian Chief . . . who has kept his people in such good relations with the whites, deserves better treatment than he has had—unless, indeed, it is going to be held by the Department that an Indian has no rights that an Agent is bound to respect.[6]

Petitions signed by citizens in behalf of Natchez were forwarded to military headquarters.[7]

Bateman kept up his side in the controversy by passing a petition around Wadsworth. It was signed by about forty residents, and in it Natchez was termed "a pretended chief": "[He is] considered by all a troublesome Indian. . . . and his late arrest by the military was not for the reason of prohibiting him from exercising his rights but for appearances and actions indicative of evil. . . . Said arrest was by the unanimous voice of this community."[8]

On February 9, 1874, Natchez was released from Alcatraz. He came home from the escapade with the new aura of chieftainship about him. He said that he had been treated well at the fort, where he had enjoyed complete liberty. He held a high opinion of General Schofield and all of the officers at the fort. As soon as the Indians heard that Natchez was back, they flocked to see him, and a big celebration was held. Even some Shoshonis came down from Battle Mountain. The Indian community had a new hero, and Bateman had lost face. He was advised by some local newspapers to "bag his head and leave the country."[9]

At the beginning of the new year, 1875, Natchez helped his father and Sarah from a carriage onto a street in San Francisco. Although the noonday traffic was busy, many pedestrians stopped to stare at the dark, wrinkled face of Chief Winnemucca, who was dressed conspicuously in a blue uniform with gold epaulets and braid and a top hat decorated with a feather. He marched straight-backed up the steps with his daughter and Doby John in pursuit. Natchez paid the coachman and followed. Sarah's brother was a tall, good-looking fellow who spoke English well and made friends easily. Sarah must have made amends with her father over her marriage to Bartlett, for now the Winnemucca family trio were in San Francisco to interview General Schofield and advise him of their latest ambitions for the Paiutes.[10]

By this time the general had had previous dealings with all three of the Winnemuccas. He listened while Natchez explained on his father's behalf that the old chief would much rather be supervised by the military than live on a reservation where the agents abused their power and stole what rightfully belonged to the Indians. Every winter had brought some new crisis to the Paiute bands who were no longer cared for by the army. They were forced from the reservations, where little or no food was provided. After one band leader, Ocheo, had agreed to go to the Yainax Reservation in southern Oregon, twenty-five of his people had died there. Captain R. F. Bernard, the commander at Fort Bidwell, could not see how this small band could survive another winter unless the commissary issued rations at the fort.[11]

Chief Winnemucca asked that land be given him near Camp McDermit, where he could look to the soldiers for protection. The old leader wanted the government to give him a start by providing implements and seeds for raising grain. He promised to settle down happily to farming with his people.[12] Schofield, of course, could make him no such promises, and he reminded his visitors that the politicians made all the decisions regarding the future welfare of the Indians. Again it was suggested that the Winnemuccas go to Senator Jones in Gold Hill, Nevada.[13] Sarah remembered how Jones had turned her and Natchez away with a twenty-dollar bill for their trouble several years earlier. Back in the hotel, however, she and Natchez agreed that they would return to the senator. Schofield had been their one hope in San Francisco, and he seemed to be powerless to help them.

On the return train the old chief sat stolidly watching the landscape of the Sierra, as they traveled over the mountains to Reno. His head dropped, and he snoozed occasionally. He had not been able to sleep in the stuffy, noisy hotel room in San Francisco, where vehicles rattled by on the streets. The floor had been uncomfortable where he had insisted on spreading his blankets.[14]

Natchez and Sarah parted company with their father at Reno and took the stage up the mountain to the Comstock diggings. When they were finally admitted into Jones's office, they found that the bewhiskered senator was more rotund than ever. He amiably offered them velvet-covered chairs. This gentleman was the owner of the Crown Point Mine and was reputed to be worth $100 million.

The Winnemuccas repeated the same request with which they had confronted General Schofield: they asked that the Paiutes be alloted land for which they could receive title and that they be taught to be farmers. They used their brother Tom as an example. He had worked in California for some years, and, since he had returned to Nevada, he had done well on his small ranch with the knowledge that he had gained.[15] They suggested that the reservation system be abolished in Nevada and that the Indians be under the sponsorship of the military, who were honest and concerned for the welfare of the Paiutes. The senator was enthusiastic about their suggestions, and he so favored their opinions that he promised to advocate them in Congress.[16]

While in Virginia City, Natchez was invited to dine with several gentlemen. Sarah was interviewed by a reporter of the Virginia City *Territorial Enterprise*, who described her as a "handsome well-formed, intelligent-looking petite young lady with dark flowing hair, spanish eyes and complexion who made use of the 'best English.'" The reporter thought that she looked twenty-two years old rather than the thirty-one that she professed to be. He commented that he had seen her mingling with her tribesmen as they were seated on the ground "engaged in playing the traditional game of 'poker'": "On such occasions she never hesitates to partake of their primitive and homely fare. . . . The friendly feeling manifested by herself towards them has greatly endeared her to the children of the desert."[17]

When they had visited Senator Jones, Sarah and Natchez had represented the Paiutes who did not choose to live on a reservation. At this time others were already committed to reservation life at Pyramid Lake, and they were worried by the recent news that the Central Pacific Railroad planned to sell the best reservation land on the open market. The railroad had acquired every other section of land along its route by an act of Congress, and, as has already been noted, the tracks ran through the most fertile part of the reservation. The company planned to sell this land to settlers: "All the improvements, buildings, ditches, fences and even the lake where the fisheries were found were included in a diagram of the area claimed by the Central Pacific Railroad," according to the report of U.S. Indian Inspector William Vandever to Indian Commissioner A. C. Barstow.[18] White squatters who had been chased off the reservation in past years were now baiting the Pyramid Lake Indians, telling them that they would soon return and take back fields and pastures for their own. Commissioner Barstow, on visiting Pyramid Lake to work out a compromise agreement with the railroad company, found few Indians on the reservation. There was an almost complete absence of houses; no teacher, preacher, blacksmith, or carpenter;

A Paiute camp near the tailings of the Ophir Mine, Virginia City, Nevada. Stove pipes emerge from the traditional smoke holes of the karnees. (Courtesy of Bancroft Library, University of California, Berkeley.)

and, worst of all, no agent. Unbeknownst to the Bureau of Indian Affairs, Agent Bateman for sometime had been living 150 miles away, near Sacramento, California. He had left his son Cephas as farmer in charge of the agency.[19] Soon after that was disclosed, Bateman resigned and nominated a Baptist compatriot, A. J. Barnes, as the new Indian superintendent for the state of Nevada. Barnes proved to be a crook of the highest order; he swindled Indians and citizens alike and was later forced out of office.

After the Winnemuccas' diplomatic efforts with politicians and military officials in San Francisco, Gold Hill, and Virginia City had not secured food for the starving bands, Chief Winnemucca and Sarah came into Camp McDermit with sixty of their people, asking for rations for the Paiutes. Sarah interpreted Winnemucca's long speech to Captain Wagner, and he in turn reported it as follows in a letter to Assistant Adjutant General Samuel Breck in California:

In a treaty entered into in 1867 between his [Winnemucca's] people and General Crook, the General had promised them food and clothing as long as they remained peaceable. They had, he said, been placed on Reservations, but that the Agents had failed to supply them with the promised food, and that some, in consequence, had left the reservations in search of game and other food. That the officers had always failed to keep their word in the treaties he had made with them, although he had never broken faith with them. That when they had been fed by the military it was as "prisoners of war" and that they had never received anything at the Indian Agencies. He said also that as he was growing old and was held responsible by his suffering people for the nonfulfillment of the promises made them, & he begged of the "Captain" (me) to use his influence to procure food for them. He did not ask this himself but for his people his women and children. . . . His people were now in a starving condition, and had only the choice between two evils left them, either to starve or to steal cattle and be shot by the soldiers. He asked again for help, all former wars, he said, had their origin in want of food; he wanted no more slaughter of his people, he was about to return to his home in Steens Mountains, but before leaving he wished to ascertain if his people would be provided for and would ask the Captain to say "Yes" or "No."

I replied to him that I had given heed to everything he had said, that I felt for the condition of his people, but that I was powerless to help them, as it was not within the province of the military to provide for the Indians, but only to protect white men and good Indians and to punish the bad. That the Government supplied the Indian Department with large sums of money to feed and clothe Indians and no doubt if they went to the Reservations and stayed there they would be well cared for. . . . There was no money from which the army could furnish their wants.

But that recently I had received instructions to issue bacon or pork to those who were starving and was now prepared to issue bacon accordingly.

Sarah, at this juncture, asked them if they would eat pork to which they gave a decided negative, adding that so long as there were plenty of cattle in the Valley, they would not eat it and that as a matter of self preservation they would have to help themselves to the cattle.

Sarah then reminded me of experiences with Pork: they had either thrown it into the Creek or used it in their fires. I replied to her, that it was to be presumed, if they were actually starving, they would have eaten the pork, that white men and soldiers had to eat it. To which she answered "I eat it too but I cannot get my people to eat it." She further proceeded to say that her poor people were starving as they had failed to collect roots or seeds last fall, under the impression that they would have been fed by the Government during the winter, and if they could only be fed for a few months it would be a matter of humanity. Her people years since had taken care of poor whites who had come among them, and they looked now to the Government or to the Community for help and if they failed in their appeals, they would be forced into the commission of depredations, in which she would join them, she was quite willing to throw off the garments of civilization she now wore and mount her pony. She remembered the time when the hills surrounding this very camp were swarming with hostile Indians and then and there the officers talked very sweetly to her.

She appealed for her people to those who had the influence, but feared that the majority of those in power would rather spend millions upon some scheme of their own than a few hundreds where humanity called as in the case of her people. She referred to the Modoc war where she said it required several hundred soldiers to defeat about 50 Modocs, and that the soldiers would never have succeeded had the Warm Spring Indians not assisted them.

I again reminded her that her people must not commit any depredations, that I and my command were here for the sole purpose of protecting the settlers and their stock, and would do so at all hazards.[20]

Later, however, Captain Wagner wrote to Breck:

Nothing has occurred which would indicate preparations for hostility on the part of the Indians. Sarah Winnemucca left here a few nights ago on the stage for Winnemucca and Chief Winnemucca accompanied by "Doby John" a sub-chief of the Humboldt band of Indians, departed here on Sunday, the 21st inst. for the north, and as I was informed by them for the Malheur Reservation, Oregon.[21]

After Sarah's departure there was a flurry of letters between General Schofield in San Francisco and his army superiors in Washington, D.C. Since the only surplus army food was pork and bacon, which made the Indians ill, it was finally decided that they would be allowed to barter it for flour with the post trader at Camp McDermit. It would then be baked into bread for the Indians at the post.[22]

On his return from San Francisco, Natchez had gone to Lovelock, Nevada. He resumed making a living for his large family by catching fish in the Humboldt River and selling them in Winnemucca, or he hired out as a ranch hand. Old Winnemucca continued his nomadic life in Oregon. Sarah stayed in Winnemucca, where within a few weeks the *Winnemucca Silver State* commented on her activities. She had gotten into a jealous tussle with another Indian woman.[23] Soon after, she was accused of cutting one Julius Argasse with a knife on the sidewalk in front of the Winnemucca Hotel.[24] Sarah had felt that her dignity was threatened because a man had touched her without permission. He had soon found that she was very able to protect herself.

The "Piute Princess," as the newspapers of the day chose to call Sarah, was put in the county jail overnight. She called in as her defense attorney M. S. Bonnifield, a man who had often befriended the Winnemuccas and the Paiutes. Her case was to be tried next day in the court of Judge Job Davis. The charge against her was assault with intent to do bodily harm. Although a large array of witnesses was subpoenaed for the defense, including several doctors and prominent church members, the case was dismissed before its merits could be evaluated because the knife, upon examination, was found to be of the smallest size.[25]

Some of the Paiutes awaited the decision outside the courthouse. When Sarah and Natchez appeared on the steps of the building, they both talked at length to those who were assembled about white justice and the merits of the court system. Sarah must have been bitter that Indians did not have the right to use the courts in a criminal case nor to testify against whites.[26] Possibly she explained to the waiting Paiutes that that was one reason why the case against her had been dropped: she would have won hands down if it had gone to trial, but, since she was an Indian, the white authorities would not deal with her case.

10

The Malheur Reservation

While riding to Camp Harney in late April, 1875, to spend time with her father, Sarah was thrown from her saddle and dragged through the sagebrush. She sustained no serious injuries.[1] At Camp Harney she stayed with the Paiutes in Old Winnemucca's lodges, enjoying the gambling games at night and the gossip of the women. One night her half brother Lee came from the Malheur agency with a letter for her. It was an invitation from Agent S. B. Parrish to become the interpreter at the Malheur Reservation.[2]

Sarah's first reaction was to say no to the proposal. She wanted no more to do with agents and reservations. Lee told her that Agent Parrish, known as "Sam" Parrish, was a good man who did well by the Paiutes at Malheur, and he encouraged her to take the position. Sarah turned to her father and asked him if he would go with her. He replied that he would, and on the next day they made the long trip over broken terrain to the Malheur agency, which was fifty miles to the east. The Malheur Reservation had been established in 1872, and it was the home for three Paiute bands under Chiefs Weahwewa, Watta-belly, and Egan.[3] Chief Winnemucca and his band of 150 had occasionally spent time there. Sarah gives us the details of the unfolding events at the Malheur Reservation in her autobiography.

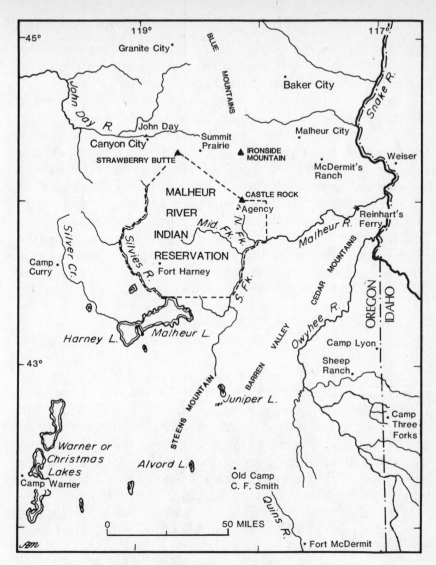

Map 2. *Malheur Reservation and Vicinity*

Agent Parrish was pleased to see Sarah. He gave her a nice room and a salary of forty dollars a month, which she gladly accepted.[4] Soon after her arrival Sarah observed how Agent Parrish treated the Indians. He called a council at which she acted as interpreter while the Paiute men, women, and children crowded around expectantly. Parrish told them that he had come to show the Paiutes how to work. He said that he could not kneel and pray for sugar, flour, and potatoes to rain down, as he was not a preacher. He drew a picture in the sand with a stick to show them his plans for building a water ditch to irrigate their fields, and he told them that crews would be needed for ditch digging and for going to the woods and cutting down trees for fences. Under his guidance the Indians would raise potatoes, turnips, and watermelon and would plant grain as well. They could raise barley and oats, but not wheat, as there was no grist mill at that time. When the crops were mature, they would belong to the Indians, because the land had been given to them by the government. Sarah saw that her people were delighted with the agent's words.[5]

Three young men were needed to learn blacksmithing, and three others to learn carpentry — trades at which they would be able to earn a living. A schoolhouse was to be built so that the young ones could learn to read and write. Parrish said that all the Numa should come to the reservation, where the government had given them a store, food, and clothes, and where they could work and earn a living. "Send out your men everywhere and have them come to this place," he told them.[6]

When the agent was finished speaking, Chief Winnemucca asked the people, "What do you all think of what this man, our new father, says?"

Chief Egan said, "I think it is very good, if he will only carry it out. There has been so much said that has never been fulfilled by our other agent."

Chief Oytes was a shaman and a follower of Smoholla, the prophet of the Dreamer religion. He considered himself to be bulletproof and kept himself apart from white ways. He announced: "I am not going to work. I and my men have our own work to do, that is, to hunt for our children."

When Sarah had translated what each leader had said, Parrish answered Oytes's statement by saying, "All right, Oytes,—you can do just as you like."

Chief Winnemucca rose and said, "My son, Natchez, tells me that if we do not work as we are told by the white people, we will not get along at all. . . . We will all work at whatever our white father says we must work at."

On the next morning all the Indians were ready to work, even those of Oytes's band though their leader was nowhere in sight. Everyone joined in, even old men, women, and children. Most had never done this kind of labor before, and there were not enough tools to go around. In the end people were on their knees, digging with their bare hands. The work continued thus for five days, until Sarah was told by Agent Parrish to bring the people again to a council.

Parrish complimented the Indians on what they had done, but told them he did not wish the old men and women to go to the fields, as it was too hard on them. He must have been aware of a new law passed by Congress that all Indians had to earn their rations (effective March 3, 1875), but he ignored it in the case of the old men. He expected the women to be preparing the meals for the workers.

At the end of six weeks the ditch was 2½ miles long and 10 feet wide. When the task was completed, Sarah again called the Paiutes together. Parrish said to them:

All my people say that you won't work; but I will show that you can work as well as anybody, and if you go on as we have started, maybe the Big Father at Washington will now give us a mill to grind our corn. Do all you can, and I know [the] government will help you. I will do all I can while I am with you. I am going to have a schoolhouse put up right away, so that your children can go to school, and, after you have cut your hay, you can go out hunting a little while and get some buckskins; I know you will like that.

They all agreed happily and went to shake the hand of Sam Parrish and his brother, Charles, as well. Charles Parrish was the reservation commissary. His wife would soon be hired as the reservation teacher.[7]

Samuel Parrish was a hard, efficient worker, and he expected results from the work of the laboring Indians. He was the son of

S. B. Parrish, a pioneer of 1840, who won the Paiutes' esteem on the Malheur Reservation. (Courtesy of the Oregon Historical Society, Portland.)

one of the early Methodist missionaries to the Indians of Oregon. He believed that the Paiutes could better their lot in the space of a few years if the white man kept his word by them, treated them with respect, and cultivated their natural interest in learning.

Sarah's autobiography tells us that the Paiutes next built a road, so that supplies could be hauled in for the winter. Summer had come and gone, and the hay had to be cut. At about this time some Indians from the Columbia River came onto the reservation to trade with the Paiutes for furs and buckskins in exchange for horses. The Paiutes were afraid of being cheated, but wished to have permission from Agent Parrish to trade the hides that they had collected, especially their beaver pelts, which were quite valuable. Oytes was all for trading without permission, and he had swapped for three horses before the day was over.

In the meantime Chief Egan told Sarah of the presence of the Columbia Indians, who, he said, often made trouble and should not come near the reservation. Winnemucca also talked to Parrish about the matter and reminded him how the Paiutes were afraid of Oytes. The shaman had told the Numa the winter before that he had the power to make them ill if they did not follow his wishes. Winnemucca said, "Last winter we had some kind of sickness, and a great many of our children died. He said it was he who was making us sick, and he told us to pay him or else we would all die. Every one of us paid him, but a great many died anyhow."[8]

Parrish discovered that Oytes had taken thirty men from the reservation and joined the Columbia Indians. The group remained away from the Malheur for almost a month. It was soon after Oytes's return that Parrish called a council to pay the laborers for their work. Parrish was liberal, paying the haymakers one dollar a day for their labor, as well as telling them that the hay that had been cut was theirs. He explained that six horses and two mules belonged to the Paiutes on the reserve. He bought the grain that was raised, paying Chief Winnemucca and Egan for it in accordance with his agreement with the people. He announced: "Now I want to tell you something more. If you work for me or any of my men, we are to pay you for it. If you cut or pile wood, we will pay you for it. If I send you to Canyon City for myself or my men, you shall be paid for it." When he asked them if they liked his law, the Paiutes all said, "Truckee, Truckee," which meant "very well."

Parrish reminded them that their potatoes would be ready to dig when they returned from hunting. Then he distributed flour, a can of gunpowder, lead, and caps to each man except Oytes. That night the people were very happy and held a fandango, a celebration of dancing and singing. They were happier than they had been for a long time. Sarah joined them in the hand game and was as deft as any of the players at hiding the sticks while moving them from hand to hand in accompaniment with a rhythmical chant.

After the big hunt the ponies of the men were laden with dried venison. All came in to the reservation but Sarah's father and a few of his people. Winnemucca sent word to Sarah that he was going to the Pyramid Lake Reservation to see the Paiutes there and to encourage them to come to Malheur. Sarah was sorry to see her father leave, for she was afraid of Oytes, as were most of the other Paiutes.[9] Oytes acted strangely. He made signs with his hands and peculiar bowing motions, while he chanted nonsensical sounds and stared at people in an odd way.[10] He shared the belief, along with the followers of young Wovoka on the Walker River Reservation and other Dreamers, that there would be a resurrection of all Indians, at which the wrongs committed against them by the whites would be righted. The Dreamers believed that the mother earth should not be plowed and therefore one should not work as a farmer. Wovoka, however, willingly worked as a ranchhand in Mason Valley, Nevada.

On the day when rations were distributed, Oytes came to Sarah and said: "I want you to talk to your father, as you call him. Tell him I and my men are going to live with our brothers; that is, the Columbia River Indians. I cannot call that white man my father. My father was black, like myself, and you are all white but me, and, therefore, tell him I quit my country."

Sarah said to Chief Egan, who was nearby, that she would go. He offered to go also. When they had ridden a distance from camp, Sarah looked back and saw Oytes. She told Egan, "I am so frightened of that man." "Don't mind him," Egan said. "If he can make you frightened of him that is all he wants, but if you are not afraid of him he will be one of the best men you ever saw." Oytes continued to follow along behind.

When they stopped at the agent's house and went in to talk to him, Sarah told Sam Parrish everything that Oytes had said. Parrish turned to Oytes:

I am heartily sorry that you have such a bad heart. Let me tell you, Oytes, if you want to get your young men into trouble, you can. I have not come here to make you do what you don't want to do. I came to tell you all that government is willing to do for you, and if you will not do it I cannot help you. I have men here to teach you all how to work, and now you want to take your men away with those Columbia River Indians. They are just like you. They don't want to work like other people. Now the sooner you go the better. I don't want to say anything more to you.[11]

The agent told Chief Egan that on the following Monday the Paiutes would be issued rations and that it would then be time for the potato digging. A pit would be dug to store the potatos for future use. An issue of clothing was also made, with which Sarah was delighted. Ten yards of calico plus ten yards of flannel for underwear were given to each woman, and unbleached muslin as well. Pantaloon goods were given to the boys, as well as handkerchiefs, shoes, stockings, and blankets. The men received shirts, pants, hats, looking glasses, and shoes, and they were able to choose the colors of the blankets and shirts that they received. The Northern Paiutes had never been treated in such a fashion before, and they never forgot their kind "father," Agent Parrish.

Although Oytes had not yet left the reservation, he received nothing. Neither did Sarah because she was on salary. Oytes came to her and complained bitterly, and later the same night he threatened the others if they would not give him some of their goods. In March, 1874, Indian Agent H. Linville had sent to Camp Harney for troops and permission to arrest Oytes because he had threatened to massacre the whites on the reservation at that time.[12] Now Oytes told the other Indians that he would kill Agent Parrish. When Sarah heard that threat, she ran to the agent and warned him. The whites on the reserve numbered twelve in all, including children. They prepared themselves for a vengeful attack. As Oytes made no move during the night, Agent Parrish sent for him the next morning. Chief Egan brought him up to the agency house.

Parrish stepped from the porch and told him: "Oytes, I have

three hundred dollars. If you will let me shoot at you, if my bolt won't go through your body the money is yours. You say bolts cannot kill you." The agent then stepped back with his gun cocked.

Oytes fell on his knees and cried: "Oh, my good father, don't kill me. Oh, I am so bad. I will do anything you say. I will do just as my men are doing [and go to work] . I will not go away if you will forgive me."

Parrish replied: "All right, Oytes; don't let me hear anymore of your talk, do you hear? You shall not fool me, and don't say anymore to your own people."

Oytes replied, "No, good father, I will not say anything more," and he and Parrish shook hands. The agent then took him to the store and gave him a blanket and a new set of clothes. He told him to return the goods that he had taken from the others.[13] After that, things went well for Agent Parrish and his charges, and there was mutual trust.

Soon after, General O. O. Howard, military commander of the Department of the Columbia, visited the Malheur Reserve. He was accompanied by his daughter, Grace, who had just graduated from Vassar College. This was the first time that the general met Sarah, and he was favorably impressed with her perfect English, her attractive appearance, and her "air of great self-respect."[14] During the night that he stayed at the reservation, the Paiutes assembled for a fandango and kept up their singing, dancing, and drumming so that the general had many wakeful hours. He was particularly worried for Grace's safety and called Sarah to the agency house to ascertain if the Indians were giving a war dance. She laughed and replied that they were merely celebrating his presence on the reservation and were performing the ritual in his honor. Howard rested more soundly during the remainder of the night.

Reporting on his observations at Malheur, Howard sent a telegram to the adjutant general: "Have just visited Malheur Indian Agency. Think it very important that present Agent be continued. Indians whites and army officers commend Parrish for successful management of remote and difficult agency. Please inform Commissioner of Indian Affairs."[15]

Despite the commendation of Howard and the warm acceptance of the Paiutes, Parrish received criticism from other quar-

Old-style nobees alongside canvas tents in a Paiute encampment. (Courtesy of Nevada Historical Society, Reno.)

ters. He had extended the limits of the reservation to ensure that the richest farming land, two hot springs where the Paiutes had traditionally bathed, and the land claimed by Chief Egan and cultivated by him would be a part of the reservation. Settlers' petitions to senators complained of the loss of land to the Indian Department, and anonymous letters of criticism in local papers did not help the standing of Parrish.[16]

Through the winter the Numa continued to work. They dug another ditch, which was 2½ miles long. One evening, when they had about half a mile to finish, Parrish called a council and told the people that they had 292 enemies in Canyon City. G. B. Curry was the leader of a group who wished to take the west end of the reservation for their own. Parrish told them, "These white men have talked to your Father in Washington, saying that you are lazy, and will not work."

Leggins and Egan said: "Our Father, you are here to talk for us. Tell our Big Father that we don't want to give up any of our reservation. The Pyramid Lake Reservation is too small for us all, and the white people have already taken all the best part of it. . . . We do not want to have white people near us. . . . We know what they are, and what they would do to our women and daughters."[17]

Parrish promised to write Washington and see what could be done. In the meantime work progressed on the school house. The carpenter finished the building in early spring. The Indian Department complained of the large number of employees on the reservation. The agent had hired his sister-in-law, Mrs. Annie R. Parrish, as teacher and Sarah Winnemucca Bartlett as her assistant.

Parrish defended his expenditures in a letter to Indian Commissioner E. P. Smith:

The number of scholars as you will observe is increasing and the indians are all taking a great deal of interest in the same. We have added an industrial branch to the school in which the boys can learn something about farming and the girls can learn to sew and make up their own clothing in good shape. My intention hereafter is, instead of making issues of cloth, to compel the women and girls to come to the school house and make up all their clothing there under the immediate instruction of the teachers and I think that enough can be saved to the government from material thus saved to almost pay the salaries of the teachers.[18]

He wrote the Department of Indian Affairs that Sarah was especially needed, as she could speak both languages.

The official opening of the new school house was on a glorious day in May, 1876. Mrs. Parrish, the well-loved teacher, brought her organ into the new building, and, with the windows thrown open, the people who gathered outside could hear the singing of the children. All the white employees sang as well. It was a joyous crowd.

Little Mattie, an orphan child and a niece of Chief Egan's, was especially enthralled by Mrs. Parrish.[19] Though she could not as yet understand the English language, Mattie recognized her as a kindhearted woman and a good teacher. The "white lily," as Mrs. Parrish was called by the children, brought to the classroom bright pictures of animals and natural scenes, upon which the students of various ages feasted their eyes. When she used a large wall map to introduce the children to the idea of the United States, the students thought that the land must be red, green, yellow, and blue, as it was on the map. Once Chief Egan himself came to the classroom and told the students that they should listen well to the teacher because it would help them greatly to speak and understand English and to know more about the white world.[20]

Sarah observed and learned a great deal from Mrs. Parrish's teaching methods. In her autobiography she explains that, after teaching in the morning, she and Mrs. Parrish cut out dresses and skirts in the afternoon for all the women of the tribe, and the women were occupied in making them up. Each of the young schoolgirls made a dress and a skirt for herself, as well as garments for the blind and those who were too old to do for themselves.[21]

Parrish was very proud of the Paiutes and what they were accomplishing. Ninety acres of newly plowed fields had been sown, and fences now protected the fields from roving stock. When a letter critical of Parrish appeared in a local paper, the agent wrote to General Howard that the "alias," or anonymous, writer was misinformed about the number of Indians on the reservation and that it was utterly false that the Paiutes had stolen horses:

Now General, you will pardon me for saying anything about the above mentioned correspondence but when I am laboring faithfully and doing the best I can to raise up and improve these indians, and make them a home that will be a comfort to themselves and a pride to the Department, it makes me mad to have some irresponsible person under an alias assail me in the daily prints and virtually call me a thief.[22]

Seven days later President Grant appointed W. V. Rinehart, former army officer, as the new agent for the Malheur Reservation. When Parrish told the Paiutes that he was leaving, they were distraught. Oytes got up and said, "We will not let our father go; we will fight for him. . . . We have made no complaints against him. We will all stand by him. He has taught us how to work, and that's what we want, and the white lily is teaching our children how to talk with the paper, which I like very much. I want some of the young men to go and tell our father Winnemucca to come here as soon as he can. I know he will think as I do. I say once more, we will not let him go."[23]

Sarah told Parrish everything that was said by the Numa. In reply he told her to tell them that it was not because he had done anything wrong that he was being sent away, but because he was not a Christian, and all the reservations were to be under the Christian men's care. "Before I go," he said, "I am going to plant for you, and help you all I can. I will give Egan and Oytes land for peas; Oytes, just on the other side of the river for him and his men, and Egan at the Warm Spring . . . and . . . Jerry Long [sic] and Sarah Winnemucca, and others, on this side of the river. . . . Your new father will not be here until the first of July." Jerry Long was a blind cousin of Sarah's. She had asked Parrish to take him on as interpreter in her stead because he had a family to support and could not do other work. She meanwhile was employed as Mrs. Parrish's assistant in the school house. The Numa set to work. Parrish told them that they could plant whatever crops they desired.

When Chief Winnemucca arrived from Pyramid Lake Reservation, Sarah took him to Parrish. The old man took the agent's hands and said, "My good father, you shall not leave me and my people. Say you will not go."

He answered: "It is not for me to say. I would like to stay, but your Big Father in Washington says that I must go, and that a better man is coming here. You will like him, I know."

Winnemucca told him: "I do not want anyone but you. I am going to see the soldier-father tomorrow. I know they will keep you here for me, or I think they can if they wish to."

Parrish said, "They can do nothing against the government."

Winnemucca sat for a long time without saying a word. Then Parrish said, "Come with me, Winnemucca, I want to give you some things."

Sarah accompanied them to the storehouse, but when they got there, she noticed her father standing in one corner of the room as if he were lost. When Parrish asked him what kind of clothes he wanted, Winnemucca replied: "I don't want anything if you are not going to stay with me. I don't want anything from you, because it will make me feel so badly after you are gone."[24] Sarah had to explain to her father that the agent would not understand if he did not take the gifts, for that was the way of white people if they were to part; the whites even kept pictures of those who had died. The old man then accepted the clothing.

On the next day Sarah, Chief Winnemucca, Egan, and Oytes went to see the officers at Camp Harney. Sarah and her father stayed with a friend, a Mrs. Kennedy, until they could speak to the commanding officer, Major John Green. When the major received them, he thought that they had come to complain about their agent in the same way that they had about the previous one. Instead Winnemucca said:

We all like our good agent Parrish. . . . There can be no better man than he, and why send him away? Oh, my good soldier-father, talk on paper to our Big Father in Washington, and tell him not to take him away. I have a reservation at . . . Pyramid Lake. For so many years not one of the agents ever gave me or my people an old rag. I am just from there. My people have nothing to live on there but what little fish they catch, and the best land is taken from them. A great many of my people . . . say they will come here to make homes for themselves.[25]

The major agreed to send a letter to Washington and tell the officials what the Paiutes had said. Then he turned to Sarah for more information. Although he was quite sympathetic with the

Indians' plight, there seemed to be little that he could do. He did, however, make the following report on May 26, 1876, to the assistant adjutant general of the Department of the Columbia:

I have the honor to report that the Indian Chief Winnemucca paid me a visit yesterday, and the first question he asked was whether I knew why Mr. Parrish (Indian Agent) was to be removed: I told him I did not know the reason. He then went on to say that Mr. Parrish was doing so much for the Indians in the way of teaching them how to raise crops, that he thought it would be a great wrong to remove him when he was doing so much good. He described how much work had been done at the Agency since Mr. Parrish had assumed control. Winnemucca also says: That if they had had such an agent as Mr. Parrish, the war with General Crook would not have occurred; that all the Indians like him except two. . . . It seems to me strange to remove an agent who is doing so much for the Indians and one whom they are so unwilling to lose.[26]

Sarah and her father returned to the reservation and told Parrish what had transpired. He laughed, but Sarah was apprehensive about what might come. On June 28, 1876, Major Rinehart arrived, and, after Parrish had spent a day showing him the reservation and the plots of land belonging to their various owners, he said good-bye to the Numa. That was the last they saw of him.

11

Trouble at Malheur

During the summer of 1876, Sarah concerned herself with the problems that inevitably were to come between the Paiutes and the new agent at Malheur. She also attended to some personal business. She had married Edward Bartlett more than four years before, and in all that time they had lived together less than one month. Now she had fallen in love again, with a man named Joseph Satwaller, and she had decided to file for a divorce from Bartlett. Little is known of Satwaller except that he was a resident of Grant County, Oregon, where the Malheur Reservation was located.

Sarah started proceedings against Bartlett on July 10, 1876. A summons for her husband was printed in the *Dalles City* (Oregon) *Mountaineer* for a six-week period, since Grant County had no regularly published newspaper. Bartlett did not appear, and on September 21 the divorce was granted in the circuit court of Grant County. Charles Parrish, the former agent's brother, acted as Sarah's counsel. Although Sarah had not been allowed her day in court in the assault case in Winnemucca, Nevada, she was able to file divorce proceedings. Civil cases involving Indians were regarded differently from criminal cases, which were traditionally handled by the federal government.

At the divorce proceedings Sarah testified that she had sent

Bartlett money through the Wells Fargo & Co. express, but he had never written her, and that he never sent her money. She was quoted as saying: "We never quarrelled any before we separated. I was kind to Defendent, during our marriage and he was kind to me only he spent my money. And Defendent took my jewelry worth about $700.00 and pawned it for $200 at a pawnbrokers shop and spent it. I never got a cent of it. This was jewelry I had before I was married."[1] Sarah paid the court costs of $69.62 to regain the name Sarah Winnemucca.

Major W. V. Rinehart was an old soldier who had been in command of Fort Klamath in 1865, when the first Northern Paiute bands had accepted a treaty and agreed to live on the Klamath Reservation.[2] He was a proponent of an extermination style of warfare. In later dealings with General O. O. Howard, Rinehart spoke derisively of the "religious idiocy" of Howard's lenient policy toward Indians.[3] Rinehart believed in following the letter of the law and would not budge in his fervor to keep the Paiutes subservient to his disciplined administration. Authority was the principle tool with which he knew how to deal with others, and, when his authority was breached, even by a child, he became irrationally brutal. He pulled the ear of a young boy, knocked him down, and kicked him because he had laughed in response to an order. Sarah explained that the child did not understand English, but that was irrelevant to the major. Soon another boy was imprisoned and threatened with hanging because he had showed disrespect.

At the first council that Rinehart held, Egan and the other tribal leaders learned that Rinehart's attitude and policies toward them would be very different from those of the well-loved Agent Parrish.[4] Major Rinehart told them how he had come to make them good people and that the land on which they lived belonged to the government and not to the Paiutes. The government would, however, give them money for their labor, paying them one dollar a day for men, women, and boys. Rinehart said, "This is what the Big Father in Washington told me to tell you."

Egan protested, "The man who just left us told us the land was ours, and what we do on it was ours, and you come and say it is government land and not ours.[5] According to Sarah, Rinehart then became angry and said, "Egan, I don't care whether any of you stay or not. You can all go away if you do not like the way I do."

The Paiutes then went to work to test the agent and see if he would pay as he had promised. At the end of the week, on Saturday, the people walked right from the fields to the agent's office to get their money. They soon learned that Rinehart meant to pay in goods, not cash as he had promised, for he started putting up signs: blankets, six dollars; pants, five dollars; shoes, three dollars; and so on. He told Sarah, "The rations they have had are worth about four dollars a week, and then they have two dollars left to get anything they want out of the storehouse."[6]

When the Numa saw how they were to be paid, many got up and left. The white employees meanwhile were walking around in new clothes from the storehouse. Egan rose and said:

Why do you want to play with us? We are men, not children. We want our father to deal with us like men. . . . Don't say you are going to pay us money, and then not do it. If you had told us you wanted us to work for nothing, we would have done it just as well [as] if you had said, "I will pay you." . . . You did not say anything about the clothing nor about what we ate while we were working. I don't care for myself, but my men want their pay, and they will go on with their work just the same. Pay them in money, and then they can go and buy whatever they like, because our Big Father's goods are too dear. We can go to our soldier-fathers, and get better blankets for three dollars than yours. You are all wearing the clothes that we fools thought belonged to us, and we don't want you to pay anything."[7]

Rinehart lost his temper and cried: "If you don't like the way I do, you can all leave here. I am not going to be fooled with by you. I never allow a white man to talk to me like that!"

That night in council many of the leaders said that they wished to go to Camp Harney to complain about their new agent, but Sarah advised that they wait a while. The council reluctantly agreed. Soon after, Egan and Oytes's men came to have a talk with Rinehart. Egan said, "My children are dying with hunger. I want what I and my people worked for; that is, we want the wheat. We ask for nothing else, but our agent Parrish told us that would be ours."

Rinehart replied, "Nothing here is yours. It is all the government's. If Parrish told you so, he told you lies."

Sarah then asked Rinehart why he had not spoken up when Agent Parrish had been there and was showing him around. Parrish had told Rinehart where each Paiute had land and had raised crops. She had been present and had not seen Rinehart make any objection to Parrish's arrangements. "Why, if you take the government wheat, you rob the government," Rinehart replied.[8]

Egan rose and told Sarah, "I want you to tell everything I say to this man. Then he made the following speech:

Did the government tell you to come here and drive us off this reservation? Did the Big Father say, go and kill us all off, so you can have our land? Did he tell you to pull our children's ears off, and put handcuffs on them, and carry a pistol to shoot us with? We want to know how the government came by this land. Is the government mightier than our Spirit-Father, or is he our Spirit Father? Oh, what have we done that he is to take all from us that he has given us? His white children have come and have taken all our mountains, and all our valleys, and all our rivers; and now, because he has given us this little place without our asking him for it, he sends you here to tell us to go away. Do you see that high mountain away off there? There is nothing but rocks there. Is that where the Big Father wants me to go? If you scattered your seed . . . there, it will not grow. . . . Oh, what am I saying? I know you will come and say: Here, Indians, go away; I want these rocks to make me a beautiful home with! Another thing, you know we cannot buy. . . . We have no way to get money.[9]

When Egan sat down, Rinehart replied, "You had better all go and live with the soldiers. What I have told you is true, and if you don't like what the government wants you to do, well and good; if I had it my way I could help you, but I cannot. I have to do government's will."

The uneasiness and misunderstanding of the Paiutes increased when Rinehart began giving only vouchers instead of giving goods or rations in payment. His supplies fell very low because the Indian Department did not process an order that he had placed soon after his arrival until after the first snow had fallen.[10] Starvation was imminent, and it appeared to be the result of Rinehart's evil doings.

Sarah took a short trip into Canyon City before the snows were too deep for her to travel. She was accompanied by Joseph Satwaller to the courthouse, where they obtained a license and were

W. V. Rinehart, the last Indian agent at Malheur, whose tactics increased the discontent of the Northern Paiutes. (Courtesy of Oregon Historical Society.)

married on the same day, November 13, 1878,[11] in the home of Charles Parrish. Sarah did not write of this short-lived marriage in her autobiography, nor does it seem to have been generally known that she had married again. "The white Lily," Annie Parrish, was a witness, and the three Parrish children watched the ceremony, which was performed by a justice of the peace. Apparently Sarah returned to the reservation after only a short honeymoon, for she, Egan, and some other Paiutes rode to Camp Harney in the middle of November to complain about Rinehart to Major Green.[12]

When the major came to investigate the Paiutes' condition at Malheur, Egan was the chief spokesman. He told Green that the Paiutes had to work for all their issues and asked if this was the new rule of the government. He also said that no blankets were available at the agency, nor clothing of any kind, and people were very cold. They had been promised sugar for the sick, but received none. Egan observed that they never knew what to expect of the government.[13]

Major Green then explained that it was the law that all male Indians between the ages of eighteen and forty-five must work for all the goods and food that was issued to them. He told them that they ought to send their children to school so that they could learn to read and understand the law themselves. Then they would not have to depend on others to explain it to them. If they went to the agency doctor, they could get sugar if he prescribed it.[14] Most of the Indians preferred the remedies of their own medicine men.

After the council and investigation the major wrote his superiors that he could find no fault with Agent Rinehart except if "it be a fault that some of the Indians do not like him. Egan came to my tent after the interview, and said he was glad I had come, that he believed I had told them the truth and that he would go to work again with a good spirit."[15]

There was no school for the children to attend as Major Green had advised. It had been closed soon after Rinehart's coming, and Sarah no longer worked there. The agent had fired Sarah shortly before she had gone to Camp Harney with the chiefs to lodge a complaint against him. He found that she had written several letters against him, and he felt that she had kept the

Paiutes discontented. Her cousin Jerry Long was hired as interpreter in her place.

Sarah stayed at Malheur for a few weeks, trying to sell a stove
for which she had paid fifty dollars. In the end she had to leave
it to Rinehart, who enjoyed its warmth but would not pay her
for it. He wrote a letter to General Howard complaining that
Sarah was an unfaithful employee who had counseled and encouraged disobedience to the law: "The want of supplies at the
Agency and the protracted delay in procuring more was easily
turned to account by her in the attempt to engender dissatisfaction among the Indians. . . . Most of the real trouble and all the
reported or imaginary threats of the Indians are believed to have
originated with this unfaithful employee."[16]

In Sarah, who had worked diligently in the interests of her
people, Rinehart had found a scapegoat to blame for his agency's
troubles. Meanwhile, as she left the agency to join Joseph Satwaller, she undoubtedly held high hopes for her new marriage.
It was not to be a success, however, though no details of the
relationship have come down to us. Rinehart indicated in a letter
to General Howard that she and her husband lived at the Warm
Springs agency for a time.[17]

In the following months Agent Rinehart became increasingly
concerned about the bands of Paiutes who refused to come to
live on the Malheur Reservation and those who worked as farm-
hands on white ranches. It was an embarrassment to his administration that he had so few Paiutes on the reserve when he was
supposed to be issuing to at least 700 people. He went himself
to Steens Mountain to talk to Chief Winnemucca, but the old
chief would not return to the Malheur. He proudly showed Rinehart a letter that had been written for him on buckskin by Judge
Bonnifield of Winnemucca. It stated that he desired a new home
on the Owyhee River in eastern Oregon, where he proposed to
engage in farming and stock raising with all his people. The
agent wrote the Indian Department: "In his visions of the new
El Dorado on Owyhee the old man is very enthusiastic and will
likely lead most of his people away from this Reservation for a
time at least, as they seem to imbibe the spirit of his adventure
and partake of his hallucination."[18]

In June, in northern Oregon, Chief Joseph and his Nez Percé

tribe refused life on a reservation, and war ensued. At Malheur, Agent Rinehart, frightened by the prospect of hostilities, collected guns and ammunition and sent his employees to safety. The Paiutes were also alarmed. They returned to the reservation in considerable numbers. It was unsafe away from the agency during wartime because the frontiersmen needed little excuse to take a potshot at an Indian.

Chief Winnemucca, however, still did not return to Malheur, and rumors circulated that his band had crossed the Snake River and were on their way north to join the hostile Nez Percé.[19] The cavalry companies at Fort McDermit were ordered to the front. There was considerable speculation that there would be a local Indian uprising while the soldiers were occupied elsewhere. The settlers took some comfort in the knowledge that Natchez was staying on his ranch near Lovelock and working as usual. The big Indian sent a telegram to General McDowell, saying: "No truth in reports of Piute hostility. Winnemucca my father at Idaho wants me and Chiefs talk with you danger that whites may make trouble for their own benefit—Pay expenses of me & chiefs to come and talk at San Francisco—answer immediately."[20]

General McDowell declined to send for Natchez, explaining that he had no resources to pay his fare, but he thanked him for confirming his own judgment that the Paiutes would remain peaceful. In the meantime, in Idaho, Old Winnemucca conferred with Governor Mason Brayman and told him of the Paiutes' peaceful intentions. He and some of his men were feasted by the governor as guests of honor.[21] Winnemucca returned in triumph to Oregon, but he was immediately challenged there by Oytes,[22] who was jealous because Winnemucca had paraded himself among the whites in Idaho as the chief of all the Paiutes. The old man had never been accepted very wholeheartedly on the Malheur Reservation by Oytes's band, who looked down upon Winnemucca's people as the "rabbit hunters" of Nevada. Oytes was a shaman of the Wadatoka band, whose wanderings had always been centered in the vicinity of Malheur.[23] He was sympathetic to Chief Joseph and the Nez Percés. Rinehart wrote to the commissioner of Indian affairs:

It appears that those bands who have lived along the Blue Mountains [in northern Oregon] and followed the deer, antelope, and bear chase for a livelihood are disposed to look upon the rabbit hunters of the sage plains of Nevada as an inferior people, and treat them accordingly—telling them this is not their country. Prompted by a feeling of independence of their less civilized Snake Brethren, the Piutes under Winnemucca are looking out for a new home of their own.[24]

One of Winnemucca's biggest objections to living on the Malheur was the presence of Oytes, who, as we have seen, threatened other Paiutes with the power of his Dreamer cult and the practice of witchcraft, which they generally believed could cause sickness and death. Winnemucca's interpreter at this time, Charlie Thacker, had been raised and educated by a white family, but he, also, shared Winnemucca's respect for Oytes's magical abilities.[25] Rinehart sent a special agent, William M. Turner, to seek out the old chief in another effort to get him back to the Malheur. Even though Turner promised that Agent Rinehart would put a stop to Oytes's 'black art,' he too could not convince Winnemucca.[26]

Still pursuing his old dream of land on the Owyhee River, Chief Winnemucca once more visited San Francisco, accompanied by Natchez and several other Paiute leaders from Virginia City and Churchill County, Nevada. He was still vigorous; his hair, cut short, was only slightly sprinkled with gray. While interviewing General McDowell, he wore a soldier's uniform coat with a double row of buttons, cavalry pants with broad yellow stripes down the sides, a pair of huge epaulets, and his usual felt hat adorned with a large, black plume.[27]

Through Natchez, who acted as interpreter, Winnemucca explained that he was now an old man, too old to fill the onerous position of chief of a tribe numbering over 700 people, and that he wanted the government to grant him a reservation for himself and about 40 of his tribe, who were willing to cast their lot in with his. In addition to this he wanted a company of cavalry stationed on the reservation to keep the peace between him and the other Indians and between the Indians and whites. Since he was too old to fight, he would have to stand between the two factions and let them fight over his head. He wanted to have land given him, so that he could plant grain and raise stock. He had always been a good friend of the white man and had used his influence on the side of peace on all occasions when trouble seemed imminent.[28]

General McDowell told Winnemucca that he already had an

agent, Rinehart, and he would have to apply through him to the Indian Department for the land that he wanted; the military authorities could do nothing. There were at this time two companies of cavalry and one of infantry at Camp Harney; they represented all that could be spared for the region. The general advised the chief to return to his reservation at once.[29]

When the party returned to Winnemucca, Nevada, Natchez was interviewed by a reporter of the *Daily Silver State*. He observed "No Indians can get anything from the government if they behave themselves." The reporter agreed that "the Piutes for years have been peaceable and it seems that because they are so, they receive no favors from the Indian Department."[30]

Winnemucca's band and that of his friend Ocheo of Surprise Valley, California, continued to show their unwillingness to come onto the Malheur Reservation. This rankled Rinehart, who claimed that they were pulled away by the free food at Fort Bidwell and Fort McDermit and the nightly fandangos, which he called a "species of brothel-dance."[31]

These allegations of Rinehart's quickly solicited responses from the officers stationed at Bidwell and McDermit. They testified that the Indians had not been given subsistence at the military camps for years and that they seldom saw Ocheo and Winnemucca. Captain Wagner of Fort McDermit wrote, "For the past three years the 'Old Chief' with his personal band of about 50, all relations, camped portions of the time on the Owyhee River near the Idaho line—there they subsist by fishing and hunting."[32]

Wagner called in Ocheo, who made a sympathetic appeal "to be let alone," which Wagner reported as follows:

He was harming no one, he asks for no assistance from the Government or the settlers, this is his home, he was born at this very creek—pointing to a creek east of the garrision—his father and mother are buried but a hundred yards from here. He has a ranch about four miles from here, with land fenced in and under cultivation, whereon he was raising potatoes and grain: during the winter he was hunting game in Warner Valley and Mountains. General Crook and all the former officers at Camp Warner and this post told him that he was all right as long as he behaved himself. He does not want to go on a reservation, and will not go.[33]

General Crook confirmed Ocheo's statement. He warned McDowell that this band of Surprise Valley Paiutes was well armed and that the country they occupied was difficult of access. If they chose to resist, they would be as determined and as difficult to overcome as the Modocs. McDowell suggested to the War Department that they be slow to yield to any efforts that might be made toward the military to coerce Ocheo's band onto the Malheur Reservation.[34]

As for Winnemucca, he visited the Malheur once again and asked that Rinehart work on his behalf for the land he coveted on the Owyhee. Rinehart would not support him in his purpose and told the old chief, "Since you are not satisfied at Pyramid Lake Agency and do not like Malheur, now your people are vagabonds without homes or property and they soon will be without friends and regarded as worthless." He did offer him a location at the confluence of the north fork of the Malheur River with the main river, fourteen miles below the agency. Winnemucca indicated that he would consider the offer if he could have the use of agency teams and tools to build a road to the place. Rinehart agreed. On the next morning the agent discovered that Winnemucca's band had suddenly left the reservation. Oytes had as usual threatened the old man and his people. As a result it was unlikely that he would ever bring his band to the reserve.[35]

All the Paiutes on Malheur Reservation were seriously discontented. Their unhappiness was not caused by the connivings of Oytes, who was avoided as a shaman of power, but by the administration of Rinehart. The latter never deviated from his policy of giving issues only to working Paiutes, no matter how great the need.

Chief Egan expressed his animosity to a saddler in the cavalry at Fort Harney, who passed on the information to United States Senator Newton Booth, who he thought might take an interest in the Paiutes' plight. He wrote:

From what I have been able to learn, not alone from the Indians themselves, but from white men as well, the cause of the discontent in this locality, is due to the rascally treatment the Indians receive at the hands of the Agent Rinehart. . . . The Agent has upon his "Rolls" between 600 or 700 Indians, for which he draws "Government Allowances" that of this number, he issues scanty allowances to such as work for him (the Agent) upon his farm. . . . Ehgan, the "War Chief" of the Payutes. . . . cannot speak english [sic] very well, but from the interview I had with him, I am Strongly inclined to the belief that he does not

Camp Harney, Oregon, during the winter of 1872. (Courtesy of Oregon Historical Society.)

propose to bear this sort of treatment much longer. I could read his determination in his countenance.[36]

In mid-April, 1878, after a church service conducted by Rinehart, several tribal leaders, including Egan, accused the agent of concealing from them the state of affairs at the Fort Hall Reservation in Idaho. Oytes told the agent that the Paiutes were afraid that soldiers would come and take away their guns and ponies as they had those of the Bannocks at Fort Hall. Rinehart replied that General Crook was at Fort Hall investigating the trouble and that, if they wanted, he would send for him. He said that they should not listen to the reports of trappers and squawmen, but wait for the full report from the general.[37]

Meanwhile the intruders' stock were grazing on the Malheur Reservation in large numbers, and the ranchers made no secret of their intention to take up residence on the Malheur.[38] At the request of the Indian Department, Rinehart reluctantly produced figures that showed that squatters maintained 545 horses and 10,720 cattle on the reservation and that they had also cut eighty tons of hay.[39] Winnemucca, Oytes, and Egan were aware that the citizens of Harney Valley had signed a petition to acquire the most fertile land on the western boundary of the reserve.[40] The chiefs complained that the area was their only source of the camas root, a staple much like potato on which the Paiutes depended; the settlers' contention that the Indians had no use for this part of the reserve was absurd. The chiefs again took their complaint to Camp Harney.

Finally, under pressure from the military, the Indian Department requested the removal of the settlers and their stock. When news of this decision reached the squatters, Rinehart found that the ranchers, not surprisingly, were suddenly interested in leasing the land. First J. W. Scott came forward and offered $100 as a deposit on a lease for Harney Valley. On the same day a Mr. Devine of Todhunter and Devine, who had signed the settlers' petition, upped Scott's offer by a proposal to rent 500 square miles of the reservation at $200 annually. The proposal included all of Harney Valley and the Crow Camp country.[41] Two days later J. W. Scott was back with a better proposition than Devine's: $1,500 per annum, paid in advance, for the use of the same acreage that Devine had requested for a five-year period.[42] Rinehart recommended that the department accept the terms of Scott's lease because the Indians had no immediate need for the land except for hunting, root digging, and fishing, and the cattle would not intrude upon those activities. A day later Rinehart granted authority to Peter French to cut the timber on the reservation, which was to be used for building and repairs at Camp Harney.[43]

For all his faults, Agent Bateman on the Pyramid Reserve had at least consulted Young Winnemucca and other Paiutes when there were major decisions to be made regarding the reservation. Such a course never entered Rinehart's head. He considered that his charges were incapable of making such decisions concerning the land that was their home, and he maintained that they were on the reservation only "through the courtesy of the United States Government." But, as it turned out, sudden events were to lead to a new crisis, in which the eviction of squatters, or the leasing of land to cattlemen, became of minor consequence to Agent Rinehart.

12

The Beginning of Hostilities

In April, 1878, Sarah was visited by a delegation of three Paiutes from the Malheur Reservation. She had not been living with Joseph Satwaller for some time and was working for a Mrs. Charles Cooley at the head of the John Day River near Prairie City, Oregon.[1] The men told her: "We are worse off than when you were at the Malheur, if that is possible. There is so little food, the children are dying of hunger." Sarah could see the poor condition of the men themselves.

Mrs. Cooley invited the hungry men into the house, and a meal was set before them such as they had not eaten for a long time. They asked Sarah: "Please come to Camp Harney and tell the officers that we are hungry, for Jerry Long, the interpreter, is in with Rinehart; he gets plenty to eat. You are our only voice!"

Sarah reminded the men how little she had been able to help them when she had complained to the officers at Fort Harney. She told them that she would do all that was within her power, but she could not leave at that moment. Toward the end of May six more delegates came from the Malheur and begged for Sarah's help again. This time she promised she would come as soon as she could get over the snow-covered mountains with her wagon.

On the first of June two gentlemen from Canyon City came to

Sarah and asked if she would take them to the Malheur Agency,
for they had heard that she was going there. One of the men,
a Mr. Morton, had a daughter named Rosey, a pretty little girl
of twelve, who would be making the trip. Sarah agreed to take
them to Malheur for $20. They left Mrs. Cooley on June 4. After
making their way over the mountainous wagon trails, they arrived
at the Malheur Agency on the next evening. Sarah dropped her
passengers at Rinehart's house and went on to stay with her
cousin Jerry Long.

Jerry told her that many Bannock Indians were now on the
reservation and that there was trouble afoot. He sent for Egan,
Oytes, and Bannock Jack to come speak with her. Jerry had no
food, and, when the others came in, they had none either.

"Did you bring any salmon or anything to eat? Sarah went to
bed without anything to eat. We have not anything at all down
here," Jerry told them. "We have not caught any salmon for ten
days and therefore we had nothing to bring. What does that
praying agent mean by not giving us our rations?" Egan complained bitterly.

Jerry replied, "I was there yesterday to see if I could buy some
flour of him, but he won't sell me any. He told me to tell you and
Oytes that he has written to Washington about the wheat, and
just as soon as the order comes he will send to your people."[2]

Sarah went to the council tent with Jerry and was introduced
to the Bannocks. Bannock Jack asked if she had heard of the
trouble at Fort Hall, and she replied that she had not seen a newspaper for a long time. He then told her what had happened.
Two girls had been digging roots when white men came and
caught one and used her shamefully. The brother of the girl,
Tambiago, got drunk and killed a white man in retaliation. The
Bannocks were told to bring in the Indian within ten days to
serve white justice. When the fugitive was found, the Indians
returning him to the fort discovered that Colonel John Smith
had already taken away all the Bannocks' ponies and guns in
retaliation against the tribe. Jack complained that it was not as
if they had not tried to bring in Tambiago, and the guns and
ponies were not the government's to take. He asked Sarah to
write it all down and send it to Washington, which she agreed
to do.

Egan rose and made a long speech about Agent Rinehart and

how he had wronged them. He spoke with dignity and authority. He was dressed like a white farmer in a cotton suit and straw hat, with his hair cut short at the neck.[3] His appearance was in sharp contrast to that of the Bannocks, whose long, braided hair was arranged in a pompadour at the forehead, while feathers and beads hung from their fringed leather garments. Sarah noticed that all of the council looked to Egan as their leader. Oytes listened attentively to him, while crouching quietly in a corner.

Egan said that Agent Rinehart had never issued clothing since he had been at Malheur. He had taken all the stray horses and penned them up for his own and shot the Paiutes' horses if they chanced to go into his grain fields. He allowed his employees to play cards and gamble with Jerry Long and the mail carrier so that they lost any money they had earned. "Now one and all of you, my men, give our mother what little money you have. Let her go and talk for us. Let her go right on to Washington, and have a talk with our Great Father," Egan implored.

He collected $29.25 from the council and gave it to Sarah, who promised she would make the long trip for them to Washington, D.C. She told them that she would sell her horse and wagon in Elko, Nevada, where she could board the train. She had agreed to take Mr. Morton and Rosey to Silver City, Idaho, en route to Elko. The party left the agency on the morning of June 8 by way of the Barren Valley.[4]

Sarah did not know that word had been received at Fort Harney of new trouble with the Bannocks on Big Camas Prairie in southern Idaho. The warrior chief Buffalo Horn had attacked and wounded some white freighters. The Bannock chief had served as a scout for the whites under General Howard during the recent Nez Percé war, but now he was embittered because the settlers had not fulfilled their promises to remove squatters and their cattle from the Camas Prairie, as had been agreed by treaty in 1868. He had 300 or 400 warriors who were well mounted and anxious to fight.

At Malheur, Rinehart was aware that all was not right on his reservation. He was suspicious of the Bannocks who had recently come from Fort Hall, and he would not issue to them, though Egan begged that the visitors be given food. Then a courier arrived reporting the Camas Prairie depredation, and this mes-

senger was followed a few days later by a second, who reported
that the Bannocks on the Snake River had stolen government
wagons loaded with ammunition. Rinehart moved his employees
off the agency. When he found that his own Paiutes had left
to assemble at the southeastern corner of the reserve in Barren
Valley (even Jerry Long, his interpreter, had gone with them),
the agent hurriedly left for the settlements in the John Day
River valley.[5]

General Irvin McDowell was apprised of the trouble in Idaho.
He telegraphed to Camp McDermit for confirmation from Natchez and Chief Winnemucca that they would help keep the
peace. Both professed their continued friendship for the whites
and announced their intention to leave for the Malheur Reservation to talk to the Bannocks there.[6]

Jim Crowley and his son were cattlemen in Barren Valley,
along with J. W. Scott, who was now the beef contractor for the
Malheur Reservation. These men talked with the Bannock and
Paiute chiefs at the ranch of a man named Thomas Davidson.
The Indians asked Scott if he would write their grievances on
paper to send to Washington. If so, the Paiutes promised to return to the reservation despite all that had occurred with Rinehart. The chiefs dictated, and Natchez interpreted what Scott
should write for them. When they had finished, not having much
confidence in Scott's integrity, they took the paper and gave
it to Crowley to read.

They found that Scott had not voiced their grievances, but
"had painted the Indians as 'demons' and the agent as an 'angel.'"
Natchez and Old Winnemucca could barely restrain the Indians
from killing Scott on the spot.[7] Subchief Leggins of Winnemucca's
band made an earnest speech in the whites' behalf, reminding
the others that he had invited the white men, and, if they were
killed, he and the Paiutes would be blamed for it. He declared
that they would have to kill him first. Since the Bannocks wished
to influence the Paiutes to join them, the issue was not pressed.

The whites stayed until darkness. When they attempted their
escape, they were chased by the hostile Indians for fifteen miles.[8]
While being pursued, Natchez leaped from his exhausted horse
and hid in the sagebrush. Thus he finally eluded his pursuers.
Old Winnemucca, however, was captured and held prisoner by
Oytes, who had become the new leader of the Malheur Paiutes.

Chief Egan too had lost his authority, for the voices of moderation were no longer tolerated.

Crowley rushed to warn the troops at Fort Harney of a new Bannock-Paiute war alliance. Already most of the cavalry at Harney were marching eastward toward Idaho, and only a skeletal force remained at that fort. Rinehart returned with a few employees to the Malheur agency to check on its condition. When he heard the report from Crowley, he telegraphed Commissioner E. A. Hoyt to ask for troops to protect the public property because he was abandoning the agency.[9] Levi Gheen, a farmer at the Duck Valley Reservation near the Nevada border, also sent a telegram to the commissioner: "The Bannocks are murdering and plundering through the northern country— They have run the Shoshones off the Duck Valley reservation and taken possession of everything. A Shoshone just arrived [in] great excitement. I am here without means. What shall I do!"[10]

Sarah says in her autobiography that, as she, Rosey, and Mr. Morton traveled through Barren Valley, they knew nothing of an Indian war, but they did notice that the few houses along the road were vacant. On the morning of June 12, as they were coming to the summit before the descent to Fort Lyon on the Oregon-Idaho line, they met a man on horseback, who stopped to warn them that the Bannocks were warring with the whites and killing everyone in their way. He said that they had chased the stage driver as he was coming from Elko and that they had killed him and wounded a passenger, who fortunately got away on one of the stage horses. The Bannocks had captured guns and ammunition. The messenger told Sarah's party that they should hurry on to Stone House, where the settlers had congregated for some protection.

Sarah's pony, which had been trotting neatly, was now rushed ahead. The three passengers in the wagon held on, while keeping a cautious eye out for hostiles. When they drove up beside Stone House, men came out of the building with guns, wanting to know who they were. Sarah explained that they had just heard of the war from a man on the road.

Captain Reuben F. Bernard's cavalry company had followed Buffalo Horn's trail from the Camas Prairie in Idaho. They arrived at Stone House on the same day as did twenty volunteers from Silver City, Idaho, who had recently engaged the Bannocks in battle near South Mountain in Idaho. One of the volunteers, Piute Joe, claimed that he had killed Buffalo Horn in the fight, but the soldiers were skeptical of the Paiute's story. Sarah noticed that the soldiers were looking at her as if she were some fearful animal, and she felt very uncomfortable. After Bernard spoke to the captain of the citizen scouts, he introduced himself politely to Sarah and said, "The citizens say that you have a good deal of ammunition in your wagon."[11] Sarah's heart "almost bounded into her mouth." She said: "Captain, they must know or they would not say so. . . . If you find anything in my wagon besides a knife and fork and a pair of scissors, I will give you my head for a football. How can I be taking guns and ammunition to my people when I am going right away from them?"[12] The tall, black-bearded captain had been active in the campaign against the Modocs and was now in charge of Fort Bidwell. He told Sarah that he believed her.

Sarah knew, of course, that her trip to Washington, so recently proposed by Egan, was now postponed indefinitely. She asked Bernard if she might be of service to the army, as she had been employed before as an interpreter and scout and was familiar with those duties. Bernard replied that he would telegraph to General Howard at Fort Boise and see what the general proposed. He asked if Sarah knew the country well, and she informed him that she did. Later, when Bernard moved on to a place called Sheep Ranch, he assured Sarah that, if Howard wished her services, he would let her know.

Sarah had a difficult time that night, for the people at Stone House still accused her of smuggling ammunition.[13] She cried and told them to look in her wagon. Finally a Captain Hill of the volunteers spoke for her: "I know your father is a friend of the whites. If I can do anything for you, I will be most happy to do it. If you want to go to the command, I will give you a horse."[14]

On the next morning Sarah took leave of Rosey and Mr. Morton. She claims in her autobiography that Morton had proposed marriage to her and that she had declined, saying that she could only marry for love (that she was still married to Joseph Satwaller was apparently not discussed). Sarah had decided to join Bernard at Sheep Ranch and saw the opportunity to go there with some couriers who were headed in that direction because telegraph lines had been pulled down. When they arrived, Captain Bernard informed Sarah that General Howard had accepted her as a scout. He also told her that her brother Natchez was reported to be killed or captured by the Bannocks. Numb with grief, Sarah also learned that her father and other tribesmen were held unwillingly by the Bannocks. She immediately made up her mind to go to them.

Bernard reported to Howard, "Sarah Winnemucca is in my camp; she wants to go to her people with any message you or General McDowell might desire to send; thinks if she can get to the Pi-Utes with such message she could get all the well-disposed to come near the troops, where they could be safe and fed; says there is nothing at the Malheur agency with which to feed them."[15]

Howard answered: "Send Sarah with two or three friendly Indians straight to her people, and have them send a few of their principal men to you. I will see that all who behave well and come in are properly fed. Promise Sarah a reward if she succeeds."[16]

Sarah tells us that she was sent off from Sheep Ranch the next morning with two Paiutes, George and John, who reluctantly accompanied her into the hostile zone. She had been offered $500 for the return of her people. Bernard had given her a helpful note at the last: "To all good citizens in the country—, Sarah Winnemucca, with two of her people, goes with a dispatch to her father. If her horses should give out, help her all you can and oblige. Captain Bernard."[17]

The trio traveled fifteen miles to the Owyhee River crossing. There they found citizen scouts, who gave Sarah a fresh horse and something to eat. They soon struck the Bannock trail and traced it down the Owyhee for some miles to the spot where the Bannocks had camped. Sarah knew that the Bannocks had been mourning the death of Buffalo Horn, for she found broken necklaces, torn clothing, and remnants of cutoff hair along the trail. Then she found that the Indians had turned toward Barren Valley. The three traveled all day through the rocky, dry country and did not stop to rest even when daylight ceased. Finally, Sarah called a halt when their horses gave out.

George and John alternated watch while Sarah slept with her saddle for a pillow. Her horse, tied to her arm, kept waking her but there were no trees to which to stake mounts in the wasteland. At daybreak Sarah mounted and hurried on, as both the animals and their riders were almost dead for water. Heading for Jim Crowley's ranch in Barren Valley at a hard gallop, they discovered on arrival that the house had been burned to the ground. Chickens were still running around in the yard, and John suggested they catch one for breakfast, but Sarah insisted it would not be right. She drew water from the well for their coffee and found a burned-out tin can in which to make it, while the two men watered the horses.

They rode hard all day over alkali flats and tumbled lava rocks following the trail through country that was destitute of wood, water, and grass. It was at least sixty miles to any white habitation, and, when Sarah spotted a discarded clock on the trail, she knew that the Bannocks must still be ahead. They soon found a fiddle without a bow, which Sarah tied onto her saddle. Later that same day they spotted a mountain sheep, which John had the luck to kill. They were happy to take some of the meat, but in the excitement of the hunt Sarah had lost her fiddle. Five miles farther they noticed two figures on a hillside. Sarah took her handkerchief and waved, and, as the riders drew nearer, there was a call from the mountainside: "Who are you?"

"Your sister, Sarah!" Sarah replied. She had recognized Lee Winnemucca, who ran down the mountain and joined them. He told them:

Oh, dear sister, you have come to save us, for we are all prisoners of the Bannocks. They have treated our father most shamefully. They have taken from us what few guns we had, and our blankets, and our horses. They have done this because they outnumber us. . . . Here I am standing and talking to you, knowing the great danger you are in by coming here. . . . Take off your hat and your dress and unbraid your hair, and put this blanket round you, so if they should come down they would not know who it is. Here is some paint. Paint your face quick. Here, men, hide your guns and take off your clothes and make yourselves look as well as you can.

All of this was accomplished quickly.

"Where is our father?" Sarah asked.

"We are all up over that mountain. We are but six miles from here. . . . but you will be killed if you go there . . . our brother Natchez has made his escape three days ago."

When Sarah heard that last piece of news, she was overjoyed.

Juniper Lake, Oregon, with Steens Mountain in the background. Here Sarah Winnemucca successfully brought her father and other Paiutes out of a Bannock war camp, which was located in a valley beyond these precipitous slopes. (Courtesy of Robert Canfield.)

She told Lee that she had to go to their father because she had come with a message from General O. O. Howard."[18]

Lee led the way over the rocky, steep mountainside, which they had difficulty ascending. At last Sarah looked down into the hostile stronghold and was overcome with the sight. There were about 327 lodges below, and 450 warriors were in Little Valley, catching and killing cattle that they had herded before them in their plunder through the countryside. As a civilized Indian woman Sarah thought it a beautiful but terrifying sight. She asked:

"Brother, is our father's lodge inside the line? We must leave our horses here and go on foot."

Lee replied, "If you are discovered, how will you get out?"

"Oh, well, our horses are almost given out anyway; so, dear brother, we must trust to good luck. . . . Let us go quick and be back, for I have no time to lose."

They hurried down the mountain and were not distinguished from the other Paiutes by the Bannocks.[19]

Before Sarah entered her father's lodge, she waited excitedly until Lee had announced her presence. Old Winnemucca then took her in his arms and said, "Oh, my dear little girl, and what is it? Have you come to save me yet? My little child is in great danger."

Everyone in the tent whispered, "Oh, Sadie, you have come to save us!"

Sarah told them: "Yes, I have come to save you all if you will do as I wish you to and be quiet about it. Whisper it among yourselves. Get ready tonight, for there is no time to lose, for the soldiers are close by. I have come from them with this word: 'Leave the hostile Bannocks and come to the troops. You shall be properly fed by the troops.' Are you all here? I mean all the Malheur Reservation Indians?"

"Yes, all are here, and Oytes is the chief of them."

"Father, you tell the women to make believe they are gathering wood for the night and while they are doing that they can get away."[20] While Sarah was yet talking, the women left one by one with ropes in their hands, with their babies on their backs and their little ones by their sides.

Lee directed the men to catch as many horses as they could after dark and drive them to Juniper Lake. Winnemucca gave similar orders to his nephews, George, Jim and James. Now that it was night, they all left the tent. Sarah felt as if she were in a dream. She could not get along, and her father had to help her. When a horse came running, they all fell to the ground. When it stopped nearby, the rider called softly for Chief Winnemucca.

It was Lee's wife, Mattie, with a horse for them, which Sarah was very thankful to mount. They hurried back up the mountain to where they had left their horses and, upon finding them, rushed down again toward Juniper Lake, where the women were cooking the meat of the mountain sheep that had been killed earlier. After eating quickly, they hurried on their way. Children were tied to their mother's backs so that they would not fall off in their sleep.

Lee came to Sarah and told her that he was going back for more people. Jerry Long was held a close prisoner, and Egan and many of his people had not come.

Sarah replied, "Get all the people you can."

Winnemucca, Mattie, Sarah, George, and John led, while six men brought up the rear and watched to see if they were pursued. At daybreak they came to Summit Springs and called a halt. They unsaddled their horses and prepared to lie down to rest. Winnemucca insisted that Sarah have something to eat. Just then came a warning alarm. Sarah and Mattie rode bareback on their horses to meet the rider, whose mount was almost falling from under him.[21] He told them, "We are followed by the Bannocks."

Sarah told him to jump up behind her, and they hurried back to the camp with the news. The rider said that Egan and his whole band had been overtaken and forced back. He had looked back and saw Lee running. The Bannocks shot at him, and he supposed that he was killed.

Winnemucca said, "If my son is killed, I will go back and be killed by them too. If we are to be killed off for what the white people have done to them, of course we cannot help ourselves."

Sarah pleaded with her father to save himself and the others with him. She told him that she was determined to return to General Howard. Her father then agreed to continue their flight and asked that she send the troops to them as fast as possible. Mattie cried out to Sarah, "Let me go with you. If my poor husband is killed, why need I stay?"[22]

Away the two women dashed on their horses, galloping through the desolate country without water. At noon the same day they finally came to a stream called Muddy Creek, where they let their horses rest and found some white currants to eat. Then, jumping their horses across the stream, they sped on toward the soldiers' camp. At three o'clock they were at the crossing of the Owyhee River, where they were given fresh horses and hard bread by the white volunteers. Then they were off again to Sheep Ranch, whipping their mounts into a lather. Upon their arrival Captain Bernard helped them from their horses.

Sarah was so fatigued and excited that she burst into tears and could not speak for a time. Captain Bernard, Lieutenant Charles E. S. Wood, Lieutenant John Pitcher, and General O. O. Howard received her report. Sarah told them that Chief Winnemucca was on his way and that he wanted soldiers for protection from the Bannocks, who had forced back Chief Egan. She noted that the officers looked at each other as if she was lying; Lieutenant Pitcher winked at Lieutenant Wood. In contrast, General Howard had such confidence in her story that he changed his plan of operation.[23] Piute Joe was sent with the captain of the volunteers, Colonel "Rube" Robbins, and all Robbins's men to bring in Chief Winnemucca and his band. Within a few days forty of the band were found and were sent safely to Camp McDermit.[24]

The whole round trip, from 10 o'clock on June 13 to 5:30 on June 15, in the saddle day and night over hard terrain, had been a grueling ride of 223 miles.[25] Sarah was justly proud of having helped her father and her people from the hostile camp, though the Paiutes who were left behind or recaptured by the Bannocks, including Egan, had lost any chance to escape. Sarah's raid of the camp had caused them to show their true colors to the Bannocks, and they were closely held prisoners through the remainder of the war, which had only just begun.[26]

13

The Bannock Indian War

Brigadier General George Crook, Department of the Platte, was interviewed early in the Bannock War of 1878 by a reporter from the *Omaha* (Nebraska) *Herald:*

Reporter: There is much serious apprehension in regard to trouble with the Indians.

Gen. Crook: There are good grounds for it. As long as the muzzle-loading arms were in use we had the advantage of them, and 20 men could whip a hundred, but since the breech loaders came into use it is entirely different; these they can load on horse-back and now they are a match for any man. In regard to the Bannocks I was up there last Spring, and found them in a desperate condition. I telegraphed and the agent telegraphed for supplies, but word came that no appropriation had been made. They have never been half supplied. The agent has sent them off for half a year to enable them to pick up something to live on, but there is nothing for them in that country. The buffalo is all gone, and an Indian can't catch enough jack rabbits to subsist himself and family . . . What are they to do! Starvation is staring them in the face, and if they wait much longer they will not be able to fight. . . .

Reporter: It seems to me that it would be cheaper to treat the Indians justly.

Gen. Crook: Of course it would be cheaper. All the tribes tell the same story. They are surrounded on all sides, the game is destroyed or driven away, they are left to starve and there remains but one thing for them to do—fight while they can. Some people think the Indians do not understand these things, but they do and fully appreciate the circumstances in which they are placed. Our treatment of the Indian is an outrage.[1]

The Department of Indian Affairs could not let this censure go unnoticed, especially as it was fighting for its very existence at this time. Congress was considering the transfer of the Indians to the War Department from the Department of the Interior. It was publicly pointed out by Indian Commissioner E. A. Hoyt that all of the congressional appropriations for Indians did not amount to more than 4½ cents per day per Indian for subsistence.[2] That was the ready retort of Agent Rinehart also, whenever his administration of the Malheur Reservation came under fire.

Ironically three wagon teams loaded with desperately needed flour finally arrived at Malheur soon after the start of the outbreak.[3] The delay of a few weeks had brought calamitous results to the Paiutes and Rinehart. The Malheur agent had telegraphed General Howard for troops to protect the agency, but the general had replied that Rinehart should employ citizen guards for this purpose. When Rinehart then asked the Indian Department for further instructions, he waited five days without a reply.[4]

He proceeded to Canyon City and tried to employ a small guard on his own, but found it impossible to procure arms or men. He then asked Captain Evan Miles, who was en route to Camp Harney, for a small detachment of men to guard the agency. This plan was frustrated because all of Miles's men were needed by Bernard, whose company had driven the Indians beyond the agency.[5]

When he thought that danger from the hostiles was past, Rinehart sent for all his employees to return to the reserve. He found, however, that Major Joseph Stewart and his company were ensconced at Malheur, and they were soon followed by General Howard and his staff. Howard instructed Stewart to take charge of all public property, and Stewart's officers were to account for all the stocks that they took from the agency for the use of the soldiers while the agency was used as a depot for army supplies and prisoners. Rinehart was instructed to act as a guide and scout, pointing out the hiding places of the Indians. The agent grumblingly gave up his quarters and had to sleep in the hay-stacks. As it turned out, General Howard and his staff remained only a few hours; the officers and their men hurriedly arrived at the agency and just as hurriedly departed. Meanwhile Rine-hart tried in a frenzy to inventory the agency's goods before the soldiers had depleted the stocks. He finally had to leave his third attempt to his employees, after which he and they left the reservation for Canyon City.[6]

Sarah meanwhile was kept busy as a scout. She traveled with Mattie. On one occasion the two women heard some soldiers on the road. When one soldier commented, "Oh, look, they have Sarah Winnemucca a prisoner," the two women laughed.[7] When Sarah's party reached the agency, the news had just arrived that the hostiles were heading for Harney Valley and it was likely that Captain Bernard's company would overtake them. Sarah and Mattie were charged by General Howard to go to Camp Harney, accompanied by Howard's aide-de-camp, Lieutenant Melville C. Wilkinson, and two other soldiers. When they reached the last stage stop, they had to replace Mattie's horse, and they took time to eat. The lieutenant followed them into the stage house, and a white woman serving coffee looked at Sarah and said: "Well, I never thought I should feed you again. I hope they will not let you off this time."

Lieutenant Wilkinson interrupted, "You don't know what you are talking about. This is Sarah Winnemucca."

She answered: "I don't care. Rope is too good to hang her with."

The lieutenant told Sarah, "Never mind her, she is crazy," but Sarah could not eat her food.[8]

The group reached Camp Harney the next morning. Both women were so tired that they went to bed without eating. In the evening the wife of the commanding officer, Major G. M. Downey, called on Sarah to see if she needed anything, and, seeing that her dress was worn from traveling, she kindly gave Sarah one of her own.[9]

The next day, June 23, was a Sunday. Lieutenant Wilkinson, who was a minister, planned to preach to the soldiers, but at ten o'clock a courier alerted Camp Harney that Captain Ber-nard's men were in battle near Camp Curry. Although his com-pany had surprised and charged the Bannocks, the hostiles had

General O. O. Howard, who led the United States Army tracking Chief Joseph and the Nez Percés in 1877. He found himself in a similar pursuit of the Paiutes and Bannocks during the Bannock Indian War of 1878. (Courtesy of Oregon Historical Society.)

rallied, and now Bernard needed reinforcements. Three soldiers
had been killed, and three wounded; the Indian casualties were
unknown.[10] Sarah, Wilkinson, and Mattie raced their horses to
report back to Howard that same day, only to find that they had
missed him en route; he had already left for Harney with more
troops.

The main command was able to catch up with Captain Bernard near Camp Curry in a few days, but steady movement
was required. It became apparent that the hostiles intended to
reach the Columbia River region and were hopeful of picking up
allies along their escape route.[11] On June 28, Howard made this
comment in his notebook:

Move at 6 a.m. Rough trail. Wagons move 13 miles; arrive in camp
8 p.m. Bernard goes some miles farther, Bernard sends back word Indian
pony-tracks just ahead. They turn suddenly and go back. Very cold;
snowing all day. Large Indian camp at this place (About 1,500 or 2,000
Indians have been here.).[12]

Sarah and Mattie were sent to interview a Bannock Indian
woman who had been captured in the Camp Curry battle. At
first she would not talk, but in the end she told them much
that was of interest to Howard. She confirmed that Buffalo Horn
had been killed at South Mountain (as Piute Joe had claimed)
and that Oytes was now the leader. The hostiles were headed
for the Umatilla agency because the Umatillas had promised
Oytes that they would join in the war. Sarah noticed the woman's blind eyes filling with tears as she remembered her nephew
Buffalo Horn.[13]

The pursuing cavalry found itself in the deep canyon of the
South Fork of the John Day River. The wagons had much difficulty covering the terrain. They moved along the highest ridges
and then slid down the steep descent to the valley floor. Howard
later wrote: "What a diversified country! Jagged rocks, precipitous slopes, knife-edged divides, deep canyons with sides steep
and difficult, the distance from a crest to the mountain stream
that tumbled over the rocks far below being sometimes four or
five miles."[14]

As the Indians pushed northward, the settlers who found themselves in the Bannocks' path rushed to the towns or other fortifications for protection. The army seemed to be always behind

and unable to check the progress of the Indians. Citizen scouts were enlisted to watch and head them off if possible.[15] The one-armed General Howard was the object of much sarcasm from certain segments of the press and the community. This war was unfolding in a way similar to the Nez Percé War, in which Howard's troops had chased Chief Joseph for hundreds of miles, seldom engaging in conflict.[16]

A dozen volunteers from Canyon City skirmished with an advance of about fifty hostile warriors. One of the citizens was killed in this encounter, and, when the news reached Canyon City, more volunteers rallied to the front. The town itself was in an uproar.[17] Agent Rinehart, who had retreated there from the agency, found his army experience useful in the emergency. He helped build a breastwork and rifle pits for the defense of the town. He had worked about three hours when the drum roll sounded from the courthouse announcing that the Indians were sweeping up the valley.

All was chaos and panic. Over one hundred families left their homes and clambered hastily up a steep bluff west of the town to reach the mining tunnels, which were now converted into a temporary refuge. There were sixty men with forty guns, some of which were only shotguns. Water was brought up the hillside in barrels and buckets. Provisions and bedding were placed in five underground tunnels which were lighted with candles and filled with terror-stricken women and children.[18]

Toward night a messenger arrived with the news that a second party of citizens had struck the Indians twenty miles down the valley and the whites were flying before the enemy. Two men had been killed, and two farmhouses were burned. This information produced a panic that lasted the night. Reports were abroad that 200 to 300 Indians were behind the advance of 50 and that the cavalry was 100 miles away.[19] On the next morning the citizens learned with relief that the main body of hostiles had bypassed the town and were on their way north.[20] The cavalry had finally arrived on the John Day River, and the infantry was only one day's march behind.

During those tumultuous days some American newspapers were sympathetic to the plight of the Indians. The *San Francisco Call* of June 23 took Rinehart to task for starving, abusing, and lying to the Paiutes. It stated that innocent settlers, killed without warning and without any knowledge of the provocation, were paying the penalty of the agent's crimes with their lives and property. The writer was concerned that Rinehart's success in getting away with thousands of dollars' worth of plunder would encourage other agents to imitate his example.

The New York Times predicted that an Indian outbreak might be extended into a larger war, because many Indians were disaffected in southern Idaho, western Montana, and eastern Oregon: "The malconstruction of our machinery for dealing with the red race is more than ever apparent. The War Department and the Interior Department, between whom the responsibility is divided, are seldom capable of effectively assisting each other."[21]

All of the Malheur Paiutes appeared to be with the Bannocks except Old Winnemucca's band of about forty whom Sarah had brought out of the Bannock camp.[22] After a short sojourn at Camp McDermit, Winnemucca had gone to Steens Mountain, where he found a few of Egan's people who had escaped from the Bannocks during the Camp Curry battle. They told him that Chief Egan and his brother-in-law Charlie had attempted to join the soldiers during the fight, but they had been critically wounded. Now the Bannocks were compelling Egan to march with them, and he would probably die.[23] The old chief also found Ocheo and his band on Steens Mountain. They told him that they wanted to go back to Surprise Valley but were afraid of the settlers and soldiers. They had never entered the hostilities, though the Bannocks had come urging them to do so.[24]

While bivouacked near Pilot Rock, Oregon, General Howard received word that some of the hostiles were crossing the Columbia River with a large number of horses. Major J. A. Kress attacked with his men on the steamer *Spokane*, destroying an Indian camp and confiscating blankets and buffalo robes.[25] The *Spokane* continued to patrol the river while Captain Wilkinson with thirty-two men boarded the steamer *Northwest* with a gatling gun and two howitzers.[26]

Sarah and Mattie stayed with General Howard's command, sometimes riding in an army ambulance over the rough terrain. In her autobiography Sarah tells how on July 7 the general asked her if she would go to the Indians and see if they would surrender without a fight. She accepted the assignment, but, after the officers discussed the matter further, they agreed that the risks were too great for her.[27] On the next day General Howard was informed by two scouts that they had located the Indians' main camp about three miles ahead on the heights of the foothills of the Blue Mountains. At this all the cavalry drew up for battle, and Captain Bernard directed them quickly into position. They faced the Indians' stronghold, which was protected by a crest of lava and backed by timber farther up the steep mountainside.[28]

When the cavalry charged, Sarah and Mattie stayed near Howard, who told them to get behind rocks to protect themselves from the bullets that were whistling about. She heard the chiefs' singing as they ran up and down the front line, while the gatling gun and other artillery whanged into the rocky ledge where the Indians fought. Once she thought that she heard Oytes yell, "Come on you white dogs—what are you waiting there for?"[29]

Howard, in describing the battle of Birch Creek, wrote:

As we reached a high crest we saw the Indians and their ponies among the rocks. They did not act as usual, but kept moving about, some jumping up and down as if in defiance. Their conduct was like Joseph's Nez Percés at the Clear Water the year before, when with blankets tossed high over their heads they danced around, looking and acting like howling dervishes in their frenzied capers, doubtless hoping to inspire terror in our breasts.[30]

Many of the troopers' horses were hit—they lay screaming in pain as they lay on the mountainside—but the cavalry surged ahead. They finally dislodged the Bannocks, who moved on to the next height. Sarah told Mattie, "We will see a great many of our people die today, and soldiers, too." She was numbed by the thought and ran out into the open to take a position by General Howard.[31]

Soon the hostiles were forced from their new battlements. Leaving their horses and camp provisions, they backed into a dense stand of pines on the crest of the Blue Mountains, where they made another short stand. Finally they retreated through the safety of the trees, where the cavalry could not easily pursue. Sarah surmised that the fleeing women and children were moving back to their own country on the best horses.[32]

The Indians' losses during the battle could not be determined, as they picked up their dead and wounded and carried them along. A scout came running to General Howard to say that an Indian was lying tied to the tail of a horse in a stream at the bottom of a deep canyon.[33] The general sent Sarah and Mattie to investigate, but they found nothing.

Five soldiers had been wounded in the battle. About twenty horses had been killed, but 200 or 300 of the Indians' horses had been captured. One of the soldiers, badly hurt, was brought to Mattie and Sarah for them to watch. They asked him if they could do anything for him, but he shook his head. Later General Howard came with a book and read and prayed with him. At four o'clock in the morning he cried out for someone to come, and the two women rushed to his side, hoping to assist him. He looked at them, but could not speak, and died in a few minutes.[34]

In retrospect Sarah wrote:

Sometimes I laugh when I think of this battle. It was very exciting in one way, and the soldiers made a splendid chase, and deserved credit for it; but where was the killing? I sometimes think it was more play than anything else. If a white settler showed himself he was sure to get a hit from an Indian; but I don't believe they ever tried to hit a soldier, — they liked them too well, — and it certainly was remarkable that with all these splendid firearms, and the Gatling gun, and General Howard working at it, and the air full of bullets, and the ground strewn with cartridges, not an Indian fell that day.[35]

Sarah and Mattie stayed with Bernard's company, who pursued the Bannocks back to the North Fork of the John Day River. Meanwhile General Howard, fearing that some of the hostiles might cross the Snake River into Idaho, took the *Northwest* for Lewiston. While he was on the steamer, an Indian courier from the Umatilla Reservation in northern Oregon reported to him that the hostiles had burned the Umatilla agency, Cayuse Station.[36]

As soon as the Umatilla agent, N. A. Cornoyer, had seen that Cayuse was in flames, he hurried there with thirty-five of his Indians. They found that the whole force of the hostiles was coming down the mountain slopes in their direction. Cornoyer gathered the agency Indians to protect themselves and their stock, but the hostiles appeared to have no intention of attacking immediately. Instead they camped out of sight in a deep canyon.

This delay allowed time for a messenger to go to the troops to request assistance for the agency Indians, who were considerably outnumbered.[37]

Before Miles arrived just at daybreak, eleven Umatillas and about fifty Columbia River Indians had defected to the Bannocks, and, while the soldiers were eating breakfast, the hostiles reappeared, about 400 strong. The Indians hesitated in their charge when they saw the unexpected soldiers, but commenced firing at long range. They continued to do so until the cavalry and some volunteers from Pendleton drove them back into the surrounding mountains.[38]

On the morning of July 14 one of the Umatillas who had joined the hostiles sent word that, if the Umatillas were pardoned, they would send a party of Cayuse Indians to a certain place in the mountains where they would waylay Chief Egan and deliver him into the hands of the army. Miles accepted the terms, and forty-three Cayuses waited at the designated spot.[39]

Chief Egan had been born of Cayuse parents, but had been captured as a child during a Shoshoni raid and had found a home among the Northern Paiutes.[40] Already critically wounded in the Camp Curry fight, and in a desperate state of mind, he and some of his followers were called away from the Bannock camp to the proposed rendezvous by Umatilla Chiefs Umapine and Five Crows. The Cayuses seized and bound him, but a fight ensued against the Bannocks, who had discovered the plot. In the struggle Egan fought to get away and was shot and killed by one of the Umatillas.[41] On the next morning the Umatillas displayed Egan's head on a pole, along with four others. They had killed twelve men and had captured five prisoners and about 300 horses.[42]

In their pursuit of the Bannocks, General Frank Wheaton's forces later came across Egan's body, which was identified by Captain Thomas McGregor. Egan, who had always told the young men that it was folly to defy the whites, had wounds in his chest, wrist and groin. His broken wrist had been bound in willow splints and laid across a pillow on his breast. Dr. J. A. Fitzgerald, the army surgeon who examined the body, decided that Egan would have died in any case of his Camp Curry wounds.[43] The doctor was said to have sent Egan's head as a specimen to the Army Medical Museum at Washington, D.C.

One investigator found that the Army Medical Museum had no record of the head, but acknowledged receipt of the head of Egan's brother-in-law Charlie, whose body had lain nearby: "That the body of Egan was decapitated, there seems to be no doubt. What happened to the head may be conjectured."[44]

On the night when Egan died, Sarah screamed in her sleep and woke Mattie. She had dreamed of his murder. When the women learned a few days later that he was indeed dead, Mattie was unconsolable, for Egan had been her stepfather.[45]

Lieutenant Colonel James W. Forsyth, fresh from General P. H. Sheridan's headquarters in Chicago, Illinois, assumed command of Bernard's battalion. Pushing through woods and mountains, the soldiers struck the Bannock rear guard in the canyon of the North Fork of the John Day River. The soldiers slid down the trails of the gorge, and, while climbing back up, some of the pack mules lost their footing and tumbled into the chasm. About forty Indians were keeping guard at the top of the trail to protect their bedraggled main force, as the latter moved southward. The guard shot three of Forsyth's men, including a citizen courier.[46]

During the commotion of that fight one of the soldiers found an Indian baby lying face down in the dirt. She appeared to be unhurt, and Captain McGregor handed her over to Sarah and Mattie, after he had fed her gingersnaps, sugar, and water. The women were careful to preserve the baby's original clothing and beads so that, if the parents surrendered, they could identify their child. Two women had been taken as prisoners. Sarah asked one of them, whom she knew, if she would care for the child. The woman consented, and Sarah showed her how to give her condensed milk.[47]

In hot pursuit of the Bannocks the army crossed the Blue Mountains into the Granite Creek valley. There, by a strange coincidence, Sarah and Mattie found their former agent Sam Parrish watering his cattle on Little Creek. He looked up in astonishment and came to them, holding out his hands, while tears ran down his cheeks. He said: "Oh, Sarah, little did I think when I left you that it would all come to this. The poor Paiutes. I can't believe it!" Sarah told him all that had happened and rode with him for a while as he drove his cattle ahead.[48]

General Howard and his troops were camping at the crossing of the Canyon City and Malheur City wagon roads, and that

night the general asked Sarah if she would go to the Malheur
agency to see if any Indians had put in an appearance. Sarah,
Mattie, and Lieutenant Wilkinson rode with eight Indian scouts
to the agency. They found that the place had been deserted
since the early days of the war. On the next day they returned
around the east side of Castle Rock only to discover that they
had just missed General Howard. Since the women were quite
tired, they told Wilkinson that they would rest a bit before returning to the agency, where the general was headed. The lieutenant was reluctant to leave them, and not without cause. Soon
three soldiers appeared and announced, "Come, boys, here are
the girls, and the lieutenant is not with them." Sarah and Mattie
jumped on their horses and had a wild ride back to Malheur.
When Howard heard their story, the three soldiers were immediately dismissed.[49]

One of the women prisoners was sent out to find her people
and tell them to return to the reservation, where they would
be fed by the government. Before the woman left, Sarah said:
"Tell them I, their mother, say come back to their homes again.
I will stand by them and see that they are not sent away to the
Indian Territory."[50] Sarah watched the woman as she rode away
on an army horse across the high plateau toward the distant
mountains. The woman did find a few of her people and brought
them in some weeks later, but, once the Paiute bands were
back in familiar territory, they promptly scattered and remained
elusive.

On July 27, Sarah and Mattie left Howard's command to accompany Colonel Forsyth. The latter was rounding up groups of
hostiles, who would be kept as prisoners of war subject to the
order of the department commander. With Forsyth the two
women marched to Steens Mountain along the South Fork of
the Malheur River, riding sometimes as much as thirty to forty
miles a day. Some of the horses gave out in the burning sun,
and the soldiers were forced to march without benefit of water
over the wasteland. When Mattie's horse became exhausted, she
and Sarah took turns riding and walking. When they got to their
destination, they found no evidence of Paiutes.[51]

They crossed a forty-five-mile desert to old Camp C. F. Smith,
and still there were no signs of Indians. That night, however,
the women saw a signal fire of distress in the hills. Colonel

Forsyth wished to know its meaning, and, when Sarah told him that they would find a lone Indian by the fire, he did not believe her. Then citizen scouts went to the area and found the footprints of one man, who was later brought in. He proved to be an acquaintance of Sarah's, who had been a good farmer on the Malheur Reservation when Parrish was there.

Sarah was so close now to Camp McDermit that she could not bear the thought of moving on without seeing her father and other relatives. When she asked the colonel for permission to go, he asked if Mattie could talk English well enough to take her place. Sarah replied that she could. Then Forsyth insisted that she take Lieutenant John Pitcher and two soldiers with her to McDermit. The four rode at a fast trot through the night. Finally, early in the morning hours, Sarah received permission to ride ahead, and with relief she broke into a gallop, arriving at McDermit just before daybreak. We have her account of what happened when she was reunited with her father.[52]

She rode up to one Paiute camp and said, "Here, you are sleeping too much! Get up!"

One of the women jumped up and said, "Who is it? What is it?"

"Where is my brother's camp? Where is Natchez?" Sarah asked. The woman pointed out the camp, and Sarah rode up to the tent. "Halloo! Get up. The enemy is at hand!" she called.

Natchez rushed out and said, "Oh, my sister!" He helped her off her horse and said to his wife, "Jump up, wife, and make a fire, sister is so cold." Sarah had nothing on but a dress. She was given a blanket, and a fire was soon made.

Natchez said to the waking people, "I am afraid, my young men, you are not doing your duty; for I have here in my camp a warrior who has just arrived. Come . . . and see for yourselves."

Winnemucca was the first to come up. He ran to Sarah and took her in his arms. "Oh, my poor child, I thought I never would see you, for the papers said you were killed by the Bannocks. . . . When I heard you, my darling, who saved my life for a little while longer, had gone first, I thought my heart would break!"

Sarah put her face on his chest. Then Winnemucca said, "Look up, dear; let me see if it is really my child." The tears ran down the old man's cheeks, and everybody had tears in their eyes.

Sarah sat at the fire and related all that had happened since the day that they had parted. She told them who had been killed and how many prisoners the United States Army had. She told them about the baby and a blind woman who had been scalped by whites and yet lived; about Oytes and about how Egan had been murdered by the Cayuses, his own people.

The Numa said they hoped that, when the soldiers caught Oytes, they would hang him, for he was to blame for all their misery. When Sarah told them that Umapine, the Umatilla who had killed Egan, was now a scout with Colonel Forsyth, Leggins rose and said, "My brothers, I think we ought to go and kill him. We have never done them any harm, and have always been kind to them when they came on our reservation. We have given them presents. Oh, my brother Winnemucca, and you, my dear Natchez, . . . You and your sister can demand of them to give him up to us."

Then Sarah jumped up and said: "I have not told you all. At the time they took Egan, they also took a great many women prisoners, and most of them are young girls."

When Sarah sat down, Natchez spoke. First he warned the Numa that they would probably never get their women and children back by killing Umapine. He said that he would make the following speech to the Umatillas:

Friends, we have come to talk to you. Now tell us what our sub-chief, Egan, has done to you that you should kill him, and have him cooked in the way you did. Was he good to eat? . . . For four years you have come on the Malheur Reservation, and told Egan and Oytes to make war against the whites. You have called them fools for staying on the reservation to starve. . . . You are nothing but cowards; nothing but barking coyotes; you are neither persons nor men. . . . Now we cease to be friends, and after the soldiers quit fighting with the Bannocks and with Oytes' men, we will make war with you for the wrong you have done us, if you do not return our women and girls whom you have taken as prisoners. Do you know there is not money enough in the world to make me go and fight a people who have not done me any harm? You have done this year after year against your own people. . . . And what do you gain by it? . . . You are as poor as we are, we, who have never taken our own brother's scalp and fastened it on a pole and danced round it to show our white brothers how brave we are. . . .

General Howard and General McDowell . . . have asked me to furnish them twenty-five of my men as scouts for them. General Howard and General McDowell are my best soldier-fathers; yet they could not give me money enough to take up arms against any tribe of Indians.

Natchez concluded by saying:

Now, my dear children, I will go with my sister, and I will say all to the Umatillas that I have said to you, right before General Forsythe and all the officers. I think it is right and just, and I also think it is the only way we can get back our women and girls. . . .

I am afraid the soldiers will think we have come to fight them, if they see so many of us coming; therefore I think about thirty of us will be enough to go.

Meanwhile Lieutenant Pitcher had arrived. He agreed that the men could go with him and Sarah to Colonel Forsyth. Winnemucca, who had not spoken, now rose:

I am ashamed to have to speak to you, my children. . . . Where is one among you who can get up and say, "I have been in battle, and have seen soldiers and my people fight and fall." Oh! for shame, for shame to you, young men, who ought to have come with this news to me! . . . My child's name is so far beyond yours. . . . Her name is everywhere and everyone praises her. Oh! how thankful I feel that it is my own child who has saved so many lives, not only mine, but a great many, both whites and her own people. Now hereafter we will look on her as our chieftain, for none of us are worthy of being chief but her.

14

Yakima

Natchez delivered a speech to the Umatillas with Lieutenant Colonel Forsyth's command, but Umapine, the man who reportedly had killed Chief Egan, was not present. Since the scouts could not find him or his pony, it was presumed that he did not want to face the wrath of the Paiutes and had returned hurriedly to his own country.[1]

Mattie and Lee were now reunited, for Lee had escaped safely from the Bannocks and returned to McDermit along with Winnemucca. He remained with Mattie and Sarah when the rest of the warriors returned to McDermit, and the three acted as couriers for Captain Bernard, Major George B. Sanford, Colonel Forsyth, and Captain W. H. Winters during the next few weeks, as small bands were gathered and brought into the military camps.[2]

On August 13, 1878, Oytes surrendered with a party of sixty at the Malheur agency. This seemed to signal the close of the war, as only a few hostiles were unaccounted for.[3] The Bannocks returned to their country beyond the Snake River, where skirmishes between them and the army occurred as late as September and as far east as the Yellowstone country.

Sarah had been all through the camps at Fort Harney with the Indian baby, and no one could identify the child. At last she found a young couple in mourning who recognized the little one. They were overcome with joy at her return. She had been thrown from her basket on a steep incline, and her mother had not missed her until too late in the confused retreat. The grateful parents named the child Sarah.[4]

Sarah Winnemucca would not have worked so industriously gathering together the Paiute stragglers if she had known what her "kind" soldier fathers were planning. In October orders came to the officers that all the Paiutes who belonged on the Malheur Reservation were to be gathered at Fort Harney so that they could be returned to Malheur Reservation for the coming winter. Sarah was told to go to Camp McDermit and bring all her people to Camp Harney. A company of cavalry was to accompany her.[5]

When Sarah told the people what was expected, they were quite upset. "We know there is something wrong," they told her. "We don't like to go." Meanwhile the officers told them that there was nothing to fear, and Natchez said, "Our soldier-fathers will see that you are all right."

Leggins replied: "Rinehart is there yet. . . . We know how we suffered while we were there."

The Numa felt greatly troubled in their hearts. Were the soldiers going to punish even those who did not go with the Bannocks? Captain Wagner became quite angry with their questions and told them that, when soldiers received orders, they had to obey them, and it was the same for the Paiutes.[6] At the council that night the people agreed to make the trip to Harney, and on the next morning, October 4, 1878, their horses were prepared for the long trek.[7] Families and relatives were parted. All were crying and lamenting that this should happen. Natchez accompanied the 180 Paiutes as far as Camp C. F. Smith, and then he too had to return. He did not go before reaching an agreement that Leggins would be chief in the absence of Winnemucca and himself.[8]

It took seven days for the Numa to arrive at the post. Army clothing was soon issued to the men, who were pleased with the new outfits. Of course, the army could not furnish calico and muslin for the women and children and they had to do without.

The people kept wondering when they would be sent to the Malheur agency. Sarah heard that Agent Rinehart was seen there from time to time and was ordering supplies through the Indian Department.[9] The Indians were well treated at Camp Harney, but they still had an unerring suspicion that all was not

Gathering sagebrush for campfires against the winter cold. (Courtesy of Special Collections, University of Nevada, Reno.)

well. They observed new settlers moving onto the reservation, building cabins, and fencing their herds, while the military did nothing about it.

One day Sarah was called to the office of Captain M. A. Cochran, the post commander. She had such a feeling of foreboding that she trembled before him. Cochran told her that she looked ill and to sit down, because he had bad news. The Paiutes were to be taken to Yakima Reservation beyond the Columbia River.[10] Sarah reminded him that many of the people had done nothing wrong, that many had not gone with the Bannocks. For example, Leggins, who had saved the lives of several whites, had moved his band to Camp McDermit right off. She asked, "If there are any to be sent away, let it be Oytes and his men, numbering about twenty-five in all, and the few Bannocks that are with them." The captain answered that the soldiers would not take Chief Winnemucca's band, but all those who were there at Camp Harney.

"Oh, if you knew what I have promised my people, you would leave nothing undone but what you would try not to have them

sent away," Sarah cried. "My people will never believe me again."
The major promised that he would write the president and do
what he could to alleviate the situation.[11]

Sarah told the sad story to Mattie, who said, "We cannot help
it if the white people won't keep their word."

"Our people will say we are working against them and are
getting money for all this," Sarah replied.

The disconsolate women walked to the camp in the evening
and watched the singing, the dancing, and the drumming. The
Numa were happy. Sarah thought, "My poor, poor people, tomorrow or next week your happiness will be turned to weeping."
She and Mattie could not sleep.

One evening, a few weeks later, Sarah was again called to
headquarters. Mattie said that she would accompany her. Captain Cochran met them and said, "Sarah, I am heartily sorry for
you, but we cannot help it. We are ordered to take your people
to Yakima Reservation."

Sarah thought her world had ended. How could she tell her
people? "What, in this cold winter and in all this snow, and my
people have so many little children? Why they will die."

Captain Cochran had no reply, only to say that they should
tell no one until a few days before leaving.[12] When the time
arrived, Sarah was told to bring Leggins to Cochran's office. The
officer then asked who were the worst offenders during the war.
Through Sarah as interpreter, Leggins named Oytes, Bannock
Joe, Captain Bearskin, Paddy Cap, Boss, Big John, Eagle Eye,
Charley, D. E. Johnson, Beads, and a son-in-law of Oytes's called
Surger. Those men were sent for and were placed in the guard-
house. Sarah was told to tell them that they were put there for
safe keeping because the citizens of Canyon City were coming
over to arrest them.

Then Sarah had to tell the whole encampment the decision of
the army. The misery and heartbreak of the Numa were immense.
The women still had few clothes, and there were no blankets.
When Captain Cochran heard that Rinehart was getting Indian
supplies at the agency, which was only fifty-five miles away, he
wrote and asked if he would come and issue to the Paiutes at
Camp Harney, as they were suffering for want of clothing. When
he received no answer, he wrote again, but again received no

answer.[13] Apparently Rinehart did not desire to break his precedent of never issuing clothing to Indians. They received nothing from him.

Leggins's band were told that they would not go to Yakima and were not put under guard, but Oytes's, Egan's, and Tau-wa-dah's were closely watched. It was just before Christmas, and the people had one week to ready themselves for the journey. On the night of December 25 thirty prisoners of war at Camp Harney broke guard and escaped. The alarm was given before they had time to get far, and the two companies of cavalry at the post were alerted before more could follow.[14] On the next day Lee and Leggins were sent out to bring the prisoners back. Later Sarah and Mattie rode after five women who had gotten away. While the two women scouts were riding hard, Mattie's horse slipped in the snow, and she was thrown to the ground. Sarah wheeled her horse around and jumped down beside Mattie, rushing to hold her in her arms. Help was summoned from the camp, but the surgeon there did little for her.[15] In the days that were left before the trek to Yakima, Mattie lay quietly on the bed, uncomplaining. Her large eyes followed Sarah about the room as she sewed fur caps, fur gloves, and fur overshoes for the two of them. On the day of departure, January 6, 1879, Mattie was carried out to a four-horse wagon.[16] Fifty other wagons were waiting for the women, children, and old people. The men were to follow on their horses.

The journey to Yakima was 350 miles over two mountain ranges in the dead of winter and without adequate clothing. Suffering was inevitable. When the slowly moving column arrived at Canyon City, a telegram waited for Captain Winters. Inexplicably, he was to return for Leggins's band at Camp Harney.[17] The weather turned stormy, and it snowed during the two days that the wagon train waited for Leggins. During this time Mr. and Mrs. Charles Parrish came to speak to the prisoners.

Mrs. Parrish was the beloved teacher, the "white lily," who had been with them during their little time of happiness at Malheur. She remembered the names that she herself had given to the children. She cried when she saw Mattie, one of her best students, in such a helpless condition and she took the young woman's hands. Mattie wept also, for the white woman had been more than a teacher to her. The Paiutes begged Mr. Parrish to help them and not to let them be taken to a country that they did not know where the other Indians would not welcome them. He told them that there was nothing that he could do.[18] On that night an old man who could not manage for himself in the cold was left in a wagon on the road. He had frozen to death by morning when they returned for him. The citizen who owned the wagon threw his body out beside the road.

The captain sent Sarah to instruct Leggins, who had just come up, that he was to help the soldiers guard the prisoners; the "Big Father" in Washington wanted him to do this, and then his people could return to Oregon in the spring. Sarah gave Leggins this message, but he would not speak to her, nor would her brother Lee.[19] They traveled all day in the snow, and that night a woman gave birth to a baby who died soon after. The mother lived another day before she too was left by the road. Three young children died on the trip from exposure to the cold. Another woman gave birth, and she lived, but her baby did not. All this time Mattie was in considerable pain being jostled along on the rutty roads. Sarah knew that there was little hope for her recovery.

After they had crossed the Columbia River on a ferry, the exiles arrived in Yakima on January 31. They made camp thirty miles from the agency buildings, which were at Fort Simcoe. The refugees stayed at this camp for ten days, while the agent, Reverend James H. Wilbur, prepared to receive them. He had not been forewarned of their coming and had no extra food or shelter available at the time of their arrival. Meanwhile Agent Rinehart at Malheur complained because 65,000 pounds of both beef and flour lay unused at his agency.[20]

"Father" Wilbur hastily constructed a large shed 150 feet long near the agency for the 543 prisoners. The work was done by the Yakima Indians, who were regarded as "civilized." It was to this shed that the Paiutes were herded when they moved to the agency.[21] The snow was waist-deep, and there was no wood for fuel. Many more people died. When they saw the conditions in which they were to live, they lost hope.

The Paiute men still had their long, warm soldiers' overcoats, but many of these were soon lost to the Yakima Indians in gambling and trading for horses and buckskins. Leggins had a good many horses with him, and so had the other men, but they kept disappearing. The Paiutes asked the Yakimas to keep an eye out for them until it was discovered that the Yakimas themselves were taking the horses and disposing of them. Sarah's own horse, Meride, disappeared and was later found with pack sores on her back.[22] Agent Wilbur did not try to improve the relations between the two Indian groups. Sarah believed that he did not want to be bothered about the horses or the lost clothing of the Paiutes.[23]

In early spring Wilbur did put the Numa to work planting wheat on their own sixty acres. The agent also told Sarah to report to her people that seventeen wagons of clothes were on their way to them from The Dalles and that they would be distributed. The issuing day came in May. Of the lovely goods that the Paiutes had seen brought into the storehouse from the wagons, only twenty-eight little shawls were given out, plus some dress goods which were so thin that Sarah claimed one could sift flour through them. Two to three yards were given to each woman. One mother was given six yards of cloth for herself and her six children. Some of the men who had worked hardest got blankets, and a few got hats.[24] After the issue the people laughed and said: "Another Rinehart!—don't you see he is the same? He looks up into the sky and says something, just like Rinehart." The goods brought for the Paiutes were sold to whoever had money for them.

During this time Mattie's condition had deteriorated. The agency doctor, a man named Kuykendall, could not help her. (Sarah relates in her autobiography how he would give her a little sugar, rice, or tea for the sick, saying, "Give them something good to eat before they die.")[25] Mattie was unable to assist with the issue of clothing, and she suffered much before her death on May 29, 1879.[26]

Rinehart made a trip to Fort McDermit in late April to talk to Winnemucca and Natchez in an attempt to induce them to come to the Malheur Reservation with their people.[27] He reminded them that Oytes was no longer at the Malheur agency and that the fertile land would be theirs, although Ocheo would be coming also from Camp Bidwell. Winnemucca refused the offer. He was still haunted by the dream of land near Fort McDermit or on the Owyhee. Most of all he was convinced that the settlers of Grant County would kill any Indian, friend or foe, on sight. Already two of the tribe had lost their lives in this manner.[28] Then, too, squatters were on the best land of the Malheur and were determined to stay.

Rinehart seemed to be the only participant in the conversations who was not facing reality. His reservation had been without a single Indian on it for almost a year. Although it was a lost cause, he could not give up such a lucrative position easily, and he persisted for many months in his determination to get the Paiutes to return.[29] He did get Old Winnemucca and Natchez to promise that they would return to Malheur if Chief Leggins and his band were brought back from Yakima.

Leggins and the other prisoners at Yakima were not forgotten by their fellow Paiutes. Chief Winnemucca took the case of Leggins to General McDowell in San Francisco. He explained that his son Lee, who had always been friendly to the whites, was also held prisoner.[30] The general produced letters showing that Lee was not a prisoner, but free to go when and where he pleased. As for Leggins, McDowell promised to inquire into his case. Winnemucca again asked for land of his own, but the general, though he desired to grant the old man's request, had no power to do so.

Again Rinehart met with Winnemucca and Natchez. He threatened that he could compel them to go to Malheur.[31] Then, suddenly changing his tactics, he offered Natchez $100 for his assistance plus $5.00 per head for every Paiute whom he could persuade to return to the Malheur reservation.[32] Natchez refused.

When Natchez was interviewed in San Francisco in June, 1879, he talked to the reporter about the Paiutes' situation at Yakima where his sister and brother Lee were living. He had recently received a letter from Sarah, and she was teaching school. Her sixty Paiute students were doing well. They had a good crop of corn and potatoes, but twenty-one people had died since the previous winter when they had been forcibly moved to Yakima and many more were on the sick list. If General McDowell allowed him to go to Yakima, Natchez planned to take Sarah some pine nuts. She had written him that she had a real yearning for the taste of them.[33]

At Yakima, Methodist minister Wilbur was making plans for a religious revival. Important personages from the East were to come to observe his work with the Indians. Sarah, though she

bitterly denounced people who she felt did not behave as professed Christians should, had accepted the religion of the whites
and considered herself a Methodist; Father Wilbur and General
Howard wrote of her as a Christian woman.[34] She was told by
Wilbur to keep the Paiutes out of sight during the revival. She
understood that it would be an embarrassment to the agent to
explain what had happened to the clothing of her people, who
were still scantily dressed.[35] However, when it was time for the
meeting, she did the opposite of what Wilbur wanted. She
brought the Paiutes right to the agent's house and had them
sit on the benches intended for the Christian Indians. In her
autobiography she wrote, "I wanted all to see how well we were
treated by Christian people." When she saw that some of the
Numa came to the revival every day, especially the little children,
she stood at the pulpit and interpreted the words of Father Wilbur
and Bishop Erastus Otis Haven from Boston, so that the Paiutes
might hear the sermons themselves.[36] Despite this confrontation
the plight of the Paiutes did not improve under Wilbur.

By August, Natchez's plans for visiting Yakima had not materialized. When Sarah at last received her compensation from the
army for her work as a scout and courier during the Bannock
war, her people begged her to go east and talk for them. With
the means at hand Sarah promised that she would do all that
she could and told Father Wilbur that she would like to leave.
He at first would not let her go, but then he said, "Well, Sarah,
I can't keep you if you want to go. Who is to talk for your people?"
She replied, "Brother Lee can talk well enough." Then Wilbur
said that she was free to go when the religious revival was over.

Sarah left Yakima in November and went directly to Vancouver to see General Howard at his headquarters. She told him
of the misery of her people at the Yakima Reservation, their
desire to return to their homes, and her plan to go to Washington
to speak for them. Howard encouraged her in her enterprise,
giving her a letter of introduction to Washington officials.[37]

She did not know that Agent Wilbur had written to the commissioner of Indian affairs that the Paiutes now under his charge
were "contented and happy," saying, "I think it would be a child-
ish course to return them." He reminded the department that they
had spent $50,000 in removing the Indians to Yakima. He recom-
mended that the Malheur Agency be broken up and Yakima made

the Paiutes' permanent home.[38] Agent Rinehart now had run up against an antagonist with an equal talent for self-aggrandizement.

The "pernicious" fandangos for which Agent Rinehart had such contempt were held several times yearly. The numerous Paiute chiefs would agree upon a time and place, and often as many as three or four hundred people would assemble. It was a time for young people to pursue a mate, and for all the Numa to visit and have a good time storytelling and gambling. By now card playing had become as popular as the rhythmical chanting of the traditional hand game. Older Paiutes would sit around the sage-brush fires in their colorful blankets, the firelight flickering on their painted faces. Little children peeped from their rabbit-skin blankets on the outer edge of the large encirclement of scattered fires, while older children ran and jumped in play, calling to each other in the darkness.

When the first dance was called, some men formed a circle around a cedar tree set up in a large cleared area. They commenced a low chant as they moved with regular steps facing the tree, shoulder to shoulder. Gradually women and children filled the circle, and the chant continued:

> Hoe, hoe, hoe, hi-hi!
> Hi-yah, hi-yah, hi-hi!
> Hoe, hoo, hi-yah, hi-hi!

The chant and dancing might keep up all night. If a dancer tired, another replaced him, most of them with the sacred red paint daubed on their faces. It was a solemn dance of communion and hope, though it seemed monotonous to white observers.

Wovoka (or Jack Wilson, as he was called by the whites) had lain ill in his hut in Mason Valley near the Walker River Reserve. He had fallen into a coma and then into trance, where he was transported to the spirit world and received a revelation. Afterward he had reported to his fellows: "An Indian millennium is to come, when all warlike things are to be discarded and honesty, peace and good will will prevail between men of all colors."[39] In their simple dance at the fandango the Paiutes expressed a longing for the promised new era.

The Northern Paiutes now possessed two leaders who would draw national attention to the plight of native Americans. While

Wovoka, or Jack Wilson, the Paiute shaman who originated the Ghost Dance religion. (Courtesy of Nevada Historical Society.)

Sarah Winnemucca would travel the continent, Wovoka stayed in Mason Valley. The Indians came to him, riding free on the rails, to hear the wisdom of the prophet who heralded a new day.

Sarah Winnemucca would attempt a political change while Wovoka prophesied a spiritual one.

15

The "Princess" Sarah

On her arrival in San Francisco from Portland on the steamer *California*, Sarah found herself something of a celebrity. When Natchez met her, he was accompanied by several reporters, who asked for individual interviews. Sarah was described as a self-possessed young woman who had been in the public eye during the Bannock War; the San Francisco newspapers headlined her as "The Princess Sarah." One writer commented, "The fire-flash in her eyes and the dramatic action of her race invest the simple language she uses with a native eloquence which carries a certain weight with the most cautious hearer."[1] The "princess" wore at her throat a silver ornament that had been given her by Natchez. It was engraved with an inscription by the citizens of Humboldt County who were grateful for the saving of several white men's lives during the Bannock War.[2]

Sarah told one reporter: "I have just been thinking how it would do for me to lecture upon the Bannock War. I might get the California Theatre, and perhaps I could make my expenses. I would be the first Indian woman who ever spoke before white people," she explained, "and they don't know what the Indians have got to stand sometimes."[3]

The *San Francisco Chronicle* reported:

Sarah has undergone hardships and dared dangers that few men would be willing to face, but she has not lost her womanly qualities, and succeeded during her visit in coaxing into her lap two little timid "pale-faced" children, usually shy of strangers, who soon lost their fear of her dark skin, won by her warm and genial ways. She speaks with force and decision, and talks eloquently of her people. Her mission, undertaken at the request of Chief Winnemucca, is to have her tribe gathered together again at their old home in Nevada, where they can follow peaceable pursuits and improve themselves.[4]

All was not accolades for Sarah, however. The *Chronicle* reporter also described her as having "an extensive and diversified matrimonial experience, the number of her white husbands being variously estimated at from three to seven."[5] When Sarah read that report, she hastily granted an interview to a reporter on the *San Francisco Call* to refute it. In the *Call* interview she mentioned her marriage to Bartlett and subsequent divorce and a second marriage to an Indian, who grossly mistreated her.[6] Aspersions on her personal life infuriated her.

Agent Rinehart learned of Sarah's popularity in San Francisco and countered by writing to the Indian Department that she was a "low, unprincipled Indian woman of questionable virtue and veracity as well, who was formerly Interpreter at the Agency and who was discharged for untruthfulness, gambling and other bad conduct."[7] Rinehart knew that General Howard had little regard for him, and he told the commissioner of Indian affairs that Sarah had prejudiced the commanding general against him.

Sarah was encouraged by friends and army officers to lecture in San Francisco, and she spoke several times in Platt's Hall on Montgomery Street between Bush and Pine Streets. Her experience in the theater fifteen years before helped her in the dramatic performances that she presented, often to capacity audiences. A San Francisco columnist, moved by a lecture that she gave in late November, wrote:

San Francisco was treated to the most novel entertainment it has ever known, last evening, in the shape of the address by Sarah, daughter of Chief Winnemucca, delivered in Platt's Hall. The Princess wore a short buckskin dress, the skirt bordered with fringe and embroidery, short sleeves, disclosing beautifully-rounded brown arms, and scarlet leggins, with trimmings of fringe. On her head she wore a proud head dress of eagle's feathers, set in a scarlet crown, contrasting well with her flowing black locks. The lecture was unlike anything ever before heard in the civilized world—eloquent, pathetic, tragical at times; at others her quaint anecdotes, sarcasms and wonderful mimicry surprised the audience again and again into bursts of laughter and rounds of applause. There was no set lecture from written manuscript, but a spontaneous flow of eloquence. Nature's child spoke in natural, unconstrained language, accompanied by gestures that were scarcely ever surpassed by any actress on the stage. The constraint which was naturally expected by the audience in one unused to faceing the public, was nowhere visible as the Indian girl walked upon the stage in an easy, unembarrassed manner, and entered at once upon the story of her race.[8]

Sarah felt that her audiences should know something of the history of her people and their way of life. She spoke of their first contacts with whites and how they had so often been mistreated. She concluded: "Then the Indians go and harm some innocent white people in their vengeance. I do not excuse my people. But I say you cannot hold them from it unless you change your treatment of them."[9] On one occasion she observed after the war, "they told us to go on the reservation and the government would give us provisions every day. Did they do it? No—they didn't. The agents robbed us."[10]

Sarah's thoughts returned to Malheur, where her superiors had so often forced her to influence the Numa against their own best interests. She wanted her audiences, who sat in the luxury of a comfortable auditorium, to understand her position and help her people. She spoke of Rinehart, his treatment of his charges when they were on the reservation, and how, even though no Paiute had set foot at Malheur for over a year, he had a large store of supplies.

Sarah brought down the house when she spoke of how the Christian Rinehart beckoned the Paiutes to be kind and good and honest with one hand while he was busy grabbing with the other behind their backs:[11] "Mr. Rinehart is a good man probably. I think he is a good man. The biggest thief, whether a man or a woman, is good if wealthy. With the jingle in his pocket and plenty in his hand, he lives away up."[12] The audience responded sympathetically to Sarah's emotions when, in her pleadings for the return of Leggins's band, the tears streamed down her face.

After one of Sarah's lectures, J. W. Scott, the beef contractor

Sarah Winnemucca as she appeared in stage attire of her own design. (Courtesy of Nevada Historical Society.)

at the Malheur Reservation, came to her and said, "Sarah, I would like to have you help me get some of your people to go with me to the Malheur Agency." He offered her thirty dollars. Sarah thought, "The white people believe they are better than I am. They make money any way and every way they can. Why not I? I have not any. I will take it." She accepted the money, but later wrote that she regretted many times that she had done so.[13]

Natchez informed Sarah that Scott had held a council with the leading Paiutes at the Winnemucca courthouse, where Natchez, Old Winnemucca, and all the leaders had again refused to go to the reservation unless Leggins was allowed to return. Natchez had said:

You take my people to Malheur to starve them. While scouting. . . . I saw Oitz take your hair in his hand when water ran out of your eyes. I saved your life, but you would not help me. I heard you read paper two ways and we cannot trust you. You told me you are a high officer. Now, when white men who are my friends hear you, you deny it. You take my word for it, my people will not go with you. . . . They live in peace here. You come to my camp and I'll board you for nothing.[14]

Although Sarah and Natchez both believed that the Paiutes should not give up the Malheur Reservation, which abounded in fish, game, and timber, they would not claim it as long as Rinehart was there.

While she was in San Francisco, Sarah wrote and circulated a petition to the Interior Department, asking on behalf of the Paiutes that the former Malheur agent, Sam Parrish, be reinstated, or, if that was not possible, that some other honest and humane civilian or military officer be appointed as agent. This document also requested that the Paiutes who had been sent to Yakima be permitted to return to the Malheur agency, and it affirmed their innocence in the conduct of the Bannock War.[15]

For her last lecture in San Francisco, on Christmas Eve, 1879, Sarah was billed as going to Washington with an imaginary string of Indian agents' scalps:

[In the East, where people are not used] to English lectures by an Indian woman, her appearance will be likely to draw, from sheer novelty, and please by the picturesqueness of her costume, and a certain gracefulness and dramatic effect of her gestures as well as her sententious sentences, which frequently bear a striking similarity [to] the poetry of Holy Writ.

As Sarah claims to be a Methodist, this coincidence may, perhaps, be referred to her reading of the Old Testament."[16]

As she stood before her last audience, Sarah implored:

I am appealing to you to help my people, to send teachers and books among us. Educate us. Every one shuns me, and turns a back on me with contempt. Some say I am a half breed. My father and mother were pure Indians. I would be ashamed to acknowledge there was white blood in me. . . . I want homes for my people but no one will help us. I call upon white people in their private houses. They will not touch my fingers for fear of getting soiled. That's the Christianity of white people."[17]

Sarah had been rebuffed in her attempts to get help and was especially critical of her own denomination, the Methodists, whom she felt had not supported her:

You take all the natives of the earth in your bosom but the poor Indian, who is born of the soil of your land and who has lived for generations on the land which the good God has given to them, and you say he must be exterminated. (Thrice repeated, with deep passion, and received with tremendous applause.)

The proverb says the big fish eat up the little fishes and we Indians are the little fish and you eat us all up and drive us from home. (The audience reacted with sympathetic cheers to this statement.)

Where can we poor Indians go, if the government will not help us? If your people will help us, and you have good hearts, and can if you will, I will promise to educate my people and make them law-abiding citizens of the United States. (Loud applause.) It can be done—it can be done. (Cheers.)[18]

The acclaim that Sarah received in San Francisco was noticed in Washington, and, when she arrived with Natchez in Lovelock, Nevada, they discovered that a special agent from the Interior Department, J. M. Haworth, had been sent to check on the "unrest" of the Paiutes.[19] When they met with Haworth in Winnemucca, Sarah acted as interpreter for the Paiute spokesmen. Natchez was the first to speak:

The reason we do not want to go to Malheur is, that the man who is there now forced our people, by ill treatment, to go on the war path. . . . Rinehart gave me money to take my people to Malheur but I would not do it for This is the country we were born in, and I think the whites will not injure us. . . . We have no homes, and if the Government does not feel disposed to give us homes, leave us as we are, and not make promises to be fulfilled after we are dead. We do not say the Great Father does not want to give us supplies, but we know we never get any. . . . The Agent now at Truckee, Mr. Spencer, gives us some rations, and does better than all the Agents who were there before him. Now, my friend from the Great Father, I am glad to hear you talk and not make promises. If you came like Indian Agents, I would fly to the mountains, where I could not be found.[20]

Old Winnemucca had spent more time than usual within the previous year in the environs of the town of Winnemucca. In August he had attended a fandango, at which he had marched with two hundred members of the tribe from their campground to the train depot. Dressed in a breechclout and a few feathers, he had painted his arms, legs and face with yellow, red, and black. At the depot the passengers on the train from the east had been astonished at the sight of the chief, who was purportedly in his late eighties, carrying the Stars and Stripes at the head of the column, while another leader bore a white flag alongside. The Indians marched straight for the tracks, but then wheeled abruptly and returned to their camp, where they had danced the remainder of the night.[21]

Winnemucca had appeared again at the station in October, this time wearing his usual epaulets, brass buttons, and feathered top hat. The passengers who had never seen an Indian crowded around him and insisted on shaking hands. He gallantly extended his hand to the ladies, but asked the gentlemen for a cigar "for the privilege."[22]

Now, in December, Winnemucca spoke to Haworth with Sarah as his interpreter:

We say, one and all, we will have a home near McDermit, or anywhere on the Humboldt river, where we were born. Look at us. Do we appear like wild animals? My people are as capable of learning as other races. You, my brother, who has come so far to see us, I think my people can tell you in English what they think, and I hope to live to see the day when they will be educated.

There have been agents after agents, but none of them gave us land, or anything to dig up the roots of the sagebrush . . . Here I stand old, ready to go into my grave; but I have never been guilty of striking any of you down, and I know my white brothers will not strike me down . . .

There will be no trouble between the Indians and whites here, they will testify to the truth of what we tell you.

He turned to Haworth and said emphatically,

We are tired of promises. When you go home tell Washington we live here and beg bread for our children when we have no other means of getting it.

Those Indians [who] were taken without cause to Yakima, we want them sent back here, to their own country. The man who killed Buffalo Horn, the Bannock Chief [Piute Joe], is now an exile from his own country. . . . We beg of you to ask permission to have them returned; but those hostile Indians, who were on the war path, you can deal with according to your own laws.[23]

The old chief sat down and closed his eyes while Sarah finished her interpretation, but he was not asleep.

After other Paiute leaders had spoken, Natchez rose again and said:

We will talk to the point. First bring Leggin and his band to Malheur. I will then go there myself and see how things are conducted, and if these Indians want to go all right. . . . If you attempt to force us there without cause you cannot do it. This driving talk is not right, we are all human beings. Have the whites no hearts? . . . We were told the Indians would be brought back from Yakima, would meet us at Malheur in three weeks. This was six months ago and they have not come there yet. We want our liberty to go when we feel like it on the same terms as white men.

At that the other Paiutes concurred with nods of approval, and Natchez concluded by saying to Haworth: "I want you to help me. We want to hear the President talk, myself, Sarah, Father Winnemucca and Jerry Long want to go to Washington. . . . When I return I will go to Ochoho's at Bidwell and try to get him to go first to the reservation, if we are treated fairly."[24]

Agent Haworth's reply was to say that he was very glad to hear that Chief Winnemucca and the others valued an education for their people. He complimented Sarah on her efficiency as an interpreter and remarked that there were other Paiute women who were as smart as she and only lacked an education to make them her equal in every respect. Natchez chuckled and said, "My wife is smarter than Sarah."

The Winnemucca family: Sarah, Chief Winnemucca, Natchez, Captain Jim, and an unidentified boy. This photograph probably was taken in Washington, D.C., in 1880. (Courtesy of Nevada Historical Society.)

Haworth promised, "I will write to Washington to make arrangements to have Chief Winnemucca, Sarah, Natchez and Jerry Long taken there to talk to the Great Father and we will arrange to have a number of tents sent here for wickiups."[25] As the long-awaited trip finally began to materialize, Sarah felt some hope that influential people with good hearts would yet come to the aid of her people.

Before leaving for Washington, Sarah lectured in Centennial Hall at Winnemucca to a fair-sized audience and exhibited pieces of tapestry that she said she had made when she had gone to school in California. She spoke of the spiritual beliefs of the Paiutes and the importance of shamans, or medicine men, to the tribe, saying, "They are venerated more than the war chiefs." She frankly admitted that she did not know whether the Paiute or the Christian religion was the better.

A local reporter criticized Sarah's lecture, writing that she jumped too much from one subject to another and that the Paiute Princess was said to have become gloriously drunk afterward: "The Princess lived here some four or five years ago, and was in the habit of getting full every night. Probably she found some of her old acquaintances Saturday night and could not resist the temptation to indulge in her old habits. In this respect she differs from her brother Naches, who is an exemplary Indian and never drinks fire-water."[26]

Sarah did not have an opportunity to defend her reputation against this journalistic attack until after her return from Washington. After several disappointing delays she finally boarded the Central Pacific Railroad on January 13, 1880.[27] She was accompanied by Natchez, Chief Winnemucca, and Captain Jim, who replaced Jerry Long for the Paiute debut in the nation's capital. They rode a week before they arrived in Washington City. Once there, Sarah was to be confronted with a concerted effort to destroy her usefulness as a witness against the reservation system and the men who benefited from its bungling procedures.

16

Washington City

When Sarah arrived in Washington City, D.C., in January, 1880, she discovered that she and the Paiute delegation were confined by a strict schedule, which allowed them appearances only before government officials and a great amount of sightseeing. On the second day after her arrival she had an appointment with Secretary of the Interior Carl Schurz. An underling in the secretary's anteroom made fun of her tears when she pleaded with him for the return of the Paiutes from Yakima. He accused her of lecturing only for money. Secretary Schurz listened sympathetically to her presentation, or so it appeared. Then he instructed Mr. Haworth, who was with the Paiutes every minute when they were not in the Tremont Hotel, to take them around by carriage to places of particular interest in the city. When reporters wished to interview Sarah or find out where she was lecturing, she was whisked away by Mr. Haworth.[1]

Sarah was not aware that Agent Rinehart had sent affidavits to Washington, signed by nine gentlemen of Canyon City, which stated in part:

We have seen with amazement the charges brought against him [Rinehart] by an Indian woman calling herself Sarah Winnemucca; not that anything this woman can say or do amazed us, but that an intelligent public and high officials should give any credence to the statements of

such a person is startling to us. . . . That her influence with the Indians
has always been to render them licentious, contumacious and profligate.
That this woman has been several times married, but that by reason
of her adulterous and drunken habits, neither squawmen nor Indians
would long live with her; that in addition to her character of Harlot
and drunkard, she merits and possesses that of a notorious liar and
malicious schemer.[2]

Among the signatures on the affidavits was that of D. G. Over-
holt, who had been in partnership with Rinehart in the mer-
chandising business in Canyon City.

Rinehart had also obtained three affidavits at Camp Harney,
sworn and subscribed to him on January 13: one by William
Currey, a stock raiser; one by Thomas O'Keefe, a discharged
soldier; and one from his former blacksmith at Malheur, W. W.
Johnson. In an introductory letter accompanying them, Rinehart
apologized for the necessity of sending the affidavits:

It has not been deemed necessary to resort to actual proof of her true
standing in this community until the present, when it seems likely that
the Depart. may be called upon to consider hers in connection with my
own.character. . . . Comment upon these affidavits is deemed unnecessary, further than to say I believe them to be true; and, so notorious
is her ill-fame, that I feel assured I could obtain the evidence of scores
of the best men in this country, as to her general bad character.[3]

William Currey and W. W. Johnson wrote that Sarah was untruthful and "generally regarded by those who know her as a
common prostitute and thoroughly addicted to the habits of
drunkenness and gambling."[4] Thomas O'Keefe stated that Sarah
could be bought for a bottle of whiskey.[5]

The Indian Department's intrigue to keep Sarah from reporters
and other interested parties was merely an attempt to allay the
criticisms that she would make of them and their department.
It is doubtful that the affidavits reached the capital before Sarah's
departure in early February, and, since she knew nothing of
Rinehart's nefarious schemes, she did not defend herself.

Sarah did gain a short interview with a reporter from the
Washington National Republican. He wrote, "Dashing Sarah . . . in
intellect, grace and knowledge of the world, will compare favorably with many belles of Pennsylvania avenue."[6] She told him
that she still planned to lecture. Consequently Secretary Schurz

called her immediately to his office and confronted her, saying, "Sarah, so you are bound to lecture."

"People want me to," she replied.

Then he said, "I don't think it will be right for you to lecture here after the government has sent for you, and your father and brother, and paid your way here. The government is going to do right by your people now. Don't lecture now; go home and get your people on the reservation; get them located properly; and then, if you want to come back, . . . we will pay your way here and back again."[7]

Schurz told Sarah that his department had granted all that she had wished and presented her with a letter with his signature that confirmed his statement. Sarah was delighted by its contents:

> Department of the Interior
> Washington D.C.
> [January 24], 1880

The Pi-Utes, heretofore entitled to live on the Malheur Reservation, their primeval home, are to have lands allotted to them in severalty, at the rate of one hundred and sixty acres to each head of a family, and each adult male. Such lands they are to cultivate for their own benefit. The allotment will be made under instructions of their agent. As soon as enabled by law to do so, this department is to give to the Indians patents for each tract of land conveying to each occupant the fee-simple in the lot he occupies.

Those of the Pi-Utes, who in consequence of the Bannock war, went to the Yakima Reservation, and whoever may desire to rejoin their relatives, are at liberty to do so, without expense to the government for transportation. Those who desire to stay upon the Yakima Reservation and become permanently settled there will not be disturbed.

None of the Pi-Utes now living among the whites, and earning wages by their own work will be compelled to go to the Malheur Reservation. They are at perfect liberty to continue working for wages for their own benefit, as they are now doing.

It is well understood that those who settle on the Malheur Reservation will not be supported by the government in idleness. They will be aided in starting their farms and promoting their civilization, but the support given them by the government will, according to law, depend upon their intelligence and efficiency in working for themselves.

> C. Schurz
> *Secretary of the*
> *Interior*[8]

The secretary also promised Sarah that, when the Paiutes returned to Lovelock, they would be sent 100 canvas tents for their use. Sarah was to issue the tents and send the department the name of each head of family who required one.

The important day came when the Paiute representatives were to talk with the Great White Father. They were first shown through the White House, where many women had congregated to see Sarah.[9] They found her fashionably dressed, in a neat black suit with satin trimmings, and thoroughly composed. Eventually President Hayes walked in and shook hands with the Paiute delegation.

"Did you get all you want for your people?" the president asked Sarah.

"Yes, sir," Sarah replied, "as far as I know."

"That is well," he answered and went out again. It was quite a short affair, seeing President Hayes, and therefore rather a letdown for the Paiutes. It was especially disappointing to Sarah, who had imagined he would take a personal interest in her people.

When the Winnemuccas arrived home in Nevada and stopped off at Lovelock, Paiutes came from all directions to hear their report of their trip and to find out if they had been successful in settling matters. As the days passed, Natchez did not have enough food at Big Meadows to feed the throng, and they almost starved while waiting for the tents to arrive from Washington. Old Winnemucca had been treated to a new suit of clothes by Washington officials. He gave it away when he was back home, saying to Sarah: "This is all I got from the Big Father in Washington. I am the only one who got anything; I don't care for them."[10]

The longer they waited the hungrier the people became. At last Winnemucca told his people: "My dear children, every word we have told you was said to us. They have given us a paper which your mother will read to you." Sarah read the letter from Schurz slowly, so that Natchez could translate. When they had finished, Buena Vista John rose and said:

I have lived many years with white people. Yes, it is over thirty years, and I know a great many of them. I have never known one of them do what they promised. I think they mean it just at the time, but I tell you they are very forgetful. It seems to me, sometimes, that their memory is not good and since I have understood them, if they say they will do so and so for me, I would say to them now or never, and if they don't, why it is because they never meant to do, but only to say so. These are your white brothers' ways, and they are a weak people."[11]

Still the tents did not arrive, and Sarah telegraphed a reminder to Secretary Schurz, saying "Send us something to eat." The secretary wrote in reply that she should take her people to the Malheur Reservation. She would not think of taking the people, who were already starving, three hundred miles through waist-deep snow. She told the Paiutes what the letter contained. They all laughed and said: "We are not disappointed. We always said that the Big Father was just like all the white people."[12] The large number of Numa scattered to wherever they could scavenge food.

During that winter and early spring Agent John Howe of the Duck Valley Reservation, which had been set aside for the Shoshonis, noted an unusual migration of as many as 500 Paiutes who had never been on his reservation before. They called the Shoshoni chief Captain Sam their leader, and claimed to be half-blood Shoshonis. They appeared to be from Natchez's band in the vicinity of Paradise Valley, but they would not claim Natchez or Winnemucca as their leader. They said that they did not like them and that they would not go to Malheur. Captain Sam accepted them as his own, and so Howe apportioned garden tracts to the newcomers. He had to use his seed potatoes and seed wheat in order to feed the unexpected visitors.[13]

In the spring a new chief of the Paiutes was elected: Dave Numana, who was a brother of Buena Vista John and a relative of Sarah's. Natchez no longer claimed the chieftainship because he did not wish to live at Pyramid Lake, which seemed to be a new requirement.[14] There was no doubt that Natchez and Old Winnemucca had lost ground with the Paiutes when they returned from the prestigious trip to the Great White Father in Washington with nothing in their hands. Then, too, their urging of tribal members to move to the Malheur did not set well. Old Winnemucca himself, after all his crediting of white friendship and brotherhood, was as destitute as anyone. He was described as "heap-a-hungry" in Virginia City.[15]

In the meantime Sarah had a clash with the editor of the *Winnemucca Silver State* who had printed the article intimating that she was drunk before her trip to Washington. In a rage she sent a telegram from Lovelock threatening the writer.[16] Now she was arrested for sending the missive and taken before Justice Charles S. Osborn of Winnemucca. She explained that she had sent the telegram because the New York pictorial newspapers had picked up the Nevada story and had claimed that she had been drunk and brandishing a knife. The *Silver State* reported, "This falsehood aroused her anger and caused her to threaten to have the editor's blood."[17] The case was dismissed, but other newspapers also carried the article and embroidered on it.[18]

Agent Rinehart was thrown into paroxysms of indignation by a letter from the Indian commissioner appointing Sarah, the "infamous" woman, to be interpreter once again for the Malheur Reservation.[19] He quickly reminded the department of "her notoriety as an untruthful, drunken prostitute." In the same letter he wrote the commissioner:

It was publicly known, then as now, that her last occupation before coming to this Agency as Interpreter for Agent Parrish, was in a public house of ill-fame at the town of Winnemucca Nevada. . . . Among the "other sufficient causes", alluded to in my report to General Howard's Headquarters for which she was discharged from the position of Interpreter, was that one of my white employees says he saw her in bed with an Indian man in the mess-house. In view of such facts knowing as I do that this is only part of her infamous history, I am induced to venture the opinion that she is not a proper person to serve in any capacity at this or any other Indian Agency.[20]

Sarah had received notice of her appointment as interpreter at Malheur while she was still in Washington, but the minimal salary of $420 a year was certainly not attractive when she had to pay board. Yet, in spite of that and in spite of Rinehart, she had made up her mind to take the position. While staying with her brother Tom at Pyramid Lake in April, she contacted Rinehart concerning the appointment.[21] She, of course, did not know of the affidavits that Rinehart had collected against her. When he wrote back that, since "none of your people are now at this Agency, your services as Interpreter are not required: and I have so informed the Indian Office,"[22] he failed to add that he had also written the department requesting that she be discharged.[23]

Sarah, recognizing that the Paiutes would only return to Mal-

heur along with Leggins and his people, decided to visit Yakima
and bring him and the others back. Armed only with the letter
that she had received from Schurz in Washington and accompanied by a sister-in-law (probably a wife of Lee Winnemucca),
she set off on horseback in April from Pyramid Lake, traveling
northward through desolate, uninhabited country. In her autobiography Sarah emphasizes the two women's worries traveling
alone.[24]

On the evening of the fourth day they approached a house
where Sarah's cousin Joe Winnemucca was working as a ranch
hand. Joe welcomed the women and introduced them to the
white rancher, who was a friend of Chief Winnemucca. The
two men could hardly believe that the women had traveled
alone through such formidable conditions. Sarah told her cousin
of the urgency of her trip—how she was going to bring the
people back to Malheur—and read him Schurz's letter. Joe was
very glad, because his brother Frank was detained at Yakima.[25]

Joe offered to go with the women to the next ranch because
he feared for their safety there. Upon their arrival at the place
Sarah was much relieved to find a friend who said, "Why, Sarah,
what in the world are you doing away out here at this time of
the year?" He helped her from her horse, and they were well
treated. When Sarah offered to pay for meals and the night's
lodging, the ranch owner would not hear of it. In the morning
Joe rode on with them a way and turned back, thinking all
was well. The women had ridden only ten miles before they discovered three horsemen traveling rapidly in pursuit. They were
Spanish vaqueros who worked on the ranch and had spotted
them. Sarah and her sister-in-law rode for their lives, but at last
they had to rest because their horses were exhausted. They
planned how they would save each other if they were attacked.
Luckily, their pursuers had lost heart by this time; only one came
up, and he spoke politely to them. They were able to ride on
without further trouble.

At the south end of Steens Mountain they stayed several days
with a cousin of Sarah's who was married to a white man. Then
they rode in the wagon of an acquaintance to their next lodging.
There a Mr. Anderson, a United States mail contractor, was very
kind to them, reading their letter and encouraging them in their
efforts. After supper, however, Sarah felt like crying. There were

eight cowboys in the ranchhouse, and there was no private room in which the women could sleep. At last Anderson said to the stage driver, "You and I must give up our bed to Miss Winnemucca tonight and go sleep with the boys."

At last the women lay down, but they could not sleep from fear. Sarah's description of the night and her feelings conveys some of the anxieties of unprotected females on the rough frontier. Sarah felt a hand on her in the darkness, and someone said, "Sarah."

She jumped up quickly and hit the intruder in the face with her fist, crying, "Go away or I will cut you to pieces." The man ran out of the house, leaving a trail of blood.

Mr. Anderson got up and lighted a candle. "Oh, Sarah, what have you done?" he said when he saw the blood. "Did you cut him?"

"No, I did not cut him; I wish I had," she answered. "I only struck him with my hand."

They looked outside, but the man was gone and had taken his horse. "The big fool," the rancher commented. A candle burned by the bed the remainder of the night.

Mr. Anderson got up at four and rustled some breakfast for the women, as they had to make Camp Harney that day, over sixty miles.[26]

At Camp Harney, Sarah and her sister-in-law found only three women, the wives of soldiers. They were very hospitable to the two Paiute women while the latter waited ten days for the deep snows to melt on the Blue Mountains. As Sarah had no money, she tried to sell her lame horse, but without success. Her last hope was that Mr. Stevens, the storekeeper at the camp, would loan her money. She went to him with her letter of appointment as interpreter at Malheur and, thinking that she would be paid in that position, the storekeeper lent her $100. Sarah, of course, assumed that the position would be hers when she returned with the Paiutes from Yakima.

Captain Drury at Camp Harney lent them a horse. Sarah and her sister-in-law spent two difficult days riding through the drifts of snow. Once they had to swim a river with their horses. At last they arrived in Canyon City, nearly frozen. While waiting in town for the stage to The Dalles, they had an opportunity to see Sarah's former attorney, Charles Parrish, who was saddened to hear of the deaths of his wife's students at Yakima.[27]

The stage to The Dalles was only a two-seated buckboard. When the two women reached the town, they were relieved to find Lee waiting for them; Sarah had written ahead, and he had hired horses from the Yakimas. Now they were on the last leg of the journey to the reservation. When they arrived, however, Sarah did not present her letter to Agent Wilbur for several days. She explains in *Life Among the Piutes* that she had to gather her courage before going to the agent's office. Meanwhile she told Lee of the letter's contents, and rumors circulated among the people.

When she did go to Wilbur, she asked him, "Did you get a letter from Washington?"

"No," he replied.

"Well, that is strange — they told me they would write."

"Who?"

"The Secretary of the Interior, Secretary Schurz."

"Why, what makes you think they would write to me?"

"Father, they told me they would write right off while I was there. It was about my people."

"We have not heard from them."

"Father, I have a letter here, which Secretary Schurz gave me." She showed the letter to Wilbur, who after reading it appeared to be angry.

"Sarah," he told her, "your people are doing well here, and I don't want you to tell them of this paper or to read it to them. They are the best workers I ever saw. If you will not tell them, I will give you fifty dollars, and I will write to Washington, and see if they will keep you here as interpreter."

Sarah replied, "How is it that I am not paid for interpreting here so long? Was I not turned over to you as an interpreter for my people? I have worked at everything while I was here. I helped in the school-house, and . . . interpreted sermons." She told him that she ought to be paid for what she had already done.

He told her that he would do so if she did not make the Paiutes discontented with their lot, as they were progressing nicely. Sarah did not promise, but neither did she tell the Paiutes about the paper, though they knew that she had an important message. They began to doubt her motives. At last Leggins called a council and demanded that Sarah and Lee come.

Sarah stood and, holding the paper over her head, she made the following speech:

My dear children, may the Great Father in the Spiritland will it so that you may see your husbands, and your children, and your daughters. I have said everything I could in your behalf, so did father and brother. I have suffered everything but death to come here with this paper. I don't know whether it speaks truth or not. You can say what you like about me. You have a right to say I have sold you. It looks so. I have told you many things which are not my own words, but the words of the agents and the soldiers. I know I have told you more lies than I have hair on my head. I tell you, my dear children, I have never told you my own words; they were the words of the white people, not mine. Of course, you don't know, and I don't blame you for thinking as you do. You will never know until you go to the Spirit-land. This which I hold in my hand is our only hope. . . . If it is truth we will see our people in fifty days. . . . I will read it just as it is, so that you can all judge for yourselves.[28]

After the reading the people reacted with joyous shouts. Leggins said, "Now, you have heard what our mother has told us, we will get ready to go at once."

While all the others were dancing and singing and coming to thank Sarah, Oytes sat quietly in a corner with his hands over his face. Anguish was in his eyes when he raised them to Leggins. He said, "Oh, brother, ask me to go with you to our dear Mother Earth, where we can lie alongside our father's bones. Just say, 'Come,' I will be glad to go with you."

Sarah felt pity for him. She said, "This paper says all that want to go can go. I say for one, Oytes, come, go with us."

Leggins agreed. "Oytes, I have no right to say to you, 'You have done wrong and you can't go to your own country.' No, I am only too glad to hear you talk as you do. We will all go back and be happy once more in our native land."[29]

Sarah wrote a letter to Natchez, which was signed by the other Paiute leaders, outlining their plans to leave Fort Simcoe on July 3, 1880. She described the Yakima Paiutes' condition: "We don't know what time we will get to the Dalles and a good many of us will have to walk. . . . We are poorer than when we came. Poorer in clothes. Poorer in horses. Poorer in victuals; in everything. Our sick have been poorly cared for and many have died of want of something to eat." It was signed by Sarah, Lee, and Frank Winnemucca; Chief Leggins; Paddy Two Chief; and Piute Joe.[30]

Father Wilbur was the roadblock to their plans. He refused to talk to the Paiute leaders, who wished him to call a military escort to keep the settlers from attacking them on their way back to Malheur. This elderly fire-and-brimstone preacher had the previous year commended Sarah to the Indian Department for her "noble work in the school room, out of the school, instructing the Piute women and girls how to cut and make garments for the children of the Piute School, and themselves, and doing the essential service as interpreter."[31] He now told her: "I am sorry you are putting the devil into your people's heads; they were all doing so well while you were away, and I was so pleased with them. You are talking against me all the time, and if you don't look out I will have you put in irons and in prison."[32]

"I don't care how soon you have it done," she replied. "My people are saying I have sold them to you, and get money from you to keep them here. I am abused by you and by my own people, too. You never were the man to give me anything for my work, and I have to pay for everything I have to eat. Mr. Wilbur, you will not get off as easily as you think you will. I will go to Yakima City and lecture. I will tell them all how you are selling my people the clothes which were sent here for them."[33]

After this argument Sarah never saw Wilbur again. Subsequently he sent for Lee and tried to urge him to stay. When Lee returned after a session with the agent, he said, "Oh, sister, I am rich. I am going to have some land, and I am going to have a wagon, and I am going to have my own time to pay for it. It will only take one hundred and twenty-five years for me to pay for my wagon," he laughed bitterly. "He wants me to stay here, not to go away. Yes, I see myself staying here."[34]

Sarah and Lee went to Yakima City and talked to the newspaper editor there. They told him that fifty-eight Paiutes, thirty of whom were children, had died in the year that they had lived at Yakima; that so many deaths had occurred that the Paiutes were no longer permitted to bury their dead in the graveyard, and the bodies were thrown in the watercourses. The Winnemuccas told the editor that they had resolved to leave Yakima for Malheur, whether Agent Wilbur provided an escort for them or not, and asked him to tell the people of eastern Oregon through the columns of his newspaper that they would harm nothing of any white man as they passed through the country. Sarah pledged her own life for the peaceful intentions and good conduct of her people.[35] The editor wrote, "As Sarah has always been the firm friend of the whites on more than one trying occasion, we hope for the credit of the white race that the people of Eastern Oregon and Nevada will treat these Indians with friendliness."[36]

Sarah then traveled to The Dalles, where she awaited the Paiutes on the first step of their long journey back to their homeland. Meanwhile, however, Agent Wilbur had telegraphed the Indian Department in an attempt to get a reversal of the permission that Sarah had received from Secretary Schurz. He wrote the department in a follow-up letter:

Till Sarah Winnemucca returned from Washington, with the unfortunate permits obtained from the Honorable Secretary of the Interior, doubtless through misrepresentations—the Paiutes were contented, and expressed themselves as well satisfied to remain here. So far as I know only one or two cherished the expectation of returning to the Malheur —the rest seemed interested in my plans for their future, and were anxious to send their children to school—Sarah represented to them that it was the wish of the *President* for them to return, that numberless and indefinite benefits were to be bestowed on them, and that the Agent at Yakama [sic] was stealing their money, which the Department had placed in his hands for their benefit. . . . I am satisfied that her anxiety to leave this Reservation is due—not to any desire to benefit her people—but that she may be able to carry out schemes for her personal aggrandizement through a connection not at all to her credit.

I have done all in my power to benefit Sarah Winnemucca. I have concealed my knowledge of her disreputable intrigues, and on her solemn promises of amendment condoned her offenses, and bestowed every favor on her in my power, and if I have a right to look for gratitude and kind feelings from anyone, I certainly have the right to look for it from her, but am forced—in sorrow not in anger—to the conclusion that she is utterly unreliable, and that no dependence whatever can be placed on her character or word.[37]

This agent had, at the end of the year in which he had received the destitute Paiutes and had let them starve, returned $8,214.59 to the United States Treasury as the unspent balance of his budget.[38] When the belated answer to his telegram arrived, Wilbur read it with satisfaction: he was instructed to hold

Sarah's autographed picture sent to Natchez. It is inscribed, "Your loving sister Sarah Winnemucca." (Courtesy of Nevada Historical Society.)

the Paiutes at Yakima. While waiting at The Dalles, Sarah also received a telegram from the acting commissioner of Indian affairs: "We have reports from General Howard, Agent Wilbur and parties living near Malheur showing that if the Piutes attempt to march across the country from Yakima to Malheur it will be attended with great risk of life on the way. Consequently, the Secretary advised that your people remain at Yakama [sic] for the present."[39] Agent Wilbur had won.

It is unlikely that General Howard ever was moved by Sarah's appeals to him for the Numa's return to Malheur. In August, 1878, at the close of the Bannock War, Howard had even considered the feasibility of sending the Paiute prisoners to Indian Territory, or, if not there, to the Lummí Reservation on Puget Sound. He had written, "It will not do to reestablish the Malheur Agency."[40] A few months later he wrote again: "Sarah Winnemucca said to me that great complaint was kept up among the Malheurs on account of shortness of supplies, complaint never made under former agent. I think news of taking horses from Bannocks, dissatisfaction with their own change of Agent, a knowledge of the general conspiracy against whites, including Columbia Indians influenced Malheurs more than want of rations at time of outbreak."[41]

Howard never acknowledged that Egan and his band were forced into the war. In *My Life and Personal Experiences Among Our Hostile Indians*, published in 1907, two years before his death, he speaks of Egan as his chief adversary in the Bannock War. Perhaps Agent Rinehart had an inkling of the general's difficulty in distinguishing between the Paiutes who had remained staunch friends of the whites and the hostiles. Rinehart wrote to the commissioner of Indian affairs:

From the evidence I have, which is partly the reports of interested parties, I am led to conclude that the effort to establish Leggin's complicity in the recent hostilities has grown out of and is incident to the payment of the bill of expenses incurred in their removal from Harney to Yakima, which is no inconsiderable amount. If their removal was unauthorized the expenditure for their removal would necessarily be unauthorized; hence the effort to bring these people within the purview of the Department order which authorized the transfer of all the hostiles by implicating Leggins also in the hostile outbreak.[42]

17

Mrs. Hopkins

Sarah's grand hope that she could help her people at Yakima was shattered. The letter from Secretary Schurz, now folded and worn after the hard riding and perils of the journey to Yakima, seemed like a taunt to her old belief that there were white men of good will to whom her people could appeal for understanding and fairness. She herself was in a desperate situation. There was no chance that she could return with her people to the Malheur Reservation. She was out of money and in debt, with no possibility of a position as interpreter at Malheur, and she was banned from the Yakima Reservation with no means to return to Nevada. Could she appeal once more to a white man for the means to survive? General Howard was stationed sixty miles down the Columbia River from The Dalles at Vancouver Barracks. She wrote him, and he did not fail her. He sent for her to work as a teacher and interpreter among Bannock Indian prisoners.

The Indians at Vancouver Barracks were Sheepeaters and Weisers captured during the war, and Sarah found the twelve girls and six boys among them apt pupils. She wrote the secretary of the interior on behalf of the fifty-three prisoners at Vancouver to ask that they be given land so that they could commence farming, and that a special dispensation be made for the women and children who had not been issued clothing.[1] There was no reply to Sarah's letter from the secretary; possibly she did not expect one.

General Howard was pleased with Sarah's work at Vancouver Barracks and termed her service to the prisoners "invaluable." He wrote a general letter of recommendation for her, saying: "[she] gave abundant satisfaction to all who were interested in Indian children. She always appeared to me to be a true friend to her own people, doing what she could for them."[2]

In the fall of 1880, Sarah wrote to Natchez from Vancouver.

Dear Brother,

I received your letter on September 7 and am very glad to hear from you. I am glad you are all well down there. That is more than I can say of myself, as I have been very sick for three weeks. I had a fever and thought I was going to die, but no such good luck befell me. I am well again and doing duty. I do hope you will all go to the Malheur. I have not heard from Lee Winnemucca for a long time and I do not know how they are getting along at Yakima. Last time he wrote he said 15 Piutes had died since I had left there. You say you will send me some Indian sugar — our pe-ha-ve. I would like to have some but I am afraid it will cost too much to have it sent here, if it does not, send me some right away. The Indians here are most all sick. Seven are out scouting, but will soon be back if they do not run away.[3]

While Sarah was working with the children in the Indian camp, she again met the president of the United States. Sarah did not allow this second opportunity to speak with President Hayes to pass without expressing her concerns in a forceful way. While touring Vancouver Barracks, the president visited Sarah's class and shook hands with the Bannock Indian children. She followed him to his carriage and "made petition for her poor people in a trembling voice and tender manner," so that the ladies present, including Mrs. Hayes, were moved to tears. Hayes replied that he could make no promises, but that he would remember her request, which was to have her people gathered at some one place where they could live permanently and be cared for and instructed.[4] "You are a husband and father," she told him, "and you know how you would suffer to be separated from your wife and children by force, as my people still are, husbands from wives, parents from children, notwithstanding Secretary Schurz's order."[5]

This impromptu interview with the president made no change

in the conditions of the Paiutes at Yakima, nor did it hasten their removal to the Malheur. Sarah's half brother Lee was permitted to return to Oregon, accompanying Agent Wilbur, who had come with some teams of horses to remove all of the usable material and Indian goods from the Oregon reservation. The Malheur Reservation's status was still undetermined, but Rinehart now had the title "farmer in charge" and was expected to resign at an early date. On behalf of Lee Winnemucca, Rinehart wrote a letter to the commissioner of Indian affairs in which he begged for justice for Leggins's band and the others who were forceably detained at Yakima. He may have had the Paiutes' welfare at heart, but his letter can also be interpreted as a last-ditch effort to keep the Malheur agency.

When he had learned of Lee's imminent departure, Leggins had become so frenzied with the desire to return to his own country that he made a noisy protest, and Agent Wilbur had had him arrested. Rinehart wrote:

He [Leggins] has trusted and waited now for two years and a half and still they are held at Yakama. It cost the government plenty of money to break its promise and do wrong in sending them to Yakama, but it is unwilling to spend a dollar to undo that wrong or to assist and protect them on their journey back to their friends and kindred. . . . No one subject—no single matter of official duty has so profoundly engrossed my thoughts as the unwarranted removal and unjust detention of Leggins and his people in their present galling and grievous exile against their expressed will and repeated protest.[6]

When Lee returned to the settlements along the railroad in Nevada and rejoined his people in late July, he told them of the frustrations of the Paiutes who were attempting to go back to Nevada on their own. Ferriage across the Columbia River cost at least $150, which they did not have. Then they had to pass five hundred miles through settlements where no unarmed and unprotected Indian was safe. So many of their horses were stolen from them that they had not enough to carry them back. By this time Leggins had become an old man, almost blind, who had nearly given up hope.[7]

Father Wilbur held a different view of the Paiutes' adaptation to his reservation. He told the Indian Department that many had declared their intention to remain under any circumstances and that the others were only anxious to leave from a desire for change, which he said was "inherent in all savage natures." He had found most of the Paiutes to be steady workers. He had given them camas irons so that they could forage for the camas root, and he planned to take them off rations entirely except for the old and infirm and those women and children who had no able-bodied male friend to depend on. He wrote:

With feelings of profound gratitude to the Providence, that has permitted me to witness the gradual progress of the people committed to my charge, from a state of degraded barbarism to comparative civilization, from the gross blackness of heathen corruption, to the glorious light and liberty of the Gospel of the Son of God, I can realize that from month to month, and from year to year, solid progress and improvement is being made.[8]

Arthur Chapman, an experienced interpreter for the army, was sent to Yakima by General McDowell and General Miles to observe the condition of the Paiutes. His arrival was greeted with suspicion by Agent Wilbur, especially when he found that Chapman was encouraging the Paiutes to leave, meeting with the leaders in secret council, and telling them that he would have transportation ready with an escort for them at the Columbia River. In the meantime Wilbur wired the Indian Department and demanded a fixed policy toward the Paiutes: Were they to go or stay? On October 31 he received a reply: Yakima was to remain the home of the Paiutes, as the Malheur Reservation had been abandoned.[9]

When Agent Wilbur showed Chapman the telegram from the Indian Department, the interpreter was much disconcerted. He returned for another conference with the Paiutes, in which he told them that, because of the lateness of the season, the departure would be postponed until spring, when he would return for them. Wilbur was rankled that Sarah Winnemucca and Chapman were making promises to the Indians that kept them from taking any interest in working the land or sending their children to his school. He termed their actions "outside interference" in his tightly run reservation. He wrote to the Indian commissioner, "To be rid of them [the Paiutes] would be an inexpressible relief to me; yet notwithstanding the trouble, labor and anxiety they have caused me, I have faithfully tried to carry out what I understood to be the wishes of the Department."[10] Wilbur was soon to retire. It rankled him that the Paiutes had not submitted to his ordered intentions and that they were leaving his accounts not entirely on the plus side of the ledger as he would have liked.

Interpreter Chapman had been appalled at the condition in which he found the Paiutes under Wilbur's care. He had never seen people in such destitution. There was no food, not even stored in baskets in their tents. The leaders told him that sometimes they had nothing for four or five days, contrary to the statements of Father Wilbur, who said that they had plenty to eat. Sarah claims that Chapman found the clothes on their backs in rags.[11]

During the long, despairing wait for the return of Leggins's people Sarah received $500 from the army as her reward for bringing Winnemucca's band to safety during the Bannock War. When the Sheepeaters and Weiser Bannocks were ordered to return to Fort Hall, Sarah accompanied them with an army officer, a Lieutenant Mills. She took this opportunity to visit her sister Elma at Henry's Lake, Idaho. They were reunited for the first time since girlhood. Elma's husband, John Smith, was a lumberman, and, though Elma lived in a typically modest frontier cabin, she made her home comfortable and attractive. Sarah envied the peace and contentment of her sister's uneventful life, but she knew it was not for her.

Elma, who had been isolated for so long in the Yellowstone country, was excited by the prospect of a trip to Nevada for a reunion with relatives. The two sisters arrived in Winnemucca on the Central Pacific in a palace car, dressed in fashionable attire.[12] They probably visited Natchez at his home in the Big Meadows near Lovelock, where he was farming and raising his large family. Their conversations may have dealt with the disappointment of the Paiutes' loss of the Malheur Reservation and the seeming impossibility of returning the Yakima Paiutes.

Then Lee brought news that after traveling for months, Frank Winnemucca, Piute Joe, and several other Yakima Paiutes, had arrived with their families at Fort McDermit. They had made their way back through great hardship and danger to their old hunting grounds. Others also had escaped and had stopped at the Warm Springs Reservation in northern Oregon, where members of their families had been held prisoners.[13] The majority of

Leggins's band and the old chief himself were still captives at Yakima.

Sarah was now about thirty-seven years of age. She was an integrated, but complicated, person who understood the realities of her situation as well as anyone and yet had a romantic attitude toward life. She wanted to believe in the wisdom and sincerity of the whites and to have their respect. She also wanted to believe in the natural, intuitive wisdom and goodness of her people and to continue to command the Paiutes' respect.

We must understand that she walked a tightrope between two worlds. She always had the view of the precipice around her, yet she believed that she would in the end take the right steps to achieve recognition for herself as her people's savior. Morals were important to her, but the differences between the Indian and white cultures often made her behavior appear suspect. Methodism, for example, was naturally appealing to her because it supported the traditional strict moral code for relations between the sexes that her own people followed. The Paiutes' marriage vows were less formal, and polygamy was accepted among them because many female hands were needed to find and prepare food in the sparse desert environment. Sarah's brother Natchez had two or three wives and was considered a congenial husband and father. Similarly, there is no doubt that Sarah gambled, but gambling was a highly regarded pastime among her people. Her father was said to have lost (and won) many ponies playing the hand game.

Sarah certainly drank on occasion, though she deplored the effects of alcohol on her people.[14] Whether she was intoxicated from time to time cannot be proved or disproved. It is irrelevant except when the question exposed her to criticism by her contemporaries. White critics were always seizing opportunities to play down her positive attributes.

As we have seen, Sarah grew to understand power in the white men's terms, and she became adept, in collaboration with Natchez, in using it to her advantage. She was a determined woman with strong opinions, ready to defend her honor with action and words. Yet she was also high-strung and emotional, needing companionship, love, and understanding.

It is likely that it was this combination of personal qualities that led Sarah abruptly to marry again on December 5, 1881.[15] The man, Lewis H. Hopkins of Virginia, was five years her junior. He wore his light brown hair parted down the middle, sported a handlebar mustache, and was a bit of a dandy. His background and where he met Sarah are open to conjecture. Some say that they met in Montana while Sarah visited Elma.[16] Others associate Hopkins with the Indian Department and the feeding of Indians during the Bannock War, which would mean that he and Sarah were acquaintances of several years' standing.[17] Although it is unfortunate that we know few of the particulars about Hopkins's past, at least we can draw some conclusions about his character from his behavior following the marriage.

Sarah and Lewis were married at the Russ House in San Francisco by a justice of the peace, and soon after the ceremony it was announced that the couple would leave for the East on a speaking engagement.[18] Sarah was to give lectures on "The Indian Agencies" and "The Indian Question as Viewed from an Indian Standpoint." She had expanded her interests to include the conditions of all Indians and their status under the agents and the "ring" in the Indian Department. She told a San Francisco reporter that the agent at Pyramid Lake was treating her people high-handedly: "We want no more of these white hypocrites, who are not content to steal half the Government allowance, but take it all." She suggested that a head chief of each tribe act as agent on the reservations and distribute the goods and annuities.[19]

Sarah and her new husband did not go east at once. Lewis Hopkins was another white husband with habits that caused problems for Sarah. While they were yet in San Francisco, he gambled away $500. This was money that she had earned teaching at Vancouver Barracks plus some of the reward that she had acquired for her arduous efforts to save her father's band at the onset of the Bannock War.

The couple traveled to Pyramid Reservation and stayed with Sarah's brother Tom until they obtained the means to make the long trip east. Apparently Hopkins had no money of his own, nor was he interested in working. Gambling was still one of the chief pastimes on the reservation, and Lewis played poker with some of his new relatives by marriage. Once, after losing a small amount of money, he gave his place to Sarah, who lost a few

Lieutenant Lewis H. Hopkins, Sarah Winnemucca's last husband. (Courtesy of Nevada Historical Society.)

dollars as well. Lewis was quite angry with her, and according to one account, when she reminded him of the losses that she had incurred from his playing in San Francisco, he walked off threatening to leave her. Sarah drank herself into a state of forgetful sleep. When she awoke, her new husband had returned, and all was forgiven.[20]

While at the reservation Sarah observed firsthand the policies and relations with the Paiutes of the new agent, who had succeeded the well-liked James E. Spencer. His name was Joseph McMaster. When the young son of a family living near Tom's place died on New Year's Eve, the relatives wailed and mourned in their customary way. Three of the agent's men—the doctor, the carpenter, and the blacksmith—and one of their friends came to the grass hut, or *karnee*, imitating the sounds of Paiute mourning in a mocking manner. They handed Lewis a bottle of whiskey, suggesting that he pass it around to his relatives. He said, "Pass it round yourselves."

They replied, "Give some to your brother-in-law."

Lewis answered, "Give it to him yourself."[21]

This interchange, of course, showed the whites' disdain for the Paiutes' customs and feelings. They were putting Hopkins down for having as a brother-in-law an Indian to whom he could not legally give whiskey. Sarah wrote in her autobiography, "This is the kind of people, dear reader, that the government sends to teach us at Pyramid Lake Reservation."[22]

Sarah found that at Pyramid Lake the Paiutes with crops, who had planted their own seed on their own farms, were expected to give every third sack of grain and every third load of hay to the agent. If they did not, their wagons were taken from them, or they were told to leave the reservation.[23] The beef contractor for the reservation ran nothing more than a butcher shop: "Those that have money can come up and buy. Those that have none stand back and cry, often with hunger."[24]

McMaster appointed Sarah's cousin, Dave Numana, as police chief, and she wrote that he was used as a front for the agent's activities.

Sarah and Lewis Hopkins left Nevada in late February, 1882, for Elma's home at Henry's Lake. They planned to move east that spring, but it was more than a year before Sarah actually arrived in Boston.[25] W. V. Rinehart also moved at this time—to Canyon

City. The Malheur Reservation, its improvements, and animals had been sold. The land was disposed of at public auction. Rinehart was an embittered man, particularly hostile toward General O. O. Howard, who, he claimed, had never officially requisitioned to replace the Indian supplies that were taken by the army at Malheur during the Bannock War. The former agent protested that he was left with a suspension of his property accounts for $18,000.[26]

Meanwhile, Leggins's band of forty-three lodges, spurred by Arthur Chapman's promise that he would return in the spring to accompany them to their old home, made plans to escape from Yakima even if no help arrived. About three hundred Paiutes wished to return with Chapman. When the army interpreter had not arrived by late July, they asked for a permit from Father Wilbur to fish at Tumwater, Washington, on the Columbia River and made their escape attempt. They sold some horses to pay their fare, crossed the river by ferry, and then started south, hoping to live on roots, game, and fish on their journey home.

Father Wilbur sent Yakima Indian policemen after them, and they were forced back. Three of the leaders were subsequently held as prisoners at The Dalles.[27] Wilbur denied Chapman's account of the Paiutes' condition at Yakima. He admitted that he had not given them full rations and that they had no houses, but countered that they had subsistence of their own. He also stated that the Yakima Indians had cheerfully agreed to cede their land for wheat and had voluntarily given Christmas presents to the Paiutes. He blamed much of the Paiute dissatisfaction on Sarah: "Since Sarah Winnemucca had excited their hopes of a return to their old country, their feeling was such, that *should Mr. Chapman tell them he had come to escort them back,* it would require a military force to keep them."[28]

Howard was very defensive when Wilbur accused him of making false promises to the Paiutes, saying: "The return of Leggins or indeed of any of the Piutes to the Malheur reservation would have, inevitably resulted in war. Whenever I had occasion to talk with Sarah Winnemucca, or any of her people on this subject, I always urged the necessity of their abandoning all thought of returning to Malheur and of their making themselves contended (*sic*) where they were."[29]

18

Old Winnemucca

Widowed for many years, Winnemucca was married again in July, 1882, to a widow with a young child.[1] A month later reports arrived in Nevada from Camp Bidwell, California, indicating that the old chief was dying. With him were his new wife, his son Lee, and his two elderly sisters, all of whom had been traveling with him to Surprise Valley, near Camp Bidwell, to visit Chief Ocheo.[2]

Winnemucca was now over ninety years of age. He had fallen ill near Coppersmith Ranch, before his small band reached Ocheo's territory.[3] A runner was sent ahead to Ocheo, who immediately came to the aid of his friend by traveling to the place of sickness and ordering a doctoring *karnee* built. After sundown a shaman began working on the old chief, while the people sat about the fire repeating the shaman's song of power. Old Winnemucca was expected to improve after the all-night performance of the doctor. Instead he settled into a coma, from which he sometimes woke and spoke to those about him. He said that he had dreamed that his wife had poisoned him.[4] By this he did not mean literally that she had given him poison, but that she had caused an evil power to enter him.

The old man lay by the fire, wrapped in a rabbit-skin robe, his feet buried in the warm ashes. As his relatives stayed by his side, their eyes often moved to his young wife, who huddled in a corner, increasingly frightened. In the minds of the assembled Paiutes the woman was guilty of her husband's illness.

We do not know the particulars of all that occurred in the next few weeks before Chief Winnemucca's death, but anthropological studies of Paiute shamanism and sorcery help us to understand the drastic measures that were taken by the Numa to ensure the extinction of the supposed evil powers.[5]

The woman was taken to a spring by some of the other Paiutes who were assembled. While they were not looking, the alleged sorceress found a rope and attempted to hang herself from a post.[6] The band had been confident that she was guilty of causing Winnemucca's illness because she had not atoned for her dark sorcery by bathing. Now the attempted suicide proved her guilt in their eyes.[7] A council was held, and Ocheo's band agreed that the woman should be stoned, which was the customary practice against evil-intentioned shamans. Her child must die also, because it was believed that her offspring would perpetuate her dark powers.[8]

The doomed woman was taken again to the spring, where she was stripped, forced to bathe, and then sprinkled with ashes. When night fell, a circle of fires was lit on a nearby hill. The woman was brought and tied by one leg to a stump, while the Paiutes joined hands and began a monotonous chant, circling their victim. One of them stepped near the fire and began to harangue in a loud voice, while the trembling woman kneeled over her child in a protective manner, crying for mercy. The speaker finally sprang forward and tore the child from her arms, swung it around several times, and dashed its head against a pile of rocks, where it was killed instantly.[9]

The dance and chanting continued. At last the leader stopped near the woman, picked up a large rock, and hit her full force with it on the back. She shrieked and fell forward. A small trickle of blood flowed from a long gash in her side. More rocks followed, and after a few agonizing moments a large rock was brought down upon her head. Her dead body and belongings and those of her child were laid on a fire. A few of the Paiutes remained to see that all was consumed.[10]

The Numa believed that Chief Winnemucca's health would now be restored. Instead, the old man continued to lie semicon-

Chief Winnemucca, whose request to the United States government for land for his band was never realized during his lifetime. (Courtesy of Oregon Historical Society.)

scious, refusing to eat or to take healing concoctions of herbs. He was bled several times, but, as the weeks passed, his body did not respond to the age-old treatment and he became skeleton-thin. At last, on October 21, 1882,[11] Chief Winnemucca died. According to Paiute belief his spirit ascended the Milky Way, and he entered an afterlife. There he would meet his ancestors in a world where there were many animals to hunt and much bountiful land that was possessed by no one and used and respected by all.

Sarah would, of course, grieve at the loss of her father. Adding to her sense of loss was her great regret that she had not been able to help him fulfill his modest desire to acquire land for his people in a place of their own choosing. After her marriage to Lewis Hopkins, she was not able to help him monetarily or even able to be present at his deathbed. It appears that she and her new husband were in residence at Henry's Lake at the time of his death.

Sarah surely deplored the death of Winnemucca's wife, though execution by stoning was a traditional means of ridding the band of a member who had not conformed—such as a woman found in intercourse out of marriage or a shaman suspected of poisoning or harming his patients. Sarah was hardpressed to explain such a group-willed and executed fate to "civilized" society. In an article published before her father's death she was critical of the Numa: "Virtue was a quality whose absence was punished by death—either by burning alive or stoning to death. The ceremony of marriage is not so strictly carried out as in olden times. They take a woman now without much ado, as white people do, and leave them oftener than of old."[12] This article of several pages in The Californian, plus the recent publication of Helen Hunt Jackson's popular A Century of Dishonor, in which Sarah's letter of 1870 to Major Douglass appears, caused renewed interest in the East concerning this literate Indian woman. Thus, when Sarah and her husband arrived in Boston in the spring of 1883, they found many earnest sympathizers and a public that was anxious to receive her.[13]

19

A Trip to the East

Two influential Boston sisters were to be Sarah's mainstays for several years to come. First was Elizabeth Palmer Peabody, who, from the time when she first met Sarah and heard her impassioned plea for the Paiutes and other American Indians, continued faithfully to support her cause.

Outwardly Elizabeth was a chunky spinster, always dressed in the same black silk, but she had created an illustrious aura about herself from her associations with the Concord Transcendentalists, whose books she published. Her own learned lectures and writings on world history, plus her dynamic enthusiasm and support for the establishment of German kindergartens in the United States, added to her stature.

Elizabeth's sister, Mary Mann, was the widow of Horace Mann. Though not so dynamic as her impulsive, talkative sister, she was accomplished as a writer and was instrumental in organizing and supporting Elizabeth's many ventures into humanitarian causes. A third sister, Sophia Peabody, had married Nathanial Hawthorne, but she was deceased before Sarah and Lewis reached Boston in the spring of 1883.

When Sarah arrived in Boston, Elizabeth was seventy-nine years old and had suffered a slight stroke but she soon began working assiduously for the cause of the "Princess" Sarah Winnemucca. She proposed that Sarah give a series of lectures, so that subscribers would learn the history and culture of the Paiutes as well as their present circumstances. When Sarah found that she could cover only a few points in each lecture, she became determined to write about her people at length.[1] Elizabeth was willing to see that the book was published. It would be a means of introducing Sarah and her cause and also would bring in revenue.

Thus Sarah gained innumerable speaking engagements up and down the East Coast before large church gatherings and Indian Association groups. She brought a new awareness to her audiences of the plight of the American Indian: their lack of land, sustenance, citizenship, and the rights that go with citizenship. She reminded her audiences that the Indians had no representation in the United States government.

Sarah lectured in New York, Connecticut, Rhode Island, Maryland, Massachusetts, and Pennsylvania within the first few months of her stay in the East. She enjoyed creating a dramatic impression, dressed in fringed buckskin and beads, with armlets and bracelets adorning her arms and wrists. She even included the affectation of a gold crown on her head and a wampum bag of velvet, decorated with an embroidered cupid, hanging from her waist.[2]

The first lecture in Boston, where she spoke on the shortcomings of Father Wilbur, offended an influential Methodist woman, who had expected Sarah to tone down her criticisms in return for support and hospitality. Sarah did not bow to such pressure. As a result opposition started against her, including the Women's Association of the Methodist church.[3]

Sarah, however, was moving in select circles, thanks to Elizabeth Peabody and Mary Mann. John Greenleaf Whittier, Ralph Waldo Emerson, and Justice Oliver Wendell Holmes were made aware of her cause through Elizabeth, who knew everybody of consequence in New England. She was a guest of Mrs. Ole Bull, the wife of the famous musician, and spoke to the students of Vassar College by invitation of their president.[4]

One early lecture in Boston was intended for women only. Sarah spoke of the domestic education given by Paiute grandmothers to the youth of both sexes concerning their relations with each other before and after marriage. It was "a lecture which

The "Princess" Sarah, as she appeared in Boston and other cities on the East Coast. (Courtesy of Nevada Historical Society.)

never failed to excite the moral enthusiasm of every woman that heard it," according to Elizabeth.[5] The elderly woman was convinced by Sarah that the Paiutes' education of their young was based on "natural religion and family moralities."[6]

As well as lecturing, Sarah found time to write *Life Among the Piutes: Their Wrongs and Claims*, the story of her own life arranged in eight chapters. In the book she made the Paiute woman's position in councils and family life sound somewhat liberated: "The women know as much as the men do, and their advice is often asked. We have a republic as well as you. The council-tent is our Congress, and anybody can speak who has anything to say, women and all." She described how women were quite willing to go into battle alongside their husbands, if need be.[7]

Mary offered to edit Sarah's manuscript and found it difficult work. She wrote a friend:

I wish you could see her manuscript as a matter of curiosity. I don't think the English language ever got such a treatment before. I have to recur to her sometimes to know what a word is, as spelling is an unknown quantity to her, as you mathematicians would express it. She often takes syllables off of words & adds them or rather prefixes them to other words, but the story is heart-breaking, and told with a simplicity & eloquence that cannot be described, for it is not high-faluting eloquence, tho' sometimes it lapses into verse (and quite poetical verse too). I was always considered fanatical about Indians, but I have a wholly new conception of them now, and we civilized people may well stand abashed before their purity of life & their truthfulness.[8]

Doubtless, Sarah's purpose in writing and lecturing at this hard pace was partly to provide much-needed financial support for her and Lewis. Mary Mann understood, however, that her principal motive was "to influence the public mind by the details of the Indian wrongs she can give so as to induce Congress to give them their farms in severalty and give them rights to defend them in the courts." There was also an effort underway to form an association to aid Sarah's educational plans.[9]

Sarah trod on dangerous ground in most of her speeches. She said: "I have asked the agents why they did these wrong things. They have told me it is necessary for them to do so in order to get money enough to send to the great white Father at Wash-

ington to keep their position. I assure you that there is an Indian
ring; that it is a corrupt ring, and that it has its head and shoulders
in the treasury at Washington."[10]

The Council Fire and Arbitrator, a monthly journal purportedly
devoted to the "civilization" and rights of American Indians,
called Sarah "an Amazonian champion of the Army [who] was
being used as a tool of the army officers to create public sentiment
in favor of the transfer of the Indian Bureau to the War Department." The Council Fire publicized the Indian Bureau files on
Sarah and the affidavits that Rinehart had sent to prejudice officials against her on her first trip to Washington: "She is so notorious for her untruthfulness as to be wholly unreliable. She is
known . . . to have been a common camp follower, consorting with
common soldiers. It is a great outrage on the respectable people
of Boston for General Howard or any other officer of the army to
foist such a woman of any race upon them."[11]

In Nevada the Winnemucca Silver State, which was not always
kind to Sarah, came to her defense this time:

Now, because she states, before an audience in Boston, what the whites
in Nevada and on the frontier generally know to be facts, the "Council
Fire," the Washington organ of the Indian Bureau, roundly abuses her.
. . . Without attempting to refute or dispute her assertions, which it
undoubtedly knows would be futile, it endeavors to break their force
by attacking her character. It adopts the tactics of the ring organs generally, and instead of showing wherein she has misrepresented the Indian
agents, it contents itself with slandering her, ignoring the fact that it
is the Indian Bureau System not Sarah Winnemucca's character, that
the people are interested in and that is under discussion."[12]

Elizabeth Peabody and Mary Mann decided that they should
add an appendix to Sarah's book with letters of recommendation
and affirmation in defense of her character. M. S. Bonnifield, the
Winnemucca attorney, who had transmitted the Council Fire article
to the editor of the Silver State, wrote the following: "I take pleasure in saying that I have known you personally and by reputation ever since 1869. Your conduct has always been exemplary,
so far as I know. I have never heard your veracity or chastity
questioned in this community." It must have been a moment of
regret for Sarah and her defenders when a letter was received
from General Howard with the request that it not be published.

Howard had led many battles for the Union during the Civil War, losing his right arm at Fair Oaks, Virginia, in 1862. He had ridden unarmed into an Apache stronghold in 1872 to treat with Cochise. Devoted to the betterment of the Negro, he was named head of the Freedman's Bureau after the Civil War and was president of Howard University between 1869 and 1873. Now his courage left him. His reason was:

My feeling towards Mrs. Hopkins is like yours, but for reasons which are imperative with me, I cannot publish a letter in defence of her character. I will say to you that when with me, or near me, her behavior was above reproach. I think her ardent love for her people, and her profound sympathy for them, has led her into several errors with regard to them, and her desires, in this respect, are positively against my own views or recommendations [referring to the removal of Leggin's band from Yakima], but this, in no way, affects the question of Sarah's moral character. . . . Should I write I would lay myself open to be assailed by the same bad man, who is thoroughly wicked, and unscrupulous. . . . You may show this to any of your friends, but do not publish it.[13]

Upon reading this letter Elizabeth Peabody wrote in the margin in her distinctive handwriting the name unstated by Howard, "Agent Rhinehart."

If a general of the army was wary of Rinehart's wrath, one can understand Sarah's predicament. An earlier letter of General Howard's was, however, printed in the appendix of *Life Among the Piutes*, along with many statements of high regard by army officers who had worked with Sarah during the Bannock War. The commander of the Military Division of the Pacific at the Presidio in San Francisco, Major General Irvin McDowell, pointedly made it his last act before his retirement on October 15, 1882, to offer a military escort to Leggins's band back to their home near Camp McDermit.[14] McDowell's offer was duly rejected, however, by Commissioner H. Price of the Office of Indian Affairs.[15]

The policy, instituted by President Grant in 1870, to use Christian agents, rather than military men, on Indian reservations had been termed "the Quaker policy." When Sarah spoke before the Universal Peace Union, the *Council Fire* criticized that organization for placing her on their agenda. In September, 1883, the Peace Union's president, Alfred H. Love, wrote a letter to the *Council Fire* in response:

> Sarah Winnemucca came thoroughly endorsed by prominent Boston friends of peace. She was as free as anyone else to express her views. We were gainers by hearing her. She modestly waited to be heard, and when she spoke, affirmed our resolutions.
>
> We think her reference to the army meant she preferred it to the loose, uncontrolled, and unscrupulous spectators and adventurers and recreant agents. . . .
>
> I wish the Quaker policy could be better understood. It comprehends more than opposition to military surveillance. It accepts the good wherever found. . . . In reference to this person, once the Indian girl of the West, even if the statements you make be true, would it not be kind to keep them from the public. Suppose she had been attracted by the soldiers with their gay trappings, and perhaps their promises of favors; they are called Christians, she is styled savage. What wonder if she went astray? Of whom should we expect the most? Who were more to blame?
>
> I would like to see those who dare make the personal affidavits you quote. Rather should we applaud this woman for now coming forth in all of womanly dignity and earnestness and upholding justice, virtue, and peace. The true Quaker policy is to encourage the good everywhere and in every thing.

Sarah wrote: "Everyone knows what a woman must suffer who undertakes to act against bad men. My reputation has been assailed, and it is done so cunningly that I cannot prove it to be unjust. I can only protest that it is unjust, and say that wherever I have been known, I have been believed and trusted.[16]

Every effort was made by Sarah and her Boston friends to get the autobiography printed, bound, and out to the public before the next session of Congress, when the legislators expected to consider legislation for the benefit of the Indians. Subscriptions were gotten up to help defray expenses, and the price of the book was expected to be one dollar per copy. John Greenleaf Whittier subscribed for ten dollars' worth, and Mrs. Ralph Waldo Emerson for the same amount. Elizabeth found five persons who underwrote the expenses of publication for a total of $600. Thus, when Sarah sold her 600 copies, the money that she received was free and clear and helped pay her expenses.[17]

Mary and Elizabeth had always lived frugally, and now they were in modest rented rooms at 54 Bowdoin Street in Boston.

Elizabeth had earned her own living since age sixteen, and Mary, the widow of an honest politician and liberal educator, had never experienced a surplus of funds. Yet they willingly gave their limited resources to this new cause. In her typical lengthy sentences and almost undecipherable slanting scrawl, Elizabeth also wrote letters to friends and congressmen regarding her good friend Mrs. Hopkins. The following appeal to Congressman Newton Booth was typical:

I have been all my life a student of Indian history and character, a great uncle of mine who was a Revolutionary officer having married an Indian princess [who] brot up her family so nobly and wisely as to have been a lesson to her civilized relations by marriage, a family that yield now some of the most respected citizens of Michigan. . . . I hope you will think it worthwhile to look into her book the first book of Indian literature—I will send you the appendix to it which contains her credentials. . . . The degree of ignorant nonsense that prevails is comparable to what was upon the negro question *fifty years ago* and will seem as amazing fifty years hence as that does now. I shall send you her book when it comes out.[18]

In this time of absorbing productivity for Sarah, who often bedded and boarded with Elizabeth and Mary, where was Lewis Hopkins, her husband? He traveled with Sarah often, sometimes introducing his wife to her audiences, and helped with the autobiography by visiting the Boston Athenaeum and other institutions for background material.[19]

A typical scenario for one of Sarah's lectures occurred in Philadelphia in Christ Episcopal Church. At least an hour before the time appointed for the lecture, masses of people began to crowd into the church's front entrance. They continued to file in until the entire building, including the galleries, aisles, and chancel steps, was completely packed.

After the singing of a hymn the rector introduced Lewis Hopkins as the husband of "Princess Winnemucca." Lewis gave a brief sketch of his wife's history and stated the purpose of Sarah's visit to the East.[20] Sarah then flashed him an appreciative smile and told her story in such a way that the audience was overcome with emotion. For almost an hour she spoke very effectively. Afterwards people crowded around, wanting to touch the hand of this resplendent Indian woman wearing a gold crown and intri-

Mary Mann, widow of Horace Mann and editor of Life Among the Piutes: Their Wrongs and Claims, *by Sarah Winnemucca Hopkins.*

cately beaded buckskin dress. Sarah's dark eyes glowed with enjoyment at the attention. Elizabeth Peabody, who often sat on the rostrum with her protégé, commented that, although she had heard Sarah lecture fifty times, each speech was different, because she never spoke from notes, but from her heart.[21]

After her lectures Sarah would obligingly sign copies of *Life Among the Piutes* for those of her followers who wished to purchase the handsome volume. The book contained 268 pages, including the 20-page appendix. The title was stamped in gold on the spine of the green or red cloth cover (the color was different in various printings). In her editor's preface Mary Mann had written: "At this moment, when the United States seem waking up to their duty to the original possessors of our immense territory, it is of the first importance to hear what only an Indian and an Indian woman can tell. To tell it was her own deep impulse, and the dying charge given her by her father, the truly parental chief of his beloved tribe."

Senator Henry L. Dawes invited Sarah and Elizabeth to his home and arranged for Sarah to lecture there one evening. Aware that the senator could make some of her ideas into law, Sarah spoke with special animation, and Dawes was greatly moved by her speech. He took her into his study and had a long talk with her — promising he would bring her before the Indian committee of which he was chairman. He encouraged her to continue speaking, because it was desirable that she "stir hearts," as she had done that day, to press congress to consideration of the Indian question.[22]

Sarah lectured in Providence, Rhode Island; Hartford, Connecticut; New York City, Newburgh, and Poughkeepsie, New York; Dorset, Vermont; Boston, Salem, Cambridge, Germantown, and Pittsfield, Massachusetts; and Philadelphia. She circulated a petition, which was signed by almost five thousand people, asking that the Indians be given lands in severalty and rights of citizenship.[23] Plans were afoot for three representatives to present the legislation in the House. Thus the "princess" was happy, feeling that her efforts for the cause of her people might yet be successful. She bought a fine overcoat for Natchez, who, when he received it found it much too large and generously gave it to his half brother Lee, who was especially tall and broadshouldered.[24]

Elizabeth Palmer Peabody, Sarah Winnemucca's staunch supporter. Sarah's Peabody Indian School was named in her honor. (Courtesy of Massachusetts Historical Society.)

Through the Christmas season Mary Mann stayed at home collecting and mending serviceable clothes to send to the Paiutes in Nevada. Though she could not afford Christmas cards for her friends, she sent a large barrel of used goods to the Paiutes. She hoped it was not as cold in Nevada as it was in Boston, where she sat frozen by the fireside.[25] Elizabeth was expected home for the holidays. Sarah and Lewis were to move to Baltimore, where a series of lectures was planned.[26]

When the bells rang in the New Year of 1884, Sarah may have kissed Lewis without hesitation, but she may also have ignored a growing discontent in the relationship. Hopkins had helped her in Washington, visiting the Library of Congress for material for her book. He had sat on the lecture platforms, and with his gentle manners he had charmed those with whom he came in contact. At the same time the joint bank account of the Hopkinses was a temptation to Lewis's gambling propensities. He and Sarah had agreed in principle that most of the money that they collected for the cause should be reserved for a school that Sarah intended to start for Paiute children in Nevada,[27] though, of course, the expenses of traveling and accommodations had to be met before banking the remainder. Six months after they had arrived in the East the *Council Fire* had accused Hopkins of squandering funds given to Sarah for the benefit of her people in "low gambling dens in Boston." The article said, "When Sarah complained of this to her husband his reply was, 'You need not say anything; if I should tell your Boston friends what I know about you, you would not hold your head so high.' "[28]

According to Elizabeth, Sarah spoke in Baltimore sixty-six times in a variety of places, including churches of various denominations and the Young Men's Christian Association. The Methodist Episcopal Church seemed to enjoy a special claim on her presence.[29] Admission was charged, from ten to twenty-five cents, and copies of *Life Among the Piutes* were sold after the lectures. The Hopkinses were dependent on Sarah for their income,[30] and her competition in Baltimore was of the highest quality, including the Shakespearian actor Edwin Booth and Henry Ward Beecher, who was heralded as the "World's greatest orator." The autobiography, personally autographed by Sarah, was also made available through the mails for one dollar. If a purchaser so wished, he could receive an autographed picture of the "princess" for another fifty cents.[31] Lewis acted as her agent, responding personally to such requests.

In the spring Sarah heard from Natchez that the bands of Leggins and Paddy Cap had escaped from Yakima and had made their way back to the Harney Valley. Her brother wrote that he had gone to see them and that they had told him they would never return to Yakima without a fight.[32] Fortunately, Father Wilbur had retired by this time, and the new agent R. H. Milroy, was more realistic than Wilbur had been. He wrote the commissioner of Indian affairs that it was best for the Paiutes to stay in their own country, for they had never been satisfied at Fort Simcoe and had been badly treated by the Yakimas.[33] Thus one of Sarah's battles with the authorities was settled off the field by the Paiute bands themselves with little fanfare.

Elizabeth Peabody now voiced her concern about Leggins's destitute condition to Congressman J. B. Long. She had celebrated her eightieth birthday on April 13, 1884,[34] but despite almost total blindness continued her correspondence for the Paiute cause, guiding her hand by the sense of feeling. She wrote that she understood Senator Dawes was going to push a bill to acquire Camp McDermit for Leggins's band, and she asked for Long's support: "I depend upon Mr. Ranney and yourself to immediately take up the subject when it comes before the House — for if there is delay they must starve. It is a matter of life and death."[35]

Over three hundred exiles had returned. McDermit seemed to be the only unsettled country still available to them, and it was the area where Old Winnemucca had often requested a reservation. Sarah was encouraged when Adjutant General J. C. Kelton and General John Pope indicated to her that McDermit could be spared as a military reserve. Pope advised the commander in chief of the army, General Philip Henry Sheridan, to give the land to the Paiutes in severalty, making them United States citizens and allowing them to govern themselves.[36]

Elizabeth told Congressman Long that Sarah's cause was supported in Washington by the best and most intelligent citizens, many of whom had tried to stir up action. She continued:

But they tell me a subtle but powerful influence from the Interior office opposed her — casting the form of unfavourable insinuations against her personally and sometimes open accusations which can all be answered as I know — who during the whole year have been investigating her life and words and find them all reliable. Lately, the enemy has changed the tactics and endeavoured to misrepresent and fabricate monstrous lies about the tribe which are pronounced fabrications and demonstrated to be absurdly false by citizens of Nevada who have been written to — and disinterested persons who have been out there — individuals who have unexpectedly risen in her audiences and endorsed her statements and declared them under-coloured rather than exaggerated.[37]

In an article on American Indians a nephew of Horace Greeley had used the stoning of Chief Winnemucca's young wife as an example to assert that the Paiutes were blood-thirsty, drunken, lawless savages undeserving of any white man's solicitude.[38] He had conveniently forgotten the burning biers that roasted human flesh during the witch hunts in Massachusetts two hundred years before.

20

Disillusionment

Sarah's petition was presented to Congress and referred to the appropriate committees in the first session of 1884. She appeared before the senate subcommittee on Indian affairs and spoke at length, answering the pointed questions of her admirer, Chairman Dawes. She pleaded that a reservation be established at Fort McDermit and land given to each head of a family, and she asked that the annuities granted by Congress to the Paiutes be administered by the military rather than the Indian Bureau.[1]

When a House bill passed giving Camp McDermit to those Paiutes who had not yet been assigned a reservation, there was a short time of rejoicing. General Sheridan, however, soon countermanded the legislative decision by claiming that the fort was still essential for the use of the Department of War.[2] As a result, a Senate bill was passed on July 6, 1884, which gave permission to Leggins's and Winnemucca's bands to return to the Pyramid Lake Reservation, where each head of a family was to be given 160 acres of land in severalty. The legislation was to be carried out under the direction of the secretary of the interior.[3]

Sarah understood immediately that all was lost. Those Paiutes had already nominally possessed Pyramid Lake Reservation since the time of Agent Frederick Dodge in 1860. There was no arable land left there to be assigned to newcomers, and white squatters

214

had been settled on the best land along the Truckee River for decades. The whole fishery at Mud Lake, or Lake Winnemucca, was dominated by Chinese fishermen. Also there was a problem of producing crops on the small amount of usable land left to the Paiutes, because of broken dams and other irrigation difficulties. It was a preposterous solution to try to find a living for 500 more individuals on the Pyramid Lake Reservation.[4]

When she had returned to Baltimore, Sarah's personal concerns had been increased, because she had found that Lewis, for whom she had been paying a doctor and furnishing medicines[5] for several months, was not improving. It was feared that he had tuberculosis. Now she also had to acknowledge that there had been no result from her efforts in Washington except for financial aid to her immediate family and the barrels of old clothes from Boston. At least, she reminded herself, she would have the means to start her Indian school with the money in the Hopkins bank account. Then the despairing woman was notified by her bank of large drafts that Lewis had written which the precious account would not cover. Hopkins had been gambling and had even given fraudulent drafts to their acquaintances and supportive friends.[6]

Sarah wrote Elizabeth that Lewis had left and that there was little more that she could do. She begged the elderly woman to keep her position a secret, as she knew that it would only provoke further accusations against her from the Interior Department if her insolvency were known.[7] Although her heart was not in it, she would go once more to Washington to see Secretary of the Interior Henry Moore Teller, who was to carry into effect the act for Winnemucca and Leggins's bands in the Indian appropriation bill.[8] She would ask Teller if there was anything that she could do and what word she was to take back to Nevada.

After Sarah had paid her husband's medical expenses and covered his gambling debts, she had only a few hundred dollars left. Then she arrived in Washington only to discover that she could not make an appointment with Secretary Teller because he refused to see her.[9] Congress had dispersed, leaving the administration of the legislation to Teller, who planned to leave Washington to electioneer in Colorado.

Now Sarah was in real despair. She could not return to Nevada without some evidence of help for her people. It would be all too reminiscent of her previous trip to the capital, which had produced nothing but a "rag friend" from Secretary Schurz that was not worth the paper on which it was written.

There was nowhere to go but Idaho, to her sister Elma at Henry's Lake. From there she wrote Elizabeth and Mary that all was lost, for she would not be recognized as the messenger and guardian of her people.[10] Mary Mann immediately wrote to Commissioner of Indian Affairs Price, asking what Mrs. Hopkins was to do, now that an act had been passed to help the Paiutes, and what preparation was being made at Pyramid Lake for the arrival of the two bands. Commissioner Price replied that Sarah was to go out and "settle down" with these bands on the Reservation and tell them what to do, and he would "cooperate with any definite plans of Education."[11]

Adjutant General John C. Kelton wrote Sarah that General John Pope would see to it that Pyramid Lake Reservation was cleared of squatters. Finally, in August, 1884, acting under orders from Washington, Lieutenant Henry D. Huntington came onto the reservation and removed settlers, fishermen, and others, destroying their property and confiscating their boats on Pyramid Lake. The old settlers dwelling on the best lands along the Truckee River were not disturbed, however.[12]

Sarah, with much apprehension about the possible success of her mission, prepared to go to Pyramid Lake. She stopped by Lovelock to see Natchez, whose people were assembling to go into the mountains for pine nuts and game, hoping to lay aside enough for the winter. Natchez had harvested sixty acres of wheat, thirty bushels to the acre, but he had paid much of it out to other Paiutes for help in the planting and harvesting. When he had experienced a bout with pneumonia during the winter, Sarah had sent him gifts and money. Now, upon her arrival, a white neighbor made a demand on him for $195 on an unpaid bill, threatening him with imprisonment. Naturally, Sarah paid the requested amount, though her brother told her that the neighbor was lying. She did not reveal to Natchez her own financial state. When she finally returned to Wadsworth, she had only fifty dollars remaining of all that she had earned from the sale of her book and from lecturing.[13]

Joseph McMaster was still agent at Pyramid Lake when Sarah

Pine-nut harvest, Carson City, Nevada. The men have already knocked the pine nuts off the trees with their long poles. Many women, barely visible, are collecting the nuts under the trees. (Courtesy of Nevada Historical Society.)

arrived on August 29. Sarah found he and his employees were, not surprisingly, opposed to her enterprise. They swore that Winnemucca's and Leggins's bands should not come on the reservation. Furthermore, Sarah found that the fishermen and squatters removed by the military had drifted back upon the land and lake; they were ensconced as usual. It was to no purpose that money had been appropriated for the removal of the settlers, for bringing in Leggins's and Winnemucca's people and giving them lands in severalty and citizens' rights, and for providing them with tools, labor, and instruction.[14]

Sarah had no alternative but to wait and hope that something would be done. She slept in a *nobee* on the ground with a couple of blankets, having given most of her belongings and clothing to destitute friends and relatives. She returned to the old diet of pine nuts and fish.[15] The cheapest hotel in Wadsworth was fifty cents a day, and lodging in a home was five dollars a week; those were beyond her means. Mary Mann was able to raise another fifty dollars from the sale of *Life Among the Piutes*. She sent it on with the hope that it would improve Sarah's situation.[16]

Sarah found that Commissioner Price had instructed a man named Ellet to gather Leggins's band at Fort McDermit and make arrangements to bring them to the reservation. This helped her to determine to remain longer at Pyramid Lake. Late in September, when the weather suddenly turned quite cold, she became violently ill with fever and chills, and her relatives reported to Elizabeth Peabody that she was dying. Elizabeth telegraphed back that they must get Sarah into a warm room, and she promised to send not less than ten dollars a week so that she might stay and observe occurrences on the reservation.[17]

When Natchez and the other Humboldt Paiutes returned from the mountains, Sarah got up from her sickbed. With one hundred of them she and her brother went down to the reservation to see the new agent, W. D. C. Gibson. He did not invite Sarah into the agency house, though it was apparent that she was sick, and he said that he could not talk until the next day. Since it was very cold, and the wind blustery, they went down by the river and camped for the night. Again Sarah was gripped with chills. The women raked ashes out of the fire, spread sand over them, and then laid blankets down to warm her. When the bed grew cold, she got up and hovered over the fire.[18]

In the morning the agent came and said that he had had no orders respecting the bands of Winnemucca and Leggins or Sarah. Sarah was shocked at this news. When she showed him Commissioner Price's letters to Mary Mann, Gibson changed his attitude and said that the bands could come to the Pyramid reserve if they chose. Sarah told him that Leggins's band could not come unless they were sent for, as they had no money. She showed him Price's comment about cooperating in any definite plans of education. Gibson suggested to Sarah that she come and see the school on the reservation that his wife was keeping, but he did not invite Sarah to come as a teacher.[19]

Sick at heart, Sarah returned to Wadsworth. There she stayed on waiting for the special agent, Ellet, to arrive with Leggins. The position that Sarah had coveted, if she were not hired as a teacher, was that of interpreter. That was soon given again to her cousin Dave Numana, who was also chief of the Indian police. Sarah wrote Elizabeth and Mary that Gibson was similar in spirit to the old agent, McMasters, and had taken McMasters's same "gang of employees."[20] Miss Peabody complained that it seemed inconsiderate of Price to have directed Sarah to go to Pyramid Lake while not providing her with money to travel or the assurance of a salary as teacher.[21] It was difficult for Elizabeth to explain to friends why Sarah needed money for board when everyone had assumed that she, as well as her people, had been well taken care of by Congress.

Sarah waited three months before Ellet appeared at Fort Mc-Dermit to consult with Leggins's band and bring them to the Pyramid reserve. Ellet held a council with the head men at Mc-Dermit, and they protested against being taken away from the land of their birth, saying that they would herd cattle for the settlers and hunt game before coming on a reservation where they were not wanted and where there was no land for them anyway. They only asked that the government provide for them in the winter months, particularly for the old who could not work—as the military had done in the past.[22] When Commissioner Ellet arrived at Pyramid Lake to look into the preparations that had been made for the new arrivals, he was appalled to see the squatters back on the land. He recognized that, even if they were removed, there would not be enough land to support another five hundred Paiutes.[23]

When the Paiutes had lost McDermit, Sarah's cause was lost, and well she knew it. She could no longer turn to her father for comfort or use his dignified position as a rallying point for a new campaign. She was very much alone at a time when she had been put in an untenable position. Instead of the heroine's role that she had sought, she appeared to be forcing the McDermit bands to come to Pyramid so that she could acquire a salaried position. Obviously this would have been resented both by the Paiutes at Pyramid Lake and by those who had escaped from Yakima and were now at McDermit.[24]

Sarah knew that Gibson had won his lucrative position as agent through Senator Jones as a political payoff, but it was difficult to make him out as an ogre, even though he had run a gambling house in Gold Hill for six years and owned a faro bank at Virginia City. At Christmas, Gibson presented the students at the Pyramid Lake boarding school with their first Christmas tree, and he played Santa Claus, distributing candy and presents during the holidays. In the last days of December, Sarah knew that the situation was hopeless: she must move in another direction.

21

The Turning Point

Natchez was embarked on a venture of his own at the Big Meadows on the Humboldt River near the town of Lovelock, Nevada. He had lived with his family in this area since 1875. White settlers had taken most of the land, and he now felt an urgent need to acquire some of his own. In 1875 the *Humboldt Register* remarked:

The great drawback to this enterprise is that the Indians have not the means of subsistence, nor the material to work with while clearing the ranch of sagebrush and otherwise preparing the crops. Natchez is quite enthusiastic over the enterprise, and thinks that he can bring nearly all of his people, over which he has control to be steady producing civilized people, if he can receive a little encouragement from the white people. But he does not like the agency system, and will not adopt it; but if they can get a start they will select their own white man as Superintendent and Instructor—one whom they can have confidence in and trust, until they shall be able to carry the business on themselves. Natchez also wants to start a school for the education of the rising generation of his tribe, and thinks most probable that Sarah Winnemucca can be got as teacher, or that they can employ some white person as soon as they get a return from their crops. . . . The ranch is to be irrigated from the new ditch recently constructed at the Meadows, water from which will be given them on very reasonable terms. We hope they will receive from the government and our people all the assistance and encouragement requisite to make the experiment a success.[1]

Natchez went to California to interview railroad officials concerning ownership. On November 27, 1876, the *Winnemucca Silver State* announced that Natchez had received title to the land from the Central Pacific Railroad Co. He had a frame house built on a railroad section (on the east half of the southwest quarter of section 35, Township 27, north of range 31, east Mt. Diablo base and meridian)[2], then he moved in with his two wives and large family. The *Silver State* reported the status of his wheat harvests often in the next few years, saying, for example, on August 25, 1884, "Naches had a good wheat crop of 60 acres, 30 bushels to an acre."

In early 1885, Sarah planned to lecture again, in San Francisco, in order to raise money for her school for Paiute children, which she planned to establish on Natchez's ranch. Before she could leave Wadsworth for her engagement in San Francisco, an incident occurred that gave Agent Gibson at Pyramid Lake ammunition for a continuing duel of words with Sarah.

While Sarah was staying at a Mrs. Nichols's rooming house in Wadsworth, twenty dollars was stolen from her. The landlady advised Sarah to go to the police, and she did so, but they gave her no satisfaction. Sarah suspected that a Bannock who had come to borrow money from her had taken the twenty dollars while she was at dinner. She went to two of her cousins for help, and with them she found the Indian's camp. Sarah wrote: "The man abused me grossly. In a fit of ungovernable passion I struck him. My cousins never touched him. I felled him to the ground with but one slap. We then searched the premises and found the money, with the exception of 75 cents. The man admitted the theft."[3] Sarah thought no more of the incident.

In San Francisco at the Metropolitan Theatre, Sarah was billed as the first Indian to write in the English language. The *Morning Call* reported, "In the history of the Indians she and Pocahontas will be the principal female characters, and her singular devotion to her race will no doubt be chronicled as an illustration of the better traits of the Indian character."[4] Sarah informed her audience: "General Sheridan asked me a short time ago if our reser-

Natchez Overton, Sarah's brother, late in life. (Courtesy of Nevada Historical Society.)

vation did not afford us a good living. I told him that high bleak hills that only a goat could safely climb rose out of the water all around the lake; that the only arable lands were . . . on the river. He seemed astonished at the revelation, for he feels very kindly toward my people."[5]

Sarah found that her stage talents were still with her, and, though she was now forty-one years old, she riveted her audience with her dramatic presence and her words of passionate sincerity. Her listeners were immediately introduced to the agents and their doings:

If a conspiracy were formed by the most cunning men to desert and neglect the Indians on our reservations, it could not succeed better than the selfish policy of Bill Gibson, the agent, and his hungry relations. Not a cent of the $17,000 which was appropriated for the support of the Piutes has been spent for us. Where it has been side-tracked on its journey from Washington I do not know. . . . Every one connected with the agency is wholly devoid of conscience. They are there to get rich.[6]

On another occasion she said that, "if she possessed the wealth of several rich ladies whom she mentioned, she would place all the Indians of Nevada on ships in our harbor, take them to New York and land them there as immigrants, that they might be received with open arms, blessed with the blessings of universal suffrage, and thus placed beyond the necessity of reservation help and out of the reach of Indian agents."[7]

Reviews of Sarah's lectures reached such papers as the *New York Times*. Because of the public attention the Indian Department finally ordered Agent Gibson to give supplies to the Indians on the Humboldt River.[8] Yet, since Leggins's band refused to go to Pyramid Lake, Gibson received instructions from the department not to supply them, though it was well known that this was the most destitute group of all.[9] Sarah laid into Gibson again, saying that he and his employees drank "firewater" publicly in an ostentatious manner, so that the Paiutes were forced to wonder what was wrong with drinking themselves the exhilarating liquids that made them sing and dance.[10] The Indian Service did not let Sarah's attacks on Gibson pass without continuing their past aspersions on her character. The incident with the Bannock Indian was twisted so that according to the Indian Department's account Sarah and her cohorts had committed a rob-

Sarah Winnemucca, probably as she appeared on stage in her last performances in San Francisco. (Courtesy of Nevada Historical Society.)

bery and attempted to murder the Bannock. Sarah in turn did not allow this new accusation to go unnoticed and vented her anger against the department in an open letter:

Under ordinary circumstances I do not notice charges made against me by the Indian ring. They are very powerful, I know, but not powerful enough to stop me from exposing their rascality. This attack is no new thing. In 1879, I charged Agent Rhinehardt [sic] with driving my people into the Bannock War. . . . After I went East this same man wrote letters and fake affidavits and sent them to Washington. The appendix to "Life Among the Piutes" shows how I nailed those lies; and now comes Mr. Gibson and his charges, and time will show how I will settle them. . . .

For years the government has been fattening preachers, and now they have changed and are going to fatten gamblers. It is a well-known fact that this man Gibson, who charges me with gambling, etc, for years and years kept the largest gambling resort in Gold Hill, Nevada. I will do him credit of saying he is considered a square gambler. In an interview with Dr. Dan DeQuille and others in Virginia City, a few months ago, some of the gentlemen asked me what I thought of having an "old sport" for an agent. I said I was willing to try him and see what he would do, that I would rather have a gambler than a preacher with a bottle in one pocket and a Bible in the other. . . . I am only an "old squaw" and, of course, people will not believe me, but no matter: there is an "all-seeing eye" that keeps my account and I am sure Mr. Gibson's charge is not entered against me "up there." He has made a mistake if he thinks he can frighten me: I am not that stock. He can find me at any time ready to tell him to his face what he is, and on the other hand I refer to Deputy Sheriff Shields, Mrs. Nickols, and to Henry Harris, all of Wadsworth, as to the truth of my statement.[11]

On one evening, toward the end of Sarah's lecture series, Natchez appeared on the stage with her. He expressed to the audience his joy at having received 160 acres of land from the Central Pacific Railroad Company and pleaded that all of his people should receive land of their own. Probably he had received the deed from the California railroad magnate Senator Leland Stanford.[12]

Sarah later went home with Natchez to their ranch near Lovelock. His six children liked to come to her *karnee* and loved to hear her marvelous stories of her adventurous life. She began holding regular classes for them. It was her intention, supported by Elizabeth Peabody, to create a school taught by and for Indians, where they would not be separated from the Indian life-ways and languages, as they were in the government boarding schools, which were miles from their homes.[13]

Early in the spring of 1885 several members of Natchez's household contracted pneumonia. Natchez's promising eldest son Kit Carson died,[14] and Sarah was made distraught by the death. Indomitable Elizabeth Peabody ordered a new printing of *Life Among the Piutes* to encourage Sarah in her new enterprise and also raised funds to send a horse wagon, harness, and plow to Natchez. She was spending several months in Washington in the interest of her "Piute friend."[15] Under the new administration of President Cleveland, the first Democratic President in twenty-five years, she was hopeful that the federal government's Indian policy would improve and the "ring" would be removed from office.[16] Meanwhile Mary Mann suffered from dyspepsia and missed her sister. She wrote: "It seems as if the world has stopped going since Elizabeth went to Washington. Life is a perfect *rush* wherever she is. She is very much occupied there with her Indian mission. Under the new administration we feel that there is some hope for that race."[17]

When Elizabeth returned home late in May, 1885, Mary wrote a friend: "She has had much satisfaction in what she has been able to achieve for her beloved Indians (for her love for Sarah diffuses itself over the whole race). . . . I am curious to see how far E. has been battered in the strife. She declares she is well, but she is apt to believe what she wishes to." A bill before Congress to stop appropriations for the Indian schools had been beaten, and new appropriations had been made. A huge gift of seed was sent to Nevada, plus three tents and more farm equipment. Elizabeth was confident that a school building would be erected on Natchez's land and that Sarah's desire to teach would at last be fulfilled. Nevada congressmen and officials had expressed interest in such an enterprise as well.[18]

Although Sarah was a controversial figure among the Indians, as well as in the white world, she was well regarded by many Indians because of her competence in white society and as a spokesman for her people's welfare. On one occasion some Washo women saw her on the street in Carson City, where she had been lecturing, and followed her with great admiration at a respectful distance. They gathered about her hotel for another glimpse, and, as the "princess" emerged from the main entrance of the hotel, rigged out in good toggery, an exclamation of delight ran along the line of waiting women. They were well rewarded when Sarah spoke a few kind words to each; according to a local newspaper, "Their . . . faces were lighted up with joy."[19]

On another occasion, when some Paiutes were thought to have been killed by Chinese, Sarah prevailed upon the assembled Indians and prevented them from attacking the Chinatown area of Carson City.[20] She was also called upon to act as a judge in a murder case in an informal Indian court.[21] Those were isolated incidents, but they indicated a general feeling for Sarah as a leader and a spokeswoman. Unfortunately, it was still true that her dealings with Washington officials had never yielded the kinds of results that were desired by the leadership of Winnemucca's and Leggins's bands. Sarah knew that they did not understand the machinations of white politicians, and, when her word was doubted by her fellows, she could not blame them. The feeling was particularly strong among the Paiutes who had homes at Pyramid Lake that Sarah had double-dealings with them for the benefit of the McDermit bands.

In the end Sarah came to believe that she could now help her people only by teaching English to the children and giving them a basic education. She also wanted to help the children to take pride in the old attitude of concern and caring for one another and to respect the sacredness of life around them.[22] The lot of her people had not improved during the years that she had been working on their behalf. They had learned how to earn money, and they had acquired clothing and some food in payment from the whites, but they had no land of their own. The majority still lived in ragged nobees, which were partially covered by tin, canvas, and blankets thrown away in the refuse piles of the towns. Many did not wish for a more permanent kind of home; they preferred the easily kept, but drafty, nobee, and they had no desire for the objects that were so necessary in white men's homes except for an occasional table or iron kettle.

Much of the food supply was still gathered in the summer months and stored away for winter hardships. If money was acquired, it was often lost, by both the men and the women, in the excitement of the gambling games, or it was spent on liquor

Gambling at the railroad station in Reno. (Courtesy of Nevada Historical Society.)

to enchance existences that were often bleak. Some of the women, both married and single, sold their bodies to bring money into the house, but more often they worked as cleaning women and cooks in white households for a dollar a day. Sarah was upset by the seeming apathy, the docile attitude, of many of her tribe. They took what came their way; they did not strive as she had for improvement of their lot.[23]

Sarah could not contain her indignation when she considered how her people were regarded by whites as servants and low-class hangers-on instead of equal citizens and brothers. The hard circumstances in which the Paiutes lived might have been more acceptable if only the whites had paid them due respect as human beings. Thus her desire was the same as the old dreams of her father and grandfather.

Sarah's bitterness reached its zenith at the death of her oldest brother, Tom, at Pyramid Lake in May, 1885. Natchez had telegraphed her to come because Tom was very ill. She traveled in an open wagon in a rainstorm from the Wadsworth station to the reservation. There she found the sick man in a brush corral on the top of a hill, where the shaman was singing over him. Sarah had lived with her brother from time to time, but she was appalled now again at the conditions of his life. He had worked faithfully for the agents for many years, but in this last illness the agency doctor had not been called, and the white employees took no interest in his condition. Before he died, while he was still conscious, Tom dispensed his few belongings to his relatives. He left Sarah his farm and everything on it. His wife received two cows, four calves, and twelve horses. He thanked his sister for all that she had done for him over the years, saying, "I never could have made it without you."[24]

Sarah wrote:

As to the coffin I can hardly express myself. He died about 4 P.M. An hour afterwards I sent for Mr. Gibson. He came and holding out his hand to me, said, "So Sarah, your brother is dead." Out of respect to the memory of my dead brother I choked back the thought of the injury he had done me and mine, and placing my hand in his I said, "Yes sir, and we have sent to ask you to make us a coffin for him." He then began measuring him and I noticed he only measured his length, as I said, "Mr. Gibson, my brother was a hard working, sober man, and as he would have given me a decent burial, I want to give him one. Please make him a nice coffin and I will pay for it." He went away and the next morning the coffin came. No agent, no doctor, no anyone. . . . How shall I describe it? A rough pine box such as civilization uses for an outside coffin, the lid had to be nailed down. . . . For years and years he was worked from sun to sun. He never drank, he never gambled, he had a saving wife, and yet he was that poor, we had to wrap him up in a blanket and put him away. He was only an Indian, a pine box was good enough for him. He had none of the vices of civilization, but he was unfortunate. He was the brother of Sarah Winnemucca. This is no sentiment. On my last trip to Wadsworth during Mr. McMasters time, my brother came to the depot as usual to haul supplies. McMaster went up to him and said, Tom I do not want you to haul anything *your sister has been talking about me.*So instead of fighting me they cowardly fought him. A week or two since I went down to the agency to settle the affairs of the ranch, which was left to me, and Mr. Gibson refused to speak to me. Now I desire to say here that I have no personal feelings against Mr. Gibson, I have fought him and all other agents for the general good of my race, but as recent events have shown that they [the Numa] are not disposed to stand by me in the fight, I shall relinquish it. As they will not help themselves, no one can help them. "Those that would be free must strike the blow themselves."

I have not contended for Democrat, Republican, Protestant or Baptist for an agent. I have worked for freedom, I have laboured to give my race a voice in the affairs of the nation, but they prefer to be slaves so let it be. My efforts hereafter shall be for my brother alone, we have plenty of friends east that will help us to build a home at Lovelock, where I will teach a school.[25]

. . . My brother asks that the Paiutes be notified of this [that the chief was now Captain Dave Numana] so they can go to Dave to settle their disputes. Hereafter, they must not come to my brother with their troubles, as he will be farmer Natches and not Chief Natches.[26]

22

The Peabody Indian School

Through the summer of 1885, Sarah taught a group of twenty-six Paiute children whom she assembled from the vicinity of Lovelock. The citizens of the town noticed them walking through the streets in the early morning, often with a little food tied neatly in a rag, ready for a day's scholarship under a brush arbor. Natchez's farm was about two miles from town.

Sarah started the students with a military drill in which they learned to respond to rhythmic directions. Early on she taught them gospel hymns, which she interpreted to them in Paiute. She began teaching them English by asking each one to say something in Paiute. Then she would tell them how to say it in English, writing the works in chalk on the blackboard so that they could copy them and find them in their books. Sarah told Elizabeth that her students never forgot those words, but wrote them all over fences in Lovelock and told their meanings in Paiute to their proud parents. She also taught her students to draw and cipher.[1] Sarah sent examples of the children's work to Elizabeth and Mary, who were deeply interested in the advancement of each of the students.

This school that Natchez and Sarah had started fired the interest of many citizens in Nevada and on the East Coast, because it was an Indian-initiated project in contrast to the reservation farms and schools. There was great pressure on the brother-and-sister team to succeed, particularly considering the formidable obstacles that confronted them from the outset. One of the more serious problems was that Sarah was not well. She had been plagued by chills and fever every other day since her illness on the Pyramid Lake Reservation, and for the past two years she had suffered from chronic rheumatism, which caused her continual pain and half paralyzed her.[2] Elizabeth dreaded the coming winter without proper shelter for her. One of the first of the Winnemuccas' enterprises was to make adobe bricks to build a large and comfortable house.[3] They had inherited some chickens and a few steers from Tom Winnemucca, and Natchez purchased a fine span of work horses with money from Boston.[4] Through the summer he prepared the land for future crops.

When Natchez spoke with their old friend M. S. Bonnifield of Winnemucca, the lawyer told him that "it was probable that Senator Leland Stanford of California would stop and see what he had done . . . on his way to Washington next November," which greatly elated Natchez. Bonnifield also told him that, if he and Sarah showed by their works that they were capable and worthy, the president probably would make them the agents of their people, and in a few years any Indian who was industrious would be given all the land that he could till and have all the rights and privileges of white citizens. Bonnifield wrote Elizabeth, "If they make the industrial showing on their farm which I anticipate I will try and get Senator Stanford to call and see them."[5]

Miss Peabody and her friends sent $1,000 worth of goods, equipment, and money through the summer, including funds to start building the house, which was to contain the school and a room for a white teacher whom they hoped to bring from the East. The building would also serve for cooking, eating, council rooms, and a worship center.[6] Sarah kept receipts for the workmen's wages and the cost of materials and sent them to Elizabeth, so that there would be no question about how the donations were used.[7] When Natchez generously set aside six ten-acre farms from his own lands to give to landless Paiute families, Elizabeth was delighted with his action. She felt that it showed "his appreciation for the principle of individual property."[8] She was confident that the Winnemucca's small experiment would be success-ful, accomplishing in a small way what the government should have been doing on a large scale.

Because of Elizabeth's prodding, a special agent, Paris H. Fol-som, was sent to Nevada in midsummer to investigate the Paiutes' situation. He went directly to the Indians to hear their viewpoint and stayed a week at Fort McDermit talking to Leggins and Paddy Cap. He also consulted with Sarah at Lovelock on affairs pertain-ing to the welfare of the Fort McDermit bands.[9] Gibson was finally required to send blankets and other supplies to those long-suffering Paiutes.[10]

Although Sarah's school progressed, and the children learned surprisingly rapidly, there were problems of almost insurmount-able magnitude. Elizabeth had exhausted her sources of money, and still the water problem on Natchez's arid farm had not been solved. An irrigation ditch ran right through the property, but he was not eligible to use it because he could not make pay-ments. Elizabeth, who was kept abreast of events by frequent letters from Sarah, surmised that the Winnemuccas' neighbors were taking advantage of the situation, trying to force them from the property.[11] Since there was no other source of water, the only recourse was to dig a well and erect a windmill—an impossible task without more funds.

The house had not been finished, nor the windmill erected, by late October.[12] Elizabeth was increasingly concerned. Then Miss Alice Chapin, an experienced kindergarten teacher who they had hoped would come to Nevada in the spring, declined the invitation. Miss Chapin had met Sarah in the East in 1883 and had become at once a convert to her cause. "How Sarah's great solemn face looms up before me," she wrote Elizabeth. "Were I rich, very rich, I would go to Sarah and see if some way could not be followed to make things right. But I have a fancy that when my purse was empty I should flee. Misery one can not alleviate is unendurable."[13]

Elizabeth Powell Bond, an associate of Elizabeth's in the pro-motion of kindergartens, had acquired an interest in the Paiutes. After she spoke of Sarah's school to the Philadelphia Human Rights Association, she was taken aside by the president of Smith College, Laurenus Clark Seelye, who told her, "Mr. Welsh [the secretary of the Indian Rights Association] wished me to put you on your guard against the woman you spoke of yesterday. He says Professor [C. C.] Painter [the Washington agent of the association] has had evidence of the most indisputable character, that she has been engaged in transactions disreputable, and is unworthy of trust. He will give you further particulars if desired."[14]

Miss Peabody despaired of correcting the unjust sabotage of the Indian Department, but immediately wrote Professor Painter of her own knowledge of Sarah Winnemucca: that she was a wise and extraordinary woman. She told him that she had letters of commendation of Sarah's character from good citizens of Nevada who knew her well. In the meantime Indian Commissioner Price told Mr. Welch that "if any of 100 affidavits in his office were trustworthy, Sarah Winnemucca was not a proper person to associate with good people."[15] The Bureau of Indian Affairs file on Sarah Winnemucca contains only four such affidavits, written at the time of Rinehart's attempt to discredit her, by persons associated with his interests. The allegations of such high officials, however, put a check upon public appeals for money. Even a friend who felt strongly that Sarah was not at fault wrote, "As I think Mr. Hopkins behaved so badly here it would be unwise to make any extended appeal for aid in her behalf."[16]

Devoted persons like Mary Bean were a heart-warming mainstay for Sarah and Elizabeth. This elderly, fragile woman wrote Miss Peabody:

Yours of yesterday 28inst. came about five minutes since. It is a great relief to me, for two reasons. First it gives me some facts, that I can use at discretion to answer slanders with which I am so often met, when I try to advocate the cause of the Piutes and of Sarah. . . . I shall give your letter a thorough, careful reading and trust to use with discretion what you have written, including the addresses of some persons if I should need information. . . . I am not sanguine nor in anyway strong but I am patient and persevering, and I have a little faith that after the holy-days I may be able to add a mite to your bank of mercy and justice and truth.[17]

Happily, the house on the ranch was finished before Christmas. Sarah's school was now in more comfortable quarters, though it was without school desks or the other helpful conveniences of the government boarding school at Pyramid Lake run by Agent Gibson. In February, 1886, Elizabeth received encouraging news

from a group of prominent citizens of Lovelock. Miss Peabody
sent it immediately to the *Boston Transcript*:

Miss Peabody—A few of the principal residents of Lovelocks, having
heard so frequently of the Piute school and the aspirations of the Princess, concluded, after very little cogitation, to verify in person the truth
of these prodigious reports [concerning her school].

When we neared the school, shouts of merry laughter rang upon our
ears, and little dark and sunburnt faces smiled a dim approval of our
visitation. . . .

Speaking in her native tongue, the Princess requested the children to
name all the visible objects, repeat the days of the week and months of
the year, and calculate to thousands, which they did in a most exemplary
manner. Then she asked them to give a manifestation of their knowledge
upon the blackboard, each in turn printing his name and spelling aloud.
It is needless to say, Miss Peabody, that we were spellbound at the
disclosure. Nothing but the most assiduous labor could have accomplished this work. But most amazingly did I rudely stare . . . when
these seemingly ragged and untutored beings began singing *gospel hymns*
with precise melody, accurate time, and distinct pronunciation. The
blending of their voices in unison was grand, and an exceedingly sweet
treat. We look upon it as a marvelous progression; and so gratified were
we that we concluded to send this testimonial containing the names of
those present, in order that you may know of the good work the Princess is trying to consummate. . . . We feel that any further assistance
would be well deserved and profitably expended by Sarah.[18]

By the middle of March, Natchez's ranch had been surveyed
and partially fenced. Sarah wrote to a friend in New York that
her brother was busy plowing and "trusting to his friends and
Providence" to supply the seed for his harvest.[19] By April the
money for the seeds had arrived, and the same donor, Mr. Warren
Delano of New York, sent a large barrel of dress goods, clothes,
sewing notions, and vegetable seeds.[20]

Sarah wrote Elizabeth of her illness. The chills and fever would
not abate and were coupled with a worsening arthritic condition.[21]
It would have been a great help if Alice Chapin would have come
to support her.

Sarah was disturbed because the time was near when the parents of her students would take their children into the mountains
on their annual hunt for winter stores. She told Elizabeth that
already some of her best scholars had gone. As she still had hopes
that Senator Stanford might stop to see the school when he re-

Northern Paiute women gathering pine nuts near Lovelock, Nevada. (Courtesy of Nevada Historical Society.)

turned from Congress in midsummer, she wished to keep and board the students. The parents had assembled in council in her schoolroom and expressed their grief that they could not pay her themselves for their children's board.[22] Sarah hoped that Stanford would value Natchez's farm and her school so highly that he would demand money from the fund in the Indian Office appropriated for Indian education. Then they could board the children in the summer months. As it was, Natchez and his family were without bread or meat and living on pine nuts. They could not keep the students.

Elizabeth immediately began soliciting promissory notes for the "first school taught by an Indian." She was attempting to raise $100 a month, and within a week she had raised enough for April. She held high hopes of sustaining the boarders through August. In her solicitations Elizabeth wrote of Sarah, "I see that she knows, as I cannot, how the Indian mind is to be approached and set at work for that self-development which is the only real education."[23]

Natchez had demonstrated throughout his life his shrewdness in dealing with white men for the Numa's benefit, but Sarah had no confidence in his ability to handle money because of his generosity. As a consequence she handled the funds that were received. She wrote Elizabeth that Natchez never asked for money, though he sometimes looked very wistfully at it when he saw it in her hands. One day she gave him a silver dollar, which pleased him greatly, and he went out "gingling it" (as Sarah spelled the phrase). When he came home that night, Sarah asked him what he had done with it, and he replied, "Oh, I had a big time." Later an old uncle who had gone with Natchez told Sarah that her brother had bought tobacco for some of the old men with the money. Sarah reported to Elizabeth that Natchez would never be rich.[24]

Natchez's fencing proved to be inadequate. The neighbors' stock broke through and trampled on the young plants rising from the plowed ground. Sarah wrote Warren Delano, asking to borrow money for more fencing. He replied to her:

About loaning $200 to your brother on his Land, I must tell you I cannot do it—and more than that let me advise you and him not to borrow *any money*, of any body, on the farm! Just as sure as you borrow any money of *any white* man and mortgage your farm for its repayment, so *surely* will your farm be lost to your Brother and his family. Until you can get the money out of your crops, or from your kind friends, you must do the best you can without fences. Let the *children* when not in school or asleep, watch the boundarys of the farm and keep the cattle off, and when night comes the men must take turns and keep the necessary watch. But do *every* thing *possible* to take care of your farm and to avoid making any debts that will cause you to lose it. Remember the success of your school and your life depend upon your maintaining your hold and cultivating your farm. For your Brother to fail in this and lose his farm would enable your adversaries to scoff at you and say it is of no use to try to help the Indians. I know the case is a hard one but your brother must try to work it out.[25]

Mr. Delano's advice was followed, as there was no other choice.

The Peabody Indian School, as Sarah called it continually interested local whites, who visited it and commended Sarah's work.[26] She took her pupils to Winnemucca, where observers, impressed with their knowledge, said that her school should be assisted by the Indian Bureau.[27] Yet, as far as the United States government was concerned, Sarah's school did not exist. The schools at Hampton, Virginia, and Carlisle, Pennsylvania, in the

East were run entirely by whites, and the Indian students could not use their own languages from the time they arrived. They were separated, often by thousands of miles, from their families and heritage. General Samuel Chapman Armstrong, the head of the Hampton Institute, believed that the sooner Indian children were taken from their parents, their languages, and their cultures the sooner they would be "Americanized." He refused to listen to Elizabeth's vindication of Sarah's character, nor would he concede a trace of merit to her program for teaching the children.[28] However, a western journalist wrote: "We believe that the Indian Department should found an Indian school in Nevada and put Sarah at the head of it. . . . She has ample culture, and she knows the Indian character thoroughly, while it is easy to believe that her example will be of great value in encouraging her pupils. When Indians have a white teacher there must naturally seem a great gulf between them."[29]

Sarah realized herself that her fluency in three Indian languages was of vital importance to the quality of education of her students. She wrote to the *Winnemucca Silver State:*

It seems strange to me that the Government has not found out years ago that education is the key to the Indian problem. Much money and many precious lives would have been saved if the American people had fought my people with Books instead of Powder and lead. Education civilized your race and there is no reason why it cannot civilize mine. Indian schools are failures at many agencies, but it is not the fault of the children, but of the teacher and interpreter. Most of teachers have but one object, viz. to draw their salary. I do not think that a teacher should have no salary. But I think they should earn it first and then think of it. The most necessary thing for the success of an Indian school is a good interpreter, a perfect interpreter, a true interpreter. . . . I attribute the success of my school not to my being a scholar and a good teacher but because I am my own Interpreter, and my heart is in my work.[30]

Sarah's hopes of supporting funds from the United States government were short-lived. During the summer of 1886 an official from Washington arrived at the ranch and told the Winnemuccas that they could not receive any aid from the Reserved Fund for Indian Education unless Sarah surrendered the directorship of her school and unless Natchez gave up the ownership of his land.[31] Of course, Sarah refused to abandon her work and the original purpose of her school. Her brother certainly had strived too long for his small amount of acreage to let it go to the Indian Department.

Sarah and Natchez were in sore need of encouragement when Alice Chapin, the hoped-for teacher from the East, arrived in mid-July. She began working with Sarah, giving her moral and physical support. She had not fathomed the difficulties facing the Indian woman until she came to Nevada and saw for herself. Sarah's health particularly concerned her. Alice administered quinine for the malarial bouts of chills and fever and saw immediate improvement in her patient.[32] As she observed Sarah's school and her teaching methods, she kept up a steady stream of correspondence with Elizabeth, giving her details of the school's progress.

Miss Chapin, a normal school teacher with years of experience, was favorably impressed with Sarah's work. Though Sarah's students had only benches without backs, which they used as tables while kneeling on the floor, they were interested in learning. They produced superior work compared with the public-school students with whom Miss Chapin was familiar. She was pleased to find that they were in the second reader. Sarah read every lesson in English and in Paiute and used both languages in discussions of the subject matter.[33] Alice sent Elizabeth specimens of the students' writing and drawing. The old woman enthusiastically showed her friends the results of their contributions.

Each day, after a morning of academic subjects, Sarah taught the children to work about the ranch. The boys tended the garden and cared for the stock, and the girls cooked and sewed. Elizabeth called this "a vanguard of the 'New Education' in which doing leads thinking, and gives definite meaning to every word used."[34] Sarah's foremost objective was to make her students teachers—to use the older ones as assistants and substitutes and to encourage them to undertake their own self-education as she had done.[35]

As far as the farm production was concerned, Alice Chapin found that the lack of adequate fences and water were still the worst difficulties. The hoped-for windmill and well had not materialized. Natchez contracted to furnish thirteen men (including himself) for one month's work on a dam and ditches, in return for water from the irrigation canal that flowed through his land. Unfortunately, he did not receive a written agreement to this

Northern Paiute Indians near Bishop, California. (Courtesy of Nevada Historical Society.)

arrangement. While Natchez's sixty-eight acres of wheat were maturing, representatives of the water company told him that he must keep his gates open, so that they could get to their ditches (some of which they had built on Natchez's land without his permission). Miss Chapin noticed that the white neighbors kept their gates shut, and, since Natchez's gates were open, the neighbors' cattle came on the land. An old uncle had to sit by the gates and drive them away — the remedy that Warren Delano had recommended.[36] Alice sought out the managers of the water company in Lovelock and discovered that Natchez did not have to leave the gates open. Thus the old man was freed for other work.

Meanwhile Natchez was accused of stealing and killing some cattle belonging to a neighboring farmer. These unfounded accusations, of course, angered Sarah, who wrote a letter to a local newspaper:

Lovelock, Nev. July 28. People without giving any proof have insinuated that Naches Winnemucca, of Lovelock, has killed beef not his own on his farm or up in the mountains, no where in particular. If any one knows anything about it let him come forward and tell it face to face like a man. If he has seen him kill or can prove anything, let him prove it in court. But if there is no proof, except that he is an Indian, and it is safe to slander him, then those who value their words will not say what they have no proof of.[37]

The coming harvest was looking promising when the water company turned off Natchez's water. Miss Chapin investigated why they had done so. The company claimed that the Paiutes had not worked enough on the irrigation ditches. "Indians are so lazy, we don't want them around," they said, and for illustration they used the old man who had sat all day by the open gate, protecting Natchez's fields. Miss Chapin's explanations did no good, and she realized that this maneuver had been planned all along to discredit the enterprise.[38]

Natchez still had no mower to cut the wheat. Fifteen Paiute men and women were hired, to be paid in grain. Some of the crop would also be needed to pay the men who had worked on the irrigation dam. Sarah notified Elizabeth that the literary exercises of the school would be suspended for a month while the

Wheat harvesting at Lovelock, Nevada. The women are using the traditional baskets for seed gathering. (Courtesy of Nevada Historical Society.)

children helped with the harvest. At the same time Alice Chapin had to return to the East, and Sarah took a needed rest.

When Elizabeth received a letter from Sarah some days later, she was shocked to read her message: to send no more money, "not one cent." A mutual friend had written Sarah that Elizabeth was giving away the provision for her old age in order to keep the boarding school going. Elizabeth wrote back immediately that this was not the case, saying, "the work I was doing for her was the greatest pleasure I had ever enjoyed in my life!"[39]

Sarah in the meantime wrote again, saying that "on account of our ill luck" she and Natchez were going away to earn some money. Elizabeth should not write again until she received a new address. The old woman was heartsick waiting for further word, wondering about the unexplained ill luck and concerned for the welfare of her Paiutes and the Peabody School.[40]

On September 25, Elizabeth was surprised by a telegram from Sarah asking for $200. Miss Peabody could not meet this need, and she sent the request on to Warren Delano, who had often helped in the past.

I was almost willing to say I would advance the money, . . . but a few hours thought have led me [to think] that *it is well*, not only for you, but possibly for Sarah herself, that you cannot meet her call. If Sarah had kept you advised of her doings and her doings had been such as to lead up to some need of money, the surprise would have been avoided and a reasonable ground for an answer yea or nay would have been presented — but the call for an immediate $200 to be placed at a point remote from her house [Elko, Nevada] and from her legitimate work, justifies a fear, a suspicion that there is some thing not quite right, if not wrong. It leads me to conjecturing various things: has she met her vagabond husband, Hopkins? or is it *possible* that there is truth in some of the scandalous reports of vicious habits: of drinking and gambling etc. etc. which have been so positively urged?

If I *knew* all about Sarah and her affairs and could be entirely satisfied that she is all you and I would like to know her to be, I might perhaps strain a point and lend her the $200 — but as the matter stands I harden my heart against the application.[41]

23

Hopkins Again

Sarah stood before her people at a fandango near Lovelock and spoke. Except for a whimpering baby the Numa listened attentively. The September wind blew small whirlwinds of dust across the cleared dance place behind the crowd, but Sarah's strong voice carried well across the wide space. "These are the days of civilization," she told them. "We must all be good, sober and industrious and follow the example of our white brothers. We must become educated and give our children an education so that they may become farmers, mechanics and business men. We must build houses and earn an honest living."[1]

She told them that the Apaches had been fighting the soldiers in the mountains in the Southwest, on the borders of Mexico, but now their fighting was done. Their old ways were no more, and they would have to become farmers. Their leaders, Naiche and Geronimo, were in jail and would doubtless be hanged. She concluded, "Now we Paiutes know the white people are our friends and will help us if we help ourselves."[2]

After the fandango Sarah and Natchez set out with the wagon team. They headed northeast for the settlement of Rye Patch, where Natchez would work as a vaquero and Sarah had work as a housekeeper for a Mrs. Mary Wash. They now had only one dollar between them.[3]

Sarah remembered how, a few weeks before, the Paiute men and women workers on Natchez's ranch had come from harvesting the fields and demanded to be paid in silver coins instead of grain. A white neighbor had told them that Sarah was receiving $100 a month from Elizabeth Peabody and had said that Sarah was cheating them, since the money had been sent to pay the workers. The money, of course, had been intended to run the boarding school and had been used for that purpose; there was no silver to pay the harvesters. Hence the telegramed appeal for money that Elizabeth had not been able to meet and that Warren Delano had refused.[4] The white farmers had succeeded in turning the Numa against the Winnemuccas. As it turned out, this resulted in a loss in the sale of the crop. After Sarah had worked at Rye Patch for a few weeks, she returned to Lovelock and at last wrote the anxious Miss Peabody:

If we could have borrowed $200 for two months . . . we could have paid them in money, and then sold the rest of the crop for $30 a ton. But it was the game to force us to sell the crop to the storekeepers for $17 a ton, which (thanks to the Spirit Father for so much) paid all our debts, but left nothing over; and I could not feed on love, so could not renew the school; and I was perfectly discouraged and worn out.[5]

Natchez's little daughter Delia had been ill with consumption since her older brother Kit Carson had died of pneumonia. Now she too was dying. Sarah helped care for the child, who had been placed in a small *nobee,* as was the custom. At Delia's death, in early November, 1886, the strength that she had given the child abandoned Sarah, and she wrote Elizabeth that she was glad that Delia was "safe in heaven." She expressed the hope that the "Spirit Father may soon let me die": "So, darling, do not talk any more on my behalf, but let my name die out and be forgotten: Only, don't you forget me, but write to me sometimes, and I will write to you while I live.[6]

With her characteristic enthusiasm Elizabeth would not let Sarah's mood daunt her, and she immediately began canvassing friends for new funds. She felt:

[It was] a natural but temporary reaction of Sarah's nerves, and I see that she is still her whole noble self in this energetic action for personal independence, which I shall make known at once to all her friends, sure that it will challenge them to help her through another year until another harvest. Meantime I believe that the entire change of work will prove a recreative rest, and her people will plainly see by it that it is not true that she had been living irrespective of them on the $100 a month, and that her enthusiastic scholars will not fail to bring their parents back to their confidence and gratitude to her.[7]

Elizabeth had 200 more copies of *Life Among the Piutes* printed. She also published a 36-page pamphlet, entitled *Sarah Winnemucca's Practical Solution of the Indian Problem*. In it she described Sarah's philosophy of education for Indian children and pleaded for support of her cause.[8] This she mailed to congressmen and influential friends of the Indians.

Sarah repaired her winter clothing and found more housekeeping work. She did not return to the ranch until November. By then her health and courage had improved, bolstered by Elizabeth's zeal. The Peabody School was reopened as a day school.[9] Later, in the first part of 1887, it was again a boarding school, for by then Elizabeth had found half a dozen friends who each sent $12 weekly for its upkeep.[10] Soon Sarah had forty-five students, and her health and vital spirit seemed to have returned.[11] She found that the children had lost some of their newly acquired skills, but review and exercises soon brought them back. Elizabeth noted that some of the Paiute children attending Agent Gibson's school at Pyramid Lake wished to change to the Peabody Indian School. She felt that this was a real mark of success, considering that the government-sponsored school had so much more monetary backing and more facilities.[12]

An inadequate water supply and lack of fencing still plagued Natchez. Sarah complained in a local paper that hogs and a lot of cattle had been running on their land since harvest: "We drive them out, but it does no good, as those who own them drive them in again. What shall I do? Will someone please advise me?"[13] This appeal in the *Winnemucca Daily Silver State* was a good maneuver on Sarah's part, as it gave notice to every one of her neighbors that she knew what was going on and that future trespassing would confirm her allegations.

From her new residence in Jamaica Plain, Massachusetts, Mary Mann wrote a friend that her sister was quite happy about "her" Indian, who was doing wonders.[14] Earlier Mary had written to the same woman, "She still rules the ascendant with E. and scarcely less with me though there is not so much of the fanatic in me as in E."[15] Mary had been feeble all winter. Although she enjoyed the visits of her grandson, it tired her extremely every time he spent the day with her.[16] In January a close friend of Mary's died and remembered her in her will. This set Mary to considering the provisions of her own will. As it turned out, the doctors' bitter medicines, which she took faithfully, though without much hope, did not save her. The widow of Horace Mann died on February 11, 1887. She left her own small legacy to Sarah, an Indian woman whom she may not have loved "fanatically," but whom she had supported in her quiet, steadfast way from the time when she had first met her.[17]

After her sister's death Elizabeth Peabody felt that she was not separated from her but nearer than ever, and she believed that Mary Mann hovered over Sarah Winnemucca as well. She told a friend that Sarah had become independent with her model school on her brother's farm, thanks to Mary's contributions. One hundred dollars had even unexpectedly come from Japan. She felt that surely the shade of Mary had brought all of this about.[18]

In February, 1887, Congress had passed the Dawes Act, which had long been supported by the Protestant churches engaged in missionary work among the Indians, the Indian Rights Association, and the liberal wing of the Republican Party. Humanitarian advocates of the lands-in-severalty act supported it because they believed that the Indians were capable of adapting to white civilization and that, if they did prove incapable, they would likely die out. White settlers in the West wanted the large parcels of land on the Indian Reservations that the Dawes Act would open to white settlement after the Indian heads of families were each allotted 160 acres. The Indian owners were not to be allowed to sell the lands allotted to them for a period of twenty-five years, but then they were to be given title to their farms and receive their citizenship. At the end of twenty-five years their tribal ties, which were believed to contribute to lack of industry and lack of individual responsibility, would supposedly be forgotten. It was expected that the Indians would then be assimilated into the great American "melting pot."

Sarah had had a great deal of influence on Senator Dawes at the time he wrote his bill. She and Natchez wanted the Numa to adapt to the white man's world and to succeed under the new system, which seemed to them a natural and hopeful alternative to the hated reservations. Aided by their well-meaning friends in the East, they could not foresee the problems of alienation, the loss of Indian lands to acquisitive whites, and the breakup of vital tribal support that the act would bring.

Sarah and Elizabeth were much upset by one facet of the Dawes Act that they never could condone: Indian children were required to be educated in white, English-speaking schools, whether their parents approved or not. Boarding schools were to be established far from the reservations, where children would be isolated from their parents and not allowed to go home for holidays. It was forbidden to speak their native languages. Anything relating to Indian religions and culture was to be disdained and discredited by the white teachers. Elizabeth and Sarah were in agreement that these schools would "repress creative self-respect and the conscious freedom to act" that was necessary for the well-being of Indian youth.[19]

A few months after the passage of the Dawes Act a gentleman, named Mr. Davis, came to the Peabody Indian School and asked Sarah to turn over her students to him. He proposed to transport them to Grand Junction, Colorado, where a boarding school for Indian children had been established. Sarah would have nothing to do with his plan, and she told Davis that she would never send the students without their parents' consent. As it turned out, a dozen Paiute children were taken from Pyramid Lake to the Colorado Industrial School, and three Paiute boys from the vicinity of Lovelock as well.[20] Lee Winnemucca was in San Francisco at the time and came home to find that one of his sons had been removed to Colorado.

Sarah and Natchez soon decided to promote their school as an industrial school for the Paiutes. Natchez proposed to give forty acres of his land for the purpose. Sarah would make another trip to the East in the hope that she could convince government officials to support their new plans. The school would prepare young Indians for specific jobs, such as carpentry, blacksmithing, and shoemaking. Some industrial-arts schools had already been established on reservations, but none had been set up in Humboldt County. It was Sarah's belief that the Indian students would learn rapidly at almost any school with proper treatment, but the right place to teach them was in their own communities, where the country was familiar and where they would be near their parents and tribal associations.

The *Winnemucca Daily Silver State* supported Sarah's ambitious project, saying, "Experience has taught her what her young people need and the Government should make an appropriation and place her at the head of an Indian industrial school—There are some 400 Indian children in the county to be educated and Sarah believes in educating them at home."[21] The newspaper gave a tribute to Elizabeth: "That grand old lady—Miss Peabody. England claims Gladstone, the grand old man in the Irish cause, and America can truly claim in her the grand old lady in the cause of education."[22]

Sarah made her pilgrimage to the East, but she did not gain the attention and recognition that had accompanied her former efforts. The Indian Association continued to promote the cause of the eastern Indian boarding schools, such as the Carlisle Indian School and Hampton Institute.[23] The nation had salved its conscience for the time being on the Indian question, and now it was felt to be time to get on with other national business. Sarah was defeated before she began. Her concept is a controversial ideal even a century later: that Indians should run their own local schools with nominal white help and should preserve and promote their own value systems.

The tangible result of the trip was that Sarah saw Lewis Hopkins, and they were reconciled. Perhaps this had been one of her intentions in returning east, to see Lewis and have the marriage settled one way or another. Her friends had been dismayed by the first trouble in Baltimore in 1884 and had been encouraging her to divorce Hopkins. Mrs. Delano, for example, had written to Elizabeth in June, 1884:

I cannot but feel pity for him, he must suffer and dispise [sic] himself to have fallen so low. He evidently appreciated his wife's character and loved her. He must suffer to see how he has made her suffer who was so devotedly attached to him. I thought they were equally attached to each other. I fear her enemies will take advantage of his misconduct to prove that she is equally base and false.... When writing will you please convey to her my love and sympathy.[24]

In the same letter, however, she stated: "I hope he will receive the imprisonment that his crime deserves which will make it impossible for him to follow her. I own myself greatly disappointed in him, for I thought I understood his character as a talented, clever, and honorable man."[25] In January, 1885, she wrote Elizabeth, "So long as she is his wife he will rob her of all the money she earns."[26]

When the Hopkinses returned to Nevada and came to the ranch, the usually placid and friendly Natchez got his back up. He would not speak to Lewis, and the rest of the family also ignored his presence. Natchez was embittered toward his brother-in-law, who he felt was only exploiting Sarah and gaining her sympathy because of his wan smile and frail appearance.[27] It seems probable that Lewis's health required him to rest, while Sarah would have been busy teaching and also cooking, sewing, cleaning, and drudging about the ranch like Natchez's wives.

Elizabeth shared the concern of Sarah's other friends that Hopkins was a phony. In due course Sarah wrote her about the bad feeling between Lewis and Natchez and begged to borrow money from Warren Delano so that her husband might get some medical attention. This time, she promised, they were about to realize a fair price for their wheat, and she would borrow against that. Delano wrote Elizabeth, "I do not believe that Hopkins is really very sick! I have the same opinion of him that *Nachez* has and believe that his weakness, loss of voice, his cough &c &c are all assumed or exaggerated to frighten the poor woman, and when he has got her last dollar the fellow will be himself again and up to some mischief."[28]

When the harvest was completed, Natchez had raised 400 sacks of wheat. He was proud of this achievement and felt that his venture into the whites' capitalist economy had proved successful. Hopkins in the meantime had suddenly come to life. He paid some workers to load the wheat and took it to Winnemucca, where he sold it. He then offered a small amount of what he received to Natchez as his share. Sarah apparently went along with this action. Natchez angrily refused the money on the grounds that the wheat had been raised on his land by his and his wives' labor and therefore all of the money belonged to him — all or nothing.[29] Soon after Hopkins left for San Francisco, taking the proceeds of the harvest with him.

When an article sympathetic to Natchez's plight was published in the *Silver State*, a neighbor of Sarah's wrote an irate letter to the editor. The neighbor claimed that, when Sarah had left the farm in Natchez's charge to go east, he had promptly quit the premises himself, and, if it had not been for his white neighbors, there would not have been a harvest at all.[30] This assertion, while it upheld Sarah's conduct in the trouble with Natchez, was not fair to her brother. He had farmed and produced good harvests for many seasons before Sarah ever appeared on the scene.

The letter continued:

Sarah has fed and clothed Natchez for years, fenced the ranch, cleared the land, plowed and leveled it, furnished seed, made irrigating ditches, paid harvesting and threshing bills, furnished sacks and paid for hauling the grain to market. After all this expense she offered him [Natchez] $75, which he refused to take, saying he wanted it all or nothing.

It is true, Sarah sent her husband to Oakland to place him under a doctor's care, he having been very ill for 6 months past and his life dispared of, and did not go herself as she sent nearly every dollar she had to the physician. This was a humane act on her part and should be placed on record on behalf of her race. Natches cannot get treated in Lovelock today for a sack of flour, while Sarah has unlimited credit.

Pale Face.[31]

Lewis Hopkins had not only caused dissension between Sarah and Natchez and taken the profits so zealously hoped for by generous friends but also caused the collapse of Sarah's Peabody Indian School. Sarah must have been torn making such a choice, fully knowing the consequences. She saved only enough from Lewis to pay back the debt to Warren Delano.[32] News of the rupture between brother and sister soon reached the East, and Mr. Delano complained of sadly shattered nerves over the whole affair. He wrote Elizabeth:

Poor Woman, she is in sad straits, not to be blamed, but greatly to be pitied and helped—but how to help her is the problem . . . . Sarah must try to suppress her feelings and resume her good work, but to do this she must be reconciled to her Brother and we must use any influence we have to bring Natchez around to a better mood and from all I have heard of him I think he may not be found unreasonable. He owes his improved condition and circumstances very largely to Sarah and her friends whose continued good offices will doubtless be for his future benefit.[33]

Lewis Hopkins returned to the ranch in a few weeks. He had run through the Winnemuccas' money, and the doctors in Oakland had been unable to arrest his tuberculosis. He died on

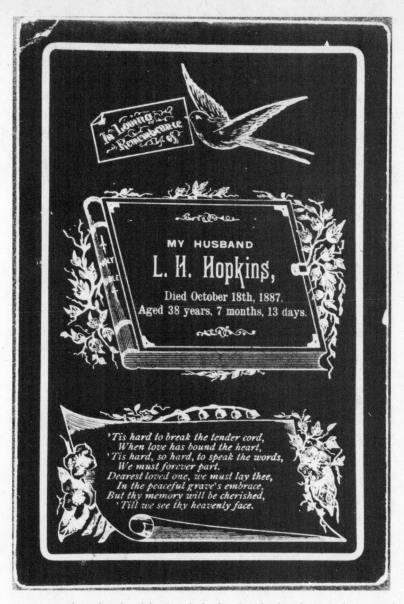

A memorial card ordered by Sarah for her late husband, an indication of her continued regard for him. (Courtesy of Nevada Historical Society.)

October 18, 1887, and was buried in the Lone Mountain Cemetery at Lovelock.[34] Sarah had a special card printed for her family
and friends, as was the custom of the day, containing a sentimental poem in her husband's memory. In March, Elizabeth had
been confident that her Indian work was successfully finished,
since Sarah had received several sums from Mary's estate and
other sources.[35] Now, six months later, the status of the Indian
project that had occupied Elizabeth's later years was once more
precarious.

24

Henry's Lake

The winter of 1887–88 was a time of looking back for Sarah, even though she was only forty-three years old. She was bitterly disappointed that the model farm and school, for which she and Natchez had worked so hard, had received no official attention and no commendation from officials such as Senator Stanford. The Peabody Indian School now obtained little money from eastern sympathizers. Sarah had given up the idea of an industrial school, since she had not received the necessary support from the government.

According to Elizabeth "the surplus of the money donated without solicitation to enable Sarah to carry on the boarding school, she has appropriated to make Natchez a partner in the water company, and so permanently secure irrigation."[1] Elizabeth knew this was a wise decision, for water would always be a problem in the Nevada desert. As it was, Elizabeth felt that there was a fair chance for the Paiute enterprise to become self-supporting. It was Sarah's plan to go on by herself and continue the day school, "which costs her nothing but her time and the strength of her heart and mind."[2] Twenty-four students remained.[3]

Elizabeth did feel that Sarah had made some mistaken judgments of character, undoubtedly referring to her attachment to Hopkins.[4] Still Elizabeth was not disappointed in her protégé.

With her usual vivacity Miss Peabody published another pamphlet on the Peabody Indian School[5] and sent it to Senators Stanford, Long, Dawes, and William S. Holman and to other congressmen, to induce them to write an amendment, in favor of the school, to an appropriation that was to be made for Indian education.[6] Elizabeth's plea was:

Will not somebody propose in Congress, this coming session, that appropriation be made to enable Sarah to put up some lodging houses and take to board these four hundred children? (Those Paiutes of school age in Nevada.) It would not cost so much as any of the government or denominational schools do, and would have none of their disadvantages, being wholly Indian work.[7]

Elizabeth's effort stirred some interest on the part of Congressman Holman,[8] but nothing came of it. Sarah made up her mind that she would not expect or ask for help from the East again. Congress was not receptive, and Elizabeth had worked too hard and too long for the cause. Nonetheless, it seemed ironic that Sarah's approach to Indian education had been spurned by Washington when there were so many Indian parents begging Sarah to take their children.

In the spring of 1888, Major General Howard made a visit to the Peabody Indian School.[9] When he spoke to Natchez, he learned that the Paiute farmer still supported the continuance of his sister's enterprise.[10] Howard could not promise them that he could influence the government to support the school. It is possible that he was able to tell them at that time that the army was intending to abandon Fort McDermit and that the military reservation would soon be turned over to the Paiutes. The Interior Department was to take possession of Fort McDermit on July 24, 1889, and some of its buildings served as headquarters for the new McDermit Indian Reservation. Part of the land that Old Winnemucca had always desired was at last to be officially possessed by some of his people.

Summer came, and the children left school with their parents for their seasonal wanderings to gather food. There was little correspondence now between Sarah and Elizabeth; the old woman had her kindergarten interests and lectured at the Concord School of Philosophy.[11] Sarah knew that her dream had ended, and she regretfully realized too that Natchez would have difficulty sustaining himself independently on the ranch. She must have felt some pride that despite all the hardships and difficulties she had kept the Peabody School going for almost four years.

Several small newspaper items give us the only clues concerning Sarah's activities from the time when she closed her school until she again joined her sister, Elma Smith. In late February, 1888, she was located in Lovelock, where she was bested in a game of casino.[12] On September 18, 1889, she and Natchez accompanied some other members of the tribe, who took a handout breakfast from a hotel kitchen. The "princess" had been attending a fandango in Elko, and she excused herself, saying that "when among the Indians she had to conform to their maners and customs."[13] A week later a notice appeared in the *Elko Independent* that no one could purchase Natchez's farm without notifying Sarah, as she owned a part interest in it.[14]

Sarah may have made several trips to visit her sister Elma, probably wintering in Nevada and returning to Idaho in the summer. She would have taken the Central Pacific to Salt Lake City and then entrained northward to Monida, Montana, the closest station to Henry's Lake, Idaho.[15] The first night's stopover, after a ride by sleigh or wagon over the rutted roads, was in a primitive hostel at Lakeview. On the second day the trail passed the northern shore of Henry's Lake and then wound by the Sherwood General Store, which also served as a hotel for the sparsely inhabited countryside.

This was Bannock Indian country. If Sarah was present at the death of Elma's husband, John B. Smith, on January 19, 1889,[16] she would have seen the painted Bannocks, who came to bury their friend in their bright regalia, their ponies decorated with bells and beadwork. Joseph Sherwood, the store owner, who acted as the local postmaster and coroner, had laid Smith out and built a wooden casket. On the next day more Bannocks arrived on their ponies, and the Indians collected on a hillside, wailing and lamenting the sudden passing of Smith. After the burial Elma would have returned to her cabin, which was about two miles down the road and closer to the shores of the lake.[17]

Elma was well situated, compared to other pioneer women. Her husband John had worked hard during his life, and he left her his savings and the home. Elma had taken in two white teenagers, Will and Ed Staley, who were orphans.[18] When spring came, at least on days when Sarah felt well, we can imagine her wandering with the two boys through the flower-strewn meadows, watching the moods of the mountains about the lake and the glorious sunsets across the water. Occasionally Elma was called away for midwife duties. Then Sarah may have taken charge of the boys. She may have taught them their lessons or accompanied them down the road to the Dick Rock Ranch, where the owner kept some tame buffalo that he had raised and was training to pull a buggy. The boys would have enjoyed the shenanigans of the cowboys working on the ranch, who took hunting parties of city people into the mountains of the Yellowstone country.[19]

Food was plentiful at Henry's Lake, even in the winter months when snow lay heavily on the ground. Friends might bring fish, caught through holes in the lake ice, or meat from the hunt. In summer the two sisters picked wild berries for preserves and wine making.

Mary Ann Garner, who would later become Joseph Sherwood's second wife, moved with her family to Henry's Lake in 1890. As a girl of nineteen she enjoyed the companionship of the two Paiute sisters. She accompanied Sarah and Elma on their excursions through the woods, picking huckleberries and other fruits, and she visited in their home. Mary Ann's father, who was an excellent shot, was out hunting one day in the woods. He sighted an antelope and brought it down. Then his heart sank because he recognized it as one of Elma's pets by the red ribbon that was tied about its neck.[20]

When young Will Staley disappeared mysteriously, and not even the body was found, the neighbors were suspicious of the Indian women. Whispers grew loud that perhaps Will had been poisoned—after all, they said, the Indians knew about poisonous plants. Mary Ann did not share the neighbors' suspicions, and she reminded them that they were perfectly willing to call in Elma when a new baby was expected.[21]

One evening in the fall of 1891, Joseph Sherwood was disturbed by rapid hoofbeats on the road and a sudden pounding on his door. He had already closed the store and was in his family quarters, sitting down to a late dinner. It was postponed, however, when a neighbor appeared and told him that there had been another death at Elma's place. The date was October 17,

1891.[22] Joseph hurried into his coat and came along in his buggy as soon as he could hitch the horse.

Sarah was laid out on the bed, her eyes already closed. Sherwood, in his position as the local coroner, learned from Elma that they had eaten a large dinner and had had some chokecherry wine. Sarah had gasped and suddenly collapsed, and that was all. The storekeeper-druggist-undertaker decided that Sarah had died of too much wine, the same cause of death that he had determined for John Smith.[23] Natchez arrived too late for the Bannock ceremonies. He found Sarah's grave near that of John Smith, with the dirt piled high in a sharp-edged wedge. There was no marker, and there is none today. Only two months after Sarah's death Natchez sold his 160 acres in the Big Meadows[24] and moved with his family to the Pyramid Lake Reservation. There he died in 1907, five days after the death of his last wife.[25] In 1905 the buyer of his land sold in turn to a conglomerate. The lost Paiute dream thus became a part of a large ranch with quantities of dairy and stock cattle. The corrals were equipped with modern machinery, and irrigating and drainage systems brought water to the buildings and land at the turn of a faucet.[26]

Elma Smith loaned money to Ed Staley to buy a place at Henry's Lake, and she lived with him there for a while on the Staley Ranch. At the time of her death in 1920 there were no longer any Indians left in the vicinity to mourn her as they had her sister Sarah in 1891.[27]

The New York Times carried Sarah's death notice and printed a review of her zealous, adventurous life of forty-seven years.[28] Colonel Frank Parker wrote how she had saved him and others during the Bannock War. He observed, "She was the only Indian on this coast who ever took any prominent part in settling the Indian question, and as such her memory should be respected."[29]

General Howard, in writing a short biography of Sarah, emphasized, "She did our government great service, and if I could tell you but a tenth part of all she willingly did to help the white settlers and her own people to live peaceably together I am sure you would think, as I do, that the name of Toc-me-to-ne [or Shellflower] should have a place beside the name of Pocahontas in the history of our country."[30]

Ironically, Sarah's life did not catch the attention of the public in the years to come as the stories of Sacajawea and Pocahontas

Elma Winnemucca Smith, Sarah's sister, in 1919, the year before her death. (Courtesy of Nevada Historical Society.)

had. She had not helped to find a new trail through the wilderness, nor did she save the life of an early colonist. Perhaps in the future, however, Sarah Winnemucca's leadership for brotherhood and human rights and her tremendous efforts for peace between races will be recognized and celebrated. In one of the last passages of her autobiography Sarah had written:

Those who have maligned me have not known me. It is true that my people sometimes distrust me, but that is because words have been put into my mouth which have turned out to be nothing but idle wind. Promises have been made to me in high places that have not been kept, and I have had to suffer for this in the loss of my people's confidence. I have not spoken ill of others behind their backs and said fair words to their faces. I have been sincere with my own people when they have done wrong, as well as with my white brothers. Alas, how truly our women prophesied when they told my dear old grandfather that his white brothers, whom he loved so much, had brought sorrow to his people. Their hearts told them the truth. My people are ignorant of worldly knowledge, but they know what love means and what truth means. They have seen their dear ones perish around them because their white brothers have given them neither love nor truth. Are not love and truth better than learning? My people have no learning. They do not know anything about the history of the world, but they can see the Spirit-Father in everything. The beautiful world talks to them of their Spirit-Father. They are innocent and simple, but they are brave and will not be imposed upon. They are patient, but they know black is not white.[31]

Notes

Chapter I. Early Years

1. Julian H. Steward and Erminie Wheeler-Voegelin, *Paiute Indians*, vol. 3, *The Northern Paiute Indians*. Two main premises of that study are that the Paiutes had no single great chief, but instead had small-band leaders, and that they had no sense of being a large separate tribe in aboriginal times.

2. *Reese River Reveille* (Austin, Nev.), September 2, 1884, p. 1, col. 1.

3. Old Winnemucca was also called Poito or Mubetawaka ("man with hole in his nose") for the bone that he wore through the septum of his nose. Young Winnemucca was also called Numaga. Robert F. Heizer, *Notes on Some Paviotso Personalities*, p. 2.

4. *Nevada State Journal* (Reno), February 12, 1873, p. 1, col. 2.

5. Moses Schallenberger, *The Opening of the California Trail: The Story of the Stevens Party from the Reminiscences of Joseph Schallenberger*, ed. George R. Stewart (Berkeley: University of California Press, 1953), pp. 19-21, 64-66.

6. Joseph Aram, "The Reminiscences of Captain Aram," in Colonel James Thompkins Watson, "Across the Continent in a Caravan," *Journal of American History* 1 (1907):627-29.

7. Sarah Winnemucca Hopkins, *Life Among the Piutes: Their Wrongs and Claims*, ed. Mrs. Horace Mann, p. 20.

8. Robert J. Heizer and Thomas R. Hester, eds., *Notes on Northern Paiute Ethnography: Kroeber and Marsden Records*, p. 32. Also Hopkins, *Life Among the Piutes*, pp. 25, 29.

9. Hopkins, *Life Among the Piutes*, p. 12.

10. Ibid., p. 18.

11. Ibid.

12. Hopkins, *Life Among the Piutes*, p. 21.

13. Also spelled *pe-har-ve*. The clumps of sugar that formed naturally on the outside of the cane were shaken off and rolled into balls that often included

the wasps and other insects that were attracted to the sugar. Early settlers found the sugar delicious until they discovered that fact.

14. Hopkins, *Life Among the Piutes*, p. 23.

15. Ibid., pp. 27–33.

16. California Historical Landmark 437 is on the site of the ferry, which was established by John Doak and Jacob Bonsall in 1848 and was the first ferry on the San Joaquin River. After passing through Stockton, Doak had crossed the San Joaquin River at the present Mossdale Fork, following an Indian trail to San Jose. Hiram Scott bought out Doak in 1849. V. Covert Martin, *Stockton Album Through the Years*, pp. 77–78.

17. Hopkins, *Life Among the Piutes*, pp. 34–35.

18. V. Covert Martin, *Stockton Album Through the Years*, pp. 77–78.

19. Hopkins, *Life Among the Piutes*, pp. 41–43.

20. John Reese, unpublished manuscript, Bancroft Library, University of California, Berkeley.

21. James F. Downs, *The Two Worlds of the Washo: An Indian Tribe of California and Nevada*, pp. 73–76.

22. Hopkins, *Life Among the Piutes*, p. 42.

23. William Wright [Dan DeQuille], *The Big Bonanza*, p. 10.

24. Frederick Dodge to Jacob Forney, January 4, 1859, Letters Received, Office of Indian Affairs, Utah Superintendency, 1859–1880, Record Group 75, M234, National Archives, Washington, D.C.

25. Wright, *The Big Bonanza*, p. 192, and the account of Captain Juan in California on p. 204.

26. *Nevada State Journal*, February 12, 1873. See also *San Francisco Chronicle*, November 14, 1879: "My brothers Tom and Naches here went to work for four years on a ferryboat."

27. *Nevada State Journal*, February 12, 1873: "I went to California, and in Stockton met Mrs. Roach and was adopted into her family."

28. Sarah is mistaken in dating her residence with Major Ormsby in Genoa to 1858. By that time the major and his family had moved to Carson City, Nevada. The Williams-McMarlin affair, which she observed while she was with the Ormsbys, is also dated by Angel to 1857. Myron Angel, ed., *History of Nevada*, p. 551.

29. Hopkins, *Life Among the Piutes*, pp. 58–59.

30. "The most of these Indians have evidently once lived in California, which accounts for their knowledge of the English language, many of them have become domesticated, and are employed by the settlers of the Carson Valley as herdsmen and laborers on their farms." Garland Hurt, "Report to His Excellency Brigham Young Gov. and Ex-officio Supt. of Indian Affairs, Territory of Utah," in James H. Simpson, *Report of Explorations Across the Great Basin of the Territory of Utah for a Direct Wagon Route from Camp Floyd to Genoa in Carson Valley in 1859*, p. 228.

31. Hopkins, *Life Among the Piutes*, p. 59. For another account see Myron T. Angel, ed., *History of Nevada*, p. 551.

32. Hopkins, *Life Among the Piutes*, p. 60.

33. Ibid., p. 61.

34. Ibid., p. 63.

35. Ibid.

36. Ibid., pp. 64, 66.

Chapter 2. The Pyramid Lake War

1. William Wright, *The Big Bonanza*, p. 11.

2. Ibid., p. 9.

3. Angel, ed., *History of Nevada*, p. 551.

4. U.S. Office of Indian Affairs, *Report of the Joint Special Committee: Condition of the Indian Tribes*, p. 517.

5. Frederick Dodge to Jacob Forney, January 4, 1859, Letters Received, Office of Indian Affairs, Utah Superintendency.

6. Robert F. Heizer, *Notes on Some Paviotso Personalities*, p. 6; Omer C. Stewart, "The Northern Paiute Bands," *Anthropological Records* 2, no. 3:129, 130.

7. Statement of William Weatherlow to William Willson Lawton, Notary Public, October 27, 1860, RG 75, M234, National Archives.

8. Wright, *The Big Bonanza*, pp. 7 and 9.

9. Frederick Dodge to Jacob Forney, January 4, 1859, Letters Received, Office of Indian Affairs, Utah Superintendency.

10. Frederick Dodge to Commissioner Greenwood, February 18, 1859, Letters Received, Office of Indian Affairs, Utah Superintendency.

11. James H. Simpson, *Report of Explorations Across the Great Basin of the Territory of Utah*, p. 9.

12. Wright, ed., *The Big Bonanza*, p. 33.

13. Angel, ed., *History of Nevada*, p. 554.

14. Sarah Winnemucca Hopkins, *Life Among the Piutes: Their Wrongs and Claims*, ed. Mrs. Horace Mann, p. 64.

15. Frederick Dodge to A. B. Greenwood, Commissioner of Indian Affairs, November 25, 1859, Letters Received, Office of Indian Affairs, Utah Superintendency.

16. William T. Whitney manuscript, California Historical Society, San Francisco, pp. 18-19.

17. Angel, ed., *History of Nevada*, p. 148.

18. Statement of Weatherlow to Lawton, October 27, 1860, RG 75, M234, National Archives.

19. Ibid.

20. Statement of Ira A. Eaton to F. W. Lander, superintendent of U.S. Wagon Road Expedition, October 23, 1860, Selected Correspondence and Papers from the Utah Superintendency File, 1860-1870, RG 75, M234, National Archives.

21. Angel, ed., *History of Nevada*, p. 151.

22. Ibid.

23. Hopkins, *Life Among the Piutes*, p. 16.

24. Angel, ed., *History of Nevada*, p. 151.

25. Ibid., p. 153.

26. Ibid., pp. 155, 156.

27. Hopkins, *Life Among the Piutes*, p. 72; Sessions S. Wheeler, *The Desert*

Lake: The Story of Nevada's Pyramid Lake, p. 61, 64.

28. Angel, ed., *History of Nevada,* p. 158.

29. Ibid., p. 163.

30. Statement of Weatherlow to Lawton, October 27, 1860, RG 75, M234, National Archives.

31. Ibid.

32. Frederick Lander, superintendent of U.S. Wagon Road, to the Honorable A. B. Greenwood, commissioner of Indian affairs, October 31, 1860, with enclosures, Selected Correspondence and Papers from Utah Superintendency File, 1860–1870, RG 75, M234, National Archives.

33. Ibid.

34. Ibid.

35. U.S. Office of Indian Affairs, *Report of the Joint Special Committee* (1867), p. 518.

36. *Sierra Democrat* (Sacramento, Calif.), 1860, Bancroft Scraps, vol. 93, pp. 17–18, Bancroft Library, University of California, Berkeley.

37. U.S. Office of Indian Affairs, *Report of the Joint Special Committee* (1867), p. 519.

Chapter 3. Growing Up Proud

1. This account of the death of Truckee is based on Hopkins, *Life Among the Piutes: Their Wrongs and Claims.* The date that Sarah gives would indicate that Truckee died before the Pyramid Lake War. It does not agree with other sources, which show October, 1860. See C. D. Irons, *Edwards Tourists' Guide and Directory of the Truckee Basin* (1883), pp. 98–99; Wright, *The Big Bonanza,* p. 269; *Gold Hill* (Nev.) *News,* May 6, 1876.

2. Hopkins, *Life Among the Piutes,* p. 67.

3. Ibid.

4. Ibid.

5. Hopkins, *Life Among the Piutes,* p. 69.

6. Bancroft Scraps, vol. 93, p. 10, Berkeley. This article describes the honesty and the virtuous manner of the Paiutes in dealing with their white neighbors.

7. Hopkins, *Life Among the Piutes,* p. 70.

8. *Nevada State Journal,* February 12, 1873, p. 1, col. 2.

9. *San Francisco Morning Call,* November 22, 1879, p. 4, col. 1.

10. *Notre Dame Quarterly,* issues for 1914 and 1915.

11. *Notre Dame Quarterly,* June, 1936, p. 32.

12. On June 4, 1977, I interviewed and corresponded with Sister Mary Dominica McNamee, historian of the College of Notre Dame, Belmont, California. She wrote:

There is no entry for her [Sarah Winnemucca] in our archives, school lists, and no photo. We have looked closely into this matter. If the story is true, she must have been in the boarding school at that early date, but the absence of her name even in the accounts would indicate that the Sisters doubted whether they could keep her. The complaint of the wealthy lady would be no surprise to them. If there was one point of agreement between the Spanish and American girls at the time it was unwillingness to live under the same roof with an Indian. . . . Though the Sisters were strong for the native, they had no funds; in order to support schools for natives, they had first to open a boarding school for the elite. Then they opened three "poor schools" in San Jose, but that was after Sarah's time.

13. James W. Nye to the Honorable Caleb B. Smith, Secretary of the Interior, August 14, 1861, Letters Received, Office of Indian Affairs, Utah Superintendency.

14. "Governor Nye and the Indians," *Carson City* (Nev.) *Silver Age*, May 27, Bancroft Scraps, vol. 93, p. 16.

15. Jacob T. Lockhart to the Honorable W. P. Dole, Commissioner of Indian Affairs, June 25, 1863, Letters Received, Office of Indian Affairs, Utah Superintendency.

16. Angel, ed., *History of Nevada*, p. 169.

17. *Humboldt Register* (Winnemucca, Nev.), June 13, 1863.

18. John C. Burche to Governor James W. Nye, August 1, 1864, Letters Received, Office of Indian Affairs, Utah Superintendency.

Chapter 4. On Stage

1. Sarah Winnemucca, "The Pah-Utes," *The Californian*, September, 1882, p. 256. Norton I, "Emperor of the United States," was an eccentric gentleman of wide reputation who strode the streets of San Francisco during this period, wearing gold braid and a sword. He used his own imperial currency and was often accompanied by two dogs, Bummer and Lazarus.

2. Margaret G. Watson, *Silver Theatre*, pp. 323, 324.

3. Bancroft Scraps, vol. 93, p. 10.

4. Ibid.

5. Ibid.

6. *San Francisco Daily Alta California*, October 22, 1864.

7. Ibid., p. 1, col. 1, "City Items."

8. *Daily Alta California*, October 23, 1864, p. 1, col. 1, "City Items."

9. Bancroft Scraps, vol. 93, p. 27.

10. Ibid., p. 10.

Chapter 5. Pyramid Lake Reservation

1. Hopkins, *Life Among the Piutes*, p. 77.

2. Bancroft Scraps, vol. 93, p. 11; Angel, ed., *History of Nevada*, p. 170.

3. Hopkins, *Life Among the Piutes*, p. 78.

4. *Virginia Union* (Virginia City, Nev.), March 17, 1865, Bancroft Scraps, vol. 93, p. 12.

5. *Virginia Union*, March 15, 1865, Bancroft Scraps, vol. 93, p. 28.

6. Bancroft Scraps, vol. 93, p. 11.

7. Angel, ed., *History of Nevada*, p. 172.

8. Ibid., p. 173.

9. Ibid.

10. *Humboldt Register*, January 3, 1866.

11. For more information on Black Rock Tom and the Nevada Indian wars of 1865 and 1866, see Sessions S. Wheeler, *The Nevada Desert*, chapter 3, "The Black Rock Desert—Indian Stronghold," pp. 56-92, and appendix B, pp. 163-68.

12. Hopkins, *Life Among the Piutes*, p. 79.

13. Ibid., p. 85.

14. *Humboldt Register*, January 20, 1866.

15. *Humboldt Register*, March 17, 1866.

16. Angel, ed., *History of Nevada*, p. 174.

17. *Humboldt Register*, May 5, 1866.

18. *Humboldt Register*, February 10, 1866.

19. *Humboldt Register*, March 31, 1866.

20. George F. Brimlow, "The Life of Sarah Winnemucca: The Formative Years," *Oregon Historical Society Quarterly*, June, 1952, p. 118.

21. Hopkins, *Life Among the Piutes*, p. 79.

22. *Humboldt Register*, February 3, 1866.

23. Agreement with H. G. Parker, superintendent of Indian affairs, State of Nevada, November 20, 1866, Letters Received, Office of Indian Affairs, Nevada Superintendency, 1861-1880, RG 75, M234, National Archives.

24. Contract between Clark W. Thompson, Superintendent of Indian Affairs and Undersecretary of the Interior, and William N. Leet, Gold Hill, Nevada, May 27, 1867, Letters Received, Office of Indian Affairs, Nevada Superintendency.

25. Hopkins, *Life Among the Piutes*, pp. 76-77.

26. Resolution of the Nevada state legislature passed March 6, 1867, Letters Received, Office of Indian Affairs, Nevada Superintendency.

27. U.S. Office of Indian Affairs, *Report of the Joint Special Committee: Condition of the Indian Tribes* (1867), p. 521.

28. Hopkins, *Life Among the Piutes*, pp. 79-80.

29. Ibid., p. 81.

30. Ibid., p. 82.

31. Ibid.

32. Hopkins, *Life Among the Piutes*, p. 83.

33. Ibid., p. 84.

34. Ibid.

35. Ibid.

36. Ibid., p. 85.

37. Ibid.

38. *Reese River Reveille*, July 8, 1867; A. J. Liebling, "Lake of the Cui-ui Eaters," part 3, *The New Yorker*, January 15, 1955, p. 35; Lieutenant J. M. Lee to H. Douglass, December 20, 1869, Letters Received, Office of Indian Affairs, Nevada Superintendency. Angel names James Flemming as having died near Williams Station (*History of Nevada*, p. 160).

39. *Annual Report of the Commissioner of Indian Affairs to the Secretary of the Interior for the year 1868*, p. 145.

40. Quoted from the *Susanville Sagebrush*, August 17, 1867, in the *Reese River Reveille*, September 2, 1867.

Chapter 6. Camp McDermit

1. Hopkins, *Life Among the Piutes*, p. 99. In *Life Among the Piutes*, Seward is called "Major" Seward, but the *Official Army Register* shows him as a captain.

2. W. V. Rinehart, unpublished manuscript, Bancroft Library.

3. Hopkins, *Life Among the Piutes*, p. 100.

4. Ibid., pp. 100–103.

5. Ibid., p. 103.

6. Ibid., p. 92.

7. Ibid.

8. Lalla Scott, *Karnee: A Paiute Narrative*, pp. 32–33.

9. Hopkins, *Life Among the Piutes*, pp. 90–91.

10. Steward and Wheeler-Voegelin, *Paiute Indians*, vol. 3, *The Northern Paiute Indians*, p. 260.

11. Ibid., p. 163.

12. Ibid., p. 261.

13. Jacob T. Lockhart to N. G. Taylor, Commissioner of Indian Affairs, July 21, 1868, Letters Received, Office of Indian Affairs, Nevada Superintendency.

14. U.S. Office of Indian Affairs, *Annual Report of the Commissioner of Indian Affairs to the Secretary of the Interior for the Year 1868*, pp. 146–47.

15. H. G. Parker to Hon. N. G. Taylor, Commissioner of Indian Affairs, December 10, 1868, Letters Received, Office of Indian Affairs, Nevada Superintendency.

16. *Humboldt Register*, May 1, 1869.

17. Franklin Campbell to Commissioner of Indian Affairs, June 9, 1865, Letters Received, Office of Indian Affairs, Nevada Superintendency.

18. J. C. Kelton, Assistant Adjutant General, to Department of the Interior, Special Order 219, September 11, 1869, Letters Received, Office of Indian Affairs, Nevada Superintendency.

19. Sarah Winnemucca to Major H. Douglass, April 4, 1870, Letters Received, Office of Indian Affairs, Nevada Superintendency.

20. *Harper's Weekly*, May 7, 1870, p. 291, col. 3.

21. Helen Hunt Jackson, *A Century of Dishonor*, appendix, p. 395.

22. Major H. Douglass to Commissioner E. S. Parker, May 31, 1870, Letters Received, Office of Indian Affairs, Nevada Superintendency.

23. The *Humboldt Register*, May 14, 1870, reported Douglass's efforts as follows: Indians Pacified—Major Douglas and Lieut. Lee, Special Indian Agents for Nevada arrived in town on last Sunday and have so far been quite successful in pacifying the Chiefs and Warriors of the Piutes, that for the present at least, no fears of an outbreak by the savages are apprehended by our citizens. The agents left here a few days ago for the Big Meadows down the Humboldt, where they are now having a big talk with the natives. Natchez, who claims to be the Winnemucca or Big Chief of the tribe is at

the Meadows, and a shrewder specimen of redskin does not exist in Nevada.

24. Report by Major H. Douglass, United States Army, to Superintendent of Indian Affairs of conversation with Paiute Indians at Camp McDermit, Nevada, May 8, 1870, Letters Received, Office of Indian Affairs, Nevada Superintendency.

25. Major H. Douglass to the Honorable E. S. Parker, Commissioner of Indian Affairs, November 30, 1870.

Chapter 7. Marriage and New Agents

1. Sarah Winnemucca to Commissioner E. S. Parker, August 9, 1870, Letters Received, Office of Indian Affairs, Nevada Superintendency.

2. Ibid.

3. A correspondent of the *Sacramento Record* writing from Winnemucca, *Alta California* (San Francisco), August 29, 1870, Bancroft Scraps, vol. 93, p. 54.

4. Wright, *The Big Bonanza,* p. 202.

5. *San Francisco Morning Call,* January 22, 1885.

6. *Nevada State Journal,* February 12, 1873.

7. George Balcom to E. S. Parker, Commissioner of Indian Affairs, March 5, 1871, Letters Received, Office of Indian Affairs, Nevada Superintendency.

8. George Balcom to E. S. Parker, Commissioner of Indian Affairs, March 15, 1871, Letters Received, Office of Indian Affairs, Nevada Superintendency.

9. George Balcom to E. S. Parker, Commissioner of Indian Affairs, April 14, 1871, Letters Received, Office of Indian Affairs, Nevada Superintendency.

10. George Balcom, Telegram, March 27, 1871, Letters Received, Office of Indian Affairs, Nevada Superintendency.

11. George Balcom to E. S. Parker, Commissioner of Indian Affairs, April 8, 1871, Letters Received, Office of Indian Affairs, Nevada Superintendency.

12. George Balcom, Telegram to E. S. Parker, Commissioner of Indian Affairs, April 29, 1871, Letters Received, Office of Indian Affairs, Nevada Superintendency.

13. George Balcom to E. S. Parker, Commissioner of Indian Affairs, April 29, 1871, Letters Received, Office of Indian Affairs, Nevada Superintendency.

14. Sarah claimed that C. A. Bateman, the agent at Walker River, was the instigator of this "wild Indian" affair, but this could not have been the case, as Bateman's arrival at Carson City from the east was announced on April 29. Hopkins, *Life Among the Piutes,* p. 86.

15. C. A. Bateman to E. S. Parker, Commissioner of Indian Affairs, June 18, 1871, Letters Received, Office of Indian Affairs, Nevada Superintendency.

16. C. A. Bateman to E. S. Parker, Commissioner of Indian Affairs, July 8, 1871, Letters Received, Office of Indian Affairs, Nevada Superintendency.

17. Captain R. F. Bernard to Major Samuel Breck, Assistant Adjutant General, U.S.A., Headquarters, Department of California, June 23, 1871, Letters Received, Office of Indian Affairs, Nevada Superintendency.

18. E. O. C. Ord, Brigadier and Brev. Major General, endorsement to above letter, July 1, 1871, Letters Received, Office of Indian Affairs, Nevada Superintendency.

19. Hopkins, *Life Among the Piutes*, p. 90.

20. Ibid.

21. C. A. Bateman to H. R. Clum, Acting Commissioner of Indian Affairs, August 20, 1871, Letters Received, Office of Indian Affairs, Nevada Superintendency.

22. Sarah Winnemucca to General E. O. C. Ord, July 1, 1871, endorsed by Ord and included in transmissions to Adjutant General by Major General Schofield, July 5, 1871, Letters Received, Office of Indian Affairs, Nevada Superintendency.

23. George Balcom to H. R. Clum, Acting Commissioner of Indian Affairs, August 17, 1871, Letters Received, Office of Indian Affairs, Nevada Superintendency.

24. C. A. Bateman to H. R. Clum, Acting Commissioner of Indian Affairs, August 20, 1871, Letters Received, Office of Indian Affairs, Nevada Superintendency.

25. *Sacramento* (Calif.) *Union*, May 16, 1872.

26. C. A. Bateman to H. R. Clum, Acting Commissioner of Indian Affairs, November 10, 1871, Letters Received, Office of Indian Affairs, Nevada Superintendency.

27. Franklin Campbell, quoted in James Mooney, *The Ghost Dance Religion and the Sioux Outbreak of 1890*, p. 3.

Chapter 8. **The Modoc War**

1. Lt. Col. O. L. Hein, U.S. Army, Retd., *Memories of Long Ago* (New York: G. P. Putnam, 1925), p. 67.

2. *Humboldt Register*, March 1, 1873.

3. *Nevada State Journal*, February 12, 1873.

4. Hopkins, *Life Among the Piutes*, pp. 86–87.

5. C. A. Bateman to F. A. Walker, Commissioner, February 17, 1872, Letters Received, Office of Indian Affairs, Nevada Superintendency.

6. *Humboldt Register*, June 8, 1872.

7. Ibid., June 22, 1872.

8. *Nevada State Journal*, February 12, 1873.

9. *Humboldt Register*, July 27, 1872.

10. Ibid., August 3, 1872.

11. C. A. Bateman to F. A. Walker, October 26, 1872, Letters Received, Office of Indian Affairs, Nevada Superintendency.

12. Keith A. Murray, *The Modocs and Their War*, pp. 66–67, 71.

13. Ibid., p. 41.

14. *Humboldt Register*, April 19, 1873.

15. Wheaton to A. A. General, Department of the Columbia, May 6, 1873, Modoc War Official Correspondence, Bancroft Library.

16. Wheaton to Lt. James A. Rockwell, April 16, 1873, Modoc War Official Correspondence, Bancroft Library.

17. Steward and Wheeler-Voegelin, *Paiute Indians*, vol. 3, *The Northern Paiute*

Indians, p. 163; and Thomas S. Dunn from Camp Warner, May 23, 1873, Modoc War Official Correspondence, Bancroft Library.

18. *Portland Daily Bulletin*, April 23, 1873, Modoc War Official Correspondence, Bancroft Library.

19. Wheaton to A. A. General, Department of the Columbia, May 6, 1873, Modoc War Official Correspondence, Bancroft Library.

20. Smohalla was a prophet and teacher of the Sokulk, or Wanapum, tribe, who were related to the Nez Percés. He had been exposed to Catholic teaching in his boyhood. After a quarrel with a rival chief he had left his country on the Columbia River in eastern Washington, wandering as far as Mexico and returning to his home through Nevada. One wonders if he preached his new religion to the Paiutes on this journey, thus influencing Wodziwob, whose visions were similar. He maintained that he had been to the spirit world and returned with a message for all Indians, which was that the Native Americans must return to their primitive mode of life, refuse the teachings and claptrap of the white man, and in all their actions be guided by the will of the Indian god, as revealed to Smohalla and his priests. Chief Joseph of the Nez Percés was a devoted believer of Smohalla's teachings. Frederick Webb Hodge, ed., *Handbook of American Indians North of Mexico*, vol. 2, p. 602.

21. Wheaton to Assistant Adjutant General, Department of the Columbia, May 6, 1883, Modoc War Official Correspondence, Bancroft Library.

22. 2d Lt. J. P. Jocelyn to Maj. Thomas S. Dunn, May 26, 1873, Letter Book 3A, Modoc War Official Correspondence, Bancroft Library.

23. Telegram from Gen. W. T. Sherman to Gen. J. C. Davis, June 3, 1873, Modoc War Official Correspondence, Bancroft Library.

Chapter 9. Law and Order

1. *Carson Daily Appeal* (Carson City, Nev.), February 8, 1874.

2. Don D. Fowler and Catherine S. Fowler, eds., *Anthropology of the Numa: John Wesley Powell's Manuscripts on the Numic Peoples of Western North America, 1868-1880*, p. 16. There is a photograph of Natchez on p. 18 of this study. Vocabulary lists given by him at Salt Lake City in May, 1873, are on pp. 210-15. A collection of tales told by him is on pp. 215 and 218-20. See also *Carson Daily Appeal*, July 24, 1873, p. 3, col. 1.

3. *San Francisco Alta California*, November 18, 1873, Bancroft Scraps, vol. 93, pp. 54-55.

4. *Carson Daily Appeal*, February 1, 1874, reprinted from *Humboldt Register* (Winnemucca, Nev.).

5. *Daily Alta California*, January 30, 1874, p. 1, col. 2.

6. *Carson Daily Appeal*, February 3, 1874.

7. *Daily Alta California*, January 30, 1874, p. 1, col. 1.

8. Petition to the Honorable Edward P. Smith, February, 1874, Letters Received, Office of Indian Affairs, Nevada Superintendency.

9. Bancroft Scraps, vol. 93, p. 43.

10. *Virginia City* (Nev.) *Chronicle,* January 11, 1875, Bancroft Scraps, vol. 93, p. 55.

11. R. F. Bernard, 1st Cavalry Captain, Camp Bidwell, to Assistant Adjutant General, Department of California, May 17, 1874, Letters Received, Office of Indian Affairs, Nevada Superintendency.

12. *Virginia City* (Nev.) *Chronicle,* January 11, 1875, Bancroft Scraps, vol. 93, p. 55.

13. Ibid.

14. Ibid.

15. Ibid.

16. *Virginia City* (Nev.) *Territorial Enterprise,* January 14, 1875.

17. Ibid.

18. Vandever to Commissioner of Indian Affairs, June 11, 1875, Letters Received, Office of Indian Affairs, Nevada Superintendency.

19. Barstow to the Honorable E. P. Smith, October 15 and 19, 1875, Letters Received, Office of Indian Affairs, Nevada Superintendency.

20. Wagner to Assistant Adjutant General of the United States Army, Washington, D.C., February 16, 1875, Letters Received, Office of Indian Affairs, Nevada Superintendency.

21. Wagner to Breck, February 23, 1875, Letters Received, Office of Indian Affairs, Nevada Superintendency.

22. Breck to Commanding Officer, Camp McDermit, Nevada, February 27, 1875, Letters Received, Office of Indian Affairs, Nevada Superintendency.

23. *Winnemucca Silver State,* March 16, 1875, Bancroft Scraps, vol. 93, p. 34.

24. *Silver State,* March 27, 1875.

25. *Reese River Reveille,* April 1, 1875, p. 3, col. 2; *Silver State,* March 29, 1875.

26. Elmer R. Rusco, "The Status of Indians in Nevada Law," in Ruth M. Houghton, ed., *Native American Politics: Power Relationships in the Great Basin Today* (Reno: University of Nevada, Bureau of Governmental Research, 1973), p. 63.

Chapter 10. **The Malheur Reservation**

1. *Silver State,* April 28, 1875.

2. Hopkins, *Life Among the Piutes,* chapter 6, "The Malheur Agency."

3. George F. Brimlow, *The Bannock Indian War of 1878,* p. 31.

4. Hopkins, *Life Among the Piutes,* p. 105.

5. Ibid., p. 106.

6. Ibid., p. 107.

7. Ibid., p. 109.

8. Ibid., p. 110-11.

9. Ibid., p. 112.

10. "They all held to that peculiar religious creed called 'Dreamers' and practised all the peculiar rites of that strange belief—such as drumming and dancing, bowing and making strange signs, not unlike some of the Orthodox Christians." W. V. Rinehart to Mrs. F. F. Victor, March 6, 1874, Bancroft Library.

11. Hopkins, *Life Among the Piutes*, p. 113.

12. H. Linville to Major Elmer Otis, March 7, 1874, Letters Received, Office of Indian Affairs, Oregon Superintendency, RG 75, M274, National Archives.

13. Hopkins, *Life Among the Piutes*, pp. 112-15.

14. Oliver Otis Howard, *My Life and Personal Experiences Among Our Hostile Indians*, p. 377.

15. O. O. Howard, Department of Columbia, telegram to Adjutant General, October 12, 1875, Letters Received, Office of Indian Affairs, Oregon Superintendency.

16. Samuel B. Parrish to the Honorable E. P. Smith, Commissioner of Indian Affairs, April 26, 1875, Letters Received, Office of Indian Affairs, Oregon Superintendency; petition to the Honorable James K. Kelly from numerous citizens of Baker County, Oregon, November 11, 1875, Letters Received, Office of Indian Affairs, Oregon Superintendency.

17. Hopkins, *Life Among the Piutes*, p. 116.

18. Samuel B. Parrish to the Honorable E. P. Smith, Commissioner of Indian Affairs, April 4, 1876, Oregon Superintendency, Letters Received, Office of Indian Affairs.

19. Mattie later married Lee Winnemucca, and she and Sarah were close companions until Mattie's untimely death in 1879.

20. O. O. Howard, *Famous Indian Chiefs I Have Known*, pp. 255-58.

21. Samuel B. Parrish to Hon. E. P. Smith, April 4, 1876, Letters Received, Office of Indian Affairs, Oregon Superintendency.

22. Parrish to General O. O. Howard, April 27, 1876, Letters Received, Office of Indian Affairs, Oregon Superintendency.

23. Hopkins, *Life Among the Piutes*, pp. 117-18.

24. Ibid., pp. 119-20.

25. Hopkins, *Life Among the Piutes*, pp. 121-22.

26. Green to Assistant Adjutant General, Department of Columbia, May 26, 1876, endorsed by General O. O. Howard, Letters Received, Office of Indian Affairs, Oregon Superintendency.

Chapter 11. **Trouble at Malheur**

1. Documents of divorce proceedings of *Sarah Winnemucca* v. *Edward C. Bartlett*, September 21, 1876, Grant County Courthouse, Canyon City, Oregon.

2. W. V. Rinehart to Mrs. F. F. Victor, March 6, 1874, Bancroft Library, University of California, Berkeley.

3. W. V. Rinehart to Mrs. F. F. Victor, April 10, 1881, Bancroft Library.

4. Hopkins, *Life Among the Piutes*, p. 125. Most of the account of Rinehart's activities is taken from Sarah's book.

5. Hopkins, *Life Among the Piutes*, p. 124.

6. Ibid., p. 125.

7. Ibid., pp. 125-26.

8. Ibid., p. 133.

9. Ibid., pp. 133-34.

10. W. V. Rinehart to Commissioner of Indian Affairs, October 28, 1876, Letters Received, Office of Indian Affairs, Oregon Superintendency.

11. Marriage certificate of Sarah Winnemucca and Joseph Satwaller, November 3, 1876, Grant County, Oregon.

12. Major John Green to Assistant Adjutant General, Department of Columbia, November 16, 1876 (with endorsements by Adjutant General H. Clay Wood, Brigadier General O. O. Howard, and Major General Irwin McDowell), Letters Received, Office of Indian Affairs, Oregon Superintendency.

13. Ibid.

14. Ibid.

15. Ibid.; Major John Green to Assistant Adjutant General, December 20, 1876, Letters Received, Office of Indian Affairs, Oregon Superintendency.

16. W. V. Rinehart to General O. O. Howard, December 23, 1876, Letters Received, Office of Indian Affairs, Oregon Superintendency.

17. Ibid.

18. W. V. Rinehart to Commissioner of Indian Affairs, April 14, 1877, Special File no. 268 ("Sarah Winnemucca"), Bureau of Indian Affairs, M574, National Archives.

19. "The Indian Uprising," *Daily Silver State*, June 21, 1877.

20. *Daily Silver State*, June 23, 1877; telegram from Natchez Overton to General McDowell, June 23, 1877, Letters Received, Office of Indian Affairs, Oregon Superintendency.

21. *Daily Silver State*, June 23 and 29, 1877.

22. *Daily Silver State*, July 19, 1877.

23. O. C. Stewart, "The Northern Paiute Bands," *University of California Anthropological Record* 2 (1939), no. 3:132.

24. W. V. Rinehart to Commissioner of Indian Affairs, April 14, 1877, Special File no. 268, Bureau of Indian Affairs.

25. William M. Turner to the Honorable W. V. Rinehart, September 10, 1877, Letters Received, Office of Indian Affairs, Oregon Superintendency.

26. Ibid.

27. *San Francisco Chronicle*, November 29, 1877.

28. Ibid.

29. Ibid.

30. *Daily Silver State*, December 12, 1877.

31. W. V. Rinehart to Commissioner of Indian Affairs, March 23, 1878, Letters Received, Office of Indian Affairs, Oregon Superintendency.

32. Captain Henry Wagner, 1st Cavalry, to Assistant Adjutant General, February 8, 1878, Letters Received, Office of Indian Affairs, Oregon Superintendency.

33. Captain Henry Wagner, 1st Cavalry, to Assistant Adjutant General, March 11, 1878, Letters Received, Office of Indian Affairs, Oregon Superintendency.

34. Irvin McDowell to Adjutant General of U.S. Army, April 16, 1878, Letters Received, Office of Indian Affairs, Oregon Superintendency.

35. W. V. Rinehart to Commissioner of Indian Affairs, April 16, 1878, Letters Received, Office of Indian Affairs, Oregon Superintendency.

36. John J. Burke, Saddler, Company A, 1st Cavalry, to Congressman Newton

Booth, March 22, 1878, Letters Received, Office of Indian Affairs, Oregon Superintendency.

37. W. V. Rinehart to Major Danielson, March 25, 1878, and Rinehart to Commissioner of Indian Affairs, April 16, 1878, Letters Received, Office of Indian Affairs, Oregon Superintendency.

38. W. V. Rinehart to Commissioner of Indian Affairs, December 18, 1877, Letters Received, Office of Indian Affairs, Oregon Superintendency.

39. W. V. Rinehart to Commissioner of Indian Affairs, February 27, 1878, Letters Received, Office of Indian Affairs, Oregon Superintendency.

40. Petition to the President of the United States signed by approximately 70 settlers near or on Malheur Reservation; and Captain George M. Downey, 1st Infantry, April 20, 1878, endorsed by General O. O. Howard and General Irvin McDowell, Letters Received, Office of Indian Affairs, Oregon Superintendency.

41. W. V. Rinehart to Commissioner of Indian Affairs, May 18, 1878, Letters Received, Office of Indian Affairs, Oregon Superintendency.

42. W. V. Rinehart to Commissioner of Indian Affairs, May 20, 1878, Letters Received, Office of Indian Affairs, Oregon Superintendency.

43. W. V. Rinehart to Commissioner of Indian Affairs, May 21, 1878, Letters Received, Office of Indian Affairs, Oregon Superintendency.

Chapter 12. **The Beginning of Hostilities**

1. Thomas E. Cooley's memories in "I Always Wondered," by Jo Southworth, *Blue Mountain Eagle* (John Day, Ore.), January 4, 1973: "The scouts found Sally Winnemucca out in the mountains, after she had been deserted by her husband." Also, Hopkins, *Life Among the Piutes*, p. 137. Sarah says that she spent the winter at Mrs. Courley's.

2. Hopkins, *Life Among the Piutes*, pp. 140–41.

3. General O. O. Howard, *Famous Indian Chiefs I have Known*, p. 269.

4. Hopkins, *Life Among the Piutes*, p. 146.

5. W. V. Rinehart to Commissioner of Indian Affairs, June 7, 1878, Letters Received, Office of Indian Affairs, Oregon Superintendency.

6. General Irvin McDowell, telegram to General Sherman, June 4, 1878, Letters Received, Office of Indian Affairs, Oregon Superintendency.

7. Elizabeth P. Peabody, *Sarah Winnemucca's Practical Solution of the Indian Problem*, p. 30–31.

8. W. V. Rinehart to Commissioner of Indian Affairs, May 12, 1879, Special file no. 268, Bureau of Indian Affairs.

9. W. V. Rinehart, telegram to Commissioner Hoyt, June 10, 1878, *New York Times*, June 14, 1878.

10. Levi Gheen, telegram to Commissioner of Indian Affairs, June 7, 1878, Letters Received, Office of Indian Affairs, Nevada Superintendency.

11. Hopkins, *Life Among the Piutes*, pp. 148–49.

12. Ibid., p. 149.

13. Some newspapers carried a story that Sarah had been arrested in Jordan Valley while attempting to smuggle ammunition to the hostile Indians. *New York Times*, June 17, 1878, p. 1, col. 6.

14. Hopkins, *Life Among the Piutes*, p. 150.

15. General O. O. Howard, *My Life and Personal Experiences Among Our Hostile Indians*, p. 388.

16. Ibid.

17. Hopkins, *Life Among the Piutes*, p. 154.

18. Ibid., pp. 157-58.

19. Ibid., p. 159. Critics look upon Sarah's account of this adventure in her autobiography with skepticism, but the various Bannock bands were not organized as a single military unit, and, while they were occupied killing cattle in this safe refuge, they would not have been on their guard. Since the prisoners' guns and horses had been taken from them, there was no need to watch them closely unless there was an alarm.

20. Hopkins, *Life Among the Piutes*, p. 160.

21. An interesting aspect of Sarah's work as a scout with the army is the style of riding that she chose. One might assume that she rode astride, considering the number of miles that she traveled and the necessity for speed and hard work. Sarah insists that she rode sidesaddle, wearing a riding dress and a hat, throughout her work. That, in fact, was the style for ladies of the day, and Sarah was very eager to impress her ladylike qualities upon her public. Hopkins, *Life Among the Piutes*, p. 152, 158.

22. Ibid., p. 163.

23. Howard, *My Life and Personal Experiences Among Our Hostile Indians*, pp. 391.

24. W. V. Rinehart, telegram to Commissioner of Indian Affairs, July 7, 1878, Letters Received, Office of Indian Affairs, Oregon Superintendency.

25. Hopkins, *Life Among the Piutes*, p. 164. Also, Howard, *My Life and Personal Experiences*, p. 391.

26. The *New York Times* account of Sarah's experience was printed on June 17, 1878, p. 1, col. 6. It bore the headline "A BRAVE INDIAN SQUAW," and the lead sentence read, "Sarah, Daughter of the Piute Head Chief, Penetrates to the Hostiles' Camp and Rescues her Father and Brothers—Movements of the Indians." The report was very consistent with Sarah's autobiography, which was written four years later, but it had two very interesting additions. Sarah was quoted as saying that her brother George (whom she calls her cousin in her book) accused her of destroying her tribe by inducing some to escape, because he thought that those left behind would be doomed without a chance of getting away from Oytes and the Bannocks. Also, more information is given on Chief Egan: "She describes Eagle of Light, the Nez Perce renegade chief, whose son was with Joseph last year taunting Egan with cowardice. Egan, the brave war chief of the Piutes, sat on his horse and exhorted the hostiles to leave them and not draw soldiers upon them. He said: 'Why do you bring war upon my people? I will not fight.' The tears were streaming down his cheeks. 'You coward,' said Eagle of Light, striking at him with his knife."

Chapter 13. The Bannock Indian War

1. *New York Times*, June 23, 1878, p. 5, col. 6, reprinted from the *Omaha* (Neb.) *Herald*, June 18, 1878.

2. *New York Times*, June 25, 1878, p. 1, col. 1.

3. W. V. Rinehart to Commissioner of Indian Affairs, June 28, 1878, Letters Received, Office of Indian Affairs, Oregon Superintendency.

4. Ibid.

5. Ibid.

6. Ibid.

7. Hopkins, *Life Among the Piutes*, p. 165.

8. Ibid., p. 168.

9. Ibid., p. 169.

10. Ibid.

11. Howard, *My Life and Personal Experiences Among Our Hostile Indians*, pp. 399–400.

12. Howard to McDowell, October, 1878, House Executive Document 1, Ser. 1843, 45th Congress, 3rd Session, Part 2, p. 219, quoted in Brimlow, *The Bannock Indian War of 1878*.

13. Howard, *Life Among Our Hostile Indians*, p. 401; Hopkins, *Life Among the Piutes*, p. 170.

14. Howard, *Life Among Our Hostile Indians*, p. 400.

15. W. V. Rinehart to Commissioner of Indian Affairs, July 1, 1878, Letters Received, Office of Indian Affairs, Oregon Superintendency.

16. Ibid.

17. Ibid.

18. Ibid.

19. Ibid.

20. Ibid.

21. *New York Times*, July 6, 1878, p. 4, cols. 3 and 4.

22. W. V. Rinehart, telegram to Commissioner of Indian Affairs, July 7, 1878, Letters Received, Office of Indian Affairs, Oregon Superintendency.

23. Captain H. C. Hasbrouck to Assistant Adjutant General, Military Division of the Pacific, July 9, 1878, Letters Received, Office of Indian Affairs, Oregon Superintendency.

24. Ibid.

25. *New York Times*, July 9, 1878, p. 1, col. 3.

26. Ibid., July 10, 1878, p. 1, col. 3.

27. Hopkins, *Life Among the Piutes*, pp. 174–75.

28. Ibid., p. 175. Also Howard, *Life Among Our Hostile Indians*, pp. 404–405.

29. Hopkins, *Life Among the Piutes*, p. 176; Howard, *Life Among Our Hostile Indians*, pp. 404–405.

30. Hopkins, *Life Among the Piutes*, p. 175.

31. Howard, *Life Among Our Hostile Indians*, pp. 404–405.

32. Ibid., pp. 175–76.

33. Ibid., p. 177.

34. Ibid., p. 178. Also Brimlow, *Bannock Indian War*, p. 143.

35. Hopkins, *Life Among the Piutes*, p. 177.

36. Brimlow, *Bannock Indian War*, p. 146.

37. N. A. Cornoyer to Commissioner of Indian Affairs, July 19, 1898, Letters Received, Office of Indian Affairs, Oregon Superintendency.

38. Ibid.

39. Ibid.

40. Howard, *Famous Indian Chiefs I Have Known*, pp. 259-60.
41. Ibid., p. 277.
42. Brimlow, *Bannock Indian War*, pp. 150-54.
43. J. F. Santee, "Egan of the Piutes," *Washington Historical Society Quarterly*, January, 1935, pp. 22-24.
44. Ibid.
45. Howard, *Famous Indian Chiefs I Have Known*, p. 241.
46. Hopkins, *Life Among the Piutes*, pp. 178-79.
47. Ibid., pp. 180-81.
48. Ibid., p. 181.
49. Ibid., pp. 181-82.
50. Ibid., p. 182.
51. Ibid., p. 186.
52. Ibid., pp. 188-93.

Chapter 14. **Yakima**

1. Hopkins, *Life Among the Piutes*, p. 195.
2. Ibid., p. 196.
3. *New York Times*, August 14, 1878, p. 1, col. 6.
4. Hopkins, *Life Among the Piutes*, pp. 199-200.
5. Ibid., p. 200.
6. Ibid., pp. 200-201.
7. Commander Corliss of Fort McDermit, telegram to Adjutant General, October 4, 1878, Letters Received, Office of Indian Affairs, Oregon Superintendency.
8. Hopkins, *Life Among the Piutes*, p. 201.
9. Letters of Capain M. A. Cochran, November 18 and December 6, 1878, in *Annual Report of the Commissioner of Indian Affairs to the Secretary of the Interior for the Year 1879*, p. 129.
10. Hopkins, *Life Among the Piutes*, p. 203.
11. Ibid., p. 204.
12. Ibid., p. 205.
13. Letters of Captain M. A. Cochran, November 18 and December 6, 1878, *Annual Report of the Commissioner of Indian Affairs . . . 1879*, p. 129.
14. *Daily Silver State*, January 2, 1879.
15. Hopkins, *Life Among the Piutes*, pp. 206-207.
16. W. V. Rinehart, unpublished manuscript, Bancroft Library.
17. Hopkins, *Life Among the Piutes*, p. 207.
18. Ibid., pp. 207-208.
19. Ibid., p. 208.
20. W. V. Rinehart to Commissioner of Indian Affairs, March 3, 1879, Special File No. 268, Bureau of Indian Affairs.
21. James H. Wilbur to Commissioner of Indian Affairs, February 6, 1879, Letters Received, Office of Indian Affairs, Oregon Superintendency.
22. Hopkins, *Life Among the Piutes*, pp. 210-11.
23. Ibid., p. 211.

24. Ibid., pp. 211–12.

25. Ibid., p. 214.

26. Ibid., p. 212.

27. W. V. Rinehart to Commissioner of Indian Affairs, May 12, 1879, Special File no. 268, Bureau of Indian Affairs.

28. *Daily Silver State*, June 25, 1879.

29. Ibid., June 13, 1879.

30. Ibid., June 6, 1879.

31. Ibid., June 13, 1879.

32. Ibid., June 14, 1879.

33. *Daily Silver State*, July 15, 1879.

34. Hopkins, *Life Among the Piutes*, p. 216. Also, General O. O. Howard to General B. Whittlesey, November 7, 1879, Letters Received, Office of Indian Affairs, Oregon Superintendency.

35. Hopkins, *Life Among the Piutes*, p. 214.

36. Ibid.

37. Ibid., p. 216.

38. James Wilbur to Commissioner of Indian Affairs, July 21, 1879. Letters Received, Office of Indian Affairs, Oregon Superintendency, Special File no. 268, Bureau of Indian Affairs.

39. James Mooney, *The Ghost Dance Religion and the Sioux Outbreak of 1890*, p. 3.

Chapter 15. **The "Princess" Sarah**

1. *San Francisco Call*, November 22, 1879.

2. *San Francisco Chronicle*, November 23, 1879, p. 1, col. 5.

3. *San Francisco Chronicle*, November 14, 1879.

4. *San Francisco Chronicle*, November 23, 1879, p. 1, col. 5.

5. *San Francisco Chronicle*, November 14, 1879.

6. *San Francisco Call*, November 22, 1879.

7. W. V. Rinehart to Commissioner of Indian Affairs, February 6, 1879, Special File no. 268, Bureau of Indian Affairs.

8. *Daily Silver State*, November 28, 1879, reprinted from *San Francisco Chronicle*.

9. Ibid.

10. *Alta California*, November 26, 1879, p. 1, col. 3.

11. *Daily Silver State*, November 28, 1879.

12. *Daily Alta California*, November 26, 1879, p. 1, col. 3.

13. Hopkins, *Life Among the Piutes*, p. 217.

14. *Daily Silver State*, November 6, 1879.

15. *Daily Silver State*, December 16, 1879.

16. *Daily Alta California*, December 24, 1879, p. 1, col. 5.

17. Ibid.

18. *Daily Alta California*, December 4, 1879, p. 1, col. 3.

19. *Daily Silver State*, December 30, 1879.

20. Ibid. After legal action had forced the departure of Agent A. J. Barnes from the Pyramid and Walker River reservations, the American Baptist Home

Mission Society had difficulty filling the position. William Garvey held it for only five months before he was suspended. Then on September 17, 1879, James E. Spencer assumed the charge. Spencer was not only competent but also honest, and he treated the Paiutes with respect and kindness before his untimely death of pneumonia on November 26, 1880. He found trustworthy farmers and traders to work on the reservations, attempted the removal of white cattlemen and sheepherders, started the building of two school buildings (one each on the Walker River and Pyramid reservations), and built a working flume designed by a civil engineer. He worked alongside the Indians in digging ditches and in building the flume. Wading in the icy waters of the Truckee may have brought on his final illness. This information is derived from numerous letters that Spencer wrote to the commissioner of Indian affairs in 1879 (Letters Received, Office of Indian Affairs, Nevada Superintendency, RG 75, M234, National Archives).

21. *Daily Silver State*, August 23, 1879.
22. *Daily Silver State*, October 2, 1879.
23. *Daily Silver State*, December 30, 1879.
24. Ibid.
25. Ibid.
26. *Daily Silver State*, January 5, 1880.
27. *Daily Silver State*, January 14, 1880.

Chapter 16. **Washington City**

1. Hopkins, *Life Among the Piutes*, p. 219.
2. John Muldrick, Phil Mitschan, William Hall, Edwin Hall, J. W. Church, J. H. Wood, F. C. Sels, D. G. Overholdt, and William Luce to the Honorable T. H. Brents, January 14, 1880, Special File no. 268, Bureau of Indian Affairs.
3. W. V. Rinehart to the Honorable E. A. Hoyt, January 15, 1880, enclosing three affidavits by William Currey, Thomas O'Keefe, and W. W. Johnson (all dated, sworn, and subscribed to Rinehart, January 13, 1880), Special File no. 268, Bureau of Indian Affairs.
4. Ibid.
5. Ibid.
6. *Daily Silver State*, January 31, 1880, reprinted from *Washington National Republican*.
7. Hopkins, *Life Among the Piutes*, p. 221.
8. Ibid., pp. 223–24. The letter was also paraphrased in the *Silver State*, February 2, 1880.
9. Ibid., p. 222.
10. Ibid.
11. Ibid., p. 225.
12. Ibid., pp. 224–25.
13. John Howe to the Hon. R. E. Trowridge, Commissioner of Indian Affairs, May 1 and 6, 1880, Letters Received, Bureau of Indian Affairs.
14. *Silver State*, June 2, 1880.
15. *Daily Silver State*, May 5 and 6, 1880.
16. *Daily Silver State*, February 16, 1880.

17. *Daily Silver State*, February 17, 1880.

18. *Baker City* (Ore.) *Bedrock Democrat*, from *Esmeralda* (Nev.) *Herald*, in John Muldrick et al. to Hon. T. H. Brent, January 14, 1880, Special File no. 268, Bureau of Indian Affairs.

19. W. V. Rinehart to Commissioner of Indian Affairs, March 20, 1880, Special File no. 268, Bureau of Indian Affairs.

20. Ibid.

21. Sarah Winnemucca to W. V. Rinehart, April 4, 1880, Special File no. 268, Bureau of Indian Affairs.

22. W. V. Rinehart to Sarah Winnemucca, April 20, 1880, Special File no. 268, Bureau of Indian Affairs.

23. W. V. Rinehart to the Honorable R. E. Trowbridge, Commissioner of Indian Affairs, April 20, 1880, Special File no. 268, Bureau of Indian Affairs.

24. Hopkins, *Life Among the Piutes*, p. 226.

25. Ibid., p. 227.

26. Ibid., pp. 231–32.

27. Ibid., pp. 232–33.

28. Ibid., p. 236.

29. Ibid., p. 238.

30. *Daily Silver State*, July 10, 1880.

31. James H. Wilbur to Commissioner of Indian Affairs, July 9, 1879, in Katherine Turner, *Red Men Calling on the Great White Father*, p. 166.

32. Hopkins, *Life Among the Piutes*, p. 239.

33. Ibid.

34. Ibid., pp. 239–40.

35. Turner, *Red Men Calling*, p. 171.

36. Ibid., p. 172.

37. James H. Wilbur to Commissioner of Indian Affairs, June 29, 1880, quoted in Turner, *Red Men Calling*, p. 173.

38. United States Office of Indian Affairs, *Annual Report of the Commissioner of Indian Affairs to the Secretary of the Interior for the Year 1879*, p. 159.

39. Howard, *My Life and Personal Experiences Among Our Hostile Indians*, p. 420.

40. Brig. Gen. O. O. Howard to Assistant Adjutant General, Presidio, S.F., August 21, 1878, Letters Received, Office of Indian Affairs, Oregon Superintendency.

41. Brig. Gen. O. O. Howard to Adjutant General, Presidio, S.F., October 8, 1878, Letters Received, Office of Indian Affairs, Oregon Superintendency.

42. W. V. Rinehart to Commissioner of Indian Affairs, May 12, 1879, Special File no. 268, Bureau of Indian Affairs.

Chapter 17. **Mrs. Hopkins**

1. Sarah Winnemucca to the Honorable Secretary of the Interior, March 28, 1881, in Hopkins, *Life Among the Piutes*, p. 244.

2. O. O. Howard to Whom It May Concern, April 3, 1883, in Hopkins, *Life Among the Piutes*, p. 249.

3. *Silver State*, October 9, 1880.

4. *Portland Oregonian*, October 8, 1880.

5. Hopkins, *Life Among the Piutes*, p. 246.

6. W. V. Rinehart to Commissioner of Indian Affairs, July 10, 1881, Special File no. 268, Bureau of Indian Affairs. *Silver State*, July 14, 1881.

7. Ibid.; *Silver State*, July 23, 1881.

8. James H. Wilbur to Commissioner of Indian Affairs, May 31, 1880, Special File no. 268, Bureau of Indian Affairs.

9. Ibid., November 21, 1881.

10. Ibid., October 27, 1881.

11. Hopkins, *Life Among the Piutes*, p. 243. Wilbur tried to counter Chapman's observations to the military by writing himself to the Honorable H. Price, Commissioner of Indian Affairs, on February 28, 1882, Special File no. 268, Bureau of Indian Affairs.

12. *Silver State*, September 29, 1881.

13. *Daily Silver State*, November 30, 1881.

14. Sarah Winnemucca Hopkins, "The Pah-Utes," *The Californian* 6 (1882): 256.

15. *Silver State*, December 8, 1881. The *San Francisco Examiner* of December 8, 1881 (quoted in *New York Times*, December 18, 1881, p. 5, col. 2) states that Sarah was married on the Monday, which would indicate December 5, 1881. Records of marriages and divorces in San Francisco prior to July 1, 1904, were destroyed by the general conflagration on April 1, 1906. Consequently, it would be difficult to confirm whether Sarah divorced Joseph Satwaller before her marriage to Hopkins.

16. Patricia Stewart, "Sarah Winnemuca," *Nevada Historical Society Quarterly* 14 (1971): 31.

17. *New York Times*, December 18, 1881, p. 5, col. 2; *Silver State*, December 8, 1881.

18. *Silver State*, December 8, 1881.

19. *New York Times*, December 18, 1881, p. 5, col. 2.

20. *Daily Silver State*, January 9, 1882.

21. Hopkins, *Life Among the Piutes*, p. 94.

22. Ibid.

23. Ibid., p. 95.

24. Ibid., p. 99.

25. *Silver State*, February 20, 1882; *Reno* (Nev.) *Evening Gazette*, April 10, 1883.

26. W. V. Rinehart, unpublished manuscript, Bancroft Library. Probably Rinehart was held personally responsible for paying for the property.

27. *Daily Silver State*, August 1, 1882.

28. James H. Wilbur to Hon. H. Price, Commissioner of Indian Affairs, February 28, 1882, Special File no. 268, Bureau of Indian Affairs.

29. Brig. Gen. O. O. Howard to Adjutant General of Army, December 16, 1882, Special File no. 268, Bureau of Indian Affairs.

Chapter 18. Old Winnemucca

1. *Daily Silver State*, September 27, 1882.

2. *Daily Silver State*, October 8, 1882.

3. *Reno* (Nev.) *Evening Gazette*, October 25, 1882, p. 3, col. 1.

4. *Daily Silver State*, October 31, 1882.

5. Beatrice Blythe Whiting, *Piute Sorcery*, p. 69.

6. *Reno Evening Gazette*, October 27, 1882.

7. R. F. Heizer, *Executions by Stoning Among the Sierre Miwok and Northern Paiute* (Berkeley, Calif.: Kroeber Anthropological Society, 1955), pp. 44-48.

8. *Daily Silver State*, September 27, 1882.

9. *Reno Evening Gazette*, November 16, 1882.

10. Ibid.

11. Ibid.; *Silver State*, October 31, 1882.

12. Sarah Winnemucca Hopkins, "The Pah-Utes," *Californian* 6 (1882):252-55.

13. *Reno Evening Gazette*, April 10, 1883.

Chapter 19. A Trip to the East

1. Hopkins, *Life Among the Piutes*, editor's preface. Also, Elizabeth P. Peabody, *The Piutes: Second Report*, p. 7.

2. *Boston Evening Transcript*, May 3, 1883, p. 2, col. 6.

3. Elizabeth P. Peabody, *Sarah Winnemucca's Practical Solution of the Indian Problem*, p. 24.

4. Peabody, *The Piutes: Second Report*, p. 7.

5. Ibid., p. 5.

6. Peabody, *Sarah Winnemucca's Practical Solution*, pp. 8-9.

7. Hopkins, *Life Among the Piutes*, p. 53.

8. Mary Mann to Miss Eleanor Lewis, April 25, 1883, Olive Kettering Library, Antioch College, Yellow Springs, Ohio.

9. Ibid.

10. *Boston Evening Transcript*, May 3, 1883, p. 2, col. 6. Thomas Tibbles, a white writer married to a Ponca Indian woman (Susette La Flesche), had recently written of the "Hidden Power" by which Indians were kept as the helpless wards of the agents, their self-respect lost while the contractors on the reservation became affluent.

11. *Council Fire and Arbitrator* 6 (May, 1883): 69.

12. *Silver State*, June 19, 1883.

13. General O. O. Howard to Mrs. Mary Mann, September 13, 1883, Olive Kettering Library, Antioch College.

14. Hopkins, *Life Among the Piutes*, pp. 250-51.

15. Ibid., pp. 256-57.

16. Ibid, p. 258.

17. Elizabeth P. Peabody to the Honorable J. B. Long, January 11, 1884, Massachusetts Historical Society, Boston.

18. Elizabeth P. Peabody to Congressman Newton Booth [1883], Olive Kettering Library, Antioch College.

19. Hopkins, *Life Among the Piutes*, p. 76.

20. *Silver State*, November 7, 1883.

21. Elizabeth P. Peabody to the Honorable J. B. Long, March [27?], 1884,

Massachusetts Historical Society.

22. Elizabeth P. Peabody to Edwin Munroe Bacon [1883], Olive Kettering Library, Antioch College.

23. Mary Mann to Miss Eleanor Lewis, December 24, 1883, Olive Kettering Library, Antioch College.

24. *Silver State*, December 13, 1883.

25. Mary Mann to Miss Eleanor Lewis, December 24, 1883.

26. *Silver State*, December 5, 1883.

27. Peabody, *The Piutes: Second Report*, p. 8.

28. *Council Fire and Arbitrator* 6 (May, 1883):135.

29. Advertisements for Sarah's lectures appeared in the *Baltimore Sun* under "Special Notices" during the winter of 1884.

30. Peabody, *The Piutes: Second Report*, p. 7.

31. Lewis H. Hopkins to a subscriber for Sarah's book, May 10, 1884, Museum and Library of Maryland History, Maryland Historical Society, Baltimore.

32. *Daily Silver State*, September 7, 1883.

33. R. H. Milroy to the Honorable H. Price, Commissioner of Indian Affairs, August 11, 1883, Special File no. 268, Bureau of Indian Affairs.

34. Kate Douglas Wiggin raised $1,000 among advocates of the kindergarten movement for Elizabeth Peabody's eightieth birthday. Elizabeth eventually sent $800 of this money to help Sarah Winnemucca in her work for the Indians. Louise Hall Tharp, *The Peabody Sisters of Salem* (Boston: Little, Brown and Co., 1950), p. 168.

35. Elizabeth P. Peabody to the Honorable J. B. Long, January 11, 1884, Massachusetts Historical Society.

36. Elizabeth P. Peabody to the Honorable J. B. Long, March [27?], 1884, Massachusetts Historical Society.

37. Ibid.

38. M. Jarvis to Mrs. Mary Mann, April 17, 1884, Olive Kettering Library, Antioch College.

Chapter 20. **Disillusionment**

1. Peabody, *The Piutes: Second Report*, p. 8; Elizabeth P. Peabody to Hon. J. B. Long, January 11, 1884, Massachusetts Historical Society; *Silver State*, April 25 and 29, 1884.

2. Elizabeth P. Peabody to the Hon. John B. Long, May, 1884, Massachusetts Historical Society.

3. Ibid.

4. On July 3, 1880, Agent Spencer had written to Commissioner of Indian Affairs R. E. Trowbridge, "You are doubtless aware that after the lakes and the mountains, the deserts and the railroad subsidies are subtracted from these reserves, there remains hardly enough good grain or pastureland to give to each head of family desiring a ranch, ten acres" (Letters Received, Bureau of Indian Affairs, Nevada Superintendency).

5. Elizabeth P. Peabody to Hon. J. B. Long, January 21, 1885, Massachusetts

Historical Society.

6. Elizabeth P. Peabody to the Hon. John B. Long, January 21, 1885, Massachusetts Historical Society.

7. Peabody, *The Piutes: Second Report*, p. 18.

8. Ibid., p. 9.

9. Elizabeth P. Peabody to Hon. J. B. Long, January 21, 1885, Massachusetts Historical Society.

10. Ibid.

11. Ibid.

12. *Daily Silver State*, August 20, 1884.

13. Elizabeth P. Peabody to Hon. J. B. Long, January 21, 1885, Massachusetts Historical Society.

14. *Christian Register*, January 15, 1885, p. 38.

15. Elizabeth P. Peabody to Hon. J. B. Long, January 21, 1885, Massachusetts Historical Society.

16. Ibid.

17. Ibid.

18. Ibid.

19. Ibid.

20. Ibid.

21. Ibid.

22. *Silver State*, December 8, 1884.

23. *Territorial Enterprise*, December 12, 1884.

24. *Silver State*, July 14 and 21, 1884; *Territorial Enterprise*, December 12, 1884.

Chapter 21. **The Turning Point**

1. *Humboldt Register*, November 16, 1875.

2. *Silver State*, May 7, 1885.

3. *San Francisco Morning Call*, February 22, 1885, p. 1, col. 6.

4. Ibid., January 22, 1885.

5. Ibid.

6. Ibid.

7. *San Francisco Morning Call*, February 4, 1885, p. 3, col. 7.

8. *New York Times*, January 23, 1885, p. 2, col. 5.

9. *Daily Silver State*, February 9, 1885.

10. *San Francisco Morning Call*, February 4, 1885, p. 3, col. 7.

11. Ibid., February 22, 1885, p. 1, col. 6.

12. Ibid., February 11, 1885, p. 3, col. 8; Elizabeth P. Peabody, *The Piutes: Second Report*, pp. 11–12.

13. Elizabeth P. Peabody, *The Piutes: Second Report*, p. 3.

14. *Silver State*, March 12, 1885.

15. Elizabeth P. Peabody to Miss Eleanor Lewis, March 20, [1885], Olive Kettering Library, Antioch College, Yellow Springs, Ohio.

16. Mary Mann to Miss Eleanor Lewis, March 29, 1885, Olive Kettering Library, Antioch College.

17. Ibid.

18. D. Allen, Attorney at Law, to Elizabeth Peabody, May 5, 1885, Olive Kettering Library, Antioch College.

19. *Reese River Reveille*, September 17, 1884.

20. *Reese River Reveille*, November 20, 1884.

21. *Reese River Reveille*, January 6, 1886.

22. *Christian Register*, January 15, 1885, p. 38.

23. *Daily Silver State*, June 23, 1885; *Reno Evening Gazette*, June 26, 1885.

24. *San Francisco Call*, May 24, 1885.

25. *Daily Silver State*, June 23, 1885.

26. *Reno Evening Gazette*, June 26, 1884.

Chapter 22. The Peabody Indian School

1. Elizabeth P. Peabody, *The Piutes: Second Report*, p. 13.

2. Elizabeth P. Peabody to Commissioner of Indian Affairs, October 12, 1885, Special File no. 268, Bureau of Indian Affairs.

3. M. S. Bonnifield to Elizabeth P. Peabody, July 1, 1885, Special File no. 268, Bureau of Indian Affairs.

4. M. S. Bonnifield to Elizabeth P. Peabody, July 1, 1885, Special File no. 268, Bureau of Indian Affairs. Attorney Bonnifield wrote Elizabeth that Natchez had inherited a fine span of work horses from his brother Tom. Elizabeth knew better, as she and her friends had contributed the money for them. She wrote a note in the margin of the letter correcting the error.

5. Ibid.

6. Elizabeth P. Peabody to Commissioner of Indian Affairs, October 12, 1885, Special File no. 268, Bureau of Indian Affairs.

7. Peabody, *The Piutes: Second Report*, pp. 13-14.

8. Ibid.

9. *Daily Silver State*, July 14, 1885.

10. *Daily Silver State*, December 17, 1885.

11. Elizabeth P. Peabody to Commissioner of Indian Affairs, October 12, 1885, Special File no. 268, Bureau of Indian Affairs.

12. *Daily Silver State*, October 22, 1885.

13. Alice Chapin to Elizabeth P. Peabody, [July, 1885], and August 15, 1885, Olive Kettering Library, Antioch College.

14. Elizabeth Powell Bond to Elizabeth P. Peabody, December 9, 1885, Olive Kettering Library, Antioch College.

15. Elizabeth Powell Bond to Elizabeth P. Peabody, December 19, 1885, Olive Kettering Library, Antioch College.

16. Amelia B. James to Elizabeth P. Peabody, December 15, 1885, Olive Kettering Library, Antioch College.

17. Mary Y. Bean to Elizabeth P. Peabody, December 29, 1885, Olive Kettering Library, Antioch College.

18. Elizabeth P. Peabody, *Sarah Winnemucca's Practical Solution*, pp. 10-11.

19. Warren Delano to Elizabeth P. Peabody, March 24, 1886, Olive Kettering

Library, Antioch College.

20. Warren Delano to Sarah Winnemucca Hopkins, April 8, 1886, Olive Kettering Library, Antioch College (copy to Elizabeth P. Peabody).

21. Warren Delano to Elizabeth P. Peabody, April 9, 1886, Olive Kettering Library, Antioch College.

22. Peabody, *Sarah Winnemucca's Practical Solution*, p. 14.

23. Ibid., p. 12.

24. Mary Mann to Eleanor Lewis, May 23, 1886, Olive Kettering Library, Antioch College.

25. Warren Delano to Sarah Winnemucca Hopkins, May 6, 1886, Olive Kettering Library, Antioch College (copy to Elizabeth P. Peabody).

26. *Reese River Reveille*, June 9, 1886.

27. *Reese River Reveille*, July 10, 1886.

28. Warren Delano to Elizabeth P. Peabody, May 24, 1886, Olive Kettering Library, Antioch College.

29. Peabody, *Sarah Winnemucca's Practical Solution*, p. 22.

30. Sarah Winnemucca to *Silver State*, July 9, 1886.

31. Peabody, *Sarah Winnemucca's Practical Solution*, p. 22.

32. Ibid., p. 17.

33. Ibid.

34. Ibid., p. 18.

35. Peabody, *The Piutes: Second Report*, p. 15.

36. Peabody, *Sarah Winnemucca's Practical Solution*, p. 21.

37. *Reese River Reveille*, August 2, 1886.

38. Peabody, *Sarah Winnemucca's Practical Solution*, p. 21.

39. Ibid., p. 33.

40. Ibid.

41. Warren Delano to Elizabeth P. Peabody, September 27, 1886, Olive Kettering Library, Antioch College.

Chapter 23. **Hopkins Again**

1. *Reese River Reveille*, September 24, 1886.

2. Ibid.

3. Peabody, *Sarah Winnemucca's Practical Solution*, p. 34.

4. Ibid.

5. Ibid.

6. Ibid.; *Reese River Reveille*, November 15, 1886, p. 1, col. 3.

7. Peabody, *Sarah Winnemucca's Practical Solution*, p. 35.

8. Ibid.

9. *Reese River Reveille*, November 15, 1886.

10. Elizabeth P. Peabody to Miss Eleanor Lewis, January 18, 1887, Olive Kettering Library, Antioch College.

11. Mary Mann to Miss Eleanor Lewis, January 26, 1887, Olive Kettering Library, Antioch College.

12. Elizabeth P. Peabody, *The Piutes: Second Report*, p. 16.

13. *Silver State*, December 1, 1886.

14. Mary Mann to Miss Eleanor Lewis, January 26, 1887, Olive Kettering Library, Antioch College.

15. Mary Mann to Eleanor Lewis, November, 1886, Olive Kettering Library, Antioch College.

16. Ibid.

17. Elizabeth P. Peabody to Miss Eleanor Lewis, March 27, [1887], Olive Kettering Library, Antioch College.

18. Ibid.

19. Peabody, *Sarah Winnemucca's Practical Solution*, p. 8.

20. *Daily Silver State*, April 25 and 27, 1887; Peabody, *The Piutes: Second Report*, p. 16. On the copy of her pamphlet now owned by Yale University Library, New Haven, Connecticut, Miss Peabody wrote on page 18: "Which their parents are pressing on her to take, having been frightened because the despotic agent of Pyramid Lake Reservation has forced 10 or 12 children to go against shrieking protests of their mothers to a Colorado Industrial School to learn of teachers who do not know Indian languages which disheartened and demoralized the children besides breaking the parent's hearts."

21. *Silver State*, June 3, 1887.

22. Ibid.

23. *Christian Union*, October 6, 1887. The "Special Supplement on American Indians" in that issue is a sampling of the leading ideas and institutions of the period dealing with the subject.

24. Sylvia H. Delano to Miss Elizabeth P. Peabody, June 21, 1884, Olive Kettering Library, Antioch College.

25. Ibid.

26. Sylvia H. Delano to Miss Elizabeth P. Peabody, January 29, 1885, Olive Kettering Library, Antioch College.

27. Warren Delano to Miss Elizabeth P. Peabody, October 12, 1887, Olive Kettering Library, Antioch College.

28. Ibid.

29. *Daily Silver State*, September 21, 1887.

30. Letter to the Editor of the *Daily Silver State*, September 23, 1887.

31. Ibid.

32. Warren Delano to Elizabeth P. Peabody, October 12, 1887, Olive Kettering Library, Antioch College.

33. Ibid.

34. *Silver State*, October 20, 1887, p. 3, cols. 1 and 3.

35. Elizabeth P. Peabody to Miss Eleanor C. Lewis, March 27, 1887, Olive Kettering Library, Antioch College.

Chapter 24. Henry's Lake

1. Peabody, *The Piutes: Second Report*, p. 15.

2. Ibid., p. 16.

3. Ibid., p. 15.

4. Ibid., p. 18.

5. Elizabeth P. Peabody, *The Paiutes: The Second Report of the Model School of Sarah Winnemucca* (Cambridge: John Wilcox and Son, 1887), 18 pages.

6. Elizabeth P. Peabody to Senator John B. Long, December 4, 1887, Massachusetts Historical Society.

7. Peabody, *The Piutes: Second Report*, p. 18.

8. Ibid.

9. *Elko* (Nev.) *Daily Independent*, March 26, 1888.

10. Ibid.

11. Robert L. Straker's Horace Mann bibliography, Olive Kettering Library, Antioch College.

12. *Carson Morning Appeal* (Carson City, Nev.), February 29, 1888, p. 3, col. 2.

13. *Elko Independent*, September 30, 1889, p. 3, col. 1.

14. *Elko Independent*, November 8, 1889.

15. Conversations with Samuel Eagle of El Cerrito, California, historian of the West Yellowstone area, on July 30, 1976, and February 10 and 28 and March 13 and 19, 1977.

16. Interview and correspondence with Mrs. R. W. Talbot of Henry's Lake, Idaho, daughter of Joseph and Mary Ann Garner Sherwood; letters from Mrs. Talbot to author, dated September 10 and December 17, 1974, and June 6, 1976, in the author's possession.

17. Interview and correspondence with Mrs. R. W. Talbot, Henry's Lake.

18. Conversations with Samuel Eagle, El Cerrito, California.

19. Interview and correspondence with Mrs. R. W. Talbot, Henry's Lake.

20. Interview and correspondence with Mrs. R. W. Talbot, Henry's Lake.

21. Conversations with Samuel Eagle, El Cerrito, California.

22. Conversations with Samuel Eagle, El Cerrito, California; *Bozeman* (Mont.) *Chronicle*, October 28, 1891, p. 1.

23. Correspondence with Mrs. R. W. Talbot, Henry's Lake, Idaho.

24. Letters to the author from Ruth Tipton, clerk for Gladys Aul, recorder and auditor of Humboldt County (Book 30, Deeds, p. 254), April 28, 1976, and November 28, 1978, in the author's possession.

25. Gilbert Natchez, a son of Natchez born about 1880, came to the University of California at Berkeley in 1914 to assist in editing Dr. W. L. Marsden's Northern Paiute texts (see Bibliography under T. T. Waterman and W. L. Marsden) and left a Paiute vocabulary. He was a landscape painter of some note.

26. Allen C. Bragg, *Humboldt County 1905*, pp. 93–94.

27. Interview and correspondence with Mrs. R. W. Talbot, Henry's Lake, Idaho.

28. *New York Times*, October 27, 1891, p. 1, col. 4.

29. Frank J. Parker, editor of the *Walla Walla Statesman*, quotes in *Reno Weekly Gazette and Stockman*, November 26, 1891.

30. Oliver Otis Howard, *Famous Indian Chiefs I Have Known*, p. 237.

31. Hopkins, *Life Among the Piutes*, pp. 258–59.

Bibliography

BOOKS AND ARTICLES

Angel, Myron T., ed. *History of Nevada*. Oakland, Calif.: Thompson and West, 1881.

Aram, Joseph. "The Reminiscences of Captain Aram," in Col. James Thompkins Watson, "Across the Continent in a Caravan." *Journal of American History* 1 (1907):627–29.

Bidwell, John. *A Journey to California, 1841: First Emigrant Party to California*. Berkeley: Friends of the Bancroft Library, 1964.

Bragg, Allen C. *Humboldt County 1905*. Winnemucca, Nev.: North Central Nevada Historical Society, 1976.

Brimlow, George F. *The Bannock Indian War of 1878*. Caldwell, Idaho: Caxton Printers, 1938.

———. *Harney County, Oregon, and Its Range Land*. Portland, Ore.: Binfords and Mort, 1951.

———. "The Life of Sarah Winnemucca: The Formative Years." *Oregon Historical Society Quarterly*, June, 1952.

Council Fire 6 (May, 1883):69.

Council Fire 6 (September, 1883):134.

Dana, Julian. *The Sacramento, River of Gold*. New York: Farrar and Rinehart, 1939.

Dangberg, Grace. "Wovoka." *Nevada Historical Society Quarterly* 11, no. 2 (Summer, 1968).

Downs, James F. *The Two Worlds of the Washo: An Indian Tribe of California and Nevada*. New York: Holt, Rinehart and Winston, 1966.

Egan, Ferol. *Sand in a Whirlwind: The Paiute Indian War of 1860*. Garden

City: Doubleday and Company, 1972.

Forbes, Jack D. *Native Americans of California and Nevada, A Handbook.* Healdsburg, Calif.: Naturegraph Publishers, 1969.

Fowler, Don D., and Catherine S. Fowler, eds. *Anthropology of the Numa: John Wesley Powell's Manuscripts of the Numic Peoples of Western North America, 1868-1880.* Washington, D.C.: Smithsonian Institution Press, 1971.

Harnar, Nellie Shaw. *Indians of Coo-yu-ee Pah (Pyramid Lake).* Sparks, Nev.: Dave's Printing and Publishing, 1974.

Heizer, Robert F. *Notes on Some Paviotso Personalities.* Anthropological Papers, no. 2. Carson City: Nevada State Museum, 1960.

────── and Thomas R. Hester, eds. *Notes on Northern Paiute Ethnography: Kroeber and Marsden Records.* Berkeley: University of California, Department of Anthropology, Archaeological Research Facility, 1972.

Hermann, Ruth. *The Paiutes of Pyramid Lake: A Narrative Concerning a Western Nevada Indian Tribe.* San Jose: Harlan-Young, 1972.

Hodge, Frederick Webb, ed. *Handbook of American Indians North of Mexico.* 2 vols. Bureau of American Ethnology Bulletin no. 30. Washington, D.C.: Government Printing Office, 1912.

Hopkins, Sarah Winnemucca. *Life Among the Piutes: Their Wrongs and Claims.* Edited by Mrs. Horace Mann. Boston and New York: privately printed, 1883. Reprint. Bishop, Calif.: Chalfant Press, 1969.

Howard, Oliver Otis. *Famous Indian Chiefs I Have Known.* New York: Century Company, 1908.

──────. *My Life and Personal Experiences Among Our Hostile Indians.* Hartford, Conn.: A. D. Worthington Co., 1907.

──────. "Toc-me-to-ne, American Indian Princess." Part 2. *St. Nicholas Magazine* 25 (May–Oct. 1908).

Intertribal Council of Nevada. *Life Stories of Our Native People, Shoshone, Paiute, Washo.* 1974.

──────. *Personal Reflections of Shoshone, Paiute, Washo.* 1974.

Jackson, Helen Hunt. *A Century of Dishonor.* New York: Harper, 1881.

James, Edward J. and Janet W. James, eds. *Notable American Women, 1607-1950: A Biographical Dictionary.* 3 vols. Cambridge, Mass.: Harvard University Press, 1971.

Johnson, Edward C. *Walker River Paiutes: A Tribal History.* Salt Lake City: University of Utah Printing Service, 1975.

Kelly, Isabel T. "Ethnography of the Surprise Valley Paiute." *American Archaeology and Ethnology.* Berkeley: University of California, 1932.

Liebling, A. J. "The Lake of the Cui-ui-Eaters," in "The Reporter at Large." *New Yorker.* Parts 1–4. January 1, 8, 15, and 22, 1955.

Lowie, Robert H. "Shoshonean Ethnography." *American Museum of Natural History Anthropological Papers* 20, Part 3 (1924).

Madsen, Brigham D. *The Bannock of Idaho*. Caldwell, Idaho: Caxton Press, 1958.

Martin, V. Covert. *Stockton Album Through the Years*. Stockton, Calif., 1959.

Miller, William C., ed. "The Pyramid Lake Indian War of 1860." *Nevada Historical Society Quarterly* 1, nos. 1–2 (1957).

Mooney, James. *The Ghost Dance Religion and the Sioux Outbreak of 1890*. Chicago: University of Chicago Press, 1965.

Murray, Keith A. *The Modocs and Their War*. Norman: University of Oklahoma Press, 1959.

Natches, Gilbert. "Northern Paiute Verbs." *American Archaeology and Ethnology* 20 (December 1, 1923).

Park, Willard Z. "Paviotso Shamanism." *American Anthropologist* 36 (January–March, 1934).

Peabody, Elizabeth P. *The Piutes: Second Report of the Model School of Sarah Winnemucca*. Cambridge, Mass.: John Wilcox and Son, 1887.

———. *Sarah Winnemucca's Practical Solution of the Indian Problem*. Cambridge, Mass.: John Wilcox and Son, 1886.

Scott, Lalla. *Karnee: A Paiute Narrative*. Reno: University of Nevada Press, 1966.

Simpson, James H. *Report of Explorations Across the Great Basin of the Territory of Utah for a Direct Wagon Route from Camp Floyd to Genoa in Carson Valley in 1859*. Washington, D.C.: Government Printing Office, 1876.

Steward, Julian H. "Ethnography of Owens Valley Paiute." *Publications in American Archaeology and Ethnology* 33 (September 6, 1933).

———. "Myths of the Owens Valley Paiute." *American Archaeology and Ethnology* 34 (1937).

——— and Erminie Wheeler-Voegelin. *Paiute Indians*. New York: Garland Publishing, 1974. Vol. 3. *The Northern Paiute Indians*.

Stewart, Omer C. "The Northern Paiute Bands." *Anthropological Records* 2, no. 3. Berkeley: University of California, 1939.

Stewart, Patricia. "Sarah Winnemucca." *Nevada Historical Society Quarterly* 14, no. 4 (Winter, 1971).

Tharp, Louise Hall. *The Peabody Sisters of Salem*. Boston: Little, Brown and Co., 1950.

Tibbles, Thomas. *The Hidden Power*. New York: Carleton and Company, 1881.

Turner, Katherine C. *Red Men Calling on the Great White Father*. Norman: University of Oklahoma Press, 1951.

Underhill, Ruth. "The Northern Paiute Indians of California and Nevada." *United States Department of the Interior Bulletin*, 1941.

United States Department of the Interior, Bureau of Indian Affairs.

Bureau of Indian Affairs Planning Support Group. *The Burns-Paiute Colony: Its History, Population and Economy.* Report No. 227. Billings, Mont.: October, 1974.

——. *Fourth Annual Report of the Board of Indian Commissioners.* Washington, D.C.: Government Printing Office, 1872.

——. *Annual Report of the Commissioner of Indian Affairs to the Secretary of the Interior.* 1867–1893. Washington, D.C.: Government Printing Office.

——. *Report of the Joint Special Committee: Condition of the Indian Tribes.* Washington, D.C.: Government Printing Office.

Waterman, T. T., and W. L. Marsden. "Phonetic Elements of Northern Paiute Language." *American Archaeology and Ethnology* 10 (November 15, 1911).

Watson, Margaret G. *Silver Theatre.* Glendale, Calif.: Arthur Clarke Co., 1964.

Wheat, Margaret M. *Survival Arts of the Primitive Paiutes.* Reno: University of Nevada Press, 1967.

Wheeler, Sessions S. *The Desert Lake: The Story of Nevada's Pyramid Lake.* Caldwell, Idaho: Caxton Printers, 1967.

——. *The Nevada Desert.* Caldwell, Idaho: Caxton Printers, 1971.

Whiting, Beatrice Blyth. *Paiute Sorcery.* Viking Fund Publications in Anthropology, no. 15. New York: 1950.

Wright, William [Dan De Quille]. *The Big Bonanza.* New York: Alfred A. Knopf, 1947.

——. *Washoe Rambles.* Los Angeles: Westernlore Press, 1963.

PERIODICALS

Alta California (San Francisco)
Baltimore Sun
Bancroft Scraps, vol. 93, "Nevada Indians," Bancroft Library, University of California, Berkeley
Boston Evening Transcript
Carson Daily Appeal (Carson City, Nev.)
Daily Alta California (San Francisco)
Daily Bulletin (Portland, Ore.)
Daily Silver State (Winnemucca, Nev.)
Elko (Nev.) *Independent*
Gold Hill (Nev.) *News*
Humboldt Register (Winnemucca, Nev.)
Nevada State Journal (Reno)
New York Times
Notre Dame Quarterly (College of Notre Dame de Namur, San Jose,

Calif.), 1913 and 1914
Reese River Reveille (Austin, Nev.)
Reno Evening Gazette
Reno Weekly Gazette and Stockman
Sacramento (Calif.) *Daily Union*
Sacramento (Calif.) *Record Union*
Sacramento (Calif.) *Union*
San Francisco Bulletin
San Francisco Call
San Francisco Chronicle
San Francisco Morning Call
San Francisco Post
Sierra Democrat (Sacramento, Calif.)
Silver State (Winnemucca, Nev.)
Territorial Enterprise (Virginia City, Nev.)
Virginia Chronicle (Virginia City, Nev.)

MANUSCRIPT MATERIALS

Mann, Mary. Personal correspondence. Olive Kettering Library, Antioch
    College, Yellow Springs, Ohio.
Peabody, Elizabeth Palmer. Personal correspondence. Olive Kettering
    Library, Antioch College, Yellow Springs, Ohio; and Massachusetts
    Historical Society, Boston, Massachusetts.
Rinehart, W. V. Unpublished manuscript and correspondence. Ban-
    croft Library, University of California, Berkeley.
United States Office of Indian Affairs. "The Case of Sarah Winne-
    mucca." Special File no. 268. M 574. National Archives.
——. Nevada Superintendency. Letters Received, 1861–80. Record
    Group 75, M 234. Microfilm rolls 538–45. National Archives.
——. Oregon Superintendency. Letters Received, 1874–78. Record
    Group 75, M 234. Microfilm rolls 619–26. National Archives.
——. Utah Superintendency. Letters Received, 1859–80. Record
    Group 75, M 234. Microfilm rolls 899–906. National Archives.
United States War Department. Official Correspondence, Modoc In-
    dian War. Bancroft Library, University of California, Berkeley.
Whitney, Wm. T. Unpublished manuscript. California Historical So-
    ciety, San Francisco.

Index

American Baptist Home Mission Society: 63, 71
Ammunition: 50, 56
Anderson, Mr. (U.S. mail carrier): 178-79
Apache Indians: 205; see also names of leaders
Aram, Capt. Joseph: 4, 10
Argasse, Julius: 92
Armstrong, Gen. Samuel Chapman: 239

Balcom, Flora: 68
Balcom, George: 68-73
Baltimore, Md.: 211, 215, 250
Bannock Indians: 22, 37, 45, 46, 121, 124-27, 129-30, 132-35, 137, 139, 142-45, 150, 152, 185, 187, 222, 226, 257; relationship to Northern Paiutes, 3; parley with Old Winnemucca, 34-35; ponies and guns taken from, 121, 124; capture government ammunition, 126; capture Old Winnemucca, 126, 129; Bannock-Paiute war alliance, 127; encamped in Little Valley, 132; recapture Egan, 133-34; war of, 135-49; battle of Camp Curry, 137, 139, 141; battle of Birch Creek, 142; surrender of, 150; prisoners at Vancouver Barracks, 186-87; return to Fort Hall, 190; see also Bannock War
Bannock Jack (from Fort Hall, Idaho): 124
Bannock Joe (prisoner of war): 153
Bannock War: 158, 162, 166, 174, 185, 190, 192, 195, 205, 226, 259

Baptist missionaries as agents: 68-74, 77, 84-86
Barnes, A. J.: 90
Barren Valley, Ore.: 125-26, 129-30
Bartlett, First Lieut. Edward C.: 65, 67, 76, 109-10
Bartlett, Sarah Winnemucca: see Sarah Winnemucca
Bateman, C. A.: 70-74, 77, 84, 90, 122
Bateman, Cephas: 90
Battle Mountain, Nev.: 76, 85-86
Beads (prisoner of war): 153
Bean, Mary: 235
Bear Flag Rebellion: 4, 6, 10
Beecher, Henry Ward: 211
Benicia, Calif.: 25
Bernard, Capt. Reuben F.: 87, 127-29, 134, 136-37, 142-43, 150; message of, 129; see also Camp Curry
Big Camas Prairie, Idaho: 125
Big John (prisoner of war): 153
Big Meadows, Nev.: 5, 28, 34, 49, 175, 190, 259
Birch Creek, battle of: 142
Black Rock Tom (Smoke Creek Paiute): 11, 46 & n.
Blue Mountains, Ore.: 116, 142, 145, 179
Bond, Elizabeth Powell: 234
Bonnifield, M. S.: 92, 115, 204, 233
Bonsall, Jacob: 7 & n., 9; Bonsall ferry: 7 & n., 11 & n., 29-30
Booth, Edwin: 211

297